T0210975

Lecture Notes in Computer Science 13882

Founding Editors

Gerhard Goos
Juris Hartmanis

Editorial Board Members

The series Lecture Notes in Computer Science (LNCS), including its subseries Lecture Notes in Artificial Intelligence (LNAI) and Lecture Notes in Bioinformatics (LNBI), has established itself as a medium for the publication of new developments in computer science and information technology research, teaching, and education.

LNCS enjoys close cooperation with the computer science R & D community, the series counts many renowned academics among its volume editors and paper authors, and collaborates with prestigious societies. Its mission is to serve this international community by providing an invaluable service, mainly focused on the publication of conference and workshop proceedings and postproceedings. LNCS commenced publication in 1973.

Anna Brunstrom · Marcel Flores · Marco Fiore
Editors

Passive and Active Measurement

24th International Conference, PAM 2023
Virtual Event, March 21–23, 2023
Proceedings

 Springer

Editors
Anna Brunstrom 🆔
Karlstad University
Karlstad, Sweden

Marcel Flores 🆔
Edgio
Scottsdale, AZ, USA

Marco Fiore 🆔
IMDEA Networks Institute
Madrid, Spain

ISSN 0302-9743   ISSN 1611-3349 (electronic)
Lecture Notes in Computer Science
ISBN 978-3-031-28485-4   ISBN 978-3-031-28486-1 (eBook)
https://doi.org/10.1007/978-3-031-28486-1

This Springer imprint is published by the registered company Springer Nature Switzerland AG
The registered company address is: Gewerbestrasse 11, 6330 Cham, Switzerland

Preface

We are excited to present the proceedings of the 24th Annual Passive and Active Measurement PAM Conference. With this program, PAM continues its tradition as a venue for thorough and compelling, but often early-stage and emerging, research on networks, Internet measurement, and the emergent systems that they host. This year's conference took place on March 21–23, 2023. Based on learnings from recent years, this year's PAM was again virtual, both to accommodate the realities of modern travel, and to ensure the accessibility of the conference to attendees who may not otherwise be able to travel long distances.

This year we received 80 double-blind submissions from over 100 different institutions of which the Technical Program Committee (TPC) selected 27 for publication, resulting in a similar sized program to previous years. As with last year, submissions could be of either long or short form, and our ultimate program featured 18 long papers, a notable increase over last year. This year also featured the option to submit papers to an explicit replication track, in which submissions could explicitly explore past findings with new experiments and conditions. We received 8 such submissions, 4 of which ultimately were accepted. The 27 papers of the final program illustrate how network measurements can provide important insights for different types of networks and networked systems and cover topics such as applications, performance, network infrastructure and topology, measurement tools, and security and privacy. It thus provides a comprehensive view of current state-of-the-art and emerging ideas in this important domain.

As with last year, we conducted a call for TPC participation, and built a TPC that included a mix of experience levels, backgrounds, and geographies, bringing both well established and fresh perspectives to the committee. Each submission was assigned to four reviewers, with each reviewer providing an average of just under 5 reviews. All but 8 papers received the assigned reviews, while the remaining 8 were evaluated based on 3 reviews, but had a clear consensus. Again following in the footsteps of previous years, we established a Review Task Force (RTF) of experienced community members who were able to guide much of the discussion amongst reviewers. Following in recent PAM tradition, the TPC meeting was again held virtually and asynchronously through lively and in depth discussions amongst the reviewers and the RTF. Finally, 19 of the accepted papers were shepherded by members of the TPC who were reviewers of each paper. As program chairs, we would like to extend a big thank you to our TPC and RTF members for volunteering their time and expertise with such dedication and enthusiasm.

Special thanks to our hosting organization this year, IMDEA Networks Institute. Particular thanks to our web chair Orlando Martinez-Durive, the publications chair Aristide Akem, and the virtual arrangements chair, Antonio Bazco Nogueras. Thanks to the PAM steering committee for their guidance in putting together the conference. Further thanks to last year's TPC chairs, Cristel Pelsser and Oliver Hohlfeld, who offered considerable guidance and learnings from last year's experience, and to Brandenburg Technical University for hosting the submission site. Finally, thank you to the researchers in the networking and measurement communities and beyond who submitted their work to PAM and engaged in the process.

March 2023

Anna Brunstrom
Marcel Flores
Marco Fiore

Organization

General Chair

Marco Fiore   IMDEA Networks Institute, Spain

Program Committee Chairs

Anna Brunstrom   Karlstad University, Sweden
Marcel Flores   Edgio, USA

PAM Steering Committee

Marinho P. Barcellos   University of Waikato, New Zealand
Fabian E. Bustamante   Northwestern University, USA
Michalis Faloutsos   University of California, USA
Anja Feldmann   Max Planck Institute for Informatics, Germany
Oliver Hohlfeld   University of Kassel, Germany
Jelena Mirkovic   University of Southern California, USA
Giovane Moura   SIDN Labs, The Netherlands
Cristel Pelsser   UCLouvain, Belgium
Steve Uhlig   Queen Mary, University of London, UK

Program Committee

Abhishta Abhishta   University of Twente, The Netherlands
Alessandro Finamore   Huawei Technologies, France
Alessio Botta   University of Napoli Federico II, Italy
Andra Lutu   Telefonica, Spain
Andrea Morichetta   Vienna University of Technology, Austria
Anja Feldmann   Max Planck Institute for Informatics, Germany
Anna Sperotto   University of Twente, The Netherlands
Arani Bhattacharya   Indraprastha Institute of Information Technology,
                                    IIIT, Delhi, India
Arash Molavi Kakhki   ThousandEyes/Cisco, USA
Carlos Ganan   ICANN, The Netherlands

Casey Deccio	Brigham Young University, USA
Cise Midoglu	Simula Metropolitan Center for Digital Engineering (SimulaMet), Norway
Daphné Tuncer	Ecole des Ponts ParisTech, France
Dimitrios Koutsonikolas	Northeastern University, USA
Esteban Carisimo	Northwestern University, USA
Fabian Bustamante	Northwestern University, USA
Faraz Ahmed	Hewlett Packard Labs, USA
Gareth Tyson	Hong Kong University of Science and Technology, China
Georgios Smaragdakis	TU Delft, The Netherlands
Giovane Moura	SIDN Labs and TU Delft, The Netherlands
Giuseppe Caso	Ericsson Research, Sweden
Ha Dao	National Institute of Informatics, NII, Japan
Haoyu Wang	Huazhong University of Science and Technology, China
Johan Mazel	ANSSI, France
Kyle Schomp	ThousandEyes/Cisco, USA
Lars Prehn	Max Planck Institute for Informatics, Germany
Maciej Korczynski	Grenoble Alpes University, France
Matt Calder	Meta/Columbia University, USA
Matteo Varvello	Nokia, USA
Matthias Wählisch	Freie Universität Berlin, Germany
Mirja Kühlewind	Ericsson Research, Germany
Morgan Vigil-Hayes	Northern Arizona University, USA
Moritz Müller	SIDN and University of Twente, The Netherlands
Muhammad Usman	Karlstad University, Sweden
Nitinder Mohan	Technical University of Munich, Germany
Olaf Maennel	Tallinn University of Technology, Estonia
Oliver Gasser	Max Planck Institute for Informatics, Germany
Oliver Hohlfeld	University of Kassel, Germany
Ozgu Alay	University of Oslo, Norway
Paul Schmitt	University of Hawaii, USA
Philippe Owezarski	LAAS-CNRS, France
Polly Huang	National Taiwan University, Taiwan
Ramin Sadre	UCLouvain, Belgium
Ricky K. P. Mok	CAIDA/UC San Diego, USA
Roland van Rijswijk-Deij	University of Twente, The Netherlands
Romain Fontugne	IIJ Research Laboratory, Japan
Sarah Wassermann	Vade, France
Shuai Hao	Old Dominion University, USA
Simone Ferlin-Reiter	Red Hat AB/Karlstad University, Sweden

Sina Keshvadi	Thompson Rivers University, Canada
Solange Rito Lima	University of Minho, Portugal
Soudeh Ghorbani	Johns Hopkins University, USA
Stephen Strowes	Fastly, USA
Suranga Seneviratne	University of Sydney, Australia
Thiago Garrett	University of Oslo, Norway
Thomas Krenc	UC San Diego/CAIDA, USA
Taejoong Chung	Virginia Tech, USA
Valerio Luconi	Istituto di Informatica e Telematica Consiglio Nazionale delle Ricerche, Italy
Vasileios Giotsas	Lancaster University, UK
Wei Sun	University of California San Diego, USA
Yuedong Xu	Fudan University, China
Zachary Bischof	Georgia Tech, USA

Local Organization Chairs

Antonio Bazco-Nogueras	IMDEA Networks Institute, Spain
Aristide Tanyi-Jong Akem	IMDEA Networks Institute, Spain
Orlando E. Martinez-Durive	IMDEA Networks Institute, Spain

Contents

VPNs and Infrastructure

Measuring the Performance of iCloud Private Relay

Martino Trevisan[1]($\boxtimes$), Idilio Drago[2], Paul Schmitt[3], and Francesco Bronzino[4]

[1] University of Trieste, Trieste, Italy
`martino.trevisan@dia.units.it`
[2] University of Turin, Turin, Italy
[3] University of Hawaii, Honolulu, USA
[4] Univ Lyon, EnsL, UCBL, CNRS, LIP, Lyon, France

Abstract. Recent developments in Internet protocols and services aim to provide enhanced security and privacy for users' traffic. Apple's iCloud Private Relay is a premier example of this trend, introducing a well-provisioned, multi-hop architecture to protect the privacy of users' traffic while minimizing the traditional drawbacks of additional network hops (e.g., latency). Announced in 2021, the service is currently in the beta stage, offering an easy and cheap privacy-enhancing alternative directly integrated into Apple's operating systems. This seamless integration makes a future massive adoption of the technology very likely, calling for studies on its impact on the Internet. Indeed, the iCloud Private Relay architecture inherently introduces computational and routing overheads, possibly hampering performance. In this work, we study the service from a performance perspective, across a variety of scenarios and locations. We show that iCloud Private Relay not only reduces speed test performance (up to 10x decrease) but also negatively affects page load time and download/upload throughput in different scenarios. Interestingly, we find that the overlay routing introduced by the service may increase performance in some cases. Our results call for further investigations into the effects of a large-scale deployment of similar multi-hop privacy-enhancing architectures. For increasing the impact of our work we contribute our software and measurements to the community.

1 Introduction

The privacy of Internet users has become one of the most discussed issues in the field of networking. New protocols and services are being developed with strong privacy guarantees, while privacy-enhancing technologies are opening opportunities for new markets. iCloud Private Relay (PR) is a new service recently created by Apple that is integrated into the company's operating systems (i.e., MacOS, iOS, iPadOS). Initially launched in 2021, it offers users the possibility of forwarding traffic via a multi-party relay [19], offering a service that in many ways resembles a VPN but differs in privacy guarantees. The architecture results in no party (neither Apple nor their infrastructure partners) holding *both* user identity and the contacted servers, whereas a VPN architecture simply shifts trust to the

© The Author(s), under exclusive license to Springer Nature Switzerland AG 2023
A. Brunstrom et al. (Eds.): PAM 2023, LNCS 13882, pp. 3–17, 2023.
https://doi.org/10.1007/978-3-031-28486-1_1

VPN which has access to both. The seamless integration of the service in the Apple OSes, its low cost ($0.99 per month for the cheapest plan) and its low entry barrier suggest that a large adoption of the service is very likely, with an anticipated major impact on Internet traffic [16] moving forward.

iCloud Private Relay works with a multi-party relay architecture: The client operating system connects to an ingress proxy (operated by Apple) using an encrypted connection over QUIC [4]. The ingress proxy routes the client traffic to an egress proxy (currently operated by one of Akamai, Cloudfare, and Fastly) that forwards the traffic to the destination server requested by the user. With this architecture, the ingress and egress proxies can only see the client's or the server's IP address, respectively, but never both. Equally, eavesdroppers (e.g., ISPs) can observe the traffic of multiple users to/from ingress and egress proxies and thus cannot easily profile individual users' activity from the traffic [26].

The possibility of a major adoption of the service in the short term raises questions about its impact on the internet. Similar privacy protection mechanisms, such as VPNs, onion routing [24] and Tor [10] have been studied in terms of both performance and privacy [2,13]. For example, the authors of [6] uncover the websites a user is visiting when connected via Tor by relying on side channels such as packet sizes and timing. Similarly, multiple authors [2,15] have studied the impact of privacy-enhancing technologies on Internet performance. For PR, however, we are aware of a single study focusing on the service [16], which focused on describing the system architecture and its deployment footprint, neglecting implications on performance and user-perceived quality of experience.

In this work, we focus on the impact of iCloud Private Relay on web performance. We set up active experiments using Apple devices and design multiple workloads to assess the effects of PR on different scenarios. We deploy our testbed across multiple locations and gather several metrics associated with users' Quality of Experience (QoE), such as page load time, throughput, and latency. Apple notes [3] that iCloud Private Relay can negatively affect web speed tests as such tests routinely use "several simultaneous connections to deliver the highest possible result", but goes on to claim that "actual browsing experience remains fast." Therefore we design our experiments to assess these claims, including speed tests and web browsing with and without PR in place.

Our results show that iCloud Private Relay does impact performance. We confirm a significant reduction in the throughput measured with speed tests, e.g., with up to 10-fold slower download throughput when using PR. We notice a performance penalty in web browsing too, observing a 60% increase in page load time in some cases. Performance impairments also occur in cases where a single connection is used to download a large file, thus questioning the claim that several simultaneous connections are the root cause of performance penalties. Interestingly, the selection of the egress proxy operator appears to have crucial implications on performance. We also observe that client traffic over PR outperforms traffic over an unmodified connection in some cases, suggesting that the system's overlay routing can result in more optimal paths.

Overall, our study is a first step towards understanding the impact of large-scale, well-provisioned, privacy-enhancing services such as iCloud Private Relay

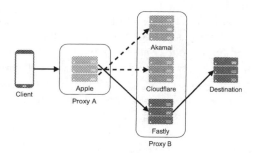

Fig. 1. Overview of the iCloud Private Relay architecture. Client traffic passes through two proxies: i) Proxy A operated by Apple; and ii) Proxy B operated by one of Akamai, Cloudflare, or Fastly.

on Internet performance. To increase the impact of our study and allow for reproducible comparisons, we release our measurements and source codes [1].

2 Background and Related Work

2.1 iCloud Private Relay Architecture

Apple launched the PR service during its Apple Worldwide Developers Conference (WWDC) in 2021 [4]. The service employs a multi-hop proxy architecture, also known as a Multi-Party Relay (MPR) [19]. The architecture provides privacy benefits by decoupling the users' network identity (i.e., the client IP address) from their Internet usage (i.e., the destination servers). This is accomplished by the client setting up two nested tunnels: the first to an ingress proxy (Proxy A in Fig. 1), operated by Apple, which provides authentication and localization; the second to egress proxy (Proxy B in Fig. 1) operated by one of Apple's infrastructure partners (currently including Akamai, Cloudflare, and Fastly), which in turn connects to the destination server(s) on the client's behalf. Proxy A only has visibility into the client's IP address and cannot inspect the encrypted and tunneled web traffic. Proxy B knows the servers that the clients connect to, but cannot see the client's IP address. Likewise, the destination server does not see the client IP addresses as connections are initiated by Proxy B. PR is currently limited to Apple-specific applications (i.e., Safari).

The PR architecture relies on well-known web protocols rather than custom protocols. The connection to Proxy A uses QUIC by default, with a fallback to HTTP/2 and TLS if the QUIC connection fails or is blocked. The connection to Proxy B defaults to HTTP/3 and MASQUE [17,18], which allows building efficient QUIC connections over a QUIC proxy. If HTTP/3 is not supported, the connection to Proxy B falls back to the classical HTTP CONNECT over TLS.

The PR does not act as a classical VPN and handles the traffic coming uniquely from the Safari web browser. Only HTTP(S) browser traffic goes through the PR, while we notice that, in the case of audio/video calls, WebRTC traffic (RTP, DTLS, and STUN/TURN protocols) is not captured by the PR. The traffic of other applications in the system uses classical routing too, including other browsers and mail clients. Interestingly, the `curl` command-line facility uses PR, but only for clear-text HTTP traffic. The fact that only some applications support PR is a problem, since PR may give users a false sense of privacy while routing only a share of their traffic to the PR tunnel.

Moreover, the usage of such an architecture will impact the efficacy of existing Internet services. For instance, services that rely on client IP address information for localizing content (i.e., IP geolocation) no longer have access to clients' actual IP addresses. Other services that require insight into user traffic, such as middleboxes that provide content filtering (e.g., corporate networks or parental control services) will be unable to access user content. Lastly, the additional hops introduced by the service may hamper performance, as we investigate in this paper.

2.2   Related Work

Onion routing [24] and Tor [10] are perhaps the most similar systems compared with PR in terms of privacy goals for Internet traffic. These systems enhance users' privacy by obfuscating sender and receiver endpoints using ad-hoc "circuits" to transit user traffic. iCloud Private Relay differs in that it utilizes fewer relay hops (Tor's default is three, PR uses two), and the relays are operated on well-provisioned commercial infrastructure rather than on volunteers' systems. PR also differs from Tor in that it uses the standard HTTP and QUIC protocols rather than a custom protocol, arguably making PR more difficult to block and/or censor.

Several works have studied these privacy-enhancing services, investigating possible attacks against users' privacy. Different website fingerprinting techniques, for example, have been tested against the Tor network in [6,22,27]. In terms of performance, some studies [2,15] benchmark popular VPN services as well as Tor, finding major impairments in some scenarios. We share a similar goal with these related efforts, focusing on iCloud Private Relay.

A single work studied specifically PR [16]. The authors analyzed the network infrastructure that iCloud Private Relay has been deployed on and highlighted the geographic footprint of the service. In contrast, we study PR from the Internet performance point of view, shedding light on possible impairments users face when using the service. Indeed, our work focuses on performing an empirical evaluation of the impact on performance caused by the PR architecture, differently from [16] which focuses on the study of PR's architecture, uncovering its ingress and egress points location (geographically and network wise).

3   Testbed and Dataset

We design three measurement campaigns aiming at quantifying iCloud Private Relay performance from different perspectives. Our experiments have been performed from three locations using three identical Apple MacBook Pro laptops running macOS Monterey. We deployed the laptops at three University networks, connecting them to the Internet through Gbit/s Ethernet links. Two laptops are deployed in large European cities, Lyon in France and Trieste in Italy. The third laptop is deployed in Hawaii (USA). Note that, although our study does uncover some of the potential impacts that PR has on network performance, our locations cannot be considered representative of the entire internet. Instrumenting more locations for extending our findings, e.g., by hosting probes in distributed cloud infrastructure, is left for future work.

We fully automate the experiments through custom-made testbed scripts. Common to all measurement campaigns is a script in the *AppleScript* format that automates the activation and deactivation of the Private Relay functionality of the laptop. All these scripts are contributed to the community to allow others to extend and validate our findings. We set up PR with the default option that preserves user location as much as possible.

Ethical Considerations. During our measurements, we took care to avoid harming the crawled web services. Considering that the targets of our analysis were some of the most popular websites and CDNs in Western countries, our belief is not to have caused an overload on the servers or any undesirable side effects.

3.1 Throughput Measurements

Active throughput measurements are a common tool to measure the speed of the slowest segment (the bottleneck) between a test device and a server deployed in the network. Modern speed tests commonly aim to deploy their servers in a region close to end-users, under the assumption that the bottleneck will be located at the access network. While these tests are not always representative of the user's experience [25], they can spot the performance impact caused by i) traversing additional middleboxes, i.e., iCloud PR's proxies, and ii) taking a different path between the user and the test infrastructure of the speed test service.

We perform active throughput measurements using Ookla's Speed Test service [14], one of the *de facto* standards for Internet speed test measurements. We instrument our machines to automatically perform speed tests by accessing Ookla's web page. Doing so requires i) accessing the web page; ii) detecting Ookla's privacy banner and accepting it (in Europe, not in the US); and iii) starting the test by clicking on the "GO" button. We automate this process using Selenium [20] tools and instrumenting the Safari browser. We run 200 speed tests from each location, half with PR enabled and half without PR.

3.2 Bulk Downloads

Architecturally, PR achieves privacy by decoupling information on users and the services they access. When iCloud Private Relay is enabled, all Safari traffic goes through the system by default. This has implications not only for web browsing but also for downloads of large files – i.e., performing bulk downloads of data through HTTP. We measure PR performance on bulk downloads using the `curl` command-line tool. When Private Relay is enabled, `curl` traffic uses it, allowing us to easily test HTTP downloads in isolation. We use `curl` to download a 1 GB file several times. We select a 1 GB test file made available on the Hetzner CDN, a standard file used for evaluating content distribution speeds [11]. From each location, we download the test file 200 times with and without Private Relay and record the download time.

3.3   Web Measurements

iCloud Private Relay is mainly designed to allow web browsing with stronger privacy guarantees. Our goal is ultimately to study to what extent Private Relay impacts the user's perceived performance and, in turn, its implications for web QoE. To this end, we instrument Safari to visit a set of web pages automatically and collect statistics regarding page loading. We target the 100 most popular websites in each country according to the public ranking provided by SimilarWeb analytics [21].

We use the BrowserTime toolset to automate the visits to the websites and the collection of the statistics [23]. For each website, we run five visits with and without PR enabled. Out of each visit, we collect statistics about each HTTP transaction carried out during the page loading. Essential to our analysis, we collect the Page Load Time (also called `onLoad` time) that we use as a practical proxy for measuring the web performance. Page Load Time represents the time elapsed between the beginning of the visit and the instant when the last object of the web page is retrieved. The Page Load Time has previously been shown to be correlated with users' QoE [9].

Finally, note that in our experimental campaign, we do not measure explicitly the end-to-end RTT. Indeed, our measurement infrastructure cannot observe the layer-4 RTT, as we rely on browser instrumentation. Measuring the RTT poses some challenges in the case of tunneled traffic (such as PR), e.g., one could instrument the SO kernel to monitor TCP statistics. This is by no means trivial, in particular considering the proprietary software offering PR. We thus focus on user-perceived quality, showing higher-level metrics such as Page Load Time or Throughput, leaving these additional aspects for future work.

4   Results

We now present results across the three workloads. We observe that, in general, PR negatively impacts performance, particularly for scenarios that require long-lasting network flows, i.e., bulk download and speed test measurements. Further, in these experiments, PR usage results in a higher level of variability in performance, even for stable and fast Ethernet network connections. Interestingly, these takeaways do not apply across all results: in one case, i.e., bulk download in France, we observe that PR outperforms an unmodified connection.

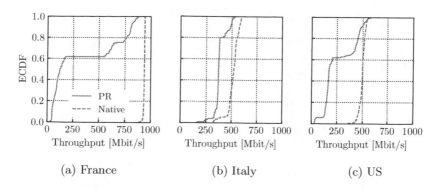

Fig. 2. Download throughput measured with speed test measurements.

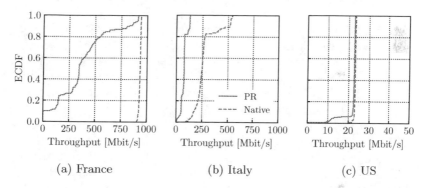

Fig. 3. Upload throughput measured with speed test measurements. Note the different x-scale for the US.

4.1 Throughput

We first evaluate the performance impact of PR on active throughput measurements using Ookla's infrastructure. Overall, we expect performance to be, at the very least, impacted by the overhead of the PR tunnels, as disclaimed on Apple's support website [3]. Here, we look to quantify this overhead, shedding light on the incurred performance penalties.

Figures 2 and 3 show the Empirical Cumulative Distribution Function (ECDF) for the downstream and upstream throughput with and without PR, respectively. Overall, we observe that performance is drastically impacted across the vast majority of scenarios, both for downstream and upstream throughput. This impact is particularly significant for our France measurement location (Figs. 2a and 3a), where measurements experience a median speed reduction of 87% and 63% respectively. The sole scenario that does not present an evident reduction in performance is the uplink throughput in our US measurement location, where performance is capped at around 23 Mbit/s for both experiments. This suggests that the bottleneck, in this case, is most likely to be found in the

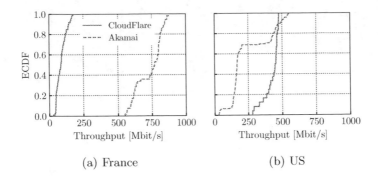

(a) France   (b) US

Fig. 4. Download throughput with PR and different Proxy B operators.

path between the client and Proxy A. In sum, PR seemingly does not impact performance when the client-side connections are the bottleneck.

Interestingly, we observe that speed tests performed when PR is enabled result in a much higher performance variability. For example, we observe that in multiple configurations, in particular for downstream experiments in France and the US (Fig. 2a and 2c, respectively), experiments result in bimodal speed distributions, possibly caused by either ephemerally congested paths or congested proxies that negatively impact performance in a subset of experiments.

We investigate this aspect further in Fig. 4, where we dissect throughput distribution according to Proxy B selected as the egress node by PR. Sattler et al. [16] found that Proxy B selection changes multiple times in a day. For France, we observe that all speed tests achieving throughput below 200 Mbit/s are those using a Cloudflare-owned Proxy B, while the faster ones are all using Akamai's Proxy B. In the US, we observe the opposite scenario, with CloudFlare Proxy B leading to better performance compared with Akamai, even if the two distributions partially overlap. We do not report the figure for Italy as all experiments for this case resulted in an Akamai Proxy B egress, leading to the performance shown in Fig. 2. We also observe that when PR is in place, the Ookla's measurement server is often further from the user than without PR for both Italy and France. With native connection, the speed test is served from a server within 120 km, while, with PR, the server is 200–300 km far away. We detail this in the Appendix. In a nutshell, the choice of egress node has paramount implications on the achieved throughput, and this choice is not under the user's control.

Overall, these results appear to confirm Apple's disclaimer that PR can negatively impact speed test performance. Apple justifies this performance loss to the normal behavior of speed test experiments. In particular, they state that "Private Relay uses a single, secure connection to maintain privacy and performance. This design may impact how throughput is reflected in network speed tests that typically open several simultaneous connections to deliver the highest possible result." To verify whether the performance loss experienced can be solely linked to the use of multiple connections, in the next section, we replicate

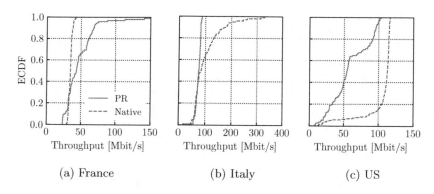

Fig. 5. Average download speed during downloads of a large file.

the performance comparison in a scenario where only a single connection is used, i.e., the single file bulk download over HTTP.

4.2 Bulk Download

We now compare the performance achieved with and without PR downloading a large 1 GB file from a CDN. Figure 5 shows the obtained results for our three locations. We observe that, although to a different extent, the US and Italy locations still experience a similar negative performance impact when downloading the file via PR, even when using a single network flow.

For the US case, we see that PR reduces performance by 53% in the median case. For the Italian case, we notice that median throughput is usually similar with and without PR, except for the tail of the distributions. In particular, in this case, PR performance is very stable, never exceeding around 80 Mbit/s. In contrast, similar tests without PR can exceed 300 Mbit/s. We conjecture that, for the Italian location, the traffic traversing PR takes a path where traffic cannot exceed 80 Mbit/s. This can be due to congestion or route peering arrangements, even if we cannot precisely pinpoint the root causes for these differences.

Most interestingly, we observe that for our experiments in France, results show very similar behavior, but with inverse outcomes, i.e., PR downloads experience *higher* throughput while non-PR traffic is capped at around 35 Mbit/s. We investigate this behavior further using traceroute and we observe that the selected CDN node changes when connected to PR and, consequently, packets follow different routes. More precisely, we observe that, when PR is not enabled, packets traverse an operator (GEANT) that is otherwise not observed when using PR. This suggests that, when not using PR, packets encounter a bottle-necked link, which is at the root of the impaired performance. Effectively, the presence of PR-induced overlay routing overrides default routes taken by client traffic in the French location. These results call for further investigation of the routing of traffic when PR is enabled, which we leave for future work.

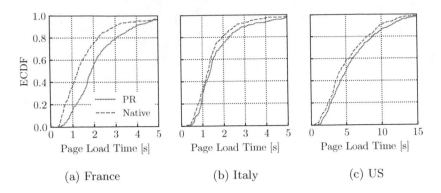

Fig. 6. Page Load Time distribution.

4.3   Web Browsing

Lastly, we study the performance impact that the use of PR has on web browsing. To this end, we measure the Page Load Time for the top-100 ranked websites in each of the three test locations. According to Apple's claim, web experience should remain "fast" even with PR active, while our results suggest that performance varies. Figure 6 shows the distribution of Page Load Time for the three locations, with and without PR active.

At a first glance, we observe that PR consistently introduces an additional delay to page loading regardless of the location. The performance impact is particularly evident in France, where the median Page Load Time increases by almost 60%. For the other locations, we observe a more moderate increase of 7% and 17% for Italy and the US, respectively. Interestingly, our measurements show that TLS handshake time increases by 9–14% when using PR, depending on the location. This increase likely impacts the page-loading process negatively, but only partially explains the performance degradation with PR.

Overall, while web performance is not as heavily impacted as throughput measurements, the claim that the architecture of PR exclusively impacts speed tests might be reductive. More detailed experiments might be required to shed light on the root causes of the additional page load times. We speculate that these results are caused by the additional overhead caused by the traversal of multiple middleboxes and the necessarily longer path packets must travel. Network latency is known to impact web QoE directly [8,12], and even a small deterioration in page load time has a large impact on the web ecosystem [7].

5   Discussion and Open Questions

We now elaborate on the limitations of our findings and possibilities for future work. In general, answering the questions listed below requires further measurements from different locations. While our measurements include several campaigns, they cannot be considered representative of the whole Internet. Indeed, we will extend our measurements in future work by deploying new probes i) in other locations – e.g., by leveraging cloud infrastructure in more countries, and ii) in heterogeneous scenarios – e.g., by deploying probes in wireless and cellular networks. Ultimately, we contribute our scripts to the community to allow others to validate and extend our results in autonomy, considering novel scenarios.

5.1 Overriding Routing

In Sect. 4.2, our results illustrate how the use of PR can lead to better performance compared to native connectivity in particular cases. We find that overlay routing appears to result in the avoidance of a congested network when using PR in one particular case. This result demonstrates one of the potential impacts that Multi-Party Relay architectures can have on network performance: The chosen traffic paths are dictated by the combination of the user's ISP, Apple, and Apple's infrastructure partners for Proxies B, rather than simply the user's ISP and the destination server. In effect, at the ISP, packet routing mechanisms with PR will significantly diverge from existing patterns. Where, today, ISPs observe a fan-out pattern, routing client traffic to the many destination networks on the Internet, networks with high usage of PR in the future will see a many-to-one pattern, with all client traffic routing to a single destination network (Apple or whoever is operating the ingress proxy of a multi-party relay).

Indeed, our initial experience while running measurements in mobile networks in France and Italy shows that performance metrics (with and without PR) are more susceptible to variations throughout the day. Additional factors, such as the cellular network load during the day, make the study of PR on mobile networks largely more complex. Longitudinal measurements in such environments are needed to draw robust conclusions and we will pursue that in future work.

5.2 Localization

iCloud Private Relay is designed to prevent destination servers from observing client IP addresses. Clearly, this design negatively impacts the ability of IP geolocation services to map clients to their geographical location. These services are widely used by content providers to localize users and determine access rules based on geographical constraints. The PR architecture aims to minimize this issue by roughly localizing the client using Proxy A, and carefully selecting the Proxy B egress based on the location that the client is purported to be. This would preserve, at least roughly, the geographic location of the user from the server's point of view. To support IP geolocation services in mapping the users' geographical location, Apple publishes Proxy B IP addresses along with the location of the users aggregated through them [5].

In many cases, low-fidelity location information is sufficient to provide localized content. Unfortunately, some services require very accurate location information to serve content (e.g., live streaming of sporting events), which may not be possible using services such as PR. Further study is required to study the tradeoff between privacy and usability in terms of localization. Additionally, previous work [16] has shown that the IP-to-location mappings offered by Apple's partners are not always a direct representation of the physical location of the proxy holding the given IP. This is done to overcome the lack of PR proxies in certain regions of the world. This could impact performance for users who connect to the PR infrastructure from locations that are not physically served by it. The network paths would be extended beyond their geographical location, adding latency to communications and crossing national borders.

5.3   Cost

While the PR design seems beneficial for privacy, the real benefits have been left unquantified and largely unexplored. Future work is necessary to understand the benefits offered by such as system. This is particularly true considering the inherent tradeoffs that Multi-Party Relay architectures have on network traffic and the capability required to process it: In PR, clients' traffic passes through multiple middleboxes in order to achieve the privacy guarantees associated with decoupling network identity from behavior. This has implications on performance, at the center of this paper, as well as on energy consumption (e.g., due to the additional servers and the multiple layers of encryption they have to handle). For example, by nesting encrypted channels as the PR architecture does, Proxy A could be wasting significant computing resources "double encrypting" traffic. To avoid this overhead, QUIC-Aware Proxying Using HTTP has been proposed, where Proxy A simply moves the traffic along the path towards Proxy B without double encryption [17,18]. Other similar optimizations are likely to be introduced as the architecture becomes more mature and more widely adopted.

6   Conclusions

Apple's iCloud Private Relay is one of the recent attempts at deploying Multi-Party Relay architectures at scale. Given Apple devices' pervasiveness and the company's push towards privacy, it is possible that this architecture will be quickly adopted as the *de facto* standard for privacy-oriented network architectures. In this work, we present a first study of the impacts that PR architecture can have on users' performance. Through experiments across three locations in France, Italy, and the US, we find that PR not only impacts active throughput measurements but also negatively affects page load time and file download, indicating potential impacts on the users' web QoE. We show for example that PR substantially changes the paths taken by traffic (e.g., during speed tests), impacting performance. Our paper sheds light on new problems and calls for further research on how to avoid them when deploying privacy-preserving services.

This work opens up a number of potential future venues to explore Multi-Party Relay architectures such iCloud Private Relay, not solely in terms of performance, but also across multiple dimensions such as privacy-costs tradeoffs, content access, and the impact on network routing at large. To engage the community to search for the answer to these questions, we release the source code of the software used to perform the experiments presented in this paper.

Appendix

In this Appendix, we break down the distance between the user and Ookla's speed test measurement servers, with and without PR. In the following two tables, we show the measurement server chosen by Ookla, detailing its location and distance from the testing location. We report data for the Italian and French locations and separate the cases with and without PR. We omit the US location as, in all cases, the measurement server is located at the same location, i.e., Hawaii.

When PR is in place, it is more likely that the speed test server is far away from the client. For example, for the Italian location, without PR, speed tests are served within 120 km, while with PR, servers are at 200 km or more from the client.

Ookla obviously cannot identify the true location of the users, since its servers observe only egress IP addresses. Indeed, hiding the users' IP addresses is the ultimate goal of PR and, as such, these differences are expected. We here show that the servers selected by Ookla when PR is enabled deliver poorer throughput figures, and our conjecture is that the root causes for such performance penalties are in the path from clients to the selected servers.

The same situation may occur with other services relying on IP geolocation, such as content providers and CDNs. Our measurements, while preliminary, show that the introduction of the PR tunnels impact performance (see our discussion on future work in Sect. 5) (Table 1).

Table 1. Share of Speed Tests served from servers in different locations. The distance from the client is reported in brackets.

	Ljubljana (70 km)	Venice (120 km)	Conegliano (120 km)	Milan (200 km)	Rome (400 km)
Native	12.7%	81.8%	5.5%	0.0%	0.0%
PR	0.0%	0.0%	0.0%	98.9%	1.1%

(a) Italy

	Lyon (0 km)	Marseille (270 km)	Nice (300 km)
Native	100.0%	0.0%	0.0%
PR	0.0%	85.2%	14.8%

(b) France

References

1. https://github.com/marty90/icloud-private-relay-experiments
2. Alsabah, M., Goldberg, I.: Performance and security improvements for tor: a survey. ACM Comput. Surv. **49**(2), 1–36 (2016)
3. Apple. About iCloud Private Relay, December 2021. https://support.apple.com/en-us/HT212614
4. Apple. iCloud Private Relay Overview, December 2021. http://www.apple.com/privacy/docs/iCloud_Private_Relay_Overview_Dec2021.PDF
5. Apple. Prepare Your Network or Web Server for iCloud Private Relay. https://developer.apple.com/support/prepare-your-network-for-icloud-private-relay/, December 2021
6. Arp, D., Yamaguchi, F., Rieck, K.: Torben: a practical side-channel attack for deanonymizing tor communication. In: Proceedings of the ASIA CCS, pp. 597–602 (2015)
7. Fast Company. How one second could cost amazon $1.6 billion in sales, December 2021. https://www.fastcompany.com/1825005/how-one-second-could-cost-amazon-16-billion-sales
8. Cui, H., Biersack, E.: On the relationship between QOS and QOE for web sessions. EURECOM, Sophia Antipolis, France, Technical report, RR-12-263 (2012)
9. da Hora, D.N., Asrese, A.S., Christophides, V., Teixeira, R., Rossi, D.: Narrowing the gap between QoS metrics and web QoE using above-the-fold metrics. In: Beverly, R., Smaragdakis, G., Feldmann, A. (eds.) PAM 2018. LNCS, vol. 10771, pp. 31–43. Springer, Cham (2018). https://doi.org/10.1007/978-3-319-76481-8_3
10. Dingledine, R., Mathewson, N., Syverson, P.: Tor: the second-generation onion router. In: Usenix Security Symposium (2004)
11. Hetzner. Test-files, December 2021. https://speed.hetzner.de
12. Mandalari, A.M., et al.: Measuring roaming in Europe: infrastructure and implications on users' QOE. IEEE Trans. Mob. Comput. **21**(10), 3687–3699 (2021)
13. Mani, A., Wilson-Brown, T., Jansen, R., Johnson, A., Sherr, M.: Understanding tor usage with privacy-preserving measurement. In: Proceedings of the Internet Measurement Conference 2018, IMC 2018, New York, NY, USA, pp. 175–187 (2018). Association for Computing Machinery
14. Ookla. Speedtest, December 2021. https://speedtest.net
15. Pudelko, M., Emmerich, P., Gallenmüller, S., Carle, G.: Performance analysis of VPN gateways. In: 2020 IFIP Networking Conference (Networking), pp. 325–333 (2020)
16. Sattler, P., Aulbach, J., Zirngibl, J., Carle, G.: Towards a tectonic traffic shift? Investigating Apple's new relay network. In: Proceedings of the 22nd ACM Internet Measurement Conference, IMC 2022 (2022)
17. Schinazi, D.: Proxying UDP in HTTP. RFC 9298, August 2022
18. Schinazi, D., Pardue, L.: HTTP Datagrams and the Capsule Protocol. RFC 9297, August 2022
19. Schmitt, P., Iyengar, J., Wood, C., Raghavan, B.: The decoupling principle: a practical privacy framework. In: ACM SIGCOMM Workshop on Hot Topics in Networking (HotNets), November 2022
20. Selenium: Selenium automates browsers. that's it!, December 2021 https://www.selenium.dev
21. SimilarWeb. Effortlessly analyze your competitive landscape, December 2021. https://www.similarweb.com/

22. Sirinam, P., Imani, M., Juarez, M., Wright, M.: Deep fingerprinting: undermining website fingerprinting defenses with deep learning. In: Proceedings of the CCS, pp. 1928–1943 (2018)
23. sitespeed.io. Documentation v16. https://www.sitespeed.io/documentation/browsertime/, December 2021
24. Syverson, P.F., Goldschlag, D.M., Reed, M.G.: Anonymous connections and onion routing. In: Proceedings. 1997 IEEE Symposium on Security and Privacy (Cat. No. 97CB36097), pp. 44–54. IEEE (1997)
25. Trevisan, M., Drago, I., Mellia, M.: Impact of access speed on adaptive video streaming quality: a passive perspective. In: Proceedings of the 2016 Workshop on QoE-Based Analysis and Management of Data Communication Networks, Internet-QoE 2016, New York, NY, USA, pp. 7–12 (2016)
26. Trevisan, M., Soro, F., Mellia, M., Drago, I., Morla, R.: Does domain name encryption increase users' privacy? SIGCOMM Comput. Commun. Rev. **50**(3), 16–22 (2020)
27. Wang, T., Cai, X., Nithyanand, R., Johnson, R., Goldberg, I.: Effective Attacks and provable defenses for website fingerprinting. In: Proceedings of the USENIX Security, pp. 143–157 (2014)

Characterizing the VPN Ecosystem in the Wild

Aniss Maghsoudlou[1]([✉]), Lukas Vermeulen[1], Ingmar Poese[2], and Oliver Gasser[1]

[1] Max Planck Institute for Informatics, Saarbrücken, Germany
{aniss,lvermeul,oliver.gasser}@mpi-inf.mpg.de
[2] BENOCS, Berlin, Germany
ipoese@benocs.com

Abstract. With the increase of remote working during and after the COVID-19 pandemic, the use of Virtual Private Networks (VPNs) around the world has nearly doubled. Therefore, measuring the traffic and security aspects of the VPN ecosystem is more important now than ever. VPN users rely on the security of VPN solutions, to protect private and corporate communication. Thus a good understanding of the security state of VPN servers is crucial. Moreover, properly detecting and characterizing VPN traffic remains challenging, since some VPN protocols use the same port number as web traffic and port-based traffic classification will not help.

In this paper, we aim at detecting and characterizing VPN servers in the wild, which facilitates detecting the VPN traffic. To this end, we perform Internet-wide active measurements to find VPN servers in the wild, and analyze their cryptographic certificates, vulnerabilities, locations, and fingerprints. We find 9.8M VPN servers distributed around the world using OpenVPN, SSTP, PPTP, and IPsec, and analyze their vulnerability. We find SSTP to be the most vulnerable protocol with more than 90% of detected servers being vulnerable to TLS downgrade attacks. Out of all the servers that respond to our VPN probes, 2% also respond to HTTP probes and therefore are classified as Web servers. Finally, we use our list of VPN servers to identify VPN traffic in a large European ISP and observe that 2.6% of all traffic is related to these VPN servers.

1 Introduction

Virtual Private Networks (VPNs) provide secure communication mechanisms, including encryption and tunneling, enabling users to circumvent censorship, to access geo-blocked services, or to securely access an organization's resources remotely.

The COVID-19 pandemic changed Internet traffic dramatically. Studies investigating the impact of the COVID-19 pandemic on Internet traffic show that streaming traffic being tripled around the world due to remote work, remote learning, and entertainment services [11,27,31]. VPN traffic has been no exception to this major traffic shift. After the COVID-19 pandemic, the VPN traffic observed in a large European IXP nearly doubled [18]. In a campus network,

A. Brunstrom et al. (Eds.): PAM 2023, LNCS 13882, pp. 18–45, 2023.
https://doi.org/10.1007/978-3-031-28486-1_2

even a more dramatic increase of 20x has been reported [27], which shows a prominent growth of remote work and e-learning. Additionally, several articles find that remote work is here to stay [21,48]. According to recent statistics from SurfShark [44], 31% of all Internet users use VPNs.

In order to facilitate network planning and traffic engineering, Internet Service Providers (ISPs) have an interest in understanding the network applications being used by their clients, and how these applications behave in terms of traffic patterns and volume. Therefore, detecting and characterizing VPN traffic is an important task for ISPs. Certain VPN protocols use known port numbers for their operation, e.g. port number 4500 is used for IPsec, and port number 1723 is used for SSTP. Thus, the traffic using protocols over the known port numbers can easily be detected as VPN traffic. However, some VPN protocols, e.g. SSTP, and in some occasions, OpenVPN use port number 443 which is commonly used for secure web applications. This makes it challenging to distinguish between web and VPN traffic.

Moreover, VPN users might share sensitive private or corporate data over VPN connections. As the number of cyber attacks has almost doubled after the pandemic [9], it makes Internet users even more aware of their privacy and the security of their VPN connections. Therefore, investigating the vulnerabilities of the VPN protocols helps to highlight existing shortcomings in VPN security.

Previous studies focused on detecting VPN traffic using machine learning [15,39], or DNS-based approaches [2,18]. Some studies have also analyzed the commercial VPN ecosystem [29,47]. However, to the best of our knowledge, this is the first work which conducts active measurements to detect and characterize VPN servers in the wild.

In this paper, we aim to detect, characterize, and analyze the deployment of VPN servers in the Internet using active measurements along with passive VPN traffic analysis. Specifically, this work makes the following main contributions:

- **VPN server deployment:** We perform active measurements to the complete IPv4 address space and an IPv6 hitlist for 4 different VPN protocols both in UDP and TCP. We find around 9.8 million IPv4 addresses and 2.2 thousand IPv6 addresses responsive to our probes.
- **VPN security evaluation:** We analyze the detected IP addresses in terms of TLS vulnerabilities, certificates, and geolocation. We observe that the United States is the most common location among our detected IP addresses. We also find that more than 90% of SSTP servers are vulnerable to a TLS attack and nearly 7% of the certificates are expired.
- **VPN traffic analysis:** We analyze passive traffic traces from a large European ISP, we find that 2.6% of the traffic uses our list of VPN servers as either source or destination address. Moreover, we use rDNS data along with DNS records from a large European ISP to compare our results with previous work looking into VPN classification [18]. We find that using our methodology, we find 4 times more VPN servers in the wild.
- **VPN probing tool:** We develop new modules for ZGrab2 [52] to send customized VPN probes. We make these modules publicly available [56] to foster further research in the VPN ecosystem.

2   Background

VPNs establish cryptographically secured tunnels between different networks and can be used to connect private networks over the public network. Thus, a proper VPN connection should be encrypted in order to prevent eavesdropping and tampering of VPN traffic. The tunneling mechanism of a VPN connection also provides privacy since the traffic is encapsulated. Therefore, users remotely accessing a private network appear to be directly connected.

While the exact tunneling process varies depending on the underlying VPN protocol, it is quite common to categorize VPNs in two different groups:

– **Site-to-site VPNs**: In this configuration, a VPN is used to connect two or more networks of geographically distinct sites. This is common for companies with branches in different locations.
– **Remote access VPNs**: This kind of VPN connection is mainly used by individual end-users in order to connect to a private network.

2.1   VPN Usage

The usage of VPNs has evolved over the past three decades. David Crawshaw [13] gives a very comprehensive overview of how and why VPNs changed over the years. While in the earlier days of the Internet, they were primarily used by companies to connect their geographically distinct offices, VPNs nowadays provide a variety of use cases for individuals as well and are used by millions of end-users around the globe. Use cases include:

– **Privacy preservation**: The encrypted VPN tunnels provide end-users the means to preserve their privacy.
– **Censorship circumvention/accessing geo-blocked content**: Specific services might be censored in some countries or geographically restricted. By connecting to a VPN server in a different country, it is still possible to access such content since it would now appear as if the user was located in a different country.
– **Remote access**: It is common to use VPNs to remotely access restricted resources or to connect with an organization's network. This usage scenario has gained importance especially during the COVID-19 pandemic among employees and students alike due to remote working.

Different usage patterns, the general understanding of the functionality of VPNs, and awareness of potential risks vary between different demographic groups. Dutkowska-Zuk et al. [17] studied how and why people from different demographic backgrounds use VPN software primarily comparing the general population with students. They found that the general population is more likely to rely on free, commercial VPN solutions to protect their privacy. Students, on the other hand, rather resort to VPN software for remote access or to circumvent censorship and access geographically blocked services with an increased use of institutional VPNs. Generally, they found that, while most VPN users are concerned about their privacy, they are less concerned about data collection by VPN companies.

Especially during the COVID-19 pandemic, VPNs increasingly gained significance. The pandemic and the resulting lockdowns caused many employees and students to work and study remotely from home. Feldmann et al. [18] analyzed the effect of the lockdowns on the Internet traffic. Their work included the analysis of how VPN traffic shifted during the pandemic. They detected a traffic increase of over 200% for VPN servers identified based on their domain with increased traffic even after the first lockdowns. These findings highlight the rising significance of VPNs. With progressing digitalization, VPN traffic can be expected to increase even further.

2.2   VPN Protocols

We want to cover as many protocols as possible including some of the most prominent ones like OpenVPN and IPsec. The functionality of a VPN connection establishment varies depending on the underlying VPN protocol. Table 1 gives an overview of all the VPN protocols we consider with general information on their underlying protocols. Among them, especially PPTP, which was the first actual VPN protocol standardized in 1999 (see RFC 2637 [22]), can be considered rather outdated and it is not recommended to be used anymore [13,38].

WireGuard is the most modern protocol at the moment. It is much more simplistic than, e.g., OpenVPN or IPsec and incorporates state-of-the-art cryptographic principles.

Table 1. Overview of VPN protocols showing the transport protocol, port, (D)TLS encryption, and possible detection.

VPN protocol	Transport protocol	Port	(D)TLS-based	Server detection possible
IPsec/L2TP	UDP	500	✗	✓
OpenVPN	UDP & TCP	1194, 443	✓	Partially
SSTP	TCP	443	✓	✓
PPTP	TCP	1723	✗	✓
AnyConnect	UDP & TCP	443	✓	✗
WireGuard	UDP	51820	✗	✗

3   Methodology

In this section, we introduce our methodology for our passive and active measurements. We perform Internet-wide measurements in order to detect VPN servers in the wild and create hit lists of identified VPN servers. Based on those results, we conduct follow-up measurements to fingerprint the VPN servers and further analyze them in terms of security. Finally, we look for the detected IP addresses in the traffic from a large European ISP to find out the amount of VPN traffic.

3.1 VPN Server Detection

Our measurements to detect VPN servers include the whole IPv4 address range as well as over 530 million non-aliased IPv6 addresses from the *IPv6 Hitlist Service* [20,58]. We send out the connection initiation requests that are used in the connection establishments of the different VPN protocols. For UDP-based protocols, we use ZMap [53] (ZMapv6 for IPv6 [12]), a transport-layer network scanner, to directly send out UDP probes. If the VPN protocol is TCP-based, we first use ZMap to find targets with the respective open TCP ports using TCP SYN-scans. We then use ZGrab2 [52] to send out the actual VPN requests. ZGrab2 works on the application layer. It can be used complementary to ZMap for more involved scans. It also allows us to implement custom modules needed for our VPN requests over TCP and TLS.

We identify an address as a VPN server based on the responses we receive to our initiation requests. If the parsed response satisfies the format of the expected VPN response, the target is classified as a VPN server. To completely detect the VPN ecosystem for a specific server, we might have to take several server configurations into account and perform multiple measurements for a single protocol accordingly. Apart from that, for some protocols and configurations, we require knowledge of cryptographic key material which we do not have since we perform measurements in the wild. Therefore, we cannot detect the entirety of the VPN ecosystem with our method. The last column of Table 1 summarizes for which protocol we are able to detect VPN servers. When OpenVPN servers specify the so-called *tls-auth* directive, an HMAC signature is required in all control messages. This means that we can only craft requests without HMACs and hence detect only a subset of all OpenVPN servers.

As mentioned above, for some protocols, it might also be necessary to consider different configurations. For IPsec, e.g., we suggest seven different cipher suites in the initiation request. Apart from that, we have to specify a key exchange method in the OpenVPN requests. Out of the two possible key exchange methods, namely *key method 1* and *key method 2*, key method 1 is considered insecure and is therefore deprecated [41]. We therefore specify key method 2 in our initiation requests and then perform a follow-up scan where we suggest the deprecated key exchange method to identified OpenVPN servers to investigate how many of them might still support key method 1.

3.2 TLS Analysis

For the TLS-based VPN protocols, which include SSTP and OpenVPN over TCP, we perform follow-up measurements to further fingerprint the servers and assess them in terms of security. For that, we collect TLS certificates of the VPN servers to analyze them for expiry, check for self-signed certificates and investigate how many of them are snake oil certificates. We characterize a certificate as a snake oil certificate if the common name (CN) of the subject and issuer are both specified as *localhost* or *user.local*. For the certificates signed by a Certificate Authority (CA), we collect the most common issuing organizations. We gather domain names corresponding to the responsive IP addresses using reverse DNS (rDNS) look-ups, and collect certificates with and without the Server Name Indication (SNI) extension using these domain names and compare them against each other. SNI can be used by the client in the TLS handshake in order to specify a hostname for which a connection should be established. This might be necessary in cases where multiple domain names are hosted on a single address. Finally, we test if the servers are susceptible to the *Heartbleed* [50] vulnerability as well as a series of TLS downgrade attacks. The Heartbleed attack is based on the Heartbeat Extension [49] of the OpenSSL library. In TLS downgrade attacks, we try to force a server to establish a connection using an outdated SSL/TLS version or using insecure cipher suites by suggesting those outdated primitives in the TLS handshake. Table 8 summarizes all the vulnerabilities and their requirements, i.e., what we have to test for or the version or cipher suite to which we try to downgrade the TLS connection. For instance, in order to check if a server is vulnerable to the FREAK attack, we suggest any SSL/TLS version and only RSA_EXPORT cipher suites in the TLS handshake.

3.3   Fingerprinting

We try to infer more information on the VPN servers based on our connection initiation requests as well as from follow-up measurements in order to further categorize them.

One aspect we examine is the server software deployment. For SSTP and PPTP, we can extract information on the software vendor directly from the responses to our initiation requests.

Furthermore, we perform OS detection measurements on a subset of 1000 VPN servers for each protocol using *Nmap* [34], a network scanner that can be used for network discovery among other things. We use Nmap's *fast* option and target 100 instead of 1000 ports to decrease runtime and parse the results for the most common open ports and OS guesses. With those results, we can learn more about the VPN server infrastructure and potential other services running on the same servers.

3.4   VPN Traffic Analysis

The active measurement in Sect. 3.1 provides us with a list of IP addresses, namely VPN hitlist, which are responsive to at least one VPN protocol initiation request. We look for these IP addresses in the DNS records gathered from the DNS resolvers at a large European ISP during a 1-hour period to learn about the domain names these IP addresses are associated with. We do not expect to find all the detected IP addresses in these DNS responses. Therefore, for any remaining IP address, we use reverse DNS resolution to find the corresponding domain names.

Then, we look for the IP addresses from our VPN hitlist on over a week of network flow data from the ISP to find out the amount of traffic associated with the VPN hitlist and compare the results with a port-based VPN traffic detection, and also a state-of-the-art approach.

3.5 Ethical Considerations

Active Scanning. We follow best current practices [28,43] to avoid potential harm to the networks we scan. We make sure that our prober IP address has a meaningful DNS PTR record pointing to our Web server which allows for requesting an opt-out from being scanned. We also limit our scanning rate and perform probing in a randomized order. We plan to notify the VPN providers about their servers' vulnerabilities.

ISP Data. All the data related to the ISP is processed on the ISP's premises. We do not copy, transfer, or store any data outside the dedicated servers that the ISP uses for its NetFlow analysis.

4   Active Measurements of the VPN Server Ecosystem

In this section, we go through the results from our Internet-wide active measurement using different VPN protocols. We discuss the characteristics of the responsive servers such as geographical locations, VPN protocols, etc. Then, we analyze their vulnerabilities and try to fingerprint them based on the gathered information.

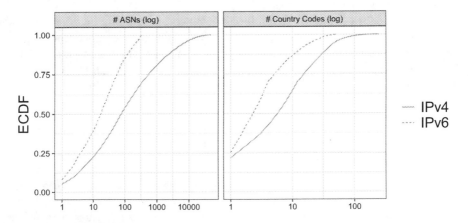

Fig. 1. Cumulative distribution of number of ASes (left) and number of countries (right) corresponding to the responsive IPs.

4.1 Responsive Servers

In total, we find 9,817,450 responsive IPv4 addresses with our probes that we can identify as VPN servers.

rDNS. We investigate the reverse DNS records corresponding to the responsive IPv4 addresses. We aggregate results on the second-level domain and sort them based on the number of responsive IPs that they correspond to. We find that all the top 10 domain names belong to telecommunication companies (e.g., Open Computer Network, a large Japanese ISP, and Telstra, an Australian telecommunications company). Next, we filter all rDNS records which contain *vpn* in their second-level domain names in order to detect commercial VPN providers. We find a single domain related to PacketHub which manages IP addresses for several companies, including NordVPN, a major commercial VPN provider. This domain name ranks 60th among all rDNS second level domains.

AS Analysis. Figure 1 shows the distribution of ASes to which our responsive IP addresses belong. The responsive IP addresses are originated by 49625 and 334 ASes in total, while top 10 ASes contribute to 22% and 38% of the IP addresses, for IPv4 and IPv6 respectively, as shown in Fig. 1. Top 10 ASes for IPv4 responsive addresses are all telecommunication companies, while out of the top 10 ASes for IPv6 responsive addresses, 8 are telecommunication companies and 2 are academy-related ASes. Tables 2 and 3 further summarize the top 10 AS numbers as well as the AS names or organizations and the number of VPN servers that are registered within the respective AS. As can be seen, most top ASes are large ISP networks.

Moreover, we investigate the top ASes for commercial VPN providers. As shown by Ramesh et al. [47] it is quite common for commercial VPN providers to use shared infrastructure. 27 providers, including popular companies such as NordVPN, Norton Secure VPN, or Mozilla VPN, use the same AS, namely AS 9009 operated by M247 Ltd. This AS is also visible in our measurements and it ranks 14th with 74,894 identified VPN servers (0.76% of all addresses). Furthermore, Ramesh et al. [47] find that some IP blocks in AS 16509 (Amazon) are shared across Norton Secure VPN and SurfEasy VPN. AS 16509 lands on rank 20 of our list being shared by almost 60,000 VPN servers (0.6% of all addresses). Another AS known to be used by VPN providers is AS 60068—again operated by M247 Ltd.— which is used by NordVPN and CyberGhost VPN. It ranks on place 178 of our list with 6,898 VPN servers (0.07% of all addresses). Overall, we find that although the top ASes are dominated by large ISPs, a considerable number of VPN servers are located in ASes used by commercial VPN providers.

Geolocation. We use Geolite Country Database [51] to determine the location of the responsive IP addresses. Figure 2 shows a heatmap of the number of responsive IPv4 addresses per country. We observe that responsive IP addresses are scattered all over the world, in total over 241 and 52 countries for IPv4 and IPv6, respectively. However, 64% and 86% of IP addresses belong to the top 10 countries for IPv4 and IPv6 respectively. Top 3 countries contributing to IPv4 responsive addresses are the United States, China, and UK, while top 3 countries for IPv6 are the United States, Japan, and Germany.

Table 2. IPv4: AS numbers, AS names and number of VPN servers belonging to the ASes.

AS number	AS name	VPN servers
4134	ChinaNet	515,830
7922	Comcast	356,327
1221	Telstra	257,821
3320	Deutsche Telekom	242,433
4766	Korea Telecom	228,863
4713	NTT Communications	145,286
7018	AT&T	137,698
4837	China Unicom	133,861
3462	HiNet	119,612
20115	Charter Communications	97,109

Table 3. IPv6: AS numbers, AS names and number of VPN servers belonging to the ASes.

AS number	AS name	VPN servers
7922	Comcast	183
63949	Akamai	159
12322	Proxad Free SAS	138
7506	GMO Internet Group	89
9009	M247 Ltd	63
9370	Sakura Internet Inc	58
14061	DigitalOcean	55
2516	KDDI Corporation	54
7684	Sakura Internet Inc	39
680	DFN-Verein	36

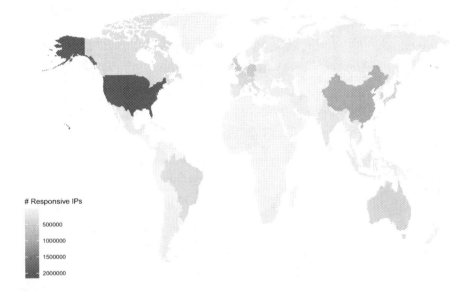

Fig. 2. Geographical distribution of responsive IPv4 addresses per country.

4.2 VPN Protocols

We are able to detect servers for IPsec, PPTP, OpenVPN without tls-auth, and SSTP. Table 4 summarizes our findings. Our IPsec UDP probes yield by far the most responsive VPN servers. It might seem surprising that we find such a large number of PPTP servers in contrast to OpenVPN and SSTP considering that PPTP is far more outdated and OpenVPN is one of the most prominent VPN protocols. However, we have to keep in mind that we can only detect a subset of the whole OpenVPN ecosystem since some configurations require knowledge of cryptographic key material as explained in Sect. 3.1. Apart from that, SSTP can only be used for remote access connections, whereas PPTP used to be the most widely deployed VPN protocol. We can assume that a large number of the detected PPTP servers are quite outdated, yet still running.

Table 4. Number of detected VPN servers per protocol.

VPN protocol	Detected servers
IPsec	7,008,298
PPTP	2,424,317
OpenVPN	1,436,667
SSTP	187,214

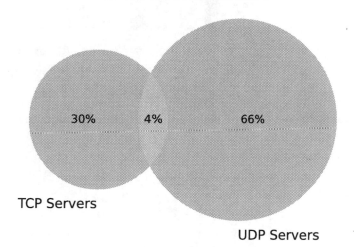

TCP Servers

UDP Servers

Fig. 3. Intersection of OpenVPN UDP and TCP servers.

Out of the around 1.4 million OpenVPN servers, 1,011,178 were detected over UDP and 482,956 over TCP. Considering that the TCP version of OpenVPN is generally rather considered as a fallback option, this disparity is to be expected. Figure 3 visualizes the intersection of those two address sets in a Venn diagram. We can see that the majority of the servers supports only a single transport protocol.

Overlap Between Protocols. In the next step, we compare the IP address sets for the four protocols to depict their intersections and to find out how many of the servers support more than one VPN protocol. Figure 4 summarizes those findings in an upset plot. The horizontal bars on the left visualize the sizes of the four protocol sets. The vertical bars represent the different intersections and the sets to be considered are indicated by the black dots below the vertical bars. The first bar on the left, e.g., represents the number of VPN servers supporting both PPTP and IPsec with roughly 550,000 servers making up for around 5.7% of the whole detected VPN server ecosystem. The second bar on the right, on the other hand, represents the number of servers supporting all four protocols, which is close to zero with only around 2.8 thousand servers.

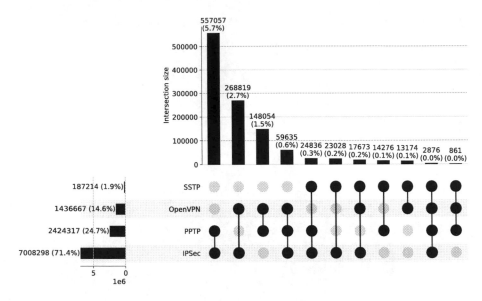

Fig. 4. VPN protocol summary: Number of detected VPN servers for each protocol and the intersection between all protocols.

We can see that the majority of all VPN servers support only one of the four protocols we consider in this work. Since commercial VPN providers usually offer a variety of different VPN protocols to choose from, it is possible that a large percentage of the servers supporting several protocols are commercial. This might be the case especially for the ones supporting three or four protocols. We investigate the rDNS records corresponding to the servers supporting all the four protocols, and find that there are no commercial VPN provider in the top 10 s-level domains. All in all, we find that commercial VPN providers account for only a fraction of the entire VPN server ecosystem considering the supported protocols.

Different Protocol Versions. Some VPN protocols might include different versions or configurations, like OpenVPN, for instance. We therefore try to trigger VPN responses from OpenVPN servers suggesting the outdated key exchange method key method 1. We also try to trigger responses with random HMAC signatures.

We find that only 84 of the roughly 1.4 million servers accept our random signature. Apart from that, none of the detected servers support the insecure key exchange method. While most of the servers ignored our requests, we still received around 6,500 responses specifying the default key exchange method key method 2. We can therefore conclude that key method 1 is truly deprecated in the OpenVPN ecosystem.

4.3 Security Analysis

TLS Certificate Analysis. We collect TLS certificates for the TLS-based VPN servers which include SSTP and OpenVPN over TCP and consider only unique certificates. For that, we compare the certificate fingerprints, i.e., the unique identifier of the certificate, to make sure we do not consider the same certificate more than once. Some certificates, however, do not include a fingerprint. Therefore, the number of certificates that we analyze in the end might be higher than the number of unique certificates. For OpenVPN, we find 129,143 unique certificates with a fingerprint for 312,095 servers. The most frequently occurring certificate is collected over 10,000 times and is issued for *www.update.microsoft.com*. For SSTP, there are 104,988 fingerprints for 184,047 servers. We detect a certificate issued for **.vpnauction.com* 2561 times and one for **.trust.zone* 1194 times. These are commercial VPN providers that seem to use the same certificate for all of their VPN servers. While we are able to collect certificates for nearly all of the SSTP servers, we only receive TLS certificates for around 65% of the detected OpenVPN servers. This is most likely caused by the fact that OpenVPN performs a variation of the standard TLS handshake during connection establishment. Therefore, some of the servers might not respond when trying to initiate a regular TLS handshake.

Table 5. Expired, self-issued, and self-signed TLS certificates for OpenVPN and SSTP.

	OpenVPN TCP	SSTP
Expired	6080 (3.8%)	13,370 (9%)
Self-issued	109,965 (69%)	39,889 (28%)
Self-signed	109,825 (69%)	34,725 (24%)
All certificates	158,705	143,517

Table 5 summarizes the results of the certificate analysis and contains the number of certificates that we analyzed after filtering out unique certificates and certificates without fingerprints. We detect a large number of self-issued or self-signed certificates for both protocols. Out of the self-issued certificates, we characterize only around 4.7% as snake oil certificates for SSTP and close to zero for OpenVPN with around 0.4%. However, 33% of the self-issued SSTP certificates contain *softether*, an open-source and multi-protocol VPN software, in the CN fields. 13% specify an IPv4 address in the CN sections. Upon looking at the organization field, we find over 21,000 different organizations where almost 14,000 specify no organization at all. For the OpenVPN certificates, we find that around 77% of the self-issued certificates include the *Fireware web CA* as CNs specifying *WatchGuard* as organization. For the rest, we detect more than 21,000 different organizations.

Table 6. Certificate issuer distribution for OpenVPN servers.

Issuer	Certificates
Stormshield	8966
Let's Encrypt	7463
Sectigo Limited	2610
Digicert Inc.	1897
GoDaddy.com, Inc.	1332

Table 7. Certificate issuer distribution for SSTP servers.

Issuer	Certificates
DigiCert, Inc.	45,156
Sectigo Limited	12,795
GoDaddy.com, Inc.	10,958
N/S	9139
Let's Encrypt	7801

Looking at the organization fields of the CA-signed certificates, we can learn more about the signing authorities. Considering SSTP, we filter out 2502 different organizations for almost 100,000 CA-signed certificates. Table 7 contains the top five organizations accounting for 87% of all signings. We examine the issuer CNs for the certificates that do not specify an organization, yet we could not find any meaningful information with 7,531 different issuers and the most frequently occurring CN being *CA* with 159 signings. For OpenVPN, the organizations are a lot more heterogeneous with 14,548 organizations in total. The top five organizations in Table 6 account for only around 50% of all signings.

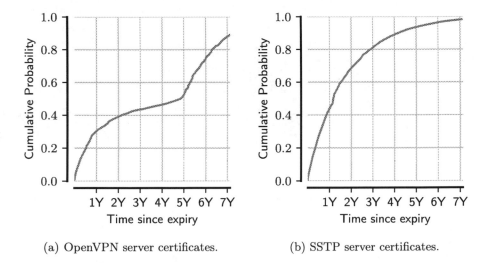

(a) OpenVPN server certificates.   (b) SSTP server certificates.

Fig. 5. Distribution of expiry time (time between day of expiry and Aug. 15, 2022) for expired certificates.

Since we also detect a quite significant number of expired certificates, we examine the date of their expiry more thoroughly. Figure 5 shows ECDFs for the time that has passed since the dates of expiry and the 15th of August, 2022. In general, over half of the SSTP certificates expired over a year ago. For

OpenVPN it is even around 70%. It is possible that those certificates belong to outdated, forgotten VPN servers.

TLS Vulnerability Analysis. The results of our TLS vulnerability analysis for the TLS-based VPN protocols can be found in the last two columns of Table 8 where we count the occurrences of susceptible servers. We detect a larger number of vulnerable servers for RC4, Poodle and ROBOT for both protocols, yet only a few outliers for the rest. SSTP is much more likely to show signs of vulnerability for all three attacks with over 90% of the servers being susceptible to ROBOT. This is most likely caused by the fact that SSTP is based on an outdated version of SSL and highlights why SSTP is not recommended to be used anymore.

Table 8. Requirements for TLS vulnerabilities and number of vulnerable servers per protocol.

	TLS version	Cipher suites	Other requirements	OpenVPN	SSTP
RC4 [5]	All	RC4	None	32,294	84,892
Heartbleed [50]	All	All	OpenSSL Heartbeat	232	10
Poodle [40]	SSL 3.0	All	None	7,005	24,917
FREAK [16]	All	RSA_EXPORT	None	31	1
Logjam [3]	All	DHE/512-bit export	None	8	0
DROWN [8]	SSLv2	All	None	0	0
ROBOT [10]	All	TLS_RSA	None	95,301	174,986
Raccoon [37]	TLS $\leq$ 1.2	TLS_DH	None	0	0

The Effect of Not Using SNI. As we target only IP addresses in our follow-up TLS measurements without the SNI extension, we want to investigate the effect of not using SNI. Therefore, we first perform an rDNS resolution for our IP addresses and find 259,910 domain names for about 480,000 OpenVPN TCP servers and 86,630 domain names for roughly 180,000 SSTP servers. We now collect certificates with the SNI extension and then re-run the TLS scans without SNI for the respective addresses for whose domains we could gather certificates.

Table 9 shows the results of the comparison of those two types of certificates and the number of certificates we could collect. Two certificates mismatch when the fingerprints differ. We then compare different fields and summarize the mismatch occurrences in the table. If those fields match and the certificate has only been renewed, we do not count it as a mismatch.

While the results for both protocols are similar, relatively speaking, we find more mismatches for SSTP. About 3% mismatch for OpenVPN, whereas for SSTP 5.5% mismatch. To confirm that those mismatches are caused by using SNI in the TLS handshakes, we perform a second measurement without SNI and compare the certificates with the other non-SNI results. Without SNI, we find less than half as many mismatches for SSTP and more than three times fewer mismatches for OpenVPN.

Considering the overall number of certificates from our large-scale measurements compared to the ones we collected with SNI and keeping in mind the mismatches we detected in the two non-SNI measurements, we can conclude that not using SNI affects less than 1% of the certificates for both protocols and the effect is therefore negligible.

Table 9. Comparison of Certificates Collected with and without SNI

	OpenVPN	SSTP
SNI Certificates	84,212	45,405
no SNI Certificates	81,379	45,026
Certificate Mismatches	2491	2515
Authority Key ID Mismatches	2051	1463
Subject Key ID Mismatches	2407	2379
Subject SANs Mismatches	2008	1677
Issuer CN Mismatches	1933	1476
Subject CN Mismatches	2021	1627

4.4 Fingerprinting

Server Software. For SSTP and PPTP, we can infer the server-side software from the responses we receive to our initiation requests. For SSTP, we find that around 80% of all detected servers use *Microsoft HTTPAPI 2.0*. Around 19% use *MikroTik-SSTP* and less than 1% use something else or specify nothing at all.

However, the PPTP vendor software is a lot more heterogeneous compared to SSTP. Table 10 shows the different software vendors we detect in the VPN server responses. While there are four prominent vendors, over 15% of the PPTP servers rely on 183 different types. This can have potential security implications on the PPTP ecosystem. Assuming there was some kind of new vulnerability, the rollout of a security update to counter this vulnerability would be significantly slower compared to SSTP with fewer software vendors. A similar phenomenon where vendor fragmentation leads to slower update rollout can also be observed in the Android ecosystem. Thomas et al. [54] showed that almost 60% of all devices ran insecure Android versions in July 2015. This share declines only slowly after the discovery of a major vulnerability. They found out that the bottleneck of this issue lies with the manufacturers and results in 87.7% of all devices being exposed to at least 11 critical vulnerabilities. Jones et al. [26] considered manufacturers between 2015 and 2019 and further showed that the median latency of a security update is 24 days with an additional latency of 11 days before an end-user update.

Nmap OS Detection and Port Scans. In our Nmap OS detection measurements, we first have a look at the most common ports for all four protocols. Figure 6 summarizes the most frequently occurring open ports. As expected, the default HTTP(S) ports 443 and 80 are the most common ports, with the exception of the PPTP servers for which the default PPTP port TCP/1723 obviously

Table 10. Software vendors for detected PPTP servers.

Vendor	Percentage
Linux	32.3%
MikroTik	30.6%
Draytek	21.1%
Microsoft	6.9%
Cananian	2.0%
Fortinet PPTP	1.4%
Yamaha Corporation	1.4%
Cisco Systems, Inc.	1.2%
Others (162)	3.2%

is the most widely used port. As Ramesh et al. [47] pointed out, specific open ports do not pose security risks by themselves, yet, they might still be abused in order to identify and exploit particular services [23].

For the OS detection, we filter out the first guesses for every target and look at the most common OSes and version ranges:

- **IPsec:** We receive 48 unique first guesses for 126 hosts out of 722 responsive IPsec servers. Out of those, 40 guess the Linux Kernel ranging from version 2.6.32-3.10. In general, Linux is the most common OS with 67 guesses. However, Microsoft was barely guessed as an OS vendor with only nine guesses.
- **PPTP:** For 792 responsive hosts, Nmap was able to guess an OS for 216 addresses with 56 unique guesses. Linux was once again the primary occurrence. Out of those guesses, 88 specified Linux 2.6.32-3.10, where the majority mewlie below version 3.2, however. As for IPsec, we have very few results for Microsoft with only 15 guesses. For the PPTP servers, there were more hardware guesses compared to the other protocols with 36 guesses specifying some kind of hardware device.
- **OpenVPN:** The most frequent guesses are almost exclusively Linux again in 33 unique guesses for 89 out of the 763 responsive hosts. 39 specify Linux ranging from 3.2-4.11, i.e., the versions are not quite as outdated as for PPTP and IPsec. We received only a single guess for Microsoft products.
- **SSTP:** The SSTP scans result in 44 different guesses for 178 out of 948 responsive hosts. This time, we have more results for Microsoft products with a total of 49 guesses. The most prominent vendor is Linux again, however, with 101 guesses where 53 range from Linux versions 2.6.32-3.10.

4.5   IPv6

VPN Server Detection. Targeting roughly 530 million IPv6 addresses in our ZMapv6 port scans, we could detect 1,195,510 responsive hosts on port TCP/443

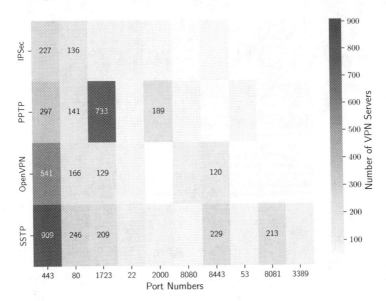

Fig. 6. Heatmap of most frequently detected open ports per VPN server.

which we target in our follow-up ZGrab2 scans for SSTP and OpenVPN over TCP. We could not find any responsive addresses on port TCP/1723, the default PPTP port. Since port TCP/1723 is used exclusively for PPTP and the protocol is very outdated, it is not too surprising that there are no IPv6 servers supporting PPTP. Apart from that, we do not get any responses on the UDP ports 500 (IPsec) and 1194 (OpenVPN over UDP).

Out of the roughly 1.2 million hits on port TCP/443, we could identify 2070 addresses as OpenVPN servers and 949 as SSTP servers with a total of 2221 VPN servers supporting IPv6. While those results seem very low, we have to keep in mind that the rollout of IPv6 is still very slow in general. IPv6 is also not yet supported by most commercial VPN providers.

As also observed in IPv4 results in Sect. 4.2, none of the OpenVPN servers accepted our OpenVPN key method 1 requests with only 11 servers still responding with the secure key exchange method. Additionally, of the overall IPv6 VPN servers we detect, around 36% support both protocols, i.e., compared to IPv4, the overlap is higher.

Investigating the rDNS records corresponding to the responsive IPv6 addresses, we observe that the top 10 domains belong to hosting providers, cloud providers, and research networks. Similar to the IPv4 results, we do not find a domain name belonging to a commercial VPN provider among the top 10 domains. By filtering second-level domains to match *vpn* we find the commercial VPN provider WhiteLabel VPN, ranking 25th among the top domains.

Therefore, we infer that most of the VPN servers that support IPv6 are, in fact, not commercial VPN providers.

TLS Certificate Analysis. The results of the TLS certificate analysis are similar to IPv4. We could collect certificates for around 75% of the identified OpenVPN servers with 816 unique fingerprints. Combined with the certificates that do not contain a fingerprint, we analyze a total of 1882 certificates. We collected certificates for every SSTP server resulting in 747 certificates after filtering out 207 unique fingerprints. Less certificates are expired this time with only 3.3% for OpenVPN and 2.1% for SSTP. This time, only 29% of the OpenVPN certificates are self-signed. For SSTP, more certificates are self-signed for the IPv6 servers with over 70% of all certificates. Out of those, we characterize roughly 2% as snake oil certificates for both protocols. Furthermore, about two thirds of the self-signed certificates for both protocols were issued by softether.

When examining the signing organizations for the CA-signed certificates, we find that around 85% (709 certificates) of the OpenVPN certificates are signed by Let's Encrypt with a total of 43 organizations. For SSTP, around 73% are signed by Let's Encrypt (153 certificates). Here, we find a total of only 16 organizations.

TLS Vulnerability Analysis. The results of the TLS vulnerability analysis are very similar to the IPv4 VPN servers. For both protocols, we are only able to detect vulnerable servers for the same three prominent attacks as for the IPv4 analysis. Out of the 2070 OpenVPN servers, 31% are vulnerable to RC4 biases, 6% to Poodle and 74% to Robot. When analyzing the 949 SSTP servers, we find that 67% are vulnerable to RC4 biases, 13% to the Poodle attack and roughly 98% to ROBOT. While the results are similar to our large-scale measurements, we can conclude that the VPN servers supporting IPv6 are much more likely to show any signs of vulnerability with the vast majority being vulnerable to the ROBOT attack.

The Effect of Not Using SNI. The rDNS measurements for the IPv6 servers resulted in 410 domain names for SSTP and 813 domain names for OpenVPN over TCP. Again, we first collect TLS certificates using the SNI extension and then try the same without SNI and compare the results. We find that only around 3% of the certificates for both protocols mismatch in terms of fingerprints and important certificate fields including authority and subject key IDs, subject SANs, and CNs. When comparing those results by running a second TLS scan without SNI, we find that only around 2.5% of the OpenVPN and less than 1% of the SSTP certificates differ. Considering the overall number of certificates, the effect of not using SNI is even less significant compared to IPv4 and is therefore negligible.

VPN Server Software. Since we could not analyze the PPTP server software ecosystem this time, we can only compare the results for SSTP. The results are similar again with 91% of the SSTP servers specifying the Microsoft HTTP API 2.0. However, the rest did not specify any vendor, i.e., the IPv6 SSTP servers seem to not use MikroTik-SSTP with Microsoft being the only vendor.

Nmap OS Detection and Port Scans. As for IPv4, we perform Nmap measurements on the detected IPv6 VPN servers including 1000 random OpenVPN

TCP servers and all 949 SSTP servers. Out of those servers, 874 OpenVPN servers and 852 SSTP servers are responsive.

The most commonly used open port is TCP/443 with 838 occurrences (96%) for OpenVPN and 852 (97%) for SSTP. Compared to IPv4, the number of open HTTPS ports is much higher for OpenVPN. Here, we have to keep in mind that we can only consider OpenVPN servers over TCP. Thus, this disparity is to be expected. The second most frequently open port for both protocols, in contrast to IPv4, is TCP/22, the default SSH port. This port occurs 245 times (28%) for OpenVPN and even 391 times (46%) for SSTP. Other common ports for both protocols are ports TCP/8000 for OpenVPN (21%) and TCP/80 accounting for around 17% of the open ports for both protocols.

We receive more OS guesses for the IPv6 servers compared to IPv4. As was the case for IPv4, we filter out the first guesses for every target:

- **OpenVPN**: The measurement results in only four unique guesses for a total of 481 hosts. 93% specify Linux with 416 guessing Linux 3.X and 33 guessing version 2.6. Only 19 predictions include a Microsoft OS and only 13 an Apple product.
- **SSTP**: For SSTP, there are five unique predictions for 406 addresses. The majority specifies Linux again with 91%. Out of those, 333 guesses specify Linux version 3.X and only 36 specify version 2.6. Microsoft OSes are predicted 36 times and only a single guess specifies a macOS.

In contrast to IPv4, Nmap was able to predict an OS for a much larger percentage of our targets with an OS guess for almost half of the targets. Additionally, the predictions are a lot more homogeneous. Linux is again the most prominent vendor, however, the predicted versions are not quite as outdated as for the IPv4 servers.

5 Passive VPN Traffic Analysis

It is important for network operators and ISPs to gain insight over the volume and daily patterns of VPN traffic. In a previous study, Feldmann et al. [18] try to find the VPN traffic based on the domain names corresponding to the IP addresses observed in the traffic. For detecting VPN traffic, Feldmann et al. use domain names to infer whether the IP addresses corresponding to them carry VPN traffic. They exclude any domain name that starts with *www.*, and does not have *vpn* to the left of the public suffix. Finally, they consider the remaining domain names as VPN domain names and count the traffic that relate to these domain names as VPN traffic.

To compare our methodology with the state of the art, we apply the methodology used by Feldmann et al. [18] on our results. We use DNS responses gathered by DNS resolvers at a large European ISP, and look for those DNS responses that include the IP addresses from our VPN hitlist. We find 13% of the IP addresses from the VPN hitlist in the above-mentioned DNS responses. Therefore, we complement our DNS data with reverse DNS look-ups for all the remaining IP addresses. To refine the reverse DNS results, we exclude any domain names containing any order of the corresponding IP address bytes or octets in decimal or hexadecimal format. Overall, we end up with the domain names corresponding to 23.6% of the IP addresses from the VPN hitlist. Then, we apply the methodology used by Feldmann et al. on the resulting domain names, i.e., we extract those domain names that contain *vpn* on the left side of the public suffix [45], while excluding any domain starting with www. to exclude web servers. We observe that this methodology captures only 4.8% of our VPN hitlist. Therefore, our approach can detect 4 times more VPN servers compared to the methodology by Feldmann et al.

Finally, we look at a one-week snapshot of all the network flow traffic from the large European ISP to find out the amount of traffic that can be attributed to VPN.

To this end, we compare the amount of VPN traffic detected with three methodologies:

1. *VPN Hitlist*: the methodology proposed in this paper, i.e. sending active probes, including the responsive IP addresses in a hitlist, excluding those IP addresses that answer to web requests, i.e. HTTP GET requests, then measuring the traffic volume originated by or destined to these IP addresses.
2. *Port-based*: this methodology captures the traffic only based on port numbers, considering traffic with port numbers 500 (IPsec), 4500 (IPsec), 1194 (OpenVPN), 1701 (L2TP), 1723 (1723) both on UDP and TCP as VPN traffic.
3. *Domain-based*: the methodology proposed by Feldmann et al., i.e. filtering domain names based on certain keywords, then measuring the traffic volume originated or destined to the IP addresses corresponding to these domain names.

Figure 7 shows the traffic volume considered as VPN traffic by each of the above-mentioned methodologies. The solid black line shows the total amount of VPN traffic detected by either of the three approaches. The dashed line shows the total traffic volume in the ISP. The left Y axis shows the VPN traffic volume (including all the three approaches), and the right Y axis shows the total ISP traffic volume. All the traffic values are normalized. While normalizing, we keep the ratio between the VPN traffic and total traffic intact. Therefore, comparing the left and right axis values shows that the total traffic is roughly 25 times as much as all VPN traffic.

Compared to the *Port-based* approach, we detect twice as much traffic, and compared to the *Domain-based* approach, we detect 8 times as much using the *VPN Hitlist*.

The mean VPN traffic volume detected by all three approaches is 4.1% of the mean total ISP traffic over the week, with *VPN Hitlist* contributing to 2.6%, *Port-based* 1.3%, and *Domain-based* 0.3%.

Looking at the overlap between every two approaches, we find that only 2.7% of all the traffic detected by all three approaches is detected both by *VPN*

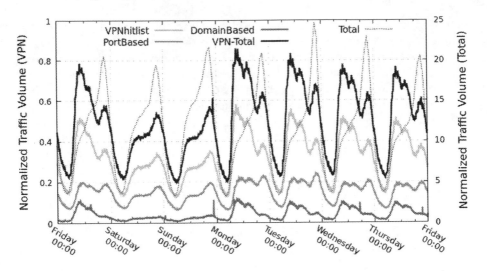

Fig. 7. Normalized VPN traffic volume for different traffic detection techniques.

Hitlist and *Domain-based.* We observe 1.2% overlap between the traffic detected by *VPN Hitlist* and *Port-based* approaches.

We observe a diurnal pattern in the VPN traffic detected by all of the three approaches. We find that VPN traffic pattern in the weekdays differs from that of weekends. It peaks at noon in the weekdays, and at night in the weekend, while the total ISP traffic always follows the same pattern, i.e. peaks at night. It could indicate the fact that the VPN traffic is mostly work-related through weekdays, while mostly entertainment-related throughout the weekend. In the domain-based approach the amount of VPN traffic detected by the *Domain-based* approach is much less in the weekends than in the weekdays. This could indicate that the *Domain-based* approach detect mostly work-related VPN servers.

We investigate the domain names corresponding to the traffic we detect using our approach and find that *vpn., mail., www.,* and *remote.* are among the most common prefixes left to the public suffix part of the domain names, with *vpn.* being the most common prefix. The fact that we observe *mail.* and *www.* might be either re-use of the same domain name for other purposes by the network operators, or a mislabeling effect from our approach caused by not answering our HTTP Get requests. Also, looking at the DNS records corresponding to the IP addresses from our hitlist, using FlowDNS—a system to correlate DNS and Netflow data at scale [36]—we find that 5 out of 10 top domains are related to commercial VPN providers and the rest are CDN domains. We observe that the most common source port/destination port combination is 4500/4500 which belongs to IPsec, also port number 1194 which is registered for OpenVPN, and at the same time 1193, which is practically used for VPN [42]. We also observe that 51820/51820 and 1337/1337 which belongs to WireGuard protocol are among the top port number pairs observed in the traffic detected by our approach. Port 51820 also falls into the range of ephemeral ports numbers (49152 to 65535) which can be temporarily used by many applications. However, due to the prominent existence of this port number in our results accompanied with port 1337, we infer that we can possibly detect some WireGuard traffic, although in our active measurement approach we cannot scan the WireGuard protocol. This might be due to the co-existence of multiple protocols in one VPN server. This shows that although in our approach we cannot scan WireGuard protocol, we can still detect some WireGuard traffic which might be due to the co-existence of multiple protocols on one VPN server. Traffic related to WireGuard protocol contributes to 8.6% of the detected VPN traffic by our VPN hitlist, while contributing to only 2% of the traffic detected by the *Domain-based* approach.

6   Discussion

In this work, we detect VPN servers in the wild by sending Internet-wide active probes using different VPN protocols. We can distinguish between VPN servers and Web servers by excluding those servers that respond to a Web request. We compare the amount of traffic detected by our approach and two other approaches over a week of traffic from a large European ISP and find out that the approach proposed by this work detects much more VPN servers compared to the state-of-the-art domain-based approach. In addition, our approach benefits from detecting VPN servers that do not use any domain name, and can also detect VPN traffic that is using unusual ports in case these servers answer VPN probe on the usual VPN port numbers. Also, to be the best of our knowledge, this is the first work to perform an Internet-wide active measurement of VPN servers in the wild.

VPN Hitlist. We send active probes according to the specification of VPN protocols including SSTP, PPTP, OpenVPN, and IPsec to the whole IPv4 address space and to an IPv6 hitlist. We make our list of detected VPN servers, namely the VPN hitlist, publicly available at vpnecosystem.github.io. This VPN hitlist can be useful for network operators to find out about the amount and patterns of VPN traffic in their networks. The VPN hitlist can also be used by fellow researchers to investigate different behaviors of the VPN servers and VPN traffic, e.g. investigating actual attacks to these servers.

Security. We also investigate the security of the OpenVPN and SSTP protocols in terms of different security aspects, including heartbleed attack, TLS certificates security, and TLS downgrade attacks. We find that SSTP servers use expired certificates 3x more than OpenVPN servers. We also find that 90% of the SSTP servers are vulnerable to ROBOT attack. Therefore, we find SSTP to be the most vulnerable protocol. This striking high percentage of vulnerable servers for some of the protocols shows, that the VPN server ecosystem is not as secure as some users believe it to be. Therefore, we hope that our analysis can highlight these security risks with using each VPN protocol and also helps network operators choose the right VPN protocols for their networks.

Limitations. Our approach builds upon receiving answers from the servers in the wild and therefore, has its limitations. If there is a VPN protocol which uses a pre-shared key in the first VPN request and does not respond otherwise, we are unable to detect it. Examples of such VPN protocols are WireGuard and Cisco AnyConnect. Therefore, we are unable to detect any VPN server which offers only these two protocols. However, we observe that 8.6% of the detected traffic is related to WireGuard which might be due to multiple protocols being served by one VPN server. In addition, certain VPN servers might only work on non-registered port numbers for better anonymization. Since in our work, we only send probes to the port numbers registered for the VPN protocols by IANA [7], we cannot detect VPN servers that work on unusual port numbers. Therefore, our list of detected VPN servers is limited to those using the supported VPN protocols and working on their registered port numbers.

Future work. In the future, our work can be complemented by including more port numbers in the active scans. Results from previous studies on predicting the services across all ports [25] can be used together with our approach to gain more coverage. Despite the above-mentioned limitations, our proposed approach detects much more VPN servers compared to the state-of-the-art domain-based approach, and also, to the best of our knowledge, is the first work to perform an Internet-wide active measurement of VPN servers in the wild.

Reproducibility. We make our analysis code and data [19], customized ZGrab2 modules [56], and our VPN hitlist publicly available[1] for fellow researchers to be able to reproduce our work and build upon it.

7 Related Work

VPN traffic classification is an open research problem, particularly challenging due to its encrypted nature. There are several studies trying to tackle this problem using machine learning approaches. Some are able to categorize the traffic into VPN and non-VPN only [32], and some provide more detailed sub-categories [4,57,59]. Zou et al. [59] identify encrypted traffic by combining a deep neural network to extract features of single packets and a recurrent network to analyze features of the traffic flow based on features of three consecutive packets. Though the model classifies some traffic incorrectly regarding sub-categories, it could achieve almost 99% accuracy when only considering VPN and non-VPN traffic. Alfayoumi et al. [4], on the other hand, also consider time-related features and subdivide traffic by also identifying applications.

All of these works require previously captured unencrypted VPN traffic to train. Previous studies have also tried to detect VPN traffic using the DNS records corresponding to the IP addresses observed in the traffic [18].

In this paper, we propose a different approach, i.e. Internet-wide active measurements, to detect VPN servers in the Internet. Internet-wide measurements

---

[1] https://vpnecosystem.github.io/.

have been previously applied for several intents including finding IPv6 responsive addresses [20], responsive IPs to abnormal traffic [35], the usage of DNS over encryption [33], and so on. However, to the best of our knowledge, this is the first work applying active measurements to detect VPN servers in the wild and detecting the traffic based on a VPN hitlist.

Investigating the security of the VPN servers is also an interesting research problem which is already addressed by several studies. For example, Xue et al. investigate the possibility and practicality of fingerprinting OpenVPN flows [1]. Tolley et al. investigate the vulnerability of known VPN servers to spoofed traffic [55]. Crawshaw [13] addresses vulnerabilities that come with some of the protocols themselves, such as outdated cryptographic cipher suites used in PPTP. In his proposal for WireGuard [14], Donenfeld talks about disadvantages in current popular VPN protocols. *VPNalyzer* requires a tool to be installed on the user's device to measure and collect data on the active VPN connections in terms different security aspects including data leakage, open ports, and DNSSEC validation [47]. Appelbaum et al. also identified vulnerabilities of commercial and public online VPN servers [6].

A large body of literature also exists that empirically examines TLS vulnerabilities including self-signed root CA injection to intercept TLS connection [24,46], and improper implementation of the protocol making version downgrade attacks possible even with new TLS 1.3 [30].

We mainly focus on potential vulnerabilities that come with VPN protocols which are built on top of SSL/TLS. Thus, we investigate SSL/TLS related features of those protocols. For some identified OpenVPN servers, we can also make assumptions on their security based on information we can infer about their server configurations. All the previous works study the security of known VPN servers, while in this paper, we measure the vulnerability of our detected VPN server in the Internet.

8   Conclusion

In this paper, we performed the first Internet-wide active measurement on the VPN server ecosystem for OpenVPN, SSTP, PPTP, and IPsec both in IPv4 and IPv6 to detect VPN servers in the wild. We detected 9.8 million VPN servers distributed globally. 10% of the detected VPN servers offered more than one VPN protocol with very few serving all the four protocols we studied. We also send active Web probes to the detected VPN servers and observed that 2% were both VPN and Web servers. Analyzing the TLS-based VPN protocols, i.e. OpenVPN and SSTP, we found that SSTP was the most vulnerable to a version downgrade attack, and certificates of OpenVPN servers had the most self-signed and self-issued certificates. We also tried to fingerprint the detected VPN servers in terms of server software vendors and operating systems. Finally, using our VPN hitlist, excluding the servers that were both VPN and Web servers, we observed that VPN traffic constitutes 2.6% of the total traffic volume in a large European ISP, which is 8x as much as that of a state-of-the-art domain-based approach, and twice as much as the trivial port-based approach. We publish our VPN hitlist, our customized ZGrab2 modules for VPN scans, and the code to our analysis for future researchers and network operators to use.

References

1. OpenVPN is open to VPN fingerprinting. In: 31st USENIX Security Symposium (USENIX Security 22). USENIX Association, Boston, MA (2022). https://www.usenix.org/conference/usenixsecurity22/presentation/xue-diwen
2. ul Abideen, M.Z., Saleem, S., Ejaz, M.: VPN traffic detection in SSL-protected channel. Secur. Commun. Netw. **2019**, 1–17 (2019)
3. Adrian, D., et al.: Imperfect forward secrecy: how Diffie-Hellman fails in practice. In: 22nd ACM Conference on Computer and Communications Security (2015)
4. Al-Fayoumi, M., Al-Fawa'reh, M., Nashwan, S.: VPN and Non-VPN network traffic classification using time-related features. Comput. Mater. Continua **72**, 3091–3111 (2022). https://doi.org/10.32604/cmc.2022.025103
5. AlFardan, N., Bernstein, D.J., Paterson, K.G., Poettering, B., Schuldt, J.C.N.: On the security of RC4 in TLS. In: 22nd USENIX Security Symposium (USENIX Security 13), pp. 305–320. USENIX Association, Washington, D.C. (2013). https://www.usenix.org/conference/usenixsecurity13/technical-sessions/paper/alFardan
6. Appelbaum, J., Ray, M., Koscher, K., Finder, I.: vpwns: Virtual pwned networks. In: 2nd USENIX Workshop on Free and Open Communications on the Internet. USENIX Association (2012)
7. Authority, I.A.N.: Service name and transport protocol port number registry. https://www.iana.org/assignments/service-names-port-numbers (2022). Accessed 25 Oct 2022
8. Aviram, N., et al.: DROWN: breaking TLS with SSLv2. In: 25th USENIX Security Symposium (2016)
9. Bitaab, M., et al.: Scam pandemic: how attackers exploit public fear through phishing. In: 2020 APWG Symposium on Electronic Crime Research (eCrime), pp. 1–10 (2020). https://doi.org/10.1109/eCrime51433.2020.9493260
10. Böck, H., Somorovsky, J., Young, C.: Return of Bleichenbacher's oracle threat (ROBOT). In: 27th USENIX Security Symposium (USENIX Security 18), pp. 817–849. USENIX Association, Baltimore, MD (2018). https://www.usenix.org/conference/usenixsecurity18/presentation/bock
11. Böttger, T., Ibrahim, G., Vallis, B.: How the internet reacted to COVID-19: a perspective from facebook's edge network. In: Proceedings of the ACM Internet Measurement Conference, pp. 34–41. IMC 2020, Association for Computing Machinery, New York, NY, USA (2020). https://doi.org/10.1145/3419394.3423621
12. Chair of Network Architectures and Services at TUM: ZMapv 6: internet scanner with ipv6 capabilities, gitHub repository (2022). https://www.github.com/tumi8/zmap. Accessed 26 Oct 2022
13. Crawshaw, D.: Everything VPN is new again: the 24-year-old security model has found a second wind. Queue **18**(5), 54–66 (2020). https://doi.org/10.1145/3434571.3439745
14. Donenfeld, J.: Wireguard: Next generation kernel network tunnel. Tech. Rep. (2017). https://doi.org/10.14722/ndss.2017.23160

15. Draper-Gil, G., Lashkari, A.H., Mamun, M.S.I., Ghorbani, A.A.: Characterization of encrypted and vpn traffic using time-related. In: Proceedings of the 2nd International Conference on Information Systems Security and Privacy (ICISSP), pp. 407–414 (2016)
16. Durumeric, Z., Adrian, D., Mirian, A., Bailey, M., Halderman, J.A.: Tracking the FREAK Attack. https://www.freakattack.com/ (2015). Accessed 19 Oct 2022
17. Dutkowska-Żuk, A., Hounsel, A., Morrill, A., Xiong, A., Chetty, M., Feamster, N.: How and why people use virtual private networks. In: 31st USENIX Security Symposium (USENIX Security 22), pp. 3451–3465. USENIX Association, Boston, MA (2022). https://www.usenix.org/conference/usenixsecurity22/presentation/dutkowska-zuk
18. Feldmann, A., et al.: The lockdown effect: implications of the COVID-19 pandemic on internet traffic. In: Proceedings of the ACM Internet Measurement Conference, pp. 1–18. IMC 2020, Association for Computing Machinery, New York, NY, USA (2020). https://doi.org/10.1145/3419394.3423658
19. Gasser, O.: Analysis scripts and raw data for VPN ecosystem measurements (2023). https://doi.org/10.17617/3.NZUPN4
20. Gasser, O., et al.: Clusters in the expanse: understanding and unbiasing IPv6 hitlists. In: Proceedings of the 2018 Internet Measurement Conference. ACM, New York, NY, USA (2018). https://doi.org/10.1145/3278532.3278564
21. Haag, M.: Remote work is here to stay. Manhattan may never be the same. The New York Times (2021). https://www.nytimes.com/2021/03/29/nyregion/remote-work-coronavirus-pandemic.html
22. Hamzeh, K., Pall, G., Verthein, W., Taarud, J., Little, W., Zorn, G.: point-to-point tunneling protocol (PPTP). RFC 2637 (Informational) (1999). https://doi.org/10.17487/RFC2637. https://www.rfc-editor.org/rfc/rfc2637.txt
23. Horowitz, M.: TCP ports to test. https://www.routersecurity.org/testrouter.php#TCPports. Accessed 13 Oct 2022
24. Ikram, M., Vallina-Rodriguez, N., Seneviratne, S., Kaafar, M.A., Paxson, V.: An analysis of the privacy and security risks of android VPN permission-enabled apps. In: Proceedings of the 2016 Internet Measurement Conference, pp. 349–364 (2016)
25. Izhikevich, L., Teixeira, R., Durumeric, Z.: Predicting Ipv4 services across all ports. In: Proceedings of the ACM SIGCOMM 2022 Conference, pp. 503–515. SIGCOMM 2022, Association for Computing Machinery, New York, NY, USA (2022). https://doi.org/10.1145/3544216.3544249
26. Jones, K.R., Yen, T.F., Sundaramurthy, S.C., Bardas, A.G.: Deploying android security updates: an extensive study involving manufacturers, carriers, and end users. In: Proceedings of the 2020 ACM SIGSAC Conference on Computer and Communications Security, pp. 551–567. CCS 2020, Association for Computing Machinery, New York, NY, USA (2020). https://doi.org/10.1145/3372297.3423346
27. Karamollahi, M., Williamson, C., Arlitt, M.: Zoomiversity: a case study of pandemic effects on post-secondary teaching and learning. In: Hohlfeld, O., Moura, G., Pelsser, C. (eds.) PAM 2022. LNCS, vol. 13210, pp. 573–599. Springer, Cham (2022). https://doi.org/10.1007/978-3-030-98785-5_26
28. Kenneally, E., Dittrich, D.: The Menlo report: ethical principles guiding information and communication technology research. Available at SSRN 2445102 (2012)
29. Khan, M.T., DeBlasio, J., Voelker, G.M., Snoeren, A.C., Kanich, C., Vallina-Rodriguez, N.: An empirical analysis of the commercial VPN ecosystem. In: Proceedings of the Internet Measurement Conference 2018, pp. 443–456. IMC 2018, Association for Computing Machinery, New York, NY, USA (2018). https://doi.org/10.1145/3278532.3278570

30. Lee, S., Shin, Y., Hur, J.: Return of version downgrade attack in the era of TLS 1.3. In: Proceedings of the 16th International Conference on Emerging Networking Experiments and Technologies, pp. 157–168 (2020)
31. Liu, S., Schmitt, P., Bronzino, F., Feamster, N.: Characterizing service provider response to the COVID-19 pandemic in the united states. In: Hohlfeld, O., Lutu, A., Levin, D. (eds.) PAM 2021. LNCS, vol. 12671, pp. 20–38. Springer, Cham (2021). https://doi.org/10.1007/978-3-030-72582-2_2
32. Lotfollahi, M., Siavoshani, M.J., Zade, R.S.H., Saberian, M.: Deep packet: a novel approach for encrypted traffic classification using deep learning. Soft Comput. **24**(3), 1999–2012 (2020)
33. Lu, C., et al.: An end-to-end, large-scale measurement of DNS-over-encryption: how far have we come? In: Proceedings of the Internet Measurement Conference, pp. 22–35. IMC 2019, Association for Computing Machinery, New York, NY, USA (2019). https://doi.org/10.1145/3355369.3355580
34. Lyon, G.: Nmap. https://www.nmap.org/. Accessed 26 Oct 2022
35. Maghsoudlou, A., Gasser, O., Feldmann, A.: Zeroing in on port 0 traffic in the wild. In: Hohlfeld, O., Lutu, A., Levin, D. (eds.) PAM 2021. LNCS, vol. 12671, pp. 547–563. Springer, Cham (2021). https://doi.org/10.1007/978-3-030-72582-2_32
36. Maghsoudlou, A., Gasser, O., Poese, I., Feldmann, A.: FlowDNS: correlating Netflow and DNS streams at scale. In: Proceedings of the 18th International Conference on Emerging Networking EXperiments and Technologies, pp. 187–195. CoNEXT 2022, Association for Computing Machinery, New York, NY, USA (2022). https://doi.org/10.1145/3555050.3569135
37. Merget, R., Brinkmann, M., Aviram, N., Somorovsky, J., Mittmann, J., Schwenk, J.: Raccoon attack: finding and exploiting most-significant-bit-oracles in TLS-DH(E). In: 30th USENIX Security Symposium (USENIX Security 21), pp. 213–230. USENIX Association (2021). https://www.usenix.org/conference/usenixsecurity21/presentation/merget
38. Microsoft: microsoft security advisory 2743314. https://www.learn.microsoft.com/en-us/security-updates/SecurityAdvisories/2012/2743314 (2012). Accessed 26 Oct 2022
39. Miller, S., Curran, K., Lunney, T.: Detection of virtual private network traffic using machine learning. Int. J. Wirel. Netw. Broadband Technol. (IJWNBT) **9**(2), 60–80 (2020)
40. Möller, B., Duong, T., Kotowicz, K.: This POODLE bites: exploiting the SSL 3.0 fallback. https://www.openssl.org/bodo/ssl-poodle.pdf (2014). Accessed 19 Oct 2022
41. OpenVPN: deprecated options in OpenVPN. https://www.community.openvpn.net/openvpn/wiki/DeprecatedOptions#Option:-key-method. Accessed 26 Oct 2022
42. OpenVPN: typical network configuration. https://www.openvpn.net/access-server-manual/typical-network-configurations/. Accessed 28 Oct 2022
43. Partridge, C., Allman, M.: Ethical considerations in network measurement papers. Commun. ACM **59**(10), 58–64 (2016)
44. Jauniskis, P.: VPN statistics: users, markets, & legality. https://www.surfshark.com/blog/vpn-users (2022). Accessed 10 Oct 2022
45. PyPi: Public suffix PyPi. https://www.pypi.org/project/publicsuffix/ (2022). Accessed 12 Oct 2022
46. Raman, R.S., Evdokimov, L., Wurstrow, E., Halderman, J.A., Ensafi, R.: Investigating large scale https interception in Kazakhstan. In: Proceedings of the ACM Internet Measurement Conference, pp. 125–132 (2020)

47. Ramesh, R., Evdokimov, L., Xue, D., Ensafi, R.: VPNalyzer: systematic investigation of the VPN ecosystem. In: Network and Distributed System Security. The Internet Society (2022). https://doi.org/10.14722/ndss.2022.24285
48. Robinson, B.: Remote work is here to stay and will increase into 2023, experts say. Forbes (2022). https://www.forbes.com/sites/bryanrobinson/2022/02/01/remote-work-is-here-to-stay-and-will-increase-into-2023-experts-say/
49. Seggelmann, R., Tuexen, M., Williams, M.: Transport layer security (TLS) and datagram transport layer security (DTLS) heartbeat extension. RFC 6520 (Proposed Standard) (2012). https://doi.org/10.17487/RFC6520. https://www.rfc-editor.org/rfc/rfc6520.txt. Updated by RFC 8447
50. Synopsis Inc: the heartbleed bug. https://www.heartbleed.com/ (2020). Accessed 29 July 2022
51. The MaxMind company: Geolite2 free geolocation data. https://www.dev.maxmind.com/geoip/geolite2-free-geolocation-data (2022). Accessed 06 Oct 2022
52. The ZMap Team: Zgrab 2.0, gitHub repository. https://www.github.com/zmap/zgrab2 (2022). Accessed 28 Sept 2022
53. The ZMap Team: Zmap: the internet scanner, gitHub repository. https://www.github.com/zmap/zmap (2022). Accessed 28 Sept 2022
54. Thomas, D.R., Beresford, A.R., Rice, A.: Security metrics for the android ecosystem. In: Proceedings of the 5th Annual ACM CCS Workshop on Security and Privacy in Smartphones and Mobile Devices, pp. 87–98. SPSM 2015, Association for Computing Machinery, New York, NY, USA (2015). https://doi.org/10.1145/2808117.2808118
55. Tolley, W.J., Kujath, B., Khan, M.T., Vallina-Rodriguez, N., Crandall, J.R.: Blind In/On-Path attacks and applications to VPNs. In: 30th USENIX Security Symposium (USENIX Security 21), pp. 3129–3146. USENIX Association (2021). https://www.usenix.org/conference/usenixsecurity21/presentation/tolley
56. Vermeulen, L.: ZGrab2 VPN modules on GitHub. https://www.github.com/vpnecosystem/zgrab2-vpn
57. Wang, W., Zhu, M., Wang, J., Zeng, X., Yang, Z.: End-to-end encrypted traffic classification with one-dimensional convolution neural networks. In: 2017 IEEE International Conference on Intelligence and Security Informatics (ISI), pp. 43–48 (2017). https://doi.org/10.1109/ISI.2017.8004872
58. Zirngibl, J., Steger, L., Sattler, P., Gasser, O., Carle, G.: Rusty Clusters? Dusting an IPv6 Research Foundation. In: Proceedings of the 2022 Internet Measurement Conference. ACM, New York, NY, USA (2022). https://doi.org/10.1145/3517745.3561440
59. Zou, Z., Ge, J., Zheng, H., Wu, Y., Han, C., Yao, Z.: Encrypted traffic classification with a convolutional long short-term memory neural network. In: 2018 IEEE 20th International Conference on High Performance Computing and Communications; IEEE 16th International Conference on Smart City; IEEE 4th International Conference on Data Science and Systems (HPCC/SmartCity/DSS), pp. 329–334 (2018). https://doi.org/10.1109/HPCC/SmartCity/DSS.2018.00074

Stranger VPNs: Investigating the Geo-Unblocking Capabilities of Commercial VPN Providers

Etienne Khan[1]([✉]), Anna Sperotto[1], Jeroen van der Ham[1,2], and Roland van Rijswijk-Deij[1]

[1] Faculty of Electrical Engineering, Mathematics and Computer Science, University of Twente, Enschede, The Netherlands
{e.khan,a.sperotto,j.vanderham,r.m.vanrijswijk}@utwente.nl
[2] National Cyber Security Centre, The Hague, The Netherlands

Abstract. Commercial Virtual Private Network (VPN) providers have steadily increased their presence in Internet culture. Their most advertised use cases are preserving the user's privacy, or circumventing censorship. However, a number of VPN providers nowadays have added what they call a *streaming unblocking service*. In practice, such VPN providers allow their users to access streaming content that Video-on-Demand (VOD) providers do not provide in a specific geographical region.

In this work, we investigate the mechanisms by which commercial VPN providers facilitate access to geo-restricted content, de-facto bypassing VPN-detection countermeasures by VOD providers (blocklists). We actively measure the geo-unblocking capabilities of 6 commercial VPN providers in 4 different geographical regions during two measurements periods of 7 and 4 months respectively. Our results identify two methods to circumvent the geo-restriction mechanisms. These methods consist of: (1) specialized ISPs/hosting providers which do not appear on the blocklists used by content providers to geo-restrict content and (2) the use of residential proxies, which due to their nature also do not appear in those blocklists. Our analysis shows that the ecosystem of the geo-unblocking VPN providers is highly dynamic, adapting their chosen geo-unblocking mechanisms not only over time, but also according to different geographical regions.

1 Introduction

Virtual Private Networks (VPN) allow us to act as part of a specific network even from a physically remote location, with the added advantage of doing so in a secure and private manner. As a consequence of this, not only are we able to access our work environment while working from home, but users all over the world benefit from better privacy or, for example, have the ability to circumvent censorship [26]. Acting as part of a physically remote network, however, also means that a user will appear to be in a different physical location than their real one, thus allowing them access to content and services that are instead typically bound to a specific geographic region. VPN providers have recently

A. Brunstrom et al. (Eds.): PAM 2023, LNCS 13882, pp. 46–68, 2023.
https://doi.org/10.1007/978-3-031-28486-1_3

added one more service to their repertoire that allows them to capitalize on this, namely a so-called *streaming unblocking service.*

VPN streaming services are born in the context of the arms race that seems to exist between VPN providers and Video-on-Demand (VOD) providers. As a consequence of non-technical constraints such as copyright negotiations, licensing and business models, VOD providers typically use geolocation mechanisms to identify if a user is allowed access to certain content. This phenomenon is known as *geo-blocking* or *geo-fencing*, and it is often negatively perceived by end users. Think about not being able to watch the new season of your favorite series that is already streaming in the US, but that lengthy copyright negotiations are holding back in other parts of the world. Since VPNs have the ability to let a user's request originate from a different geographical location, VOD providers have developed methods to detect if a user connects to their service using a VPN, and can block the request. Despite these countermeasures, VPN providers claim to be able - and we can confirm that they succeed - to bypass VOD geo-blocking and VPN detection mechanisms.

This paper investigates how VPN providers are able to bypass geo-blocking and VPN detection. We refer to this as *geo-unblocking*. The challenge in this is that VPN providers act as "black boxes", hiding from the end-user how geo-unblocking is achieved. This calls for an in-depth analysis of the VPN geo-unblocking ecosystem.

The contributions of this paper are that:

- We empirically infer a model of the VPN geo-unblocking ecosystem and identify a methodology that gives us visibility into the population of proxy hosts used to bypass geo-unblocking;
- We identify two distinct methods used by VPN providers to circumvent VOD geo-blocking and VPN-detection mechanisms;
- We characterize these methods at the network-level, shedding light on how VPN providers implement these methods and how their strategies adapt over time and over different regions.

The remainder of this paper is organized as follows. In Sect. 2 we present the relevant related work and background information. In Sect. 3 we describe the VPN ecosystem in relation to geo-unblocking. We then describe how we select relevant VPN providers in Sect. 4. In Sect. 5 we explain our methodology to identify VPN exit nodes used for geo-unblocking, and we explain how we collected our data set. Section 6 presents our results. We discuss ethical concerns regarding our study in Sect. 7. Finally, we present our conclusions in Sect. 8.

2 Background and Related Work

2.1 Background

Geo-blocking and Geolocation. Geo-blocking is the term for the procedure of prohibiting access to online resources based on the user's geographical location [27]. VOD providers make use of this, because they often do not possess the licensing rights to broadcast their content globally [11,19]. Therefore, they have to ensure that only subscribers from regions for which the license has been acquired may access the resource. In order to accurately do so, VOD providers make use of geolocation databases to map users' traffic to its geographical origin. Such geolocation databases are often maintained by commercial parties and strive to have a high accuracy, but research has shown that this data is mostly only accurate and consistent at a country level, compared to a more fine-grained province or city level [24].

Proxy/VPN Detection at VOD Providers. VOD providers are aware that their users circumvent the geographical restrictions put in place by using proxies or VPNs [4,8,10,13,15]. To deter the use of these proxies and VPNs, the VOD provider has to reliably detect their use. VOD providers do not disclose their detection methods, but we suspect that IP geolocation services are used at least partially for this [2,9,14]. Nowadays, many IP geolocation providers, e.g. NetAcuity, Maxmind, IP2Location or IPInfo offer more data than just geographical information. For example, they provide publicly available information such as the *AS number*, *ISP name*, or *reverse DNS* entry of the IP in question, but some providers are even classifying IP ranges by their usage. In those cases they provide information such as if the IP address is located at a data center or at a consumer's household as well as if the IP address is being used for proxy purposes (such as an open proxy or Tor exit node) or if it belongs to a commercial VPN service including the name of the VPN provider. We call these databases *enhanced geolocation databases*, as they provide metadata which cannot be inferred from public databases (i.e. from national or regional Internet registries). This information may allow VOD providers to more easily identify users circumventing geoblocking.

2.2   Related Work

Researching commercial VPN providers is a relatively new direction in the Internet measurement community and most current work focuses on privacy and security aspects.

In 2015, Perta et al. manually analyzed 14 providers on their privacy and security claims, and concluded that almost all providers are vulnerable to IPv6 leakage [29]. A follow-up study by Ikram et al., one year later, extended this previous work, by analyzing 283 Android VPN apps [25]. Even though the Android apps benefit from a standardized networking interface, many of the apps came with embedded malware, ad-trackers, JavaScript injection, ad-redirections and even TLS interception. Work by Khan et al. from 2018 presented a more comprehensive view of the commercial VPN ecosystem as a whole [26]. This work not only includes the previously mentioned privacy and security issues, but also investigates the VPN providers' claims regarding the physical location of the VPN servers. In their results the authors show that 5-30% (depending on the geolocation database used) of all servers are located in a different country than what is advertised and in one extreme case a provider claimed to have 190 distinct locations, but ultimately only 10 different data centers were responsible for the hosting of the servers.

Similar research has been conducted by Weinberg et al., who tried to verify advertised proxy locations with the help of geolocation [32]. They conclude that one third of all proxies are definitely not in the advertised location and another third might not be. A different study by Winter et al. tried to geolocate BGP prefixes, in order to better understand routing anomalies, outages and more [33]. One of their data points showed that a /23 network geolocated to 127 different countries (including Vatican City and North Korea). This is of course highly unlikely and only after consulting WHOIS data, it became clear that this was an IP range owned by a commercial VPN provider[1]. The most recent paper on the commercial VPN ecosystem from Ramesh et al. presents measurement software called *VPNalyzer* which can run on end-user devices to "collect 15 distinct measurements that test for aspects of service, security and privacy essentials, misconfigurations, and leakages" [30]. Their system allows for a systematic analysis of key security and privacy issues in VPN implementations in the wild.

All previously mentioned studies highlight the usage of VPNs (or proxies) to circumvent geo-blocking. Yet to the best of our knowledge, there has not been any study so far that investigated the unblocking methodologies of these providers, which we instead cover in this paper. There has been an assumption that geo-unblocking can be facilitated through the sheer amount of servers operated[2]. Our contribution to this field presents new insights, by showing that this is not necessarily the case.

3   Ecosystem

When analyzing the geo-unblocking ecosystem, the first step is to understand how geo-unblocking is carried out. In this section, we reason about how geo-unblocking can be achieved, we test our assumptions and derive a model of the geo-unblocking ecosystem.

If we consider that VOD providers use enhanced geolocation databases to detect the use of proxies or VPNs by looking at IP addresses, but also that streaming unblocking services do work, then it stands to reason that commercial VPN providers claiming to be able to bypass geolocation must use IPs which are not marked as proxy or VPN in geolocation databases.

This helps us shape a view of the geo-unblocking VPN ecosystem, and leads to the assumption that traffic to VOD providers may be routed differently via the VPN server than traffic to non VOD providers.

---

[1] The provider in question is the same provider who claimed to operate 190 distinct locations from the Khan et al. study [26].

[2] Some commercial VPN providers claim to run between 2,000 and 4,000 servers [26].

```
traceroute to example.com (93.184.216.34), 64 hops max, 72 byte packets
 1  10.8.0.1
 2  cs0-evo.nl.as25369.net
 3  ae2.10.rt0-evo.nl.as25369.net
 4  adm-b3-link.ip.twelve99.net
 5  adm-bb4-link.ip.twelve99.net
 6  prs-bb2-link.ip.twelve99.net
 7  rest-bb1-link.ip.twelve99.net
 8  ash-b2-link.ip.twelve99.net
 9  verizon-ic342246-ash-b2.ip.twelve99.net
10  ae-65.core1.dcb.edgecastcdn.net
11  93.184.216.34
```

Fig. 1. ICMP traceroute to example.com while being connected to NordVPN. RTTs have been omitted for readability.

We investigated this assumption by purchasing multiple subscriptions to common commercial VPN providers that advertise with geo-unblocking capabilities. During the setup phase for these providers we were asked to use their custom connection clients, which featured simple menus through which we could choose our VPN server's location. The source code for these applications is not made available though, so we cannot reason about the inner workings of the programs without reverse engineering. Luckily, all the providers we considered offer OpenVPN configuration files as well, meaning that we can access and investigate the exact parameters with which the OpenVPN tunnel is established. The systematic analysis of the configuration files, however, did not show anything out of the ordinary with respect to geo-unblocking, which led us to believe that the geo-unblocking mechanism must be located on the server side. We therefore used `traceroute` to get a first impression of the paths the traffic to the VOD providers could take.

Our test led to unexpected results, which were instrumental for defining a model of the VPN ecosystem. Ordinarily, one would expect that `traceroute` would trace a route from the VPN server to the VOD's homepage, likely with multiple hops depending on the relative location of the source and end point. This is the case, for example, when we issue a request to `example.com` while using a geo-unblocking VPN service (NordVPN), as shown in Fig. 1. However, when contacting a streaming provider (in this case `www.netflix.com`) using the same VPN service, we observe only a single hop as seen in Fig. 2.

From this we can draw two conclusions. Firstly, the IP address the `traceroute` terminates at clearly does not belong to the VOD provider, as the address falls in a prefix that is reserved for IETF Protocol Assignments[3]. Secondly, as a consequence of receiving these IP addresses, we infer that the commercial VPN providers are manipulating the proper DNS resolution for URLs

---

[3] https://www.iana.org/assignments/iana-ipv4-special-registry/iana-ipv4-special-registry.xhtml.

Table 1. Manipulated DNS requests from NordVPN's DNS servers for requests to Netflix's and Disney+'s homepage and CDN.

VOD Provider	VPN DNS	Cloudflare DNS
www.netflix.com	192.0.0.69	54.246.79.9
nflxvideo.net	192.0.0.69	54.155.178.5
www.disneyplus.com	192.0.0.56	23.206.113.15
disney.api.edge.bamgrid.com	192.0.0.56	18.65.39.3

belonging to VOD providers by returning IP addresses under their control. This mode of operation closely resembles what is often called a "smart" DNS Service [23]. Table 1 shows a sample of the returned IP addresses when requesting the A records for Netflix's and Disney+'s landing page and CDN network through NordVPN's DNS servers. For comparison, Table 1 also shows the expected A records for those domains when connected to NordVPN but forcing the use of Cloudflare's DNS server, thus showing that DNS manipulation is carried out.

Figure 3 shows a shortened log of trying to fetch Netflix's homepage via *curl* while being connected to NordVPN. The log shows the connection to 192.0.0.69, and also presents some rudimentary information on Netflix's TLS certificate. From this log, we inferred the following observation. If the certificate had been self-signed or expired then *curl* would have presented a warning and would not have continued unless instructed to do so. As this was not the case, and considering that the commercial VPN providers cannot terminate the TLS connection, we conclude that our connection to Netflix has been forwarded opaquely. We call these opaque forwarders *TLS forwarding proxies*.

Figure 4 depicts the principal building blocks of the geo-unblocking VPN mechanism that we identified based on our experiments so far. The figure shows the VPN user, who wants to perform geo-unblocking, on the left. The user connects to the VPN provider's gateway. The configuration of the provider then tells the client to use the VPN provider's DNS resolver. When the user connects to a streaming service, the VPN provider's resolver returns an internal IP address that presents as a transparent TLS proxy. The remainder of this paper will focus on what happens to traffic after the TLS forwarding proxies, shedding light on how VPN providers manage to achieve geo-unblocking.

```
traceroute to netflix.com (192.0.0.69), 64 hops max, 72 byte packets
1   192.0.0.69
```

Fig. 2. ICMP traceroute to Netflix.com while being connected to NordVPN. RTTs have been omitted for readability.

4   Commercial VPN Provider Selection

The commercial VPN ecosystem is ever-changing, with some providers going out of business [1], or being shut down by law enforcement due to almost exclusively offering their services for criminal purposes [3]. To fill this void, new providers take their places. Some providers stand the test of time and are a stable presence in the industry. In 2018, Khan et al. [26] identified 200 unique commercial VPN providers through three selection methods, namely: popular review site, Reddit crawl and personal recommendation. The fact that neither an exhaustive nor a more systematic approach for selection exists, highlights the size and dynamicity of this industry and also the lack of academic overview.

In this paper, we only consider commercial VPN providers that explicitly offer geo-unblocking. This requirement drastically reduces the set of possible providers. Our selection methodology takes inspiration from the methodology in [26], but rather than focusing on identifying a large number of VPN providers, we focus on building a sample among VPN providers bearing in mind the following guidelines:

- the VPN providers should appear in popular review sites;
- the VPN providers should have geo-unblocking capabilities;
- the selected VPN providers should be representative of different market shares.

With these guidelines in place we were able to execute a more targeted search for providers. We first identify a comprehensive review of existing VPN providers, namely the "VPN TIER LIST" [18]. Similarly to the popular review sites, which were used by Khan et al., the "VPN TIER LIST" maintains a ranking of commercial VPN providers, based on criteria such as pricing or if the user can

```
$ curl https://www.netflix.com -v

*   Trying 192.0.0.69:443...
* Connected to www.netflix.com (192.0.0.69) \
port 443 (#0)
...
* Server certificate:
*   subject: C=US; ST=California; L=Los Gatos; \
O=Netflix, Inc.; CN=www.netflix.com
*   start date: Dec 14 00:00:00 2021 GMT
*   expire date: Jan 14 23:59:59 2023 GMT
*   subjectAltName: host "www.netflix.com" \
matched cert's "www.netflix.com"
*   issuer: C=US; O=DigiCert Inc; CN=DigiCert \
TLS RSA SHA256 2020 CA1
*   SSL certificate verify ok.
...
```

Fig. 3. Private IP returns valid certificate for www.netflix.com

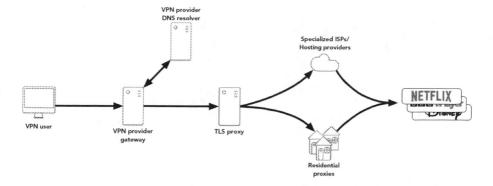

Fig. 4. Inferred geo-unblocking system

fully utilize the promised bandwidth without being throttled. The main difference though is the presence of a "streaming" criterion. This criterion rates the compatibility of a commercial VPN provider to flawlessly work with VOD providers. If we remember that VOD providers usually prohibit the use of VPNs, this compatibility rating is an indication of whether VPN providers are capable of deploying geo-unblocking methods that successfully circumvent blocking by VOD providers. Among the geo-unblocking VPN providers, we select six commercial providers that occupy different roles in the market. In particular, ExpressVPN [6] and NordVPN have been selected because they are established providers with a large market share, as can be inferred by the fact that they are able to allocate significant resources to marketing [7,21]. WeVPN, on the contrary, is a recent up-and-coming provider, which we expect to still have a limited market share. Manual investigation of CyberGhost, PrivateVPN and Surfshark places those instead as medium-sized providers. Finally, we also checked that all the selected providers actually succeed in geo-unblocking content. To do so, we followed the geo-unblocking instructions from each VPN provider as a regular user would, and tried streaming content that would otherwise be not available in our geographical area.

5 Methodology

In this section, we describe our measurement methodology, which focuses on gaining visibility behind the TLS forwarding proxies we identified in Sect. 3.

5.1 Geo-Unblocking IP Retrieval

The use of TLS forwarding proxies at most commercial VPN providers means that network path information is not available for the entire route from client to VOD CDN endpoint. Instead, we can only observe the path from our client to the host on which the proxy is running, as demonstrated in Sect. 3. To understand

```
Response
HTTP/1.1 403 Forbidden
Content-Type: application/octet-stream
...
Server: nginx
X-TCP-Info: addr=<Our Public IP>;port=58219;
```

Fig. 5. Shortened response of a GET request to Netflix's video CDN, showing the populated *X-TCP-Info* header.

how geo-unblocking takes place in VPN providers, we need a way to retrieve which IP address the VPN provider uses to connect to the VOD provider.

The analysis of the HTTP header for connections towards Netflix's CDN provided valuable information in this respect. When a connection request is issued to a Netflix CDN edge server (e.g. *ipv4-c139-ams001-ix.1.oca.nflxvideo.net*), we observed that a custom header (*X-TCP-Info*), likely set by the Netflix CDN itself, is returned. This header contains an IP address. Our hypothesis is that this IP address is actually the IP address of the host initiating the connection to the Netflix CDN.

To verify this hypothesis, we accessed Netflix's CDN from multiple vantage points under our control, such as residential wired and mobile connections, cloud providers, as well as from workstations at our institute. To simulate a VPN connection we also setup a VPN on a cloud-hosted machine under our control. In all cases, *X-TCP-Info* contains either the IP address of the host we were using for the test, or the external-facing IP of the VPN server, proving that this header contains information about the host initiating the VOD request. In addition, once connected to a geo-unblocking VPN host, we observe that the IP address returned in this header is no longer our own machine's address, but instead belongs to an unrelated autonomous system. We therefore consider this field as ground truth for the exit-node accessing Netflix, making it an invaluable source of information to map the ecosystem behind the TLS proxy (see Fig. 4).

We have also looked for this kind of header at other popular streaming providers at the time that data collection started, but we were not able to find any. Therefore, in the remainder of the paper, we will focus on Netflix as VOD service at which to direct our requests during our data collection.

Figure 5 shows a snippet of the HTTP response containing the populated *X-TCP-Info* field. Notice also, that the HTTP status code in Fig. 5 is "403 Forbidden". This is because we accessed Netflix's CDN node without providing prior authorization on purpose (i.e., without being logged in with a Netflix account). Logging in changes the HTTP status code to "200 OK", but the returned header fields are the same, including *X-TCP-Info*. We therefore strongly believe our method to be log-in status agnostic.

5.2   Testbed

To automate the retrieval of the header and the extraction of the *X-TCP-Info* field, we set up a testbed in the Netherlands which can support many concurrent VPN connections. A previous study [26] has used virtual machines for this purpose to maintain isolation between the VPNs, but this is not feasible for dozens of concurrent measurements. As a consequence we opted for a more lightweight solution, by using containers with segregated network namespaces. Within each container we establish an OpenVPN connection to a desired geographical unblocking region for every commercial VPN provider we consider. Once the VPN connection is established, we send a single HTTPS request at an interval of 30 s to Netflix's video CDN. For each request we save the following information: the time of the request, the status code of the request (i.e., OK or timeout) and the IP address of the exit-node. We then enrich the collected IP address with AS and (enhanced) geolocation information.

5.3   Geo-Unblocking Regions

Most VPN providers limit the amount of concurrent connections per account. As a result we cannot measure all geo-unblocking regions of a given VPN provider. Instead, we focused on a limited number of regions making sure that these regions are mostly supported by all chosen providers. We have selected the following four regions: USA, Japan, Germany and the Netherlands. The rationale behind these choices is as follows. We chose the USA because US-based VOD providers usually offer a larger content library for their internal market (while rights need to be negotiated for other countries), so we expect that this will draw the attention of geo-unblocking services. Japan has instead been chosen because it is a content creator for niche content, such as Anime, which could also be a reason to trigger geo-unblocking requests. Finally, Germany and the Netherlands are chosen for geographical diversity. In addition, the Netherlands has been chosen because it is known to have a generally good Internet infrastructure, both for consumers as well as for hosting. Table 2 shows that all chosen providers support these regions except CyberGhost, who do not offer geo-unblocking in the Netherlands.

Most VPN providers support at least five concurrent connections, which is why we chose to limit our vantage points to four, leaving one free connection as buffer for timed-out sessions or for debugging purposes.

6   Results

In this section, we discuss the results of the two measurement campaigns we ran. These measurement campaigns, both executed in 2022, are summarised in Table 3. We start with a general overview of our measurements, and then dig deeper into two particular mechanisms that VPN providers use to provide geo-unblocking for their customers. We end the section with an analysis of potential overlap in the backend infrastructures of VPN providers.

Table 2. Matrix showing the availability of measurements of a region per provider.

Provider \ Vantage Point	🏴	⬛	🇯🇵	〰
CyberGhost	☑	☑	☑	✕
ExpressVPN	☑	☑	☑	☑
NordVPN	☑	☑	☑	☑
PrivateVPN	☑	☑	☑	☑
Surfshark	☑	☑	☑	☑
WeVPN	☑	☑	☑	☑

Table 3. Data set overview

Measurement	Start date	End date	# samples
#1	24 February 2022	15 May 2022	3,810,624
#2	1 July 2022	29 October 2022	7,059,110

6.1 General Characterization of the Geo-Unblocking Ecosystem

We start with a general overview of our two main measurement campaigns as shown in Fig. 6. The graphs are arranged in a matrix where each row represents one of our six measured commercial VPN providers and the columns are the four distinct regions in which we measured. Each element of this matrix consists of two bar charts. The top chart represents the amount of unique IP addresses seen per day, where the bars are color-coded for IP versions, green for IPv4 and pink for IPv6. The overlaying black line visualizes the perceived IP churn, measured as the number of new IP addresses seen each day.

The bottom graphs, which are often more colorful, show a normalized view of the different autonomous systems we encountered per day. Each color represents a distinct AS and the colors are consistent across all graphs. We observed a total of 2,059 distinct ASNs and were therefore not able to give all of them a unique color. To account for this we gave the top 50 ASNs by observations in our data set a unique color, while the remaining ASNs have been colored black.

Based on these plots, we can see a few different geo-unblocking patterns. To start, we focus on the ASN usage. Some providers, for example NordVPN, PrivateVPN and Surfshark in Germany, Japan and the Netherlands, select their VPN exit nodes from a pool belonging to one or at maximum a few ASNs. Differently, providers such as Cyberghost in Germany or ExpressVPN in Germany and Japan, select their IP addresses from a large pool of ASNs.

These patterns are by no means stable over time though, nor are they the same for the same provider in different regions. For example, at CyberGhost in Japan we see their unblocking strategy switch from multiple ASNs to a single one, yet in the United States their strategy changes from a few ASNs to many. We can also see both of these behaviors occur in a single region, for example

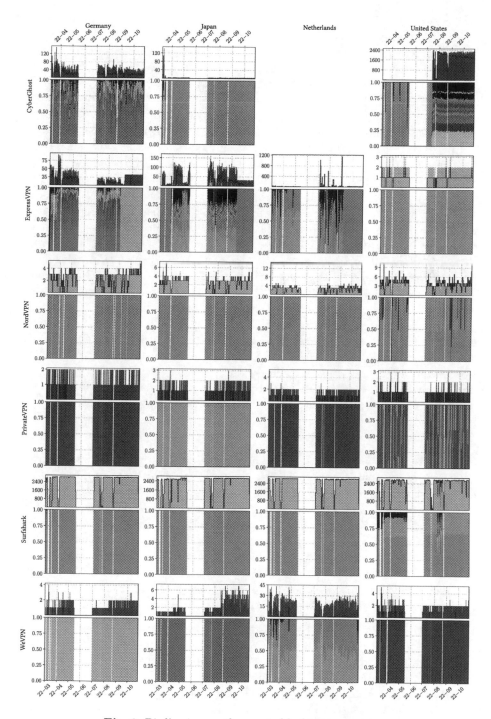

Fig. 6. Bird's view or the geo-unblocking ecosystem

ExpressVPN in Japan, where their unblocking strategy changes from one ASN to many and then reverts back to one.

The difference in ASN usage is not the only noteworthy observation. We now look at the IPv4/v6 usage and churn. Also in this case, the ecosystem shows several different approaches. In the US, CyberGhost relies on many thousands of distinct IPv4 addresses over the entire measurement period, many hundreds of which also seem to be repeating between August and November. Differently, PrivateVPN in Germany uses only 29 IPv4 addresses. These approaches are in sharp contrast to Surfshark's geo-unblocking solution. Instead of using IPv4, their preferred method is IPv6. Additionally, for every HTTPS request we sent we retrieved a unique IPv6 address, which is indicated by our churn-graph sitting on top of the unique IP graph peaks.

Lastly, we sometimes seem to observe the VPN providers "experimenting" with their settings. For example, Surfshark in the US has four distinct short-lived periods in August, during which we recorded many different ASNs mixed in with their "regulars". The IP graph in the top plot also indicates the inclusion of IPv4 addresses during these periods. Similarly, ExpressVPN in the Netherlands displays several periods during which the amount of unique IPs spikes above what is generally observed for that provider/region pairing.

These observations raise the question: *Can the different patterns be explained by VPN providers using different mechanisms to facilitate geo-unblocking?* To answer this question, we performed a detailed inspection of the IPs and ASNs we observe for each provider in each region.

For each ASN with a substantial presence in our data set, we manually obtained information on the type of service these ASNs provide, classifying these into two groups: Specialized networks or hosting providers and (apparent) residential Internet service providers.

Specialized Networks/Hosting Providers—The first mechanism we identify is the use of what we call "Specialized Networks" or "Hosting Providers". This category can be characterized as typically using a small number of ASNs (often, but not always a single one) and a small number of IPs, and the ASNs are characterized – at first glance, e.g., by inspecting their website – as residential access networks. Deeper inspection of these networks, however, reveals that they are in fact not residential access providers, but only masquerade as such. An especially interesting case in this category is PrivateVPN, which is the only provider in our set that does not use TLS proxies. Instead, it entirely relies on the specialized ISP model. We discuss this category in more detail in Sect. 6.2.

Residential ISPs – The second mechanism we identify is the use of proxies located at residential ISPs. VPN providers and regions that use this mechanism can be characterized by the use of a large(r) number of ASNs and larger numbers of unique IP addresses. The ASNs can all be categorized as legitimate ISPs that provide residential and/or business services, and the IP addresses reflect this as well (based on reverse DNS entries and geolocation). We discuss this category in more detail in Sect. 6.3.

Table 4. Unblocking behavior for each provider region

	Germany	Japan	Netherlands	United States
CyberGhost	R	R→H	n/a	H→R
ExpressVPN	R→H	H→R→H	R→(R+H)→H	R
NordVPN	H	H	H	H→(H+R)
PrivateVPN	H	H	H	H
Surfshark	H	H	H	H→(H+R)→H
WeVPN	H	H	R	R

(R = Residential, H = Specialized ISP/Hosting Provider)

Figure 6 shows that the geo-unblocking ecosystem is highly dynamic, suggesting that VPN providers are willing to put considerable effort into enabling their unblocking mechanisms. To further highlight this dynamicity, Table 4 summarizes our results in terms of the changes we observe in behavioral patters among the considered providers and geographic regions. In the table, we indicate with H a provider unblocking strategy based on the use of specialized networks/hosting providers, and with R a strategy based on residential ISPs. An arrow indicates a change in strategy. The table shows a variety of mechanism dynamics per region. What really stands out is the lack of a clear trend or overall strategy, even for each provider separately. In this, a few examples stand out. In Fig. 6 we see that ExpressVPN in the US makes use of a single ASN, which would typically indicate that this provider relies on a specialized network/hosting provider. However, in this case we were able to verify (by asking the ASN operator, a large US ISP, directly), that the IPs used for ExpressVPN operations were actually all allocated for residential use. We also observe that the same operator can choose a completely different approach in different geographical zones. This is for example the case of NordVPN in the US (hosting) compared to the other zones. PrivateVPN seems to use the same mechanism. However, this is a particular case that we will discuss in more detail in Sect. 6.2. Finally, Surfshark in the US shows only a temporary switch from a hosting mechanism, to residential and back to hosting. We speculate, given how stable their behavior in the US zone has been throughout the entire measurement, this is rather a fluke in their infrastructure than a real behavioral change.

Not only do geo-unblocking mechanisms change drastically within the same provider from measurement #1 to measurement #2, but within that same provider they are also substantially different from region to region. Such observations clearly provide hints that providers are willing to tailor their unblocking mechanisms to what works best at a specific moment in time and in a specific region. While it is hard to substantiate this without insider knowledge on how the VPN providers run their operation, we speculate that these changes are evidence of the arms race between VPN providers that want to offer geo-unblocking to their customers, and streaming providers that want to stop viewers from circumventing geo-fencing of content [5].

In the remainder of our analysis, we will provide more details on the categories of "Specialized Networks/Hosting Providers" and "Residential ISPs" in Sects. 6.2 and 6.3 respectively. The dynamics we observe suggest that the VPN provider ecosystem w.r.t. geo-unblocking is in constant evolution, probably because providers constantly look for IPs that do not appear in blocklists. This brings forward the question if providers also share these resources, or if they differentiate their infrastructure. We will look into this in Sect. 6.4.

Key Takeaways: *Analysis of regional Internet registry data for the IP addresses involved in geo-unblocking indicates that there are two main approaches to geo-unblocking: specialized networks and residential ISPs. Furthermore, we see strong indications that VPN providers adapt their behavior. This may be driven by attempts of the VOD providers to block them, or alternatively, the change in behavior may also be a result of a need to have more bandwidth available to satisfy the demand of their customers. As an external observer, however, we cannot ascertain whether either of these two is the case or not.*

6.2 Specialized Networks/Hosting Providers

We now take a deeper look at the specialized networks/hosting provider category we identified as being used by VPN providers to facilitate geo-unblocking earlier. We first look at hosting providers, in particular what we consider *non top-tier hosting providers*. These providers offer all of the services one might expect from a hosting provider, such as virtual private servers (VPS), dedicated servers or rack space to retail customers. Yet they are not one of the well-known major international players in the hosting business. The combination of these two attributes gives the VPN providers ample bandwidth to power their geo-unblocking network while also staying under the radar of enhanced geolocation database providers. Examples of these providers are Inter Connecx (AS13737 INCX Global, LLC), which operates from two data centers in the US (Detroit, MI and Kansas City, MO), and Starry DNS, which is a service provider based in Hong Kong with a small presence in the EU and US as well (AS134835 Starry Network Limited).

Key Takeaway: *It is possible for VPN providers to find lesser known hosting providers that are not listed in enhanced geolocation databases. However, this reveals an intrinsic fragility in the ecosystem as such hosting providers could be listed in those databases at any moment.*

The other subclass, *specialized ISPs*, can generally be described as IP space brokers. They often directly advertise that they monetize unused IP addresses, by renting them to interested parties or have a certain quantity of IP ranges on lease. Examples are IPXO [12] or Xantho UAB [20]. In some cases only a cryptic static landing page (if at all) informs potential customers of their services. This is the case, for example, for Trafficforce UAB (https://trafficforce.lt/), which has a very minimalist Web presence, but their IP addresses are in use in no fewer than four different VPN providers (Surfshark, NordVPN, ExpressVPN and CyberGhost).

Table 5. Matrix of PVDataNet AB and Telia Company AB's ASes and IPs per vantage point and the corresponding maintainer according to RIPE. IPs are represented by their network prefix.

Country	AS	IP	RIPE Maintainer
Germany	Telia Company AB (AS1299)	`193.104.198.0/24`	Nordic Internet Service AB
		`80.239.128.0/19`	Privat Kommunikation Sverige AB
Japan	Datacamp Limited (AS212238)	`193.234.55.0/24`	PVDataNet AB
Netherlands	Telia Company AB (AS1299)	`80.239.128.0/19`	Privat Kommunikation Sverige AB
United States	Telia Company AB (AS1299)	`193.104.198.0/24`	Nordic Internet Service AB
	PVDataNet AB (AS42201)	`45.130.86.0/24`	PVDataNet AB

What differentiates this subclass from non top-tier hosting providers is that the organisations in this category generally do not service any retail customers and have optimized their business model to monetize IP addresses.

Key Takeaway: *The use of specialised ISPs, especially those that are used by multiple VPN providers, suggests that there may exist a specialised market that caters to the needs of VPN providers for the combination of sufficient bandwidth coupled with IP addresses that are not blocked by VOD providers.*

Finally, we want to highlight one particular model that does not fit well into either category. In particular we want to spotlight a company that appears to be wholly owned and operated by PrivateVPN, for the sole purpose of appearing to be a consumer ISP. This company, called Nordic Internet Service AB came to light when we performed further investigation of the IP ranges we collected during our measurement. In particular, this concerns IP ranges that belong to either Telia Company AB (AS1299), Datacamp Limited (AS212238) or PVDataNet AB (AS42201). Looking at the administrative information in the RIPE database, the so-called maintainer object of these IP ranges shows that they are delegated to either Nordic Internet Service AB, Privat Kommunikation Sverige AB or PVDataNet AB as shown in Table 5.[4]

We consulted the Swedish companies registration office (Bolagsverket) for additional information on the companies listed as RIPE maintainers, due to their similarity in name. What we found is that the CEO for PrivateVPN Global AB and Nordic Internet Service AB is the same person. Furthermore, this person also acts as ordinary board member for PVDataNet AB. We therefore conclude that PVDataNet AB, Nordic Internet Service AB and PrivateVPN Global AB, are essentially the same entity.

---

[4] Note that, at the time of writing, some IP ranges have already been re-allocated to different providers and current RIR data might not reflect the data of this table.

Table 6. Residential ISPs with the largest amount of unique IPs per core unblocking region.

Country	AS	n
Germany	Deutsche Telekom (AS3320)	2,412
	Vodafone (AS3209)	1,143
Japan	NTT (AS4713)	1,052
	Softbank (AS17676)	724
Netherlands	Vodafone Libertel (AS33915)	347
	KPN (AS1136)	319
United States	Comcast (AS7922)	48,288
	AT&T (AS7018)	24,306

PVDataNet AB and Nordic Internet Service AB are also both registered local Internet registries (LIR) with RIPE, meaning that they can get IP address ranges assigned to them by an RIR, or have their own AS. From this publicly available information we conclude that PrivateVPN is using shell companies under their control for two specific goals. Firstly, by being a registered LIR they can easily enter the commercial Internet transit market to buy transit and IP addresses in a region they would like to geo-unblock. And secondly, by creating the impression of being a consumer ISP, they evade classification by enhanced geolocation databases, which in turn allows for geo-unblocking.

Key Takeaway: *Some VPN providers are willing to go the extra mile by seriously investing in their own dedicated infrastructure in order to circumvent VPN detection.*

6.3   Residential Proxies

The second class of geo-unblockers are residential proxies. Residential proxies, as the name suggests, run on hardware which is connected via consumer ISPs to the Internet. More research into this area is needed to understand the nature of these proxies, although other studies suggest that these proxies sometimes consist of compromised devices [22,28,31]. Residential Internet connections in general still have asymmetric network speeds, making them a sub-par solution compared to data center connectivity, which is what the first geo-unblocking solution would provide. On top of that, residential proxies might be less stable since they might be hosted on devices which are regularly turned off.

And yet, in all of our measurement regions we have identified major residential ISPs. Table 6 shows the unique IPs we identified per major residential ISP. Despite the intuition that residential proxies may be less reliable than specialized ISPs or hosting, we observe very large numbers of residential addresses being used in geo-unblocking, take for example the tens of thousands of IPs observed in two large US ISPs as shown in Table 6.

Table 7. Appearance of unique IPs which can be described as belonging to educational institutes (measurement campaign #1 and #2 combined).

Region	VPN Provider	n
Germany	ExpressVPN	17
Germany	Surfshark	2
Japan	ExpressVPN	3
United States	CyberGhost	95
United States	Surfshark	17

We not only see classic residential ISPs though. As a consequence of the fact that those proxies run on user computers, we have noticed that some geo-unblocking exit points appear in a variety of networks, even some where VOD streaming traffic might be odd. For example, we identified a residential proxy running on an IP belonging to the address space of the Ministry of Defense of a European country (which we have duly notified). Educational institutions are another example of networks where we observe VPN proxies, as we have detailed in Table 7. Those examples suggest that there are not only a few major players in the field of residential connection providers hosting VPN proxies, but that there is also a long tail of exit nodes distributed over numerous other networks.

We have been in contact with several operators of residential ISPs as well as educational networks to confirm our hypothesis that our recorded IPs largely belong to residential end-users and are not freely available to rent. The two residential ISP operators from two different countries (the US and Japan) provided us with ground truth that shows that the overwhelming majority of IPs belong to residential connections. In one case the operators indicated the occurrence of their commercial cloud in our data set ($\sim$3.7%).

In the case of the educational institutes we contacted (in two countries), we received confirmation that all but one IP were used by students or belonged to student housing, while the remaining IP belonged to the workstation of a university employee.

Key Takeaway: *The fact that VPN providers are willing to use "unreliable" residential connections means that this is still a mechanism that pays off, most likely w.r.t. evading VPN detection mechanisms.*

6.4 VPN Infrastructure Overlap

The availability of IP space that has not yet been tagged by an enhanced geolocation database (and thus aids in evading VOD VPN detection mechanisms) could be considered a precious, if not rare, commodity. This therefore brings about the question if VPN providers share their underlying unblocking infrastructure. We have investigated this by first looking into the number of unblocking IP addresses that occur at multiple VPN providers. From a total of 214,993 unique IPv4 and 1,925,327 unique IPv6 addresses, we only found an overlap of 273 IPv4 addresses

Table 8. Amount of ASNs shared between distinct number of VPN providers

Distinct ASNs	2	8	40	414	1582
Shared by N Providers	5	4	3	2	1

($\sim 0.1\%$) and no IPv6 addresses. These 273 IPv4 addresses in turn account for only $\sim 5.8\%$ of all observations (580,360 of 9,987,688). Even within this set of IPv4 addresses, the distribution is not uniform. As Fig. 7 shows, roughly 10 IPs make up half and about 40 IPs are responsible for 90% of our overlapping observations. In other words, based on these numbers we assume that it is highly unlikely that the VPN providers share a common geo-unblocking platform.

Taking a step back though and looking at a coarser-grained set of data, namely ASNs, we can see a different picture. In total, we observed 2,046 distinct ASNs of which 464 ($\sim 22.7\%$) have been found to overlap between the different VPN providers. Table 8 shows how often ASNs that overlap occur in our dataset.

Generally speaking the amount of shared ASNs resembles a heavy-tailed distribution and can be seen in Fig. 8. Just two ASNs (AS212144 (45.3%) and AS212238 (11.1%)) make up 56.4% of all overlapping observations. More importantly, though, they make up 48.8% of *all* observations in our data set. The first ASN, AS212144, Trafficforce UAB (which we discussed previously in Sect. 6.2) is shared among four of the VPN providers (NordVPN, Surfshark, CyberGhost, ExpressVPN) and the latter, AS212238, Datacamp Ltd. (which announces IP space for Trafficforce) is shared among five (PrivateVPN, CyberGhost, Surfshark, NordVPN, ExpressVPN). This can also be noticed in Fig. 6 by keeping in mind that the same ASN is plotted in the same color throughout the picture.

Key Takeaway: *The majority of overlap in infrastructure between VPN providers lies with just a few distinct ASNs that seemingly belong to a class of service provider that caters well to the need of VPN providers that want to perform geo-unblocking. Nevertheless, we also still see evidence of overlap in residential connections*

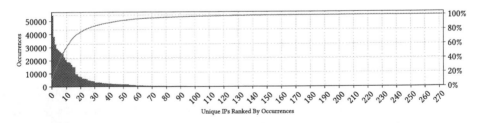

Fig. 7. Number of overlapping IPv4 addresses and amount of occurrences in our data set

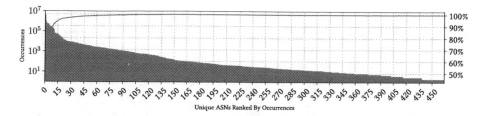

Fig. 8. Number of overlapping ASNs and amount of occurrences in our data set

7 Ethical Considerations

The work described in this paper has presented us with several different ethical dilemmas that affect many of the different stakeholders in this context. In this section we aim to provide an overview of the ethical challenges that we identified and explain how we handled them to minimize impact on the relevant stakeholders.

7.1 Ecosystem

The ecosystem of VPN providers in the context of geo-unblocking and Video-on-Demand (VOD) providers creates tensions. As described in Sect. 3 VOD providers put measures in place to restrict material due to distribution right restrictions. VPN providers in contrast advertise with geo-unblocking capabilities to allow VPN users to circumvent the restrictions put in place by the VOD providers. VOD providers in turn aim to detect the circumvention methods, which causes VPN providers to come up with alternative ways to route traffic and evade this detection.

This context presents ethical tensions:

- Users may use the VPN services to circumvent the geo-blocking measures of VOD providers, which breaks the terms of service of most of these services, and may even be illegal in some jurisdictions.
- VOD providers currently restrict content due to licensing agreements, and have put detection capabilities in place to prevent geo-unblocking. Research into this context provides them with additional information on the practices, allowing (or perhaps even forcing) them to improve their detection capabilities.
- VPN providers on the other hand advertise with the geo-unblocking capability. Our research into this practice may hurt their business practices.

7.2 VPN Provider Selection

As described in Sect. 4 the VPN ecosystem is ever-changing, in part due to catering to the criminal market. For this reason we limited our research to long-lived commercial providers that presented geo-unblocking capabilities.

While the practice of geo-unblocking in the context of VOD may be breaking terms of service, we are aware that there might also be legitimate uses of geo-unblocking.

7.3   Methodology and Results

While designing our measurement system and exploring the systems and capabilities of the VPN providers, we discovered that routes could also include personal networks. This meant that we would record personally identifiable information in recording traffic routes.

It was impossible for us to request informed consent from the users of the residential IP addresses, as there was no way for us to contact them directly. To mitigate impact on these individuals we secured our testbed which we described in Sect. 5. We secured this testbed so that only the researchers had access to the data, and further restricted access to just our university's network.

In the paper we only use aggregated results that do not identify specific users, and we will not voluntarily share the data with others. Furthermore, the recording of this personal data has been registered at the university following the official processes required by the GDPR.

An approval record from our institution's ethics board is available under registration number *redacted*.

8   Conclusion

Both streaming and VPNs are multi-billion dollar industries [16,17]. The two are constantly locked in an arms race where VPN providers are trying to offer geo-unblocking to their customers and VOD providers are trying to enforce restrictions on the content delivery to certain regions to enforce licensing agreements.

In this paper we shed first light on how VPN providers circumvent geo-blocking restrictions. Our main findings are three-fold. Firstly, VPN providers use different mechanisms for bypassing geo-blocking, making use of specialized networks/hosting providers and residential ISPs. Secondly, VPN providers use different mechanisms in different geographical regions, thus adapting their behavior to what best ensures escaping VOD detection mechanisms. Finally there are also temporal dynamics, i.e., the approaches change at different moments in time, even within the same provider. These findings paint a picture of the geo-unblocking VPN providers' ecosystem as highly dynamic and adaptable. Given the value of the market we expect this arms race to continue in a future where we might see even *Stranger VPNs*.

References

1. Tunnelr - maintenance mode - we'll be right back! (2018). https://www.tunnelr.com/
2. Digital element commemorates 20th anniversary (2019). https://www.digitalelement.com/digital_element_20th_anniversary/

3. Cybercriminals' favourite VPN taken down in global action (2020). https://www.
   europol.europa.eu/media-press/newsroom/news/cybercriminals'-favourite-vpn-
   taken-down-in-global-action
4. Hulu help center - i'm getting an anonymous proxy error (2021). https://www.
   help.hulu.com/s/article/anonymous-proxy-error
5. Netflix intensifies 'VPN Ban' and targets residential IP-addresses too (Updated)
   * TorrentFreak (2021). https://www.torrentfreak.com/netflix-intensifies-vpn-ban-
   and-targets-residential-ip-addresses-too-210811/
6. Top podcast advertisers USA 2021 (2021). https://www.statista.com/statistics/
   1273734/podcast-advertisers-usa/
7. Brands with highest youtube influencer marketing spend 2020 (2022). https://
   www.statista.com/statistics/1267365/youtube-influencer-marketing-spenders/
8. Error code 73: 'Disney+ is only available in certain regions...' (2022).
   https://www.help.disneyplus.com/csp?id=csp_article_content&sys_kb_
   id=bd59d944db08d9943142eb2ed396199a
9. Geo-blocking security & filtering — Video streaming with geo blocking (2022).
   https://www.streamingvideoprovider.com/secure-streaming/geo-blocking-
   restrcitions/
10. HBO Max — Find out what to do if you're getting an 'HBO Max isn't available in
    your region' message. (2022). https://www.help.hbomax.com/us/Answer/Detail/
    000001252
11. How Netflix licenses TV shows and movies (2022). https://www.help.netflix.com/
    en/node/4976
12. Monetize the Unused IPv4 Space. Quick Setup & Easy-to-Use (2022). https://
    www.ipxo.com/monetize-ips/
13. Netflix says 'You seem to be using an unblocker or proxy'. (2022). https://www.
    help.netflix.com/en/node/277
14. Netflix thinks I'm in a different country (2022). https://www.help.netflix.com/en/
    node/26100
15. Prime video: help (2022). https://www.primevideo.com/help/ref=atv_hp_nd_cnt?
    nodeId=GU85HKX66NVFNQ9Y
16. Streaming worldwide (2022). https://www.statista.com/study/112979/streaming-
    worldwide/
17. VPN market size worldwide 2027 (2022). https://www.statista.com/statistics/
    542817/worldwide-virtual-private-network-market/
18. VPN tier list 2022 (2022). https://www.vpntierlist.com/vpn-tier-list-2022
19. Where is Disney+ available? (2022). https://www.help.disneyplus.com/csp?
    id=csp_article_content&sys_kb_id=27544637dbb23894ac7ceacb1396197e
20. Xantho IP space lease (2022). https://www.xantho.lt/
21. Akgul, O., Roberts, R., Namara, M., Levin, D., Mazurek, M.L.: Investigating influ-
    encer VPN Ads on YouTube. In: 2022 IEEE Symposium on Security and Privacy
    (SP), pp. 876–892. IEEE, San Francisco, CA, USA (2022). https://doi.org/10.
    1109/SP46214.2022.9833633
22. Chung, T., Choffnes, D., Mislove, A.: Tunneling for transparency: a large-scale
    analysis of end-to-end violations in the internet. In: Proceedings of the 2016 Inter-
    net Measurement Conference, pp. 199–213. ACM, Santa Monica California USA
    (2016). https://doi.org/10.1145/2987443.2987455
23. Fainchtein, R.A., Aviv, A.J., Sherr, M., Ribaudo, S., Khullar, A.: Holes in the
    geofence: privacy vulnerabilities in "Smart" DNS services. Proceed. Priv. Enhan.
    Technol. **2021**(2), 151–172 (2021). https://doi.org/10.2478/popets-2021-0022

24. Huffaker, B., Fomenkov, M., claffy, k.: Geocompare: a comparison of public and commercial geolocation databases. Tech. Rep. (2011)
25. Ikram, M., Vallina-Rodriguez, N., Seneviratne, S., Kaafar, M.A., Paxson, V.: An analysis of the privacy and security risks of android VPN permission-enabled apps. In: Proceedings of the 2016 Internet Measurement Conference, pp. 349–364. ACM, Santa Monica California USA (2016). https://doi.org/10.1145/2987443.2987471
26. Khan, M.T., DeBlasio, J., Voelker, G.M., Snoeren, A.C., Kanich, C., Vallina-Rodriguez, N.: An empirical analysis of the commercial VPN ecosystem. In: Proceedings of the Internet Measurement Conference 2018, pp. 443–456. ACM, Boston MA USA (2018). https://doi.org/10.1145/3278532.3278570
27. McDonald, A., et al.: 403 forbidden: a global view of CDN geoblocking. In: Proceedings of the Internet Measurement Conference 2018, pp. 218–230. IMC 2018, Association for Computing Machinery, New York, NY, USA (2018). https://doi.org/10.1145/3278532.3278552
28. Mi, X., et al.: Resident evil: understanding residential IP proxy as a dark service. In: 2019 IEEE Symposium on Security and Privacy (SP), pp. 1185–1201. IEEE, San Francisco, CA, USA (2019). https://doi.org/10.1109/SP.2019.00011
29. Perta, V.C., Barbera, M.V., Tyson, G., Haddadi, H., Mei, A.: A glance through the VPN looking glass: IPv6 leakage and DNS Hijacking in commercial VPN clients. Proceed. Priv. Enhan. Technol. **2015**(1), 77–91 (2015). https://doi.org/10.1515/popets-2015-0006
30. Ramesh, R., Evdokimov, L., Xue, D., Ensafi, R.: VPNalyzer: systematic investigation of the VPN ecosystem. In: Proceedings 2022 Network and Distributed System Security Symposium. Internet Society, San Diego, CA, USA (2022). https://doi.org/10.14722/ndss.2022.24285
31. Tosun, A., De Donno, M., Dragoni, N., Fafoutis, X.: RESIP host detection: identification of malicious residential IP proxy flows. In: 2021 IEEE International Conference on Consumer Electronics (ICCE). pp. 1–6. IEEE, Las Vegas, NV, USA (2021). https://doi.org/10.1109/ICCE50685.2021.9427688
32. Weinberg, Z., Cho, S., Christin, N., Sekar, V., Gill, P.: How to catch when proxies lie: verifying the physical locations of network proxies with active geolocation. In: Proceedings of the Internet Measurement Conference 2018, pp. 203–217. ACM, Boston MA USA (2018). https://doi.org/10.1145/3278532.3278551
33. Winter, P., Padmanabhan, R., King, A., Dainotti, A.: Geo-locating BGP prefixes. In: 2019 Network Traffic Measurement and Analysis Conference (TMA), pp. 9–16. IEEE, Paris, France (2019). https://doi.org/10.23919/TMA.2019.8784509

TLS

Exploring the Evolution of TLS Certificates

Syed Muhammad Farhan and Taejoong Chung[✉]

Virginia Tech, Blacksburg, USA
{farhan,tijay}@vt.edu

Abstract. A vast majority of popular communication protocols such as HTTPS for the Internet employs the use of TLS (Transport Layer Security) to secure communication. As a result, there have been numerous efforts to improve the TLS certificate ecosystem such as Certificate Transparency logs and Free Automated CAs like LetsEncrypt. Our work highlights the effectiveness of these efforts using the Certificate Transparency logs as well as certificates collected via full IPv4 scans by validating them. We show that a large proportion of invalid certificates still exists and outline reasons why these certificates still exist. Additionally, we report unresolved security issues such as key sharing. Moreover, we show that the incorrect use of template certificates has led to incorrect SCTs being embedded in the certificates. Taken together, our results emphasize the continued involvement of the research community to improve the web's PKI ecosystem.

1 Introduction

TLS has become the de-facto standard for securing the Internet; it is the underlying security procedure behind popular communication protocols like HTTPS and SMTPS.

The widespread use of TLS has led to a lot of efforts from the community to make the TLS certificate ecosystem more democratic, transparent and economically feasible. Some efforts worth mentioning are the introduction of (1) ACME (specifically Let's Encrypt) [6] that allows valid certificates to be issued for free and removes the need for human intervention for certificate issuance and (2) the CT standard, which states that all compliant certificates must be published to append-only public servers so that any mis-issuance is promptly discovered, thus can be revoked.

This work presents an *audit* on the evolution of the certificate ecosystem over the last 8 years by using two sets of a large corpus of certificates; certificates collected from full IPv4 scans [20] from 2013 to 2021 and certificates logged in Google operated Certificate Transparency Logs till February 2021.

We make the following contributions. *First*, we explore how the overall *validity* of certificates has changed over time across most end-user applicable root stores. We observe that while the percentage of valid certificates has improved, a large portion of certificates are still invalid.

Second, we show that the use of template certificates to create new certificates has led to certificates presenting invalid extension data. Some certificates using template certificate fail to update key components in a certificates, which are supposed to be unique such as `subjectKeyIdentifier` and `ct_precert_scts` fields resulting in incorrect usage of these extensions.

Third, we show how the TLS certificate ecosystem has evolved over the past 8 years. We show that the overall security of certificates such as key strength has improved, and the ecosystem has become more centralized over time with a small number of CAs issuing a large percentage of total certificates.

2   Background

TLS Certificates: A TLS certificate binds a subject (domain) to a public key. These certificates are usually issued and signed by Certificate Authorities (CAs) once it successfully vets the subject. Thus, certificates usually have a certificate chain rooted in a widely-trusted set of root certificates, which are self-signed.

X.509 [12] is the most commonly used certificate management standard. X.509 certificates typically includes the subject (e.g., domain name), issuer (i.e., CA), public key, serial number (unique to a CA). It can also have additional information such as CRL Distribution Points extension [12], which allows a client to perform revocation check using URLs provided in the extension.

Invalid Certificates: A certificate can be *invalid* if it fails to meet certain rule in the RFC [12]; there can be multiple reasons that a client determines the certificate to be invalid; name a few, cryptographic errors (e.g., the signature of a certificate cannot be validated), expiration, self-signed certificates, etc.. A previous study [11] showed that the most common reason for this invalidity is certificates signed by untrusted root or self-signed and reported that 88% of invalid certificates are self-signed.

Certificate Transparency: Certificate Transparency logs [5] are public and append-only data structure, which are designed to ensure any certificate mis-issuance is caught early and can be revoked by the issuer. Over 6 billion certificates have been logged to Certificate Transparency logs to date [23].

Nowadays, Certificate Transparency sits within the wider ecosystem of the Web's PKI; CAs are expected to create a pre-certificate and log it to a CA when domain owners issue a Certificate Signing Request (CSR) to CAs. The CT, in return, sends an SCT (Signed Certificate Timestamp), which is a promise that the certificate will be added to the CT log within a predetermined timeframe. The CA then signs the final certificate and sends the certificate as well as the SCT to the domain owner. SCTs are usually embedded within a certificate, but may also be communicated through other means (e.g., an OCSP stapled response).

User agents (mostly browsers) validate SCTs when they receive a certificate to ensure that it has been logged to a Certificate Transparency log. Popular user agents have their own CT policy that determines how many and which CTs a certificate needs to be logged to be considered secure [10].

3   Related Works

Free and Automated CAs. While most measurement studies for PKI focus on valid certificates, a previous study [11] showed that a majority of certificates (88%) were invalid. The reason for these certificates being invalid was economical and a vast majority of invalid certificates originated from IoT devices. Since then, the introduction of Let's Encrypt [15] and the concept of free, automated CAs has made it increasingly easy and economically feasible to get valid certificates. Other CAs (like Sectigo [3] and cPanel [25]) soon followed suit and added support for automated certificate issuance.

Certificate Transparency. Benjamin et al. [7] explored different sources of SSL certificates and show that Certificate Transparency logs hold the largest collection of certificates. Still, CT was missing 15% of all certificates observed by the researchers; however, this research was conducted (in 2016) while Certificate Transparency was still in its infancy. Certificate Transparency became a standard industry practice and requirement for major browsers in 2018 as explained in [21]. Gasser et al. [14] focused on the syntactical compliance of certificates required by Baseline Requirements and found that nearly 900 k certificates are not compliant mainly due to a small number of CAs.

Korzhitskii et al. [16] characterized the root stores of popular Certificate Transparency logs and showed that while the CT root stores are expected to be a super-set of root stores from major browsers, most logs are missing a few root certificates from Apple, Microsoft or Mozilla root stores. Some studies [18,22] focused on the reliability and effectiveness of the CTlogs; for example, Stark et al. [22] measured the error rates and reported that it had been running with minimal breakage. However, Li et al. [18] showed that it is not practical to monitor the CT logs in a real time and process on top of them reliably due to the sheer volume of the CT logs.

4   Dataset and Methodology

4.1   Datasets

Our dataset consists of certificates collected via full IPv4 scans in project Sonar by Rapid7 [20] and the certificates logged to Certificate Transparency logs managed by Google.

IPv4 Scans: These scans are conducted by Rapid7, are open for public use, and are designed to find certificates from HTTPS endpoints. The timeline of this dataset spans from September 2013 to December 2021 with a total of 358,575,204 unique certificates observed. Scans were conducted every week from September 2013 to June 2017, every two weeks from June 2017 to January 2019, and daily afterwards. Additionally, from September 2013 to January 2018, only port 443 (the standard port for HTTPS) was scanned, while alternate HTTPS ports were also scanned afterwards. We use the number of unique certificates as the unit of measurement for this dataset as a certificate is expected to be seen in multiple scans.

Certificate Transparency: Our Certificate Transparency dataset contains certificates published to CT logs operated by Google. We limit out CT dataset to logs managed by google since Chrome's CT policy requires certificates to be posted on at least one CT logs operated by google [10]. We collect a total of 4,481,716,844 certificates spanning from the inception of CT to February 2021. Since (1) IPv4 scans cannot fetch certificates that are only available through SNI (Server Name Indication) and (2) some certificates are not for Web (e.g., DANE [13]), we expect this is the cause of 12.5 times more certificates found in the CT logs.

The volume of certificates in CT was low before 2016, after which the number of certificates logged has been growing every year. We use the CT index as the unit of measurement for this dataset.

4.2   Validation Methodology

Root Stores. When validating certificates, the first question that needs to be answered is which root store should we use. Since our goal is to find out if end-user applications will find these certificates to be valid, we use four different root stores (Apple, Microsoft, Mozilla NSS, and Android root stores) to validate all certificates collected from IPv4 scan. Previously, Zane et al. [24] showed that a vast majority of root stores used in end user applications stem from a handful of 'root' root stores.

Since our certificate transparency dataset only includes certificates logged to Certificate Transparency logs managed by google, we want to use the root store from google's CT logs. Google states that the root stores for CT should be a super set of all major root stores (Apple, Microsoft and Mozilla) to be inclusive of all certificates that may be considered valid by these entities [4]. Looking at the current snapshot of root certificates for all the CT logs in our dataset, we find that the root stores for all active CT logs managed by google are the same. We then backtrack through the entirety of the timeline that CTs have been active to ensure we have all the historical root certificates in our root store.

Validation Configuration. We use the command line version of OpenSSL to validate all certificates in our dataset and set it up to ignore time related errors and certificate revocations.

To validate certificates collected via IPv4 scans, we first isolate all CA certificates (certificates with the is_ca tag set to true) and iteratively validate them. After each iteration, we add valid CA certificates to our set of possible intermediate certificates and repeat this process until there are no new valid CA certificates. Finally, we verify all the leaf certificates using the full set of intermediate certificates.

The rules governing which certificates may be added to CT are more relaxed than those generally used to validate x509 certificates where inclusion to CT only

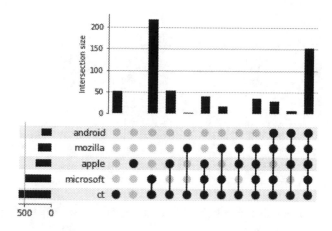

Fig. 1. Set relationship between root stores.

requires a valid chain to a root certificate [17]. To validate CT certificates, we setup OpenSSL to ignore x509 critical errors (CT pre-certificates have a poison added to make them invalid for regular use) and use the intermediate certificates logged to CT.

5   Certificate Validity

5.1   IPv4 Scanning

Unless stated otherwise, we define a certificate as valid if it is valid for any end-user root store in our dataset. After validating all certificates in our dataset, we isolate 121,062,606 unique valid certificates (33.76% of all certificates). We observe that the majority (66.23%) of certificates are *invalid* across all the root stores we use in our test; more specifically, 55.41% (131,625,055) of the invalid certificates are invalid because they are self-signed and 44.58% (105,770,334) are invalid because they are signed by another invalid certificate. This accounts for the vast majority of invalid certificates with only 1074 certificates invalid due to some other reason.

Figure 1 shows the set relationship across different root stores. We find that the CT root store contains all the root certificates from other root stores apart from one certificate that is only present in the Apple root store. We also observe that while a large number of certificates are shared between all end-application root stores, a large number of certificates are unique to the Microsoft and Apple root stores. However, there is little variation in the validity of certificates between different root stores. We find that 120,200,897 certificates (99% of the certificates valid in any root store) are valid across all end-application root stores in out dataset. This echoes the work done by Pear et al. showing that a vast majority of HTTPS servers use CAs that are trusted by all major trust stores [19].

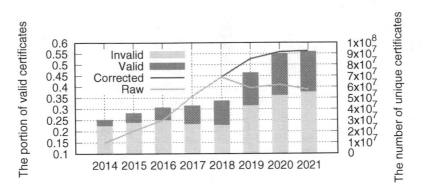

Fig. 2. The number of valid and invalid certificates via IPv4 scanning

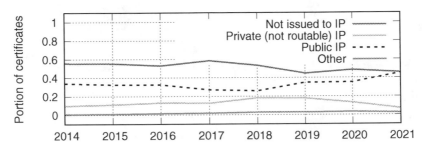

Fig. 3. The number of invalid certificates issued to IP addresses

The total number of certificates and percentage of valid certificates has been on the rise throughout our scanning period as shown in Fig. 2. We surprisingly saw a declining validity percentage after 2018, which we later found was an artifact of more frequent scanning since a large percentage of invalid certificates are seen in a single scan and are ephemeral. The corrected validity percentage (where we sample our data after 2019 to be consistent with the prior data) shows a constant increase over time. However, there remains a large percentage (45%) of invalid certificates.

Why are there still invalid certificates? Almost half of the invalid certificates are issued to IP addresses (i.e. the common name is an IP address) as highlighted in Fig. 3 (the other half has a valid FQDN); we find that the percentage of invalid certificates issued to private IPs has been on the rise for the past three years, while the percentage of invalid certificates not issued to IP addresses has been on the decline. Only a minute number of valid certificates are issued to IP addresses as CAs will generally not issue certificates without a valid domain name.

Where are Invalid Certificates Hosted? We use the common name of the certificate and the subject alternative names of the certificates to find all the domains a certificate represents. Note that some certificates are issued to IP addresses and are excluded from this analysis (and some certificates counted multiple times in different domains) Fig. 4 shows the top 5 top level domains in

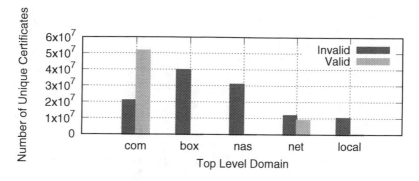

Fig. 4. Popular top level domains for valid and invalid certificates

our dataset. We observe that popular web domains like .com and .net hosting publicly accessible web pages tend to present valid certificates. Throughout the manual investigation, we find that invalid certificates for the .net domain are largely issued by Kubernetes. The .box and .nas domains (over 99.9%) are almost exclusively invalid and routers from AVM (fritz box) constitute a large majority of these certificates; thus, we believe that such invalid certificates are used for individual applications (such as using a network attached storage device). Since the .local domain is reserved for use by Internet Engineering Task Force (IETF), thus we exclusively observed them in invalid certificates. We could not identify any patterns that might tell us their source.

5.2   Certificate Transparency

Validating the certificates in the CT logs, we find that only few certificates are invalid as shown in Fig. 5. Some of these invalid certificates were added to the log due to bugs in the CT code; for example, in 2015, a bug introduced to the Google Pilot and Aviator logs accepted all certificates with unsupported algorithms [2].[1] Interestingly, these logs were not removed from the trusted set for Google Chrome. As the set of root certificates used by a CT log is arbitrary, any certificate may be added to the CT log without any consequence since any user agent will have their own root store and validate the certificate in question. The reason for the filter in Certificate Transparency is due to operational reasons like reducing the amount of spam in the logs, and keeping the log servers available at all times.

6   Certificate Authorities

6.1   IPv4 Scanning

Figure 6 tracks how domains (CNs) have been migrated across different CAs. We can infer that common names representing invalid certificates tend to be short-lived, since the percentage of invalid certificates in Fig. 6 does not match the one

---

[1] It is worth noting that these problematic certificates cannot be removed because the CT log is a Merkle-tree based structure, which is append-only.

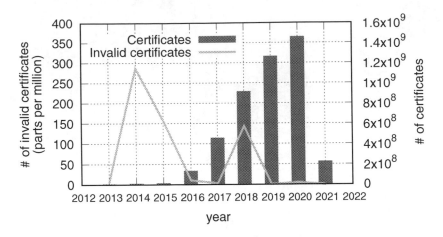

Fig. 5. The number of total (and invalid) certificates in the CT logs

in Fig. 2. We observe the growth of Let's Encrypt, which issued an insignificant amount of certificates in 2015, which is the largest issuer of certificates in 2021. Note that most domains that use Let's Encrypt and are new TLS (either new to using TLS or new domains altogether) as highlighted by the fact that we cannot find certificates for these domains before the one issued by Let's Encrypt. The increase in flow for Digicert is explained by the fact that Digicert acquired Symantec in October 2017. The decrease in flow for Comodo CA Limited between 2018 and 2019 is because it was rebranded as Sectigo in November 2018. Fortinet had a small presence up till 2017, after which we see a sharp increase in the number of certificates issued by Fortinet. This is likely an artifact of scanning since most of the Fortinet certificates are found on port 8010 and our dataset did not include this port before 2018.

Overall, centrality of issuers has increased over time where only a small percentage of certificates were issued by top CAs in 2013, but a large fraction of certificates are issued by Let's Encrypt in 2021. Additionally, we also find that only 10 keys are used to directly sign 80% of the valid certificates, which brings a security concern; if any of these keys are compromised, there will be a disproportionately large impact on the health of the ecosystem.

6.2   Certificate Transparency

We find that Let's Encrypt dominates the Certificate Transparency logs, consistently issuing 80% of the certificates logged after 2016; Note that the volume in CT was quite low prior to 2016. As shown in Fig. 7, cPanel and Sectigo also consistently log a substantial portion of certificates. Since the vast majority of the certificates from CT Logs are valid as shown in Fig. 5, we could not find any distinctive pattern in terms of the population of invalid certificates acrossthe CAs.

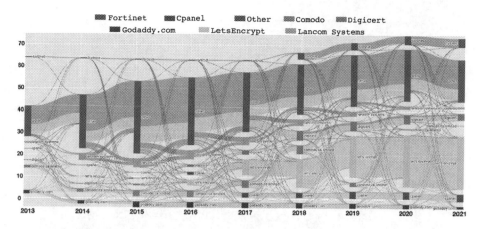

Fig. 6. Tracking yearly CA choice for all common names in the certificates from IPv4 scanning. The red flow represents invalid certificates while the blue flow represents valid certificates. (Color figure online)

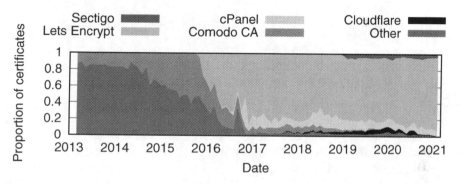

Fig. 7. Proportion of certificates logged to CTs by CA

7   Host Networks

Now, we focus on where the certificates are hosted from by looking at the IP address of hosts that serve certificates.

7.1   IPv4 Scanning

Similar to previous approach [11], we use CAIDA AS classification dataset [8] and group the certificates by the type of AS. Figure 8 shows the distribution of AS types over time for both valid and invalid certificates; we first immediately notice that invalid certificates can predominately be found on transit/access type ASes, which correspond to end-user connections; however, the portion of such certificates decreases as time goes on.

Valid certificates, on the other hand, are much less likely to be found on transit addresses. We also see a decreasing trend in the usage of transit addresses

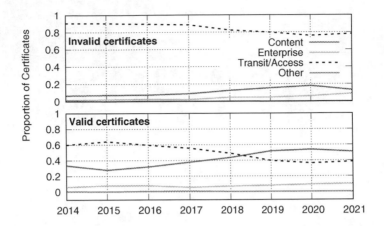

Fig. 8. Distribution of AS types over time for certificates collected through IP scanning

for valid certificates while the proportion of valid certificates hosted via content ASes is increasing.

7.2 Certificate Transparency

For the certificates collected from September 2020 to March 2022, we run DNS queries on the domain names for which certificates are posted on CT to get the A records mapped to the domain. We then follow the procedure highlighted above to get the AS number, and show the results in Fig. 9. Comparing with Fig. 8, we see a larger portion of certificates logged to CT hosted on content ASes as compared to valid certificates seen in IP scans for the same time range; this is aligned with a previous study [9], which showed that many websites are hosted at least in part by third parties, more centralized in CDNs.

8 Evolution

This section describes the major changes we observe in the IP scanned certificates.

Signature Algorithm: In early 2017, major browsers including Chrome, Firefox and Safari officially depreciated the use of SHA1 as an encryption algorithm for certificates [1] as there are significant collision attacks available for the algorithm. Almost all valid certificates shifted to using SHA256 in favor of SHA1 by 2017. The same change happened much slower for invalid certificates with a considerable portion of certificates still employing SHA1 as late as 2020.

Certificate Revocation. We rarely find a certificate revocation mechanism defined for invalid certificates. For valid certificates, we find that CRLs were very popular till 2015, after which we observe a constant decline in the percentage of valid certificates supporting CRLs. OCSP was quite popular in 2013 with 90% of

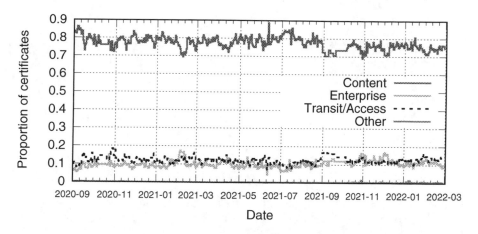

Fig. 9. AS types of certificates logged to CT logs

the valid certificates supporting it, but after 2015 practically all valid certificates support OCSP.

CT Inclusion Proofs. Figure 10 shows the inclusion in CT for Rapid7 scanned certificates over time. More than 99% of valid certificates after 2018 are included in CT logs, while a small but increasing proportion of invalid certificates have SCTs. While the rules governing Certificate Transparencies to filter certificates are more lenient than those for validity, it is unexpected to find invalid certificates with SCTs. We find that these certificates are sharing SCTs. SCTs should be cryptographically generated by the CT log and thus valid SCTs must be unique. Only 24% of invalid certificates have a unique SCT, in contrast we find no valid certificate sharing an SCT with another valid certificate. We revalidate these certificates (the ones that have unique SCTs) using the CT root store and corresponding rules and find that a majority of these may be considered valid by CT [17].

99% of the invalid certificates sharing SCTs are issued by Fortinet. In the general case we find one valid certificate who's SCT is shared by multiple invalid certificates. Moreover, other (certificate specific) extensions, like Subject Key Identifier are shared among these certificates even though they do not share a public key. We believe that these are a result of using existing valid certificates as a template to create new certificates. This explains why these certificates present invalid SCT tags and share the Subject Key Identifiers. We reached out to Fortinet for a comment but have not received a response.

9   Discussion

Free, Automated CAs like Let's Encrypt and cPanel have been the biggest source of change for the TLS certificate ecosystem. These services allow valid certificates to be issued without any real investment from the domain owner (both in terms

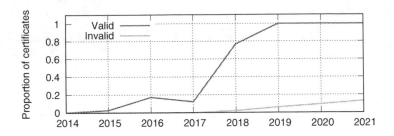

Fig. 10. Proportion of valid and invalid certificates with SCTs defined

of time and money). The improvement in validity percentage that we see is also in large part due to these Certificate Authorities. We can also attribute the decrease in validity period to these CAs.

On the other hand, these ACME-supporting CAs also put the overall ecosystem at risk. The nature of the PKI ecosystem means that any domain can be impersonated by compromising the least secure CA, and there are known attacks against the domain validation employed by these CAs. We observe that centrality in issuers has increased considerably over the course of our scans, and this is likely caused by the popularity of Let's Encrypt and cPanel. Only 10 keys are responsible for directly signing 80% of the valid certificates, which means that in case these keys are compromised, a mast majority of valid certificates should become invalid as the certificates with these keys are revoked, or are removed from trust stores. These keys are likely to be compromised when compared to keys used for root certificates, as the root certificate keys are rarely held in memory to sign other certificates, while these are continuously held in memory.

10   Conclusion

This work presents a bird's eye view of how the web's PKI ecosystem has evolved over the past 8 years. The validity of certificates has improved consistently, but a large proportion of certificates are still invalid. Over time, most indicators show that the ecosystem is moving towards better security practices. However, there are a few alarming trends including the incorrect use of template certificates causing invalid extensions and increasing centrality in issuers.

Acknowledgments. We thank the anonymous reviewers and our shepherd, Oliver Gasser, for their helpful comments. We also thank Christo Wilson and Alan Mislove for allowing us to use their computing infrastructure and Zane Ma for sharing datasets and discussion. This research was supported in part by NSF grants CNS-2053363 and CNS-2051166.

A   Ethics

This paper does not pose any ethical issues as all the data we use for analysis is collected by third parties and is available for public use.

References

1. Browser security icon updates And sha-1 deprecation — digicert. Com. https://www.digicert.com/blog/browser-security-icon-updates-sha-1-deprecation
2. incident response: november 2015 google 'pilot' And 'aviator' Logged 3 Certs With Invalid Signatures
3. Sectigo Adds Acme Protocol Support In Certificate Manager Platform To Automate Ssl Lifecycle Management. 2019. https://sectigo.com/resource-library/sectigo-adds-acme-protocol-support-in-certificate-manager-platform-to-automate-ssl-lifecycle-management
4. Certificate transparency Website. Google, March 2022. https://github.com/google/certificate-transparency-community-site/blob/4ae90f78cdd821b9cb3a68848851 86d71b529c87/docs/google/getting-started.md
5. Laurie, et al. Certificate Transparency. RFC 6962 (Proposed Standard), IETF, June 2013
6. Barnes, R., Hoffman-Andrews, J., McCarney, D., Kasten, J.: Automatic Certificate Management Environment (acme). IETF, March 2019
7. Sloot, V., et al.: Towards a complete view of the certificate ecosystem. In: Proceedings of the 2016 Internet Measurement Conference, New York, NY, USA, pp. 543–549, Association for Computing Machinery (2016)
8. Caida asclassifications Dataset. https://www.caida.org/data/as-classification/
9. Cangialosi, F.,et al.: Measurement and analysis of private key sharing in the https ecosystem. In: ACM Conference on Computer and Communications Security (CCS), Vienna, Austria, October 2016
10. Certificate Transparency In Chrome (2019). https://github.com/chromium/ct-policy/blob/master/ct_policy.md
11. Chung, T., et al.: Measuring and applying invalid SSL certificates: the silent majority. In: ACM Internet Measurement Conference (IMC), Santa Monica, California, USA, November 2016
12. Cooper, D., Santesson, S., Farrell, S., Boeyen, S., Housley, R., Polk, W.: Internet X.509 public key infrastructure certificate and certificate revocation list (CRL) profile. RFC 5280, IETF, May 2008. https://www.ietf.org/rfc/rfc5280.txt
13. Dukhovni, V., Hardaker, W.: The DNS-based authentication of named entities (DANE) protocol: updates and operational guidance. RFC 7671, IETF, October 2015
14. Gasser, O., Hof, B., Helm, M., Korczynski, M., Holz, R., Carle, G.: In log we trust: revealing poor security practices with certificate transparency logs and internet measurements. In: Passive and Active Measurement Conference (PAM) (2018)
15. Aas, J., et al.: Let's encrypt: an automated certificate authority to encrypt the entire web. In: Proceedings of the 2019 ACM SIGSAC Conference on Computer and Communications Security, New York, NY, USA, pp. 2473–2487, Association for Computing Machinery (2019)
16. Korzhitskii, N., Carlsson, N.: Characterizing the root landscape of certificate transparency logs. In: 2020 IFIP Networking Conference, Networking 2020, Paris, France, 22–26 June 2020, pp. 190–198. IEEE (2020)
17. Laurie, B., Langley, A., Kasper, E.: Certificate Transparency. RFC 6962, IETF, June 2013. https://www.ietf.org/rfc/rfc6962.txt
18. Li, B., et al.: Certificate transparency in the wild: exploring the reliability of monitors. In: ACM Conference on Computer and Communications Security (CCS) (2019)

19. Perl, H., Fahl, S., Smith, M.: You won't be needing these any more: on removing unused certificates from trust stores. Financial Cryptography and Data Security (FC), Christ Church, Barbados, March 2014
20. Project sonar. https://www.rapid7.com/research/project-sonar/
21. Scheitle, Q., et al.: The rise of certificate transparency and its implications on the internet ecosystem. In: Proceedings of the Internet Measurement Conference 2018, New York, NY, USA, pp. 343–349. Association for Computing Machinery (2018)
22. Stark, E., et al.: Does certificate transparency break the web? Measuring adoption and error rate. In: IEEE Symposium on Security and Privacy (IEEE S&P) (2019)
23. Working Together To Detect Maliciously Or Mistakenly Issued Certificates. https://certificate.transparency.dev/
24. Ma, Z., Austgen, J., Mason, J., Durumeric, Z., Bailey, M.: Tracing your roots: exploring the TLS trust anchor ecosystem. In: Proceedings of the 21st ACM Internet Measurement Conference, New York, NY, USA, pp. 179–194, Association for Computing Machinery (2021)
25. Cpanel Auto SSL. https://docs.cpanel.net/knowledge-base/security/guide-to-ssl/#autossl

Analysis of TLS Prefiltering for IDS Acceleration

Lukas Sismis[1]([✉])[ID] and Jan Korenek[2][ID]

[1] CESNET, Generála Píky 430/26, Prague 16000, Czech Republic
sismis@cesnet.cz
[2] Faculty of Information Technology, Brno University of Technology, Bozetechova 2/1, 61200 Brno, Czech Republic
korenek@vut.cz
https://www.cesnet.cz, https://fit.vut.cz

Abstract. Network intrusion detection systems (IDS) and intrusion prevention systems (IPS) have proven to play a key role in securing networks. However, due to their computational complexity, the deployment is difficult and expensive. Therefore, many times the IDS is not powerful enough to handle all network traffic on high-speed network links without uncontrolled packet drop. High-speed packet processing can be achieved using many CPU cores or an appropriate acceleration. But the acceleration has to preserve the detection quality and has to be flexible to handle ever-emerging security threats. One of the common acceleration methods among intrusion detection/prevention systems is the bypass of encrypted packets of the Transport Layer Security (TLS) protocol. This is based on the fact that IDS/IPS cannot match signatures in the packet encrypted payload. The paper provides an analysis and comparison of available TLS bypass solutions and proposes a high-speed encrypted TLS Prefilter for further acceleration. We are able to demonstrate that using our technique, the IDS **performance** has **tripled** and at the same time detection results have resulted in a **lower rate of false positives**. It is designed as a **software-only architecture** with support for commodity cards. However, the architecture **allows smooth transfer** of the proposed method **to the HW-based solution** in Field-programmable gate array (FPGA) network interface cards (NICs).

Keywords: IDS · TLS · DPDK · Prefilter · Suricata · Performance · Acceleration · Throughput · Measurements

1 Introduction

Intrusion detection/prevention systems are widely used to detect threats by careful analysis and deep packet inspection. However, as intrusion detection is a computationally intensive task, ever-increasing traffic needs more and more processing power. Insufficient processing capabilities of the IDS lead to uncontrolled packet drops and missed alerts. Apart from large traffic volumes, even encrypted

A. Brunstrom et al. (Eds.): PAM 2023, LNCS 13882, pp. 85–109, 2023.
https://doi.org/10.1007/978-3-031-28486-1_5

traffic can complicate threat-hunting by generating false detection results from matched patterns of encrypted communication streams. Additionally, the attack vectors of bad actors regularly change. A combination of the previously mentioned things leads to the fact that network administrators have limited visibility of what really happens on the network. This put requirements on IDS systems to be highly flexible, scalable, and easy to operate.

To meet the performance requirements, one could potentially transfer IDS systems completely to the hardware. However, the inability to change rules arbitrarily makes this system impractical. Additionally, limited hardware resources make it impossible to transfer the entire IDS into the hardware. This is mainly caused by complex packet parsing and detection procedures or a large set of detection rules and leads to functional trade-offs in these hardware-based systems.

We can optimize only part of the IDS by the highly-specialized hardware network interface cards (SmartNICs). These NICs can assist IDS by solving certain tasks such as TCP reassembly, inline encryption/decryption, or similar. The problem with these approaches is that they require specialized and expensive hardware. The hardware system cannot be changed, so future changes to the acceleration task are not possible. For example, SmartNIC can be capable to decrypt Secure Socket Layer (SSL) but it will not support TLS of version 1.2 and above. Additionally, to employ the SmartNIC offloads, IDS must first be capable to use them.

To meet the performance demands of the current networks, systems can either speed up the time it takes to process and analyze individual packets or reduce the amount of analyzed network traffic. SmartNICs, IDS hardware solutions, or improved pattern matching are examples of common techniques for accelerating IDS as a whole. On the other hand, network traffic bypass can be a general way to cut down the traffic that needs to be analyzed. The bypass is done on the flow level, where flow is defined as bidirectional communication between two hosts. The bypass systems can be either self-managed or directly controlled by individual intrusion detection systems. This feature is commonly integrated into the IDSes. However, relying only on IDS-induced bypass commands does not generally increase the IDS's performance enough to reach the requirements of current networks.

In an effort to improve IDS performance through the bypass technique, we analyzed the captured traffic from multiple major backbone links of the real network. We came to the conclusion that encrypted traffic contributes a major part to the overall network traffic composition. Based on these findings and an assumption that analysis of encrypted traffic by a common IDS is impossible without encryption keys, we designed a high-speed TLS Prefilter. The system is able to detect and bypass ongoing encrypted communication, which leads to a major increase in IDS performance.

The paper explains the motivation for the work as it assesses the composition of common network traffic. In the next part of the paper, the design of TLS acceleration heuristics and architecture description are shown. The last part presents a conclusion with achieved results.

2 Related Work

2.1 Software-only Solutions

The problem of meeting the throughput of current networks is the leading issue for intrusion detection systems. There are multiple approaches to how network administrators can deploy such systems. The first and most common one is a software-only-based IDS. There are multiple options to choose from, notably, IDS systems like Snort [8], Suricata [10], and Zeek (formerly Bro) [11] are the most popular. The software-only approach leads to the easiest deployment but is also tied to the most limited performance. As an example described in [19], reaching a network throughput of 100Gbps with Zeek requires a complicated deployment scheme involving multiple switches and servers, where each runs an instance of Zeek.

2.2 Hardware-Oriented Solutions

On the other hand, some research published in papers, e.g., Pigasus [22], Snort Offloader [18], propose a heavily-oriented hardware solution. The aim is to put the whole/most of the IDS into the FPGA to accelerate the overall processing performance. Snort offloader puts an entire IDS/IPS solution to the FPGA, however, it lacks certain capabilities (e.g. TCP reassembly) to be deployed in the production. Pigasus implementation is more complete than [18]. It puts most parts of the IDS into the FPGA while the CPU is used for exact pattern matching. However, due to resource constraints of FPGAs, Pigasus limits the number of rules to 10 000 and the size of the flow table to 100 000 flows. Enabled detection rules are statically inserted into the FPGA so they cannot be changed dynamically.

2.3 Solutions Using SmartNICs/GPUs

Emerging SmartNICs (NICs containing hardware accelerators) offer aid to IDS with certain use cases. NICs containing also an FPGA chip establish a foundation for experiments. Historically, there is a continuous effort to accelerate the pattern-matching part of IDS. The papers [12,13,17] put matching of regular expressions to FPGA. To a certain level, it does help with the acceleration of certain parts of pattern matching. However, due to rapidly changing attack vectors, there is a requirement for a quick ruleset change. As the regular expressions are usually part of the FPGA program, it may take hours to modify the rules because of the long FPGA compilation process. That means it may not be always preferred to use these cards for IDS acceleration.

Other papers [15] use, e.g., GPU as an accelerator to improve the speed of matching exact patterns and regular expressions. However, due to PCIe transfers between the CPU and the GPU (execution units) better performance comes with the cost of higher latency.

2.4 Traffic Bypass Solutions

Instead of accelerating IDS processing to achieve higher throughput, it is possible to reduce the amount of actually analyzed traffic. IDS is able to tell when a network flow is not interesting anymore and thus can be skipped. Having a bypass mechanism in the FPGA chip can be beneficial in filtering out the safe traffic and as a result allowing more traffic to be analyzed. A similar approach was described in papers, e.g., [16,20]. The [20] demonstrated the use of an IPS filter with the use of a custom FPGA card but with a limited speed of up to 1Gbps. However, the paper describes almost exclusively a hardware design and does not present results of overall detection quality, especially with real-world network traces. The latter paper, which described general IDS acceleration using the SDM (Software Defined Monitoring) system presents the results of flow shunting. Flow shunting as published in [14] relies on the fact that the most relevant information of the flow is in its first N bytes/packets. The paper [16] implements this concept and examines results while also suggesting a hardware-based design.

Some intrusion detection systems support traffic bypass and also have an option to alternatively set a bypass rule after the TLS negotiation (e.g. Snort [9] or Suricata[1]). The idea of the bypass is to drop bypassed packets as early as possible so that the packet path is shorter and packets spend less time in the system. In the case of Suricata IDS, bypass can be done either in the capture module before a packet enters Suricata or internally in Suricata after decoding the packet. The internal (local) bypass is for the capture modules that do not support bypass directly. As an example, we can mention the Suricata AF_PACKET packet capture method which by itself does not offer capture bypass functionality so packets can only be bypassed by Suricata after decoding the packet. However, when combined with the eXpress Data Path (XDP) filter program, packets are dropped in the kernel space and therefore earlier than with the standalone AF_PACKET [2,4].

2.5 Proposed Solution

In our work, we also utilize the technique of reducing the amount of analyzed network traffic to achieve higher performance. However, in contrast with the aforementioned papers ([16,20]), we do not rely on flow shunting. Instead, we exploit the fact that TLS connections after initial negotiation are unanalyzable for common intrusion detection systems. Due to the fact that TLS flows are generally heavy and due to the widespread use of TLS, excluding the encrypted TLS traffic can lead to major reductions in processed network traffic. Our work is implemented completely in software and works with regular commodity NICs. The primary focus is to be able to handle TLS connections up to TLS version 1.2. The overall architecture of the proposed solution puts high importance on the possible transfer of the acceleration offload into the hardware-based platform residing on the network card. This primarily divides the solution into two

---

[1] https://suricata.readthedocs.io/en/latest/performance/ignoring-traffic.html#encrypted-traffic.

independent parts - acceleration logic and IDS. For our experiments, we chose Suricata IDS for its multi-threaded, high-performance architecture and, generally, good extensibility for further additions.

Suricata IDS supports multiple capture modules for packet sniffing with capture module AF_PACKET being the most prevalent in the Suricata deployments. As mentioned previously, AF_PACKET can be extended with eXpress Data Path (XDP) filtration program running in kernel space to improve the performance of the capture module.

Suricata also contains a capture module based on Data Plane Development Kit (DPDK) [6]. Unlike other packet capture interfaces, Suricata constantly polls packets of the NIC to improve the throughput (performance) of the system. The results of this approach have been evaluated in [23] where the results of DPDK were compared to the AF_PACKET non-bypassed capture interface. We decided to have the DPDK capture module as a foundation for our work and compare our results to baseline measurements of both AF_PACKET (with XDP) and DPDK capture modules.

The paper contains an analysis of real-world network traces, a comparison of various TLS bypass methods coupled with the proposed acceleration solution, and an elaborate analysis of detection results. The analysis of the detection results proves the correctness of the results of the proposed solution.

3   TLS Traffic Analysis

Transport Layer Security (successor of SSL) is a widespread protocol securing communication and providing authentication, encryption, and data integrity for all involved clients. It uses asymmetric cryptography for the negotiation process and symmetric encryption for communication after the negotiation. In completely controlled networks, administrators might have a chance to decrypt the clients' traffic. Since intrusion detection systems normally do not have an option for decryption, performing detection on encrypted TLS becomes useless for IDS. It can only obtain information of any value from the unencrypted TCP and TLS handshakes.

To better understand how widespread TLS traffic is, we present the following analysis. To provide relevant data from real-world networks, we have collected network traces from 14 locations within the national research and education network (NREN) and from 5 commercial links. The total size of the traces was around 1 500 GB. During our further experiments, we used one of the packet capture (PCAP) traces to evaluate the performance of TLS Prefiltering methods. It contained 509 449 209 packets and spanned over almost 400 GB. The PCAP contained 14 295 620 flows at around 2.6 Gb link utilization over the duration of 1 s.

The traces from commercial and NREN links were gathered over different time periods from various metering points. All of the network traces were collected in intervals, each being 5 min long. Metering points used for the collection were located on the backbone network of a national internet service provider.

We have classified the traffic into two groups, where one group represents traffic with TLS protocol and the other group represents the remaining traffic.

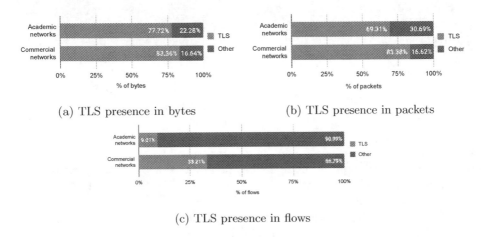

(a) TLS presence in bytes   (b) TLS presence in packets

(c) TLS presence in flows

Fig. 1. TLS analysis based on the number of bytes, packets, and flows

We provide 3 different views on the captured datasets displayed in Fig. 1, where the figures present the ratio of TLS and non-TLS traffic based on different metrics. Figure 1a is based on the number of bytes, Fig. 1b on the number of packets, and Fig. 1c on the number of flows. Figures containing byte and packet analysis (1a and b) count towards the TLS group everything related to TLS protocol (i.e. unencrypted and encrypted data). In terms of flow statistics shown in Fig. 1c, a single flow was defined by a 5-tuple. All bidirectional flows were counted as one and a flow was added to statistics after detecting the first unique direction. This means single-direction flows (flows where we only saw one direction) were also counted towards the statistic.

From the graphs in Figs. 1a and b, it is possible to observe that TLS traffic is prevalent both in terms of bytes and packets in both commercial and academic networks. The total amount of packets or bytes is in both cases above 69%. However, Fig. 1c representing a percentage of TLS flows within the traffic does not show a prevalence of TLS flows among all flows in the datasets. TLS flows occupy only one-third of the total number of flows. Taking into consideration the ratio of TLS bytes and TLS flows (1a and c), it is possible to observe that TLS flows on average contain more data than non-TLS flows and thus can be called heavier.

As mentioned previously, the graph presented in Fig. 1c shows the total number of bytes including non-encrypted parts of the TLS communication. TLS consists of several types of messages that are used during communication. All messages are framed to TLS records, which act as a basic transfer unit between the client and the server. Based on the type of the message, a sniffing application (IDS) can identify whether the payload of the TLS record is encrypted or not. TLS handshake between communicating parties follows right after the TCP handshake and is still unencrypted. During the TLS handshake, several messages are exchanged primarily for acknowledgment and verification of both sides and for agreeing on the used cryptographic algorithms and session keys for the subsequent encrypted communication. Once communication becomes encrypted, it does not downgrade back to unencrypted. The graph in Fig. 2 represents an occurrence of various TLS records within the TLS traffic of the datasets. TLS record type ApplicationData serves as the main message for encrypted communication. This type of message is not valuable for IDS as it only contains the length of the content and the encrypted message content itself. IDS can process the remaining message types to match specific fields, e.g. server name identification (SNI), or analyze JA3/JA3s hashes of the handshake messages as described in [5].

This hints that only approximately 4% of TLS traffic is actually useful for IDS and the remaining 96% can be bypassed. Taking an example of a 100 Gbps network and given the facts mentioned previously, on average, only 30% of the total network traffic (non-TLS) and 4% of TLS traffic is relevant for IDS. This reduces data throughput to only 33 Gbps of valuable traffic from the overall 100 Gbps. The results also imply that IDS can be potentially sped up by up to 3 times in our network. Obviously, the overall acceleration is dependent on the network traffic mix.

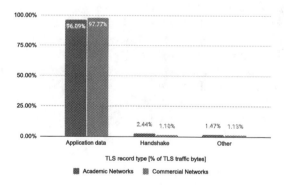

Fig. 2. Share of individual TLS record types in the TLS traffic

To provide deeper insights into the characteristics of TLS flows, Fig. 3 presents an analysis of an average length of TLS flows plotted using the Empirical Cumulative Distribution Function (ECDF). The average length of the TLS flows was calculated as an average value of ECDFs of individual datasets. The average as a metric for the TLS flow length was selected to avoid plotting ECDFs of all individual datasets and at the same time provide an overview of all available datasets. The variance of ECDFs of TLS flow length among all datasets was

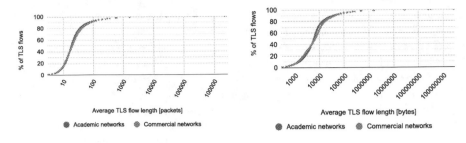

(a) ECDF plot of an average length of TLS flows in packets

(b) ECDF plot of an average length of TLS flows in bytes

Fig. 3. Empirical Cumulative Distribution Function (ECDF) plot of TLS flows

small and no dataset contained extremely different values in comparison with other datasets.

The ECDF graph is plotted both in bytes in Fig. 3b and in packets in Fig 3a. The X-axis shows the average TLS flow length on a logarithmic scale. The Y-axis shows the ratio of TLS flows. The Y-axis data points increment by 1% except for the last percent where values for 99, 99.9, 99.99, and 100 percent ratios were included. It is possible to read from the ECDF function that e.g. TLS flows with the length of 100 packets and more are on average longer than 90% of all TLS flows among all datasets.

The analysis of TLS presence in the traffic presented in Figs. 1 and 2 shows that bypass of TLS traffic can be greatly beneficial to the acceleration of IDS processing. While TLS traffic can contain long and heavy flows, further flow analysis of the TLS flows presented in Fig. 3 shows that 99% of TLS flows are rather short with about 1000 packets per flow. The remaining flows in the top 1% can be extensively long. Because of the short TLS flows, it is essential to detect packets with encrypted data as soon as possible to avoid reaching receive buffers of the IDS system. At the same time, the TLS bypass table must be fast to modify the flow entries.

4   DPDK TLS Prefilter for TLS Traffic

The analysis has revealed the dominant use of encrypted connections in real network traffic and thus a worthwhile use case for bypassing the TLS traffic by a TLS Prefilter. This section explains Prefilter architecture and its internals.

As mentioned previously, we chose Suricata [10] as an IDS for our experiments because of the high-performance multi-threaded model, ease of extensibility, and the possibility to extend the present DPDK implementation of the Suricata packet capture module. Instead of using interrupts to deliver packets to the application, DPDK drivers constantly poll the NIC for new packets. This proves to be a high-performance strategy for busy networks that comes at the cost of increased CPU load.

Figure 4 presents the high-level architecture of the proposed system. Going from left to right, the incoming traffic of the monitored network is delivered to the NIC. Afterward, packets are received by TLS Prefilter. The main responsibility of TLS Prefilter is not only to curate the received traffic by looking for newly encrypted TLS flows and bypassing the already found ones but also to pass the selected traffic to the IDS (Suricata). The bypass of individual flows is self-governed by Prefilter, i.e. Prefilter maintains a flow table of bypassed flows and solely manages its entries. Prefilter's intention is to act transparently from Suricata's point of view, meaning Suricata's operation should not be affected by the Prefilter's presence. The aim is to reduce the amount of input traffic by bypassing the encrypted TLS traffic without any major impact on Suricata detection results. With non-TLS traffic, TLS Prefilter passes to the IDS also unencrypted parts of TLS communication (e.g. TLS handshakes). Therefore, IDS can evaluate and detect e.g. on JA3(s) hashes, server name identification, or SSL certificates as it would without the presence of TLS Prefilter.

Along with achieved throughput, the impact on the Suricata's detection results is considered as one of the major metrics for this paper. While designing the architecture for TLS Prefilter, we emphasized the ease of prototyping and accessible portability to hardware platforms on the network interface cards. As a result, TLS Prefilter is not directly part of the Suricata capture module but, instead, TLS Prefilter passes packets to Suricata via DPDK ring buffers. No logic is shared between the TLS Prefilter and Suricata. Embedding the acceleration logic directly into Suricata could potentially block the transfer of the acceleration offload to the hardware platform. Once TLS Prefilter is converted to be a hardware part of the NIC, Suricata can directly read from the TLS Prefilter-accelerated NIC. Then it is possible to remove the software TLS Prefilter and save CPU cores. The proposed architecture allows rapid prototyping with new functionalities while paving the way for a possible hardware-based solution.

4.1   TLS Prefilter Internal Logic

The main concept behind TLS Prefilter is to look for encrypted TLS records and then make a decision about the bypass. The header of TLS records can be found in the packet after the TCP header. From the TLS record, it is possible to deduct whether the TLS payload is encrypted or not. Once TLS Prefilter detects an encrypted TLS payload then it can safely assume that the flow remains encrypted until the connection is terminated.

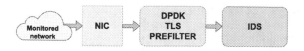

Fig. 4. DPDK TLS Prefilter location in the deployed network environment

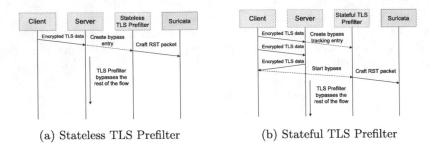

(a) Stateless TLS Prefilter   (b) Stateful TLS Prefilter

Fig. 5. Creating a bypass entry in TLS Prefilter

During our experiments and prototypes, we have come up with two solutions to TLS prefiltering that are displayed in Fig. 5. The first solution works in a stateless mode (Fig. 5a) where TLS Prefilter is analyzing packets and upon the first encrypted TLS record, TLS Prefilter creates a bypass record in its internal bypass flow table. The solution greatly helps Suricata to increase its performance. Even though the traffic analysis of the current NREN and commercial networks shows a majority of the traffic is encrypted, unencrypted services can still exist. The advantage of plain traffic is that it can be completely monitored by IDS and its pattern-matching engine. However, the naive approach of bypassing the flow on the first encrypted TLS record can possibly open a security vulnerability in these network-monitored environments. For example, monitoring of the unencrypted HTTP server can be circumvented by sending, among valid requests, also a fabricated request containing a TLS-encrypted record. After this packet, the stateless bypass-triggering logic of TLS Prefilter would bypass the flow, and Suricata (IDS) would be completely blind to the given flow.

To mitigate this issue we have converted TLS Prefilter to be stateful (Fig. 5b). That means the bypass table stores the states of each tracked flow. In this case, TLS Prefilter does not issue flow bypass based on one packet. After detecting an encrypted TLS record, TLS Prefilter creates a new record in the flow table but does not issue a bypass yet. The flow remains inspected by the IDS until TLS Prefilter receives the second encrypted TLS record but from the opposite direction. This means that even if the attacker sends a forged packet with the encrypted TLS record to the server's direction, TLS Prefilter still passes all packets of the flow to the IDS. TLS Prefilter enables the flow bypass only if the server also replies with an encrypted TLS record.

Packet Parsing and Decoding

Figure 6 presents the general flow control of the analyzed packets. Receiving a packet from the top, it first parses the packet to an internal representation. If the parsing fails (e.g. due to non-TCP or non-IPv4/6 packets), the packets are passed to the IDS. The TLS Prefilter is alternatively able to unpack packet encapsulation, e.g., VLAN protocol. Internal packet representation is formed by a 5-tuple. Flow 5-tuple is defined as pairs of source and destination addresses and

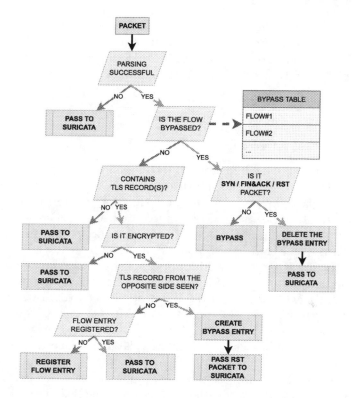

Fig. 6. TLS Prefilter decision flow diagram

ports and transport layer protocol (TCP/UDP). Even though TLS is based only on the TCP protocol and therefore the information about the transport layer protocol can be considered redundant, Prefilter follows the convention and uses the standard 5-tuple flow identification. For efficient lookups, n-tuples are unified for both directions of the communication by placing the lower IP address as the first one in the pair. The same applies to the port pairs. This allows storing only 1 entry per-flow while also performing only 1 lookup for the subsequent packets coming from both directions. After successful parsing, TLS Prefilter does a table lookup. If the packet should not be bypassed, TLS Prefilter inspects the packet for encrypted TLS records.

TLS Record Evaluation

In case the packet contains some, TLS Prefilter checks if a TLS flow has been registered in the flow table. Registering a flow means detecting the first encrypted TLS record. After the flow entry is created, TLS Prefilter also notes the direction (based on, e.g., IP addresses and ports) from which the packet came. At this point packets of the flow are still passed to the IDS as the received packet can still be forged by an attacker. If a flow entry is already present in the flow table, then TLS Prefilter has already encountered at least one TLS-encrypted packet of the given flow. The received packet is further inspected by TLS Prefilter to determine whether it comes from the opposite direction as from which the first encrypted TLS traffic has arrived. Receiving a packet from the reversed direction means both sides of the connection use an encrypted TLS protocol to communicate and therefore the flow can be bypassed.

Bypass of an Encrypted Flow

However, to prevent the sudden stop of packets of the given flow from the IDS perspective, TLS Prefilter sends 1 extra packet in the direction of the IDS. The aim of the packet is to terminate the connection within the IDS and as a result, make the IDS' flow table less polluted and make table lookups faster. TLS Prefilter crafts the packet based on the last inspected but bypassed TLS-encrypted packet. The crafting relies on the fact, that TLS is encapsulated on a transport layer in a TCP protocol. TCP protocol has mechanisms for maintaining a flow connection state (SEQ, ACK numbers) along with 2 ways of connection termination (FIN-ACK / RST header flags). Clients need to exchange 4 messages in case of the graceful ending through the FIN-ACK sequence. RST header is used in an emergency exit and receiving only one from any direction results in connection termination. TLS Prefilter uses the RST connection termination technique to craft a TCP RST packet based on the SEQ and ACK numbers of the bypassed packet and inject the packet into the IDS. This allows IDS to properly close the flow and release the flow record of the IDS' flow table to store more unencrypted flows. While IDSes typically contain a remove timeout for their flow table entries (in case the flow becomes inactive), this technique allows faster eviction of encrypted flows of the IDS flow table.

While the RST technique keeps the complexity of the IDS flow table eviction to a minimum, it comes with a downside in being dependent on the traffic. The crafted RST packet depends on SEQ/ACK numbers which are derived from the first packet to be bypassed. If the packet contains incorrect sequential or acknowledgment numbers then this will be reflected in the RST packet and the IDS will reject the processing of such packet. However, the overall IDS functionality is not affected as the bypassed flow would be removed after the flow timeout that is set in the flow table (and not right after the TLS Prefilter bypass). To completely eliminate the issue with SEQ/ACK numbers it would be better to establish a communication channel between TLS Prefilter and IDS or implement pseudo-packets to ensure management communication does not depend on the actual traffic.

Bypass Removal

Coming back to the beginning of the control flow diagram displayed in Fig. 6, if the packet's flow tuple is contained by the bypass table, TLS Prefilter analyzes TCP header flags of the matched (bypassed) packets for the closing/opening flow signs (e.g. RST/SYN/FIN+ACK flags). Flows of respective packets that contain these flags remove bypass entries from the bypass flow table. Packets not containing these flags are bypassed. Bypassed packets are then discarded by TLS Prefilter.

TLS Prefilter can delete a bypass flow entry if a packet has its SYN flag set as this is usually a sign of a new flow. If the communication continues (e.g. SYN bit set but the sequence number outside of the expected window as described in RFC 5961), TLS Prefilter removes bypass entry after receiving a such packet. This way Suricata can receive more traffic than anticipated. However, if TLS Prefilter encounters encrypted traffic from both directions of the flow again, the bypass entry would be reinserted.

Similar behavior can happen with other closing TCP flags as well. To completely eliminate the issue, TLS Prefilter could wait with the bypass entry removal until it is also confirmed with the other side of the communication. For instance, this can be detecting a packet with FIN+ACK flags that is part of the bypassed flow and only deleting the bypass entry from the table after encountering a packet from the opposite side of the communication with the same closing flags.

Comparison to Common Bypass Handling

General IDS bypass does packet accounting on the bypassed flows. By using timeouts, it periodically checks flow liveliness (if any new packets were received within the time frame). On the flow inactivity, the bypassed flow entry is removed from the IDS bypass table. As a result, when regular bypass methods are used, IDS can never determine an end of the flow accurately and only guesses the flow end based on the timeout and flow activity.

As Prefilter inspects all incoming packets, it can also detect the closing connection and based on that, delete the flow entry from the bypass flow table. It is, therefore, ready to immediately receive the next TCP handshake/TLS negotiation sequence of the given flow n-tuple. The bypass flow entry removal can also occur if a flow is bypassed but Prefilter detects a start of a new TLS negotiation. In contrast to the regular bypass methods, TLS Prefilter can accurately terminate the flow bypass and let IDS inspect the newly opened TLS connection that follows right after the old connection.

4.2   TLS Prefilter Architecture

The system architecture is illustrated in Fig. 7. Suricata supports multiple runmodes. In workers runmode, each detection thread is called a worker. Individual Suricata workers perform the whole processing pipeline and that is the packet capture, detection, and output. At the same time, for the best performance results, every worker should run on a dedicated CPU core and all workers should reside on the same NUMA node. In the IDS workers runmode, Suricata expects that the traffic is scattered among all workers but each worker receives both directions of the flow. Going from top to bottom in Fig. 7, each Suricata worker has a ring buffer from which it reads incoming packets. As running TLS Prefilter requires yet another separate CPU core(s) (as compared to running a bare IDS without the TLS Prefilter), it was crucial to amortize this cost by distributing packets in 1:N relationship, meaning from a single Prefilter core the packets are scattered to multiple IDS cores/workers. The distribution operation had to take into account the previously mentioned workers' requirement (bi-directional flow capture by one worker). The distribution problem has been solved by Receive side scaling (RSS) [1] on the NIC card and symmetric RSS [21]. The number of NIC queues is determined by the number of subscribed IDS workers.

Avoiding resource sharing was an important objective in the TLS Prefilter design process. As can be seen in Fig. 7, each core of Prefilter operates on the designated NIC queues, has separate rings for the assigned Suricata workers, and has a unique bypass flow table. The bypass flow table is realized as a fast hash table with a flow key and flow data as a key-value pair.

We started to experiment with different types of hash tables and finally selected the Least Recently Used (LRU) hash table. The LRU hash table on the inability to insert an entry into the hash table bucket (i.e. on the full hash table bucket), replaces the least recently used entry with the inserting one. This provides a simple mechanism to evict stale flows with new ones. LRU hash table does not guarantee that all flows will be bypassed all the time. In case an active flow is evicted, then it is bypassed with the pair of the following encrypted TLS records. This attribute of the hash table can be manually adjusted by the size of the flow bucket. However, the lightweight operation of the LRU hash table proved to provide the best throughput while also keeping the detection results consistent.

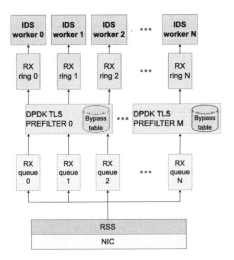

Fig. 7. DPDK TLS Prefilter's overall architecture

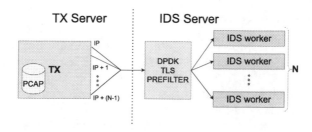

Fig. 8. DPDK TLS Prefilter test topology

5   Results

For the performance evaluation, we selected a standard server with 2 NUMA nodes where each NUMA node contains an Intel Xeon Silver 4114 CPU with a maximal speed of 2.20GHz. Experiments have not utilized hyper-threaded cores of the CPU, therefore it only ran on the 10 physical cores of the CPU. In all experiments, we concentrated all required applications on 1 NUMA node. Each NUMA node then contains 32GB of memory. Packets were received through 1 port of the dual-port 100G Nvidia network interface card from the MT2892 (ConnectX-6) family. As an IDS we chose Suricata [10] for its high-performance multi-threaded characteristics. Suricata's detection engine worked with 21104 rules from the Emerging Threats Open ruleset [7] downloaded on the 14th of January of 2021. The proposed TLS Prefilter is tested on Suricata version 7.0.0-dev.

As a packet generator, we use a server equipped with a custom FPGA-based NIC with 100Gbps interfaces. Each transmission queue of the FPGA NIC has the ability to replicate the traffic with the possibility of changing some traffic attributes deterministically. In our experiments, we have utilized this feature to not only increase the speed of the transmission but also to increase the number of concurrent flows by modifying each packet's IP address when replicating. This strategy helps to maintain flow characteristics while also increasing the speed of transmission. For every running Suricata worker, we have used a separate replication. That means every Suricata worker did a detection upon a copy of the originally transmitted PCAP file. Only IP addresses were deterministically changed by the FPGA NIC. For evaluation, we used the aforementioned PCAP in Sect. 3. Using the custom FPGA card for packet transmission the previously mentioned PCAP statistics were multiplied by the number of running Suricata workers. That means if originally, the PCAP would have a million packets in 10000 flows then the receiving side with 4 Suricata workers see 4 million packets in 40000 flows.

Figure 8 represents the test's topology, where packets go from left to right i.e. the packets are transmitted from the TX server and delivered through the DPDK TLS prefilter to IDS workers. The number of TLS Prefilters can vary along with the respective number of IDS workers belonging to each TLS Prefilter instance.

5.1   Analyzed Bypass Methods

We have evaluated 7 approaches to traffic analysis by Suricata, which were distinct only in packet capture modules and bypass strategy. The packets were received either by AF_PACKET or DPDK. AF_PACKET packet capture interface was selected for its widespread use among Suricata deployments.

AF_PACKET is part of Linux since 2.2 and is very well integrated into Suricata. Linux 4.8 introduced eXpress Data Path (XDP) which brings the ability to handle packets even before they are processed by the kernel. This is considered as the most effective enhancement of the AF_PACKET packet capture interface. For this reason, we have also included this approach in our experiments. With respect to the Nvidia MLX5 NIC's abilities, we have put the XDP program into the NIC driver. The XDP bypass is driven solely by Suricata through a shared eBPF key-value map.

DPDK implementation in Suricata offers a high-performance packet capture module. From the experiments of the default AF_PACKET and DPDK modules, we can compare and set the baseline for the following alternatives. In the measurements, we included five DPDK variants that use the DPDK capture module. The first DPDK variant does not have bypass functionality activated so the configuration is the same as with the original AF_PACKET capture interface. The second measurement can bypass flows by multiple triggers, one of which is Suricata-induced TLS-encrypted traffic (the same as XDP bypass). In this case, Suricata bypasses TLS flow after it has processed the whole TLS handshake. The same technique is used in Snort SSL Dynamic Preprocessor as mentioned in [9]. In the case of the DPDK capture method, Suricata bypasses all packets internally as there is no current support for capture module bypass. However, this is not a major limitation as packets in DPDK skip kernel space and go directly to the user space application. The third DPDK measurement contains, in addition to the base ruleset (used in other measurements), payload-matching rules that emulate the same decision-making process as TLS Prefilter. The proposed optimization solutions are the last two measurements concerning the new DPDK TLS Prefilter. The graph in Fig. 9 contains both the stateless and the stateful variants as explained in Sect. 4.

From the previous paragraph, we concluded the following tested variants:

– **AF_PACKET**
– **AF_PACKET + XDP TLS bypass**
– **DPDK**
– **DPDK + internal TLS bypass**
– **DPDK + internal TLS + TLS Prefilter rules bypass** - TLS Prefilter rules bypass flows after encountering TLS-encrypted data received from both directions of the communication
– **Stateless DPDK TLS Prefilter** - bypassing flows after detecting a single TLS-encrypted packet
– **Stateful DPDK TLS Prefilter** - bypassing flows after encountering TLS-encrypted data received from both directions

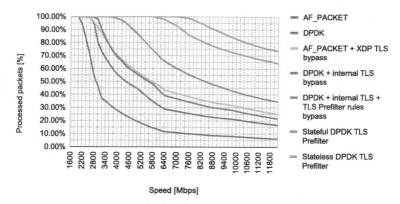

Fig. 9. Performance report of individual experiments (evaluated after a single run)

All tested variants were manually tuned to improve the performance from the default configuration. However, sections of the configuration file not related to the packet capture modules (e.g. detection settings) were shared among all experiments.

5.2   Throughput Measurements

Before any results are presented, it is important to note that the performance of Suricata/IDS, in general, varies on many factors. Of the main ones, we can mention the size of the ruleset, complexity of the individual rules, memory and NUMA placement, CPU speed, or traffic composition. For this reason, we present mainly relative measures rather than absolute values.

The first experiment was focused on measuring the Suricata throughput under increasing load. The experiment was based on 4 Suricata workers running on separate CPU cores. Each worker executed detection on the full ruleset. Figure 9 presents the results where a horizontal axis describes the speed at which packets were transmitted against Suricata and a vertical axis describes the ratio of processed packets. The ratio was calculated as the number of processed packets by Suricata in proportion to the number of transmitted packets. In the measurements that include bypass functionality, the dividend in the ratio of processed packets was calculated as the number of processed packets by Suricata plus the number of bypassed packets. Since the DPDK TLS Prefilter runs on 1 core and distributes packets to 4 Suricata workers, this measurement used 5 cores in total. From the graph, it is possible to notice that AF_PACKET with 4 workers and the complete ruleset starts to discard packets at the bandwidth of around 2 Gbps. AF_Packet in combination with the XDP filter (AF_PACKET + XDP TLS bypass) increases the throughput to 2.6 Gbps. Performance-oriented DPDK packet capture interface outperforms the default AF_PACKET capture module with a 2.4 Gbps throughput. When bypass functionality is enabled in the same way as it was used in AF_PACKET + XDP TLS bypass measurement, the

Table 1. Traffic that reached Suricata after applying individual bypass methods where 100% is all transmitted traffic

	IDS analyzed traffic [%]	
Variant	Packets	Bytes
AF_PACKET + XDP TLS bypass	90.84%	87.72%
DPDK + internal TLS + TLS Prefilter rules bypass	56.31%	44.58%
Stateless DPDK TLS Prefilter	35.26%	25.33%
Stateful DPDK TLS Prefilter	39.18%	28.18%

DPDK capture interface (DPDK + internal TLS bypass) reaches an even higher throughput of 2.8 Gbps per 4 Suricata workers. On top of that, the next variant (DPDK + internal TLS + TLS Prefilter rules bypass) with a set of bypassing rules that emulates the TLS Prefilter in Suricata pushes the performance to 3.8 Gbps.

The performance of Suricata paired with DPDK TLS Prefilter in the next two measurements increases to up to 7 Gbps. This means that Suricata can handle over three times more traffic compared to the commonly deployed Suricata setup running on the AF_PACKET packet capture interface. The stateless mode of TLS Prefilter almost doubles the performance of standalone Suricata running with DPDK packet capture interface, has Suricata-induced TLS bypass and bypass rules triggered after detecting encrypted TLS records from both sides of the communication (DPDK + internal TLS + TLS Prefilter rules bypass variant). Suricata with TLS Prefilter running in stateful mode reach a performance of 6 Gbps. This again triples the performance of the AF_PACKET capture interface and increases the performance by almost 60% compared to the most performant standalone Suricata setup running on DPDK (DPDK + internal TLS + TLS Prefilter rules bypass). Stateful processing took some toll on the performance but, in our opinion, is required to prevent evasion of network monitoring by the IDS. Bad actors are therefore not able to easily trigger the Suricata bypass by forging a TLS encrypted packet as it is possible in the stateless mode. Additionally, we see a huge opportunity in transferring the stateful mode to the hardware platform.

With regards to the results of the measurement displayed in Fig. 9 we have also examined how many packets Suricata avoids thanks to individual bypass methods. For this measurement, we were only interested in the variants with enabled bypass and those are:

- AF_PACKET + XDP TLS bypass
- DPDK + internal TLS + TLS Prefilter rules bypass
- Stateless DPDK TLS Prefilter
- Stateful DPDK TLS Prefilter

Table 1 summarizes how much of the transmitted traffic the IDS is required to process. From the relationship between the amount of bypassed packets and bytes, it is possible to observe that encrypted TLS packets are larger than average. It can be also noted that Suricata with the internally-controlled TLS bypass (AFP + XDP bypass variant) has the lowest bypass rate of all examined variants. This is most likely caused by strict requirements for triggering bypass from the IDS-side as it requires processing a complete TLS handshake and only issues bypass if IDS considers it as a valid handshake. Other variants bypass around the same amount of traffic.

To better interpret the data presented in Fig. 9, we transformed them to the performance per one CPU core. This is shown in Fig. 10 where individual capture interfaces are sorted in ascending order. The results for the DPDK TLS Prefilter also account for 1 extra core. From Fig. 10 it is possible to observe the differences between the performance of individual experiments. Comparing the achieved results of the stateful DPDK TLS Prefilter with the other variants we can notice a more than doubled increase in performance from the default AF_PACKET capture interface. Compared with the AF_PACKET or DPDK capture modules with the enabled bypass functionality, the one core of the stateful DPDK TLS Prefilter can also handle about double the amount of the traffic bandwidth. In other words, this means the DPDK TLS Prefilter requires only half the number of cores compared to the existing capture interfaces. Compared to the standalone Suricata running with DPDK capture interface, TLS internal bypass, and bypass rules (DPDK + internal TLS + TLS Prefilter rules bypass), stateful TLS Prefilter boosts the performance by over 26%.

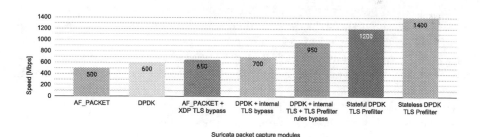

Fig. 10. Per-core performance report (evaluated after a single run)

Table 2. Estimated number of cores required to cover specified throughput

Variant	Speed [Gbps]		
	10	40	100
AF_PACKET + XDP TLS bypass	16	62	154
DPDK + internal TLS	15	58	143
DPDK + internal TLS + TLS Prefilter rules bypass	11	43	106
Stateful DPDK TLS Prefilter	9	34	84

Table 2 helps to visualize how many CPU cores would Suricata need in a regular network to reach common network speeds of 10, 40, and, 100 Gbps. The results are always rounded up. The table shows that Suricata with a DPDK TLS Prefilter can reach at least 40 Gbps using a commodity NIC and a regular 36-core Xeon CPU. Without the DPDK TLS Prefilter, it would be required to use a load balancer and a set of Suricata servers. Even though the table shows a theoretical estimate of cores required to analyze the specified speeds, we see a great acceleration opportunity in having the TLS Prefilter directly embedded inside the NIC's hardware.

Based on results presented in Figs. 9 and 10 and Table 1 we have presented the main differences between the current commonly used Suricata bypass solution (AF_PACKET + XDP TLS bypass) and our newly proposed stateful TLS Prefiltering method. Both the XDP program and TLS Prefilter receive packets prior to Suricata. This proves to be a suitable place to discard unwanted packets. However, the two solutions are distinct not only in the bypass-decision process but also in the architecture.

XDP program is running in kernel space and has a hash-based flow table shared with Suricata that runs in the user space. To secure thread consistency, the flow table needs to contain locks. The solution leads to the lock contention. Since the XDP program relies on Suricata-induced bypass, Suricata is required to perform flow record insertion to bypass new flows, lookup to evaluate flow activity, and deletion to remove stale flows. XDP program then performs lookup and update operations based on the incoming packets.

During the analysis of the results, we have also looked at a possible explanation for worse results of the AF_PACKET + XDP TLS bypass variant mentioned in the [2]. XDP program runs asynchronously to Suricata operation and passes packets to Suricata through receive buffers. At the same time, the bypass process in the XDP program is dependent on Suricata-induced bypass. As a result, Suricata bypass decisions are reflected in the XDP bypassing process with a certain delay. It is therefore possible that by the time the bypass decision is propagated to the XDP bypass table, the receive buffers already contain packets of the bypassed flows. This problem is potentially significant with short flows where the whole flow is inserted into Suricata's receive buffer earlier than the bypass decision is reflected in the XDP program. The problem seemed relevant as the analysis in Fig. 3a shows that 90% of flows are shorter than 100 packets. However, further analysis showed that while this problem was present, it has not proved to be the main cause of the worse performance results of the AF_PACKET + XDP TLS bypass variant. The rate of bypassed packets that were delivered to Suricata (and instead should be bypassed) was around 1% of the total number of bypassed packets. These packets were then bypassed by Suricata internal bypass as mentioned in Subsect. 2.4.

As the TLS Prefilter bypass decision does not depend on Suricata, subsequent packets of the flow are bypassed as soon as the first packet triggers the bypass decision. As a result, this completely avoids the aforementioned issue. With regard to data consistency, individual cores of the TLS Prefilter contain separate

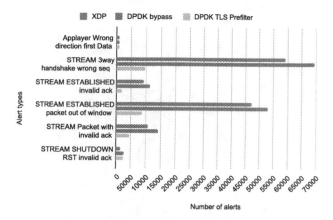

Fig. 11. Reported alerts (N > 5000) after 50 million packets (evaluated after a single run)

bypass tables. The bypass tables are solely managed by the TLS Prefilter cores and as a result, do not need to contain any synchronization mechanism.

5.3 Detection Quality Analysis

Along with performance experiments, we have also evaluated the correctness of the solution. The evaluation was focused on comparing the number of generated alerts. In this test, we enabled the full ruleset and replayed 50 million packets from the original PCAP on Suricata on each variant of the measurement. While there were generated more types of individual alerts, we selected only alerts that were generated at least 5000 times. These can be seen in Fig. 11. Upon reviewing Fig. 11, a reader might be intuitively under impression that with DPDK TLS Prefilter, Suricata actually loses visibility during traffic analysis. This can stem from the fact the XDP version produces more alerts of almost every displayed alert type. Upon problem investigation, we have found the root cause for this difference. This is mainly caused by reordered packets causing Suricata to report, e.g., a wrong ACK number. But even after Suricata received the remaining packets, it continued to report the same alert for every incoming packet i.e. Suricata has not adjusted to the new ACK numbers. This problem is illustrated in Fig. 12 where packets of the flow are transmitted row by row while the actual order of the packets should be as indicated by the red number in the top left corner. After these packets, Suricata generates the wrong SEQ number for all remaining packets of the flow. The highlighted packet is the point where DPDK TLS Prefilter bypasses the flow and as a result, cuts off Suricata from generating more invalid alerts. We can conclude that this step of the DPDK TLS Prefilter does not deteriorate the Suricata visibility, but rather increases it by not generating false alerts. Network administrators are less burdened with redundant alerts.

The only heavy-hitter alert type that DPDK TLS Prefilter generates slightly more than the baseline is an invalid acknowledgment number for the RST packet.

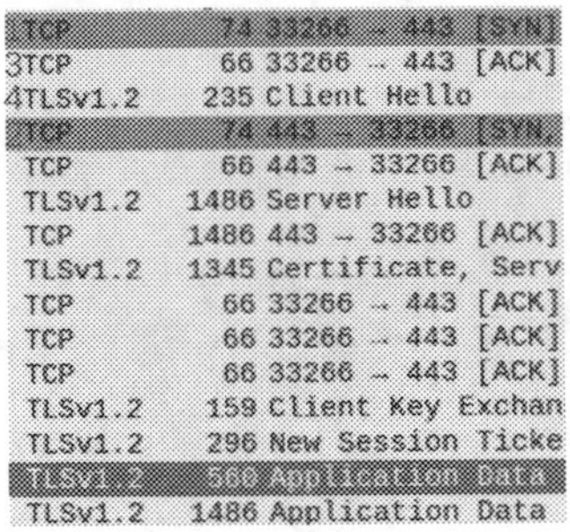

Fig. 12. False alert example due to reordered packets

This can stem from the fact that during flow termination (as the flow starts to be encrypted), the DPDK TLS Prefilter uses the ACK/SEQ numbers to generate the RST packet. In case the packet has an incorrect SEQ/ACK number, the DPDK TLS Prefilter unaware of this fact, sends the crafted packet to Suricata. Sending the crafted RST packet is a TLS Prefilter optimization to evict encrypted flow from Suricata sooner than Suricata would bypass the flow based on flow inactivity.

The presented analysis of the alerts showed only general Suricata engine-related events. To perform an analysis of the TLS Prefilter impact on Suricata and Emerging Threats, it was necessary to use a different dataset as the dataset used in the previous measurements did not produce any ET alerts. For this reason, we have also evaluated TLS Prefilter against malware traffic which can trigger rules from the Emerging Threats ruleset. The next analysis includes AF_PACKET + XDP TLS bypass and TLS Prefilter and was done on a publicly available traffic capture of Dridex malware [3]. Dridex malware communicates over TLS. The presence of Dridex on the network can be detected with ET rules focusing on JA3 hash and SSL certificate. These are parts of the TLS protocol which can be obtained or derived from an unencrypted TLS handshake.

The analyzed Dridex traffic capture contains 4294 packets. Table 3 presents the results of individual variants after analyzing the traffic capture. Variant "Full inspection, no bypass" was reading packets from the PCAP directly and executed full detection analysis to provide baseline results for the following bypass variants. Suricata with AF_PACKET + XDP TLS bypass as a capture module bypassed 2889 packets and generated 14 alerts. Suricata in combination with TLS alerts bypassed 2934 packets and also generated 14 alerts.

The generated alerts were the same in both measurements. The same pair of alerts was hit multiple times during the analysis of the Dridex traffic capture. The signature IDs of the generated alerts were 2028765 and 2023476. They detected the Dridex malware by inspecting the SSL certificate and JA3 hash.

Table 3. Suricata results after analyzing Dridex traffic capture

Variant	Alerts	Analysed packets	Bypassed packets
Full inspection, no bypass	14	4294 (100%)	4051102 (100%)
AF_PACKET + XDP TLS bypass	14	1405 (32.72%)	2889 (67.28%)
Stateful DPDK TLS Prefilter	14	1360 (31.67%)	2934 (68.33%)

Based on these findings we can conclude that DPKD TLS passes all necessary traffic to Suricata and does not impact Suricata's visibility/correctness in a negative way. From the earlier analysis of Suricata engine alerts it is possible to observe that DPDK TLS Prefitler can even save Suricata from generating invalid alerts by cutting off the encrypted traffic.

6   Conclusion

The paper introduced an acceleration of IDS/IPS by bypassing encrypted TLS traffic, which is useless for matching signatures to detect suspicious behavior. The goal is to reduce CPU load by decreasing the amount of network traffic using TLS prefilter.

We captured and analyzed real-world network traces from both commercial and research (NREN) networks. The analysis has shown that at most only 30% of the traffic is non-TLS. The remaining 70% of the data is the TLS traffic. The TLS traffic is then divided into a 4:96 ratio, where 4% is unencrypted (e.g. TLS handshake) and the rest is encrypted traffic. It means that from 100 Gbps of network data, only 33 Gbps is analyzable by the IDS. This is based on the fact that the processing of the encrypted traffic is useless for the detection systems.

We have examined and analyzed multiple available methods that can be used for encrypted TLS bypass. Then we designed and developed a new prefilter architecture to test IDS acceleration concepts without the need of modifying the actual IDS. The architecture is modular and focused on a software-only solution to be compatible with commodity network interface cards. Prefilter is completely separated from the IDS and as a result, allows to transfer of the acceleration solution to the hardware.

In our work, we have focused on TLS Prefilter, which analyzes the incoming traffic and bypasses encrypted TLS flows. From the intrusion detection systems, we have selected Suricata for its fast multi-thread architecture and good extensibility options. Performance-measuring tests based on real-world network traces show that TLS Prefilter increases the performance of the Suricata setup up to almost three times compared to the commonly deployed Suricata configurations. The measured Suricata configurations ran on multiple cores. In our tests, we were able to build a very similar solution solely in Suricata. However, TLS Prefilter compared to this solution increases the overall Suricata per-core performance by 27%.

We were able to achieve the results in a software-only architecture running on commodity cards. During our acceleration experiments, we emphasized the IDS detection results. As can be seen from the results, our work does not negatively impact the detection results and TLS Prefilter even helps to produce far fewer false positive alerts directed to the network administrator. We also believe the hardware solution based on TLS Prefilter can even further increase Suricata performance.

References

1. Scalable networking: eliminating the receive processing bottleneck-introducing RSS (2004)
2. Suricata and xdp (2019). https://www.slideshare.net/ennael/kernel-recipes-2019-suricata-and-xdp
3. Dridex malware traffic capture (2020). https://www.malware-traffic-analysis.net/2020/06/03/index.html
4. Introduction to eBPF and XDP support in suricata (2021). https://www.stamus-networks.com/hubfs/Library/Documents%20(PDFs)/StamusNetworks-WP-eBF-XDP-092021-1.pdf
5. TLS fingerprinting by JA3(s) method (2021). https://www.github.com/salesforce/ja3
6. DPDK support in suricata (2022). https://www.suricata.readthedocs.io/en/latest/configuration/suricata-yaml.html#data-plane-development-kit-dpdk
7. Emerging threats open ruleset official webpage (2022). https://www.rules.emergingthreats.net/open/suricata/rules/
8. Snort official webpage (2022). https://www.snort.org/
9. SSL dynamic preprocessor (SSLPP) (2022). https://www.snort.org/faq/readme-ssl
10. Suricata official webpage (2022). https://www.suricata.io/
11. Zeek official webpage (2022). https://www.zeek.org/
12. Baker, Z.K., Prasanna, V.K.: High-throughput linked-pattern matching for intrusion detection systems. In: 2005 Symposium on Architectures for Networking and Communications Systems (ANCS), pp. 193–202 (2005). https://doi.org/10.1145/1095890.1095918
13. Ceška, M., et al.: Deep packet inspection in FPGAs via approximate nondeterministic automata. In: 2019 IEEE 27th Annual International Symposium on Field-Programmable Custom Computing Machines (FCCM), pp. 109–117 (2019). https://doi.org/10.1109/FCCM.2019.00025
14. González, J., Paxson, V., Weaver, N.: Shunting: A hardware/software architecture for flexible, high-performance network intrusion prevention, pp. 139–149 (2007). https://doi.org/10.1145/1315245.1315264
15. Jamshed, M.A., et al.: Kargus: a highly-scalable software-based intrusion detection system. In: Proceedings of the 2012 ACM Conference on Computer and Communications Security. p. 317–328. CCS 2012, Association for Computing Machinery, New York, NY, USA (2012). https://doi.org/10.1145/2382196.2382232
16. Kučera, J., Kekely, L., Piecek, A., Kořenek, J.: General ids acceleration for high-speed networks. In: 2018 IEEE 36th International Conference on Computer Design (ICCD), pp. 366–373 (2018). https://doi.org/10.1109/ICCD.2018.00062

17. Mitra, A., Najjar, W., Bhuyan, L.: Compiling PCRE to FPGA for accelerating snort IDS. In: Proceedings of the 3rd ACM/IEEE Symposium on Architecture for Networking and Communications Systems, pp. 127–136. ANCS 2007, Association for Computing Machinery, New York, NY, USA (2007). https://doi.org/10.1145/1323548.1323571

18. Song, H., Sproull, T., Attig, M., Lockwood, J.: Snort Offloader: a reconfigurable hardware NIDS filter. In: International Conference on Field Programmable Logic and Applications, pp. 493–498 (2005). https://doi.org/10.1109/FPL.2005.1515770

19. Stoffer, V., Sharma, A., Krous, J.: 100G Intrusion Detection, August 2015. https://www.cspi.com/wp-content/uploads/2016/09/Berkeley-100GIntrusionDetection.pdf. Accessed 27 May 2022

20. Weaver, N., Paxson, V., Gonzalez, J.M.: The shunt: an FPGA-based accelerator for network intrusion prevention. In: Proceedings of the 2007 ACM/SIGDA 15th International Symposium on Field Programmable Gate Arrays, pp. 199–206. FPGA 2007, Association for Computing Machinery, New York, NY, USA (2007). https://doi.org/10.1145/1216919.1216952

21. Woo, S., Park, K.: Scalable TCP session monitoring with symmetric receive-side scaling (2012)

22. Zhao, Z., Sadok, H., Atre, N., Hoe, J.C., Sekar, V., Sherry, J.: Achieving 100Gbps intrusion prevention on a single server. In: 14th USENIX Symposium on Operating Systems Design and Implementation (OSDI 20), pp. 1083–1100. USENIX Association (2020). https://www.usenix.org/conference/osdi20/presentation/zhao-zhipeng

23. Šišmiš, L.: Optimization of the Suricata IDS/IPS, Master's thesis, Faculty of Information Technology (FIT), Brno, Czech Republic (2021)

DissecTLS: A Scalable Active Scanner for TLS Server Configurations, Capabilities, and TLS Fingerprinting

Markus Sosnowski(✉) ⓘ, Johannes Zirngibl ⓘ, Patrick Sattler ⓘ,
and Georg Carle ⓘ

Technical University of Munich, Munich, Germany
{sosnowski,zirngibl,sattler,carle}@net.in.tum.de

Abstract. Collecting metadata from Transport Layer Security (TLS) servers on a large scale allows to draw conclusions about their capabilities and configuration. This provides not only insights into the Internet but it enables use cases like detecting malicious Command and Control (C&C) servers. However, active scanners can only observe and interpret the behavior of TLS servers, the underlying configuration and implementation causing the behavior remains hidden. Existing approaches struggle between resource intensive scans that can reconstruct this data and light-weight fingerprinting approaches that aim to differentiate servers without making any assumptions about their inner working. With this work we propose DissecTLS, an active TLS scanner that is both light-weight enough to be used for Internet measurements and able to reconstruct the configuration and capabilities of the TLS stack. This was achieved by modeling the parameters of the TLS stack and derive an active scan that dynamically creates scanning probes based on the model and the previous responses from the server. We provide a comparison of five active TLS scanning and fingerprinting approaches in a local testbed and on toplist targets. We conducted a measurement study over nine weeks to fingerprint C&C servers and analyzed popular and deprecated TLS parameter usage. Similar to related work, the fingerprinting achieved a maximum precision of 99 % for a conservative detection threshold of 100 %; and at the same time, we improved the recall by a factor of 2.8.

Keywords: Active scanning · TLS · Fingerprinting · C&C servers

1 Introduction

Transport Layer Security (TLS) is currently the *de facto* standard for encrypted communication on the Internet [18]; thus, providing a good common base to analyze, compare, and relate servers. The protocol is influenced by libraries, hardware capabilities, custom configurations, and the application build on top, resulting in an a server specific TLS configuration. A large amount of metadata from this configuration can be collected because in the initial TLS handshake clients and servers must exchange their capabilities such that a mutual

© The Author(s) 2023
A. Brunstrom et al. (Eds.): PAM 2023, LNCS 13882, pp. 110–126, 2023.
https://doi.org/10.1007/978-3-031-28486-1_6

cryptographic base can be found. There are at least two possibilities to collect this metadata: on the one hand, TLS server debugging tools like testssl.sh [33] or SSLyze [10] perform resource intensive scans that dynamically adapt to the server and can reconstruct a human-readable representation. On the other hand, active TLS fingerprinting approaches like JARM [4] or Active TLS Stack Fingerprinting (ATSF) [31] use a small set of fixed requests that are designed to be good in differentiating TLS server configurations. Their light-weight approaches enable them to be used for Internet-wide scans; *e.g.*, `censys.io` already provides JARM fingerprints [8].

Related works have shown that collecting and analyzing TLS configurations from a large amount of servers enables further use cases, *e.g.*, monitoring a fleet of application servers [4] or detecting malicious Command and Control (C&C) servers [4,31]. To be able to collect this data, the respective scanning approach needs to be efficient, to both reduce the time it takes to collect the data and the impact the scan has on third parties.

However, using a fixed set of probes will always leave open the possibility for redundant data to be collected and for useful information to be overlooked; therefore, the performance of subsequent applications (*e.g.*, detecting C&C servers) might not reach their full potential. An alternative is to exhaustively scan a server until the full TLS configuration can be reconstructed. However, current tools are not efficient enough to be used on a large scale.

This work investigates whether a dynamically adapting scan can be implemented efficient enough to be used on a large scale and if this provides a benefit over existing work and tools. We propose DissecTLS as an efficient tool to collect TLS server configurations and provide the following contributions:

(i) a model of the TLS stack on a server that explains its behavior towards different requests and that can be used to craft TLS Client Hellos (CHs) on a per-server level to reconstruct its underlying configuration;

(ii) a comparison of five popular TLS scanners regarding their capabilities to detect different configurations and their scanning costs performed both in a controlled testbed environment and on toplist servers;

(iii) a measurement study of one top- and two blocklists over nine weeks comparing a C&C server detection using fingerprinting tools and this work, complimented with an overview of common TLS parameters; and

(iv) published measurement data [29], scanner, and comparison scripts [30].

2   Methodology

During the initial handshake of the TLS protocol, clients and servers share several pieces of information related to their capabilities to negotiate a mutual encryption base. Part of this can be configured by the user (*e.g.*, ciphers the server is allowed to select), only limited by the actual capabilities of the software and hardware. However, TLS servers only react to clients; therefore, reveal only a portion of their internal configuration with every response (*e.g.*, the server

Table 1. Model of TLS configuration properties on a server and their representations.

Property	Representation
Supported TLS versions	set
Cipher suites	
Supported groups	priority list / set[a]
ALPNs	
Selected extension values[b]	map(id → value)
Inappropriate Fallback support	bool
Order of TLS extensions	DAG[c] / set
Error behavior	one of {TCP, TLS, Ignore}

[a] Only sets can be collected if the server uses the client preferences.
[b] EC Point Formats, Signature Algorithms (Cert), and Heartbeat.
[c] A directed acyclic graph (DAG) is used if the server responds consistently.

selects only a single cipher from the list of proposed ciphers). This means, multiple requests (i.e., CHs) must be sent to collect the full amount of information hidden in the TLS stack. It is not feasible (regarding time and resources) to send every possible CH to a server. Thus, every active TLS scanner uses a strategy to select CHs depending on the information it wants to collect. With DissecTLS we aim to reconstruct the configuration that cause the observed TLS behavior in a scalable manner that can be used even for Internet-wide scans. Therefore, we need to reduce the number of requests as far as possible. This is achieved by defining a general model of the TLS configuration on a server and use the minimum number of requests necessary to learn the parameters of the model. Additionally, we defined the output such that it can be used for fingerprinting; i.e., exclude session, timing, and instance related data. Depending on the previous responses from a TLS server we use the model to craft the most promising CH that should reveal new information about the server.

The following sections will explain our model of the TLS stack, how we represent its features, and how our scanner is implemented on an abstract level.

2.1   Modeling the TLS Configuration on Servers

To design a scan that is able to extract the parameters of a TLS stack configuration, these parameters need to be defined first. We analyzed popular web server configurations (e.g., provided by Mozilla [23]), TLS server debugging tools (testssl.sh [33] and SSLyze [10]), passively captured TLS handshakes, and the TLS 1.2 and 1.3 specification [27,28] to derive the model from Table 1. This model reflects our understanding of TLS and how it is applied in the Internet. It is not complete as discussed in Sect. 6.

TLS servers support a set of versions and either answer with the correct version, abort the handshake, or attempt a downgrade to a lower version. There are three priority lists used in the handshake where the client offers a list of options and the server selects one according to its internal preferences. Iteratively removing each parameter from new requests that was previously selected by the server, the full list of length n can be scanned with $n + 1$ requests. This is the optimal approach using the "lowest number of connections necessary [...]" for one host", explained by Mayer et al. [20]. However, if the server prefers client preferences, only a set of supported parameters can be acquired instead of a priority list. Clients can inform the server about their own priorities through the order of parameters in the CH. We tested whether servers respect this priority as follows: after learning at least two parameters, we also learned which one the server selected first. Then, we send a new CH where the order of the two is reversed; we know a server prefers its own preferences if this had no influence on the selection. We scan cipher suites, supported groups, and Application Layer Protocol Negotiations (ALPNs) with the currently 350, 64, and 27 possible values listed by IANA [17], respectively. Some servers provide the full list of supported groups [27] directly as extension, in these cases we do not explicitly scan them. However, the presence of a pre-computed key share can influence the priorities of the supported groups; hence, we collect the preference without a pre-computed key share and afterwards test whether the presence influenced the decision. Support of most TLS extensions is indicated by their presence or absence and does not need a particular logic, they just need to be triggered in the CH with their presence. Others need specific logic because they modify the encryption (Encrypt Then Mac and Extended Master Secret), are mutually exclusive with other extensions (Record Size Limit and Max Fragment Size), or multiple values can be send (Heartbeat). Sometimes, the content of extensions is of interest because it reveals information about the server capabilities, and in these cases we store the raw byte content. The man-in-the-middle inappropriate fallback protection needs special logic because it only makes sense to send the signaling cipher [21] if multiple TLS versions are detected. Lastly, servers can respond differently in cases of problems, some report an error on the Transmission Control Protocol (TCP) layer, some send TLS alerts, and others just ignore the problematic part of the handshake (e.g., using a default value). An example is shown in Appendix A.

In summary, this model is an abstract and human-readable representation of the TLS stack on a server that can explain its behavior in TLS handshakes.

2.2 Representing Multiple Observations of Extension Orders

The order of extensions is not defined in the TLS standard; however, we argue most servers have a consistent order as result how they are implemented in the code. We confirmed this by checking the source code of the Golang TLS library we modified to implement our tool. Moreover, in Sect. 4.2 we found that more than 99% of the servers in the study responded with a consistent order.

The presence of extensions depends on the request and not all extensions can be observed at the same time (e.g., the key share extension is only present in a TLS 1.3 handshake). This means, every response from the server reveals part of the order and multiple observations can be combined to reconstruct the

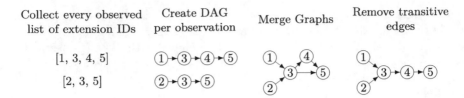

Fig. 1. Example for merging multiple observations of TLS extensions into a single format. If the graph contains cycles after merging, the extension order is inconsistent.

internal order on the server as close as possible. We created a DAG for each observation, merged these graphs and removed duplicate and transitive edges. If the graph contains cycles after merging; this means, the observations were inconsistent and the extension order cannot be reconstructed. An example for this process is illustrated in Fig. 1.

In conclusion, a DAG allows to represent multiple observations of extensions in a compact format that is as close as possible to the internal server order.

2.3   Implementation of DissecTLS

DissecTLS is implemented as feature of the TUM goscanner [15], which is a TLS scanner for Internet-wide measurements. It is based upon a modified version of the Golang TLS library that can send custom CHs and extract handshake data.

We designed DissecTLS to use as few requests as possible. To achieve this, the logic of the scan is divided into several scan tasks and each task is responsible for one or a few related parameters. The tasks are designed to collect information in parallel. Every task modifies the next CH depending on its current state and, after receiving the response, updates the server parameters with the new information. This is repeated until an error occurs; then, each task that could have caused the error is toggled on or off until one remains and the cause is found (*e.g.*, whether a missing cipher or the wrong TLS version was responsible). The task causing the error must resolve it (*e.g.*, mark the cipher scan as complete or a TLS version as unsupported) and the scan is continued normally. In general, the more specific a server was (*e.g.*, it sent a "protocol version" TLS alert instead of a TCP reset), the faster the cause can be identified. Some servers did not respond with error messages but let the TCP connection time out, we treat these cases not as an error in favor of reducing the load in case of real timeouts.

In summary, with help of our model we implemented a scanner that uses a minimal amount of requests that allow us to reconstruct the TLS configuration.

3   Comparison of TLS Scanners and Their Ability to Detect Different TLS Stack Configurations on Servers

Active TLS scanners are designed to extract information from servers. We compared their performance doing so by measuring their ability to distinguish differ-

Table 2. Detected number of Nginx configurations for each test case. An ideal scanner detects every alteration made on the server and finds "Goal" number of configurations.

Test Case	DissecTLS	DissecTLS (lim.)	ATSF	JARM	SSLyze	testssl.sh	Goal
TLS Versions	15	15	13	11	15	14	15
Cipher Suites	1 956	359	115	11	63	1 956	1 956
ALPNs	2	2	2	2	1	2	2
Preferences	2	2	2	2	1	2	2
Session Tickets	2	2	2	2	2	2	2
Used CHs per Server							
Minimum	8.0	8.0	9.0	9.0	423.0	9.0	
Average	14.3	10.0	10.0	10.0	450.1	132.7	
Maximum	42.0	15.0	12.0	10.0	455.0	224.0	

ent TLS server configurations. Without analyzing the scanner output we argue that whenever a scanner is able to differentiate two different TLS configurations, the scanner has detected the relevant piece of information. The more configurations it can differentiate, the more valuable is its output. However, we also measured the costs of the scanner by counting the amount of requests it needed to perform the scan. The lower the costs are, the more servers can be scanned in the same time and the lower the impact is on individual servers. An ideal scalable approach collects a high amount of information with low costs.

We compared testssl.sh [33], SSLyze [10], JARM [4], ATSF [31], and this work. We selected them because from our knowledge they are the relevant representatives that either fingerprint or reconstruct the TLS configuration. We configured our approach in two versions, one tries to fully reconstruct the TLS configuration (DissecTLS), the other completes using 10 handshakes (DissecTLS lim.). We interpret the textual output of each scanner as its representation of the server. If two outputs are equal, they detected no difference in the configuration. We were able to directly use the output of JARM, ATSF, and this work. We had to remove information regarding timing (*e.g.*, scan time), sessions (*e.g.*, cryptographic keys), and server instances (*e.g.*, the domain name) from the output of testssl.sh and SSLyze to get stable results for the same TLS configuration. Additionally, we disabled the vulnerability detection of these tools.

3.1   Scanner Comparison in a Local Testbed

In our local testbed we compared the TLS scanners based on a ground truth. We challenged them in different scenarios where we systematically made alterations to a server and checked whether the scanners were able to detect it.

The experiment was designed as follows: we selected a parameter we could configure on the TLS server (Test Case), launched an Nginx 1.23 docker container for each configuration we could generated for this parameter, and scanned the containers with every scanner. We used tcpdump [32] to measure the number of CHs the scanners were using. The results can be seen in Table 2. An ideal scanner is able to differentiate all variations we have configured (listed under "Goal"). Nginx allowed to configure four TLS versions, resulting in 15 working combinations ($2^4 - 1$). We only used six TLS 1.2 ciphers because this number was still scannable in a reasonable time. These six ciphers resulted in 1 956 configurations (every permutation of every combination of the six ciphers). ALPNs, Server Preferences, and Session Tickets were scanned either en- or disabled. The table shows that only DissecTLS and testssl.sh were able to detect every alteration we made on the server. DissecTLS (lim.) tried to detect the TLS versions, then data in extensions, and lastly the ciphers; hence, it usually detected only the first few ciphers from the server and could not detect configurations that differ in the lower cipher priorities. Testssl.sh could not detect one case where only TLS 1.3 was enabled because at the time of the experiment it included an OpenSSL version that was not TLS 1.3 capable. SSlyze was not able to detect the order of ciphers, therefore, could not detect any permutation we performed on the ciphers. The two fingerprinting approaches ATSF and JARM were not able to detect every alteration on the servers. This was expected as they use a fixed number of requests. However, as this experiment is artificial, it is possible that the obtained fingerprints are still good enough for fingerprinting use cases. Regarding the scanning costs, the picture is reversed. The fingerprinting tools and the limited version of DissecTLS used the least number of requests, DissecTLS slightly more, and testssl.sh and SSlyze being the most costly. We expect testssl.sh and SSLyze to be used on a small scale where scanning costs do not matter; however, we can see that the former is more optimized and uses fewer requests to collect more information. We can see a difference in JARM and ATSF regarding the maximum number of used CHs: both initially use 10 CHs, but the latter completes handshakes; therefore, we sometimes observe an additional CH from the scanner as response to a Hello Retry Request (servers can send them to request a different key share from the client). DissecTLS makes use of this TLS feature to reconstruct the supported group preferences of the server in case no key share is present because its presence might influence the decision. Therefore, we observe up to 15 CHs for the maximum of 10 handshakes.

To conclude, DissecTLS competes both with testssl.sh regarding the amount of collected information and with active TLS fingerprinting tools regarding their low scanning costs. However, this analysis only includes a single TLS implementation and artificial test cases; therefore, to get a more complete view the next section compares the scanners in a more realistic setting on toplist servers.

3.2   Scanner Comparison on the Top 10k Toplist Domains

This section compares the five TLS scanners on the top 10k domains from the Tranco [19] toplist. Because the ground truth is unknown, only their performance to differentiate servers can be compared. The scan took 6 days to complete because of the low request rate testssl.sh and SSLyze were able to achieve.

The number of configurations each tool was able to detect and the number of requests necessary to collect this information can be seen in Table 3. DissecTLS was able to detect the most configurations, followed by Testssl.sh. However, this

Table 3. Comparison of TLS scanners regarding the number of detected configurations and Client Hello usage on the resolved (IPv4 and IPv6) top 10k Tranco domains.

	DissecTLS	DissecTLS (lim.)	ATSF	JARM	SSLyze	testssl.sh
Configurations	3 450.0	1 839.0	1 956.0	1 325.0	2 738.0	3 235.0
Total CHs	530.6k	235.6k	238.5k	209.4k	9.5M	3.4M
Average CHs	24.0	10.7	10.8	9.5	430.0	154.9
Total Scanned Targets						22 075

Table 4. Overview of the collected data for the Top- and Blocklist study.

Input source	Total Samples	Distinct Targets	Unique Domains	Successful Scans		
				DissecTLS	ATSF	JARM
Tranco Toplist	15.8M	2.8M	1.1M	14.4M	13.1M	14.3M
abuse.ch Feodo Tracker	4 040.0	812.0		1 725.0	2 126.0	768.0
abuse.ch SSLBL	1 034.0	223.0		27.0	42.0	26.0

does not mean a scanner collected only a super-set from another, as discussed in Sect. 6. This work uses just a sixth of the requests compared to testssl.sh, with 24 CHs on average. JARM used less than 10 requests on average because sometimes the TCP connection failed and no CH was sent. In contrast to the last section, the limited version of DissecTLS performed a bit worse than ATSF. Apparently, our approach only detects the finer details that help to differentiate TLS configurations when it completes the scan.

This sections showed that the dynamic scanning approach from testssl.sh, DissecTLS, and SSLyze is superior to the fixed selection of CH regarding collected data. However, this comes with increased scanning costs. We argue that only JARM, ATSF, and DissecTLS are resource efficient enough to be used for large-scale measurements. Additionally, in the following we refrain from limiting the number of requests of DissecTLS. While roughly doubling the scanning costs it provides a more complete; hence, a more useful view on the TLS stack.

4   Measurement Study on Top- and Blocklist Servers

This section transfers the findings from the previous section to a larger scale where we collected more than 15 Million data samples with each scanner (data available under Ref. [29]). However, we only used DissecTLS, ATSF, and JARM for this study because testssl.sh and SSLyze did not scale well enough for this use case.

We scanned servers from the complete Tranco [19] toplist and two C&C server blocklists: the abuse.ch Feodo Tracker [1] and the abuse.ch SSLBL [2]. We collected nine weekly snapshots starting from July 01, 2022. Table 4 presents an overview of these measurements. We resolved domains from the toplist and

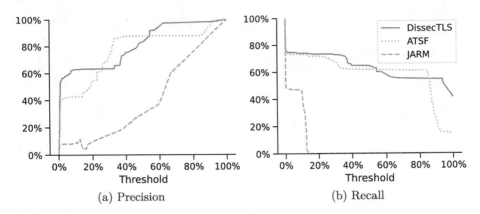

(a) Precision   (b) Recall

Fig. 2. Precision and Recall for classifying C&C servers each week based on the data collected in previous weeks. Using the fingerprints from the respective scanner as input.

scanned each combination of IPv4 and IPv6 address together with the domain as Server Name Indication. We call each IP and domain name combination a target. The two blocklists only list IP addresses; hence, the number of targets is equal to the number of entries on these lists. We count a "success" if the respective scanner produced an output. For DissecTLS and ATSF this is the case if a TCP connection could be established. JARM additionally needed the server to respond at least once with a Server Hello. DissecTLS and JARM implement a retry mechanism on failed TCP handshakes, together with the different success definition, this can explain the variations in the success rates.

4.1 Fingerprinting C&C Servers

Althouse *et al.* [4] and Sosnowski *et al.* [31] describe the fingerprinting of malicious C&C servers as one of the major use cases of their respective approach. Like the fingerprinting tools, DissecTLS collects data from the TLS stack and its output can be used for fingerprinting. In the following, we performed a C&C server classification based on the data collected with JARM, ATSF, and DissecTLS from the weekly top- and blocklist measurements. This allowed us to compare the different data collection approaches regarding a C&C server detection.

Each scanned target is labeled as C&C server (positive) or toplist server (negative) based on whether the IP address was listed on one of the blocklists in the respective week. In case of ambiguity, the blocklist took preference. Then, we made a prediction for each target based on the data and labels from previous weeks. The prediction worked as follows: each week n, we calculated the rate how often a fingerprint was observed from C&C servers versus toplist servers during weeks $[1..n-1]$ and predicted a "C&C server" if this rate was above a configurable threshold. A threshold of 50% means that at least every second server with a specific fingerprint would need to be labeled as C&C server so that this fingerprint results in a "C&C server" prediction. We performed this classification with the fingerprints from JARM, ATSF, and DissecTLS. Figure 2 compares the precision and recall defined as $\frac{TP}{TP+FP}$ and $\frac{TP}{TP+FN}$ ($TP :=$ "true positives", $FP :=$

"false positives", $FN :=$ "false negatives"), respectively. Intuitively, precision is the rate of correct classifications and recall the fraction of C&C servers we were able to identify. It shows that the classification based on ATSF or DissecTLS performed quite similar with a high precision that reached the maximum at the most conservative detection threshold of 100%. However, the high precision is only achieved through a lower recall of 15% and 42%, respectively. JARM fingerprints were not descriptive enough to identify the C&C servers on our two blocklists and together with the lower success rate this resulted in a low recall.

In conclusion; DissecTLS, ATSF, and JARM collect TLS data that can be used to detect C&C servers. DissecTLS and ATSF achieved a precision that is more than 99% for the 100% threshold. Moreover, DissecTLS achieved a 2.8 times higher recall than ATSF for said threshold. Additionally, we argue that DissecTLS collects more valuable data because it provides a human-readable representation of the TLS stack as described in the next section.

4.2   Human-Readable TLS Server Configurations

Until this section this work analyzed TLS configurations as a single unit; however, DissecTLS produces an output (see example in Appendix A) that can be used to understand how a server is configured. This can help to explain why fingerprinting was possible. In Appendix B we present statistics from the top- and blocklist servers that can deepen our understanding of TLS parameter usages on the Internet. We have analyzed the support for different TLS versions; computed a popularity ranking of cipher suites, supported groups, and ALPNs; analyzed whether servers prefer client preferences or not; and looked how many servers supported deprecated cipher categories.

In conclusion, an exhaustive TLS scanning approach can be used for fingerprinting but additionally provides valuable insights into the TLS ecosystem.

5   Related Work

Fingerprinting TLS clients in passive network traces is a well established discipline, shown by multiple related works [3,5–7,16]. This concept has been adapted by Althouse et al. [4] and Sosnowski et al. [31] through active scanning to be able to fingerprint servers. Both approaches use a fixed set of 10 requests that "have been specially crafted to pull out unique responses in TLS servers" [4] and "empirically optimized to provide as much information as possible" [31], respectively. They capture variations of the TLS configuration in their fingerprints; however, they do not actively search for them; additionally, the explainability of their output, or fingerprint, is low and it is difficult to understand what has caused the specific fingerprint. Both works show that they can find malicious C&C servers on the Internet. A fundamentally different approach is proposed by Rasoamanana et al. [26], they define a State Machine describing TLS handshakes and argue that the transitions between states can be used to fingerprint specific implementations; especially, if these transitions are not conform to the TLS specification and, sometimes, even pose a security vulnerability. Their focus on the behavior of the library in the context of erroneous input does not consider the parameters that are the cause of the non-erroneous behavior. Dynamically scanning TLS servers is a common practice in the context of analyzing and debugging servers with tools like testssl.sh [33] or SSLyze [10]. Both make assumptions how the TLS on the server works and adapt their scanning to this model. However, they focus on the configurable part of the server, do not export every fingerprintable information, and are not optimized for Internet-wide usage (e.g., use more than 100 requests to scan a single server). Mayer et al. [20] showed that cipher suite scanning can be optimized to use 6% of the connections compared to related works. However, they ignore the rest of the TLS configuration.

6   Discussion

This work proposes an exhaustive but optimized TLS scanning approach that can be used for large-scale Internet measurements and for TLS fingerprinting. The following paragraphs discuss several aspects we found worth mentioning.

C&C TLS Configurations. In general, configurations we could relate to C&C servers had just slight alterations in their parameters compared to common configurations (e.g., the position of a single cipher). However, we collected interesting results (see Appendix A) from several servers labeled as Trickbot, according to the Feodo Tracker [1]. These servers supported TLS 1.0 and downgraded higher versions, which is already a rare behavior. In contrast to the low TLS version, the ciphers were strong and some used a modern key agreement, *i.a.*, X25519 (standardized 2016 [14] - 8 years after TLS 1.2 [28]). This led us to the conclusion that this was a modern server where some modern features were disabled.

Completeness of the Testbed. Every TLS scanner from Sect. 3.1 was capable to detect more configurations than the ones we have tested, e.g., TLS versions prior to TLS 1.0 or other cipher suites. We selected the tested values because they were configurable on the Nginx server. Some features, e.g., the extension order, cannot be configured. Our choice of the six ciphers was arbitrary and it is possible that there are combinations of ciphers where the performance of the scanners is different. However, our tool sends 350 different ciphers and the analysis shows that it can effectively identify permutations of those on the server.

Completeness of the TLS Server Model. Sections. 3.2 and 3.1 showed that DissecTLS and testssl.sh were able to detect the most TLS configurations. However, looking into their output, no scanner provided a super-set of the other; hence, our proposed model cannot be complete. We manually investigated cases where testssl.sh was able to differentiate configurations while DissecTLS was not, and vice versa. Both scanners rely on consistent server responses; however, Sosnowski et al. [31] reported inconsistent behaviors for 1% of their fingerprinted targets. If servers behave inconsistently, both scanners might have collected an incomplete view of the TLS stack and reported different configurations on each connection attempt. We expect testssl.sh is a bit more resilient to this behavior due to its excessive but thoroughly scanning in contrast to limiting the amount of CHs as possible. DissecTLS was able to find more configurations than testssl.sh; *i.a.*, through differentiating the error behavior and by merging the observed extensions into a single DAG. However, testssl.sh detected more details sometimes: *e.g.*, it was able to detect variations for non-elliptic TLS 1.2 Diffie-Helman Key Exchange Mechanism (KEM) key sizes, collected cipher priorities per TLS version, detected typical server failures like being unable to handle certain CH sizes, differentiated whether a session resumption was implemented through IDs (legacy) or tickets, and used a service detection (*e.g.*, detecting Hypertext Transfer Protocol). To support these cases with DissecTLS, we would need to increase the number of sent CHs and implement the missing TLS features in the library. Whether the additional data would provide a benefit for use cases like the C&C detection is an open question for future work because we could not include testssl.sh in our C&C server detection study (Sect. 4.1), due to its limited scalability. To conclude, neither scanner collected a super-set from the other and we argue that it is impossible to build an ideal scanner without knowledge about every TLS implementation and how TLS will evolve in the future.

Ethical Considerations All our active Internet measurements are set up following best scanning practices as described by Durumeric *et al.* [12]. We used rate limiting (overall and per-target), dedicated scan servers with abuse contacts, informative reverse DNS entries and websites that inform about our research, maintained a blocklist, and provided contact information for further details or scan exclusion. Our work does not harm individuals or reveal private data as covered by [11,24] and focuses on publicly reachable services. The core design principle of our approach was to reduce the impact on third parties by minimizing the number of requests while maintaining an useful level of data quality.

7   Conclusion

This work proposes a scalable active scanning approach to reconstruct the TLS configuration on servers. The approach is compared with four active TLS scanners and fingerprinting tools. While we are able to collect a comparable amount of information to single server TLS debugging tools, we also keep up with the performance of scalable active TLS fingerprinting tools using around twice the number of requests. Our approach collects more data than the fingerprinting tools and produces human-readable representations of a TLS configuration, improving the explainability of the approach. We performed a nine week measurement study of top- and blocklists, analyzed common TLS parameter usages, and fingerprinted potentially malicious C&C servers. Similar to related work, the fingerprinting achieved a precision of more than 99% for the most conservative detection threshold of 100%; however, at the same time DissecTLS achieved a recall 2.8 times higher than the related ATSF [31]. This was achieved by a scan that dynamically adapts based on a TLS stack model and previously learned information. The model was used to explain server responses and to craft new requests that should reveal new data. This paper shows that an exhaustive TLS parameter scanner can be implemented efficiently enough to be used on a large scale. Moreover, it can replace existing active TLS fingerprinting approaches because it provides a similar fingerprinting performance but additionally produces a valuable dataset. In the future, it can help to acquire a global view on the TLS parameter usage to deepen our understanding of the TLS ecosystem.

A   Example DissecTLS Output

Table 5 shows an example output we have collected from a TLS server that was labeled as Trickbot on the Feodo Tracker [1]. For better readability the output was enhanced with the parameter names from IANA [17]. We could determine the order of the ciphers and supported groups; therefore, the shown values are a priority list. We could not determine the ALPN preferences from the server because it supported only one option. The extension order was consistent across all observations and the resulting DAG had no branches.

Table 5. Example DissecTLS output obtained from a server labeled as Trickbot.

Property	Value
supported TLS versions	TLS 1.0 support
	TLS 1.1 downgrade
	TLS 1.2 downgrade
	TLS 1.3 downgrade
cipher suites (priority list)	TLS_ECDHE_RSA_WITH_AES_256_CBC_SHA
	TLS_ECDHE_RSA_WITH_AES_128_CBC_SHA
	TLS_RSA_WITH_AES_256_CBC_SHA
	TLS_RSA_WITH_AES_128_CBC_SHA
	TLS_RSA_WITH_CAMELLIA_256_CBC_SHA
	TLS_RSA_WITH_CAMELLIA_128_CBC_SHA
cipher Preference	server
supported groups (priority list)	x25519
	secp256r1
group preference	server
with key share	client
ALPN (set)	http/1.1
ALPN preference	unknown
extension data	EC Point Format → [uncompressed
	ansiX962_compressed_prime,
	ansiX962_compressed_char2]
order of TLS extensions (DAG)	renegotiation_info → max_fragment_length →
	ec_point_formats → session_ticket → ALPN →
	encrypt_then_mac → extended_master_secret
version error behavior	Ignore
cipher error behavior	TLS Alert
groups error behavior	Ignore
ALPN arror behavior	Ignore

B   Additional TLS Server Parameter Statistics

This section adds several statistics we have obtained while analyzing the data from the measurement in Sect. 4.2. We find them interesting; however, not necessary to support the findings of the paper.

Table 6. Support for different TLS versions from successfully scanned targets.

	TLS 1.0	TLS 1.1	TLS 1.2	TLS 1.3
Success	62.83%	65.24%	99.57%	74.57%
Abort	37.61%	35.03%	0.32%	0.00%
Downgrade	0.02%	0.21%	0.15%	25.90%

Support for the TLS versions can be seen in Table 6. Although TLS 1.0 and 1.1 is deprecated since 2021 [22], we saw a high amount servers supporting it. Some servers even downgraded the handshake by responding with a lower version than the one we requested. This was expected for TLS 1.3 because the TLS 1.3 CHs is basically a TLS 1.2 CH with special extensions. A server that does not understand these extensions should continue with a TLS 1.2 handshake. However, we rarely observed this behavior also for other versions.

We collected cipher suites, supported groups, and ALPNs as priority lists. This enables combining them to get the overall most popular values as shown in Table 7 (full list available under [30]). This problem is similar to a voting problem where multiple individuals can vote with a list of descending preference and can be solved with scoring rules as discussed by Fraenkel *et al.* [13]. We decided to use the Dowdall rule, which favors parameters with top preferences. This way parameters of a low priority, usually only kept for backward compliance, are given a low score. The ranking worked as follows: from each priority list the parameters $[p_1, \ldots, p_n]$ are scored with $[1, \frac{1}{2}, \ldots, \frac{1}{n}]$, the scores for each parameter are summed up, and ranks based on the highest scores are computed. We analyze the parameters independent of the TLS version; hence, the TLS 1.3 ciphers are ranked above the others because, in general, higher versions are preferred over ciphers.

Some servers selected the cipher suites, supported groups or ALPNs based on the preference of the client. This leaves security decisions open to the client but can be beneficial to the user if the client has limited hardware capabilities. However, in our measurements we saw this was rarely the case and most servers preferred their own priorities as shown in Table 8. This is different if a client already pre-computed a TLS 1.3 key share for one of the supported groups; then, 29% of the servers used the key share to avoid an additional round trip.

An important security feature on servers is the support against version downgrade attacks. If this is not given, even when security issues are fixed in a newer TLS version, a downgrade can reopen these attack vectors. Such a downgrade could be achieved, *e.g.*, by a man-in-the-middle attacker blocking connections

Table 7. Most preferred TLS parameters (IANA names [17]) ranked separately with the Dowdall rule and total distinct values. Each scanned target was used as vote.

Rank	Cipher Suites	Supported groups	ALPNs
1	aes_256_gcm_sha384	x25519	h2
2	chacha20_poly1305_sha256	secp256r1	http/1.1
3	aes_128_gcm_sha256	secp384r1	http/1.0
4	ecdhe_rsa_with_aes_128_gcm_sha256	secp521r1	spdy/3
5	ecdhe_rsa_with_aes_256_gcm_sha384	x448	spdy/2
6	ecdhe_ecdsa_with_chacha20_poly1305_sha256	brainpoolP512r1	http/0.9
7	ecdhe_ecdsa_with_aes_128_gcm_sha256	brainpoolP384r1	acme
8	ecdhe_rsa_with_aes_256_cbc_sha384	secp256k1	tls/1
9	ecdhe_rsa_with_aes_128_cbc_sha256	brainpoolP256r1	h2c
10	ecdhe_ecdsa_with_aes_128_cbc_sha	sect571r1	h3
Total	152	45	13

Table 8. Server preferences and downgrade protection in relation to number of targets where the parameter could be successfully determined.

	Parameter Determined	Values	
Cipher suite preference	2334678	4.63%	(client)
Supported Group preference	2125081	5.58%	(client)
with Key Share	1661825	28.60%	(client)
ALPN preference	1899399	0.03%	(client)
TLS downgrade protection	2101497	98.68%	(protcted)

for a higher TLS version expecting the client will attempt to reconnect with a lower version. Table 8 shows most servers were protected.

Several servers still support categories of deprecated ciphers [9, 25] as shown in Table 9. These ciphers are known to be insecure; however, they are not per-se a security vulnerability because an attacker would still need to force a client and server to agree on them.

Table 9. Servers supporting at least one deprecated cipher suite per category. Percentages are in relation to the successfully scanned targets.

	Null	Export	Anonymous	RC4	Any
Targets	376	1403	1606	36281	36694
	0.02%	0.06%	0.07%	1.56%	1.58%

References

1. abuse.ch: Feodo Tracker. https://feodotracker.abuse.ch/. Accessed 28 Oct 28 (2022)
2. abuse.ch: SSL Certificate Blacklist. https://sslbl.abuse.ch/. Accessed 28 Oct 2022
3. Althouse, J., Atkinson, J., Atkins, J.: TLS Fingerprinting with JA3 and JA3S (2019). https://engineering.salesforce.com/tls-fingerprinting-with-ja3-and-ja3s-247362855967
4. Althouse, J., Smart, A., Nunnally Jr., R., Brady, M.: Easily identify malicious servers on the internet with JARM (2020). https://engineering.salesforce.com/easily-identify-malicious-servers-on-the-internet-with-jarm-e095edac525a
5. Anderson, B., McGrew, D.: OS fingerprinting: new techniques and a study of information gain and obfuscation. In: 2017 IEEE Conference on Communications and Network Security (CNS) (2017). https://doi.org/10.1109/CNS.2017.8228647
6. Anderson, B., McGrew, D., Kendler, A.: Classifying Encrypted Traffic With TLS-Aware Telemetry. FloCon (2016)
7. Anderson, B., McGrew, D.A.: Accurate TLS fingerprinting using destination context and knowledge bases. CoRR (2020). https://doi.org/10.48550/arXiv.2009.01939
8. Censys: JARM in Censys Search 2.0 (2022). https://support.censys.io/hc/en-us/articles/4409122252692-JARM-in-Censys-Search-2-0. Accessed 14 Oct 2022
9. Dierks, T., Rescorla, E.: The Transport Layer Security (TLS) Protocol Version 1.1. RFC 4346 (2006). https://doi.org/10.17487/RFC4346
10. Diquet, A.: SSLyze. https://github.com/nabla-c0d3/sslyze. Accessed 13 Oct 2022
11. Dittrich, D., Kenneally, E., et al.: The Menlo Report: Ethical principles guiding information and communication technology research. US Department of Homeland Security (2012)
12. Durumeric, Z., Wustrow, E., Halderman, J.A.: ZMap: fast internet-wide scanning and its security applications. In: Proceedings of the USENIX Security Symposium (2013)
13. Fraenkel, J., Grofman, B.: The Borda Count and its real-world alternatives: comparing scoring rules in Nauru and Slovenia. Aust. J. Pol. Sci. (2014). https://doi.org/10.1080/10361146.2014.900530
14. Friedl, S., Popov, A., Langley, A., Emile, S.: Transport Layer Security (TLS) Application-Layer Protocol Negotiation Extension. RFC 7301 (2014). https://doi.org/10.17487/RFC7301
15. Gasser, O., Sosnowski, M., Sattler, P., Zirngibl, J.: Goscanner (2022). https://github.com/tumi8/goscanner
16. Husák, M., Cermák, M., Jirsík, T., Celeda, P.: Network-based HTTPS client identification using SSL/TLS fingerprinting. In: 2015 10th International Conference on Availability, Reliability and Security (2015). https://doi.org/10.1109/ARES.2015.35
17. IANA: Transport Layer Security (TLS) Parameters. https://www.iana.org/assignments/tls-parameters/tls-parameters.xhtml. Accessed 13 Oct 2022
18. Labovitz, C.: Internet traffic 2009–2019. In: Proceedings of the Asia Pacific Regional Internet Conference on Operational Technologies (2019)
19. Le Pochat, V., Van Goethem, T., Tajalizadehkhoob, S., Korczyński, M., Joosen, W.: Tranco: a research-oriented top sites ranking hardened against manipulation. In: Proceedings of the 26th Annual Network and Distributed System Security Symposium (2019). https://doi.org/10.14722/ndss.2019.23386

20. Mayer, W., Schmiedecker, M.: Turning active TLS scanning to eleven. In: De Capitani di Vimercati, S., Martinelli, F. (eds.) SEC 2017. IAICT, vol. 502, pp. 3–16. Springer, Cham (2017). https://doi.org/10.1007/978-3-319-58469-0_1
21. Moeller, B., Langley, A.: TLS Fallback Signaling Cipher Suite Value (SCSV) for Preventing Protocol Downgrade Attacks. RFC 7507 (2015). https://doi.org/10.17487/RFC7507
22. Moriarty, K., Farrell, S.: Deprecating TLS 1.0 and TLS 1.1. RFC 8996 (2021). https://doi.org/10.17487/RFC8996
23. Mozilla: SSL configuration generator (2022). https://ssl-config.mozilla.org. Accessed 13 Oct 2022
24. Partridge, C., Allman, M.: Addressing ethical considerations in network measurement papers. In: Proceedings of the 2015 ACM SIGCOMM Workshop on Ethics in Networked Systems Research. Association for Computing Machinery (2016). https://doi.org/10.1145/2793013.2793014
25. Popov, A.: Prohibiting RC4 Cipher Suite. RFC 7507 (2015). https://doi.org/10.17487/RFC7465
26. Rasoamanana, A.T., Levillain, O., Debar, H.: Towards a systematic and automatic use of state machine inference to uncover security flaws and fingerprint TLS stacks. In: Computer Security - ESORICS (2022). https://doi.org/10.1007/978-3-031-17143-7_31
27. Rescorla, E.: The Transport Layer Security (TLS) Protocol Version 1.3. RFC 8446 (2018). https://doi.org/10.17487/RFC8446
28. Rescorla, E., Dierks, T.: The Transport Layer Security (TLS) Protocol Version 1.2. RFC 5246 (2008). https://doi.org/10.17487/RFC5246
29. Sosnowski, M., Zirngibl, J., Sattler, P., Carle, G.: DissecTLS Measurement Data. https://doi.org/10.14459/2023mp1695491
30. Sosnowski, M., Zirngibl, J., Sattler, P., Carle, G.: DissecTLS: Additional Material (2023). https://dissectls.github.io/
31. Sosnowski, M., et al.: Active TLS stack fingerprinting: characterizing TLS server deployments at scale. In: Proceedings of the Network Traffic Measurement and Analysis Conference (TMA) (2022)
32. The Tcpdump Group: tcpdump. https://www.tcpdump.org. Accessed 27 Oct 2022
33. Wetter, D.: Testing TLS/SSL encryption. https://testssl.sh/. Accessed 27 Oct 2022

Applications

A Measurement-Derived Functional Model for the Interaction Between Congestion Control and QoE in Video Conferencing

Jia He$^{(\boxtimes)}$, Mostafa Ammar, and Ellen Zegura

Georgia Institute of Technology, Atlanta, GA, USA
jhe332@gatech.edu, {ammar,ewz}@cc.gatech.edu

Abstract. Video Conferencing Applications (VCAs) that support remote work and education have increased in use over the last two years, contributing to Internet bandwidth usage. VCA clients transmit video and audio to each other in peer-to-peer mode or through a bridge known as a Selective Forwarding Unit (SFU). Popular VCAs implement congestion control in the application layer over UDP and accomplish rate adjustment through video rate control, ultimately affecting end user Quality of Experience (QoE). Researchers have reported on the throughput and video metric performance of specific VCAs using structured experiments. Yet prior work rarely examines the interaction between congestion control mechanisms and rate adjustment techniques that produces the observed throughput and QoE metrics. Understanding this interaction at a functional level paves the way to explain observed performance, to pinpoint commonalities and key functional differences across VCAs, and to contemplate opportunities for innovation. To that end, we first design and conduct detailed measurements of three VCAs (WebRTC/Jitsi, Zoom, BlueJeans) to develop understanding of their congestion and video rate control mechanisms. We then use the measurement results to derive our functional models for the VCA client and SFU. Our models reveal the complexity of these systems and demonstrate how, despite some uniformity in function deployment, there is significant variability among the VCAs in the implementation of these functions.

1 Introduction

Video Conferencing Applications (VCAs) represent an increasingly significant amount of Internet application and bandwidth usage [35]. Schools and businesses have turned to video conferencing in support of safe COVID practices and also for efficiency and convenience. In VCAs, a signaling server first allows clients to coordinate their activities and perform session management. Once a session is established the clients transmit video and audio to each other, either directly in peer-to-peer mode or indirectly through a video bridge. The dominant type of commercial video bridge is a Selective Forwarding Unit (SFU), which forwards

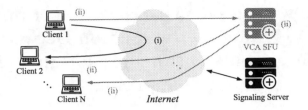

Fig. 1. High-level architecture of a video conference with N clients. Video traffic originating at Client 1 shown: (i) peer-to-peer connection between two clients (ii) in SFU mode, the SFU will forward the video from Client 1 to all other clients.

videos from each client to other clients without decoding [44]. SFUs can manipulate videos prior to forwarding using techniques such as subsampling and layer selection which can be applied to the encoded video. A high-level overview of a video conferencing session is given in Fig. 1.

VCAs can be bandwidth intensive because of their extensive use of video. Commercial systems carry the video on top of UDP, with congestion control implemented in the application. Recognizing the important role of congestion control, there is a long history of effort dedicated to building application layer congestion control on top of UDP (e.g., [4,11,15]) with more recent efforts geared towards specific use in VCAs [13]. Congestion control mechanisms present in commercial VCAs are typically not shared publicly, though some open-source, production-quality VCAs do exist [3,25].

The main goal of congestion control is to determine an application sending rate that does not congest the shared network path used by the application. After congestion control functions determine an acceptable target sending rate, the application must enforce this target rate through *video rate control*. The application can adjust the rate of the video being sent using video encoding at the sending client or through layer selection and/or subsampling at the SFU[1]. Congestion control in VCAs, therefore, has a direct impact on video quality and, in turn, the VCA user's quality of experience (QoE). Understanding the user-perceived QoE is important for network operators as it helps with efficient bandwidth provisioning, though in this paper we show that congestion control and video rate control can differ between VCAs, potentially complicating the matter of estimating QoE. Researchers have reported on the throughput and video metric performance of specific VCAs using structured experiments. Yet prior work rarely examines the interaction between congestion control mechanisms and rate adjustment techniques that produces the observed throughput and QoE metrics. Understanding this interaction at a functional level paves the way to explain observed performance, to pinpoint commonalities and key functional differences across different VCAs, and to contemplate opportunities for innovation. This is the aim of this paper.

---

[1] In principle, the total client sending rate includes video, audio, and control data (e.g., RTCP packets). In this paper, we focus only on video data as it is the most bandwidth intensive.

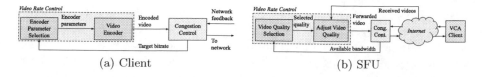

(a) Client   (b) SFU

Fig. 2. Interaction between congestion control and video rate control.

Our starting point is the high-level interaction shown in Fig. 2 between congestion control and video rate control in both the client and in the SFU. Figure 2(a) illustrates that the target rate determined by the congestion control function at a VCA client is used to determine video encoding parameters. These parameters are then fed into the video encoder which outputs video at or below the desired target rate. Figure 2(b) shows the interaction between congestion control and video rate control within an SFU. The SFU receives video from all clients and forwards them to other clients according to their available download bandwidth. As coarse-grained rate control, all SFUs we examine can select which videos to forward to each client [19]. After this selection, the SFU uses additional mechanisms to manage the forwarded video rate without decoding.

This paper aims to deepen understanding of this interaction between congestion control, video rate control, and end user video quality in VCAs beyond the high-level structure shown in Fig. 2. The interaction between these three is complicated, and the proprietary nature of commercial VCA systems restricts visibility into key details. We know that WebRTC [13] and the open source Jitsi [25, 26] use Google Congestion Control (GCC). Prior work [9, 28, 30] has ascertained the presence of congestion control in VCA clients and was able to fit their operation within the general structure of the GCC mechanisms [8]. We add to this literature in two ways. First, we conduct a measurement study, outlined in Sect. 3, of several VCAs (WebRTC/Jitsi, Zoom, and BlueJeans) to fully understand the different congestion control methods (Sect. 4) and video rate control methods (Sect. 5). The measurements are extended to include multiple clients and device types in Sect. 6.

Altogether, the results obtained from our measurement study allow us to develop functional models of the VCA client and VCA SFU, which is one of the primary contributions of this paper. The results allow us to make several observations key to the functional models including, among other things, the different congestion control algorithms employed by the VCAs, such as how BlueJeans is unresponsive to changes in latency but highly sensitive to packet loss, while Zoom is insensitive to packet loss and does respond to latency. Similarly, the VCAs prioritize different video quality metrics at highly constrained bandwidth. For example, Zoom commits to a maximum quantization parameter (QP), while WebRTC/Jitsi prioritize maximizing the frame rate.

The differences among VCAs observed from our measurements highlight the need for a generalized functional model. To that end, in Sect. 7, we derive the generalized functional models of the VCA client and VCA SFU from the measurement results, along with data from publicly available documents and source code. Our models reveal additional details and complexity in these systems and demonstrate how, despite some uniformity in function deployment, there is significant variability among the VCAs in the implementation of these functions. We believe our more detailed models can better serve the research community as we continue to investigate the design and performance of VCAs.

1.1 Ethical Considerations

The experiments presented in this work were highly controlled and did not involve any real users. There was no personal or private information sent or received as part of any experiment. This work raises no ethical concerns.

2 Related Work

The surge in video conferencing use in recent years allow us to split prior work into two groups; those from before this surge [1,3,16,24,42,43], and those from after it [9,27,28,30,34]. In general, previous studies cover VCAs that were popular at the time of publication. For example, Xu et al. [42] and Yu et al. [43] from 2012 and 2014 cover Skype and FaceTime, whereas more recent work studies VCAs like Zoom [9,27,28,30,34], Microsoft Teams [27,30], and WebEx [9,28]. "Legacy" VCAs, such as Skype, are typically not subject to examination in more recent work, reflecting their decline in use in favor of newer products such as Zoom and Microsoft Teams. Notably, interest in WebRTC remains consistent in both groups of prior work [1,3,24,28,30].

VCA measurements typically involve subjecting various VCAs to different network conditions and recording the results. These results are often presented as measurements of throughput and video metrics, typically the video resolution and frame rate. A recent study aimed to infer models for congestion control [28] but without exploring the fully functional dependence between congestion control and video QoE. In typical studies, measurements are often taken in a highly controlled laboratory environment, though Fund et al. [16] perform their measurement campaign in two different outdoors settings, one urban and one suburban/rural, with the user devices connected to WiMAX base stations in the vicinity. Varvello et al. [39] evaluate the performance of Zoom, Webex and Google Meet using clients distributed around the world.

The VCAs studied and measurements taken in this paper result are most directly related to work by MacMillan et al. [30]. In that work, the authors study Zoom and WebRTC-based VCAs and consider measurements of the video metrics without considering the underlying architectures. However, in our work we focus on measurement for the purpose of building a generalized understanding of critical parts of the VCA, rather than to measure performance of specific VCAs. Sander et al. [34] focus on improving Zoom's performance in the presence of competing flows by implementing different queuing policies at the bottleneck, and discuss Zoom's insensitivity towards packet loss and queuing delay. We observe similar results for packet loss, but show that Zoom will respond to network latency above a certain threshold. This paper focuses on developing an understanding of the congestion control to explain the competition behaviors, with some examples in Appendix A. Furthermore, while we consider multiple VCAs, direct comparisons of the benefits or drawbacks of each [27] is outside of the scope of this work. To achieve the desired understanding of VCA behavior, we consider the time-varying effects of bandwidth limitation along with packet loss and latency on the sending rate and video metrics. The video metrics we consider include the quantization parameter (QP) used by the Zoom encoder, which to the best of our knowledge has not been previously studied.

In summary, we believe this paper to be the first to present a generalized functional structure of VCAs, using measurements designed to determine the specifics of the interaction of the congestion control and video rate control, the two key components governing overall VCA QoE. We anticipate that the models presented in this work will aid research into VCAs and end user QoE by explaining behavior seen but not elaborated on in prior work.

3   Measurement Design

In this section we describe the measurement design. We first provide a breakdown of the possible test conditions and describe those relevant to our goal of building the generalized models. Second, we describe the experimental testbed that will enable measurement under the defined set of test conditions.

3.1   Test Conditions

The space of possible VCA measurements is multidimensional. We consider the following dimensions: (i) choice of VCA, (ii) type of video, (iii) network conditions, (iv) type of data collected, (v) number of clients, (vi) background traffic, and (vii) device type. A summary of these dimensions and selected values is given in Table 1, and further details are provided in Sects. 4.1 and 5.1.

We perform measurements with Zoom, BlueJeans, Jitsi, and a custom, basic WebRTC program. Zoom and BlueJeans are commonly used closed-source production VCAs. Jitsi and the custom application provide production and baseline examples, respectively, of systems built around the open-source WebRTC. Jitsi itself is also open-source. Each VCA uses one of two encoders (H264 or VP8), and provides different stream subsampling methods (described in Appendix B) for the SFU, as well as different congestion control and video rate control methods. We send a "talking head" video through the VCA during measurements, which represents a typical video from a user webcam.

We apply different levels of adverse bandwidth limitation, packet loss, and latency to provoke a response from the VCA congestion control or video rate control. These network conditions could be experienced by users in under-provisioned locations, such as rural areas [14], or in highly loaded access networks. Even in well-served areas, cellular providers are known to shape video traffic via bandwidth limitation to reduce congestion at the radio edge [12]. To study the response

Table 1. Summary of the considered test conditions and the values selected for each.

Dimension	Selected values
VCA	Zoom, BlueJeans, WebRTC/Jitsi
Video type	Low-motion "talking head"
Network conditions	Adverse conditions for bandwidth, latency, and loss
Collected data	Packet traces, in-app video metrics
Number of clients	2 for most measurement, 4–6 for others
Background traffic	Minimize on the measurement devices
Device type	Laptop, phone, tablet

of the congestion or video rate control, we collect packet traces and video metrics available in the VCA statistics or in conference recordings.

Two laptop clients are used for the majority of measurements, as this is sufficient to understand the congestion control and video rate control on the client side. To fully understand the SFU, we take measurements with additional clients to examine how the SFU works when multiple videos are to be forwarded to a single client. The background traffic on each client is kept to a minimum to avoid competition with other flows. Measurements with competing TCP flows are presented in Appendix A, but they do not help directly inform the functional models. Lastly, as it is known that device type can impact video conferencing performance and QoE [9,39,40], we use phone and tablet clients alongside the laptops in SFU mode to understand their effect.

3.2   Testbed

The testbed used for measurements reflects the high-level architecture in Fig. 1 and must support two clients, with support for more in select experiments. Furthermore, the testbed supports video conferencing in both peer-to-peer and SFU-mediated modes, as the two are important for fully understanding the VCA client and SFU, respectively. For measurements taken in peer-to-peer mode, only Clients 1 and 2 and the Signalling Server, typically located within the network owned by the VCA developer [31], are involved. The signalling server is only used to establish the peer-to-peer video call and is uninvolved after this. The SFU measurements make use of Clients 1 and 2 as well as the VCA SFU for forwarding videos. Some measurements will also include additional clients.

While we desire minimal background traffic on the devices themselves, this is not necessarily a realistic environment in practice. Therefore, to provide a semi-realistic environment that we can model the VCAs within, the measurements were taken with the two laptops connected to an uncontrolled WiFi access point (AP). This access point was found to deliver a minimum of 10 Mbps upload and download to each device at all times, which is sufficient for all of the considered VCAs to send and receive video at maximum bitrate. Furthermore, packet loss at the AP is minimal, and the latency is stable even during peak periods, such as evenings and weekends. These properties ensure that all effects under the various applied network conditions can be reliably observed, which is further guaranteed using repeated measurements.

We are not able to control the traffic condition at the Zoom or BlueJeans SFU, though we assume in our measurements that the SFU experiences minimal congestion. We believe this to be a fair assumption, given the large cloud-based networks that Zoom and BlueJeans control. We find that the clients typically connect to Zoom SFUs located in or around New York City, as reported by the Zoom application. The precise location of the BlueJeans SFU could not be ascertained, though we suspect it is the eastern USA from traceroutes to the SFU IP address. The Jitsi SFU is set up on a Google Cloud VM located in the us-east1-b datacenter region in South Carolina. As the Jitsi SFU runs on a VM which we control, we can ensure background traffic is kept to a minimum.

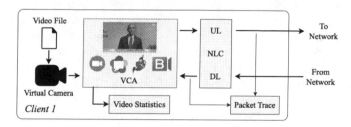

Fig. 3. Architecture of Client 1. Client 2 only uses the VCA and virtual camera input.

Both Clients 1 and 2 run Mac OS with native Zoom and BlueJeans applications (version 5.10.4 and 2.35.0, respectively), and Chrome version 100, which is used for Jitsi and WebRTC. We note that VCAs are subject to frequent software updates, which may bring slightly different behavior to the VCAs over time. Given the relatively short time period over which measurements were taken, we do not anticipate such effects to impact the accuracy of the measurements or derived models. Different operating systems can also influence the behavior of native VCA apps [30,39]. In addition, we observed over the course of our measurements that the administrator-controlled settings for the enterprise VCAs, particularly Zoom, could impact how the VCAs can be used. For example, over Summer 2022, we noticed that peer-to-peer mode calls could not be established on the Zoom accounts provided by our institution, but accounts from a different institution would permit peer-to-peer calls under the same conditions.

All measurements are taken on Client 1, which has additional software running as shown in Fig. 3 to support automated measurement and data processing. We apply the network conditions on Client 1; we use Network Link Conditioner (NLC), available as part of the Xcode developer tools on Mac OS. NLC allows the bandwidth, packet loss rate, and latency to be changed on upload and download independently. Both clients use a virtual camera to display a talking head video, a still from which is shown in Fig. 3. This video was chosen for its typicality and realistic resolution of 1280×720. The VCAs are operated in full-screen mode during the two-client measurements. The measurement process was fully automated using the Selenium library [32] and the Chrome WebDriver [10] for WebRTC/Jitsi, and using the PyAutoGUI library [38] for Zoom and BlueJeans. The automation code is made open source on GitHub [20].

Client 1 performs two types of data logging. The first is collecting packet traces using Tshark. We note that packets are collected after NLC operates in the uplink (UL) and the downlink (DL); this operating principle is important for putting the results in later sections into context. Secondly, video statistics data is logged. This logging varies depending on the VCA; for WebRTC and Jitsi, the data is collected from the Chrome instance running the VCA using the developer tools at `chrome://webrtc-internals`. Zoom and BlueJeans provide statistics within the application itself; these are extracted via recording the screen area containing the statistics and processing this screen recording with the Tesseract text recognition software [17], with appropriate error-checking and correction to ensure accurate reconstruction of results. Zoom provides statistics on the frame rate, resolution, and bitrate; BlueJeans only provides the resolution.

Zoom's built-in local recording feature produces videos that are high-fidelity representations of the exact video that was sent or received, and thus can be used to analyze the quantization parameter (QP) as well. The recording is processed using an FFMpeg-based tool [33] to extract the QP for each frame; the tool also outputs whether the frame is an I-frame or a P-frame. While BlueJeans supports cloud-based recordings, they are post-processed to add black borders when the video degrades from maximum resolution, and thus it is impossible to determine if the QP is faithful to the encoder's configuration.

4   Congestion Control Study

We begin developing the functional models by examining the VCA congestion control algorithms. In this section we present the results of measurements taken with Zoom and WebRTC operating in peer-to-peer mode, and then the results for Zoom, Jitsi, and BlueJeans operating in SFU mode.

4.1   Measurements

We measure congestion control by applying a network condition to an otherwise stable network environment, and then removing it. This gives insight into two critical parts of the congestion control: what network conditions elicit a response, and how the sending rate increases once the network condition is removed.

The three considered network conditions are the available bandwidth, packet loss rate, and latency. For each condition, we specify four values, for a total of 12 experiments. During each experiment, the VCA is started and left to stabilize under no applied condition for two minutes, after which the measurement begins. During these two minutes, the VCA will achieve the maximum sending rate.

After $t = 60$ s from the start of measurement, the network condition is applied, after which it is removed at $t = 240$ s. The measurement continues for three more minutes until $t = 420$ s. This gives seven-minute measurements, which are repeated five times for each network condition. When studying the VCA client's congestion control, the network conditions are applied to Client 1's upload; to study the SFU congestion control we apply the network condition to Client 1's download. Using the five repeats, we are able to compute an average and standard deviation of the VCA sending rate over time. Thus, each graph with results represents 35 min of measurement for each VCA.

4.2 Peer-to-Peer Mode Congestion Control

Figure 4 shows throughput plots for Zoom and WebRTC under the bandwidth, latency, and packet loss conditions. To conserve space, nine out of the 12 network conditions are shown.

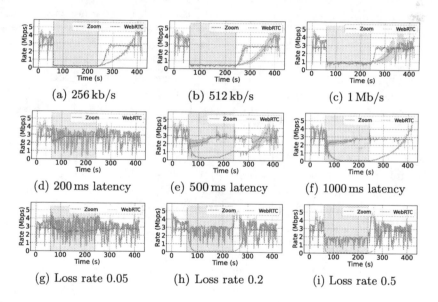

Fig. 4. Response of Zoom and WebRTC peer-to-peer clients to different network conditions. (a)-(c) upload bandwidth limits, (d)-(f) additional upload latency, (g)-(i) upload loss rates.

We note that there are differences in the sending rate for each VCA even in the absence of induced network conditions. Zoom's sending rate varies considerably over time with peaks between 3.5 and 4 Mb/s, while WebRTC has a much more stable sending rate that rarely exceeds 2.8 Mb/s.

Bandwidth. Removal of the 512 kb/s bandwidth limit in Fig. 4(b) shows that Zoom takes over 160 s to return to its original sending rate of around 3.7 Mb/s; WebRTC returns to its original peak sending rate in only around 40 s. Zoom also exhibits a step-like sending rate increase.

Latency. Unlike WebRTC's GCC which responds to delay variation, Zoom responds to the actual delay value, and only does so above a certain threshold, at most 500 ms. The response is severe, with the sending rate dropping to less than 300 kb/s when 500 ms of latency is added.

Packet Loss. While WebRTC's GCC uses a loss rate threshold of 10% before reducing the sending rate, we find a small response at 5% loss rate. This may be due to NLC's probabilistic packet drop mechanism causing packet loss rates above 10% at some points. Figures 4(g) and 4(h) show how GCC's sending rate decreases further when the packet loss rate is higher.

We note that the observed drop in Zoom's sending rate is equal to the loss rate. Given that the packet trace is recorded after NLC as described in Sect. 3.2 and shown in Fig. 3, we are observing only the packet loss enforced by NLC, rather than Zoom lowering its sending rate. The lack of the step-like increase upon removal of the packet loss is further evidence that Zoom's congestion control algorithm is insensitive to packet loss, even at a loss rate of 50%.

The ability of Zoom to function in the presence of such extreme loss rates may be due to forward error correction (FEC) data that is included with the video stream [29]. Observation of the received video shows intermittent freezing, but the picture quality and resolution remain high.

Overall, the measurements taken for WebRTC match well with the GCC algorithm as described in the literature. We learn that Zoom in peer-to-peer mode exhibits three notable behaviors: (i) a slow, step-like sending rate increase function with a step multiplicative factor of 1.2, (ii) a severe response to latency above 500 ms, and (iii) no response to extremely high packet loss rates. We note that properties (i) and (iii) are highly similar to the TCP BBR algorithm [7], which has been gaining popularity on the Internet [6]. Though the time between each bandwidth probe event for Zoom is much longer than for BBR, Zoom's probing gain value of 1.2 is very similar to BBR's 1.25. It seems likely that Zoom uses a BBR-like congestion control algorithm, which contradicts studies that find a fit between Zoom's congestion control and GCC [28].

Zoom's lack of response to packet loss means it behaves essentially opposite to loss-based TCP congestion control. Therefore, in the presence of competing TCP flows, Zoom is likely to starve the TCP flows, as long as the latency does not increase beyond the threshold at which Zoom lowers its sending rate. This effect has been noted in previous work [9,28], and we confirmed this behavior with measurement shown in Appendix Sect. A. Appendix Fig. 15 shows how the Zoom network flow is unhindered by up to ten concurrent TCP flows started at the same time, instead managing to *increase* its sending rate while the TCP flows are active.

Lastly, Zoom takes a considerably longer time to recover its sending rate compared to WebRTC, as can be seen most clearly in Fig. 4(a). At face value, this means the user needs to wait almost 90 s longer for Zoom to reach the same sending rate as WebRTC after recovery from a drop in network bandwidth.

4.3   SFU Mode Congestion Control

We run identical measurements to study the congestion control when operating in SFU mode, using Zoom, Jitsi, and BlueJeans. We consider the congestion control at the client and SFU separately.

Client Behavior   We run an identical set of measurements, changing upload bandwidth, latency, and packet loss as in Sect. 4.2. The results for nine out of the 12 conditions are shown in Fig. 5. For Jitsi, clients make use of the browser WebRTC implementation using GCC.

Bandwidth. Zoom shows a similar step-like increase function as previously observed. Compared to Zoom, Jitsi and BlueJeans both have a faster rate increase. BlueJeans has the fastest recovery time, around ten seconds faster than Jitsi and over a minute faster than Zoom. Additionally, BlueJeans has a highly fluctuating sending rate for 40 s after it returns to the original sending rate when the upload limit is more severe.

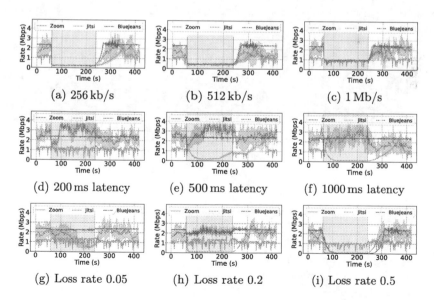

Fig. 5. Response of Zoom, Jitsi, and BlueJeans clients to network conditions while in SFU-mediated mode. (a)-(c) upload bandwidth limits, (d)-(f) additional upload latency, (g)-(i) upload loss rates.

Latency. Zoom has a similar response to the peer-to-peer case when 500 ms latency is added, including how the sending rate will begin to recover before this additional latency is removed. This particular effect is further investigated from the perspective of the video metrics in Sect. 5.2. This may occur as Zoom realizes the latency has not decreased as a result of reducing the sending rate. Jitsi has a similar transient response to latency changes as WebRTC has in peer-to-peer mode. BlueJeans is notable as it has no observable response to latency changes, except for small transients when the latency is added and removed.

Packet Loss. When the packet loss rate increases, there is an increase in Zoom's sending rate, as opposed to remaining unchanged in the peer-to-peer case. This is possibly because Zoom is adding a larger amount of FEC code for resilience to packet loss. The ability of Zoom to add FEC was noted previously in [30] and is explained further in patents held by Zoom [29]; these results show that the Zoom client itself is also capable of adding FEC. Jitsi starts to show a response to loss above 5%, which becomes more severe as the loss rate increases. BlueJeans does not have a significant response to packet loss except for the 50% case; before this point we are measuring the reduction in effective sending rate due to NLC's packet drops, as explained in Sects. 3.2 and 4.2 for Zoom. At 50% packet loss in Fig. 5(i), there is a pronounced reduction in BlueJeans' sending rate. This figure also shows that after packet loss, BlueJeans takes over 30 s longer than Jitsi to start recovering sending rate.

BlueJeans stands out among the three VCAs in that it has a purely loss-based congestion control. Zoom and Jitsi have responses to both loss and delay when the SFU is being used.

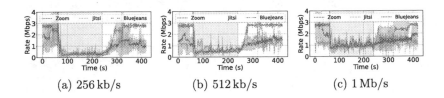

(a) 256 kb/s   (b) 512 kb/s   (c) 1 Mb/s

Fig. 6. VCA SFU responses to client download bandwidth.

SFU Behavior. The SFU also performs congestion control on forwarded videos, leveraging the SVC or simulcast mechanisms described in Appendix B. By limiting the download bandwidth of Client 1, we can measure the response of the SFU's congestion control.

Figure 6 shows the results of measurements taken similarly to the ones in Sects. 4.2 and 4.3. We can see that the Jitsi SFU uses a similar multiplicative rate increase as the client uses, and also takes around 40 s to complete the rate increase. However, with higher download limits, we observe some variance in the measurement results. This is likely caused by the SFU's video selection algorithm, which is choosing a different resolution simulcast stream or different frame rate subsampling for each of the five measurement runs.

The Zoom SFU behaves almost identically to the client, whereas the Blue-Jeans SFU does not keep a steady sending rate, and takes longer to recover from a bandwidth constraint than the client. The SFU takes around one minute to recover to the original sending rate; the client takes around 20 s.

Remarks. The first notable difference is how Zoom in SFU mode uses a significantly lower sending rate when no network conditions are applied. The reason for this is likely to reduce congestion at the SFU, though we do observe that this is an institutional configuration setting, as accounts from a different institution were capable of the same sending rate in both SFU and peer-to-peer mode. We report the results for the reduced sending rate case to best illustrate this markedly different mode of operation. BlueJeans uses a maximum resolution of 1280×720 even though it also operates in SFU mode like Zoom. Consequently, the bandwidth usage is almost double that of Zoom.

We see that whether the video conference is held in peer-to-peer mode or via the SFU, the Zoom and WebRTC/Jitsi clients have mostly the same congestion control, aside from the lower sending rate for Zoom in SFU mode. Instead, we see significant differences between the VCAs; BlueJeans stands out as having no response to latency increase, and Zoom stands out having little response to packet loss, with the client *increasing* its sending rate when in SFU mode.

5   Video Rate Control Study

We now focus on the video rate control methods used by the VCAs. We again carry out two separate studies of VCAs operating in peer-to-peer mode and SFU mode, to examine what differences the two modes of operation and the different VCAs have. Our goal as before is to reveal the presence of various functions and their interactions.

5.1   Measurements

Unlike the measurements described in Sect. 4.1, we keep a constant network condition applied for the duration of the measurements. By adjusting the available bandwidth or the latency of this constant condition, we are able to study how the three video quality metrics are affected: (i) frame rate, (ii) resolution, and (iii) quantization parameter (QP). These will give insight into how the video rate control is responding to different target encoding bitrates provided to it by the congestion control.

Repeated measurements were taken for a range of upload bandwidth limits between 96 kb/s and 2 Mb/s on Client 1. We also took measurements with upload latency values between 200 and 1,200 ms for Zoom in particular, as the results in Sects. 4.2 and 4.3 show that Zoom responds to high, long-term latency. Each measurement consists of five minutes with the network condition held in steady state; we take five repeats for each test condition, leading to each plotted point representing 25 min of data. Each measurement repeat is given two minutes to stabilize before data is collected. The average and standard deviation for each video metric is computed over the entire 25 min of data.

We observe that the receiver's window size impacts the quality of the received video for Zoom. Therefore, in a call with Client 1 and Client 2, if Client 2 changes its window size, it can cause Client 1 to send a lower maximum video quality. This occurs in both peer-to-peer and SFU mode. We ensure the Zoom window on both clients is of sufficient size to allow for the maximum video quality.

5.2 Peer-to-Peer Mode Video Rate Control

Here, we present the results for measurements with limited upload bandwidth and different upload latencies.

Upload Bandwidth Limit. Figure 7 presents the video metrics as a function of the measured video sending bitrate. Note, the minimum possible video sending rate for Zoom was measured to be 150 kb/s; if this bandwidth is not available, Zoom sends no video.

Frame rate. WebRTC clearly prioritizes keeping the frame rate at 30 (same as the source video) as much as possible, with only a slight decrease observed at extremely low sending rates below 100 kb/s. Zoom on the other hand starts to reduce the frame rate when the video sending rate is below 500 kb/s.

Resolution. Both Zoom and WebRTC show a very similar, almost-linear relationship between the average resolution and video sending rate. Zoom requires a slightly lower sending rate for a given resolution. Both VCAs reach the maximum video resolution of 1280×720 (same as the source video) at around 750 kb/s video sending rate.

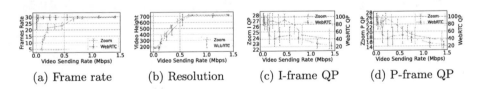

(a) Frame rate   (b) Resolution   (c) I-frame QP   (d) P-frame QP

Fig. 7. Client sent video quality metrics in peer-to-peer mode, when adjusting the available upload bandwidth.

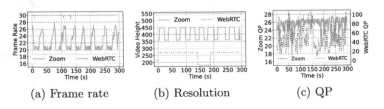

(a) Frame rate   (b) Resolution   (c) QP

Fig. 8. Video quality metrics over time with upload bandwidth limited to 256 kb/s.

QP. Note that Zoom and WebRTC use different encoders with different QP scaling. As a consequence of WebRTC's preference of maintaining 30 FPS, the QP can reach values above 90, leading to a significant loss of picture quality. Zoom reaches a plateau around 27 for I-frames and 25 for P-frames, achieved by reducing the frame rate as seen in Fig. 7(a).

Figure 8 illustrates how the frame rate, resolution, and QP change over time with an upload bandwidth of 256 kb/s. The frame rate and QP can change by small amounts over time, most clearly seen in Zoom's frame rate and WebRTC's QP. However, these small changes will occur around a clear target value. For example, Fig. 8(a) shows two distinct frame rate levels for Zoom.

Conversely, the resolution for Zoom and WebRTC takes discrete values, and typically changes on a much longer time scale compared to the frame rate and QP. This suggests that, given a specific target bitrate, the encoder is able to minutely adjust the frame rate and QP to meet it as best as possible, but will settle on one of a small set of available resolutions.

Remarks. We note that Zoom and WebRTC have taken different approaches on how the encoder responds to low target bitrates. The video metrics measurements in Fig. 7 show that WebRTC considers frame rate to be more important than QP at low bandwidths, whereas Zoom considers the opposite. Therefore, these two VCAs behave very differently in low bandwidth regimes, with WebRTC offering smooth frame rate but extremely low picture quality, and Zoom offering low frame rate and moderate picture quality.

Figure 8 shows how Zoom's frame rate and resolution have a periodic character at the 256 kb/s upload bandwidth limit. This is also shown by the relatively high variance at lower sending rates in Fig. 7. Furthermore, the periods of higher frame rate appear to coincide with the periods of lower resolution, and vice versa. Periodic changes in quality are not ideal, and this behavior may be caused by a combination of the low bandwidth limit and a limited set of target resolutions and frame rates that Zoom chooses from. Specifically, the upload bandwidth of 256 kb/s seems to lie between the minimum bandwidths which support 640×360, 26 frame/s and 800×450, 20 frame/s targets.

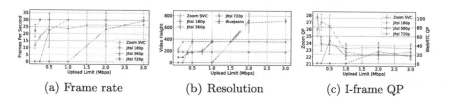

(a) Frame rate   (b) Resolution   (c) I-frame QP

Fig. 9. Client sent video quality metrics in SFU mode.

Lastly, results for Zoom under different latency conditions are presented in Appendix Sect. C. The discrete levels of average sending rate as a function of latency shown in Fig. 16(d) suggest that the Zoom congestion control has four modes of sending rate reduction in response to latency: (i) no reduction, (ii) a limited, temporary reduction, (iii) an increased but still temporary reduction, and (iv) a severe and long-term reduction. Each of these operation modes has a clear threshold in terms of the additional upload latency. Furthermore, within operation mode (iii), the time taken for the sending rate to recover varies as a function of the additional latency.

5.3   SFU Mode Video Rate Control

Client Behavior. Figure 9 shows the metrics for video sent by the VCA clients as a function of the available upload bandwidth. Zoom's SVC stream is shown, along with Jitsi's three simulcast streams. Chrome's built-in WebRTC statistics page provides metrics for each of Jitsi's simulcast streams. The BlueJeans application provides information regarding the resolution of the current video; it is likely this represents the resolution of the highest bitrate simulcast stream. The individual simulcast streams cannot be measured for BlueJeans.

Figures 9(a) and 9(b) show that the Zoom client will send video with a maximum resolution of 640×360 and frame rate of 26 frames/s when the upload bandwidth is 512 kb/s or greater. In the peer-to-peer case, the sent video reaches 1280×720 and 30 frames/s. Figure 9(c) shows how Zoom uses additional bandwidth above 512 kb/s to reduce the QP.

The three simulcast streams for Jitsi each turn on at certain upload bandwidths. The 320×180 stream is always on, while the 640×360 stream is enabled at 512 kb/s and the 1280×720 stream is enabled at 2 Mb/s. Interestingly, Fig. 9(a) shows that the video streams require additional bandwidth to reach 30 frames/s beyond the amount needed to enable them. This is a different result compared to the WebRTC peer-to-peer case, where 30 frames/s was achieved in all but the lowest bandwidth cases. The QP for the 640×360 and 1280×720 streams also does not exceed 50, showing that the bandwidth thresholds for enabling the simulcast streams are chosen to achieve some minimum picture quality rather than achieve the maximum frame rate. We found that the 320×180 and 640×360 streams have a maximum sending rate of around 200 kb/s and 700 kb/s respectively, and each successive stream will not turn on until the lower quality stream is sent at its maximum rate. The resolution of the highest bitrate BlueJeans stream in Fig. 9(a) shows a step increase, demonstrating how successive simulcast streams are enabled as bandwidth increases.

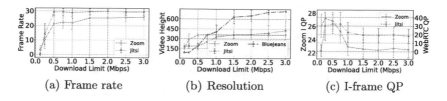

(a) Frame rate   (b) Resolution   (c) I-frame QP

Fig. 10. Client received video quality metrics in SFU mode.

SFU Behavior. To understand how the SFU decides what video quality to forward, we take similar measurements to Sect. 5.3 with the download rate limited on Client 1. Figure 10 shows the video metrics as a function of the applied download limit. Overall, the quality metrics for the forwarded video from Zoom's SFU are similar to those for the encoded video from the Zoom client. The main difference is a slight reduction in frame rate and resolution at lower bandwidths. This suggests that the Zoom SFU has almost the same flexibility via subsampling as the client does via encoder parameter selection.

Jitsi achieves a stable 30 frames/s at 512 kb/s download bandwidth as seen in Fig. 10(a), which is higher than the frame rate achieved by Zoom. However, at 128 kb/s, the frame rate is almost zero on average, while Zoom will still be able to forward video. This is likely a consequence of the limited frame rate subsampling options available to Jitsi's SFU [26]. The zero frame rate is also what causes the close-to-zero measured QP in Fig. 10(c). Figure 10(b) shows that the average resolution does eventually exceed Zoom's maximum of 640×360, which is expected as Jitsi has a 1280×720 simulcast stream. The high variance suggests that the received video resolution changes frequently over time, which implies that the Jitsi SFU is switching between simulcast streams very often.

BlueJeans' resolution is also prone to switching as shown by the variance in Fig. 10(b), however it is not as prevalent as in Jitsi. The BlueJeans SFU is able to forward the maximum resolution stream consistently once the download bandwidth reaches 3 Mb/s.

Remarks. We find Zoom's SFU behaves very similarly to the Zoom client in the presence of bandwidth limits, as seen in Figs. 9 and 10. This shows that the SVC mechanism used by Zoom allows for stream selection at the SFU which is almost as flexible as the client's encoder. The same does not hold for the simulcast systems Jitsi and BlueJeans; for example, the resolution sent by the BlueJeans client at 1.5 Mb/s is lower than the resolution that can be received at 1.5 Mb/s, likely due to the overhead from sending multiple simulcast streams.

The received video quality metrics measurements in Fig. 10 show that the Jitsi SFU is unstable even at 3 Mb/s client download rate. The client should be able to download the maximum bitrate simulcast stream at this point, but the Jitsi SFU still switches it with a lower bitrate stream. This unintended behavior manifests as a received video that changes quality often, possibly degrading QoE.

All SFU will be prone to such a problem, especially if the network bandwidth is close to the threshold between two available bitrate streams.

6 SFU with Multiple Users

The experiments in Sects. 4 and 5 involve only two users in the setup described in Fig. 1. In this section, we consider video conferencing sessions in SFU-mediated mode with more than two users. These experiments demonstrate certain behaviors of the SFU, including how it considers different device types, and how it chooses which videos to forward to a client with constrained download bandwidth. These insights cannot be provided by the two-user experiments.

6.1 Experimental Setup

The additional devices available are an older laptop from 2014 running Mac OS, a 2017 iPad Pro, and a 2015 iPhone 6S. Every device used the native VCA available for the platform, and was connected to the same access point. These devices reflect a range of commonly used form-factors and different device age.

Client 1 is used similarly to Fig. 3, with a few modifications. First, the packet trace is not collected, as unknown packet formats make it difficult to filter the trace to correlate packets and clients[2]. Secondly, the video statistics collection is performed manually for Zoom, as it only displays the statistics for the *currently focused video*. We continue to use NLC to adjust the download rate on Client 1, as in Sect. 5.3. The SFU will measure the available download rate for the client in order to decide which videos to send and at what quality.

VCAs display videos to users in one of two modes; single-speaker or gallery mode. The *currently focused video* is the video which is shown in single-speaker mode, or the current speaker's video in gallery mode. Therefore, we can collect the Zoom video statistics for a specific device by unmuting it and keeping all other devices muted. The same method does not work for Blue-Jeans', which seems to report the highest resolution out of all displayed videos. Jitsi is able to use the same measurement collection method used previously, as `chrome://webrtc-internals` provides one report for each received video stream.

6.2 Observations

We consider two effects in our experiments. The first is the impact of device type on the recorded statistics. Secondly, we try to understand how the SFU decides which videos to send, and at what quality to send those videos.

---

[2] The Zoom packet structure determined by Michel et al. [31] could aid this process.

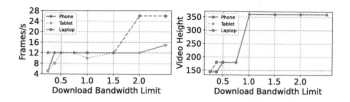

Fig. 11. Received frame rate and resolution with different device types on Zoom.

Impact of Device Type. Device type may have an impact on VCA performance as described in [9,40]. Therefore, we can evaluate whether there are any differences between the three device types: laptop, tablet, and phone.

Zoom. Figure 11 shows the received frame rate and video resolution for the three additional devices on a Zoom call with Clients 1 and 2. Client 1 was kept in gallery mode for this experiment. The video resolution received from each device type generally follows the same trend, though at the lowest download bandwidths, it appears that the laptop gets some priority in bandwidth allocation. However, for frame rate, there is a significant difference; even at higher bandwidths, the phone and tablet will only be received at 15 frames/s maximum.

In single-speaker mode, we found that all devices had the same behavior. This shows that the phone and tablet are capable of sending at the maximum 26 frames/s that was found in the two-client video call for Zoom. However, the SFU intervenes to limit the forwarded video from the phone and tablet to 15 frames/s if the client receiving the forwarded video is in gallery mode.

BlueJeans. While the reported video statistic for BlueJeans is difficult to control, we observed that a 320×180 resolution video was received from the phone client in gallery mode, while all others were 640×360. The frame rate, while not reported in the BlueJeans application, appeared to be the same for all devices.

Jitsi. There was no observed impact of device type for Jitsi.

SFU Decisionmaking. Section 5.3 describes how the SFU adjusts the video quality metrics of the forwarded video streams in response to download bandwidth constraints at the receiving client. If multiple client videos are available for forwarding, the SFU must also make decisions on which videos to forward to a receiving client. Combined with the adjustment of per-stream video quality metrics, this represents the full congestion control at the SFU. Known decision making processes such as Last-N [19] are based on the measured download bandwidth for the receiving client, as well as a priority queue based on when each client last spoke (produced sound through their microphone).

In all three VCAs, we found that the SFU will only decide which videos to forward when the receiving client is in gallery mode, displaying multiple other client videos at once. In single-speaker mode, all SFUs will forward the currently focused video at maximum possible quality. Typically, they will forward only thumbnail videos at the lowest possible resolution for the remaining video participants, which may be displayed as small insets in the VCA interface.

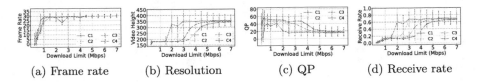

| (a) Frame rate | (b) Resolution | (c) QP | (d) Receive rate |

Fig. 12. Jitsi received video quality metrics as a function of download bandwidth when receiving four client videos (C1–C4) simultaneously.

Zoom. The limited information available within the application and packet traces mean an observational approach must be taken. Client 1's download bandwidth is limited between 0.5 and 7 Mbps with the other five available devices connected with video on. Notably, Zoom does not turn off any received videos; at lower bandwidth, some videos may freeze for an extended time but will remain visible. At moderate bandwidths, we observed that Zoom will allocate the maximum possible quality to the currently focused video, and then share remaining bandwidth fairly between all others.

BlueJeans. As BlueJeans also provides limited information in the application and packet trace, the same approach as Zoom is taken. Like Zoom, BlueJeans does not turn off received videos even at very low bandwidths. However, unlike Zoom, BlueJeans has a more clear prioritization of videos; the currently focused video will receive the most bandwidth possible, but then successive videos will receive a bandwidth share in order of when they were last active in audio. So the remaining bandwidth after the currently focused video is not shared equally, it is prioritized similarly to Jitsi's Last-N algorithm.

Jitsi. Jitsi's Last-N algorithm is well described [19]. Furthermore, the Jitsi source code describes how bandwidth is allocated to videos according to the Last-N prioritization [25, 26]. Altogether, the decisionmaking process is very similar to BlueJeans. However, the `chrome://webrtc-internals` statistics allow us to evaluate how Last-N impacts the received video quality metrics.

Figure 12 shows how the video metrics for each of the four received video streams change as a function of download bandwidth. The Last-N algorithm is clear in the plots for resolution, QP, and video bitrate; each video stream increases in quality in turn. However, for the frame rate, all three videos are being received at the maximum 30 frames/s as soon as 1.5 Mbps download rate is reached. This matches the general behavior of WebRTC and Jitsi as described in Sects. 5.3 and 5.3 where the frame rate is maximised with greater priority than the resolution and QP.

Altogether, the three studied SFU-mediated VCAs have similar behavior when deciding which videos to forward and at what quality. All use a prioritization based on which client was last active in audio; this client becomes the currently focused video in gallery mode. Zoom will share the remaining bandwidth fairly among other clients, whereas BlueJeans and Jitsi will allocate bandwidth to clients prioritized according to audio activity.

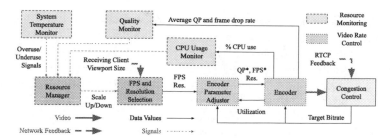

Fig. 13. Functional model for the peer-to-peer VCA client.

7   VCA Functional Models

In this section, we leverage the results presented in Sects. 4, 5, and 6 to derive the functional models for a VCA client and VCA SFU. These functional models will expand on the high-level depictions in Fig. 2. In addition to the measurement results, we will also include findings from a study of the Chromium WebRTC and Jitsi open-source code [18,25].

7.1   VCA Client

Using our results from Sects. 4 and 5, along with a review of the WebRTC open-source code, we can elaborate on the simple functional diagram of the client depicted in Fig. 2(a). In this section, we focus specifically on the *peer-to-peer* client, as it does not involve simulcast or SVC-based encoding, a complexity which we cover in Sect. 7.2.

Figure 13 shows the outcome of piecing together the measurement results and code survey into a coherent functional model. There are three distinct components in the functional model: (i) *resource monitoring*, indicated by the green boxes with dashed outline, (ii) *congestion control*, indicated by the yellow box with solid outline, and (iii) *video rate control*, indicated by the blue boxes with dotted outline.

Resource Monitoring. The resource monitoring component relies on three "monitors" which constantly measure certain system parameters. These three monitors are explicitly defined in Chromium WebRTC, and we postulate that they are also used in other VCAs. The first monitor is the *system temperature monitor*, which can generate an overuse signal to the VCA to reduce video quality to ease processing load and reduce device temperature. Curiously, in the Chromium code, we find that this monitor is enabled by default only on Chrome OS and Mac OS, further highlighting potential differences between VCA behavior on different operating systems.

The second is the *CPU usage monitor*, which provides similar feedback to the system temperature monitor. While Zoom's source code is unavailable for review, we note that the Zoom statistics view does report CPU usage, suggesting that this parameter is at least monitored by Zoom. CPU utilization on mobile devices can reach 100% on two cores in typical VCA usage [9], meaning that the CPU usage monitor, like the system temperature monitor, is particularly important for mobile devices.

The third monitor is the *quality monitor*, which monitors the average QP and frame drop rate reported by the encoder. The encoder may drop frames when it has insufficient bitrate to encode frames at the target video metrics. If the frame drop rate or QP are above or below certain thresholds, this monitor will generate an overuse or underuse signal. The Chromium WebRTC source specifies an upper threshold for frame drop rate of 0.6 and a QP of 95 for signaling overuse, and a lower QP threshold of 29 for signaling underuse. This monitor is particularly important as it ultimately derives from the target bitrate provided by the congestion control, meaning that under typical VCA use, this is the monitor that governs much of the VCA operation.

All three monitors feed their signals into the *resource manager*, which aggregates the incoming signals and produces a scale up or scale down signal, ensuring only the most important signal is processed if multiple are active. The scale up/down signal is used by the *FPS and resolution selection* to adjust the target frame rate and video resolution used by the encoder. While the architecture of this resource monitoring component is inferred in large part from the Chromium WebRTC source, we believe that a functionally similar system is employed by Zoom and BlueJeans, and VCAs generally. This is indicated largely by the results in Sects. 5.2 and 5.3, which show that the VCAs have a discrete set of target frame rates and resolutions.

Congestion Control. The congestion control component of the model maintains the high-level view as in Fig. 2. While a unified VCA congestion control model based on GCC has been proposed [28], we find through the results in Sect. 4 that the congestion control behavior is vastly different between VCAs. Zoom experiences reduced sending rates in the presence of stable high latency and BlueJeans has no response to latency at all; these modes of operation are incompatible with the GCC model, which responds to the *change* in latency [8,13,22,24]. A similar point can be made for packet loss response; Zoom effectively does not have any, but BlueJeans and WebRTC/Jitsi have a very clear reduction in sending rate for moderately high levels of packet loss.

Another distinction between the VCAs is how their sending rates increase over time when network conditions improve. As noted in Sect. 4.2, Zoom has a step-like increase in sending rate over time. Furthermore, as seen in Fig. 5(b), this stepped increase function can exceed the typical maximum video sending rate, suggesting that Zoom is actively probing for bandwidth, rather than employing a multiplicative rate increase function as used by GCC.

Altogether, the differences in measured congestion control responses in Sect. 4 demonstrate the infeasibility of generalizing VCA congestion control. Even within only the subset of specific VCAs covered in this study, we observed highly incongruent techniques for congestion control. Therefore, we include the

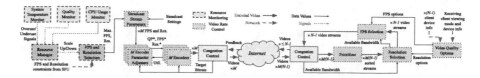

Fig. 14. Functional model for the VCA SFU and client.

congestion control as a unified block in the functional model, which uses RTCP
network feedback to make adjustments to the target video encoding bitrate.

Video Rate Control. The video rate control is split into two parts, the *encoder
parameter adjuster*, and the *encoder* itself. The *encoder parameter adjuster*
accepts a target frame rate and resolution from the *FPS and resolution selection*
and makes adjustments to the targets as well as generates the QP. The objective
of this is to most closely match the target bitrate that is provided by the congestion control. As seen in Fig. 8, the QP and frame rate can be finely adjusted
over time to match the target bitrate as best as possible, but the resolution takes
a set of discrete values and does not change on such a small timescale. Therefore, as illustrated in Fig. 13, the resolution emerges from the *encoder parameter
adjuster* unchanged, whereas the final frame rate may be different from the target, indicated by the asterisk notation.

The *encoder* uses the resolution, frame rate, and QP provided by the *encoder
parameter adjuster* to produce the video that will be sent over the network. The
encoder also uses the target bitrate produced from the congestion control to
compute the utilization, which it feeds back to the *encoder parameter adjuster*.
This forms the first of three closed feedback loops that the encoder drives. The
second feedback loop involves the encoder's CPU utilization, and the third feedback loop involves the frame drop rate and the QP. These two feedback loops
connect back to the system monitors.

Section 5 shows how Zoom and WebRTC/Jitsi share a similar control for the
video resolution as a function of the available bandwidth, but opposite behavior
for frame rate and QP. At low bandwidths, Zoom will drop the frame rate to
maintain a reasonable QP, while WebRTC/Jitsi will maximize the QP to maintain a high frame rate. Therefore, while each VCA may employ a different policy
or algorithm to control the video metrics for the video rate control, they all make
use of the general functionality described in Fig. 13.

7.2   VCA SFU

The VCA SFU model also derives from measurement results in Sects. 4 and 5. In
addition, the observations from Sect. 6 will be vital for understanding some specific components of the SFU. Figure 14 presents the complete functional model
of a VCA client and SFU operating in tandem. This functional model represents
the singular VCA SFU and one of N connected clients, all of whom are functionally identical. The VCA client follows the same structure as Fig. 13, with some

differences specific to operation in SFU mode. We develop the SFU side of the model to be as analogous to the client side as possible, and so it is split into the *congestion control* and *video rate control* components, with the associated boxes colored and bordered as in Fig. 13.

Changes to the Client Model. The client now includes M encoders and encoder parameter adjusters to support simulcast streams at M different resolutions. Zoom, with its single SVC stream, has $M = 1$. In our measurements and examination of the source code, we observe $M = 3$ for Jitsi. We are not able to determine specific parameters for BlueJeans. Additionally, the client may also receive feedback from the SFU providing additional constraints for what resolution and frame rate to send. These constraints are based on the SFU's knowledge of how the client's video is being displayed by other clients. As observed for Zoom, if all other clients are displaying a particular client's video in a small viewport, then that client has no need to send high quality video and the SFU will provide parameters to constrain the quality of the video being sent.

We note that the measurement results in Sects. 4.3 and 5.3 show that the congestion control and video rate control mechanisms on the client side are generally identical between peer-to-peer and SFU modes. Therefore, we retain the same congestion control and video rate control components as in the peer-to-peer model.

SFU Congestion Control. Section 4.3 shows that the SFU also performs congestion control when forwarding video to a client. As on the client side, the SFU must implement congestion control by adjusting the video metrics for the videos it forwards. Furthermore, the SFU can choose to not forward all videos if there is insufficient bandwidth to do so. Therefore, the foremost job of the SFU congestion control is to generate an available bandwidth for the video rate control to use for decision making. This is equivalent to the target encoding bitrate generated by the congestion control on the client side.

The specific behaviors of the SFU congestion control seen in Sect. 4.3 typically mirror those of the client, and so we are left with the same conclusion that generalizing the SFU congestion control is infeasible. With the observation that each VCA's SFU will implement its own specific congestion control algorithm, typically similar to the client's, we use the same unified block as on the client.

SFU Video Rate Control. The video rate control on the SFU side of the model can be viewed as a step-by-step procedure. First, the $M(N - 1)$ received client videos are processed by the *prioritizer*, which orders the videos according to a specific criteria. For Jitsi, the Last-N algorithm which prioritizes by most recent speakers is used [19], and we observed similar behavior for BlueJeans as described in Sect. 6.2. Zoom uses a similar algorithm, but instead attempts to share the remaining bandwidth fairly after allocating the most recent/pinned speaker as much bandwidth as possible. We note the prioritization process can be done in a centralized manner by the SFU and applied to the video rate control for all receiving clients.

After video prioritization, the SFU will run *resolution selection* for each of the $N-1$ client videos that are to be forwarded using the available bandwidth estimated by the congestion control. For VCAs which use simulcast, this will involve the selection of one out of the M simulcast streams that were received. For VCAs that use SVC-based encoding, this will involve a subsampling procedure. In any case, the number of videos which emerge from the *resolution selection* will be $N-1$. The SFU will then run *FPS selection* for each of the $N-1$ video streams, again taking the available bandwidth into account. *FPS selection* can typically be performed via subsampling on all VCAs, as it is supported by H.264, VP8, and VP9, the most common encoders used.

The available options for resolution and frame rate are determined by several factors, including the devices used by the $N-1$ sending clients and receiving client, and the receiving client's viewing mode. All will be known by the SFU as a result of signaling operations. The effect of different device types for Zoom is shown in Fig. 11, and the video metrics for each of four received streams at a bandwidth-limited client are shown in Fig. 12. This figure clearly shows the prioritization method, with four distinct traces for each client. We note that the SFU must perform all of its video rate control on the encoded video streams, as the decoding would put an unscalable computational load on the SFU.

8   Concluding Remarks

VCAs deploy congestion control and video rate control functionality at both the client and SFU. In both instances, target rates are determined by congestion control functions and then used to influence the rate of video transmitted by the clients and the SFU. The adjustment of the video rate has direct consequences on the video quality metrics such as frame rate and resolution. Given this baseline level of understanding, we constructed more detailed functional models for the VCA client and SFU which are based predominantly off of a directed measurement campaign using a subset of commonly used VCAs. We believe these models, along with the accompanying measurement results, provide a level of understanding which was previously unavailable in related literature.

We expect the functional models will serve to inform further research into video conferencing. We will use the functional models in our future work to relate the congestion control mechanisms employed by different VCAs to end user quality of experience, which is an important functionality for network operators in order to best provision network services to maximize end user QoE.

Acknowledgement. This work was supported by NSF grant NETS-1909040. We thank the PAM reviewers and our shepherd for their valuable feedback.

A   Competition with TCP

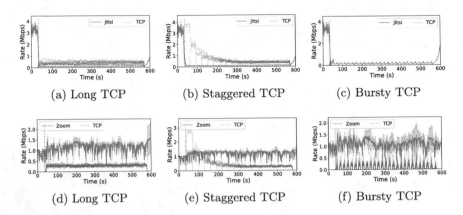

Fig. 15. Competition with different types of TCP flows. (a-c) Jitsi, (d-f) Zoom in SFU mode.

As Zoom has been reported to take a majority share of the bandwidth when competing with TCP [28,30,34], we took measurements with different types of TCP flows to compare and explain results using the functional models and measurements in Sect. 4.

Table 2. Summary of subsampling methods for the considered SFU-mode VCAs.

VCA	Simulcast	SVC	Subsample FPS	Subsample Res.	Codec	Alternate Codecs
Zoom	No	Yes	Yes	Yes	H.264	None
Jitsi	Yes	No	Yes	No	VP8	VP9, H.264
BlueJeans	Yes	No	Yes	No	VP8	None

The testbed was used in two-person SFU mode with Zoom and Jitsi as in Sect. 4.3. In all cases, a total bandwidth limit of 4 Mb/s was applied to the upload of Client 1. After 30 s of measurement, ten TCP flows begin in various patterns: (i) started at the same time with nine minute duration, (ii) started at 30 s intervals, all finishing at the nine minute mark, and (iii) started and stopped at the same time every 20 s.

Figure 15 shows the results of these measurements. Figures 15(a), 15(b), and 15(c) all show that Jitsi immediately gives up practically all of its bandwidth in the presence of TCP. In particular, Fig. 15(b) shows that this occurs with only a single TCP flow sharing the link at the 30 s mark. This behavior is likely caused by GCC's sensitivity to changes in delay; once GCC gives up some bandwidth, TCP takes it, compounding the response. Conversely, Figs. 15(d), 15(e), and

15(f) show that Zoom sending rate actually increases in TCP's presence. This is likely a consequence of how it decides to add FEC as described in Sect. 4.3, the general insensitivity that Zoom has to packet loss, and the high threshold for responding to latency.

B   Video Subsampling Methods

As mentioned in Sect. 1, the SFU is able to adjust the quality of forwarded video streams via subsampling. The exact method used for this differs between the considered VCAs, as described below, and summarized in Table 2.

Zoom uses a custom implementation of H.264 Scalable Video Coding (SVC) [2, 23, 36] to encode base and enhancement video layers. The SFU can then add/drop layers before forwarding to clients. Because H.264 SVC is used, subsampling of both the resolution and the frame rate is available to the SFU in Zoom as an orthogonal technique to adjust video bit rate [21, 37, 44, 45].

Jitsi and BlueJeans use video *simulcast*, in which the VCA client sends multiple independent video streams at different resolutions. Jitsi uses simulcast when the VP8 encoder is used. In particular, the Jitsi clients make use of three simulcast streams, with resolution scaling factors of 1, 2, and 4. At 1280×720 native video resolution, this means the two other streams will be 640×360 and 320×180. Blue-Jeans also uses the VP8 encoder, implying use of simulcast, though there are no means of measuring the individual video streams. In a VCA with simulcast, the SFU chooses which one of the received video streams to forward, which determines the resolution. Additionally, it may choose to adjust the frame rate without re-encoding. Note that resolution changes without re-encoding are not possible with the VP8 codec [5, 41], demanding the use of simulcast.

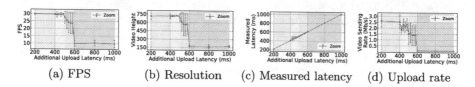

(a) FPS   (b) Resolution   (c) Measured latency   (d) Upload rate

Fig. 16. Client sent video quality metrics in peer-to-peer mode, when adjusting the upload latency. The colors indicate the distinct modes of operation.

C   Zoom Video Rate Control under Different Latency Conditions

Figure 16 presents the video metrics for Zoom as a function of the additional latency on the upload. Overall, the sent video metrics begin to see an impact at 400 ms additional upload latency, and beyond 600 ms additional latency, there are no further impacts.

Frame Rate and Resolution. We group the consideration of both of these metrics as they share a very similar response to the additional upload latency. The most notable feature is the evolution of high variance in the measurement results for added latencies above 500 ms. We observe that much of the measured variance is not due to fluctuation in the frame rate or resolution; instead it is caused by Zoom returning to the maximum resolution and frame rate some time after the experiment starts. The time at which this occurs is a function of the latency; the higher the latency, the longer Zoom takes to begin recovering its sending rate. At higher latencies beyond 600 ms, the recorded variance is low. This is either because the time taken for Zoom to begin recovering is longer than the measurement duration, or because Zoom keeps the low sending rate indefinitely if the latency is beyond this value.

Measured Video Sending Rate. The measured video sending rate corresponds well to the frame rate and resolution trends. Specifically, there appear to be two intermediate levels of video sending rate; the first averaging around 2.25 Mb/s between 400 and 500 ms added latency, and the second averaging around 1.5 Mb/s between 500 and 600 ms. Beyond 600 ms, a flat 100 kb/s sending rate is used, which corresponds to what is observed in Fig. 4(f).

QP. The method for obtaining Zoom's QP outlined in Sect. 3.2 is incompatible with latency measurements. This is because starting a screen recording in the Zoom application prompts a sudden, very large spike in latency. Once this spike dissipates, the Zoom application begins sending at the maximum rate, even when the steady-state latency is above 1,000 ms. We are uncertain if this is intended behavior to maintain maximum quality for recording purposes, or if this is a bug. In any case, we are unable to ascertain the Zoom QP for these measurements.

References

1. Amirante, A., Castaldi, T., Miniero, L., Romano, S.P.: Performance analysis of the Janus WebRTC gateway. In: Proceedings of ACM Workshop on All-Web Real-Time Systems (2015)
2. Amon, P., Li, H., Hutter, A., Renzi, D., Battista, S.: Scalable video coding and transcoding. In: Proceedings of IEEE International Conference on Automation, Quality and Testing, Robotics (2008)
3. André, E., Le Breton, N., Lemesle, A., Roux, L., Gouaillard, A.: Comparative study of WebRTC open source SFUs for video conferencing. In: Principles, Systems and Applications of IP Telecommunications (IPTComm) (2018)

4. Arif, A.S.M., Hassan, S., Ghazali, O., Nor, S.A.: The relationship of TFRC congestion control to video rate control optimization. In: Proceedings of IEEE International Conference on Network Applications, Protocols and Services (2010)
5. BlueJeans: Technical Specifications for Services (2021). https://support.bluejeans.com/s/article/BlueJeans-Technical-Specifications
6. Cao, Y., Jain, A., Sharma, K., Balasubramanian, A., Gandhi, A.: When to use and when not to use BBR: an empirical analysis and evaluation study. In: Proceedings of ACM Internet Measurement Conference (2019)
7. Cardwell, N., Cheng, Y., Gunn, C.S., Yeganeh, S.H., Jacobson, V.: BBR: congestion-based congestion control. ACM Queue **14**, 20–53 (2016)
8. Carlucci, G., de Cicco, L., Holmer, S., Mascolo, S.: Analysis and design of the google congestion control for web real-time communication (WebRTC). In: Proceedings of ACM International Conference on Multimedia Systems (2016)
9. Chang, H., Varvello, M., Hao, F., Mukherjee, S.: Can you see me now? A measurement study of Zoom, Webex, and Meet. In: Proceedings of ACM Internet Measurement Conference (2021)
10. Chromium: ChromeDriver - WebDriver for Chrome (2022). https://chromedriver.chromium.org/home
11. Chundong, S., Chaojun, L., Shaohua, L.: Research on congestion control algorithms for real-time audio and video stream. In: Proceedings of IEEE International Conference on Computer and Communications (2018)
12. Cisco: Cisco Ultra Traffic Optimization (CUTO) Data Sheet (2021). https://www.cisco.com/c/en/us/products/collateral/wireless/ultra-traffic-optimization/datasheet-c78-744385.html
13. De Cicco, L., Carlucci, G., Mascolo, S.: Congestion control for WebRTC: standardization status and open issues. IEEE Commun. Stand. Mag. **1**(2), 22–27 (2017)
14. Federal Communications Commission: FCC Proposes Higher Speed Goals for Small Rural Broadband Providers (2022). https://www.fcc.gov/document/fcc-proposes-higher-speed-goals-small-rural-broadband-providers-0
15. Floyd, S., Handley, M., Padhye, J., Widmer, J.: Equation-based congestion control for unicast applications. In: Proceedings of ACM Conference on Applications, Technologies, Architectures, and Protocols for Computer Communication (2000)
16. Fund, F., Wang, C., Liu, Y., Korakis, T., Zink, M., Panwar, S.S.: Performance of DASH and WebRTC video services for mobile users. In: Proceedings of IEEE Packet Video Workshop, pp. 1–8 (2013).https://doi.org/10.1109/PV.2013.6691455
17. Google: Tesseract Open Source OCR Engine (2022). https://tesseract-ocr.github.io/
18. Google Git: WebRTC Native Code Package (2022). https://webrtc.googlesource.com/src/
19. Grozev, B., Marinov, L., Singh, V., Ivov, E.: Last N: relevance-based selectivity for forwarding video in multimedia conferences. In: Proceedings of ACM Workshop on Network and Operating Systems Support for Digital Audio and Video (2015)
20. He, J., Ammar, M., Zegura, E.: Automation Code (2023). https://github.com/jh4001/PAM2023_Automation
21. High Scalability: A Short On How Zoom Works (2020). https://highscalability.com/blog/2020/5/14/a-short-on-how-zoom-works.html
22. Holmer, S., Lundin, H., Carlucci, G., de Cicco, L., Mascolo, S.: A Google Congestion Control Algorithm for Real-Time Communication (2017). https://datatracker.ietf.org/doc/html/draft-ietf-rmcat-gcc-02

23. International Telecommunications Union: H.264: Advanced video coding for generic audiovisual services (2016). https://www.itu.int/rec/dologin_pub.asp?lang=e&id=T-REC-H.264-201602-S!!PDF-E&type=items
24. Jansen, B., Goodwin, T., Gupta, V., Kuipers, F., Zussman, G.: Performance evaluation of WebRTC-based video conferencing. ACM SIGMETRICS Perform. Eval. Rev. **45**(3), 56–68 (2018)
25. Jitsi: Github repository (2022). https://github.com/jitsi
26. Jitsi: Selective Forwarding Unit implementation of the Jitsi Videobridge (2022). https://github.com/jitsi/jitsi-videobridge/blob/master/doc/sfu.md#bandwidth-estimations
27. Kumar, R., Nagpal, D., Naik, V., Chakraborty, D.: Comparison of popular video conferencing apps using client-side measurements on different backhaul networks. In: Proceedings of ACM Symposium on Theory, Algorithmic Foundations, and Protocol Design for Mobile Networks and Mobile Computing (2022)
28. Lee, I., Lee, J., Lee, K., Grunwald, D., Ha, S.: Demystifying commercial video conferencing applications. In: Proceedings of ACM International Conference on Multimedia (2021)
29. Liu, Q., Jia, Z., Jin, K., Wu, J., Zhang, H.: Error resilience for interactive real-time multimedia application. U.S. Patent #10348454 (2019)
30. MacMillan, K., Mangla, T., Saxon, J., Feamster, N.: Measuring the performance and network utilization of popular video conferencing applications. In: Proceedings of ACM Internet Measurement Conference (2021)
31. Michel, O., Sengupta, S., Kim, H., Netravali, R., Rexford, J.: Enabling passive measurement of zoom performance in production networks. In: Proceedings of ACM Internet Measurement Conference (2022)
32. Muthukadan, B.: Selenium with Python (2022). https://selenium-python.readthedocs.io/
33. Robitza, W., Goring, S., Lebreton, P., Trevivian, N.: ffmpeg_debug_qp (2022). https://github.com/slhck/ffmpeg-debug-qp
34. Sander, C., Kunze, I., Wehrle, K., Rüth, J.: Video conferencing and flow-rate fairness: a first look at Zoom and the impact of flow-queuing AQM. In: Proceedings of Passive and Active Measurement, pp. 3–19 (2021)
35. Sandvine: 2022 Global Internet Phenomena Report (2022)
36. Schwarz, H., Marpe, D., Wiegand, T.: Overview of the scalable video coding extension of the H.264/AVC standard. IEEE Trans. Circuits Syst. Video Technol. **17**(9), 1103–1120 (2007)
37. Streaming Media: Q&A: Zoom CTO Brendan Ittelson (2021). https://www.streamingmedia.com/Articles/Editorial/Featured-Articles/QA-Zoom-CTO-Brendan-Ittelson-145024.aspx
38. Sweigart, A.: PyAutoGUI - GitHub (2022). https://github.com/asweigart/pyautogui
39. Varvello, M., Chang, H., Zaki, Y.: Performance characterization of videoconferencing in the wild. In: Proceedings of ACM Internet Measurement Conference (2022)
40. Vucic, D., Skorin-Kapov, L.: QoE Assessment of mobile multiparty audiovisual telemeetings. IEEE Access **8**, 107669–107684 (2020)
41. WebRTC Glossary: Temporal Scalability (2022). https://webrtcglossary.com/temporal-scalability/
42. Xu, Y., Yu, C., Li, J., Liu, Y.: Video telephony for end-consumers: measurement study of Google+, IChat, and Skype. In: Proceedings of ACM Internet Measurement Conference (2012)

43. Yu, C., Xu, Y., Liu, B., Liu, Y.: Can you SEE me now? A measurement study of mobile video calls. In: Proceedings of IEEE Conference on Computer Communications (2014)
44. Zoom: Zoom: Architected for Reliability (2019). https://explore.zoom.us/docs/doc/Zoom_Global_Infrastructure.pdf
45. Zoom: Here's How Zoom Provides Industry-Leading Video Capacity (2022). https://blog.zoom.us/zoom-can-provide-increase-industry-leading-video-capacity/

Effects of Political Bias and Reliability on Temporal User Engagement with News Articles Shared on Facebook

Alireza Mohammadinodooshan$^{(\boxtimes)}$ and Niklas Carlsson

Linköping University, Linköping, Sweden
{alireza.mohammadinodooshan,niklas.carlsson}@liu.se

Abstract. The reliability and political bias differ substantially between news articles published on the Internet. Recent research has examined how these two variables impact user engagement on Facebook, reflected by measures like the volume of shares, likes, and other interactions. However, most of this research is based on the ratings of publishers (not news articles), considers only bias or reliability (not combined), focuses on a limited set of user interactions, and ignores the users' engagement dynamics over time. To address these shortcomings, this paper presents a temporal study of user interactions with a large set of labeled news articles capturing the temporal user engagement dynamics, bias, and reliability ratings of each news article. For the analysis, we use the public Facebook posts sharing these articles and all user interactions observed over time for those posts. Using a broad range of bias/reliability categories, we then study how the bias and reliability of news articles impact users' engagement and how it changes as posts become older. Our findings show that the temporal interaction level is best captured when bias, reliability, time, and interaction type are evaluated jointly. We highlight many statistically significant disparities in the temporal engagement patterns (as seen across several interaction types) for different bias-reliability categories. The shared insights into engagement dynamics can benefit both publishers (to augment their temporal interaction prediction models) and moderators (to adjust efforts to post category and lifecycle stage).

Keywords: User interactions · Bias · Reliability · Temporal dynamics

1 Introduction

Despite 74% of all Americans believing that the propagation of online misinformation is a big problem [9], a very large fraction of users today obtains their news via social media [16]. In this environment, news articles are often propagated based on other users' interactions with the news (e.g., through likes, comments, and sharing of posts linked to various news articles). Indeed, users' interactions (and their engagement) with different news are becoming the big driver for which news are most likely to be viewed by others, and hence also which news are given the best chance to impact other users' views of the world, including their opinions and thoughts on various current issues.

With increasing (political) polarization [11] and news articles often having vastly different reliability levels, it is therefore important to measure and understand whether there are fundamental disparities in the users' interaction dynamics with news articles that have different levels of reliability and political bias. In this paper, we provide a rigorous temporal analysis in which we identify cases of statistically significant disparity in the user interaction dynamics with different classes of news articles. Our findings provide insights into how and when to better protect against and/or slow down the spread of misinformation.

Combined Impacts, Granularity Levels, and Per-Article-Based News Classification: While reliability represents the degree of factual reporting, bias refers to the tendency for journalists to favor one political side or another in their reporting, sometimes even without being aware that they are doing so. Prior research has established a link between the bias and reliability of news articles and how people engage with and distribute them. For example, by focusing on the reliability factor, Vosoughi et al. [20] showed that false information spreads substantially farther, faster, deeper, and more widely than the truth. Examining the bias parameter, Wischnewski et al. [22] discovered that users are more inclined to share hyperpartisan news pieces that coincide with their own political views. Limited works like [3] have considered both these parameters but studied them independently. There are even fewer studies that consider both parameters in combination. The primary exception is the work by Edelson [4], which findings indicate, among other things, that while misinformation generates less engagement than non-misinformation, it can nonetheless account for a significant percentage of the overall engagement (e.g., 37.7% on the far left).

Regardless of the bias or reliability parameter, there are also big differences in the granularity that each parameter has been classified and whether all news articles of a news outlet have been classified the same or individually. Both these aspects impact the applicability of the results. First, while a few works used several levels for the studied factors (e.g., [13]), most previous studies analyzed data at the binary level, including the only other work that considers both bias and reliability in combination. In their work, they label news as either reliable or not reliable [4]. Second, while most prior works (including the work by Edelson [4]) give the same bias/reliability score for all news articles published by a publisher, only a few papers have used the ratings of individual news articles. We argue that this is of significant importance for the generalization of the result. Otherwise, for example, political, sports, or science news published by Fox News would all receive the same reliability and political bias classification. In practice, two news articles from the same publisher or even by the same author can have significantly different ratings.

In summary, the majority of prior research is based on the ratings of publishers (not news articles), considers only bias or reliability (not both combined), use a limited news article classification (e.g., binary), focuses on a limited set of user interactions, and ignores the users' engagement dynamics over time.

Main Contribution: This paper addresses the above shortcomings of the current literature by presenting the first temporal analysis of the user interaction dynamics with news articles of varying degrees of (political) bias and reliability. We consider a spectrum of user interactions and study the impact of bias and reliability in combination. In contrast to prior works studying the interaction dynamics as part of the political conversations (in online social networks) during elections and other events [7, 8, 18], our focus here is instead on the roles that the bias and reliability play in the dynamics. Another novel aspect of our temporal analysis is that we compare the temporal dynamics seen using different classes of interactions with the news, including likes and shares of posts linking the news articles. Only a few works have considered all types of user interactions (e.g., Edelson et al. [4]) but none of them consider the relative dynamics or the impact of bias and reliability on the dynamics. Finally, we examine the predictability of the total amount of user engagement that news articles of different classes may receive based on the interactions it has received thus far.

Temporal Dynamics and Research Questions: To study the temporal dynamics at the granularity and scale needed to address the above limitations of prior works, we obtain and study temporal traces of all types of user interactions for around 18K news articles that have been individually scored based on their bias and reliability. For the news article labeling, we use data from Ad Fontes Media, and we use CrowdTangle to obtain temporal data for all classes of user interactions with all Facebook posts discussing or linking the labeled news articles. Using several carefully designed prepossessing steps, we then study the observed temporal dynamics and address the following research questions:

RQ1 How do the bias and reliability of a post affect the temporal dynamics of a user's engagement with it?

RQ2 Using its intermediate interactions as a predictive criterion, how does the bias and reliability of a post affect the prediction of the total engagement it will receive?

RQ3 How do the temporal dynamics of user engagement differ across different interaction types, and how does this variation relate to the bias and the reliability of the post?

Empirical Example Findings: Our analysis uncovers several interesting observations. In comparison to left-leaning posts, right-leaning posts receive more interactions per post. Considering the reliability, the "Most unreliable" and "Most reliable" news receives the minimum number of interactions per posting. Considering the temporal dynamics of interactions, our findings show that the temporal interaction level is best captured when bias and reliability are evaluated jointly. We highlight different joint bias-reliability classes that deviate from the temporal dynamics of the bias or reliability classes they belong to. In terms of interaction changes over time, the "most reliable" posts and the "most unreliable" posts exhibit opposite trends. Here, the "most reliable" news is experiencing a faster decrease (than average) in the interaction rates, whereas the "most unreliable" news experience a faster than average increase in the interaction rates, as seen over time.

We find that when examining just the number of likes that a post receives within the first hour of publication, the reliability of the post is positively associated with the normalized (over the total number of interactions) number of likes received. In other words, during this period of time, the posts that are considered "most reliable" receive the highest number of likes. Finally, when considering the outlet-specific analysis, we find that despite Fox News and the New York Times having different political biases, in both cases, relatively unbiased posts receive greater interaction rates during the initial stages compared to their biased posts.

Example Beneficiaries: Various stakeholders can benefit from our contributions. Researchers will benefit from our quantitative analysis of the temporal dynamics of user engagement with various types of news, including our use of statistical tests to back up example findings captured in the different stages of our time-series analysis. We share the code used to produce the results,[1] allowing others to reproduce and expand on our findings. Among practitioners, Facebook content moderators may use knowledge about the statistical disparities highlighted here between the user interactions with reliable and unreliable news to better focus their resources during the different stages of a post's lifetime. Furthermore, news content providers may incorporate the mentioned temporal patterns into their engagement prediction models.

Roadmap: The remainder of the paper is organized as follows. Section 2 describes how we collect and analyze the data. Here, we also provide detailed definitions of the normalized metrics computed and used. Section 3 presents our results for the complete dataset, as well as the outlet specific results. In Sect. 4, we explore the extent to which we can predict the maximum interaction volume based on the intermediate number of interactions. Sections 5 and 6 discuss related works and limitations, respectively. Ethical considerations are discussed in Sect. 7, before we conclude the paper in Sect. 8.

2   Methodology and Dataset

We first describe our methodology and dataset. Section 2.1 describes the news article selection and the labeling of articles. Section 2.2 describes the filtering we applied to have a clean dataset. Section 2.3 describes how we collected the Facebook posts sharing each news article, as well as temporal data of the user interactions associated with each such post. In Sect. 2.4, we determine time thresholds

---

[1] https://github.com/alireza-mon/pam2023.

Table 1. Bias classes and their intervals.

Bias class	Far left	Skews left	Balanced Bias	Skews right	Far right
Bias range	[−42, −18]	(−18, −6]	(−6, 6)	[6, 18)	[18, 42]

(based on the number of total interactions between consecutive time thresholds) that together define a sequence of time buckets with equalized (total) number of interactions per time bucket. For our (later) temporal analysis, we use these bucketized time sequences of the interactions associated with different subsets of news articles (where each subset contains the articles with a specific bias/reliability label). In Sect. 2.5, we explain the normalization process we use to provide a fair head-to-head comparison between different subsets. Section 2.6 provides a summary of the final dataset.

2.1 News Article Selection and Bias/Reliability Labeling

There exist several independent evaluation efforts to asses the bias and/or reliability of individual news articles and/or news sources. Examples include Media Bias Fact Check[2], Ad Fontes Media[3], AllSides[4], and NewsGuard[5]. Of these, we selected to use data from Ad Fontes Media for the following primary reasons: (1) they evaluate individual news articles, (2) each evaluated article is scored with regard to both bias and reliability, (3) the dataset contains over 30K articles covering over more than 1,500 sources, and finally (4) they provide a transparent strategy, published and explained in a white paper [14].

For each news source, Ad Fontes Media selects sample articles that are prominently featured on each source's website over multiple news cycles. To prioritize popular news sources, they rank the news sources and organize them into tiers that are given different sample frequencies. Specifically, they label approximately 15 articles per month for the top-15 sources, seven articles per month are labeled for the next 15 sources, the rest of the top-200 sources are assigned approximately five new labeled articles per quarter, and the following 200 articles (ranks 201–400) are updated approximately five times per six months. As mentioned in their white paper [14], they attempt to strike a balance between rating new sources and updating current ones with more recent samples. As a result, the dataset consists of news articles spanning both a broad range of news sources and capturing many samples from popular new sources seen over time.

Each article in the Ad Fontes Media dataset is evaluated with regard to both bias and reliability by at least three human analysts with a balance of right, left, and center self-reported political perspectives. The bias scores reported by Ad Fontes Media range from −42 to +42, with greater negative values indicating a

---

[2] https://mediabiasfactcheck.com
[3] https://adfontesmedia.com
[4] https://www.allsides.com
[5] https://www.newsguardtech.com

Table 2. Reliability classes and their intervals.

Reliability class	Most Unreliable	Unreliable	Reliable	Most Reliable
Reliability range	[0, 16)	[16, 32)	[32, 48)	[48, 64]

more leftward bias and positive values leaning toward the right party. For the reliability scores, they use grades from 0 to 64, with 64 being the most reliable news. Note that 42 and 64 (not usual numbers used for scales) are arbitrarily selected by Ad Fontes Media, as described in [15]. For the analysis presented here, we binned the bias scores into belonging to one of five bias ranges and we binned the reliability scores into four reliability ranges. Ranges and assigned labels are provided in Tables 1 and 2, respectively. Due to the smaller sample size of extremely biased news articles (both to the left and right) we used larger bin sizes for articles labeled as "Far left" [−42, −18] or "Far right" [18, 42].

2.2   Preprocessing of News Articles

We first and on August 2, 2022 received resources evaluated by Ad Fontes Media and their corresponding bias and reliability values. Second, we used Ad Fontes Media's search functionality to prune the dataset to include only news articles. After removing television shows and podcasts, the dataset contained 27,547 articles. Third, through manual examination, we identified and removed several videos and television shows from the remaining results (e.g., some shows from https://www.rushlimbaugh.com). Fourth, to reduce the effects of potential long-term trends/biases, we restricted the final dataset to articles published after 2018. To determine the publication date of each news article, we calculated the minimum of the following four values:

- The news article's earliest archived date on web.archive.org.
- The publication date of the article is extracted from the article page using the htmldate python package, which applies heuristics on HTML code and linguistic patterns to derive a page's publishing date.
- The minimum post date of all Facebook posts sharing the URL.
- The minimum post date of all tweets sharing the URL.

Finally, we excluded news pages that did not refer to news articles but rather pages reporting on an event over a period of time[6]. Following these steps, the dataset contained 27,329 articles from 986 domains.

Before trying to identify social media posts pointing to a news article, it is important to note that not all links to an article will look the same. To ensure that we find as many posts referencing the identified articles as possible while avoiding false positives, we next calculated the canonical form of the URL of each news article. By canonical form, we mean the minimum form of the URL that uniquely identifies any shared version of the URL. As an example, we identified several campaign query parameters used to augment numerous URLs that we could remove. Appendix A.1 explains our procedure to compute the canonical form of the URLs.

---

[6] E.g., reuters.com/subjects/myanmar-reporters.

2.3   Temporal User Engagement of Related Facebook Posts

We next used the CrowdTangle API to collect (1) all their Facebook posts including one of the news article URLs, as well as (2) the temporal data of users' interaction with these posts. The CrowdTangle platform [6], which is owned by Facebook, indexes the posts and engagement data for around 7 million pages, including "more than 50K likes pages, all public Facebook groups with 95k+ members, all US-based public groups with 2k+ members, and all verified profiles" [6], as well as any pages added to a CrowdTangle list by those with access to it. For collecting the Facebook posts, we opted to use the "/Links" endpoint of the CrowdTangle API. This ensured us that all shortened versions of the URLs were also collected. To collect the maximum number of posts related to each article, we passed the canonical form of the URL to this end point. In addition, we strived to account for instances in which query strings were included in the URLs' canonical form.

The data collection was done on or after Sept. 1 (2022) for all posts published before Sept. 1. By including only articles published before Aug. 2, our methodology ensures that at least 4 weeks had passed since the publication date of any articles included in our dataset. Since most posts sharing news articles occur soon after an article is posted, the 4-week gap (between the collection of articles and posts) allows us to collect (the 21 days) temporal interaction data for all posts associated with the studied news articles. Similarly, the 4-week threshold also ensures that we can catch most of the posts linking an article. In this study, we removed any articles that did not have any published posts. After this filtering, the dataset included 21,872 labeled articles for which we extract the temporal interaction data.

Using CrowdTangle, we compile temporal user interaction data for the number of likes, shares, comments, and emoji-based interactions such as Like(s), Wow(s), Sad(s), Angry(s), Love(s), and Haha(s). For each of the above metrics, as well as for the total interactions (across all actions allowed by users), Crowd-Tangle breaks the first (approximately) 21 days after the post is published into 74 roughly exponentially increasing time steps and provides the number of user interactions for each of the user interactions at each of these time steps. The increasingly sparse sample rate used by CrowdTangle is most likely motivated by most posts being short-lived and the interaction rates quickly reducing over time. We illustrate this in Fig. 1, where we show the cumulative fraction of all interactions that have taken place after some time since the posting time of each studied post in our dataset (with time on log scale).

For most posts, we have temporal data for the full 21-day period (the maximum age at the final data point for any posts observed in our dataset was 23 days). In addition to this temporal data, we also extract other post-related data from CrowdTangle, including the date that the post was published.

Here, it should be noted that a user sharing a post essentially pushes the post to the timeline of their friends and followers, and their statistics do not include the shares of a post (on the original shares of a post). For comments

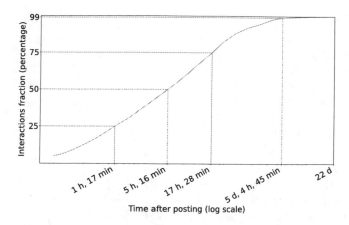

Fig. 1. Cumulative fraction of interactions (min: minutes, h: hours, and d: days).

statistics, the API counts all comments on the post and all first-level replies to those comments.

2.4   Time Partitioning

For studying the temporal dynamics of the posts, we break up the 21-day time period into smaller time buckets and then study the dynamics of user interactions over each of these time-bucket sequences. For the analysis presented here, we used four time buckets and selected the time thresholds used to define the bucket sizes so that each bucket had roughly the same total number of interactions. More specifically, we selected the time thresholds so that they represent the points where 25%, 50%, and 75% of the overall interactions (sum of over all interaction types) have been observed by CrowdTangle (and apply linear interpolation when thresholds fall between sample points). The determined threshold values are shown and highlighted (using red lines) in Fig. 1. As expected, the decreasing interaction rates, result in increasing time bucket sizes.

While we observe approximately straight-line behavior for part of the parameter range, we note that the above selection process does not require any assumptions about the actual probability distribution. This selection also helps provide fair head-to-head comparisons (using statistical tests) between the interaction differences observed during the four different stages, effectively maximizing the information gains from comparing the interaction dynamics of the users across the four phases.

2.5   Capturing Engagement Dynamics

By picking time buckets of equivalent size in terms of interaction volume, we can better compare the number of user interactions of each type in each time bucket. For our primary comparisons, we first define a metric called the Total

Interactions Covered Ratio (TICR), defined as the percentage of total interactions that a post receives which are covered within a specific period of time. For example, if a post receives a maximum of 600 interactions over the full timeline and 200 interactions between hours 1 and 5 (following its publication), then the TICR is 33% for this period.

After computing the TICR values for all the times that the current post has been probed on, we calculate the average observed over the successful probes done within each time bucket. This procedure is repeated for all time buckets and posts.

At this stage, we removed any post that was not probed at least once during each of the four buckets or that received fewer than ten interactions in total (including the ones with zero interactions). This helps remove noise from non-popular posts and improves the stability of the results.

Finally, after the above per-post filtering, we removed any article without any remaining posts. Table 3 provides summary statistics for the final dataset.

Table 3. Dataset summary statistics.

Articles#	Domains#	Posts#	Total interactions#	Bias mean	Reliability mean
17,966	953	106,325	81,891,888	−1.08 (std:10.11)	40.47 (std:8.59)

We next use the bias-reliability labels of the articles associated with each post to compute statistics for each bias-reliability pair and time bucket. For most of our analysis presented here, we report the mean values observed for each time bucket and interaction type, as well as perform statistical tests on the relative mean values.

2.6   Dataset Summary

Given the above steps, for each bias-reliability class and for each interaction type, we have the bucket-based temporal sequences of the user interactions to the posts associated with news articles of that class. Figures 2a and b summarize the number of articles we have in each bias and reliability class and the number of posts for which we have completed such sequences, respectively, as broken down per bias-reliability category. In addition to five categories for bias and four categories for reliability, we include one column and one row for the aggregate statistics combining all categories of reliability and bias, respectively. With this design, the overall observed articles (17,966) and posts (106,325) are shown in the top-right corners of the first two sub-plots, respectively.

While there are some categories (primarily the "most unreliable less biased" articles and the "most reliable" but extremely biased articles) for which we only have a small number of articles with complete stats, we often have enough posts for our analysis also for these categories. In fact, most categories have a significant number of posts per article on average (Fig. 2c). In terms of the normalized

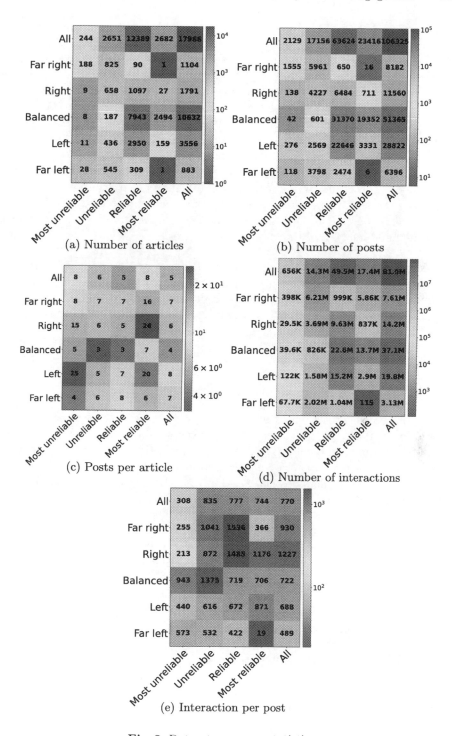

(a) Number of articles

(b) Number of posts

(c) Posts per article

(d) Number of interactions

(e) Interaction per post

Fig. 2. Dataset summary statistics.

number of posts that shared them, the eleven articles in the most unreliable-left and the reliable-right classes were the most successful, as shown in this figure. Moreover, we observe that, among all classes of reliability, the two extreme classes are shared the most.

We also provide summary statistics for the total number of interactions (irrespective of interaction type), calculated as the sum of all interactions.[7] As shown in Fig. 2d, 81.9 million interactions have been recorded for the posts included in our final dataset. As expected, the interactions are correlated with the number of posts. To determine objectively which class performs better in terms of interactions per post, we present the normalized number of interactions (over the number of posts) in Fig. 2e. As is noticeable, the right party (both "far right" and "right") receives more interactions. Regarding reliability, however, it is shown that the "most unreliable" news are the least engaging for users. We next present the results and analysis of the temporal sequences.

> **Key Observations:** In comparison to left-leaning posts, right-leaning posts receive more interaction per post. In terms of reliability, the "Most unreliable" news receives the minimum interaction per posting.

3   Results

3.1   High-level Analysis of the All Interactions Dynamics

Let us first consider the cases when all interactions are aggregated into one interaction metric, calculated as the sum over all interaction types. Figure 3 shows the temporal interaction dynamics of this metric in terms of TICR. Here, we again show the five categories of the bias and an "All" category (that combines all observations regardless of bias) as rows in each sub-plot and show the four categories of the reliability plus an aggregate "All" category (that combines all observations regardless of reliability) as columns. The four sub-plots, going from left to right, show the results for the time buckets containing all sample points (as described in Sects. 2.3 and 2.5) associated with the following time buckets: (1) 0 to 1 h and 17 min, (2) 1 h and 17 min to 5 h and 16 min, (3) 5 h and 16 min to 17 h and 28 min, and (4) 17 h and 28 min until the end of the timeline of each post we study (typically 21 days). We use a timeline with green markers to illustrate this bucketization. As expected from the definition of TICR (Sect. 2.5) and our selection of time bucket thresholds (Sect. 2.4), the TICR value for the "all news" case (i.e., the right-top-most cell) of each bucket is 25%.

In each bucket, the mean TICR value for all posts belonging to the respective class and bucket is depicted (using heatmap colors). To capture the variances of each class and thereby quantify the reliability of the mean reported for each group, the coefficient of variation of the mean (cv_{mean})(i.e., standard error of

---

[7] For example, if a post receives 6 likes, 2 comments, 3 shares, and no other interactions, the value of the total interactions for this post is 11.

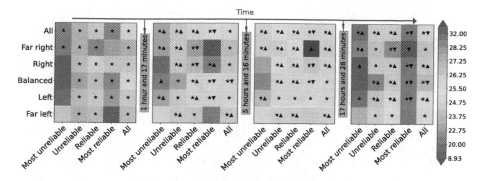

Fig. 3. Temporal dynamics of the total interactions (⋆: coefficient of variation of the mean is smaller than 4%, ▲ and ▼: has deviation from the previous time bucket with p-value < 0.05).

the class divided by its mean) of that class in percentage is computed. Then, we mark the class with an asterisk (⋆) if cv_{mean} is smaller than a threshold. In the following, we decided on the value of 4% as the threshold. Accordingly, the classes for which the cv_{mean} is higher than 4% (due to not having enough samples or having high variances) do not receive the asterisk.

Regarding selecting 4% as the cv_{mean} threshold used for the above statistical tests, we first note that this value is small. For example, for the general population, which has a mean of 25, this threshold is equal to a standard error of 1.0. The use of such a small threshold allows the comparison of all classes to be made in a more reliable way. Furthermore, we have found that with this selection, any two classes with "asterisks" within the same time bucket whose TICR values are at least 0.2 units apart (from each other) always have statistically significantly different means at the 90% confidence level. This finding has been validated for all category pairs and time buckets using t-tests for comparing the means of these classes, and the p-values are always less than 0.1[8].

To come to the above thresholds, we performed pairwise comparisons between all the classes for each bucket using different example thresholds. For each case, this corresponds to calculating a 30 × 30 table of pairwise tests, in which each cell include the p-value (capturing the statistical significance of the pairwise mean comparisons). Clearly, showing this table – even for a single bucket (and example threshold) – takes a lot of space. For this reason, we instead simply report the determined thresholds (in our case 4% and 0.2 point difference) and mark the classes that satisfied the 4% criteria with an "asterisks". As an example, if we turn our attention to the first bucket, we note that the "most reliable" group's

---

[8] Here, we use independent samples t-test when the classes are independent and dependent samples t-test when the classes are not independent. Examples when the dependent test is used, include cases when a class is compared to its parent bias or parent reliability class (that it belongs to); e.g., comparison between the "right-unreliable" class and the "right" (over all biases).

TICR mean is higher than that of the "unreliable" class (with more than a 0.2 difference) and that both classes are marked with an "asterisks". Therefore, we can say that these two classes have statistically different means.

More than comparing the interaction levels of classes within the same time bucket, it is also interesting to capture the changes in the interaction level of one class between the time intervals. To cover this aspect, we annotated the cells of the figure with an arrow for any class in a bucket for which the difference between its mean in this bucket and its mean in the previous bucket is statistically significant at the 95% confidence level (i.e., the p-value of the paired t-test is smaller than 0.05). Here, the direction of the arrow indicates whether this variation is increasing (▲) or decreasing (▼). As an example, we note that the "most reliable" class receives these temporal significance indicators between the first two buckets. This class (which was outperforming the other classes in terms of receiving user interactions in the first bucket) hence performs more similar to the other classes in the second bucket. For this group, the decrease pattern between the second and the third bucket is also significant, although the change is not as high. This is mainly due to this class having many samples (23,416 posts) and therefore more easily passing the t-test. The decreasing pattern of this class also continues in the last bucket, but with a sharper slope.

We make several other observations from Fig. 3. As an example, there is a positive correlation between the reliability level of news and the level of interaction they receive in the first bucket. Here, more reliable posts receive interactions at a higher rate during the first hour after posting. In contrast, for the bias parameter, the two extremely biased classes (i.e., "far right" and "far left") receive less interaction rate than the unbiased (balanced) class in this bucket. In the final bucket, the pattern is reversed, suggesting that unbiased postings are more successful in the early stages of their lifespan compared to strongly biased posts. Notably, even in the fourth bucket, unbiased postings receive higher interaction volume because their total interaction (the denominator of the TICR values) is significantly more than those of the other two extremely biased classes (37M vs. 7M and 3M interactions). This is one of the reasons why we chose to provide the temporal dynamics of the TICR values as opposed to the actual interaction values, as the TICR values capture these dynamics more precisely.

Another important observation we want to highlight is that for some classes, identifying the class that a sample trend belongs to is easier to profile when we look at the bias-reliability class not the reliability or bias class independently. As an example, consider the "most unreliable - left" class which receives statistical significance, and "asterisk" in the third bucket. Both of the means of the bias and reliability classes it belongs to is statistically different than this class. This observation suggests that the interaction level is best captured when bias and reliability are evaluated jointly. Another observation worth mentioning is regarding the temporal changes of the most unreliable news. This class has an increasing pattern in terms of the rate of change they experience (for all buckets, it is statistically significant). We have seen the exact opposite trend when it comes to the "most reliable" news sources.

> **Key Observations:** The "most reliable" posts and the "most unreliable" posts experience opposite trends in the interaction changes over time. In the first hour following the publication of the post, there is a positive correlation between the reliability of the post and the level of interaction it receives.

3.2   Temporal Dynamics of Different Interactions

We now turn our attention to each individual interaction types, including shares, likes, and comments. In order to capture how much of the total interactions is covered by each of the interactions in each time bucket, we use the same denominator as total interactions for each of these interaction types. As an example, if a post receives a maximum of 600 total interactions during our timeline of study and receives 90 likes during the first time bucket, we say that the TICR of likes for this period is 15%.

Shares: With sharing having perhaps the most direct effect on what news people may be exposed to, we start our analysis with shares. The TICR scores for the number of shares (of posts linking articles) are shown in Fig. 4. First, note that the average TICR value for all posts (the top-right cell in each table) has decreased from 25% to approximately 4% in each bucket (due to normalizing over the total interactions). Comparing the top-right cells in Figs. 4-6, we note that the fraction of shares is almost the same as the number of comments but smaller than the number of likes.

Second, while it should not be expected that the top-right cell of all buckets to have equal values when considering individual interaction classes, we note that they are almost the same (in the range of 4-4.5%). Since we picked the bucket thresholds to have roughly the same number of total interactions over all posts to each bucket (but not necessarily the same volume for each interaction type), this suggests that shares as an aggregate (over all classes of news articles) represents a relatively stable fraction of the total number of interactions.

Third, across all buckets, the "most unreliable" class is the clear winner. When compared to the other classes of reliability (first row) and even all classes of bias (last column), they receive a greater proportion of the shares during all buckets. Although this pattern could not occur for the "total interactions", it is feasible here since TICR values here are normalized over the total interactions. Referring back to the "total interactions", for which this class saw the lowest ratio of interactions in the first two buckets(when compared with the other reliability classes), we, therefore, expect the number of likes (Fig. 5) and comments (Fig. 6) to be comparatively less (than for the other reliability classes) for these two time buckets. This shows that the "most unreliable" news often is relatively more shared early, despite not seeing as many likes and comments, but that this evens out over time.

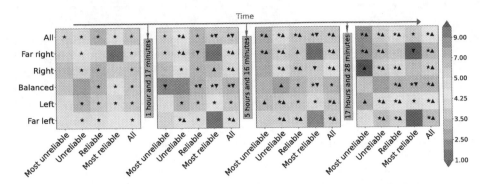

Fig. 4. Temporal dynamics of the total interactions covered for shares (⋆: coefficient of variation of the mean is smaller than 4%, ▲ and ▼: has deviation from the previous time bucket with p-value < 0.05).

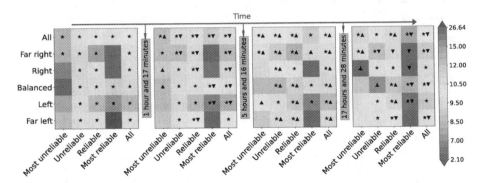

Fig. 5. Temporal dynamics of the total interactions covered for likes (⋆: coefficient of variation of the mean is smaller than 4%, ▲ and ▼: has deviation from the previous time bucket with p-value < 0.05).

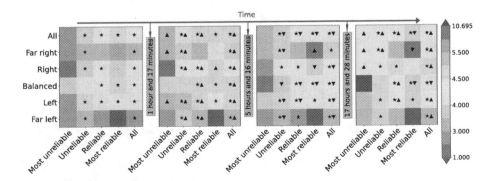

Fig. 6. Temporal dynamics of the total interactions covered for comments (⋆: coefficient of variation of the mean is smaller than 4%, ▲ and ▼: has deviation from the previous time bucket with p-value < 0.05).

Fourth, some classes consistently (throughout the four time buckets) see a larger relative sharing fraction than the other classes. For example, the two extreme bias classes ("far right" and "far left") perform better than the remaining bias classes in all buckets. Moreover, for both of these extreme bias classes as well as for the "most unreliable" group, the trend of shares rate is increasing as time goes on. As a result of this trend, the last bucket exhibits a negative correlation between the total number of interactions covered for shares and the reliability of news, with the "most unreliable" news seeing relatively more late sharing.

Fifth, we observe several classes with relatively different temporal dynamics than the bias and reliability classes they belong to. As an example, we can clearly observe that for the third bucket, the "unreliable-right" class has a markedly different pattern than both the corresponding bias and reliability classes that it belongs to. This suggests that it is important to consider both these parameters in combination when predicting the sharing of the news in a bucket.

> **Key Observations:** Among all the reliability classes, the "most unreliable" posts experience the greatest gains in terms of share rates. During the late stages of the posts' lifetime (17 hours after publishing), there is a negative correlation between reliability levels and share rates. The most reliable postings receive the least normalized number of shares.

Likes: A more passive way to (indirectly) impact how visible posts on Facebook is to like various posts. One reason for this is that posts with many likes are more likely to occur higher up in the timelines of friends. A like also represents a user's (in most cases positive) interaction with the news. Figure 5 shows the temporal dynamics of the total interactions covered for the number of likes. First, again it is evident that considering bias and reliability simultaneously will yield more reliable results. As an example, in the second bucket, the "unreliable-balanced" class deviates from the bias and reliability classes it belongs to.

Second, in the first bucket, a positive correlation is observed between the reliability level and the rate of likes in the early stages of the posts' lifetime (initial hour). In other words, during the initial time period, people more frequently like reliable news. This is in contrast to the share rates (Fig. 4), which happens more for unreliable posts during the very first stages of the posts' lifetime.

These observations may suggest that the sharing patterns and like patterns are substantially different and depend on the reliability and bias of the news. Yet, some similarities between their patterns can also be observed. For example, if we consider "all" posts, both metrics observe an increase in the third bucket.

> **Key Observations:** During the first hour following the publication of a post, there is a positive correlation between the post's reliability and the number of likes it receives. Throughout this period the "most reliable" posts experience the most like rates.

Comments: Similar to likes, comments provide an indirect way of exposing friends to various posts. However, in contrast to likes, a single user can give several comments on the same posts. Here, we treat all comments the same but note that the somewhat larger fraction of comments in part may come from users making several comments on the same post.

Figure 6 displays the temporal dynamics of TICR values for the number of comments. There are multiple observations to be made from this figure. First, the "most reliable" group, which was not successful in terms of shares, performs the best in the first three buckets of comment results. As a result, for a typical post in this category, we expect to see a higher normalized rate of comments during the first 17 h after publishing it. Second, we observe (from the last columns) that the two extreme bias classes perform poorly, except in the final bucket of the "far-right" class. This is the opposite of the pattern we have observed for the shares of these classes. Third, we again observe deviations for several of the bias-reliability classes from the bias or reliability classes that they belong to. An example of this is the "unreliable- right" class in the last bucket.

Other Interaction Types: While Facebook also allows other interaction types, these typically see smaller interaction volumes and, therefore may have a less clear impact on the dissemination patterns of news. We include results for some of the other used interactions in Appendix A.2.

3.3   Outlet-Specific Results

In addition to examining the temporal patterns of interactions across different types of news, we have also studied how bias and reliability of the news published by specific media outlets impacted people's interactions with the posts sharing that news over time.

For this analysis, we selected six outlets with the goal to achieve a fair comparison of popular outlets with different political biases. First, we selected the top-10 outlets with the most articles in our dataset to ensure that each selected outlet had sufficient samples for statistical significance. Second, we omitted yahoo.com which is among the top-10 outlets as it is more known as a news aggregator (rather than a news source). Third, from the remaining outlets, we selected to provide the analysis results for (1) two right-biased outlets (Fox News and New York Post), (2) two left-biased outlets (The New York Times and CNN), and two outlets that could represent (mostly) unbiased news sources (NPR and

Reuters). For the classification of the outlets, we used Ad Fontes Media outlet-based ratings.[9] Table 4 lists these sources and high-level statistics extracted from our dataset, including their bias class (from Ad Fontes ratings), the number of articles in our data, the number of posts sharing these articles, the number of interactions related to these posts, the number of posts per article, the number of interactions per post, and their popularity in terms of their monthly visits.

Table 4. Statistics of the outlets (†: M stands for million, ‡: Website monthly visits reported by similarweb.com (Oct. 2022)).

Outlet	N.Y.Times	Fox News	CNN	N.Y.Post	NPR	Reuters
Bias Class	Left	Right	Left	Right	Unbiased	Unbiased
Articles No	300	209	206	135	176	125
Posts No	6354	2797	2501	3085	2582	777
Interaction No	4.74 M†	6.18 M	3.45 M	1.68 M	3.88 M	0.48 M
Post per Article	21	13	12	23	15	6
Interaction per Post	746	2209	1378	543	1499	615
Monthly Visits‡	618.60 M	280.30 M	569.10 M	144.20 M	115.50 M	89.30 M

We next present temporal analysis results for the total interactions of articles published by The New York Times (left-biased), Fox News (right-biased), and NPR (unbiased). Results for the other three outlets are found in Appendix A.3. Furthermore, using the code we publish, interested researchers can conduct similar analyses for the remaining media outlets we studied, although not all of the results will be statistically significant.

The New York Times: Figure 7 shows the results for The New York Times. We note that the white boxes represent categories of news for which we did not have data. As perhaps expected, for The New York Times, we did not have data for any of the right-biased categories (irrespective of reliability).

First, note that we are reporting the TICR statistics for the total interactions. As discussed previously, given the selection of bucket thresholds, we anticipate around 25% of TICR of the total interactions for all buckets when considering the overall population (reported in the top-right cell of each bucket). However, when considering individual publishers, this is not necessarily the case. For example, as seen in Fig. 7, the user engagement with posts linking news articles by The New York Times that are older than 17 h is lower than average. Instead, posts linking their news appear most successful during the third bucket (5–17 h after posts first appear). Second, a definite association between interactions with The New York Times news related posts receive and their reliability can also be seen when we focus on the early stages of postings (first two buckets) and late stages

---

[9] Ad Fontes Media provides evaluations of both publishers and individual articles.

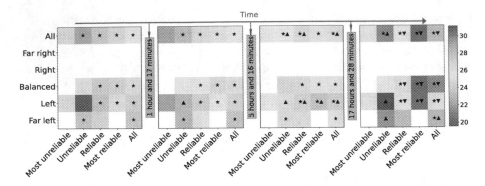

Fig. 7. Temporal dynamics of total interactions for The New York Times (white boxes: no data available, ⋆: coefficient of variation of the mean is smaller than 4%, ▲ and ▼: has a deviation from the previous time bucket with p-value < 0.05).

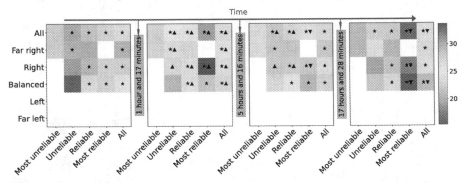

Fig. 8. Temporal dynamics of the total interactions covered for Fox News (white boxes: no data available, ⋆: coefficient of variation of the mean is smaller than 4%, ▲ and ▼: has a deviation from the previous time bucket with p-value < 0.05).

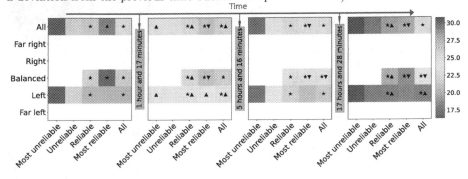

Fig. 9. Temporal dynamics of the total interactions covered for NPR (white boxes: no data available, ⋆: coefficient of variation of the mean is smaller than 4%, ▲ and ▼: has a deviation from the previous time bucket with p-value < 0.05).

(17 h onward) and exclude the most unreliable news (which has only six articles in our dataset). Here, the first stages' correlation is positive, whereas for the late stage this correlation is highly negative. While aiming to receive early engagements, it is clear that the reliability of the news plays a significant factor in the actual interaction levels achieved.

When considering bias, it is clear that less biased news receives higher interactions in the early time slots (although The New York Times belongs to the left party). Again, the trend of deviation of a class from the reliability and bias class that it belongs to can be seen in different buckets. As an example during hours 1 to 5 (after publishing a post), a typical post belonging to the "most reliable-left" class does not follow the pattern of the "most reliable" nor the "left group".

Fox News: Figure 8 shows the temporal results for Fox News. For the first and the last bucket, similar to The New York Times, we see a correlation between reliability engagement, when again discarding the non-significant results of the "most unreliable" class. After around five hours, the "most reliable" class loses its first-place ranking to the "unreliable" group. The large increase in unreliable news after 5 h is statistically supported. Again, we can see a big, normalized decline in the most reliable news 17 h after posting. Similarly to what we have observed for The New York Times, we may observe that in the earliest phases of a post's lifetime, balanced news is more engaging than biased ones, although Fox News itself is a right-biased biased news outlet. Here, statistical evidence supports the divergence we see for the bias class from the average population, until 5 h after posting.

> **Key Observation:** In spite of Fox News and the New York Times being biased publishers, for both, related unbiased posts receive a higher interaction rate than biased ones in the first hour following posting.

NPR: Finally, we used NPR as an example of an outlet with very limited bias. As seen in Fig. 9, again balanced news receives higher interaction rates than the unbiased ones in the very first bucket, and the trend changes in the last bucket. The biased news published by this outlet tends to receive the most interaction during the late stages of the posts' lifetime. Moreover, the statistically significant decreasing pattern of the interaction rate with the "most reliable" news is worth noting.

4   Prediction of the Maximum Interaction's Volume

Another interesting aspect when comparing bias-reliability classes is the extent to which a post's maximum interaction value (denominator of TICR) is predictable from the post's interaction at each moment. To quantify the proportion of the variation in the denominator of TICR that can be explained by the current interaction a post has received, we next present a correlation-based analysis.

Table 5. Minimum time required for reaching high correlations between the current and ultimate interactions (m: minutes, h: hours, and d: days).

| | | Reliability | | | | | | | | | |
| | | Most unreliable | | Unreliable | | Reliable | | Most reliable | | All | |
		$r^2 > .6$	$r^2 > .8$	$r^2 > .6$	$r^2 > .8$	$r^2 > .6$	$r^2 > .8$	$r^2 > .6$	$r^2 > .8$	$r^2 > .6$	$r^2 > .8$
Bias	Far left	15 m	21 m	25 m	1 h, 51 m	15 m	15 m	31 m	31 m	15 m	31 m
	Left	15 m	15 m	25 m	2 h, 13 m	31 m	2 h, 13 m	15 m	37 m	31 m	1 h, 17 m
	Balanced	9 h, 35 m	1 d, 10 h	15 m	13 h, 48 m	6 h, 39 m	16 h, 33 m	21 m	1 h, 51 m	1 h, 17 m	11 h, 30 m
	Right	15 m	15 m	21 m	1 h, 51 m	25 m	2 h, 40 m	18 m	18 m	21 m	2 h, 13 m
	Far right	15 m	15 m	15 m	15 m	15 m	18 m	15 m	37 m	15 m	15 m
	All	15 m	31 m	15 m	53 m	37 m	11 h, 30 m	21 m	1 h, 4 m	31 m	6 h, 39 m

First, we divide the time axis into exponentially increasing time buckets. For the first bucket, we use a size of 15 min, and then we use a factor of 1.2 to increase the bucket sizes. Then, in each bucket and for each group, we compute the coefficient of determination (r^2) as the squared value of the Pearson correlation coefficient between the current interaction values of the posts of the class and the total interaction they receive in the future. Finally, we recorded the moments in which the (r^2) reached .6 and .8, respectively. Table 5 summarize the results. While more advanced prediction models might be used in practice, not limiting the discussion to a particular predictive model provides quantifiable insights into the extent to which we can rely on predictive models to estimate the total number of interactions from the current value of the interaction a post received (even with simple models). We next share some of our key observations.

First, note that in most classes a Pearson correlation coefficient of 0.8 (r^2 of 0.6) is achieved within one hour of posting, suggesting that the total number of interactions is relatively well predicted very early. Second, if all posts are taken into consideration, this can be accomplished within 30 min of posting. Third, considering all reliability classes (last row), we can see that we can achieve this level of predictability within around 40 min of posting. Fourth, as we examine all bias classes in the last column, we can see that the biased classes are able to reach this level earlier than the unbiased classes.

Fifth, note that reaching the high value r^2 level of 0.8 for the general population (last row and last column of the table) is feasible within 7 h after the posting. With regard to our definition of 4-bucket thresholds, we can say that for all the classes except for 3 we can reach the 0.6 level of r^2 in the first bucket. In the second bucket, it is also feasible to achieve an r^2 level of 0.8, except for the six classes. Finally, we note that for all classes except one, we can reach the r^2 level of 0.8 before the fourth bucket, allowing us to apply patterns observed in this bucket more broadly.

5   Related Work

This paper relates to the works modeling and understanding the behavior of users, their interactions with various kinds of news and contents, and the factors that play roles in this context. For example, Aldous et al. [1] focus on the topic and emotional factors and analyze their effects on posting on five social media platforms (Facebook, Instagram, Twitter, YouTube, and Reddit) to demonstrate that user engagement is strongly influenced by the content's topic, with certain topics being more engaging on a particular platform. Their work shows that the engagement level is impacted differently on various platforms and by different topics. They also demonstrate that post emotion is indeed a significant factor. Karami et al. [10] demonstrate how social engagement may be used as a distinguishing characteristic between false and true news spreaders. However, they do not consider the temporal patterns of different user interactions in their study.

The most comparable work to ours is the recent work by Edelson et al. [4]. Their large-scale study explores how consumers engage with news inside the Facebook news ecosystem, as well as with specific pieces of news from unreliable suppliers and also between the suppliers and their audiences. However, their methodology is distinct from ours in that they base their study on publisher ratings rather than independent bits of news, they use binary classes for reliability, and they do not account for the temporal dynamics of the user interactions. Galen et al. [21] carried out a similar investigation as Edelson et al. on Reddit rather than Facebook. They also employ publisher-based rankings and demonstrate that low-factual content receives 20% fewer upvotes and 30% fewer cross-posting exposures than neutral or more factual information.

In another line of research, Allcott et al. [2] examine how users engage with fake news information and websites. Their findings indicate that through the end of 2016, user interactions with fraudulent information increased consistently on both Facebook and Twitter. Since then, engagements on Facebook have decreased significantly while continuing to increase on Twitter. Another group of studies related to our work are the ones which examine the temporal dynamics of user interactions but in different contexts. For example, Vassio et al. [19] examine how influencer-generated material draws interactions over time. Their findings indicate that while the growth rate of interactions naturally decays with time, the decay rate differs substantially between posts and social media platforms. As another related work and with a different methodology from the above works, in [12] the authors use NLP techniques to analyze over 2,5 million social media comments. The results show that Social media misinformation is largely disregarded by users.

6   Limitations

Our study has four main limitations that the researchers should consider when generalizing the findings. First, we dropped the posts with less than 10 total interactions from our study. While these types of postings constitute a significant portion of the total number of posts on Facebook, they make up a very small fraction of the total interactions (less than 5% in our dataset) and typically are of little interest to both Facebook content moderators (wanting to ban large interactions with misinformation) and also content publishers.

Second, similar to some other works (e.g., [4], we limited the study to news postings and interactions on Facebook public forums (the most popular social media platform [17]). Therefore, interactions with news articles on other social media platforms and on the publisher's website were not considered. We consider a combined analysis that also takes into account these aspects as an interesting future work. It should also be noted that our study is based on the CrowdTangle dataset and does not consider every public page on Facebook. Yet, CrowdTangle covers many pages from the whole public pages distribution. As as example, they index more than 99% of the pages with more than 25K followers [5].

Third, despite the t-test results indicating that the results are significant for several classes, the significance of the results may differ between different classes. To help interpret the significance of individual results the interested reader can consider also the number of articles in our dataset for each specific class. To help the interested reader to reproduce the results and more easily consider such additional dimensions, we will share our code. Here it should also be noted that we utilized the TICR distributions of the posts, not the aggregated results across the articles. One reason for this is that the number of posts for the flagged classes was sufficient for the findings to frequently have p-values less than 0.05.

Finally, The study focuses on the impact of bias and reliability on user engagement but does not account for other potential factors such as the relevance, timeliness, or credibility of the news source, as well as the user's individual preferences and views. Further research can consider these factors and their impact on user engagement, as well as investigate the effects of alternative labeling methods or different time frames compared to those used in the current study.

7   Ethical Considerations

All data was collected via public APIs while adhering to the rate limits of the companies hosting the data. The study is done at the aggregate level and no specific individuals are revealed. The likelihood of a substantial portion of the analyzed posts having been removed from Facebook is low due to the 28-day temporal separation between the publication date of the article and the date of data collection.

8   Conclusions

This paper presented a large-scale investigation of the temporal dynamics of various user interactions with Facebook posts belonging to different classes of bias and reliability. Using a carefully designed methodology, our investigation has answered and provided statistically supported insights into the research questions outlined in the introduction. For example, we demonstrated that user engagement with news for various classes of bias and reliability varies over time and highlighted these differences (RQ1). We have also done a study for different interaction types and observed that various interactions for the same class have different temporal interaction patterns (RQ3). Various statistically significant patterns were identified in the answers to the above questions which examine the four dimensions of this study: bias, reliability, time, and interaction type.

First, the results illustrate the importance of incorporating time into future research. As an example, we saw that the "most reliable" posts and the "most unreliable" posts exhibit opposite trends in terms of total interaction dynamics. The results also show that the temporal patterns of user interaction varied among the various user interactions, highlighting that users tend to interact differently with news of different levels of bias and reliability. A key benefit of this identification is that it allows users to profile temporal engagement patterns with varying types of news, including Facebook content moderators, by identifying different temporal patterns for different classes of interactions (e.g., shares, likes) to different posts. Moreover, this study highlights the importance of incorporating bias and reliability concurrently in future studies by showing that bias-reliability classes have statistically significant differences from bias and reliability classes with which they are associated.

As all of the temporal patterns addressed in our research are dependent on the total interactions covered metric, which requires direct access to the value of the total interactions a post receives, we have quantified the predictability of total interactions from intermediate interaction values. Except for a few specific classes, there are strong correlations between the current and total engagement that a post receives within a few hours after its posting. Additionally, we have quantified this effect for various classes (RQ2).

To conclude, as the first study to address all four dimensions of bias, reliability, time, and interaction type in a single investigation, this work quantified the effect of these factors on the interaction level dynamics a post receives.

Acknowledgements. The authors express their gratitude to CrowdTangle for providing the Facebook data. They also extend their thanks to the four anonymous reviewers for their insightful comments that helped improve the paper.

A   Appendix

A.1   Procedure of Computing the Canonical Form of an Article Url

The following procedure is taken to transform URLs to canonical form. We begin by converting all text to lowercase. We then delete the protocol schema (e.g. 'http://') and remove any prefix instances of the strings 'www.' that may be present. Next, we remove any # signs from the URL except for the domains that it could not be removed from the canonical form (e.g., some of *edsource* or *npr* domains URLs). Then, we remove all URL query parameters except for the domains for which this was part of their canonical form (e.g., for some of *abcnews.go.com* domain URLs). As an example, the canonical form of the URL "https://www.nytimes.com/2020/10/24/technology/epoch-times-influence-falun-gong.html?referringSource=articleShare" that we used to collect posts were "nytimes.com/2020/10/24/technology/epoch-times-influence-falun-gong.html".

A.2   Temporal Dynamics of the Other Forms of Interactions

In Sect. 3.2 we studied the temporal dynamics of "likes", "shares", and "comments" as the most common interactions users make with Facebook posts. With the same conventions discussed in Sect. 3.2, we here present the results for 2 other common interactions which are "angry", and "haha" in Figs. 10, 11. Researchers interested in extracting the statistical analysis results for other types of interactions may use our code. Several observations can be drawn from these results. First, among all the time buckets for the "angry" results, biased posts outperform balanced posts when we simply consider the aggregated bias classes (the rightmost column). In other words, biased posts make users angrier than unbiased posts. Second, the general trend for "angry" interactions for the whole population (the top right cell) is that it increases during middle buckets and then decreases after around 17 h after posting. In other words, angry interactions with posts are more likely to happen during the second and third time buckets. Third, when we consider the left group, the most reliable class gets the most "angry" interactions. A fourth observation is that, when focusing on the "haha" interaction dynamics, there is a general tendency toward decreasing interaction rates for the whole population (right topmost cell). In other words, compared to the other buckets, a greater number of "haha"s is received during the first hour following posting. It should be noted that most of the classes that received arrows and therefore have significant trend changes follow this decreasing pattern. Finally, when we consider just the aggregated bias classes (the right columns), it is apparent that the "right" class received higher rates of "haha"s during all buckets and compared to the other bias classes which have significant means.

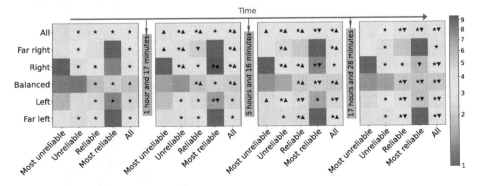

Fig. 10. Temporal dynamics of the total interactions covered for angry counts (⋆: coefficient of variation of the mean is smaller than 4%, ▲ and ▼: has deviation from the previous time bucket with p-value < 0.05).

A.3   Temporal Dynamics of CNN and the New York Post and Reuters

The temporal dynamic results for CNN (as our second left-based example) and New York Post (as our second right-based outlet) and Reuters (as the second least biased publisher) are presented in Figs. 12, 13 and 14. In contrast to the other biased example outlets, we observed both right-biased and left-biased articles published by New York Post.

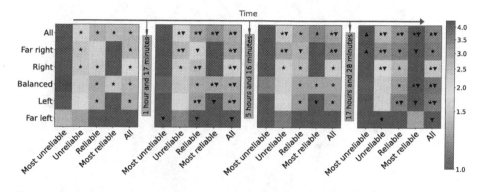

Fig. 11. Temporal dynamics of the total interactions covered for haha counts (⋆: coefficient of variation of the mean is smaller than 4%, ▲ and ▼: has deviation from the previous time bucket with p-value < 0.05).

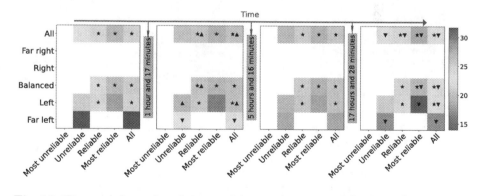

Fig. 12. Temporal dynamics of the total interactions covered for CNN (⋆: coefficient of variation of the mean is smaller than 4%, ▲ and ▼: has deviation from the previous time bucket with p-value < 0.05).

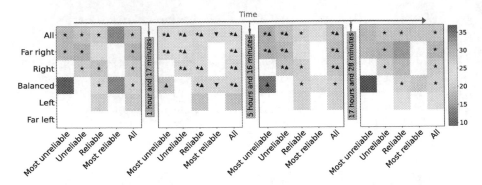

Fig. 13. Temporal dynamics of the total interactions covered for The New York Post (⋆: coefficient of variation of the mean is smaller than 4%, ▲ and ▼: has deviation from the previous time bucket with p-value < 0.05).

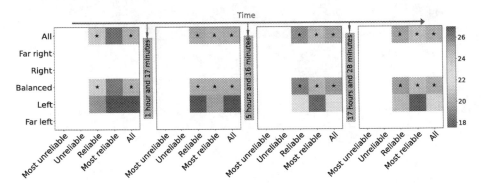

Fig. 14. Temporal dynamics of the total interactions covered for Reuters (⋆: coefficient of variation of the mean is smaller than 4%, ▲ and ▼: has deviation from the previous time bucket with p-value < 0.05).

References

1. Aldous, K.K., An, J., Jansen, B.J.: What really matters?: characterising and predicting user engagement of news postings using multiple platforms, sentiments and topics. Behaviour & Information Technology, pp. 1–24 (2022)
2. Allcott, H., Gentzkow, M., Yu, C.: Trends in the diffusion of misinformation on social media. Res. Polit. **6**(2), 205316801984855 (2019). https://doi.org/10.1177/2053168019848554
3. Barfar, A.: Cognitive and affective responses to political disinformation in Facebook. Comput. Human Behav. **101**, 173–179 (2019). https://doi.org/10.1016/j.chb.2019.07.026
4. Edelson, L., Nguyen, M.K., Goldstein, I., Goga, O., McCoy, D., Lauinger, T.: Understanding engagement with U.S. (mis)information news sources on Facebook. In: Proceedings of the ACM SIGCOMM Internet Measurement Conference, IMC, pp. 444–463 (2021). https://doi.org/10.1145/3487552.3487859

5. Elena: what data is CrowdTangle tracking? https://help.crowdtangle.com/en/articles/1140930-what-data-is-crowdtangle-tracking (2021)
6. Elena: crowdtangle-about us. https://help.crowdtangle.com/en/articles/4201940-about-us (2022)
7. Ferrara, E., Interdonato, R., Tagarelli, A.: Online popularity and topical interests through the lens of Instagram. In: Proceedings of the 25th ACM conference on Hypertext and social media, pp. 24–34 (2014)
8. Ferreira, C.H., et al.: On the dynamics of political discussions on Instagram: a network perspective. Online Soc. Netw. Media **25**(2020), 100155 (2021). https://doi.org/10.1016/j.osnem.2021.100155
9. Gallup and knight foundation: Americans views 2020: trust, media and democracy. a deepening divide. Tech. rep., Knight Foundation (2020). https://knightfoundation.org/reports/american-views-2020-trust-media-and-democracy/
10. Karami, M., Nazer, T.H., Liu, H.: Profiling fake news spreaders on social media through psychological and motivational factors. In: Proceedings of the 32nd ACM Conference on Hypertext and Social Media, pp. 225–230 (2021)
11. Kubin, E., von Sikorski, C.: The role of (social) media in political polarization: a systematic review. Ann. Int. Commun. Assoc. **45**(3), 188–206 (2021)
12. Metzger, M.J., Flanagin, A.J., Mena, P., Jiang, S., Wilson, C.: From dark to light: the many shades of sharing misinformation online. Media Commun. **9**(1), 134–143 (2021)
13. Mitra, T., Gilbert, E.: CREDBANK: a large-scale social media corpus with associated credibility annotations. In: Proceedings of the 9th International Conference on Web and Social Media, ICWSM 2015, pp. 258–267 (2015)
14. Otero, V.: Ad fontes media's multi-analyst content analysis white paper (2021). https://adfontesmedia.com/white-paper-2021
15. Otero, V.: Ad Fontes media's multi-analyst content analysis white paper (2021). https://adfontesmedia.com/white-paper-2021
16. Shearer, E.: 86% of Americans get news online from smartphone, computer or tablet | Pew Research Center (2021). https://www.pewresearch.org/fact-tank/2021/01/12/more-than-eight-in-ten-americans-get-news-from-digital-devices/
17. statista: most popular social networks worldwide. https://www.statista.com/statistics/272014/global-social-networks-ranked-by-number-of-users (2022)
18. Trevisan, M., Vassio, L., Giordano, D.: Debate on online social networks at the time of COVID-19: an Italian case study. Online Soc. Netw. Media **23**(April), 100136 (2021). https://doi.org/10.1016/j.osnem.2021.100136
19. Vassio, L., Garetto, M., Chiasserini, C., Leonardi, E.: Temporal dynamics of posts and user engagement of influencers on Facebook and Instagram. In: Proceedings of the 2021 IEEE/ACM International Conference on Advances in Social Networks Analysis and Mining, pp. 129–133 (2021)
20. Vosoughi, S., Roy, D., Aral, S.: The spread of true and false news online. Science **359**(6380), 1146–1151 (2018). https://doi.org/10.1126/science.aap9559
21. Weld, G., Glenski, M., Althoff, T.: Political bias and factualness in news sharing across more than 100,000 online communities. In: Proceedings of the International AAAI Conference on Web and Social Media, vol. 15, pp. 796–807 (2021)
22. Wischnewski, M., Bruns, A., Keller, T.: Shareworthiness and motivated reasoning in hyper-partisan news sharing behavior on Twitter. Digit. Journal. **9**(5), 549–570 (2021). https://doi.org/10.1080/21670811.2021.1903960

Measurement Tools

Efficient Continuous Latency Monitoring with eBPF

Simon Sundberg[1]([⊠]) [iD], Anna Brunstrom[1] [iD], Simone Ferlin-Reiter[1,2] [iD],
Toke Høiland-Jørgensen[3] [iD], and Jesper Dangaard Brouer[3]

[1] Karlstad University, Karlstad, Sweden
{simon.sundberg,anna.brunstrom}@kau.se
[2] Red Hat, Stockholm, Sweden
sferlinr@redhat.com
[3] Red Hat, Copenhagen, Denmark
{toke,brouer}@redhat.com

Abstract. Network latency is a critical factor for the perceived quality of experience for many applications. With an increasing focus on interactive and real-time applications, which require reliable and low latency, the ability to continuously and efficiently monitor latency is becoming more important than ever. Always-on passive monitoring of latency can provide continuous latency metrics without injecting any traffic into the network. However, software-based monitoring tools often struggle to keep up with traffic as packet rates increase, especially on contemporary multi-Gbps interfaces. We investigate the feasibility of using eBPF to enable efficient passive network latency monitoring by implementing an evolved Passive Ping (ePPing). Our evaluation shows that ePPing delivers accurate RTT measurements and can handle over 1 Mpps, or correspondingly over 10 Gbps, on a single core, greatly improving on state-of-the-art software based solutions, such as PPing.

Keywords: Passive monitoring · Network latency · eBPF

1 Introduction

That network latency is an important factor of network performance has long been known [8]. Various studies have shown that users' Quality of Experience (QoE) for many different applications, such as web searches [3], live video [32] and video games [31], is strongly related to end-to-end latency, where network latency can be a major component. For highly interactive applications envisioned for the Tactile Internet or Augmented and Virtual Reality (AR/VR), reliable low latency will be even more crucial [24]. It is therefore of great interest to Internet Service Providers (ISPs) to be able to monitor their customers' network latency at large. Furthermore, network latency monitoring has a wide range of other use cases like: verifying Service Level Agreements (SLAs), finding and troubleshooting network issues such as bufferbloat [28], making routing decisions [34], IP geolocation [12] and detecting IP spoofing [18] and BGP routing attacks [4].

A. Brunstrom et al. (Eds.): PAM 2023, LNCS 13882, pp. 191–208, 2023.
https://doi.org/10.1007/978-3-031-28486-1_9

There exists many tools for actively measuring network latency by sending out network probes, such as `ping` [16], IRTT [11], and RIPE Atlas [22]. While active monitoring is useful for measuring connectivity and idle network latency in a controlled manner, it is unable to directly infer the latency application traffic experience. The network probes may be treated differently from application traffic by the network, due to for example active queue management and load balancing, and therefore their latency may also differ. Furthermore, many active monitoring tools require agents to be deployed directly on the monitored target, which is not feasible for an ISP wishing to monitor the latency of its customers.

Passive monitoring techniques avoid these issues by observing existing application traffic instead of probing the network. Additionally, passive monitoring can often run on any device on the path that sees the traffic, not limited to end hosts. Several tools for passively inferring TCP round trip times (RTTs) already exist: `Tcptrace` [25] can compute TCP RTTs from packet traces, but is unable to operate on live traffic. `Wireshark` and the related `tshark` [9] can operate on live traffic, but are unsuitable for continuous monitoring over longer periods of time, due to keeping a record of all packets in memory. On the other hand, `PPing` [21] uses a streaming algorithm, which allows for continuous monitoring of live traffic. However, like most other software based passive network monitoring solutions, `PPing` relies on traditional packet capturing techniques such as `libpcap`. Packet capturing imposes a high overhead and is unable to keep up with the high packet rates encountered on modern network links [17].

To enable passive network monitoring at higher packet rates, several recent works [7,10,23,35] propose solutions based on P4 [6]. While these P4-based solutions can achieve high performance, they require hardware support for P4, commonly found in Tofino switches. It could be possible to modify such P4 programs to compile with Data Plane Development Kit (DPDK), however, this would compromise on the guaranteed performance provided by the hardware. Beyond DPDK and P4, there are many more Linux devices relying on kernel network stacks that could still benefit from monitoring network latency. Examples include commodity web servers, routers, traffic shapers and Network Intrusion Detection Systems (NIDS), which use the Linux network stack for their normal operation.

In recent years, the introduction of eBPF [29] in the Linux kernel added the ability to attach small programs to various hooks that run in the kernel. This makes it possible to inspect and modify kernel behavior in a safe and performant manner, without having to recompile a custom kernel. eBPF is in general well suited for monitoring processes in the kernel, and the BPF Compiler Collection (BCC) repository already contains two tools to passively monitor TCP RTT: `tcpconnlat` and `tcprtt`. While these tools expose RTT metrics in an efficient manner, they rely on the RTT estimations from the kernel's own TCP stack, and can therefore only run on end hosts.

While retrieving statistics from the kernel certainly has its uses, Linux Traffic Controller (tc) BPF and eXpress Data Path (XDP) [13] hooks go a step further and essentially enable a programmable data plane in the Linux kernel [30]. eBPF programs attached to tc and XDP hooks can process and take actions on each packet early in the Linux network stack, without the overhead from cloning the packet and exposing it to a user space process like packet capturing does. XDP and tc-BPF have been used to implement for example efficient flow monitoring [1], load balancers [19] and a Kubernetes Container Network Interface (CNI) [14]. Of particular relevance for this work, [33] proposes an in-band network telemetry approach for measuring one-way latency. It uses eBPF to add timestamps to a fraction of the packet headers. However, this approach requires full control over the part of the network that should be monitored as well as synchronized clocks between source and sink nodes.

In this paper we instead propose using eBPF to efficiently inspect packets and use a streaming algorithm, such as the one used by PPing, to calculate the RTT for the packets as they traverse the kernel. Such a solution can continuously monitor network latency from any Linux-based device that is able to see the traffic in both directions of a flow. Also, our proposal does not require the control of any other device in the network or end hosts. Furthermore, it avoids the overhead of packet capturing, and it does not require any modifications to the Linux kernel or special hardware support. To show the feasibility of this approach, we make the following contributions:

- We implement an evolved Passive Ping (ePPing), inspired by PPing, but using eBPF instead of traditional packet capturing.
- We evaluate the accuracy and overhead of ePPing, demonstrating that it provides accurate RTTs and can operate at high packet rates with considerably lower overhead than PPing, being able to process upwards of 16x as many packets at a third of the CPU overhead.
- We identify that reporting a large number of RTT values makes up a significant part of the overhead of ePPing, and implement simple in-kernel sampling and aggregation to mitigate it.

The design and implementation of ePPing is covered in Sect. 2, while the accuracy and performance of ePPing is evaluated in Sect. 3. Finally, we summarize our conclusions in Sect. 4.

Ethical Considerations This work does not raise any ethical issues as all experiments have been performed in a controlled testbed with no real user traffic. However, the presented ePPing tool reports IP addresses and ports, which in other contexts may contain sensitive information. Like any tool that can collect and report IP addresses, great care should therefore be taken to ensure that such information does not leak to unauthorized parties before deploying ePPing in a public network.

2   Design and Implementation

The principle behind ePPing and most other passive latency monitoring tools is to match replies to previously observed packets and to calculate the RTT as the time difference between these. How `ePPing` performs this task is illustrated in Fig. 1. First, each incoming or outgoing packet is parsed for a packet-identifier that can be used to match the packet against a future reply ①. If such an identifier is found, the current time is saved in a hash map using a combination of the flow tuple and the identifier as a key to uniquely identify the packet ②. Then the program checks if the packet contains a suitable reply identifier, which it can use to match with a previously seen packet in the reverse direction, and queries the hash map ③. If a match is found, the RTT is calculated by subtracting the stored timestamp from the current time ④. Finally, the RTT report is pushed to user space ⑤, which prints it out ⑥. Additionally, `ePPing` also keeps track of some state for each flow, e.g., number of packets sent and minimum RTT observed.

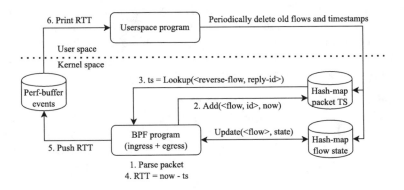

Fig. 1. Overview of ePPing design.

Both `ePPing` and `PPing` use the TCP timestamp option [5] as identifiers. With TCP timestamps, each TCP header will contain two timestamps: TSval and TSecr. The TSval field will contain a timestamp from the sender, and the receiver will then echo that timestamp back in the TSecr field. One can thus use the TSval value as an identifier for an observed packet and later match it against the TSecr value in a reply. It should be noted that TCP timestamps are updated at a limited frequency, typically once every millisecond. Thus, multiple consecutive packets may share the same TSval, which is therefore, especially at high rates, not a reliable unique identifier. To avoid mismatching replies to packets and getting underestimated RTTs, we only timestamp the first packet for each unique TSval in a flow and match it against the first TSecr echoing it. By only using the edge when TCP timestamps shift, the frequency rather than the accuracy of the RTT samples is limited to the update rate of TCP timestamps. Note that matching the first instance of a TSval against the first matching TSecr, combined with the algorithm for how the receiver sets the TSecr, means that the calculated RTT will always include a delay component of delayed ACKs [5]. We further discuss the implications of using TCP timestamps as identifiers to passively monitor the RTT in Appendix A.

Although primarily designed for TCP traffic, the fundamental mechanism ePPing is based on, to match replies of previously timestamped packets, is not limited to TCP. As a way to demonstrate this possibility, we have also implemented support for ICMP echo request sequence numbers as identifiers. This means that ePPing can also passively monitor latency for common ping utilities. Other possible extensions for future work include the DNS transaction ID [20] or the QUIC spin bit [15].

While the underlying logic for passively calculating RTTs is very similar between ePPing and PPing, the main difference between them is where this logic runs, i.e., how it is implemented. PPing is a user space application and relies on traditional packet capturing, i.e., copying packets from kernel to user space. Once copied to user space, PPing can parse the packet headers to retrieve the necessary packet identifiers, e.g., the TCP timestamps. In contrast, ePPing implements most of its logic in eBPF programs running in kernel space, as shown by Fig. 1. By attaching its eBPF programs to the tc-BPF and XDP hooks, ePPing can parse packet headers directly from the kernel buffers, without any copying. The logic for parsing and timestamping packets, matching replies and calculating RTTs is implemented in the eBPF programs. The user space component is only responsible for loading and attaching the eBPF programs, printing out RTTs pushed by the eBPF programs, and periodically flushing stale entries in the hash maps.

Therefore, by moving most of the logic to kernel space and thereby avoiding the costly packet capturing and related copying of packets, ePPing is able to operate with lower overhead, significantly outperforming PPing at high packet rates. ePPing is available as open source [27], and the exact build used in this work together with the experiment scripts and measurement data is archived at [26].

3   Results

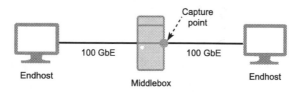

Fig. 2. Testbed setup.

To evaluate ePPing, we run a number of experiments to evaluate the accuracy of the reported RTT values as well as the runtime overhead. All experiments are performed on a testbed setup as depicted in Fig. 2. The testbed consists of two end hosts (Intel i7 7700, 16 GB RAM, kernel 5.16) connected via 100 Gbps links to a middlebox (Intel Xeon E5-1650, 32 GB RAM, kernel 5.19), which forwards traffic between the end hosts. In all experiments, the (partial) RTT between the middlebox and receiver end host is passively monitored from the interface on the middlebox facing the receiver, unless otherwise specified.

The network offloads Generic Receive Offload (GRO), Generic Segmentation Offload (GSO) and TCP Segmentation Offload (TSO) are disabled on the middlebox, but left enabled on the end hosts. With this, we force the middlebox to process every packet. This is not necessary for PPing or ePPing, however, it provides a more accurate view of how packets traverse the wire. Furthermore, disabling the offloads makes it easier to fairly compare performance across a varying amount of concurrent flows, as the offloads tend to become less effective as the rate per flow decreases. With the offloads left enabled, the middlebox would have inherently performed much better for a few flows with very high packet rates compared to if the same packet rate is distributed across many flows, even without passive monitoring.

Section 3.1 focuses on the accuracy of the RTTs reported by ePPing by comparing them to the RTTs reported by PPing, which also relies on TCP timestamps, and tshark, which instead calculates the RTTs from the sequence and acknowledgement numbers. Section 3.2 covers the overhead ePPing incurs on the system compared to PPing, thereby evaluating if implementing a similar algorithm in eBPF programs instead of relying on packet capturing is a feasible way to extend passive latency monitoring to higher packet rates.

3.1 RTT Accuracy

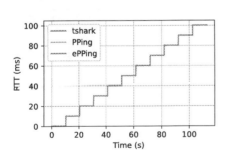

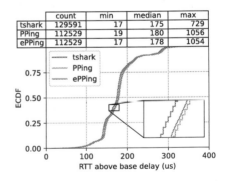

(a) RTTs reported over the duration of the test.

(b) The distribution of RTTs after subtracting configured delay.

Fig. 3. RTT values reported by tshark, PPing and ePPing for a single TCP flow with 0 to 100 ms of additional latency added in 10 ms steps.

To evaluate the accuracy of the RTT values ePPing reports, we use iperf3 to send data at a paced rate of 100 Mbps over a single flow from the sender to the receiver end host. To test that ePPing is able to accurately track changes in RTT, we apply a fixed netem delay, which is increased in 10 ms steps every 10 s, going from 0 to 100 ms, see Fig. 3a. In addition to running ePPing at the capture point, we capture the headers of all packets by running tcpdump on the same interface. PPing, tshark and tcptrace calculate the TCP RTT values from the capture file, but tcptrace is omitted from the results as it yields identical RTT values as tshark. To avoid small latency variations from the CPU aggressively entering different sleep states, we use the tuned-adm profile *latency-performance* on the middlebox during these tests.

Figure 3a shows a timeseries of the RTT values calculated by each tool. All tools provide RTT values closely following the configured netem delay. Figure 3b instead shows the distribution of how much higher the reported RTT values are compared to the configured netem delay, to avoid the scale of RTT values to dwarf the variation. However, in both Figs. 3a and 3b the magnitude of the RTT values and their variation are much larger than the differences between the tools. Therefore, Fig. 4 shows the pairwise difference between each RTT value for ePPing compared to PPing and tshark, respectively. Note that tshark reports an RTT value for every ACK, whereas PPing and ePPing only produce an RTT for ACKs with a new TSecr value, thus providing 13 % fewer RTT samples than tshark in this experiment (see the count field in Fig. 3b). Therefore, Fig. 4b only includes the RTT values from tshark that correspond to those from PPing and ePPing, i.e. the ones from the first ACK with each TSecr value. Furthermore, differences below 1 μs may be due to rounding as the RTT values from tshark and PPing have microsecond resolution.

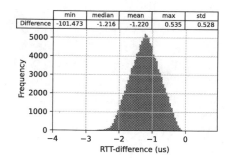

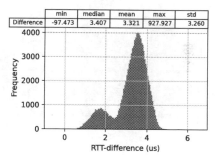

(a) Difference between ePPing and PPing.   (b) Difference between ePPing and tshark.

Fig. 4. Pairwise difference between RTT values reported by ePPing compared to other tools.

Overall, ePPing reports slightly lower RTT values than PPing. This is expected as the XDP hook used by ePPing for ingress traffic is triggered before the packet enters the rest of the Linux network stack, and can be captured by tcpdump. On the other hand, ePPing provides RTT values that are around 1 to 5 μs higher than those from tshark, which is explained by tshark calculating the RTT in a different way. Both PPing and ePPing use TCP timestamps, and will therefore always include the additional latency caused by delayed ACKs. Meanwhile, `tshark` instead matches sequence and acknowledgement numbers, which will often exclude this delay component. We have verified that the differences between `ePPing` and `tshark` correspond to the additional latency component from delayed ACKs. While the difference in how delayed ACKs are handled result in very small differences in Fig. 4b, it can create larger differences for some particular traffic patterns. In Appendix A we further discuss how relying on TCP timestamps affect the calculated RTT values.

3.2   Monitoring Overhead

The motivation behind implementing `ePPing` in eBPF was to reduce overhead and thus allow it to work at higher packet rates. Therefore, we measure what impact `ePPing` has on the forwarding performance when running on a machine that is under high packet processing load. This is done by measuring the throughput `iperf3` is able to achieve when sending TCP traffic from the sender to the receiver end host. The test is first performed without any passive monitoring on the middlebox to establish a baseline, and is then repeated with either `ePPing` or `PPing` running at the capture point. We run each test 10 times for 120 s, but discard the results from the first 20 s as a warm-up phase to let cache usage and CPU frequency scaling stabilize. We then repeat the tests using 1, 10, 100 or 1000 TCP flows to evaluate how performance is affected by the number of flows.

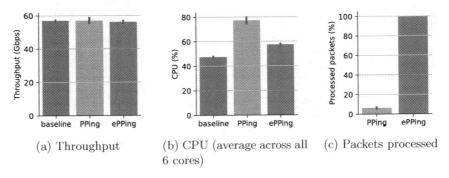

(a) Throughput   (b) CPU (average across all   (c) Packets processed
                              6 cores)

Fig. 5. Forwarding performance without monitoring (baseline), with PPing and with ePPing for 10 concurrent `iperf3` flows, when middlebox uses all CPU cores.

Figure 5 shows the performance that is achieved with 10 concurrent flows, which is when the end hosts are able to push the traffic at the highest rate in our experiments. While Fig. 5a shows that neither `PPing` or `ePPing` has a considerable impact on the forwarding throughput, Fig. 5b shows that `ePPing` has much lower CPU overhead. With a baseline utilization of 47 %, `ePPing` only increases it to 57 %, while `PPing` increases it all the way to 77 %. Meanwhile, Fig. 5c shows that despite `PPing` having roughly 3 times higher CPU overhead than ePPing, PPing is actually only processing just over 6 % of the packets. This is due to the packet capturing being unable to keep up with the high packet rate, and therefore missing the majority of the packets. In contrast, ePPing runs in line with the rest of the network stack, and sees every packet, meaning it processes roughly 16 times as many packets. While not apparent from Fig. 5, also note that PPing is implemented as a single-threaded user space application, and is therefore limited to how fast a single core can process all the logic. While the user space component reporting the RTT values in ePPing is also single-threaded, the eBPF programs that contain the logic for calculating the RTT values run on the cores that the kernel assigns to process each packet, thus distributing the load across multiple cores in the same manner as the normal network stack processing.

Table 1. Average packets per second processed on single core at capture point when only forwarding (baseline scenario).

No. flows	Packet rate (Mpps)		
	Tx	Rx	Total
1	1.86	0.04	1.90
10	1.86	0.09	1.95
100	1.72	0.21	1.92
1000	1.64	0.29	1.93

Although the results in Fig. 5 are promising, the end hosts are usually the bottleneck here, especially as we increase the number of flows. These experiments are consequently unable to push the middlebox and ePPing to their limits. We therefore constrain the middlebox to using a single CPU core in the remaining experiments, moving the bottleneck to the middlebox CPU. This means that the middlebox is already using all of its CPU capacity just forwarding the traffic, and any additional overhead from the passive monitoring results in decreased throughput. Furthermore, we emphasize the total packet rate (sum of transmitted and received packets) rather than the throughput. Packet rate is more relevant for the performance of PPing and ePPing, as their logic has to run per packet, and also stays more consistent across a varying number of flows as Table 1 shows. As the number of flows increases, the number of ACKs sent back by the receiver increases (seen by the increase in received packets at the middlebox). This results in less capacity to forward data packets by the middlebox (decrease in transmitted packets), and thereby a lower throughput, while the total packet rate handled remains similar.

Figure 6a summarizes the impact PPing and ePPing have on the forwarding performance of the middlebox when it is constrained to a single core. Both ePPing and PPing now have a considerable impact on the forwarding performance, but ePPing clearly sustains a higher packet rate than PPing, at least at a limited number of flows. As the number of flows increases, the packet rate with ePPing drops from 1.53 to 1.13 Mpps. The reason for this drop in performance as the number of flows increases is that, due to the limited update rate of TCP timestamps, the number of potential RTT samples that ePPing has to process increases with number of flows. This is evident in Fig. 6b, which shows that while ePPing reports the expected 1000 RTT values per second for a single flow, at 1000 flows this increases to roughly 125,000 values per second.

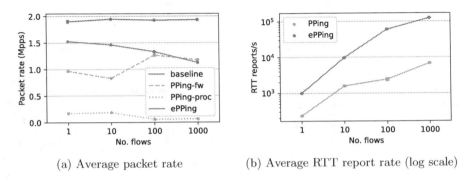

(a) Average packet rate   (b) Average RTT report rate (log scale)

Fig. 6. Middlebox performance when just forwarding (baseline), with PPing or ePPing on a single CPU core. PPing misses most packets and thus processes (PPing-proc) packets at a much lower rate than they are forwarded (PPing-fw).

Meanwhile, the forwarded packet rate with PPing actually appears to increase slightly with number of flows (0.97 Mpps at one flow, 1.18 Mpps at 1000 flows), but this is merely due to the packet capturing missing a larger fraction of packets. The packet rate actually handled by PPing drops from approximately 170 kpps at 1 and 10 flows, to just 60 kpps at 100 and 1000 flows, meaning ePPing processes packets at approximately an 18 times higher rate than PPing at 1000 flows. PPing missing the majority of packets results in it also missing many RTT samples, which can be seen by the much fewer RTT values reported by PPing in Fig. 6b. Furthermore, the algorithm for matching packets to replies that PPing and ePPing uses, relies on matching the first instance of each TSval to the first matching TSecr. As PPing does not see every packet, it cannot guarantee this, and it may therefore introduce small errors in its RTT values.

However, limiting the load by sampling, as PPing in practice does by missing packets, can be a valid approach. The high rate of RTT values reported by ePPing may not be necessary, or even desirable, for many use cases. We therefore implement sampling for ePPing, and evaluate if it can be an effective way to reduce the overhead. While it would be possible to only process a random subset of the packets, similar to PPing, such an approach has several drawbacks. As already mentioned, missing packets may interfere with the algorithm for matching packets and replies, thus resulting in less accurate RTT values. Furthermore, a random subset of packets is likely to mainly yield RTT samples from elephant flows, and largely miss sparse flows. However, sparse flows often carry control traffic and other latency sensitive data, and being able to monitor their RTT may therefore be at least as important as the RTT of the elephant flows. Instead of eliminating ePPing's advantage of being guaranteed to see every packet, we opt to implement a simple per-flow sample rate limit. With the sample rate limit, ePPing must wait a time period t after saving a timestamp entry for a packet before it can timestamp another packet from the same flow. This t may either be set to a static value, or it can be dynamically adjusted to the RTT of each flow, so that flows with shorter RTTs get more frequent samples than flows with longer RTTs.

We repeat the experiments from Fig. 6, setting the sample limit t to 0, 10, 100 and 1000 ms, in practice corresponding to at most 1000, 100, 10 and 1 RTT values per flow and second, respectively. Figure 7a summarizes the results, and clearly shows that less frequent sampling greatly reduces the overhead of ePPing. Already at a sample limit of 10 ms we see great improvements. When limiting it to a single sample every 1000 ms per flow (the default rate of ping), ePPing is able to sustain a packet rate of 1.54 Mpps for 1000 flows, compared to 1.14 Mpps without sampling. The drop in forwarding performance when going from 1 to 1000 flows thus decreases from 27 % without sampling, to just 1.6 % at $t = 1000$ ms. The drawback of such coarse sampling is that the granularity of the monitoring is reduced, and one might miss important RTT variations.

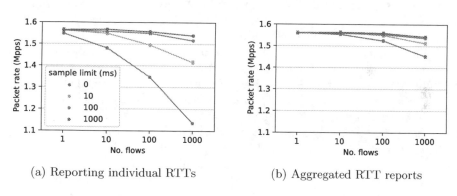

(a) Reporting individual RTTs   (b) Aggregated RTT reports

Fig. 7. Impact of different levels of per-flow sample limiting and aggregation. Note that the Y-axis does not start at 0.

As an alternative approach to sampling, aggregation can be used to reduce the overhead from frequent RTT reports. We therefore also implement a bare bones aggregation functionality to evaluate the feasibility of aggregating the RTT values directly in the kernel. When aggregation is enabled, the eBPF programs add each RTT value to a global histogram in a BPF map, instead of sending every RTT value directly to user space. Additionally, the minimum and maximum RTTs are tracked. The user space then pulls the aggregated RTT statistics once per second and prints them out. Figure 7b shows the results when repeating the experiment in Fig. 7a using the aggregation. As can be expected, with a high sample limit, and consequently few RTT values to aggregate, the aggregation yields a very modest improvement. However, for smaller sample limits the aggregation becomes more beneficial. In the scenario without any sampling, the aggregation increases the packet rate at 1000 flows from 1.14 to 1.45 Mpps. By combining sampling and aggregation, we therefore expect ePPing to be able to maintain a high level of performance, while still providing useful RTT metrics, at significantly more than 1000 concurrent flows. Due to limitations with the current testbed, we are however unable to validate performance beyond 1000 flows.

4   Conclusion

In this paper we propose using eBPF to passively monitor network latency, and demonstrate the feasibility of this by implementing evolved Passive Ping (ePPing). By using eBPF, ePPing is able to efficiently observe packets as they pass through the Linux network stack without the overhead associated with packet capturing. It does not require any modifications to the kernel or replacing the network stack with DPDK, nor any special hardware support. Our evaluation shows that ePPing delivers accurate RTTs and has much lower overhead than PPing, being able to handle over 1 Mpps on a single core, corresponding to more than 10 Gbps of throughput. We also demonstrate that sampling and aggregation of RTT values in the kernel can be used to further reduce the overhead from handling a large amount of RTT samples.

While ePPing overall performs well in our experiments, our evaluation is heavily based on bulk TCP flows generated by iperf3. In future work we intend to evaluate how ePPing fares with a more realistic workload by using traffic from an ISP vantage point. Another important aspect to consider is what impact the passive monitoring has on end-to-end latency. We are currently working on better understanding ePPing's impact on end-to-end latency. Preliminary findings indicate that while ePPing only adds a couple of hundred nanoseconds of processing latency to each packet (99th percentile of approximately 350 ns), it may under certain scenarios increase end-to-end latency by hundreds of microseconds.

Furthermore, our current implementation of ePPing has some limitations. Limitations inherent to using TCP timestamps are further discussed in Appendix A, with one of the primary ones being the lack of ability to monitor flows where TCP timestamps are not enabled. Some of the these limitations could be avoided by using sequence and acknowledgement numbers instead, although that has its own set of limitations. We are also considering adding support for other protocols, such as DNS and QUIC. Additionally, the sampling and aggregation methods we employ in this work are relatively simple, and we are working on more sophisticated ways to sample, filter and aggregate RTTs in-kernel to provide enhanced RTT metrics while maintaining low overhead.

A Effects of Using TCP Timestamps to Infer RTT

As briefly explained in Sect. 3.1, using TCP timestamps to match packets to their corresponding ACKs may yield slightly different RTTs than when matching sequence and ACK numbers. We here discuss these differences in further detail, covering the pros and cons of each approach to passively monitor network latency.

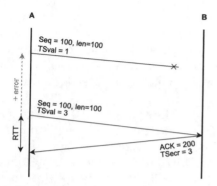 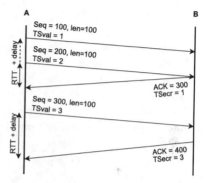

(a) Retransmission. Sequence and acknowledgement matching suffer from the retransmission ambiguity, which may cause a large over- or underestimation of the RTT. TCP timestamps can separate the original from the retransmitted packet and do therefore not have the ambiguity.

(b) Delayed ACK. TCP timestamps will always calculate the RTT between the first packet being ACKed and the ACK, always including the additional latency from a delayed ACK. Matching sequence and acknowledgement numbers will only include the additional latency if the delayed ACK was triggered by a timeout.

Fig. 8. TCP timestamps and sequence and ACK numbers: Differences.

The decision to use TCP timestamps for `ePPing` was mainly based on having a simple algorithm that avoids the TCP transmission ambiguity. As illustrated in Fig. 8a, retransmissions can cause approaches that match sequence and ACK numbers to greatly overestimate or underestimate the RTT, unless they also detect retransmissions to filter out such spurious RTT samples. However, for TCP timestamps, the retransmission will typically have a newer TSval, and, therefore, no additional precautions are needed to calculate a correct RTT.

if $SEG.TSval \geq TS.Recent$ **and** $SEG.SEQ \leq Last.ACK.sent$ **then**
$\quad | \quad TS.Recent \leftarrow SEG.TSval;$
end
Algorithm 1: RFC 7323 algorithm for how to update $TS.Recent$, which is copied into the TSecr field when an ACK is sent.

Due to how TSecr is updated, TCP timestamps also handle delayed ACKs a bit differently compared to sequence and ACK number matching: The echoed TSecr value is not necessarily the latest TSval. Rather, RFC 7323 [5] specifies that TSecr should be set to a recent Tsval, which is updated according to Algorithm 1, and essentially results in TSecr being set to the TSval from the oldest in-order unacknowledged segment. The effect of this is that RTTs based on TCP timestamps will, by design, always include the additional latency from delayed ACKs. On the other hand, matching sequence and ACK numbers will only include the delayed ACK if it is triggered by a timeout, as shown in Fig. 8b. Consequently, matching sequence and ACK numbers will usually result in RTTs that are a bit closer to the underlying network latency, whereas using TCP timestamps will result in RTTs more similar to those experienced by the TCP stack. Both methods are, however, prone to include RTT spikes caused by delayed ACKs timing out.

There are also two noteworthy drawbacks with relying on TCP timestamps: Firstly, TCP timestamps are optional, and ePPing can therefore only monitor TCP traffic with TCP timestamps enabled. A recent study [2] found that out of the most common operating systems (Android, iOS, Windows, MacOS and Linux), Windows was the only one not supporting TCP timestamps by default. A lot of traffic these days goes through mobile devices running Android and iOS, but Windows is still the dominant desktop OS, making this a noteworthy limitation. Secondly, the TCP timestamp update rate limits how frequently we can collect RTT samples within a flow. The study in [2] found that among servers for popular websites, the most common update rate was once per millisecond, which is what Linux uses since v4.13, but some updated at a slower rate of every 4 ms or every 10 ms. For most applications we deem that 1000–100 RTT samples per second per flow is plenty, but for very fine-grained analysis requiring an RTT sample for every ACK this could be problematic.

Furthermore, there are two edge cases in which matching TCP timestamps may result in slightly overestimating the RTT beyond the delayed ACK component: The first case is when a retransmission happens fast enough that the TSval is not updated from the original transmission. For example, consider if the retransmission in Fig. 8a would still use $TSval = 1$. This can only occur if the retransmission occurs faster than the TCP timestamp update rate, and may at most overestimate the RTT with the TCP timestamp update period. With TCP timestamps typically being updated every millisecond, this should be very rare in most environments outside of for example data center networks. The second case is when the TSval is updated during a delayed ACK and persists into packets being acknowledged by the next ACK. For example, consider if the third packet sent by A in Fig. 8b would still have $TSval = 2$. In that case, the RTT for the second ACK sent by B ($ACK = 400$) would incorrectly be calculated from the second packet sent by A ($Seq = 200$) instead of from the third packet sent by A ($Seq = 300$). This error can occur in the presence of delayed ACKs, and if multiple packets within a flow have the same TSval. Thus, this is also bounded to at most overestimate the RTT with one TCP timestamp period. This edge case is more likely to occur than retransmissions without updated timestamps, however, the magnitude of the error is still small compared to the spikes that can be caused by delayed ACKs.

Finally, Fig. 9 shows an example of how the different handling of delayed ACKs and overestimations due to the second edge case can impact RTTs based on TCP timestamps when compared to matching sequence and ACK numbers. Here, a modified version of the experiment from Fig. 4 is used, where the latency applied with `netem` is 50 ms and the traffic is sent in a burstier manner by using `iperf3`'s internal pacing at 50 ms intervals (-b 100M –pacing-timer 50000). Figure 9a shows the additional latency due to the handling of delayed ACKs, which is typically in the range between 0 to 100 μs, with three instances exceeding 1 ms, and one reaching 12.4 ms. Meanwhile, Fig. 9b shows the overestimation for the 582 out of the 5104 RTT samples where the second edge case occurs. These overestimations are of a similar scale as the difference due to delayed ACKs, although the maximum error is just under 1 ms. In contrast, both using TCP timestamps and matching sequence and ACK numbers result in a few RTT values of over 92 ms, exceeding the configured latency by over 40 ms, due to delayed ACKs timing out.

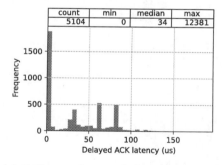 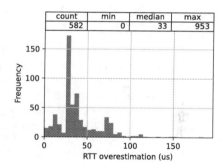

(a) Difference from including and excluding the additional latency component of delayed ACKs.

(b) Additional overestimation of RTT from TCP timestamps due to the second edge case.

Fig. 9. Difference between RTTs computed by matching TCP timestamps compared to sequence and acknowledgement numbers.

In summary, using TCP timestamps may result in slightly higher RTT values than matching sequence and ACK numbers, mainly due to different handling of delayed ACKs. While `ePPing` could be modified to instead operate on sequence and ACK numbers, it would then risk missing valid RTT samples, especially on lossy links, and would still capture the largest RTT spikes from delayed ACKs.

References

1. Abranches, M., Michel, O., Keller, E., Schmid, S.: Efficient network monitoring applications in the Kernel with eBPF and XDP. In: IEEE NFV-SDN 2021 (2021). https://doi.org/10.1109/NFV-SDN53031.2021.9665095
2. Barbette, T., Wu, E., Kostić, D., Maguire, G.Q., Papadimitratos, P., Chiesa, M.: Cheetah: A high-speed programmable load-balancer framework with guaranteed per-connection-consistency. IEEE/ACM Trans. Netw. **30**(1), 354–367 (2022). https://doi.org/10.1109/TNET.2021.3113370
3. Barreda-Ángeles, M., Arapakis, I., Bai, X., Cambazoglu, B.B., Pereda-Baños, A.: Unconscious physiological effects of search latency on users and their click behaviour. In: SIGIR 2015 (2015). https://doi.org/10.1145/2766462.2767719
4. Birge-Lee, H., Wang, L., Rexford, J., Mittal, P.: SICO: surgical interception attacks by manipulating BGP communities. In: CCS 2019 (2019). https://doi.org/10.1145/3319535.3363197
5. Borman, D., Braden, R.T., Jacobson, V., Scheffenegger, R.: TCP Extensions for High Performance. Technical report. RFC 7323, Section 3, Internet Engineering Task Force (2014). https://doi.org/10.17487/RFC7323
6. Bosshart, P., et al.: P4: programming protocol-independent packet processors. SIGCOMM Comput. Commun. Rev. **44**(3), 87–95 (2014). https://doi.org/10.1145/2656877.2656890
7. Chen, X., Kim, H., Aman, J.M., Chang, W., Lee, M., Rexford, J.: Measuring TCP round-trip time in the data plane. In: SPIN 2020 (2020). https://doi.org/10.1145/3405669.3405823
8. Cheshire, S.: It's the Latency, Stupid (2001). http://www.stuartcheshire.org/rants/Latency.html. Accessed 07 May 2022
9. Combs, G.: Tshark (2022). https://www.wireshark.org/docs/man-pages/tshark.html. Accessed 17 May 2022
10. Ghasemi, M., Benson, T., Rexford, J.: Dapper: data plane performance diagnosis of TCP. In: SOSR 2017 (2017). https://doi.org/10.1145/3050220.3050228
11. Heist, P.: IRTT (Isochronous Round-Trip Tester) (2021). https://github.com/heistp/irtt. Accessed 31 Oct 2022
12. Hillmann, P., Stiemert, L., Rodosek, G.D., Rose, O.: Dragoon: advanced modelling of IP geolocation by use of latency measurements. In: ICITST 2015 (2015). https://doi.org/10.1109/ICITST.2015.7412138
13. Høiland-Jørgensen, T., et al.: The eXpress data path: Fast programmable packet processing in the operating system kernel. In: CoNEXT 2018 (2018). https://doi.org/10.1145/3281411.3281443
14. Isovalent: Cilium - Linux Native, API-Aware Networking and Security for Containers (nd). https://cilium.io. Accessed 21 Oct 2022
15. Iyengar, J., Thomson, M.: QUIC: A UDP-Based Multiplexed and Secure Transport. Technical report, RFC 9000, Section 17.4, Internet Engineering Task Force (2021). https://doi.org/10.17487/RFC9000
16. Kuznetsov, A., Yoshifuji, H.: Iputils (2022). https://github.com/iputils/iputils. Accessed 03 May 2022
17. Li, J., Wu, C., Ye, J., Ding, J., Fu, Q., Huang, J.: The comparison and verification of some efficient packet capture and processing technologies. In: DASC/PiCom/CBDCom/CyberSciTech 2019 (2019). https://doi.org/10.1109/DASC/PiCom/CBDCom/CyberSciTech.2019.00177

18. Maheshwari, R., Krishna, C.R., Brahma, M.S.: Defending network system against IP spoofing based distributed DoS attacks using DPHCF-RTT packet filtering technique. In: ICICT 2014 (2014). https://doi.org/10.1109/ICICICT.2014.6781280
19. Meta: Katran: A high performance layer 4 load balancer (2022). https://github.com/facebookincubator/katran. Accessed 21 Oct 2022
20. Mockapetris, P.: Domain names - implementation and specification. Technical report, RFC 1035, Section 4.1.1, Internet Engineering Task Force (1987). https://doi.org/10.17487/RFC1035
21. Nichols, K.: PPing: Passive ping network monitoring utility (2018). https://github.com/pollere/pping. Accessed 21 Sep 2021
22. RIPE NCC: Home—RIPE Atlas (nd). https://atlas.ripe.net/. Accessed 20 Oct 2022
23. Sengupta, S., Kim, H., Rexford, J.: Continuous in-network round-trip time monitoring. In: SIGCOMM 2022 (2022). https://doi.org/10.1145/3544216.3544222
24. Sharma, S., Woungang, I., Anpalagan, A., Chatzinotas, S.: Toward tactile internet in beyond 5G era: recent advances, current issues, and future directions. IEEE Access. **8**, 56948–56991 (2020). https://doi.org/10.1109/ACCESS.2020.2980369
25. Shawn Ostermann: Tcptrace (2013). https://github.com/blitz/tcptrace. Accessed 03 Apr 2022
26. Sundberg, S., Brunstrom, A., Ferlin-Reiter, S., Høiland-Jørgensen, T., Brouer, J.D.: Efficient continuous latency monitoring with eBPF - Resources (2023). https://doi.org/10.5281/zenodo.7555410
27. Sundberg, S., Høiland-Jørgensen, T.: BPF-examples: PPing using XDP and TC-BPF (2022). https://github.com/xdp-project/bpf-examples/tree/master/pping. Accessed 26 Jan 2023
28. The Bufferbloat community: Bufferbloat.net (nd). https://www.bufferbloat.net/projects/. Accessed 05 May 2022
29. The Linux Foundation: eBPF - Introduction, Tutorials & Community Resources (2021). https://ebpf.io/. Accessed 03 May 2022
30. Vieira, M.A.M., et al.: Fast packet processing with eBPF and XDP: concepts, code, challenges, and applications. ACM Comput. Surv. **53**(1), 1–36 (2020). https://doi.org/10.1145/3371038
31. Vlahovic, S., Suznjevic, M., Skorin-Kapov, L.: The impact of network latency on gaming QoE for an FPS VR game. In: QoMEX 2019 (2019). https://doi.org/10.1109/QoMEX.2019.8743193
32. Wang, H., Zhang, X., Chen, H., Xu, Y., Ma, Z.: Inferring end-to-end latency in live videos. IEEE Trans. Broadcast. **68**(2), 517–529 (2022). https://doi.org/10.1109/TBC.2021.3071060
33. Xhonneux, M., Duchene, F., Bonaventure, O.: Leveraging eBPF for programmable network functions with IPv6 segment routing. In: CoNEXT 2018 (2018). https://doi.org/10.1145/3281411.3281426
34. Zhao, Z., Gao, S., Dong, P.: Flexible routing strategy for low-latency transmission in software defined network. In: ICCBN 2021 (2021). https://doi.org/10.1145/3456415.3456444
35. Zheng, Y., Chen, X., Braverman, M., Rexford, J.: Unbiased delay measurement in the data plane. In: APOCS 2022 (2022). https://doi.org/10.1137/1.9781611977059.2

Back-to-the-Future Whois: An IP Address Attribution Service for Working with Historic Datasets

Florian Streibelt[1], Martina Lindorfer[2], Seda Gürses[3], Carlos H. Gañán[3], and Tobias Fiebig[1(✉)]

[1] Max Planck Institute for Informatics, Saarbrücken, Germany
{fstreibelt,tfiebig}@mpi-inf.mpg.de
[2] TU Wien, Vienna, Austria
martina.lindorfer@tuwien.ac.at
[3] TU Delft, Delft, The Netherlands
{f.s.gurses,c.hernandezganan}@tudelft.nl

Abstract. Researchers and practitioners often face the issue of having to attribute an IP address to an organization. For *current* data this is comparably easy, using services like whois or other databases. Similarly, for historic data, several entities like the RIPE NCC provide websites that provide access to historic records. For large-scale network measurement work, though, researchers often have to attribute millions of addresses. For *current* data, Team Cymru provides a bulk whois service which allows bulk address attribution. However, at the time of writing, there is no service available that allows *historic* bulk attribution of IP addresses. Hence, in this paper, we introduce and evaluate our 'Back-to-the-Future whois' service, allowing historic bulk attribution of IP addresses on a daily granularity based on CAIDA Routeviews aggregates. We provide this service to the community for free, and also share our implementation so researchers can run instances themselves.

1 Introduction

A common issue in the network measurement domain–but also in industry fields from Threat Intelligence to traffic engineering–is attributing an IPv4 or IPv6 address to an organization. While, technically, Regional-Internet-Registries (RIRs) allocate IP addresses to organizations [16], and provide a whois [7] infrastructure to make this information accessible, common whois interfaces are impractical for bulk requests. This is mostly due to whois providing unstructured text data, which has to be appropriately parsed [35]. Furthermore, organizations may have multiple organizational objects with overlapping and semantically equivalent data, which is not bit-equivalent or hides relationships due to subsidiaries from, e.g., different countries [4]. To address the needs of, especially, the threat hunting community, Team Cymru operates a bulk whois service, which allows users to bulk-request AS attribution for thousands of requests.

© The Author(s) 2023
A. Brunstrom et al. (Eds.): PAM 2023, LNCS 13882, pp. 209–226, 2023.
https://doi.org/10.1007/978-3-031-28486-1_10

However, when working with *historic* data-sets, sometimes ranging back decades, *current* whois information may be ill suited to correctly attribute IP addresses, especially in the wake of IPv4 exhaustion [27] and the accelerating IPv4 market [11,21,22,25]. Hence, in this paper, we introduce our historic whois service–Back-to-the-Future whois–which we implemented to address these challenges, leveraging the public CAIDA Routeviews aggregates [3,29]. Our service is publicly available to the community at bttf-whois.as59645.net port tcp/43. The service provides a historic address attribution service starting in May 2005 and for IPv4 and in January 2007 for IPv6. It can be queried using a simple syntax, and provides structured JSON output, see also the website at https://bttf-whois.as59645.net.

In summary, we make the following contributions in this paper:

- We introduce 'Back-to-the-Future whois' (BTTF whois) as a public service for the research community as a simple way to historic attribute IPs.
- We document our methodology, so researchers can independently distil historic IP attribution from Routeviews or the CAIDA aggregates.
- We evaluate BTTF whois' coverage over time on a case-study, and find BTTF to perform comparably to Team Cymru's bulk whois service on recent data, while outperforming it in accuracy for historic data.

Structure: First, we introduce the datasets we use and our methodology for BTTF whois in Sect. 2. Next, we evaluate BTTF whois against Team Cumry's bulk whois in a sample case. Finally, we first discuss our results and limitations in Sect. 4, before concluding in Sect. 5.

2   Dataset and Methodology

2.1   Utilized Data

CAIDA Data for BTTF Whois. The historic whois service leverages the aggregates of the RouteViews project compiled daily by CAIDA [3]. The dataset spans the time from May 2005 for IPv4 until today, and the time from January 2007 until today for IPv6, both with a daily resolution. We use aggregates computed by CAIDA instead of aggregating the routing tables provided by the RouteViews project [29] ourselves, as the RouteViews dataset is large (tenth of TB), and aggregation of this data is already a significant task in itself.

This prefix data alone is, however, insufficient to estimate a whois service based on routing data. Routing data only maps IP addresses to ASes that announced the prefix at a specific time. However, over time, ASes may change the organization they are allocated to. Furthermore, we may find ASes that announce prefixes which are not registered to the announcing AS' organization, see for example Cogent announcing various customer prefixes,[1] see also Sect. 4.2.

We address the issue of tying ASes to organizations by leveraging the AS2ORG dataset, also published by CAIDA [4,12]. The AS2ORG dataset covers

---

[1] https://bgp.tools/as/174#prefixes.

the period from April 2004 up until today, with a quarterly resolution. However, this reduced resolution will lead to a reduced reliability of the AS2ORG mappings, meaning that changes of ownership/authority over an AS may be reflected up to three months too late, while temporary changes of a duration less than three months may remain completely unnoticed, see Sect. 4.2.

Case-Study Research Data. To evaluate BTTF whois, we have to compare its efficacy against a 'current' whois extract on a historic IP address dataset, where we can also investigate the impact of BTTF whois on the analysis results. For this purpose, we use a study by Fiebig et al. on the cloudification of universities [10]. In their study they utilize the Farsight SIE DNS Dataset [8] – specifically the A, AAAA, and CNAME records in the dataset – from January 2015 to October 2022, to identify where universities' services are hosted. The Farsight SIE dataset provides a *historic* perspective on the IP addresses, names, and services under universities' domains. For example: Finding www.example.com. IN A 198.51.100.23 from January 2015 to April 2021 would indicate that the services was hosted in TEST-NET-2 then. Finding only www.example.com. IN A 203.0.113.11 from April 2021 onwards indicates that the service moved to TEST-NET-3.

To actually attribute IP addresses found via these records to ASes, Fiebig et al. used – in earlier iterations of the paper [9] – the Team Cymru bulk whois service [33]. Using that information, they then calculate the share of universities for several countries who have at least one system under their domain colocated with one of the big three cloud providers (Amazon, Google, Microsoft, or a combination of the three), see also Fig. 1. Overall, from January 2015 to October 2022, the dataset used by Fiebig et al. spans a total of 880M DNS requests, pointing to between 500k and 6M individual IP addresses per month, adding up to 155M IPs (14M unique). Naturally, the same IP address may occur in several months. As Fiebig et al. initially used the Team Cymru bulk whois service (only containing *current* AS attributions), their work is an ideal case study to evaluate how using a historic AS attribution service influences observed results.

Team Cymru Whois Data. As a base-line, we requested bulk whois data from Team Cymru's bulk whois service for all unique addresses in January 2023. We used the Team Cymru whois to resolve all 14M unique IP addresses in the university dataset. For each IP address the bulk whois service of Team Cumry returns the currently associated AS number, the requested address, and the AS Name and location of the corresponding AS.

2.2 Methodology

In this section, we describe how we organized the CAIDA AS2ORG and AS2Prefix datasets in our service daemon to enable quick queries for individual addresses against the dataset. The major challenge–preventing a traditional RDBMS from being used–is that these datasets contain whole prefixes, instead of individual IP addresses, and relations between objects are complex. This would lead to, for example in SQL, a nested JOIN structure which limits performance of an RDBMS. To prevent this bottleneck, our implementation uses a completely in-memory prefix trie, i.e., pytricia [1].

AS2ORG Data-Structure. To use the supplied dataset to identify the AS and organization announcing a specific IP address, we first create a data-structure mapping time-frames, organizations, and ASes to each other. The challenge here is that the resolution of the supplied data is relatively low. Furthermore, we find that the supplied data regularly contains parsing errors, as it has been sourced from RIR supplied whois data, which is known to be often unstructured and to have volatile formats [20].

To handle the sparseness of the supplied data, we do have to make decisions on the margin of error that is acceptable for a whois service when making an educated guess for the organizational affiliation of an AS in between two quarterly files. There, we have to handle four cases:

– **AS2ORG unchanged:** If, in both files, the AS is mapped to the same organization, we assume that it was continuously mapped to the same organization between the two dates for which we have data.
– **AS missing from newer file (AS removed):** If an AS has been removed, we consider it to be removed from the day directly following the last quarterly file's date in which the AS could be found.
– **AS missing from older file (AS added):** If an AS has been added, we consider this AS mapping to be valid from the date of the file in which the AS first occurs (again).
– **AS2ORG changed:** If the AS2ORG mapping changes between two adjacent files, we consider this change to have come into effect on the day after the older files' collection date.

Following this approach, we can then construct a continuous mapping of ASes to organizations in our data-structure.

Prefix Tree (Trie). Next, we iterate through the list of available files by date, and add the prefixes we find to an IP trie [1]. In that trie, each added prefix holds a list at date ranges when it was observed. For each prefix in our input files, we check if the prefix exists in the trie. Here, we have to handle four cases:

– **Prefix is not in the trie:** We add the prefix to the trie, setting the 'first seen' field to the date of the collection date of the currently processing file.
– **Prefix is in the trie:**
  • **No gap to last-seen date:** If the last-seen date of the prefix is the date of the day before the collection time of the currently processing file, we update the last-seen date of the most recent date-range to the date of the currently processing file.
  • **Gap to last-seen date:** If the last-seen date of the prefix is not the date of the day before the collection time of the currently processing file, we add a new date-range to the list of date-ranges, and set the first seen date to the date of the currently processing file.

- **Originating AS changed:** If the originating AS(es; see below) changed from the last seen state, we treat the prefix as a new prefix, i.e., start a new date range associated with the new ASes.

In all cases, the prefix is attributed to the ASes we observe as announcing the prefix. There, we also have to handle several special cases:

- **Prefix originated by exactly one AS:** If a prefix is originated by exactly one AS, we add this AS as the authoritative AS.
- **MOAS prefix:** If a prefix is announced by multiple ASes at the same time, commonly known as a MOAS (Multi Origin AS) prefix, we add all these ASes to the announcement state, see the section on handling requests for details on the presentation.
- **ASSET aggregate:** ASes may aggregate prefixes received from downstream ASes. Fore example, if AS65536 announces 198.51.100.0/25 to AS65538, and AS65537 announces 198.51.100.128/25 to AS65538, AS65538 can aggregate these announcements to 198.51.100.0/24, only announcing that to its peers, while also aggregating AS65536 and AS65537 to { AS65536, AS65537 } in the AS path of that announcement. The information whether 198.51.100.0/25 was originated by AS65536 or AS65537 is lost in this process. As this is suggested to occur only on provider aggregatable IP space [6], we attribute the whole /24 to the aggregating AS, i.e., AS65538 in this case.

After having determined the ASes to which we attribute a prefix, we look up the associated AS2ORG mapping from our first datastructure and add that information to the date range. Please note that the trie data structure handles the occurrence of more specific prefixes by a branching approach, i.e., we can add 198.51.100.128/25 to the trie, even if 198.51.100.0/24 is already present. When looking up addresses, the more specific will match, and we will have to traverse the tree upward, see also below under 'Lookups'. Loading the full data set into the implementation takes around 24 h.

Filtering. Prefix announcements on the Internet are noisy. Specifically, we may regularly observe organizations announcing prefixes they are not supposed to announce [32], announce prefixes that are more specific than the maximum agreed prefix size in the global routing table (/24 for IPv4 and /48 for IPv6) [31], announce prefixes that are unreasonably short, e.g., when leaking default routes, or announce prefixes and AS numbers from reserved ranges [26] (see also IANA's registires[2,3]). Reserved prefixes are statically added to our lookup daemon, and reported as such upon lookup. Hence, when importing prefixes we are filtering all announcements less specific than a /8 for IPv6 and /18 for IPv6, and more specific than a /24 for IPv4 and /48 for IPv6. Similarly, we exclude all prefixes

---

[2] https://www.iana.org/assignments/iana-ipv4-special-registry/iana-ipv4-special-registry.xhtml.

[3] https://www.iana.org/assignments/iana-ipv6-special-registry/iana-ipv6-special-registry.xhtml.

originated by private and reserved AS numbers, i.e., 0 [18,19], 23456 [34], 64496–64511 [17], 64512-65534 [14,24], 65535 [13], 65536-65551 [17,34], 65552-131071 (IANA Reserved), 4200000000-4294967294 [24], and 4294967295 [13].

Lookups. The implementation of the historic whois service allows lookups with daily granularity. When an IP address or prefix is looked up, we first identify the most specific match. Next, we check if the prefix has been announced at the given date, i.e., if it has a date-range covering the requested date. If it does not have a corresponding date range, we traverse the tree until we either find a less specific prefix with a covering date-range or arrive at the root of the address tree. If we reach the root, we return that the prefix was not found at that date.

For the most specific prefix with a covering date range, we return the requested IP address or prefix, the requested date, and the result set. The result set contains the dates when the prefix was first and last observed for the date-range covering the requested date, with the last-seen date being null if the prefix was still being observed in the newest file imported into the daemon. Additionally we return the identified prefix and the list of ASes associated with the prefix. For each AS we also return an AS2ORG mapping, listing the ASN, the ASNAME and RIR where the ASN has been registered. Furthermore, we return all organizations associated with the AS at the time of the request, which includes the country code registered for the organization, the RIR the organization object has been obtained from, and the name of the organization.

Implementation, Infrastructure, and Performance. We implemented the historic whois system in a team using roughly three person months between May and August 2022 in Python. To handle our request load, we deployed forty instances behind a load-balancing frontend on a cluster of four hardware machines. Each instance consumes roughly 16 GB of memory (including caches) and has access to two dedicated CPU threads, leading to a total resource consumption of 80 CPU cores and 640 GB of memory, without Kernel Same-Page Merging (KSM) applied. An instance can process around 1.2K lookups a second, allowing us to perform the address resolution for the 155M addresses over 7 years in a bit more than 1.5 h given noise in actual lookup rates and a maximum parallelization factor of 40.

3   Results

In this section, we describe how we evaluate the efficacy of BTTF whois using the work of Fiebig et al. [10] as a case-study. We first introduce the results Fiebig et al. obtained by using Team Cymru's bulk whois service. We then compare the attribution of address ownership between Team Cymru's bulk whois service and BTTF whois. Finally, we revisit the results of Fiebig et al., and describe how using BTTF whois influences them.

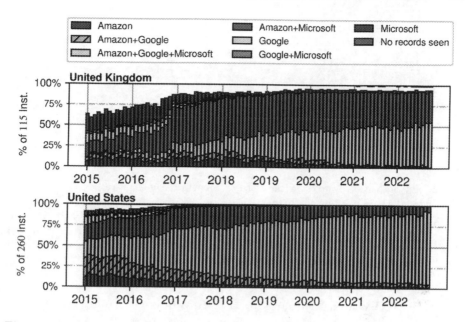

Fig. 1. Cloud use attribution for universities in the U.K. and the U.S. (January 2015–May 2022) based on Team Cymru bulk-whois data.

3.1 Universities' Cloud Usage: Team Cymru's Bulk Whois

As outlined in Sect. 2.1, Fiebig et al. use the Farsight SIE dataset to identify IP addresses to which names under universities domains point with a monthly granularity. Using Team Cymru's bulk-whois service, they then attribute these IPs to AS numbers. For their final analysis, they then calculate the share of universities in a country under whose domains at least one name ultimately points to an IP address announced by one of Amazon's, Google's, or Microsoft's ASes. Naturally, a university may have multiple names under its domain that point to addresses announced by different cloud providers. Figure 1 depicts their results from January 2015 to October 2022 for 115 U.K. universities and 260 U.S. universities, with each bar in the bar-plots representing the distribution observed during a single month.

For both, the U.S. and the U.K., they find an overall high prevalence of at least one service or site being run on Amazon, Google, or Microsoft systems. Notably, the U.S. already shows an over 90% saturation in cloud use, with the main development being that the prevalence of universities having infrastructure located at all three major cloud providers continuously rises over time. For the U.K., still around 75% of universities have at least one service in the major three clouds in January 2015, followed by a gradual increase across all platforms. Still, even in October 2022, the use of Google systems in the U.K. is lower comparison to the observed U.S. usage.

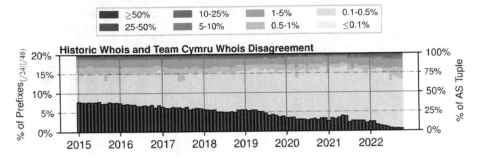

Fig. 2. Percentage of prefixes in the dataset on which the historic whois service we implemented and the data from Team Cymru's bulk whois service disagree. The shaded background indicates the distribution of disagreement over AS tuple, i.e., the tuple of the ASes to which Team Cymru attributes a prefix and the ASes BTTF attributes a prefix to. Note that, as common with centralization, only a minor fraction of AS tuples is responsible for the bulk of disagreement.

3.2   IP Attribution Comparison: BTTF Whois vs. Team Cymru

We first compare the direct attribution results between Team Cymru's bulk whois and BTTF whois. For that, we first use Team Cymru's bulk whois to attribute all 14M unique IP addresses found by Fiebig et al. (see Sect. 2.1) to ASes. We then use the BTTF whois service to attribute all addresses seen in a month to ASes based on the joined state seen on the 1st, 14th, and 28th of that month. Finally, we calculate the disagreement in attribution between the two data sources over time per /24 (IPv4) and /48 (IPv6), the minimum prefix sizes that can be successfully announced. We strictly compare the sets of ASes, only considering an exact match to be agreement. If one service returns a subset of ASes of the other, we consider this a disagreement.

The intuitive assumption for this is that Team Cymru's whois data is accurate 'as of now', while accuracy declines gradually while going further into the past as prefixes have been transferred between organizations. Based on these assumptions, there should be a high agreement between data from the historic whois service and the Team Cymru provided data for relatively recent months. However, the discrepancy should increase when we go further back in time.

As Fig. 2 depicts, this is indeed the result we obtain. While disagreement started out at around 7.67% in 2015, it continuously decreases over time, with the lowest disagreement occurring in October 2022, with 0.49%. Overall, this result aligns with our predictions in terms of reliability for the historic whois service. Hence, as it comparably reliable on data where Team Cymru's whois is reliable, we assume BTTF whois to be reliable for historic data as well.

3.3   Impact of BTTF Whois on Case-Study Analysis

For demonstrating the benefits of our historic whois service, we analyze how its different perspective on IP address ownership influences the results Fiebig et

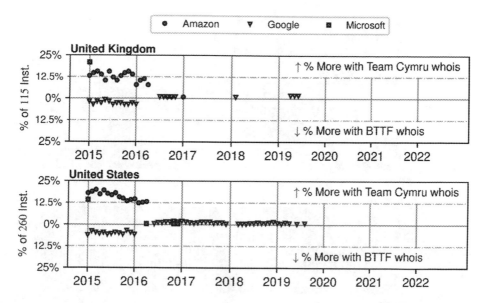

Fig. 3. Difference in cloud use attribution for universities in the U.K. and the U.S. (January 2015–May 2022) between Team Cymru bulk-whois data and historic bulk-whois data as absolute percent values as relative change considering Team Cymru as the base-line, i.e., positive values mean *more based on Team Cymru whois data*, while negative values mean *more based on historic bulk whois data*.

al. presented [10]. To this end, we compared the final cloud hosting verdict for several countries between an analysis where our historic whois service has been used and one where Team Cymru's whois has been used (see Fig. 3). Over all countries in our analysis, we only observe a significant impact in the U.K. and the U.S.. For the U.K. and the U.S., we find that, overall, the number of universities attributed to Amazon (i.e., Amazon, Amazon+Google, Amazon+Microsoft, Amazon+Google+Microsoft) are estimated higher by data from Team Cymru's whois until May 2016 by around 12.5%. Additionally, we find a minor (≤5%) underestimation for Google use in 2015, and a high overestimation of Microsoft use in January 2015 only.

Focusing on the Amazon case, we were able to attribute it to 18.0.0.0/8, the IPv4 address block formerly allocated to the Massachusetts Institute of Technology (MIT). In 2017, MIT announced its intent to sell large parts (87.5%) of this address block to Amazon [30]. The transfer of addresses was finalized in 2019, with the creation of associated route objects [2], but the networks to be sold were cleared ahead of time. As several Universities in the U.S. and U.K. had names under their domain pointing to IP addresses from MIT, and – based on *currently* accurate attribution information – these now belong to Amazon, these addresses were wrongly attributed to Amazon.

To better understand the significance of this attribution error, we compare the cloud usage graphs generated when using whois data sourced via the Team

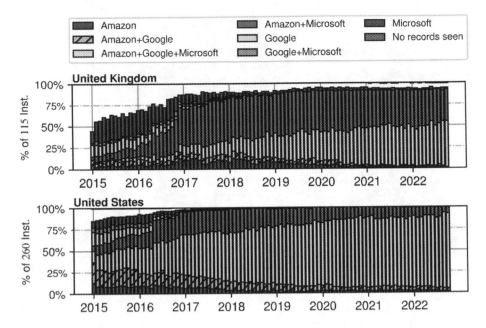

Fig. 4. Cloud use attribution for universities in the U.K. and the U.S. (January 2015–May 2022) based on historic bulk-whois data.

Cymru whois service (see Fig. 1) with the updated version relying on our historic whois (see Fig. 4). We find that for both countries, the U.S. and the U.K., using the historic whois service reveals an initially lower usage of Amazon based hosting, followed by a more rapid increase. For example, in the U.S., we find that the initial share of universities also using Amazon hosted services now hovers around 60% instead of the 75% initially observed.

In the U.K. the effect has been more pronounced. Instead of the gradual increase initially assumed based on Team Cymru's whois data, we now a lower share of Amazon service usage for the U.K. in 2015 (around 12.5% instead of 25%), increasing during 2016. Hence, by initially not using a historic whois service, Fiebig et al. missed an important growth effect in the data.

4   Discussion

In this section, we discuss lessons learned for research on historic datasets, discuss the limitations of our approach, and outline further work.

4.1   Lessons Learned for Research on Historic Datasets

In Sect. 3, we have seen the major impact incorrect address attribution can have on research results when working with historic records. Especially research that investigates research questions in which IP address ownership and control is instrumental–as the case-study work by Fiebig et al.–becomes more robust by selecting a more accurate IP address attribution methodology. Given the growing availability of historic datasets containing IP addresses, for example, the Farsight SIE dataset [8], the OpenINTEL dataset [15,28], but also historic trace-route datasets [23], or IXP datasets [5], we expect more future research to deal with historic address datasets. At the same time, the exhaustion of IPv4 [27], and the associated growth of the IP address and leasing market [11,21,22] will make real-time whois information increasingly unreliable for such historic datasets. As such, our service fills an important gap for the research community.

4.2   Limitations

Despite our successful validation of the historic whois service by demonstrating it performs comparable to established bulk whois services on recent data, there are several limitations which should be discussed. First, the utilized CAIDA data exhibits several inconsistencies in data, e.g., AS numbers having a dot in the middle. The CAIDA prefix data is an aggregate of RouteViews data. The aggregation process may occlude specific announcements, e.g., if a prefix is not yet visible at the single route collector used by CAIDA. Similarly, prefix hijacks [32] may inject routes into the aggregate table, which are then wrongly attributed to the hijacking organization. This issue could only be addressed by a more elaborate data structure, that includes Internet Registry Routing object data as well as RPKI [18] data – which is difficult to obtain in historic form – and heuristics to identify and exclude route hijacks. Given the current accuracy of the historic whois service, we consider this approach as out-of-scope.

Furthermore, there are several limitations in the AS2ORG mapping data. AS family calculation [4], i.e., grouping of ASes to a common organization if the organizational objects of theses ASes are, e.g., subsidiaries of a common corporation, are unreliable over time. Fields from the whois data provided by RIRs is not consistently parsed, and fields contain faulty data if the base format on the RIRs side changes without the parsers that generate the AS2ORG extract we rely on being adjusted. In addition, the AS2ORG maps have a quarterly granularity, which makes AS2ORG attribution unreliable when changes occur, as discussed in our methodology.

Finally, as noted before, a prefix being announce by an AS does not necessarily mean that this prefix is allocated to, or owned by said AS, see the example of announcements of AS174. Hence, our implemented historic whois service will mis-attribute prefixes that are registered to an organization that is not the organization to which the announcing AS is associated.

Nevertheless, again given the observed reliability in comparison with Team Cymru's whois service, we consider the current implementation of our historic whois service as sufficiently robust to provide historic whois data. Effectively, it is comparably accurate to the commonly used Team Cymru whois service on recent data, while providing higher accuracy in historic data, as highlighted by the case of MIT's /8 network.

4.3   Future Work

As discussed in our limitations section, our reliance on the CAIDA aggregates of the Routeviews BGP announcement collections still limits the accuracy of our data. To improve our service, it would hence be advisable to not only provide routing information based IP attribution, but also access other sources for historic whois information, and attach it to returned records if it is available. For example, RIPE NCC provides a historic non-bulk whois service. We are in conversations with relevant RIRs and registrars to obtain access to these datasets, so that our service can–along with routing based attribution information, i.e., the announcing AS–also return information from RIR databases. If these datasets become available, it would also be prudent to compare RIR information with actual routing information over the historic timeframe covered by our service.

Similarly, Routeviews data is available for a longer timeframe than the CAIDA aggregates. Hence, we also plan to aggregate Routeviews information from before the first CAIDA aggregates became available–as early as 2000–to include in our BTTF whois service.

5   Conclusion

In this paper, we introduce and evaluate BTTF whois as a public community service. This historic whois service allows more accurate estimations of IP address ownership, especially when the concerned IP address has been observed in the past. Based on a case-study, we demonstrate how the use of an accurate historic whois service allows deeper insights into datasets, and reveal developments that would remain shrouded when only relying on *current* whois information.

Nevertheless, several challenges exist, which should be resolved in further iterations of the development of our service. This includes aggregating the Route-Views dataset ourselves – especially as older data-sets are available than aggregated by CAIDA – and continuously collecting RIR provided data for generating AS2ORG maps ourselves, including addressing the issue of organizational families more reliably. Furthermore, future implementations should include IRR and RPKI data to make the implementation more robust against data noise due to prefix hijacks and the announcement of prefixes by ASes not belonging to the prefix-holder's organization.

Service Availability: You can use a publicly available instance of BTTF whois at bttf-whois.as59645.net port tcp/43. See Appendix A for usage details and https://bttf-whois.as59645.net for further information.

Acknowledgements. We thank Farsight Security, Inc. (now DomainTools) for providing access to the Farsight Security Information Exchange's passive DNS data feed. Without this data, the project would not have been possible. The authors express their gratitude to the anonymous reviewers and our shepherd Thomas Krenc for their thoughtful and encouraging input during the reviewing process. Furthermore, we thank the reviewers who accompanied *'Heads in the Clouds? Measuring Universities' Migration to Public Clouds: Implications for Privacy & Academic Freedom'* at PoPETS from 2022.2, via 2022.4, to 2023.2 for seeding the idea to implement the BTTF whois service and their continuous encouragement to pursue this work. Finally, Sebastian Lohff's input on the implementation and performance tuning were invaluable to realize the service in a production-ready manner. This work was partially funded by the German Federal Ministry of Education and Research under the project 6G-RIC, grant 16KISK027. Any opinions, findings, and conclusions or recommendations expressed in this material are those of the authors and do not necessarily reflect the views of Farsight Security, Inc., DomainTools, the German Federal Ministry of Education and Research, or the authors' host institutions and affiliations.

A BTTF Whois Short Documentation

Here, we document a) how you can use BTTF whois with a whois client, and b) how to obtain bulk results. Furthermore, we provide an overview over the returned JSON's structure.

A.1 Using BTTF Whois Manually

BTTF whois can be used with a standard whois client. The date format is YYYYMMDD.

```
% whois -h bttf-whois.as59645.net '1.1.1.1 20210101'
# This is the historic IP to AS mapping service
# Contact: <contact@as59645.net>
# Trie Status: READY - loaded 2191224 IPv4 and 345010 IPv6 prefixes
# AS2Org Status: 119641 AS and 201610 organisations loaded
# Enter HELP to get basic usage information
# NOTICE: OUTPUT FORMAT: JSON-SHORT
# READY
{
    "ipaddr": "1.1.1.1",
    "qdate": "20210101",
    "results": {
        "timestamp": 20180320,
        "until": null,
        "prefix": "1.1.1.0/24",
        "aslist": [
            13335
        ],
        "orgmapping": {
            "13335": [
                {
                    "asn": 13335,
                    "aut": {
                        "aut": 13335,
                        "aut_name": "CLOUDFLARENET-AS",
                        "org_id": "@family-471",
                        "opaque_id": "",
```

```
                              "source": "RIPE"
                    },
                    "seen": [
                        "20180703"
                    ],
                    "changed": "20180703",
                    "change_guessed": true,
                    "orgs": [
                        {
                            "org_id": "@family-471",
                            "org": {
                                "org_id": "@family-471",
                                "org_name": "Cloudflare Inc",
                                "country": "US",
                                "source": "ARIN,RIPE"
                            },
                            "seen": [
                                "20180703"
                            ],
                            "changed": "20180703",
                            "change_guessed": true
                        }
                    ]
                }
            ]
        }
    }
}
```

A.2   Using BTTF Whois for Bulk Requests

BTTF whois ingests bulk requests enclosed in a 'begin' and 'end' statement:

```
% cat ./file
begin
1.1.1.1 20210101
1.1.1.1 20120101
8.8.8.8 20210201
end
```

You can use netcat/nc to send this file to the bulk whois service and receive the results directly or redirect them to a file:

```
% cat ./file | nc bttf-whois.as59645.net 43
# This is the historic IP to AS mapping service
# Contact: <contact@as59645.net>
# Trie Status: READY - loaded 2169926 IPv4 and 319033 IPv6 prefixes
# AS2Org Status: 119005 AS and 199948 organisations loaded
# Enter HELP to get basic usage information
# NOTICE: OUTPUT FORMAT: JSON-SHORT
```

```
# READY
{"IP": "1.1.1.1", "QDATE": "20210101", "results": {"DATA_FIRST": [...]
{"IP": "1.1.1.1", "QDATE": "20120101", "results": []}
{"IP": "8.8.8.8", "QDATE": "20210201", "results": {"DATA_FIRST": [...]
# goodbye
```

A.3   BTTF Whois JSON Data Structure

Below, you can find an overview of the response fields returned by BTTF whois.

```
{ # Requested IPv4 or IPv6 address
  "IP": "1.1.1.1",
 # Date for which data was requested
  "QDATE": "20210101",
  "results": {
   # First time the most specific prefix for address has been seen
   # first with this specific set of announcing ASes
   "DATA_FIRST": 20180320,
   # Last time this entry was seen, i.e., valid until. If it is
   # null, the most specific is still visible in the most recent
   # dataset (valid NOW).
   "DATA_LAST": null,
   # List of ASNs that announced the most specific prefix for the
   # requested address.
   "asns": [
     13335
   ],
   # The most specific matching prefix from the dataset.
   "prefix": "1.1.1.0/24",
   # AS2ORG mappings for all announcing ASN.
   "as2org": [
     {
       # AS number
       "ASN": 13335,
       # AS name
       "ASNAME": "CLOUDFLARENET-AS",
       # RIR that is the data source in the AS2ORG mappings
       "RIR": "RIPE",
       # Org objects associated with the ASN
       "orgs": [
         {
           # Country code attributed to an organization
           "CC": "US",
           # RIRs that hold an instance of this ORG object
           "RIR": "ARIN,RIPE",
           # Organization name from the ORG object
           "ASORG": "Cloudflare Inc"
         }
       ]
     }
```

```
    ]
  }
}
```

References

1. Jsommers, et al.: pytricia: an IP address lookup module for Python, 30 August 2022. https://github.com/jsommers/pytricia. Accessed 30 Aug 2022
2. ARIN. WHOIS for NET-18-32-0-0-1, 7 October 2019. https://whois.arin.net/rest/net/NET-18-32-0-0-1. Accessed 01 Sept 2022
3. CAIDA. Routeviews Prefix to AS mappings Dataset for IPv4 and IPv6, 30 August 2022. https://www.caida.org/catalog/datasets/routeviews-prefix2as/. Accessed 30 Aug 2022
4. CAIDA. The CAIDA AS Organizations Dataset, all dates, 30 Aug 2022. https://www.caida.org/data/as-organizations. Accessed 30 Aug 2022
5. Chatzis, N., Smaragdakis, G., Böttger, J., Krenc, T., Feldmann, A.: On the benefits of using a large IXP as an Internet vantage point. In: Proceedings of the 2013 Conference on Internet Measurement Conference (2013)
6. Chen, E., Stewart, J.: A framework for inter-domain route aggregation. RFC 2519. IETF, February 1999. http://tools.ietf.org/rfc/rfc2519.txt
7. Daigle, L.: WHOIS protocol specification. RFC 3912. IETF, September 2004. http://tools.ietf.org/rfc/rfc3912.txt
8. Farsight Inc., Farsight - Security Information Exchange (SIE). https://www.farsightsecurity.com/solutions/security-information-exchange/
9. Fiebig, T., et al.: Heads in the clouds: measuring the implications of universities migrating to public clouds. arXiv preprint arXiv:2104.09462 (2021)
10. Fiebig, T., et al.: Heads in the clouds? Measuring universities' migration to public clouds: implications for privacy & academic freedom. In: Proceedings on Privacy Enhancing Technologies Symposium, vol. 2 (2023)
11. Giotsas, V., Livadariu, I., Gigis, P.: A first look at the misuse and abuse of the IPv4 transfer market. In: Sperotto, A., Dainotti, A., Stiller, B. (eds.) PAM 2020. LNCS, vol. 12048, pp. 88–103. Springer, Cham (2020). https://doi.org/10.1007/978-3-030-44081-7_6
12. Giotsas, V., Luckie, M., Huffaker, B., Claffy, K.: Inferring complex AS relationships. In: Proceedings of the 2014 Internet Measurement Conference (2014)
13. Haas, J., Mitchell, J.: Reservation of last autonomous system (AS) numbers. RFC 7300. IETF, July 2014. http://tools.ietf.org/rfc/rfc7300.txt
14. Hawkinson, J., Bates, T.: Guidelines for creation, selection, and registration of an autonomous system (AS). RFC 1930. IETF, March 1996. http://tools.ietf.org/rfc/rfc1930.txt
15. Hohlfeld, O.: Poster: operating a DNS-based active internet observatory. In: Proceedings of the 2018 ACM SIGCOMM Conference (SIGCOMM) (2018)
16. Housley, R., Curran, J., Huston, G., Conrad, D.: The internet numbers registry system. RFC 7020. IETF, August 2013. http://tools.ietf.org/rfc/rfc7020.txt
17. Huston, G.: Autonomous system (AS) number reservation for documentation use. RFC 5398. IETF, December 2008. http://tools.ietf.org/rfc/rfc5398.txt
18. Huston, G., Michaelson, G.: Validation of route origination using the resource certificate public key infrastructure (PKI) and route origin authorizations (ROAs). RFC 6483. IETF, February 2012. http://tools.ietf.org/rfc/rfc6483.txt

19. Kumari, W., Bush, R., Schiller, H., Patel, K.: Codification of AS 0 processing. RFC 7607. IETF, August 2015. http://tools.ietf.org/rfc/rfc7607.txt
20. Liu, S., Foster, I., Savage, S., Voelker, G.M., Saul, L.K.: Who is .com? Learning to parse WHOIS records. In: Proceedings of the 2015 Internet Measurement Conference (2015)
21. Livadariu, I., Elmokashfi, A., Dhamdhere, A.: On IPv4 transfer markets: analyzing reported transfers and inferring transfers in the wild. In: Computer Communications, vol. 111 (2017)
22. Livadariu, I., Elmokashfi, A., Dhamdhere, A., Claffy, K.: A first look at IPv4 transfer markets. In: Proceedings of the Ninth ACM Conference on Emerging Networking Experiments and Technologies (2013)
23. Luckie, M., Hyun, Y., Huffaker, B.: Traceroute probe method and forward IP path inference. In: Proceedings of the 8th ACM SIGCOMM conference on Internet measurement (2008)
24. Mitchell, J.: Autonomous system (AS) reservation for private use. RFC 6996. IETF, July 2013. http://tools.ietf.org/rfc/rfc6996.txt
25. Prehn, L., Lichtblau, F., Feldmann, A.: When wells run dry: the 2020 IPv4 address market. In: Proceedings of the ACM Conference on Emerging Networking EXperiments and Technologies (CoNEXT) (2020)
26. Rekhter, Y., Moskowitz, B., Karrenberg, D., Groot G.J.d., Lear, E.: Address allocation for private internets. RFC 1918. IETF, February 1996. http://tools.ietf.org/rfc/rfc1918.txt
27. Richter, P., Allman, M., Bush, R., Paxson, V.: A primer on IPv4 scarcity. ACM SIGCOMM Comput. Commun. Rev. 45(2) (2015)
28. van Rijswijk-Deij, R., Jonker, M., Sperotto, A., Pras, A.: A high-performance, scalable infrastructure for large-scale active DNS measurements. IEEE J. Sel. Areas Commun. 34(6) (2016)
29. RouteViews: RouteViews Project, 30 August 2022. http://www.routeviews.org. Accessed 30 Aug 2022
30. Schmidt, M.A., Executive, I.R.: Letter to: to the members of the MIT community, 20 April 2017. https://gist.github.com/simonster/e22e50cd52b7dffcf5a4db2b8ea4cce0. Accessed 01 Sept 2022
31. Sediqi, K.Z., Prehn, L., Gasser, O.: Hyper-specific prefixes: gotta enjoy the little things in interdomain routing. ACM SIGCOMM Comput. Commun. Rev. 52(2) (2022)
32. Sermpezis, P., Kotronis, V., Dainotti, A., Dimitropoulos, X.: A survey among network operators on BGP prefix hijacking. ACM SIGCOMM Comput. Commun. Rev. 48(1) (2018)
33. Team Cymru. IP to ASN mapping service. https://team-cymru.com/community-services/ip-asn-mapping/

34. Vohra, Q., Chen, E.: BGP support for four-octet autonomous system (AS) number space. RFC 6793. IETF, December 2012. http://tools.ietf.org/rfc/rfc6793.txt
35. Zhou, L., Kong, N., Shen, S., Sheng, S., Servin, A.: Inventory and analysis of WHOIS registration objects. RFC 7485. IETF, March 2015. http://tools.ietf.org/rfc/rfc7485.txt

Towards Diagnosing Accurately the Performance Bottleneck of Software-Based Network Function Implementation

Ru Jia[1,2,3(✉)], Heng Pan[1,4], Haiyang Jiang[1], Serge Fdida[3], and Gaogang Xie[5]

[1] Institute of Computing Technology, Chinese Academy of Sciences, Beijing, China
{jiaru,panheng,jianghaiyang}@ict.ac.cn
[2] University of Chinese Academy of Sciences, Beijing, China
[3] Sorbonne University, Paris, France
[4] Purple Mountain Laboratories, Nanjing, China
[5] Computer Network Information Center, Chinese Academy of Sciences, Beijing, China
xie@cnic.cn

Abstract. The software-based Network Functions (NFs) improve the flexibility of network services. Comparing with hardware, NFs have specific behavioral characteristics. Performance diagnosis is the first and most difficult step during NFs' performance optimization. Does the existing instrumentation-based and sampling-based performance diagnosis methods work well in NFs' scenario? In this paper, we first re-think the challenges of NF performance diagnosis and correspondingly propose three requirements: fine granularity, flexibility and perturbation-free. We investigate existing methods and find that none of them can simultaneously meet these requirements. We innovatively propose a quantitative indicator, Coefficient of Interference (CoI). CoI is the fluctuation between per-packet latency measurements with and without performance diagnosis. CoI can represent the performance perturbation degree caused by diagnosis process. We measure the CoI of typical performance diagnosis tools with different types of NFs and find that the perturbation caused by instrumentation-based diagnosis solution is 7.39% to 74.31% of that by sampling-based solutions. On these basis, we propose a hybrid NF performance diagnosis, to trace the performance bottleneck of NF accurately.

Keywords: Network functions · Performance diagnosis · Performance perturbation

1 Introduction

As the size of the network rapidly grows, traditional underlying network that based on custom hardware, face significant development costs combined the low flexibility and scalability. In order to resolve the issue, network providers move hardware middleboxes to software-based network functions (NFs) running on the commodity servers. The softwareization of NFs improves the operation efficiency through simpler deployment and upgrade cycles. However, software-based NFs can lead to a significant performance issue, that is difficult to diagnose.

Compared with hardware platforms, processing packets in software means complex running environments and more intense resource contention. Moreover, new large-scale network scenarios, e.g., data centers, cloud platforms and the 5G mobile network [1], introduce complicated functional requirements and make the code size of software-based NFs largely increased. For example, the popular software packet processing framework, Cisco VPP [2], contains more than 2000 source files, 450,000 code lines. When performance issue emerge, the complicated running environments and code structures make it difficult for developers to quickly locate the issue. As the result, performance diagnosis, the process of finding and explaining the performance issue in NF program, is difficult and time-consuming in production environment.

In order to explore the performance behavior and perform NF performance diagnosis, developers generally use the general-purpose performance diagnosis tools based on the CPU hardware feature, Performance Monitoring Counter (PMC). Diagnosis tools based on PMC sampling (Linux Perf [3], Intel VTune [4]) have been widely used in NF performance diagnosis, since they are easy-to-use and have low overhead. There are also a lot of research focusing on performance diagnosis on High Performance Computing (HPC) and general-purpose computing programs ([5–12]). However, NF programs are different from general-purpose programs. It brings new challenges to performance diagnosis. Therefore the NF performance diagnosis is re-considered in the work and we present three requirements critical to the issue:

1) **Fine granularity.** Due to the queues and batch operations in NFs, the performance issue are transitive cross packets. To identify the root cause, NF performance diagnosis solution should be fine-grained enough to perform packet-level performance tracing.
2) **Flexibility.** The modular architecture and high-performance requirements complicate the code structure and execution of NF. NF performance diagnosis solution should be flexible enough to handle inline functions and libraries loaded at run-time.
3) **Perturbation-free.** The performance perturbation caused by measurement is unavoidable. To reflect the original behavior as accurately as possible, performance diagnosis solution should be perturbation-free as much as possible.

Facing to these requirements for NF performance diagnosis, are these general-purpose performance diagnosis methods still suitable for NFs? Unfortunately, there is no evaluation of existing PMC-based performance diagnosis methods in NF scenarios.

We investigate two major types of PMC-based performance diagnosis methods, sampling-based and instrumentation-based methods, summarize their capabilities in NF performance diagnosis (Sect. 5). Through theoretical mechanism analysis and NF measurement verification in real scenarios, we find that, existing PMC-based performance diagnosis methods cannot meet both requirements for fine granularity and flexibility. The sampling-based approach is not mechanically capable of packet-level performance tracing. Instrumentation-based methods have the potential for packet-level performance tracing, but existing methods fail at handling libraries loaded after the startup as well as inline functions.

In addition, compared to sampling, instrumentation-based methods introduce high measurement overhead. At present, it is considered to seriously interfere with the original performance behavior of NF. But does high measurement overhead mean significant performance perturbation? There is currently no theoretical proof or experimental verification. The performance perturbation is hard to evaluate since we cannot capture the real performance data without extra measurement operations. Most of research only use the overhead to evaluate their tools ([5–12]). Based on the NF's performance characteristics, we innovatively propose an indicator, the coefficient of interference (CoI), to quantitatively evaluate performance perturbation (Sect. 6). We deploy typical performance diagnosis tools (Perf [3], TAU [10]) on different NFs in real forwarding environment, to evaluate their CoI situation. We find that, even with high measurement overhead, the perturbation caused by instrumentation-based diagnosis solution is still only 7.39% to 74.31% of that by sampling-based solutions. The instrumentation-based performance diagnosis is more perturbation-free for NF performance diagnosis.

Finally, in Sect. 7, we summarize the capabilities and limitations of existing tools for NF performance diagnosis. Based on the results of measurement and verification, we propose a hybrid solution for NF performance diagnosis, as well as suggestions for designing and implementing packet-level performance diagnosis based on existing instrumentation tools.

In summary, we make three contributions in this paper.

1) From the perspective of NF performance behavior, we re-think the challenges of NF performance diagnosis and propose three requirements for NF performance diagnosis: **fine granularity, flexibility,** and **perturbation-free**.
2) We summarize existing PMC-based performance diagnosis methods. And through mechanism analysis and experimental verification, we prove that, existing performance diagnosis methods cannot meet the requirements of fine granularity and flexibility at the same time.
3) Through the research on NF performance behavior, we propose a quantitative indicator, – **coefficient of interference (CoI)**, to evaluate the performance perturbation of performance diagnosis methods. We evaluate the CoI of typical performance diagnosis tools with different types of NFs. We argue that, high measurement overhead doesn't mean large performance perturbation, and instrumentation-based tools are more perturbation-free for NF performance diagnosis.

The rest of the paper is organized as follows: In Sect. 2, we provide the background of NF and conventional performance diagnosis. And the challenges and requirements of NF performance diagnosis are presented in Sect. 3. In Sect. 4, we introduce our experimental environment and basic evaluation methods. We investigate major PMC-based performance diagnosis methods, and evaluate them through theoretical analysis and NF measurement verification in Sect. 5. In Sect. 6, we focus on the quantitative evaluation of performance perturbation. Based on our observations, a hybrid NF performance diagnosis solution is provided in Sect. 7. Finally, we discuss related work in Sect. 8 and conclusion in Sect. 9.

2   Background

The list of features that need to be supported by network functions has grown rapidly. New network services appear with new functional requirements, new network protocols emerge and evolve. Due to the slow development cycle (typically years), the closed, static and inflexible hardware, can no longer support the complex, rapidly evolving network functions [33].

Software-based NF was proposed and rapidly gained popularity. In the past decade, software-based NF has developed from the earliest simple software switch to complex firewall, IPsec gateway, OpenFlow [20] switch, Network Intrusion Detection System (NIDS), etc. Compared to hardware, the NF softwareization introduces complicated performance issue. Resource contention in the complex run-time environment will make NF performance unstable. The inefficient code segments also degrade performance. Even though many different diagnosis tools have been designed, NF performance diagnosis and optimization is still heavily dependent on the experience of programmers. The performance diagnosis is the bottleneck of the NF development cycle, and full of challenges [13]. In this section, we first briefly describe the packet processing procedure of network functions, explain the complexity of NF performance issues in Sect. 2.1. Then we describe conventional performance diagnosis solutions, which are commonly adopted in NF performance diagnosis in Sect. 2.2.

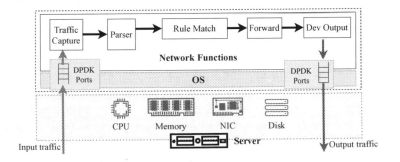

Fig. 1. NFs' packet processing procedure

2.1   NFs' Packet Processing Procedure

As the main purposes of the work is to accurately diagnose the NF performance, we illustrate the NFs' typical packet processing procedure in Fig. 1 and discuss factors that can affect NFs' performance.

1) The Traffic Capture module captures packets on the wire. High performance NF commonly adopts user-space driver frameworks, e.g., DPDK, in the module to bypass the kernel's protocol stack and move the packet processing entirely into user-space. The packets' pointers are delivered through queue data structures and the packets are processed in batch. The procedure contains massive memory operations and address calculations. Any inappropriate data structure design, e.g., unaligned memory address, is likely to cause serious performance issue.

2) The Parser module processes the network protocols, e.g., dealing with IP fragments and TCP reassembly. Due to complex logic processing and plenty of execution branches, parser module usually face high prediction error rate and low instruction cache hit rates. For example, if a branch prediction is wrong, the instructions and the correlative computational results have to be "flushed" and replaced with correct ones.

3) Then, according to the functional requirements, NF performs rule matching on packets. Rule matching is critical to most NFs (Table 1). The rule matching is computationally intensive, and usually not a simple one-dimensional numeric match. All of the rule sets, the traffic patterns, the design and implementation of algorithms, affect the CPU usage and data cache utilization of rule matching, which finally will affect the performance.

4) Depending on the result of rule matching, the packet may be rewritten, and forwarded to specified output port. The memory occupied by the packet will be modified or copied, and at last released. Frequent memory access put pressure on the cache. Data locality will seriously affect the utilization of cache, which will obvious affect the performance.

Go through NF's packet processing, the factors affecting NF performance are complex and closely related to the underlying fine-grained hardware usage. It makes the fine-grained performance diagnosis of NF extremely challenging.

2.2   Conventional Performance Diagnosis

General-purpose performance diagnosis focuses on the most common computing programs, which commonly aim to complete the computing task in the shortest time with minimal resource usage. They focus on the **overall performance of processing the entire input set**. Generally, PMC-based performance diagnosis methods accumulatively collect the performance data until the whole task is completed. They are able to identify the hottest call paths or functions during the computing of the entire input with relatively low overhead.

Different from general computing programs, NFs are required to provide long-term, stable network services, with continuous, relatively infinite input packets.

Table 1. The rule matching in NFs

NF	Algorithm	Matching Fields
NAT	IP longest prefix matching	IP header
Firewall	Packet classification	Header
OpenFlow switch	Packet classification	Header
IPsec gateway	Packet classification	header
NIDS	String matching	Full packet
Anti-Virus	String matching	Payload

In actual network operation and maintenance (O&M), network services usually have strict Service-Level Agreements (SLAs). SLAs include not only requirements for global processing capacity, such as throughput, but also strict limits on the processing performance of each packet. For example, SLAs often limit the maximum latency as T_{max}. In this case, the processing time of each input packet must be less than T_{max}. In other words, NFs need **continuously provide high-throughput packet processing, under the strict constraints of latency and packet drop rate**. In addition to global performance data, NFs also focus on packet-level performance data of each packet processing, such as latency.

Because NF is different from general-purpose programs in performance characteristics and issues, the requirements of NF performance diagnosis should be re-considered.

3   The Challenges and Requirements of NF Performance Diagnosis

According to the NF performance characteristics, we identify three challenges for NF performance diagnosis. Correspondingly, we propose three requirements for NF performance diagnosis solution: **fine-grained, flexible, and perturbation-free**.

1) **Performance issues of NFs are transitive.** The existence of queues and batch operations, make the abnormal event occurred in the processing of certain packet continue to affect several subsequent processing of packets (see Sect. 3.1). Facing to this challenges, performance diagnosis solution should be **fine-grained**, which means packet-level and function-level.
2) **The code structure and execution of modern NF frameworks is complicated.** Modern NF frameworks have complicated modular code structure and plenty of inline functions. Functional modular are usually constructed into separate dynamic libraries, and loaded on demand after the startup of the NF program (see Sect. 3.2). NF performance diagnosis solution should be **flexible** enough to handle inline functions and libraries loaded at any time.

3) **The performance perturbation is unavoidable.** Measurement operations of performance diagnosis interfere with the performance behavior of NF. The performance perturbation caused by measurement is unavoidable. The performance data collected by performance diagnosis tools cannot accurately reflect the original behavior of NF (see Sect. 3.3). To restore the original behavior accurately, performance diagnosis solution should be **perturbation-free.**

3.1   Performance Issues of NF Are Transitive.

Queue data structure, that follows the first-in-first-out principle, is a common and necessary component in NF packet processing procedure (see Fig. 1). The existence of queues brings queuing delays, and have significant impact on NF performance. Queue monitoring has always been a major task for NF performance monitoring and diagnosis. However, existing methods have a blind area for NF performance diagnosis. They cannot handle well the complex performance issues caused by queues, e.g., the transitivity of performance issues. Queuing makes a performance issue for one packet or flow to affect not only itself, but also subsequent subtle packets or flows [13]. Furthermore, modern high performance NF frameworks make widely use of batch operations, to improve the throughput of NF. The batch processing also complicates the transitivity of performance issues.

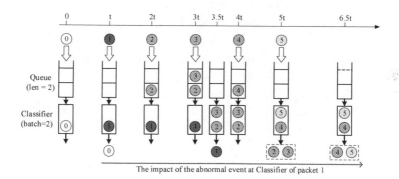

Fig. 2. The propagation of NF performance issues

Figure 2 describes the transitivity of performance issues caused by queues and batch. For simplicity, we assume the packet processing only contains one RX queue with length of 2, and one Classifier module, with the max batch size of 2. We assume that the costs of enqueue and dequeue are ignorable. As long as the queue and Classifier are idle, packets can directly go into the Classifier. Classifier can handle one packet with t, and handle a batch of two packets within $1.5t$. As shown in the top of the Fig. 2, 6 packets $p_0, p_1, \ldots, p_5$ arrive at the speed of one packet per t time. If there is no abnormal event, all packets should be processed within t, such as packet p_0. Unfortunately, an abnormal event occurs while the Classifier processing p_1, and lead to its large processing delay $(2.5t)$. Since the Classifier is blocked by the abnormal processing of p_1, subsequent three packets p_2, p_3, p_4 have to wait in the queue. Combined with the queueing delay, packet p_2 even experience a larger delay $(3t)$ than p_1. In addition, due to the batching operation of packets p_4 and p_5, even if p_5 doesn't need to queue, it experiences a delay of $1.5t$, not t. In this example, only packet p_1 triggers the abnormality, but it affects the delay of the following 4 packets. So we suppose that p_1 is the culprit, and $p_2, \ldots, p_5$ are victims.

Performance diagnosis measurements need to be able to distinguish among the processing of different packets, and find out which packets are culprits, and which packets are just victims. It means that performance diagnosis should support packet-level performance tracing. Furthermore, packet processing usually has many stages, the abnormal event can occur at any stage of the packet processing. Finding the culprit packet is not enough to pinpoint abnormal events. NF performance diagnosis should be able to identify which stage of certain packet processing the abnormal event occurred at, such as, "the abnormal event occurred at the classifier stage in the processing of packet p_1". It means that NF performance diagnosis should support function-level performance monitoring. Existing researches [13,14], which are based on queue monitoring and flow measurement, only approximately identify the culprit packets/flows, and cannot go deep into each stage of packet processing.

Based on this challenge, we propose the first requirement for NF performance diagnosis, **Fine granularity:** *NF performance diagnosis should provide packet-level and function-level performance tracing.*

3.2 The Complexity of Modern NF Frameworks

Table 2. The code statistics of modern NF and NF frameworks

Framework/NF	No. of Code lines	No. of files
VPP [2] (v19.08)	455,651	2338
Click [33] (v2.0.1)	213,388	1413
DPDK (v19.11.3)	1,548,835	2947
OVS [32] (v2.17.0)	252,429	1033

Table 3. The statistics of functions in different NFs captured by Perf-Dwarf at runtime. FW, NAT and IPsec are implemented by Cisco VPP.

NF	No. of func.	No. of inline func.	Proportion
OVS [32]	428	290	67.8%
FW	284	248	87.3%
NAT	306	248	81.0%
IPsec	311	235	75.6%

With the continuous development of NFV and software NF technology, more and more network scenarios choose to use software NFs, instead of hardware middleboxes. The emergence of new scenarios has made the functions of NF more and more complex, and the size of code has expanded rapidly. Table. 2 lists the size of modern NF frameworks. The complex code structure makes it difficult to develop new functions and diagnose performance.

In order to reduce development costs and improve the extensibility of the framework, most NF frameworks adopt a modular architecture [2,33,37]. In the most popular framework, VPP, most of the complex, non-essential functions, such as ACLs, encryption and decryption, IKEv2 protocol, etc., are implemented as separate dynamic libraries that are loaded on demand during run-time. At the same time, in order to reduce unnecessary resource usage, NF sometimes cannot occupy a large amount of memory resources. In order to reduce the memory footprint of the NF, these libraries are not directly linked to the executable during the compiling and linking. Instead, after the NF program starts, NF will read the configuration file provided by the user, and dynamically load the libraries based on demand of users(Fig. 3). This brings a new challenge for fine-grained performance diagnosis. Because there is no information in the header of executable, the diagnosis tools need the flexibility to identify modules that are dynamically loaded at any stage.

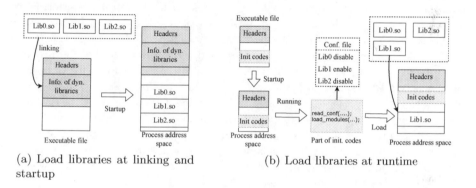

(a) Load libraries at linking and startup

(b) Load libraries at runtime

Fig. 3. Loading libraries at different stages

In addition, to improve performance, a large number of inline functions are imported in NF programs, as listed in Table. 3. These functions do not really exist as visible functions under the compilation optimization option, and do not appear in the symbol table of the executable file. It's difficult to obtain the information of inline functions directly from the header of the executable.

Based on this challenge, we propose the second requirement for NF performance diagnosis, **Flexibility:** *NF performance diagnosis should have the capacity to handle libraries loaded at any stage, and inline functions.*

3.3   Performance Perturbation Is Unavoidable

Rule matching processing is critical to NFs as it is usually the performance bottleneck (see Fig. 1). As an algorithmic problem, rule matching has been studied a lot [21–25]. However, the performance diagnosis of rule matching is still challenging, because it can not be treated as a pure algorithmic problem during the NF performance diagnosis. Due to the resource contention in the real running environment, there is a big gap between the performance behavior of rule matching in offline algorithm experiments and in online NF processing.

For example, in TupleMerge [22], which is a research on packet classification, VPP's TSS algorithm averages $2.93\mu s$ of packet classification time with a 256k rule set in offline. While in the actual forwarding environment with a 4K rule set, the time of each lookup reach $10\mu s$-$12\mu s$. Although TulpeMerge optimizes specifically for the difference between online and offline environments, compared with it average classification time of $0.64\mu s$ with 256k rule set at offline, its overhead is already between $0.55\mu s$ and $0.7\mu s$ with 4k rule set at online.

Since offline performance diagnosis cannot efficiently find performance issues in real-world system rule matching, online performance diagnosis tools is necessary. However, the interference with the original program by online measurement is unavoidable. Performance data cannot be captured without extra measurement operations. Although the PMC hardware can count the hardware performance metrics of certain process with ignorable overhead, complete performance diagnosis also requires the extra operations such as reading values from hardware PMCs to user space, constructing performance data records. All of these extra operations compete for CPU time, cache and memory, with the NF process, disrupt the performance behavior of NF execution. For example, let's consider the usage of CPU caches. SEPS'17 [30] shows that, the number of mis-predicted branches and instruction cache misses will significantly increase due to the measurement operations. In NF diagnosis, we usually need to identify the culprit packet, measurement should remain the differences of the processing of different packets. The perturbation here is more related to the interference with these differences. Due to the extra operations and resource contention, the differences of the processing of different packets will be disrupted.

Based on this challenge, we propose the third requirement for NF performance diagnosis, **Perturbation-free:** *Performance perturbation to the packet-level performance behavior, caused by online measurement should be as small as possible.*

4   Overview

Before stepping into our evaluation, we first introduce our experiment environment in Sect. 4.1, and evaluation methods in Sect. 4.2.

4.1   Experiment Environment

Because our aim is to analyze and evaluate the general performance diagnosis methods in NF performance diagnosis scenario, we build a real NF forwarding environment, as shown in Fig. 4.

We use open source DPDK-based packet processing framework, Cisco VPP, to construct our NFs. All the NFs are running at a high performance commodity server, with an Intel Xeon Platinum 8160 CPU @2.10GHz, and 128GB DDR3

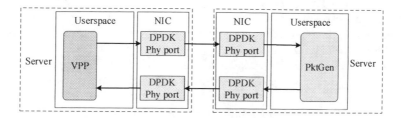

Fig. 4. NF forwarding environment

memory. Each core is equipped with a 32KB L1 data cache and a 1024KB L2 cache. A 33MB L3 cache is shared among all cores. The CentOS 7.9.2009 operation system with linux kernel 3.10 is installed on the server. The software packet generator is developed by ourselves based on DPDK, to support high performance packet sending and receiving with hardware timestamps. The packet generator is running on another server which has the same configuration with the one running NFs. To avoid the fluctuations in propagation delay, two servers are directly connected via the high performance Mellanox MT27800 NIC. The software we used are listed in Table. 4.

Table 4. The information of software used in the paper

Software	Version	Description
Cisco VPP [2]	19.08	Packet processing framework
Linux Perf [3] (*record*)	3.10	Sampling-based performance diagnosis tool
HPCToolkit [5] (*hpcrun*)	2021.03.10	Sampling-based performance diagnosis tool
TAU [10] (*tau_run*)	2.29.0	Instrumentation-based performance diagnosis tool
Score-P [8]	7.0	Instrumentation-based performance diagnosis tool

We choose three NFs, Firewall (FW), NAT, IPSec gateway (IPsec) as our target NFs. All of them are built based on Cisco VPP [2], which is one of the most popular packet processing frameworks. And to make it easy to follow, we choose the firewall NF as an example throughout the paper. Firewall is a very typical and common network function, which involves all packet processing stages described in Sect. 2.1. In Sect. 6, we also give the detailed experimental results of NAT and IPsec.

4.2   Evaluation Methods

The unique performance behavior characteristics of NF poses new challenges and requirements for performance diagnosis, as we described in Sect. 3. General-purpose PMC-based performance diagnosis tools have been widely used in the

NF performance diagnosis. However, can they meet the demand for NF performance diagnosis? Unfortunately, at present, there is a lack of verification of existing tools in NF scenarios.

In this paper, we validate and evaluate existing PMC-based performance diagnosis tools from two perspectives in real NF forwarding scenario.

– We delve into the principles of two major categories of PMC-based performance diagnosis tools. The performance diagnosis are performed on different types of NF and the information available is analyzed. Based on the principle of the tools and the information they can obtain, we analyze whether they are **fine-grained** and **flexible** enough for NF performance diagnosis, in Sect. 5.
– We propose a quantitative method for evaluating the performance perturbation of performance diagnosis tools. By evaluating the performance perturbation of existing performance diagnosis tools, we verify whether the tools are **perturbation-free**, in Sect. 6.

We evaluate two sampling-based methods (Perf [3] and HPCToolkit [5]) and two instrumentation-based methods (Score-P [8] and TAU [10]) in our NF forwarding environment. And to make it easy to follow, we choose Perf and TAU as the representatives of two categories to discuss their details. More explanations will be given in Sect. 5.2.

The rule sets and traffic patterns are all generated by ClassBench [36], which has been widely used to evaluate the performance of NF and packet processing algorithms. ClassBench produces rule sets based on seed files generated from real rule sets, and sequences of packet headers to exercise them. The software packet generator read the packet headers, and constructs 64-byte packets with random payloads.

5 Performance Diagnosis Based on PMC

In this section, we evaluate the PMC-based performance diagnosis tools, and verify whether they can meet the requirements of fine granularity and flexibility in the last section.

5.1 The Principle of PMC-Based Performance Diagnosis

First of all, we discuss the philosophy of PMC-based performance diagnosis. PMC is a set of hardware registers that can be configured to track hardware performance events, such as cache misses. Overall, PMC provides two types of performance diagnosis modes as follows.

– **Sampling mode.** PMC is configured to raise an interrupt every N times occurred events. The interrupt handler is responsible for recording the samples.
– **Counting mode.** PMC simply counts the number of events occurred from its startup. Linux provides a syscall-based API to read the registers directly.

Based on the sampling mode, the community proposes sampling-based performance diagnosis methods, whose main idea is shown in Fig. 5(a). Specifically, in the sampling-based methods, PMC is configured with a threshold value of N. As long as the counter exceeds N, PMC will raise an "overflow" event, and interrupt the kernel. Then, the interrupt handler will fetch the instruction address, PMC register values and call stack information to constitute "records", which finally are written into a ring buffer in the shared memory. The user-space measurement process will pull those "records" from the shared memory and store them into the local files for offline performance analysis.

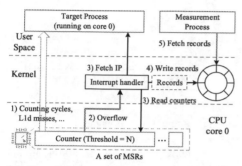
(a) Sampling-based performance diagnosis

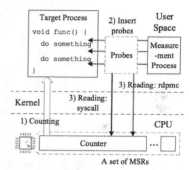
(b) Instrumentation-based performance diagnosis

Fig. 5. The principle of performance diagnosis technologies based on PMC

Meanwhile, some instrumentation-based performance diagnosis methods have been proposed based on the PMC counting mode. Figure 5(b) presents a typical work flow. Specifically, the measurement process actively constructs the probes and inserts them into a few specified location of the target program. That said, as long as the target program runs to one probe, the corresponding measurement code will be executed. Note that probes not only maintain a few metadata (e.g., location information and call stack) but also read PMC values through syscall-based *perf_event* API or the user-mode instruction *rdpmc*. In addition, probes are also responsible for structuring performance data as a record and storing it in a file.

5.2   The Capacity of Existing PMC-Based Performance Diagnosis Tools in NF Scenarios

Faced with so many PMC-based performance diagnosis tools, we next try to make it clear that whether these tools are enough for NFs. To this end, we enumerate the most popular PMC-based tools (see Table 5).

Table 5. Popular performance diagnosis tools in NF scenario

Type	Tools	Metrics	Applying to VPP
Sampling -based	Perf [3]	PMC metrics, kernel events	Directly
	HPCToolkit [5]	PMC metrics, kernel events	Directly
	Intel VTune [4]	PMC metrics, kernel events, stack data	Directly
Instrumentation-based	HPCToolkit	IO, memory consumption	Only external functions
	Intel VTune	IO, memory consumption	Only external functions
	Score-P [8]	PMC metrics, kernel events	Failed
	Callgrind [12]	Simulated hardware metrics	Limited measurement scope
	TAU [10]	PMC metrics, kernel events	Limited measurement scope
	Dyninst [34]	N&A	Only provide instrumentation library
	DynamoRio [35]	Simulated hardware metrics	Limited support

As mentioned before, we select two typical and popular tools, Perf and TAU. The underlying mechanism of the same type of diagnosis tools is similar. The major difference of sampling-based tools is the visual analysis and collection of metrics (see Table 5). From the perspective of PMC metrics, Perf is a representative sampling-based tool, which is open source and widely used. In the part of instrumentation-based tools, the differences appear in the instrumentation technology and the construction of probes. However, as we listed in Table 5, most of them don't have full support to NF performance diagnosis. For example, HPCToolkit and Intel VTune only support measuring the functions in external shared libraries. And Score-P cannot be applied to VPP framework, since VPP's complicated building environment. TAU can be directly applied to VPP framework without any modification and able to measure most of functions, so we choose TAU to represent instrumentation-based tools.

Sampling-based Perf generates time-aggregated performance data as shown in Fig. 6. Each rectangle represents a function while the shade of color indicates the number of performance events (CPU cycles) triggered by the function throughout the entire measurement task cycle. The up-to-down positions of the rectangles (functions) represent the function call sequence. Indeed, Perf is able to identify hot spot functions. However, the left-to-right positions do not reflect the function execution sequence. For example, in the flame graph, $dpdk\_input\_node\_fn\_avx2$ $\rightarrow$ $acl\_in\_l2\_ip4\_node\_fn\_avx2$ $\rightarrow$ $ethernet\_input\_node$ $\_fn$, does not mean their execution sequence. Limited by the PMC sampling mechanism, Perf cannot achieve per-packet measurement and analysis. The sampling of PMC is based on the frequency of occurrences of hardware performance events. Specifically, only when the program triggers N specified events, a sampling will be performed. Even with the call stack information, the results can only reflect the total number of the event triggered by certain function in a period of time. That said, we cannot distinguish the data of a specific function execution, let alone the data of a specific packet processing.

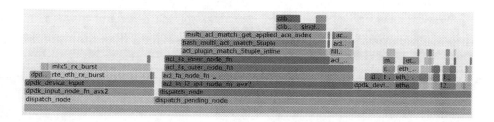

Fig. 6. The flame graph of FW based on part of data captured by Perf (cpu-cycles)

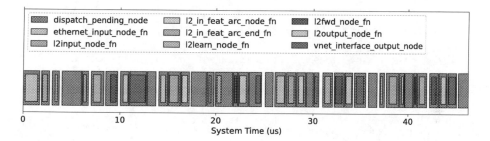

Fig. 7. The performance tracing of FW based on part of data captured by TAU (systime)

The instrumentation-based TAU tool gives a different performance view of the NF as shown in Fig. 7. For TAU, probes can be manually inserted into the NF at a specified location as required. Thus, we selected 9 functions, 8 of which are the main functions of VPP's functional modules (nodes) and the other is the dispatching function of all nodes. The probes are inserted into the entry and exit points of these functions in order to measure their execution overhead. In Fig. 7, the rectangles with different colors represent different functions, the width of the rectangle is the execution time. Since the execution of the probe and the packet processing of NF are tightly coupled, it is easy to distinguish every packet processing. For example, we can find out that there are 4 times of packet processing in Fig. 7, where each one starts from the $ethernet\_input\_node\_fn$, and ends at the next node of $vnet\_interface\_output\_node$, $dpdk\_dev\_output$. Furthermore, TAU can also fetch the time-aggregated global hot spots and call relationships via simple calculation. But instrumentation-based tools usually have two drawbacks as follow.

- *Limited measurable ranges.* Even though TAU can leverage the PMC, it cannot measure the library functions that are dynamically loaded. For example, ACL and DPDK-related modules are reported as the hot spots in Perf while TAU cannot measure them.
- *High measurement overhead.* Compared with sampling-based performance diagnosis methods, instrumentation-based methods introduce much greater overall measurement overhead. So far, it is widely believed that it will severely disrupt the performance behavior of NF, make measurements untrustworthy. However, does the high overall overhead of the measurement lead to large performance perturbation?

In summary, we argue that, neither sampling based performance diagnosis tools, nor instrumentation-based performance diagnosis tools can meet both requirements for granularity and flexibility. The sampling-based approach is not mechanically capable of packet-level performance tracing. Instrumentation-based methods have the potential for packet-level performance tracing, but lack flexibility.

6   Performance Perturbation

Intuitively, the performance diagnosis tools will introduce extra measurement overhead. But this leaves a question that whether higher measurement overhead leads to larger performance perturbation. This section replies to the question.

6.1   Performance Distribution Similarity

Capturing the performance data of NFs requires extra measurement operations, such as collecting, reading and saving performance data and so on. Indeed, these operations consume CPU and memory resources, leading to resource competition with the NFs and decreasing NF performance. Consequently, for PMC-based diagnosis tools, the values recorded in PMC registers become the original NF performance plus measurement overhead and their interplay.

To demonstrate it, we next conduct a set of experiments. Specifically, we build a typical NF (Firewall) based on VPP and evaluate its original performance as a baseline. Next, we respectively run the NF with the sampling-based and the instrumentation-based PMC tools, and record their performance results. Figure 8 shows the results. As expected, both the sampling-based and the instrumentation-based PMC tools introduce significant overhead while the instrumentation-based ones perform worse. Due to these reasons, the community tends to use the sampling-based PMC tools to diagnose the performance. However, does higher measurement overhead lead to larger performance perturbation?

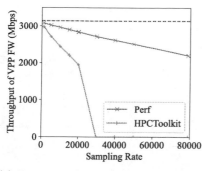
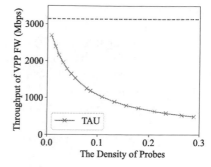

(a) Sampling-based performance diagnosis. The sampling rate is the maximum samples per second.

(b) Instrumentation-based performance diagnosis. The density of probes is the average number of probes executed during processing of each packet.

Fig. 8. The overall overhead of PMC-based performance diagnosis on VPP Firewall. The red dashed line represents the FW performance without any measurement

Key Finding–Performance Distribution Similarity with Instrumentation-Based Tools. We run the above NF again but using the "latency" as the performance metric. The latency is a packet-level performance metric that can achieve stable performance results as long as the NF runs in the same environment (e.g., rulesets, traffic patterns, and servers). With this basis, we evaluate the latency performance of the NF with/without TAU (a instrumentation-based diagnosis tool). Figure 9 shows the results. It is clear that their performance distributions are very similar.

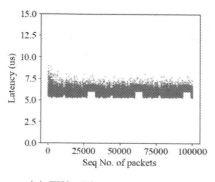
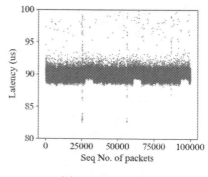

(a) FW without measurement

(b) FW with TAU

Fig. 9. The latency distribution of FW with and without measurement operations.

Theoretically, in the instrumentation-based measurement, the hot spots in the original NFs are still "hot" when running them with measurement tools.

The key reason is that those abnormal packets will lead to significant cost both in the two scenarios. That said, the abnormal events can be reserved in the measurement result. Logically, the measurement result can be viewed as a slow-down of the original performance. As shown in Fig. 9, though TAU introduces high measurement overhead increasing the average latency from $5.94\mu s$ up to $89.90\mu s$, the similarity is reserved.

We believe that high performance distribution similarity means low performance perturbation. This is because it is possible to infer to the original performance based on the measurement result.

6.2   Coefficient of Interference

Based on the prior observation, we propose a quantitative evaluation method for performance perturbation happened in NF performance diagnosis.

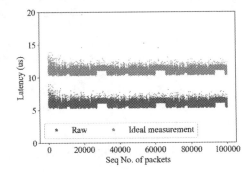

Fig. 10. Ideal measurement with incremental overhead

Let's consider an ideal zero-performance-perturbation measurement even if it still introduces measurement overhead. In such case, the measurement overhead should be constant and identical for each input packet. The latency distribution of one NF that runs with measurement operations is equal to moving that of the NF running without measurements (a.k.a isomorphic latency distribution). Figure 10 shows an example. That said, zero-performance-perturbation measurement does not change the latency distribution.

Unfortunately, the actual measurement overhead in NF is uncertain; this breaks the isomorphism of the latency distribution and leads to performance perturbation. To quantify the performance perturbation, we introduce the coefficient of interference, CoI for short.

Essentially, CoI is the quantification of the latency distribution similarity with and without the measurement. From the following three aspects, we believe that, latency distribution similarity is enough to reflect the performance perturbation. Other metrics, such as throughput and PMC hardware metrics are not suitable.

1) Latency is one of the most important performance metrics for NF, and is able to clearly characterize NF packet-level performance.

2) For NF diagnosis, we usually focus on the related performance data. For example, to identify the costliest function, we need to distinguish who has a relatively high resource consumption. To identify the reason of fluctuations, we need to identify which packet took longer process, and which part of code was unstable. Therefore, the diagnosis methods should remain the fine-grained differences (relative state) of the processing. Even if the overall overhead is high, as long as the relative state can be maintained, we can still locate the culprit. The global performance metrics, such as throughput, cannot describe fine-grained performance differences. Packet-level performance metric, latency and its distribution, can clearly describe the packet-level differences of the processing, as we described in Sect. 6.1.

3) Our goal is to evaluate performance perturbation accurately. If the measurement of the metrics used to evaluate the perturbation introduces new perturbation, the results will become unreliable. The measurement of latency can be executed in the side of packet generator, isolated from the execution of NF. In contrast, the measurement of PMC hardware performance metrics must be executed in the same environment with NF. Fine-grained PMC measurement will introduce new perturbation.

For an input packet set $P = \{p_0, p_1, \ldots, p_n\}$, $lat_M(p_i)$ is denoted as the processing latency of the packet p_i when the measurement operations are activated. Likewise, $lat(p_i)$ refers to the process latency of packet p_i without any measurement operation. We normalize the latency data, and use $E[lat_M]$ and $E[lat]$ to respectively refer to their average values. With this basis, for a packet p_i, we define its "latency distance" as follow.

$$D_i = |(lat_M(p_i) - E[lat_M]) - (lat(p_i) - E[lat])| \tag{1}$$

Thus, we further define the coefficient of interference—the sum of each packet "latency distance". Specifically, for the input packet set P, the corresponding CoI_P is calculated as follow.

$$CoI_P = \sum_{i=0}^{n} D_i \tag{2}$$

For the ideal zero-performance-perturbation measurement (see Fig. 10), the measurement overhead of each is constant. In other words, for any packet, its "latency distance" is also a constant value C while the CoI_P is zero. More details are as follow.

$$\forall p_i \in P, lat_M(p_i) - lat(p_i) = C \rightarrow E[lat_M] - E[lat] = C \tag{3}$$

$$D_i = |(lat_M(p_i) - lat(p_i)) - (E[lat_M] - E[lat])| = C - C = 0 \tag{4}$$

$$CoI_P = \sum_{i=0}^{n} D_i = 0 \tag{5}$$

It is clear that, for one NF running under the same configurations, the less the *CoI* is, the smaller performance perturbation is. Logically speaking, it is impossible to achieve the ideal zero-performance-perturbation measurement due to a few complex influence factors, such as cache contention.

6.3 The Performance Perturbation of PMC-based Performance Diagnosis Tools

Based on the quantitative evaluation method, we are able to evaluate the performance perturbation of existing PMC-based performance diagnosis tools for the NF scenario. For instrumentation-based tools, we choose TAU. This is because we failed to integrate the Score-P tool into VPP due to the complicated CMAKE compilation structure while other instrumentation-based tools also lack the full support of PMC. For sampling-based performance diagnosis tools, we choose Perf since the sampling-based HPCToolkit relies on the same PMC sampling driver, the Linux perf_event, whose behaviors are similar to Perf.

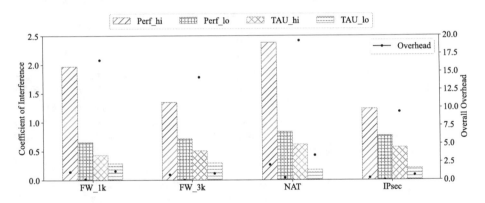

Fig. 11. The coefficient of interference of different performance diagnosis tools on different NFs

We apply these tools to 4 NFs constructed by VPP while the results are shown in Fig. 11. FW_1k is a firewall with 1k rules while FW_3k is the firewall with 3k rules. Both of the rule sets are generated by ClassBench [36]. NAT is a simple SNAT that translates the source IP addresses based on the longest prefix match rules. IPSec provides the authentication of IP packets based on the Authentication Header protocol (AH) while packets are classified by 100 5-tuple rules, and then perform authentication with the SHA1-96 cryptographic hash algorithm.

Each performance diagnosis tool can be configured into two modes: the measurement with high overhead (_hi) and the measurement with low overhead (_lo). The overall overhead in the Fig. 11 is calculated as follows. The $Latency_{with\_measurement}$ represents the average latency of NFs with the measurement. And $Latency$ represents the average latency without the measurement.

$$Overhead = \frac{Latency_{with\_measurement}}{Latency} - 1 \tag{6}$$

For all NFs, even running the sampling-based tools with low overhead, the coefficient of interference is much larger than that of TAU. For example, let's consider FW_3k in Fig. 11. The overhead of Perf_lo is very low (0.020) comparing with TAU_hi (14.240). On the contrary, the CoI of Perf_lo (0.713) is 1.412 times as much as that of TAU_hi (0.505). For all cases, the CoI in TAU is only 7.39% to 74.31% of that in Perf. In summary, even though instrumentation-based performance diagnosis tools introduce larger overall overhead than sampling-based tools, their performance perturbation is less than sampling-based tools in NF scenario.

The Reason for Why Sampling-Based Tools Lead to Large Perfor-mance Perturbation. Recall that the principle of sampling-based performance diagnosis (see Sect. 5.1) shows that the PMC sampling is based on the frequency of the triggered performance events. That said, the location where extra measurement operations are performed in the target program cannot be controlled; the number of samples happened in each packet processing is unpredictable and uneven.

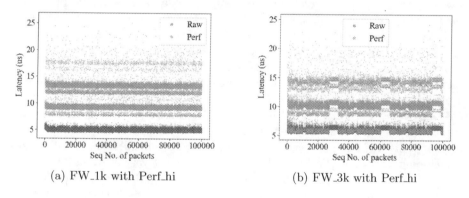

(a) FW_1k with Perf_hi   (b) FW_3k with Perf_hi

Fig. 12. The latency distribution of FW with and without measurement

To verify it, we further evaluate the latency distribution of Perf_hi (see Fig. 12). We find out the packet latency points are located into several layers. Packets in the upper layer suffer from more PMC sampling operations, leading to more measurement overhead. Worse, due to the transitivity of NF performance problems (see Sect. 3), the packets with more PMC sampling operations require more processing time so that they will increase the queuing delay of the subsequent packets. Furthermore, the PMC sampling adopts the expensive interrupt mechanism while handling one interrupt often consumes $2\mu s$ to $4\mu s$. Note that the average latency of FW_3k is only $5.89\mu s$.

In contrast, the instrumentation-based methods insert the probes at the pre-determined execution points on the processing path. And the operations performed by the probe are usually simple and fixed. Therefore, even with the large overall overhead, the performance perturbation of instrumentation-based methods is still relatively small. With this basis, we argue that the instrumentation-based performance diagnosis is more efficient than the sampling-based ones.

7   Towards Accurate NF Performance Diagnosis

Though sampling-based performance diagnosis methods can be applied into a wide range of areas (e.g., HPC), they fail to achieve fine-grained packet/batch-level time-scale performance diagnosis. On the contrary, the instrumentation-based methods are capable of fine-grained packet/batch-level time-scale performance diagnosis with small performance perturbation. However, the scope of the instrumentation-based methods is limited, which also are not easy to use. Based on our prior analysis on the two types of performance diagnosis methods, we next discuss how to build a hybrid solution that can achieve accurate NF performance diagnosis.

First-Glance Profiling: Hotspot Analysis via Sampling-Based Tools. Most of sampling-based tools don't need any modification to the NF programs. Developers can directly employ them to perform the performance diagnosis even with little knowledge of the target NF. Compared with the instrumentation-based methods, sampling-based methods are able to capture almost all executed functions, including those inline functions. Therefore, at the first glance, we argue that the sampling-based performance diagnosis methods should be used to identify the hot functions or call paths.

In-Depth Performance Diagnosis: Instrumentation-Based Tools Associated with Packet Lifecycle Infos. After identifying the hot functions or call paths during the packet processing, the instrumentation-based performance diagnosis tools can be used to achieve packet-level performance tracing. Altogether with the lifecycle information (e.g., Sending/Receiving time), we can further obtain the detailed processing progress for each packet. Next we use an example to illustrate it (see Fig. 13).

The top of Fig. 13 presents the basic packet processing modules while the middle portion shows multiple packet processing. Note that each packet processing starts from the *ethernet_input_node_fn* node, and ends at the next node of *vnet_interface_output_node*. The bottom of the Fig. 13 refers to the packet life-cycle infos (Sending/Receiving time), while each line corresponds to one packet and the color represents its latency. In this example, there is a batch with 7 packets that are required to be processed by the NF. We also find out the first packet has long queuing latency while the last packet suffers form the abnormal execution of *dispatch_pending_node*.

Efficient Instrumentation-Based NF Performance Diagnosis Method is Required. To restate, the existing instrumentation-based tools have a lot of drawbacks. TAU is the only tool that can be applied to VPP for NF performance

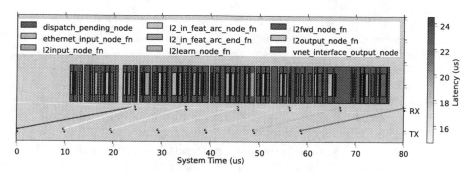

Fig. 13. The mapping between the performance tracing data and the RX&TX times-tamps

diagnosis, but it still fails to measure the library functions that are dynamically loaded when running NFs. In addition, for multi-core multi-thread programs, only the PMC on the master core can be manipulated correctly. Thanks to the modern instrumentation technology, it has already supported the instrumentation for run-time multi-core multi-threading processes. With this basis, we can effectively alleviate the limitations of TAU. In addition, the probe also has a large optimization space, such as replacing the syscall-based *perf_event* with the user-mode instruction supported by the newer Linux kernels.

Based on the above design principles, we plan to design a packet-level performance diagnosis method based on modern instrumentation technology, and build well-defined lightweight measurement probes in the future.

8 Related Work

Performance Diagnosis Inside Software NFs. Some works [15,16] employ static code analysis technique, such as Symbolic Execution (SE), to analyze the behavior of NFs under the simulation environment. These are efficient for correctness checking. But for performance diagnosis, they are not reliable, since hardware-level commercial techniques (such as Intel SmartCache) are difficult to simulate. Other researchers [13,14,17–19] use queue monitoring and flow measurement to approximately identify performance problems through mathematical modeling and theoretical analysis. Unfortunately, these methods can only work in either the NF location problem for the VNF service chains or identifying the flows that lead to the performance issues. That said, they are not able to perform fine-grained performance diagnosis for NFs.

Accuracy Assessment of Performance Diagnosis. Weaver, V. M. [26], D. Z [27] have proven that the performance data measured by PMC is accurate. However, besides the measurement of PMC hardware, PMC-based performance diagnosis methods require additional operations, such as reading PMC registers, recording address and stack information, which probably lead to performance perturbation.

Evaluation of Performance Perturbation. Overall, there are two types of evaluation methods for performance perturbation caused by performance diagnosis. One is based on the global overhead. For example, some works [6,7,28–30] employ the differences in the execution time and memory footprint of the programs when they run with/without measurement operations, to evaluate the accuracy of the measurement. Unfortunately, these differences only reflect the overall performance rather than the performance perturbation. The other is based on case studies. Specifically, some early works on general performance diagnosis methods [5,8–10] directly measure standardized benchmarks (SPEC, etc.). FVSAMPLER [6], DrCCTProf [7] and other HPC performance diagnosis methods perform diagnosis and manual code optimization for standardized benchmarks and common HPC programs, and use the results of optimization to define their accuracy. However, the manual fashion is time-consuming and error-prone.

9   Conclusions

The softwareization of network functions (NFs) effectively increases the flexibility of development and management, but inevitably sacrifice processing performance due to the complex run-time experiment and intense resource contention (e.g., Cache). Therefore, how to accurately diagnose performance bottlenecks in NFs for performance improvement is very significant. Since the complicated NF frameworks and running environment, NF performance diagnosis is difficult and costly. In this paper, we focus on the specific performance behavior of NF, re-think the challenges and requirements of NF performance diagnosis. We argue that, NF performance diagnosis methods should be fine-grained, flexible, and perturbation-free. With these requirements, we investigate general-purpose PMC-based performance diagnosis methods, which have been widely used in NF performance diagnosis. Through theoretical mechanism analysis and NF measurement verification in real scenarios, we find that, existing PMC-based methods cannot simultaneously meet the requirements to granularity and flexibility. We also innovatively propose a quantitative evaluation method for the performance perturbation caused by the measurement. And through the experiments on two typical PMC-based performance diagnosis, we argue that, high measurement overhead does not mean large performance perturbation, and instrumentation-based tools are more perturbation-free for NF performance diagnosis. In the end, we also give a hybrid solution for NF performance diagnosis. And we plan to design and implement an efficient packet-level performance diagnosis method for software network functions in the future.

Acknowledgments. We thank our shepherd Simone Ferlin-Reiter and the anonymous reviewers for their insightful feedback. This work is supported in part by the National Key R&D Program of China (Grant No. 2019YFB1802800), and in part by the National Natural Science Foundation of China (Grant No. 61725206).

References

1. Faqir, Z.Y., Michael, B., Sibylle, S., Fabian, S.: NFV and SDN-Key technology enablers for 5G networks. IEEE J. Sel. Areas Commun. **35**(11), 2468–2478 (2017)
2. Cisco: vector packet processing (2022). https://wiki.fd.io/view/VPP
3. Linux Community: perf: Linux profiling with performance counters (2009). https://perf.wiki.kernel.org/index.php/Main_Page
4. Intel Corporation: intel VTune performance analyzer (2022). https://www.intel.com/content/www/us/en/develop/documentation/vtune-help/top.html
5. Laksono, A.S.B., Michael, F., Mark, K., Gabriel, M., John, M., Nathan, R.T.: HPCTOOLKIT: tools for performance analysis of optimized parallel programs. Concurr. Comput. Pract. Exper. **22**(6), 685–701 (2009)
6. Pengfei, S., Shuyin, J., Milind, C., Xu, L.: Pinpointing performance inefficiencies via lightweight variance profiling. In: Proceedings of the International Conference for High Performance Computing, Networking, Storage and Analysis, SC2019, pp. 1–19. Association for Computing Machinery, Denver, Colorado (2019)
7. Qidong, Z., Xu, L., Milind, C.: DrCCTProf: a fine-grained call path profiler for ARM-based clusters. In: Proceedings of the International Conference for High Performance Computing, Networking, Storage and Analysis, SC2020, pp. 1–16. IEEE Press, Atlanta, GA, USA (2020)
8. Andreas, K., et al.: Score-P: a joint performance measurement run-time infrastructure for Periscope, Scalasca, Tau, and Vampir. In: Brunst, H., Müller, M., Nagel, W., Resch, M. (eds.) Tools for High Performance Computing 2011. LNCS, pp. 79–91. Springer, Heidelberg (2011). https://doi.org/10.1007/978-3-642-31476-6_7
9. Markus, G., Felix, W., Brian, J.N.W., Erika, Á'., Daniel, B., Bernd, M.: The Scalasca performance toolset architecture. Concurr. Comput. Pract. Exper. **22**(6), 702–719 (2010)
10. Sameer, S.S., Allen, D.M.: The TAU Parallel Performance System. Int. J. High Perform. Comput. Appl. **20**(2), 287–311 (2006)
11. David, B., et al.: Caliper: performance introspection for HPC software stacks. In: Proceedings of the International Conference for High Performance Computing, Networking, Storage and Analysis, SC2016, pp. 550–560. IEEE Press, Salt Lake City, UT, USA (2016)
12. Nicholas, N., Julian, S.: Valgrind: a framework for heavyweight dynamic binary instrumentation. In: Proceedings of the 28th ACM SIGPLAN Conference on Programming Language Design and Implementation, PLDI2007, pp. 89–100. Association for Computing Machinery, San Diego, California, USA (2007)
13. Junzhi, G., Yuliang, L., Bilal, A., Aman, S., Minlan, Y.: Microscope: queue-based performance diagnosis for network functions. In: Proceedings of the 2020 Conference of the ACM Special Interest Group on Data Communication, SIGCOMM2020, pp. 390–403. Association for Computing Machinery, Virtual Event, USA (2020)
14. Yiran, L., Liangcheng, Y., Vincent, L., Mingwei, X.: PrintQueue: performance diagnosis via queue measurement in the data plane. In: Proceedings of the 2022 Conference of the ACM Special Interest Group on Data Communication, SIGCOMM2022, pp. 516–529. Association for Computing Machinery, Amsterdam, Netherlands (2022)
15. Luis, P., Rishabh, I., Arseniy, Z., Jonas, F., Katerina, A.: Automated synthesis of adversarial workloads for network functions. In: Proceedings of the 2018 Conference of the ACM Special Interest Group on Data Communication, SIGCOMM2018, pp. 372–385. Association for Computing Machinery, Budapest, Hungary (2018)

16. Rishabh, I., Luis, P., Arseniy, Z., Solal, P., Katerina, A., George, C.: Performance contracts for software network functions. In: 16th USENIX Symposium on Networked Systems Design and Implementation, NSDI2019. USENIX Association, Boston, MA, USA (2019)
17. Xiaoqi, C., et al.: Fine-grained queue measurement in the data plane. In: Proceedings of the 15th International Conference on Emerging Networking Experiments And Technologies, CoNEXT2019, pp. 15–29. Association for Computing Machinery, Orlando, Florida (2019)
18. Vimalkumar, J., Mohammad, A., Yilong, G., Changhoon, K., David, M.: Millions of little minions: using packets for low latency network programming and visibility. In: Proceedings of the 2014 Conference of the ACM Special Interest Group on Data Communication, SIGCOMM2014, pp. 3–14. Association for Computing Machinery, Chicago, Illinois, USA (2014)
19. John, S., Oliver, M., Adam, J.A., Eric, K., Jonathan, M.S.: Scaling hardware accelerated network monitoring to concurrent and dynamic queries with *flow. In: Proceedings of the 2018 USENIX Conference on Usenix Annual Technical Conference, ATC2018, pp. 823–835. USENIX Association, Boston, MA, USA (2018)
20. Nick, M., et al.: OpenFlow: enabling innovation in campus networks. SIGCOMM Comput. Commun. Rev. $38(2)$, 69–74 (2008)
21. Srinivasan, V., Suri, S., Varghese, G.: Packet classification using tuple space search. SIGCOMM Comput. Commun. Rev. $29(4)$, 135–146 (1999)
22. James, D., et al.: TupleMerge: fast software packet processing for online packet classification. IEEE/ACM Trans. Networking $27(4)$, 1417–1431 (2019)
23. Xinyi, Z., Xie, G., Xin, W., Penghao, Z., Li, Y., Kavé, S.: Fast online packet classification with convolutional neural network. IEEE/ACM Trans. Netw. $29(6)$, 2765–2778 (2021)
24. Sorrachai, Y., James, D., Alex, X.L., Eric, T.: A sorted partitioning approach to high-speed and fast-update OpenFlow classification. In: 2016 IEEE 24th International Conference on Network Protocols, ICNP2016, pp. 1–10. IEEE, Singapore (2016)
25. Kirill, K., Sergey, I.N., Ori, R., William, C., Patrick, E.: Exploiting order independence for scalable and expressive packet classification. IEEE/ACM Trans. Networking $24(2)$, 1251–1264 (2015)
26. Vincent, M.W., Sally, A.M.: Can hardware performance counters be trusted? In: 2008 IEEE International Symposium on Workload Characterization, pp. 141–150 (2008)
27. Dmitrijs, Z., Milan, J., Matthias, H.: Accuracy of performance counter measurements. In: 2009 IEEE International Symposium on Performance Analysis of Systems and Software, ISPASS2009, pp. 23–32. IEEE, Boston, Massachusetts (2009)
28. Todd, M., Amer, D., Matthias, H., Peter, F.S.: Understanding Measurement Perturbation in Trace-based Data. In: 2007 IEEE International Parallel and Distributed Processing Symposium, IPDPS2007, pp.1–6. IEEE, Long Beach, California (2007)
29. Matthias, W., et al.: Detection and visualization of performance variations to guide identification of application bottlenecks. In: 2016 45th International Conference on Parallel Processing Workshops, ICPPW2016, pp. 289–298. IEEE, Philadelphia, PA, USA (2016)
30. Lehr, J.-P., Iwainsky, C., Bischof, C.: The influence of HPCToolkit and Score-p on hardware performance counters. In: Proceedings of the 4th ACM SIGPLAN International Workshop on Software Engineering for Parallel Systems, SEPS2017. Association for Computing Machinery, Vancouver, BC, Canada (2017)

31. Srikanth, K., Ratul, M., Patrick, V., Sharad, A., Jitendra, P., Paramvir, B.: Detailed diagnosis in enterprise networks. In: Proceedings of the ACM SIGCOMM 2009 Conference on Data Communication, SIGCOMM2009, pp. 243–254. Association for Computing Machinery, Barcelona, Spain (2009)
32. Ben, P., et al.: The design and implementation of open vSwitch. In: 12th USENIX Symposium on Networked Systems Design and Implementation, NSDI2015, pp. 117–130. USENIX Association, Oakland, CA (2015)
33. Eddie, K., Robert, M., Benjie, C., John, J., Marinus, F.K.: The click modular router. ACM Trans. Comput. Syst. **18**(3), 263–297 (2000)
34. Buck, B., Hollingsworth, J.K.: An API for runtime code patching. Int. J. High Perform. Comput. Appl. **14**(4), 317–329 (2000)
35. Derek, B., Qin, Z., Saman, A.: Transparent dynamic instrumentation. In: Proceedings of the 8th ACM SIGPLAN/SIGOPS conference on Virtual Execution Environments, VEE2012, pp. 133–144. Association for Computing Machinery, London, England, UK (2012)
36. David, E.T., Jonathan, S.T.: ClassBench: a packet classification benchmark. IEEE/ACM Trans. Networking **15**(3), 499–511 (2007)
37. Sangjin, H., Keon, J., Aurojit, P., Shoumik, P., Dongsu, H., Sylvia, R.: SoftNIC: a software NIC to augment hardware. Technical Report No. UCB/EECS-2015-155 (2015). http://www2.eecs.berkeley.edu/Pubs/TechRpts/2015/EECS-2015-155.html

Network Performance

Evaluation of the ProgHW/SW Architectural Design Space of Bandwidth Estimation

Tianqi Fang[(⊠)], Lisong Xu, Witawas Srisa-an, and Jay Patel

University of Nebraska-Lincoln, Lincoln, USA
{tfang,xu,witty}@cse.unl.edu, jpatel9@huskers.unl.edu

Abstract. Bandwidth estimation (BWE) is a fundamental functionality in congestion control, load balancing, and many network applications. Therefore, researchers have conducted numerous BWE evaluations to improve its estimation accuracy. Most current evaluations focus on the algorithmic aspects or network conditions of BWE. However, as the architectural aspects of BWE gradually become the bottleneck in multi-gigabit networks, many solutions derived from current works fail to provide satisfactory performance. In contrast, this paper focuses on the architectural aspects of BWE in the current trend of programmable hardware (ProgHW) and software (SW) co-designs. Our work makes several new findings to improve BWE accuracy from the architectural perspective. For instance, we show that offloading components that can directly affect inter-packet delay (IPD) is an effective way to improve BWE accuracy. In addition, to handle the architectural deployment difficulty not appeared in past studies, we propose a modularization method to increase evaluation efficiency.

Keywords: Bandwidth estimation · Programmable hardware · Evaluation

1 Introduction

Bandwidth estimation (BWE) is an essential functionality used in various network fields ranging from cloud applications to congestion control [3,4,27,33,46]. For example, BWE can improve the performance of Hadoop by optimizing the bandwidth utilization among a group of virtual machines (VMs) [27]. However, inaccurate BWE can cause packet loss and degraded throughput [24,46]. Therefore, how to improve BWE accuracy is an ever-lasting research topic.

While researchers and engineers have conducted many studies and evaluations of BWE, most of them focus on either the algorithmic designs and parameters of BWE [34,41,42,44,48] or the impact of network conditions on BWE [10,22,42], but the architectural optimizations have not been addressed adequately. Nevertheless, as networks become faster (e.g., 10 Gbps, 100 Gbps) and more complex nowadays, the architectural aspects of BWE become increasingly important [31]. Consider time precision as an example. BWE relies heavily

A. Brunstrom et al. (Eds.): PAM 2023, LNCS 13882, pp. 257–283, 2023.
https://doi.org/10.1007/978-3-031-28486-1_12

on packet timing measurement. On faster networks, packet transmission time becomes shorter, which makes measurement more sensitive to timing errors caused by interrupt coalescing [35] or OS scheduling [25] of software-based architectures. In addition, concurrency issues of software-based architectures can also interfere with BWE accuracy [14].

In the paper, we aim to fill the gap above by systematically evaluating the architectural design space of BWE, especially in the trend of programmable hardware (ProgHW)/software (SW) co-designs. The comparison between our work and related works is shown in Fig. 1. Recently, one of the major architectural upgrades is that pure SW-based network stacks have gradually been replaced by ProgHW/SW co-designs, such as Azure SmartNIC [18], Microsoft Catapult [36] or AWS F1 [43]. This new ProgHW/SW paradigm can provide a group of design choices unavailable in the past to improve BWE accuracy in high-speed networks. Although a few works have used ProgHW to improve timing measurement accuracy [19,20,46], some important questions have not been studied carefully, and we aim to answer them in the paper. For example, compared with BWE optimization techniques, what are the gains and costs of ProgHW-based designs? Considering the variety of BWE components, what are the trade-offs and cost-efficiencies of different ProgHW/SW combinations?

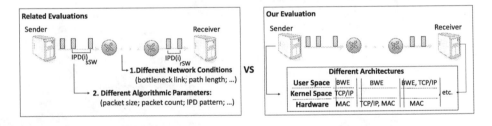

Fig. 1. Comparison between related works and our work

The main cause for the inadequate architectural evaluation is that the evaluation of the ProgHW/SW space is more laborious and challenging than evaluations carried out on pure SW. There are two reasons. First, the evaluation period of ProgHW/SW often takes much longer time than that of pure SW. Compared with SW-level compilation, ProgHW-level compilation or ProgHW offloading has many extra steps, such as netlist synthesis, place and route, and timing, power, and area constraints. These extra steps are time-consuming. Second, ProgHW/SW space provides more combinations than pure SW, which increases the workload of the architectural comparison. Specifically, for one endpoint, a different BWE algorithm may have different components, and each component can choose to stay at either ProgHW or SW to make up a different architecture. For two endpoints, a sender and a receiver can use different architectures to execute BWE. These diverse combinations increase the number of evaluation cases.

We deal with the ProgHW/SW evaluation challenges by leveraging an insight: most factors that impact BWE performance can be attributed to a single factor: inter-packet delay (IPD), and architectures of different BWE algorithms have many common components related to IPD. Therefore, we classify and study different ProgHW/SW architectures based on how they impact IPD. IPD describes the difference among packet latencies, which differentiates our classification from other works that focus on the absolute values of packet latencies [21,47]. In addition, we modularize the BWE components that process and transmit IPD information and reuse those modules in different architectures, thereby saving time from ProgHW-level compilation and reducing evaluation difficulty.

Our contributions are summarized as follows:

- In terms of the evaluation object, we build an IPD-based classification to systematically evaluate different ProgHW/SW architectures of BWE. Furthermore, we study topics that have not been addressed well, such as heterogeneous combinations and the comparison between SW-level and ProgHW-level optimization techniques. In addition, we make several new findings as follows:
  - If the limited supply of cloud ProgHW only allows one end (sender or receiver) to be deployed with a new BWE ProgHW/SW configuration, then deployment on the receiver alone can achieve a similar effect to the two-end configuration and can only consume half the ProgHW resources at the same time.
  - Although ProgHW/SW designs and pure SW designs have comparable performance in low-speed networks, the former show much better performance in high-speed networks. Specifically, in a 100 Gbps network, ProgHW/SW designs can improve average IPD accuracy by 45% (max: 64%) and average BWE accuracy by 20% (max: 35%).
  - Although offloading modules from SW to ProgHW can have better timing accuracy, offloading more does not necessarily achieve better performance in BWE. We find that the offloading of modules that directly update IPD can maximize BWE accuracy.
- In terms of the evaluation methodology, we propose an IPD-modular method that improves the evaluation efficiency by multiple times.
- We implement BWE modules in ProgHW and make them meet the requirements of BWE evaluations and be portable across different architectures.

The paper is organized as follows: Sect. 2 introduces our motivation and the background of BWE. Section 3 presents our IPD-based classification of architectures. Section 4 presents the implementation details of our modularization. Section 5 evaluates ProgHW/SW architectural space for BWE. Section 6 summarizes related works and Sect. 7 concludes the paper.

2   Motivation and Background

In this section, we first present our motivation to evaluate the ProgHW/SW architectural space of BWE and then introduce the working principles of different BWE types, in which **we show that most BWE algorithms have a close relation with IPD, which bases our classification and modularization of ProgHW/SW architectures**.

2.1   Motivation

Our motivation to do the ProgHW/SW architectural evaluation can be summarized into three points:

1) As network speed keeps growing, algorithmic optimizations alone do not meet BWE accuracy requirements anymore, and architectural factors have an increasing impact. For example, the work [23] suggests a technique of increasing measurement samples to improve BWE accuracy based on the law of large numbers. However, the study [25] shows that this technique can only keep timing error within a few microseconds in typical Linux architectures, which is not acceptable in current multi-gigabit speed where packet gaps are at sub-microsecond level.
2) The prevalence of ProgHW brings up a set of new architectural optimizations infeasible in the past, such as TCP/IP offloading, or BWE functions offloading, but existing evaluations lack a systematic comparison among those new architectures. For example, Emmerich et al. [17] only analyze kernel-bypass architectures. Besides, most evaluations also miss a comparison between ProgHW designs and traditional BWE optimizations, such as BASS [48].
3) Several topics of ProgHW designs have not been addressed sufficiently in existing works. First, although a few works leverage ProgHW to improve packet transmission accuracy [19, 20, 46], the costs of such practice are inadequately discussed. Balancing benefits and costs has practical value at the current stage. Compared with SW, developing and deploying BWE algorithms on ProgHW/SW often take much longer time. For example, we find that compiling a typical BWE algorithm pathload [23] only takes a few seconds on SW, but it takes 8–9 hours on a ProgHW/SW architecture to complete. The reason is that ProgHW compilation does not only need to translate a high-level language to a netlist but also needs to guarantee the closure of timing, power, and area. Second, heterogeneous combinations are less-studied where the sender and the receiver have different architectures. This topic is important because high-end ProgHW is limited and expensive at the current time [30], and there might not be enough ProgHWs for both endpoints.

2.2   Bandwidth Estimation Background

Network bandwidth is an attribute of a network path, and it specifies how fast a user can send data through this path. Bandwidth is useful information, but it is often hard to obtain from routers due to technical and privacy issues, so people develop various BWE algorithms that can estimate this information from endpoints.

   This part presents the working principles and classification of major BWE algorithms. Please refer to Table 1 for definitions of symbols. There are three metrics for bandwidth: capacity (bw-capa), available bandwidth (avai-bw), and achievable throughput [24]. Capacity is the maximum rate that a network path can support. In a real network path, some portion of capacity may be occupied

Table 1. Symbols and notations

Format	
$Symbol(i)_l$	i denotes the i-th packet and l denotes any of four locations: sSW (sender's SW), rSW (receiver's SW), sHW (sender's NIC port), and rHW (receiver's NIC port)
$\Delta Symbol(i)_l$	$Symbol(i+1)_l - Symbol(i)_l$
Symbol	
$t(i)_l$	Measured timepoint of i-th packet at location l
$t(i)_l^R$	Real timepoint of i-th packet at location l
$tdr(i)_l$	Clock drift at l: $t(i)_l - t(i)_l^R$
$d(i)_{SW}$	Measured delay of i-th packet from sender to receiver by SW: $t(i)_{rSW} - t(i)_{sSW}$
$d(i)_{HW}$	Measured delay of i-th packet from sender to receiver by HW: $t(i)_{rHW} - t(i)_{sHW}$
$d(i)^R$	Real delay: $t(i)_{rHW}^R - t(i)_{sHW}^R$
$IPD(i)_l$	$IPD(i)_l = \Delta t(i)_l = t(i+1)_l - t(i)_l$
$\Theta IPD(i)_{SW}$	$IPD(i)_{rSW} - IPD(i)_{sSW}$
$\Theta IPD(i)_{HW}$	$IPD(i)_{rHW} - IPD(i)_{sHW}$
$n(i)_s^R$	Real delay from SW to ProgHW on sender
$n(i)_r^R$	Real delay from ProgHW to SW on receiver

by cross traffic, then the rest capacity for our usage is called available bandwidth. While the first two metrics only consider network speed, the achievable throughput also considers an endpoint's processing speed and protocols. In a nutshell, achievable throughput indicates the maximum throughput that a system can achieve under a given protocol, network speed, and processing speed.

From the perspective of working principles, BWE algorithms can be classified into the packet-pair type and the packet-train type as shown in Fig. 2. The details of each algorithm in Fig. 2 can be found in [25]. The two types differ in timing features but share a basic idea: a sender sends out a set of packets with a pre-defined timing feature. If the sending rate exceeds the bandwidth, a receiver will detect a change in the timing feature when those packets arrive. BWE algorithms iteratively adjust sending rates to find the turning point where the change occurs, and the turning point is the estimated bandwidth value.

We first define IPD as follows. Examples of IPD such as $IPD(i)_{sSW}$ and $IPD(i)_{rSW}$ are shown in Fig. 2.

Definition 1. *Inter-packet Delay (IPD) is the timing delay between any two consecutive packets.*

For the **packet-pair** type, a pair of packets are sent out back-to-back or in a pre-defined IPD value. Then, a receiver captures the receiving IPD and compares it with the pre-defined IPD to infer bw-capa or avai-bw. The formal expression is as follows:

Definition 2. *A packet-pair BWE algorithm is a function of the difference between the receiving and sending IPDs. Assume there are n pairs of packets (i.e., 2×n packets) in transmission, the estimated value BW is as follows:*

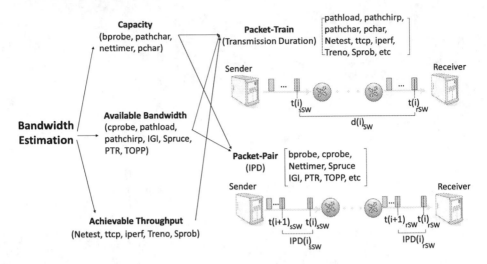

Fig. 2. Bandwidth estimation classification

$$BW = f(\Theta IPD(1)_{SW}, \Theta IPD(3)_{SW}, \cdots, \Theta IPD(2n-1)_{SW})$$

For the **packet-train** type, a sequence of packets are transmitted from a sender to a receiver. For the i-th packet, the difference between its receiving timepoint $t(i)_{rSW}$ and sending timepoint $t(i)_{sSW}$ is called its delay $d(i)_{SW}$. The packet-train type analyzes the change in each packet's delay to estimate the bandwidth. This type includes different patterns of probing rate such as constant rate [23] or exponential rate [38]. The formal expression is as follows:

Definition 3. *A packet-train BWE algorithm is a function of changes in packet delays from the sender to the receiver. Assume there are n packets in transmission, the estimated value BW is as follows:*

$$BW = f(\Delta d(1)_{SW}, \Delta d(2)_{SW}, \cdots, \Delta d(n-1)_{SW})$$
$$where \; \forall i \in [1, n), \Delta d(i)_{SW} = IPD(i)_{rSW} - IPD(i)_{sSW}$$

We observe that the delay change $\Delta d(i)_{SW}$ of the i-th packet can be expressed by the difference between the receiver's IPD and the sender's IPD: $IPD(i)_{rSW} - IPD(i)_{sSW}$. We can derive this expression by using timepoints as follows:

$$\Delta d(i)_{SW} = (t(i+1)_{rSW} - t(i)_{rSW}) - (t(i+1)_{sSW} - t(i)_{sSW})$$
$$= IPD(i)_{rSW} - IPD(i)_{sSW}$$

As shown above, there is an important observation that most BWE algorithms rely on relative timing or changes in timing rather than absolute timing. Furthermore, the relative timing features of both BWE types can be converted into a unified form: IPD, which motivates our ProgHW/SW architectural evaluation to focus on IPD rather than absolute timing quantities.

3   Our Classification of Bandwidth Estimation Architectures

In this section, we first present our IPD-based classification of ProgHW/SW architectures for BWE. Meanwhile, we explain the functionality of each module in those architectures. The implementation details of those modules are shown in Sect. 4. Then, we analyze the timing context of ProgHW/SW architectures and explain how to keep IPD accuracy in such context.

According to our investigation of different types of BWE, we have an important insight that the factors that impact BWE performance can be attributed to a single factor: IPD, and architectures of different BWE types share many components in common to process and transmit IPD. Therefore, we study different architectures based on how they impact IPD, and we modularize those common components to reduce the evaluation difficulty caused by the time-consuming ProgHW-level compilation. The insight is further discussed in Sect. 3.2.

3.1   IPD-based Architectural Classification

We identify and modularize common BWE components that process and transmit IPD information, and our classification of different ProgHW/SW architectures is based on different allocations of those modules. Specifically, there are three modules for the sender: packet generator, IPD modulator, and IPD transceiver, and three modules for the receiver: IPD gauge, IPD transceiver, and IPD processor. In a BWE process, a sender uses an IPD modulator to set predefined timing features, and a receiver uses an IPD gauge and an IPD processor to measure and analyze the change in those timing features. We will illustrate those modules by using the traditional SW architecture of type 1.

Type 1 (No IPD Optimization). This type does not involve any specialized optimization to improve IPD accuracy. One feature of type 1 is that most BWE modules locate in user space. The traditional SW architecture is a representative of this type, whose architecture is shown in Fig. 3. There are several steps in a complete procedure of BWE. On a sender, the packet generator generates a sequence of packets. Then, the sender's IPD modulator specifies the IPD information of packets through a system timer. Next, these packets pass through the IPD transceiver whose major component is the TCP/IP stack, and they reach the MAC (Ethernet) TX port. After being transmitted through the network path, these packets reach a receiver. On the receiver, the IPD transceiver uploads IPD information, and then the IPD gauge module measures the IPD of packets. Lastly, the measured IPD is used by the IPD processor to infer network bandwidth.

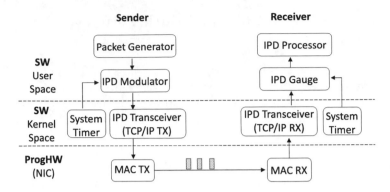

Fig. 3. Type 1 (No IPD Optimization)

Type 1 architecture finds it difficult to keep IPD accuracy because of many timing-noise factors. For the system timer, there is a timestamp counter (TSC) in the kernel space, which is accessed by timing operations such as the system call function *gettimeofday*. On the sender, after sending one packet, the process keeps polling TSC to wait for a specified IPD. Once that IPD is reached, the sender timestamps and sends the next packet. On the receiver, once the packet arrives, the process gets the arrival time by reading the current value of TSC. The TSC access operation on both ends generates about 1–2 μs timing noise [25]. The IPD transceiver may generate timing noise of several microseconds, and it covers the TCP/IP stack, PCIe switching, and other transceiving services. The BWE functions or other daemon services may also disturb the accuracy of the timing [37]. Because of these inaccuracy factors, it becomes increasingly difficult for the traditional SW architecture to measure IPD accurately with the trend of faster network speed and shorter IPD.

Type 2 (IPD Noise Mitigation). The feature of this type is that both IPD modulator and IPD gauge are still in user space as type 1, but architectures are improved to mitigate timing noise. There are several choices to do the mitigation: TCP/IP stack offloading, kernel bypass, or BWE functions offloading as shown in Fig. 4. Both TCP/IP stack offloading and kernel bypass aim to reduce the number of data copies in packet transmission so that timing is more stable, and performance is better. The difference between these two is that TCP/IP offloading moves TCP/IP stack down to ProgHW while kernel bypass moves it up to user space. TCP/IP offloading has several related works [7,39].

BWE functions offloading, to the best of our knowledge, has rarely been studied, so we implement our custom version of this architecture by offloading the packet generator and IPD processor modules down to ProgHW. The implementation details are presented in Sect. 4. BWE functions offloading is based on TCP/IP offloading, which means that TCP/IP stack is also offloaded to ProgHW in the BWE functions offloading architecture.

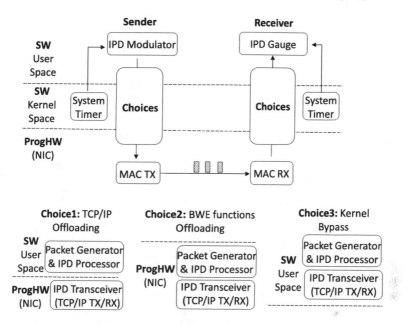

Fig. 4. Type 2 (IPD noise mitigation)

Type 3 (IPD HW Modulation). The feature of this type is that both the IPD modulator and IPD gauge are placed close to NIC port. The purpose of such placement is to restore IPD information tampered by the timing noise of the ProgHW-SW transmission path. Specifically, both the IPD modulator and IPD gauge modules adopt a HW timer rather than a SW timer to improve timing stability. On the sender, ProgHW modulates the IPD of packets according to the IPD specification of SW. On the receiver, ProgHW records receiving IPD and sends the IPD information to SW.

This type uses the combination of stream control signals and the timer of ProgHW to achieve accurate IPD modulation and gauge [16, 20]. Specifically, on the sender, a HW timer is used to measure the delay of packet transmission. Then, the delay is compared with a specified IPD. If the delay is smaller, stream control signals block the following packets until the specified IPD is reached. On the receiver, a look-up table is dedicated to storing IPD information of packets. The receiving IPD information is then uploaded to the IPD processor (Fig. 5).

3.2   ProgHW/SW Timing Context Analysis

In this part, we analyze the timing context of ProgHW/SW architectures and provide a criterion to keep IPD accuracy. We first build up a model to summarize timing-noise factors and then explain how our criterion addresses those factors.

As shown in Fig. 6, we use an example of transmitting packets from sender to receiver to illustrate the ProgHW/SW timing context. Please refer to Table 1

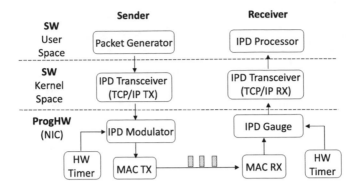

Fig. 5. Type 3 (IPD HW modulation)

for definitions of symbols. Because of timing-noise factors in ProgHW/SW, timing measurement is sometimes inaccurate. If a SW-based design aims to measure delay $d(i)^R$ of packets transmission from sender to receiver, its measured value $d(i)_{SW}$ may differ from the real value $d(i)^R$. Specifically, a packet is first transmitted from SW to ProgHW and experiences timing noise $n(i)_s^R$. Then, the sender's ProgHW sends the packet out and the receiver's ProgHW captures it. Lastly, the packet is uploaded to the receiver's SW and experiences receiving timing noise $n(i)_r^R$. The difference between the measured value and real value (i.e., measured error): $d(i)_{SW} - d(i)^R$ can be expanded as $(n(i)_s^R + n(i)_r^R) + (tdr(i)_{sSW} + tdr(i)_{rSW})$, where $n(i)_s^R$ and $n(i)_s^R$ are generated by timing-noise factors such as system scheduling, data copy, and many others [25,32]. One thing worth noting is that both $n(i)_s^R$ and $n(i)_s^R$ are variables, so they may vary for different packets.

Clock Drift: Another timing-noise factor comes from clock drift such as $tdr(i)_{sSW}$ or $tdr(i)_{rSW}$. Because of imperfections and accessing noise in a real-world timer, there might be a difference between a real-world timer and an ideal reference timer [15]. In the ProgHW/SW timing context, there are four timers (a sender's SW and ProgHW, and a receiver's SW and ProgHW) and they usually have different frequencies and accessing manners. Therefore, clock drift will happen if the four timers are not synchronized with each other. However, it is difficult to achieve synchronization by traditional methods such as NTP. The reason is that packet transmission time is nanosecond-level while NTP takes milliseconds.

Because of timing-noise factors shown in Fig. 6, SW timing could differ from real timing in packet transmission, and it is difficult to make those two the same. Fortunately, it is unnecessary to keep absolute timing accurate. According to Definition 2 and 3, major BWE algorithms depend on relative timing values rather than absolute timing values to carry out estimation. Therefore, the timing accuracy requirements of both the packet-pair and the packet-train BWE types are based on relative timing values. Specifically, their requirements shown below

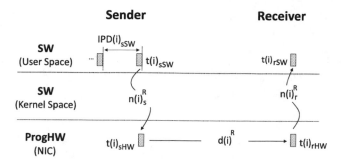

Fig. 6. ProgHW/SW timing context

state that the specified or measured relative timing values are equal to the real values.

Definition 4. *Packet-pair timing accuracy requirement: Assume there are n pairs of packets (2×n packets) in transmission, the requirement is shown below.*

$$\forall i \in [1,n], k = 2i - 1 \quad \Theta IPD(k)_{SW} = \Theta IPD(k)^R$$

Definition 5. *Packet-train timing accuracy requirement: Assume there are n packets in transmission, the requirement is shown below.*

$$\forall i \in [1,n), \Delta d(i)_{SW} = \Delta d(i)^R$$

Furthermore, we observe that the timing accuracy requirements of both types can be converted into a unified form: the accuracy of IPD. For the packet-pair type, its relative timing value is already IPD. For the packet-train type, its relative timing value: delay $\Delta d(i)$ can be expanded to a function of IPD. This expansion is shown in Theorem 2. In a nutshell, our IPD-based criterion states that a ProgHW/SW architecture can meet the timing accuracy requirements of both types by synchronizing IPD between ProgHW and SW on both sender and receiver. We formalize our criterion with two theorems shown below.

Assumption 31. The clock jitter in ProgHW is negligible for IPD measurement. Formally, if there are n packets in transmission, then we have

$$\forall i \in [1, n-1], tdr(i+1)_{sHW} - tdr(i)_{sHW} = 0$$
$$tdr(i+1)_{rHW} - tdr(i)_{rHW} = 0$$

Note that clock jitter is different from clock drift. Clock jitter means temporal timing variation while clock drift means spatial timing variation. According to the past study [11], the clock jitter of ProgHW is around several picoseconds, which accounts for less than 0.1% of IPD measurement.

Theorem 1. $\forall i \in [1,n]$, $k = 2i - 1$, if $IPD(k)_{sSW} = IPD(k)_{sHW}$ and $IPD(k)_{rSW} = IPD(k)_{rHW}$, then the Packet-pair timing accuracy requirement (Definition 4) can be satisfied.

Proof. To satisfy the requirement, we need to prove that $\Theta IPD(k)_{SW} = \Theta IPD(k)^R$ for all pairs of probing packets. We first expand $\Theta IPD(k)_{SW}$ and $\Theta IPD(k)^R$ as follows.

$$\Theta IPD(k)_{SW} = IPD(k)_{rSW} - IPD(k)_{sSW}$$
$$\Theta IPD(k)^R = IPD(k)_{rHW} - IPD(k)_{sHW}$$
$$+ \Delta tdr(k)_{sHW} - \Delta tdr(k)_{rHW}$$

According to Assumption 31, the values of $\Delta tdr(k)_{sHW}$ and $\Delta tdr(k)_{rHW}$ can be both zero. Therefore, If $IPD(k)_{sSW} = IPD(k)_{sHW}$ and $IPD(k)_{rSW} = IPD(k)_{rHW}$, then $\Theta IPD(k)_{SW} = \Theta IPD(k)^R$.

Theorem 2. $\forall i \in [1, n)$, *if* $IPD(i)_{sSW} = IPD(i)_{sHW}$ *and* $IPD(i)_{rSW} = IPD(i)_{rHW}$, *then the Packet-train timing accuracy requirement (Definition 5) can be satisfied.*

Proof. To satisfy the requirement, we need to prove that $\Delta d(i)_{SW} = \Delta d(i)^R$ for all probing packets. We first expand $\Delta d(i)_{SW}$ and $\Delta d(i)^R$ as follows.

$$\Delta d(i)_{SW} = d(i+1)_{SW} - d(i)_{SW}$$
$$\Delta d(i)^R = d(i+1)^R - d(i)^R$$

The One-way delays $d(i+1)_{SW}$ and $d(i)_{SW}$ can be expressed in the form of timepoints:

$$d(i+1)_{SW} = t(i+1)_{rSW} - t(i+1)_{sSW}$$
$$d(i)_{SW} = t(i)_{rSW} - t(i)_{sSW}$$

Therefore, their difference can also be expressed in the form of timepoints:

$$\Delta d(i)_{SW} = (t(i+1)_{rSW} - t(i)_{rSW}) - (t(i+1)_{sSW} - t(i)_{sSW})$$
$$= IPD(i)_{rSW} - IPD(i)_{sSW}$$

Following the similar deduction procedure and considering Assumption 31, we can get

$$\Delta d(i)^R = IPD(i)_{rHW} - IPD(i)_{sHW}$$

Therefore, If $IPD(i)_{sSW} = IPD(i)_{sHW}$ and $IPD(i)_{rSW} = IPD(i)_{rHW}$, then $\Delta d(i)_{SW} = \Delta d(i)^R$.

As shown above, synchronizing IPD between ProgHW and SW is critical to achieving timing accuracy for different BWE algorithms because of the relative timing feature of BWE. Architectures of type 3 satisfy the criterion, but type 1 and 2 do not strictly follow the criterion.

4   Implementation of Modules

According to Sect. 3, different architectures share many modules in common to process and transmit IPD information, and this section introduces our implementation details of those modules. We have two requirements for those modules: (1) they are portable across different architectures, and (2) they are suitable for BWE evaluations. The IPD transceiver module [7, 8] and packet generator [16, 40] of existing works satisfy those requirements, but the IPD modulator, IPD gauge, and IPD processor do not, so we focus on the last three. We use our IPD processor to make up the architecture of BWE functions offloading (type 2), and we use our IPD modulator and IPD gauge to make up the architecture of IPD HW modulation (type 3).

4.1   Preliminaries of FPGA

To better understand the implementation details, we present an introduction of two ProgHWs used in our work: NetFPGA-SUME [50] and Alveo U280 FPGA [2]. FPGA is a widely used ProgHW. NetFPGA-SUME and Alveo U280 are network-oriented FPGAs for high-speed networking development.

The layouts of NetFPGA and Alveo are presented in Fig. 7. Both FPGAs use a group of modules to build up specified functionalities. For NetFPGA, the MAC RX and MAC TX modules transfer packets between a network and a FPGA while the DMA RX and DMA TX modules transfer packets between a FPGA and a host computer. Besides, the MAC RX and MAC TX modules have four copies. The User Data Path module serves as a flexible packet buffer where users can design their custom functionalities. For Alveo U280, TCP/IP is often implemented on the Network Kernel module. The CMAC and GT kernels cooperate to achieve 100 Gbps network speed and they usually operate at 200 MHz or more. The User Kernel module is open for users to create custom designs such as BWE algorithms.

FPGA designs have two types of communication: the communication between a host computer and a FPGA, and the communication among modules on a FPGA. The former uses peripheral component interconnect express (PCIe) interface while the latter uses Advanced Extensible Interface (AXI). AXI has two types: AXI-Lite and AXI-Stream. AXI-Lite is used to configure the registers of each module and AXI-Stream is used to control the transmission of packets (i.e., data). The AXI-Lite master module in Fig. 7 serves as an arbiter for different AXI-Lite signals. For more details on AXI, please refer to [1]. Packets are buffered in a data structure called first-in&first-out buffer (FIFO), whose control signals are often combined with AXI-Stream to regulate the start and end of a new packet.

There are two types of memory resources that are widely used in packet transmission. The first one is on-chip memory named Block RAM (BRAM), and the other is external memory resources including high bandwidth memory (HBM) and Double Data Rate (DDR) memory.

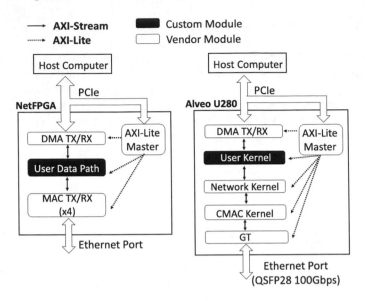

Fig. 7. Layout of NetFPGA (Left) and Alveo U280 (Right)

4.2   Implementation Details

To make modules portable across different architectures, all of these modules follow a unified interface: AXI. Specifically, we use AXI-Stream to control the transmission of packets, and AXI-Lite to set parameters, such as sending rate or packet count.

The IPD processor module has rarely been studied in the context of ProgHW, and we implement a key BWE function, named pair-wise comparison test (PCT) to build this module. PCT is used to examine if the BWE sending rate saturates the available bandwidth of a network path. Specifically, if the ratio approaches a threshold between the number of receiving IPDs that are larger than sending IPDs and the total of receiving IPDs, the sending rate is considered to be larger than the available bandwidth, and a BWE algorithm will begin turning down its sending rate to avoid network congestion. In addition, we design two counters on the receiver side. One is used to count the total number of receiving IPDs, and the other is used to count the number of receiving IPDs larger than sending IPDs. We compare two counters to check if the PCT condition is satisfied. Furthermore, we use the direct access mechanism in PCIe for IPD transfer between the host memory and the FPGA board. This way consumes fewer memory resources than creating a dedicated global memory for transfer. Then, we build up the architecture of BWE functions offloading (type 2) by combining our IPD processor with the IPD transceiver from the design [7] for NetFPGA-SUME and from the design [8] for Alveo U280.

For the IPD modulator and IPD gauge, we refer to the design: Combov [20], and we make two changes to suit BWE evaluations. First, we enlarge the packet

FIFO size of these modules. The default size is 8 packets × 64 bytes, which is not large enough to hold hundreds of packets in some packet-train BWE algorithms, such as pathload [23]. Thus, we resize the FIFO to 1000 packets × 1500 bytes which are larger than the maximum value of most BWE algorithms. Second, to avoid overflow, we set a proper bit width for both sender's and receiver's IPD arrays. These arrays are used to store sending and receiving IPDs. According to our study, both the packet-train and the packet-pair types spend less than 30 min doing estimation and the default timing precision of two FPGA boards is 8 ns [2, 50], which means that the width should be at least 38 bits to store IPDs (30 mins ×60 × 10^9/8 ns < 2^{38}). In addition, for the IPD modulator, we use the read-valid signal of AXI-Stream to make sure that packet transmission follows the specified IPD. For the IPD gauge, we use the transmission-last signal of AXI-Stream to record the arrival time of a new packet. We use our implementation of IPD modulator and IPD gauge to build the IPD HW modulation architecture (type 3). Besides, we use BRAM to implement packet FIFOs for packet transmission among FPGA modules.

5   Evaluation

This section presents evaluations of both our IPD-modular evaluation method and the ProgHW/SW architectural space of BWE. Our ProgHW/SW source code of the experiments is available at [9]. This work does not raise any ethical issues.

5.1   Evaluation Environments

We use Alveo U280 FPGA [2] and NetFPGA-SUME [50] to examine different ProgHW/SW architectures. Alveo U280 FPGA is used for 100 Gbps experiments in Open Cloud Testbed (OCT) [30]) while NetFPGA-SUME is used for less than or equal to 10 Gbps experiments in our local testbed built with mininet version 2.2.2. Specifically, we deploy two Alveo U280 FPGA boards on two VMs of OCT and each is equipped with 32 Virtual CPU cores and 64GB RAM. We deploy NetFPGA-SUME on a Dell Precision 3630 machine with Intel Xeon-E5 16 Cores and 64GB RAM. The network topology of NetFPGA-SUME is shown in Fig. 8 where two nodes on the top generate cross traffic and two nodes on the bottom run BWE algorithms and optionally run other concurrent applications. The testbed for Alveo U280 is similar to Fig. 8 with two differences. First, the bottleneck link is a Dell Z9100 100G switch. Second, because a user can create no more than two nodes in OCT, there are no cross-traffic nodes (i.e., no Node2 and Node3 in Fig. 8). The Operating system is Ubuntu 2020.4 LTS with the Linux kernel 5.4. To compile ProgHW source code, we use Xilinx Vivado Design Suite v2020.1. We choose two representative BWE algorithms: bprobe [13] of the packet-pair type and pathload [23] of the packet-train type for our experiments.

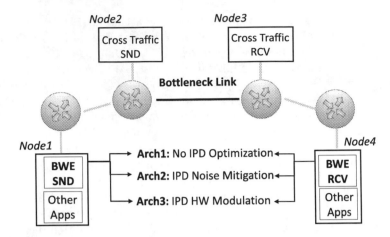

Fig. 8. Experiment network topology

5.2 Evaluation of IPD-Modular Method

In this section, we compare the efficiency of our modular evaluation method against the dedicated evaluation method of past works [34,42]. The dedicated evaluation method means that we compile every design for every new study case. In contrast with that, our method converts common components of different BWE algorithms into several modules that can be reusable in different ProgHW/SW architectures. In this way, if modules of two architectures overlap, we only need to compile those common modules once and reuse them for the other architecture. For example, as shown in Sect. 3, the architectures of BWE functions offloading and TCP/IP offloading share ProgHW-based TCP/IP stack, so we only need to compile ProgHW-based TCP/IP once. The compilation time (hrs: hours) comparison is shown in Table 2. The compilation of IPD modulator and IPD gauge in Combov takes 2 h. In addition, the main difference between the packet-pair and the packet-train types is on packet generator and IPD processor modules, so we spent another 2 h recompiling these two for the packet-train type after finishing the packet-pair type.

Summary: The IPD-modular method greatly reduces total compilation time. Spotting and reusing common components among different BWE designs can save time from ProgHW recompilation. As the number of studied algorithms and architectures goes up, the advantage of the IPD-modular evaluation method can become bigger.

5.3 Evaluation of ProgHW/SW Architectures

Group1 - IPD Accuracy and Cost Effectiveness of Different Architectures: In this group, we evaluate how well different ProgHW/SW architectures keep IPD accuracy. We use the hardware timestamp functionality in FPGAs to specify IPD values and set the clock cycle to 8 ns in this experiment. Results

Table 2. Evaluation efficiency comparison

BWE type	Arch	Dedicated eval.	IPD-Mod eval.
Packet-pair (bprobe)	BWE Func Offloading	9 h	9 h
	TCP/IP Offloading	8 h	/
	Combov	8 h	2 h
Packet-train (pathload)	BWE Func Offloading	9 h	2 h
	TCP/IP Offloading	8 h	/
	Combov	8 h	/
Total		50 h	13 h

(Note: "/" means no need to do recompilation)

are shown in Fig. 9. We use the formula below to define the IPD measurement error (IPD_{err}) where #IPD is the number of measured IPD samples. For each experiment set, we collect 40 samples. Furthermore, we check the cost efficiency of each architecture by metrics of offloading workload and ProgHW resources consumption. ProgHW resources are described by three key metrics: the number of Look-up Tables (LUTs), Flip-flops (FFs), and BRAMs. The results are shown in Table 3.

$$IPD_{err} = \sqrt{\frac{1}{\#IPD} \cdot \sum_{i=1}^{\#IPD} (IPD[i] - IPD_{actual})^2}$$

For both sender and receiver, according to Fig. 9, IPD noise mitigation (type 2) and IPD HW modulation (type 3) have better IPD accuracy than the pure SW architecture, especially in short IPD (e.g., 120ns). The advantage of type 2 comes from the kernel-bypass effect, which requires less data copy from SW to ProgHW. However, this effect cannot completely remove the IPD noise of systems. Type 3 shows better IPD accuracy than type 2, and the former can keep IPD error within 1%. The main reason is that accessing the ProgHW timer is more stable than accessing the SW timer. From the experiment, we find that IPD restoration is more effective than noise mitigation, and this result is consistent with our analysis in Sect. 3.2. In addition, we also find that type 3 does not completely remove IPD measurement errors. This is because the type 3 design needs 1 clock cycle to read the measured IPD to a register. In terms of cost effectiveness, we find that more offloading does not necessarily lead to better performance in ProgHW/SW designs. As shown in Table 3, although Combov uses 70% fewer resources than BWE functions offloading architecture, it can achieve 20% more accurate IPD than BWE functions offloading. Thus, we suggest engineers prioritize offloading modules that can directly update or recover IPD.

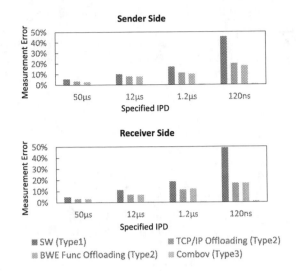

Fig. 9. IPD measurement error of different architectures

Group1 - Summary: In terms of IPD accuracy, type 3>type 2>type 1. In addition, more offloading does not necessarily have better performance. Specifically, although TCP/IP offloading and BWE functions offloading consume nearly 10 times more ProgHW resources than Combov, the former architectures are less accurate than the latter.

Group2 - BWE Accuracy of Different Architectures: In this group, we check if the IPD accuracy improvement of ProgHW/SW architectures can benefit BWE performance. We evaluate both the packet-pair and the packet-train types. This group of experiments do not involve concurrent applications. Influences of cross traffic and concurrent applications will be discussed in the following experiment groups. Besides, the actual available bandwidth equals the capacity of the bottleneck link. In addition, we include DPDK [5], one of the most widely used kernel-bypass frameworks as a reference in this group. The size of the packets is 1408 bytes, and the data width of AXI-Stream is 512 bits. Figure 10a and 10b show the BWE performance of different ProgHW/SW architectures. The x-axis represents the actual available bandwidth, and the y-axis represents the estimation value.

From Fig. 10a and 10b, we find that higher IPD accuracy can lead to higher BWE accuracy on both the packet-pair and the packet-train types. In the 100 Gbps network, Combov of type 3 can even improve bprobe accuracy by 35% from pure SW architecture. In addition, we find that type 2 and type 3 can reduce BWE estimation variance. For example, in the 1 Gbps network, Combov of type 3 can keep the variance from the specified value within 60 Mbps while the variance of pure SW reaches 200 Mbps. This is because of the timing-stability

Table 3. Resources consumption and offloading workload comparison

	Combov (mod. & gauge offloading)	TCP/IP offloading	BWE func. offloading
Offloading code lines	100	1500	1800
LUTs	14013	137286	146493
FFs	53623	222838	233761
BRAMs	26	468	480

feature of ProgHW. We also find that relocating TCP/IP alone (e.g., TCP/IP offloading or DPDK) is not enough to achieve the best BWE accuracy. The reason is that relocating TCP/IP cannot completely remove timing noise in user space. However, the main advantage of DPDK is that it generally requires less time for development and deployment since it is a SW-based solution. Furthermore, we find that the packet-pair type gets more performance improvement than the packet-train type in type 2 and 3. This is probably because the packet-pair type only uses a single IPD sample rather than multiple samples to estimate bandwidth, so the packet-pair type is more sensitive to timing noise compared with the packet-train type.

Group2 - Summary: In terms of BWE accuracy, type 3 achieves the best performance for both the packet-pair and the packet-train types, and the advantage of ProgHW-based architectures becomes bigger as networks become faster. In addition, although DPDK has comparable average performance to TCP/IP offloading, the latter can achieve a smaller estimation variance.

Group3 - Heterogeneous Combinations: This group studies the BWE performance of heterogeneous combinations where the sender and receiver have different architectures. This study is important for users to save costs and effectively use ProgHW resources. At the current stage, high-end ProgHW is expensive, and its supply is limited [30], so there might be a situation where not every endpoint can be equipped with an expected ProgHW/SW configuration.

We use Combov (type 3) in this group. Experiment results are shown in Fig. 11. We use the formula below to define the BWE measurement accuracy (BWE_{acc}) where #BWE is the number of measured BWE samples. For each experiment set, we collect 20 samples. According to Fig. 11, the heterogeneous combination of SW sender and Combov receiver can achieve at least 80% performance of the architecture where both endpoints are equipped with Combov.

$$BWE_{acc} = 1 - BWE_{err}$$

$$BWE_{err} = \sqrt{\frac{1}{\#BWE} \cdot \sum_{i=1}^{\#BWE} (BWE_i - BWE_{actual})^2}$$

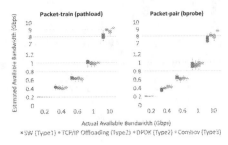

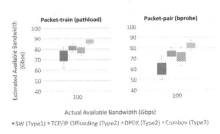

(a) Bandwidth Estimation of Different Architectures (≤ 10Gbps)

(b) Bandwidth Estimation of Different Architectures (100Gbps)

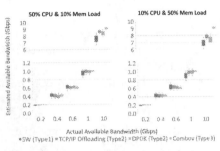

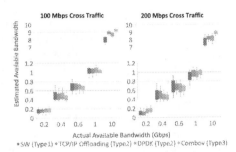

(c) Bandwidth Estimation (pathload) with Concurrent Applications

(d) Bandwidth Estimation (pathload) with Cross Traffic

Fig. 10. Bandwidth estimation experiment results

One possible explanation for this phenomenon is that the duty of the sender and the receiver is different. The sender aims to saturate avai-bw by continuously increasing the rate to transmit packets. The receiver uses IPD information to calculate bandwidth. The SW-based sender uses interrupt coalescing [35] and the Combov sender uses packet buffering. Both those techniques can achieve fast rate to saturate avai-bw, so the sender replacement does not have a significant difference. However, interrupt coalescing on the receiver can damage each packet's timing information, which reduces BWE accuracy. If limited ProgHW resources only allow one endpoint to use ProgHW, then deployment on the receiver may achieve better performance than on the sender.

Group3 - Summary: The receiver side has a larger impact on BWE performance than the sender side in terms of ProgHW/SW configurations. This finding is useful to save costs. Specifically, we can assign ProgHW/SW configurations to the receiver alone to achieve comparable performance to the two-end configurations.

Group4 - Impact of Concurrent Applications: BWE programs sometimes inevitably share CPU and memory resources with other applications on the same machine. In this group, we evaluate how different ProgHW/SW architectures perform with the existence of concurrent applications. We use LookBusy [6] to sim-

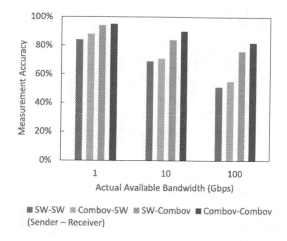

Fig. 11. BWE accuracy of heterogenous combinations

ulate both CPU-intensive and I/O-intensive applications. We set 50% CPU load and 10% memory load for a CPU-intensive application and 10% CPU load and 50% memory load for an I/O-intensive application. The results are shown in Fig. 10c.

We find that type 3 can greatly resist the influence of either CPU-intensive or memory-intensive applications compared with the other two types. One possible reason is that its IPD restoration mechanism can correct timing errors caused by concurrent applications in SW. Type 2 can also resist the influence to some extent. Type 2 offloads components down to ProgHW, so it becomes less dependent on CPU for network-related operations. In addition, we find that memory-intensive applications are more impactful than CPU-intensive applications on SW. Specifically, the former degrades SW performance by 26% while the latter degrades it by 16%.

Group4 - Summary: Type 3 can resist the influence of concurrent applications while DPDK and TCP/IP offloading of type 2 have degraded accuracy in such influence.

Group5 - Impact of Cross Traffic: A real-world network path is usually shared among many network applications which can generate cross traffic to interfere with BWE traffic. In this group, we study how different ProgHW/SW architectures perform with the existence of cross traffic. We use D-ITG 2.8.1 to generate cross traffic with a constant rate, and the packet size is 500 bytes. We set the transmission rate of cross traffic to be 100 Mbps and 200 Mbps. The results are shown in Fig. 10d.

We find that the introduction of cross traffic degrades BWE performance for all three types, but type 2 and 3 still show better performance than type 1. Furthermore, according to Fig. 10d, we find that BWE performs poorly when the transmission rate of cross traffic is comparable to available bandwidth. For example, if available bandwidth is 200 Mbps, and cross traffic is 200 Mbps, more

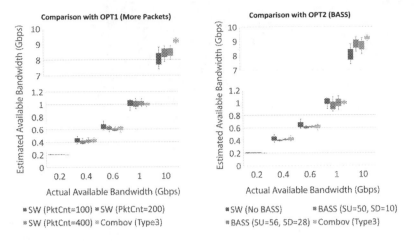

Fig. 12. Comparison with BWE optimizations

than 40% estimation error is produced. One possible reason is that the irregular insertion of cross packets into probing packets can interfere with BWE.

Group5 - Summary: Type 2 and 3 show better BWE accuracy than type 1 under the influence of cross traffic.

Group6 - Comparison with BWE Optimizations: In this group, we compare two common optimizations of BWE with the ProgHW-based architecture: Combov. The first optimization is to increase packet count (denoted by *PktCnt*) [23]. The idea is that more samples can reduce measurement variance based on the law of large numbers. The second optimization, named BASS [48], is to smooth measurement spikes. These spikes are outliers in measurement, and they may disturb bandwidth calculation. We use SU to denote the index of spike detection and SD to denote the index of spike confirmation.

According to the results shown in Fig. 12, more packets can reduce measurement variance, but they only have a small improvement (around 6%) to the BWE accuracy. For the spikes smoothing optimization: BASS, it shows better BWE accuracy than Combov in networks with less than 1 Gbps speed, but it is not as good as Combov if the network speed goes above 1 Gbps. Nevertheless, those two optimizations are SW-based, and their deployments are easier than ProgHW deployments.

Group6 - Summary: Compared with the ProgHW-based solution, in low-speed networks (<1 Gbps), two SW-level optimizations can achieve similar or even better BWE accuracy, but they show poorer accuracy in high-speed networks (≥1 Gbps).

6   Related Work

6.1   Related Evaluations of Bandwidth Estimation

Researchers and engineers have conducted many evaluations to improve BWE accuracy, and these works have three classes.

The first class evaluates different algorithmic mechanisms and parameters. For example, Strauss et al. [45] evaluate the performance of pathload, IGI, and spruce under 100Mb/s bandwidth. They find that spruce is more accurate than the other two. Yin et al. [48] propose a spike smoothing strategy to improve BWE accuracy on 10 Gbps networks. Alok Shriram et al. [42] and Xiliang Liu et al. [34] study BWE performance under different parameter settings such as different measurement timescales and flow sizes. To reduce the architectural bias of BWE, Alok Shriram et al. [41] establish a generic implementation framework. Their experiments focus on how different sampling intensities affect the performance of BWE algorithms. They observe that $50ms$ measurement timescale can significantly improve performance.

The second class focuses on how BWE performs under different network conditions. For example, Aceto et al. [10] propose a unified architecture to tackle inaccuracy issues caused by heterogeneous network environments. Shriram et al. [42] evaluate different BWE methods in both high-speed datacenter and OC-48 networks. Hu et al. [22] investigate network paths with less than 100 Mbps bottleneck links.

The third class analyzes the influence of architectural components of BWE. For example, Jin et al. [25] conclude that major BWE algorithms cannot accurately estimate the high-speed bandwidth (>1 Gb/s) because of the limited capabilities of traditional SW systems. Their work also gives a detailed breakdown analysis of system factors such as the interrupt rate, the system timer accuracy, or the PCI bandwidth. Liao et al. [32] and Larsen et al. [28] provide an in-depth discussion of the influence of PCI switching, driver, and DMA engine. They find that the driver and buffer release can produce up to 54% overhead. Kagami et al. [26] propose a passive BWE method for the data plane in Software-Defined Network (SDN). This method improves the BWE accuracy by 10%. Furthermore, a few works leverage ProgHW to improve BWE, such as minProbe [46], Caliper [19], and Combov [20], but most of them only discuss limited design types like traffic synthesizers.

In addition, some other works try to improve the evaluation accuracy and fidelity instead of directly studying BWE algorithms. To mitigate the timing noise of the host system, Strauss et al. [45] collect measurements from multiple probe streams and use OS kernels to improve the timestamp accuracy. To reduce the bias of testing scenarios, Hui Zhou et al. [49] test BWE under more comprehensive internet paths to reveal the difficulties of major BWE algorithms. Kagami et al. [26] offload BWE to the data plane to improve evaluation quality.

6.2   Programmable Hardware Designs

There are some ProgHW/SW designs for traffic generation, but few of them are dedicated to BWE. In terms of the methods of controlling timing, ProgHW/SW designs can be classified into two types: HW-timing type and packet-insertion type. HW-timing type means that the hardware timer is used to either set the IPD of sending packets or record the receiving time of each packet. In contrast with the sub-millisecond timing accuracy of SW design [12], one of the main advantages of this type is that it supports nanosecond-level timing accuracy. For example, Netthread [40] and SPG [16] can accurately replay pre-recorded traffic. However, some designs of this type are not suitable for high-speed BWE. For example, the HW timing module of NIC-based designs [17] can only control the average bit rate, which is unsuitable for the varying-IPD BWE algorithms such as pathchirp [38]. As for the packet-insertion type, the sending IPD is determined by inserting an extra packet between two valid packets. MoonGen [17], SoNIC [29], and minProbe [46] belong to this type, which balances well between the timing accuracy and design flexibility. But the main problem of this type is that the specified IPD may get disturbed by interrupt coalescing. If the extra packets and valid packets appear in different interrupt batches, the pre-defined IPD will not hold anymore.

7   Conclusion

In the paper, we provide an IPD-based modular method to systematically classify and evaluate ProgHW/SW space of BWE. This evaluation method shows higher efficiency than traditional evaluation methods. Furthermore, we make some new findings from the architectural evaluation. According to our experiment results, the IPD HW modulation architecture shows the best improvement in BWE performance. Specifically, it can increase IPD accuracy by 45% and BWE accuracy by 20–30% in a 100 Gbps network. We also find that the receiver side affects BWE more than the sender side. In the future, we plan to extend ProgHW/SW space study to more types of BWE algorithms.

Acknowledgement. The work presented in this paper was supported in part by NSF CNS-1616087 and CNS-2135539.

References

1. AXI Reference Guide (2020). https://www.xilinx.com/support/documentation/ip_documentation/ug761_axi_reference_guide.pdf
2. Alveo U280 Product Brief (2021). https://www.xilinx.com/products/boards-and-kits/alveo/u280.html
3. Apache Hadoop (2021). https://hadoop.apache.org/
4. AWS High Performance Computing (2021). https://aws.amazon.com/hpc/
5. Intel. Intel DPDK: Data Plane Development Kit (2021). https://dpdk.org/
6. Lookbusy - a synthetic load generator (2021). https://www.devin.com/lookbusy/

7. TCP/IP Socket Opencores (2021). https://opencores.org/projects/tcp_socket
8. Vitis with 100 Gbps TCP/IP Network Stack (2022). https://github.com/fpgasystems/Vitis_with_100Gbps_TCP-IP
9. FPGABandwidth (2023). https://github.com/ftqtfff/FPGABandwidth
10. Aceto, G., Botta, A., Pescapé, A., D'Arienzo, M.: Unified architecture for network measurement: the case of available bandwidth. J. Netw. Comput. Appl. **35**(5), 1402–1414 (2012)
11. Aloisio, A., Giordano, R., Izzo, V.: Jitter issues in clock conditioning with fpgas. In: NPSS Real Time Conference, pp. 1–6. IEEE (2010)
12. Botta, A., Dainotti, A., Pescapé, A.: Do you trust your software-based traffic generator? IEEE Commun. Maga. **48**(9), 158–165 (2010)
13. Carter, R.L., Crovella, M.E.: Measuring bottleneck link speed in packet-switched networks. Perf. Eval. **27**, 297–318 (1996)
14. Chou, P.A., Miao, Z.: Rate-distortion optimized streaming of packetized media. IEEE Trans. Multimedia **8**(2), 390–404 (2006)
15. Chowdhury, D.D.: Packet timing: network time protocol. In: NextGen Network Synchronization, pp. 103–116. Springer, Cham (2021). https://doi.org/10.1007/978-3-030-71179-5_7
16. Covington, G.A., Gibb, G., Lockwood, J.W., McKeown, N.: A packet generator on the NetFPGA platform. In: The 17th IEEE Symposium on Field Programmable Custom Computing Machines, pp. 235–238 (2009)
17. Emmerich, P., Gallenmüller, S., Raumer, D., Wohlfart, F., Carle, G.: Moongen: a scriptable high-speed packet generator. In: Proceedings of the 2015 Internet Measurement Conference, pp. 275–287 (2015)
18. Firestone, D., et al.: Azure accelerated networking: SmartNICs in the public cloud. In: The 15th USENIX Symposium on Networked Systems Design and Implementation (NSDI), pp. 51–66 (2018)
19. Ghobadi, M., Salmon, G., Ganjali, Y., Labrecque, M., Steffan, J.G.: Caliper: precise and responsive traffic generator. In: The 20th Annual Symposium on High-Performance Interconnects, pp. 25–32. IEEE (2012)
20. Groleat, T., et al.: Flexible, extensible, open-source and affordable FPGA-based traffic generator. In: Proceedings of the 1st Edition Workshop on High Performance and Programmable Networking, pp. 23–30 (2013)
21. Haecki, R., et al.: How to diagnose nanosecond network latencies in rich end-host stacks. In: USENIX Symposium on Networked Systems Design and Implementation (NSDI), pp. 861–877 (2022)
22. Hu, N., Steenkiste, P.: Evaluation and characterization of available bandwidth probing techniques. IEEE J. Sel. Areas Commun. **21**(6), 879–894 (2003)
23. Jain, M., Dovrolis, C.: End-to-end available bandwidth: measurement methodology, dynamics, and relation with TCP Throughput. ACM SIGCOMM Comput. Commun. Rev. **32**(4), 295–308 (2002)
24. Jin, G., Tierney, B.: Netest: a tool to measure the maximum burst size, available bandwidth and achievable throughput. In: International Conference on Information Technology: Research and Education (ITRE), pp. 578–582. IEEE (2003)
25. Jin, G., Tierney, B.L.: System capability effects on algorithms for network bandwidth measurement. In: Proceedings of the 3rd ACM SIGCOMM Conference on Internet Measurement, pp. 27–38 (2003)
26. Kagami, N.S., da Costa Filho, R.I.T., Gaspary, L.P.: CAPEST: offloading network capacity and available bandwidth estimation to programmable data planes. IEEE Trans. Netw. Serv. Manag. **17**(1), 175–189 (2019)

27. LaCurts, K., Deng, S., Goyal, A., Balakrishnan, H.: Choreo: network-aware task placement for cloud applications. In: Proceedings of the Conference on Internet Measurement Conference, pp. 191–204 (2013)
28. Larsen, S., Sarangam, P., Huggahalli, R., Kulkarni, S.: Architectural breakdown of end-to-end latency in a TCP/IP network. Int. J. Parallel Program. **37**(6), 556–571 (2009)
29. Lee, K.S., Wang, H., Weatherspoon, H.: Sonic: precise realtime software access and control of wired networks. In: USENIX Symposium on Networked Systems Design and Implementation (NSDI), pp. 213–225 (2013)
30. Leeser, M., Handagala, S., Zink, M.: FPGAs in the Cloud. Authorea (2021). https://doi.org/10.22541/au.163647170.02504770/v1
31. Li, Y., et al.: HPCC: high precision congestion control. In: Proceedings of the ACM Special Interest Group on Data Communication, pp. 44–58. Association for Computing Machinery (2019)
32. Liao, G., Znu, X., Bnuyan, L.: A new server I/O architecture for high speed networks. In: The 17th International Symposium on High Performance Computer Architecture, pp. 255–265. IEEE (2011)
33. Lin, W., Liang, C., Wang, J.Z., Buyya, R.: Bandwidth-aware divisible task scheduling for cloud computing. Softw. Pract. Exp. **44**(2), 163–174 (2014)
34. Liu, X., Ravindran, K., Loguinov, D.: Evaluating the potential of bandwidth estimators. In: The 4th New York Metro Area Networking Workshop (NYMAN) (2004)
35. Moreno, V., del Rio, P.M.S., Ramos, J., Garnica, J.J., Garcia-Dorado, J.L.: Batch to the future: analyzing timestamp accuracy of high-performance packet I/O engines. IEEE Commun. Lett. **16**(11), 1888–1891 (2012)
36. Putnam, A., et al.: A reconfigurable fabric for accelerating large-scale datacenter services. In: 2014 ACM/IEEE 41st International Symposium on Computer Architecture (ISCA), pp. 13–24 (2014)
37. Ramos, J., del Río, P.S., Aracil, J., de Vergara, J.L.: On the effect of concurrent applications in bandwidth measurement speedometers. Comput. Netw. **55**(6), 1435–1453 (2011)
38. Ribeiro, V.J., Riedi, R.H., Baraniuk, R.G., Navratil, J., Cottrell, L.: Pathchirp: efficient available bandwidth estimation for network paths. In: Passive and Active Measurement Workshop (2003)
39. Ruiz, M., Sidler, D., Sutter, G., Alonso, G., López-Buedo, S.: Limago: an FPGA-based open-source 100 GbE TCP/IP stack. In: International Conference on Field Programmable Logic and Applications (FPL), pp. 286–292. IEEE (2019)
40. Salmon, G., Ghobadi, M., Ganjali, Y., Labrecque, M., Steffan, J.G.: NetFPGA-based precise traffic generation. In: Proceedings of NetFPGA Developers Workshop, vol. 9. Citeseer (2009)
41. Shriram, A., Kaur, J.: Empirical evaluation of techniques for measuring available bandwidth. In: International Conference on Computer Communications (INFO-COM), pp. 2162–2170. IEEE (2007)
42. Shriram, A., et al.: Comparison of public end-to-end bandwidth estimation tools on high-speed links. In: Dovrolis, C. (ed.) PAM 2005. LNCS, vol. 3431, pp. 306–320. Springer, Heidelberg (2005). https://doi.org/10.1007/978-3-540-31966-5_24
43. Skhiri, R., Fresse, V., Jamont, J.P., Suffran, B., Malek, J.: From FPGA to support cloud to cloud of FPGA: state of the art. Int. J. Reconfig. Comput. **2019** (2019)
44. Sommers, J., Barford, P., Willinger, W.: Laboratory-based calibration of available bandwidth estimation tools. Microprocess. Microsyst. **31**(4), 222–235 (2007)

45. Strauss, J., Katabi, D., Kaashoek, F.: A measurement study of available bandwidth estimation tools. In: Proceedings of the 3rd ACM SIGCOMM conference on Internet measurement, pp. 39–44 (2003)
46. Wang, H., Lee, K.S., Li, E., Lim, C.L., Tang, A., Weatherspoon, H.: Timing is everything: accurate, minimum overhead, available bandwidth estimation in high-speed wired networks. In: Proceedings of the 2014 Conference on Internet Measurement Conference, pp. 407–420 (2014)
47. Yasukata, K., Honda, M., Santry, D., Eggert, L.: Stackmap: low-latency networking with the OS stack and dedicated NICs. In: USENIX Annual Technical Conference (USENIX ATC 2016), pp. 43–56 (2016)
48. Yin, Q., Kaur, J., Smith, F.D.: Can bandwidth estimation tackle noise at ultra-high speeds? In: IEEE 22nd International Conference on Network Protocols, pp. 107–118 (2014)
49. Zhou, H., Wang, Y., Wang, X., Huai, X.: Difficulties in estimating available bandwidth. In: International Conference on Communications, vol. 2, pp. 704–709. IEEE (2006)
50. Zilberman, N., Audzevich, Y., Covington, G.A., Moore, A.W.: NetFPGA SUME: toward 100 Gbps as research commodity. IEEE Micro 34(5), 32–41 (2014)

An In-Depth Measurement Analysis of 5G mmWave PHY Latency and Its Impact on End-to-End Delay

Rostand A. K. Fezeu[1]($\boxtimes$)(ID), Eman Ramadan[1](ID), Wei Ye[1](ID),
Benjamin Minneci[1](ID), Jack Xie[1], Arvind Narayanan[1](ID), Ahmad Hassan[1](ID),
Feng Qian[1](ID), Zhi-Li Zhang[1](ID), Jaideep Chandrashekar[2](ID),
and Myungjin Lee[3](ID)

[1] University of Minnesota, Twin Cities, USA
{fezeu001,ye000094,minne078,xie00056,hassa654,fengqian}@umn.edu,
{eman,arvind,zhzhang}@cs.umn.edu
[2] InterDigital, Los Altos, USA
Jaideep.Chandrashekar@InterDigital.com
[3] Cisco Systems, San Jose, USA
myungjle@cisco.com

Abstract. 5G aims to offer not only significantly higher throughput than previous generations of cellular networks, but also promises millisecond (ms) and sub-millisecond (ultra-)low latency support at the 5G physical (PHY) layer for future applications. While prior measurement studies have confirmed that commercial 5G deployments can achieve up to several Gigabits per second (Gbps) throughput (especially with the mmWave 5G radio), are they able to deliver on the (sub) millisecond latency promise? With this question in mind, we conducted to our knowledge the first in-depth measurement study of commercial 5G mmWave PHY latency using *detailed physical channel events and messages*. Through carefully designed experiments and data analytics, we dissect various factors that influence 5G PHY latency of both downlink and uplink data transmissions, and explore their impacts on end-to-end delay. We find that while in the best cases, the 5G (mmWave) PHY-layer is capable of delivering ms/sub-ms latency (with a minimum of 0.09 ms for downlink and 0.76 ms for uplink), these happen rarely. A variety of factors such as channel conditions, re-transmissions, physical layer control and scheduling mechanisms, mobility, and application (edge) server placement can all contribute to increased 5G PHY latency (and thus end-to-end (E2E) delay). Our study provides insights to 5G vendors, carriers as well as application developers/content providers on how to better optimize or mitigate these factors for improved 5G latency performance.

Keywords: mmWave · 5G · PHY Layer · Latency · Sub-millisec · End-to-end · Network measurement · 5G Latency Dataset · AWS WaveLength · AWS Local Zone · AWS Regional Zone

The original version of this chapter was revised: An error in the presentation of Jaideep Chandrasheker's affiliation was corrected. The correction to this chapter is available at https://doi.org/10.1007/978-3-031-28486-1_28

1   Introduction

The past few years have seen a rapid commercial deployment of 5G networks. With enhanced mobile broadband services (eMBB), 5G promises to offer much higher bandwidth than previous generations of cellular networks to consumers. Existing measurement studies [10,20,23,29,33] have found that 5G radio technologies can in general achieve higher throughput performance than 4G LTE. For example, with line of sight (LoS), mmWave 5G radio can deliver up to several Gbps of *downlink* (DL) bandwidth [20,29,33] and up to hundreds of Mbps *uplink* (UL) bandwidth [23], albeit their performance can fluctuate wildly.

Motivations for this Study. From the perspective of new applications which require mission critical communications, what is perhaps more exciting is the promise of 5G to offer millisecond (ms) or even sub-millisecond (PHY-layer) latency support to applications [Sect. 7.5 in [3]][1] *e.g.*, through the so-called *Ultra Reliable Low Latency Communication* (URLLC) services [Sect. 7.9 in [3]] [4,17,27]. These applications include but are not limited to, Autonomous Vehicles (AVs) and drones supported with edge-assisted cooperative driving/flying intelligence, Augmented/Virtual reality (AR/VR), and "metaverse", all which require extreme low latency and very high reliability to make crucial decisions.

Background of 5G Measurement Studies and Research Gap. Recently, several measurement studies have been conducted to assess the latency performance of current 5G deployments and their impact on applications [23–25,29,32–35,44]. These studies have shown that 5G E2E latency performance is affected by factors such as sporadic coverage, link quality disturbances due to User Equipment (UE) mobility, handovers, and poor interactions across the 5G network stack. Furthermore, they have focused solely on UL or DL separately, from an E2E perspective. However, they cannot be used to infer the latency of 5G in PHY-layer (*i.e.*, both UL and DL) and identify issues that could prevent 5G from delivering its expected latency performance on the PHY-layer nor what factors can significantly affect the delay in PHY-layer.

Objectives of this Study. In this paper, we present a measurement study of today's commercial mmWave 5G latency on the PHY-layer. Using AT&T and Verizon (VZW)'s mmWave 5G networks as case study, we seek to quantitatively answer the following critical, yet unaddressed questions: 1) Is today's commercial 5G network capable of delivering millisecond/sub-millisecond ($\leq$ 1ms) latency on the PHY-layer? If so, what is the best achievable PHY-layer latency in DL and UL? 2) Quantitatively, what are the important factors of the 5G Radio Access Network (RAN) that can significantly affect PHY-layer latency? 3) What factors are inherent in the design of the 5G RAN architecture, which may not be easily controlled or mitigated, and what factors are due to the current 5G network configuration or implementation of the cellular carriers, which may be further improved or even eliminated in future 5G deployments? 4) How do other factors

---

[1] The one-hope (UE to gNB) target for URLLC "should be 0.5ms for UL, and 0.5ms for DL".

such as the placement of the application server and packet payload affect the latency of 5G PHY-layer and therefore the E2E delay experienced by applications? We answer these questions through a close look analysis of 5G mmWave PHY-layer key performance indicators (KPIs) with the aim of quantifying the impact of various factors and configurations. Our approach is laid out as follows: First, we aim to quantitatively understand the PHY-layer latency and study it under the "best-case" scenario (Sect. 4). Second, we quantify the impact of several factors that impact the PHY-layer latency (Sects. 5 and 6). Lastly, we explore the latency benefits and drawbacks of deploying services on edge nodes supported by mmWave 5G (Sect. 7). Based on our knowledge, our paper is the first to answer the question, "Is sub-millisecond PHY-layer latency achievable with today's commercial 5G"? And what impact does several factors like 5G smartphone radio ON-OFF cycle and server placement have on the PHY-layer and E2E delays. Next, we summarize our key findings and contributions.

F1. **Today's Best Achievable PHY-layer Delay** (Sect. 4). Our analysis shows that the best achievable mmWave 5G PHY-layer latency is 0.85 ms which occurs about 2.27% of the time. Sub-millisecond ($\leq$ 1ms) PHY-layer latency is guaranteed only 4.42% of the time, with PHY-layer latency reaching up to 3.08 ms about 22.36% of the time (Sect. 4.1). This delay is limited by network side UL scheduling with control overhead contributing to the largest share (about 81%) compared to data overhead, as a result of scheduling requests and backoffs on the busy shared radio channel (Sect. 4.3).

F2. **Impact of Channel Conditions** (Sect. 5). A UE periodically (based on the configurations) reports the DL channel condition to the base station by calculating the value of the channel quality indicator (CQI), which is a number from 1 to 15, where 15 indicates the best channel condition. When the CQI value drops, transmitted data might be corrupted, requiring re-transmission (ReTx). Our experiments show that: 1) The PHY-layer latency when exactly one ReTx occurs is 1.33 ms, making sub-millisecond ($\leq$ 1ms) PHY-layer latency not achievable. 2) As the number of ReTxs increases, the overhead of the PHY-layer data increases 3.5 times the overhead of the control (Sect. 5.1). 3) On average, there is a 2ms additional overhead delay on the PHY-layer when the CQI drops noticeably (Sect. 5.2).

F3. **Impact of Mobility and Handovers (HOs)** (Sect. 6). As mmWave is directional, highly susceptible to many impairment factors, and has shorter coverage ranges, mobility not only affects the channel condition experienced by a UE, but also causes HOs in some situations. All these further impact the latency on the PHY-layer. We find that: 1) When a UE is walking with good channel conditions (*i.e.*, high CQI value) and no HOs occur, the additional PHY-layer overhead due to mobility is 0.51 ms (Sect. 6.1). 2) When there is a HO, the minimum additional PHY-layer overhead is 2 ms (Sect. 6.2).

F4. **Impact of UE Sleep Cycle** (Sect. 7.2). As a way to reduce power consumption on 5G smartphones, 5G supports *discontinuous reception* (DRX). The operations of DRX modes depend on the UE's *state*. We focus only on the *connected* state (CDRX), namely, the UE has established a connection with the base station. In such a state, the UE radio antennas go through *ON* and *OFF* cycles (*i.e.,* awake and asleep states). Two scenarios can occur; 1) The DL transmission occurs while the UE is awake, no additional delay is incurred (best case). 2) The network has data, but the UE is asleep (worst case). Our results show that there is an additional overhead of 6.4 ms (on average) to the PHY-layer latency in the worst case.

F5. **Impact of Packet Payload Size** (Sect. 7.3). We use PING packets to mimic different application payload sizes. We find that the packet payload size has little to no impact on the PHY-layer delay. Our results show that the same time is taken to transmit a ping packet with 100 bytes and 1200 bytes payload. This is because when the payload size of the PING packet increases, the network adopts more hybrid ARQ (HARQ) process IDs [1] that work in parallel to send and receive data between the UE and the base station.

C1. We present an in-depth and thorough analysis which allows for the quantitative revelation of the status quo of today's mmWave 5G PHY-layer delay, identifying carrier specific configurations and poor design choices which hinders 5G's promise of sub-millisecond PHY-layer delay.

C2. We study several factors that impact the latency on the PHY-layer and quantify them, showing that 5G network configurations and server placement decisions can significantly impact the PHY-layer delay and thus E2E latency.

C3. We make all our data as well as other artifacts used in our study publicly available to enable research continuation within the community: https://github.com/FarRoss/5gPHYLatency

Ethical Considerations. This study was carried out by paid and volunteer students. We purchased several dedicated smartphones for experiments only and several unlimited plans from AT&T and Verizon mmWave 5G carriers. No personal identifiable information (PII) was collected or used, nor were any human subjects involved. This study is consistent with the Wireless Network Customer Agreement. This work does not raise ethical issues.

2 Main Measurement Campaign and Challenges

In this section, we present our measurement methodology, experimental platform and setup, data collection approach, equipment, and tools used during this study.

Commercial 5G Networks. We judiciously select two urban areas in two densely populated large metropolitan cities in the U.S., which are two cities with the first mmWave 5G deployments launched in April 2019. **Area 1)** A four-way intersection with three dual-panel faced 5G towers. **Area 2)** A four-blocks loop near the U.S. Bank Stadium in downtown Minneapolis with three 5G base stations. Each block is about 90 m. These two outdoor urban areas are very busy with heavy traffic, several restaurants, coffee shops, railroad crossings, and outdoor parks. At the time of this study, high band/mmWave (24.25–27.5 GHz) 5G deployment is supported by three major U.S. cellular carriers (AT&T, T-Mobile, and Verizon (VZW)) using Non-Standalone mode (NSA) [5]. NSA adopts a dual connection mode in which 4G acts as an anchor for the control plane functionality and to ensure continuous data connectivity. On the other hand, Standalone mode (SA) relies on 5G for all control and data plane activities. Since mmWave deployments are not continuous and have coverage holes, using mmWave with SA 5G can lead to loss of connectivity during mobility. Additionally, any future SA mmWave 5G deployments will most likely use the same 5G RAN technologies. Thus, we believe that our finding will also be valid for future mmWave SA 5G deployments. Mid-bands (3.3-3.8 GHz) and low-bands (700 MHz, n28) have not been deployed yet, thus, beyond the scope of this study. Refer to recent work [22] for a study of the mid-band 5G in Europe. Most of our controlled experiments are focused specifically on **Area 1**.

5G UE and Measurement Tools. We use four phones, two S20s (Exynos 990 Qualcomm SM8250 Snapdragon 865 5G) and two S21 Ultras (Exynos 2100 Qualcomm SM8350 Snapdragon 888 5G) [8]. We believe that these phones represent the state-of-the-art 5G smartphones at the time we conducted the measurement study with powerful communication modems, Mali-G77 MP11 and Mali-G78 MP14, respectively. Moreover, smartphone chip-sets do not affect the network performance at the TCP and application layers [44].

To access the 5G New Radio (NR) stack and PHY-layer KPIs from chipset's diagnostic interfaces (*Diag*), we use a professional tool called *XCAL* [6]. XCAL runs on a laptop connected to smartphones via USB or USB-C (Fig. 1). It monitors, decodes, and deciphers signaling messages and the 5G RAN protocol stack interactions between the UE and gNB following the 3GPP Rel-15 standard. For our controlled experiments, we choose traceroute and ICMP-based PING packets of 32 bytes because of two reasons; 1) It is readily available in Android smartphones and does not require rooting devices. 2) To avoid any limitations due to lack of radio resources using bigger packet sizes. However, we also study the impact of larger packet sizes on PHY-layer and E2E delay (See Sect. 7).

Cloud Server. To explore the benefits of deploying services on the edge, we perform our latency measurements using the Amazon Web Services (AWS) cloud platform [2]. We selected three AWS *nodes* to interact with the UE as shown in Fig. 1 (i) An AWS Wavelength (WL) node is the nearest edge and is directly connected to the VZW's 5G core network. It provides a commercially available 5G edge cloud service through VZW's 5G in the same geographical location as the UE. (ii) An AWS Local Zone (LZ) node is the second-nearest edge located in the same geographical location as the UE. Unlike WL, LZ is not directly connected to VZW's 5G core network. (iii) An AWS Regional (RG) node is the farthest away from a UE but is also located in the same geographical region as the. UE[2] Other main operators, like AT&T and T-Mobile are not directly connected to an edge platform. Therefore, we use VZW to measure the latency for the best-case scenario using a WL node.

---

[2] Our definition of region in this paper is as per AWS, and it is a cluster of a minimum of 3 data centers.

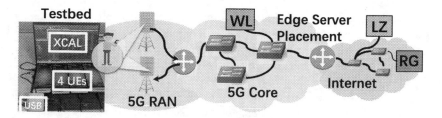

Fig. 1. Measurement Setup and Edge Server Placement.

Challenges. In this study, we face three main challenges; **[C1]** Internet-side buffering, congestion, and data transportation policies of the carrier network can negatively affect the E2E round-trip time (RTT). We minimize this impact by using a WL node. To ensure high-speed connectivity, we conducted several test runs using the Ookla speed test [9], and 5G Tracker [31] to measure the 5G performance. We validate the results are within the expected 5G performance before we start each experiment. **[C2]** We have no visibility into the commercial cellular carrier network. We use XCAL to overcome this challenge. The major advantage of XCAL compared to other wireless network analyzers such as MobileInsight [26] and 5G-Tracker [31] is its ability to decode 5G signaling messages. **[C3]** We need to monitor and trace a PING packet in the 5G RAN stack of the UE down the PHY-layer to the gNB and identify when the gNB sends a packet to the UE. To do this, we leverage consecutive PING echo request intervals. Specifically, 1) we monitor the PHY-layer activities with and without data transfer and 2) we enforce the reception of the PING echo reply from the server between consecutive PING echo requests. Unless otherwise mentioned, we use 1000 ms as the PING intervals. This approach also avoids the case when two or more PING echo replies are sent to the UE at once due to network-side buffering/congestion. During no data periods, our observation of the PHY-layer control channels show that, based on the network configurations, the UE sends (periodic, semi-periodic, or aperiodic) reports to the network which aid in resource allocation and scheduling decisions [Sect. 5.2 in [14]]. Simply put, this approach is like a heartbeat with varying beat intervals, where the corresponding echo requests/responses are the beats. This helps establish the time spent in each phase, as explained later in Fig. 5. Another issue we faced is that XCAL reports the data per channel. Since UE and gNB communicate using several channels, domain knowledge is required to correlate the different events and establish the timeline to trace the UL vs. DL packets. We discuss this in more details later (See Sect. 3).

Experiments and Data Collection. With the above methodology, we conducted several controlled experiments on 5G, resulting in 192+ hours of experiments. Our experiments span different hours (morning, rush hours, night) and days (including weekends). The state of UE Radio Resource Control (RRC) [Sect. 5 in [15]] may further skew the measurement results [33], *i.e.*, if the UE is in RRC_IDLE or RRC_Inactivity state when sending a packet, an additional delay is incurred to transition to RRC_Connected before sending the PING request. The UE will always be in RRC_Connected state when receiving the PING echo reply, as the length of RRC_Connected is 320 ms [33] which is far greater than the worst RTT (100 ms) observed in our experiments. Before each experiment, we close/stop all background apps, disable background-app refresh, and turn off the WiFi interface. To avoid delay overhead during transitions from RRC_IDLE or RRC_Inactivity to RRC_Connected state, we first play a random YouTube video for 30 s, then immediately close the YouTube app, wait 2 s, and then start the experiment. This ensures that the UE is in the RRC_Connected state before sending the echo request. To minimize the UE-side factors that may affect our measurements, we placed the smartphones on a flat surface during stationary experiments and kept them attached to a car phone holder for driving experiments.

3   5G PHY Processing and Factors

In this section, we introduce the 5G NR, 5G RAN, and zero in on the 5G PHY-layer, and outline its key operations. The goal is two-fold: 1) introduce the key PHY-layer interactions used in 5G NR defined by the 3GPP standards that are most relevant to our study to justify our results and insights; and perhaps more importantly, 2) dissect the various components of 5G PHY processing, and identify the major factors which may influence 5G PHY latency, and consequently the E2E latency experienced by applications running on a UE or a remote server.

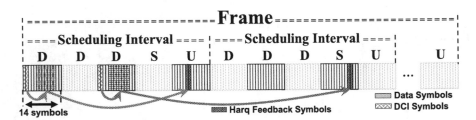

Fig. 2. Illustration of Frame and Scheduling Intervals.

Like 4G and its predecessors, 5G is a *scheduling* system: when a UE can receive or transmit data is completely controlled by the base station (4G eNB or 5G gNB) through Medium Access Control (MAC) scheduling. The MAC layer multiplexes and segments the upper layer data (*e.g.*, user traffic) into transport blocks [Sect. 6.1.1.1 in [14]] of *dynamic* sizes (See Sect. 4.3 for more details). Then it passes the transport blocks down the PHY-layer to be transmitted through dedicated DL and UL transport channels.[3] 5G NR introduces *flexible* subcarrier spacing (SCS), from 15 kHz (same as in 4G LTE), to 30 kHz (mid-band), and 120 kHz (mmWave), to accommodate diverse UE capabilities and meet varying

---

[3] The primary physical channel for the DL transmissions (base station to UE) is PDSCH (physical downlink shared channel), and for the UL transmissions (UE to base station) is PUSCH (physical uplink shared channel).

bandwidth and latency requirements of applications. The wider SCS not only allows for higher channel bandwidth, but also enables lower latency through a shorter *slot* time, *i.e.,* from 1 ms in 15 kHz down to 0.125 ms in 120 kHz (mmWave). A *slot* is defined as the basic (time) unit in which radio transmissions are commonly scheduled [Sect. 4.3.1 in [12]] (See Sect. 4). Our study focuses on 5G mmWave, as it can (potentially) provide both high bandwidth and low latency.

During each *slot*, one data chunk[4] is transmitted over the radio interface to/from the UE. The scheduling configurations are exchanged via the *downlink control information* (DCI)/the *uplink control information* (UCI) carried in the Physical DL Control Channel (PDCCH)/Physical UL Control Channel (PUCCH) respectively, as part of the PHY-layer control signaling (See Fig. 2). 5G mmWave uses *time division duplex* (TDD) which means both the DL and UL share the same carrier frequency (physical transport channel) [16]. However, the transmissions of DL and UL are scheduled at different times, *e.g.,* using different *slots* on the same frequency. We expand on these points below.

Slots and Scheduling. The 3GPP standards allow flexible scheduling of which *slots* are dedicated for DL vs. UL transmissions [Sect. 5 in [16]]. However, we find that current commercial 5G deployments still use a "fixed" pattern. For example, as illustrated in Fig. 2, VZW mmWave 5G uses a 5-*slots* pattern, DDDSU for DL/UL transmission scheduling: The first three *slots* ("DDD") are reserved for DL transmission only, the last *slot*, ("U") is reserved for UL transmission only, while the fourth *slot*, ("S") is *flexible* – it can be used either for DL or UL transmission, or both. *For DL Transmission (data sent from gNB):* the scheduling information carried in the DCI specifies which symbols within "D" (and "S") *slots* are used to carry data; it also indicates which symbols in the "U" (and "S") *slots* may be used to carry UL transmissions, including UCI. DCI is typically carried in the first 1-3 symbols in a "D" or "S" *slot*, while UCI is carried in the last symbol in a "U" or "S" *slot*. While the UE is *active* in a "Connected" state, it monitors the physical channels to see if there is DL data and/or control traffic for it. *For UL Transmission (data sent from UE):* the UE first sends a *scheduling request* in either the "U" or "S" *slot* which only informs the network that the UE has data to transmit. The UE later sends the Buffer State Report (BSR) [Sect. 5.4.5 in [13]], which informs the network the UL data volume. With the BSR information, the network then explicitly *grants* the UE resources. Lastly, the UE prepares and transmits the data using the scheduled future UL *slots*. As a result, we can deduce that this configuration enables asymmetric traffic between UL and DL demands. Thus, UL transmissions likely incur longer latency than DL, which is also confirmed by our results in Sect. 4.

Channel Conditions (CQI), Modulation and Coding Schemes (MCS). A UE periodically reports to the gNB the DL channel condition using the channel quality indicator (CQI), a number from 1 to 15, where 15 indicates the best

---

[4] Assuming no spatial multiplexing, which is the case of VZW 5G mmWave. However, with spatial multiplexing, at most 2 Transport Blocks can be transmitted per *slot*.

channel condition [Sect. 5.1.6 in [14]]. The gNB uses this CQI value to determine which modulation (*e.g.,* QPSK, 32QAM, or 64QAM) and coding rate (*e.g.,* the number of redundant bits) to use to encode the data. This is collectively referred to as the Modulation and Coding Schemes (MCS) [Sect. 5.1.3 in [14]]. The MCS value informs a UE on how to decode a DL transmission or how to encode a UL transmission. The main take-away is the following: higher CQI generally leads to higher MCS – *if* there is sufficient data buffered to warrant it; and higher MCS means more information bits (*i.e.,* more data from the upper layer) is carried per *slot*. As the MAC layer multiplexes data from multiple "logical" channels (*e.g.,* RRC messages, multiple concurrent user sessions), an IP packet from an application server to a UE (or vice versa) can be segmented into multiple data chunks, therefore requiring multiple *slots* for the packet to be delivered to the user (or server), incurring longer latency even under "ideal" channel conditions.

Hybrid ARQ (HARQ) Re-transmission Processes. As in 4G, 5G employs a hybrid ARQ (HARQ) mechanism that combines forward error correction (FEC) coding and automatic re-transmission (ReTx) request (ARQ) to recover errors. At either the gNB or UE, the MAC layer is responsible for re-transmitting a data chunk upon receiving a negative acknowledgment (NACK). For DL, a UE has to explicitly ACK or NACK every transmission. For UL, the gNB implicitly "NACKs" corrupted received data for the UE to (re)transmit (Sect. 5.1). Under poor channel conditions, transmitted data chunks are likely to be corrupted, and require ReTxs. This is reflected by the *block-level error rate* (BLER) [13]. As ReTxs require additional *slots*, poor channel conditions and higher BLERs can significantly increase the latency experienced by users.

DRX Mode in *Connected State: CDRX.* Both 4G and 5G support *discontinuous reception* (DRX) for the UE power management. The operations of DRX modes depend on which *state* the UE is in. We focus only on the *Connected* state (CDRX), namely, the UE has established a connection with the gNB [1]. In such state, the UE goes through *active* and *sleep* cycles to save power. Only when active, the UE searches for data, receives, or transmits data. Therefore, if data from an application session arrive at the gNB while the UE is asleep, the gNB has to wait until the next active cycle to signal the UE and allocate DL radio resources for DL transmission, which further increases the latency (Sect. 7.2).

Mobility and Handovers. mmWave 5G is directional, highly susceptible to many impairment factors, and has shorter coverage ranges. Therefore, UE mobility not only affects the channel conditions experienced, but also causes handovers (HOs) in some situations, further affecting the E2E latency experienced by users/applications (Sect. 6).

4   5G PHY-layer Latency: Best Cases

Throughout this section, we define the best-case as: the UE is stationary, in RRC_Connected state, and facing a 5G base station. This is because the channel conditions *i.e.,* CQI values ≥ 12 which indicates high MCS [Sect. 5.2.2 in [14]] (See Sect. 5) and no ReTxs occur. We summarize all the latency definitions in Table 1.

4.1 Quantifying Best-Case PHY Latency

PHY-layer latency, T_{Phy} is defined as the time taken to send a PING echo request in the UL, (T_{UL}) and receive the corresponding echo reply in the DL, (T_{DL}) on the physical layer. *i.e.,* $T_{Phy} = T_{UL} + T_{DL}$. To compute T_{Phy}, we carefully trace every PING packet on the UE side down the 5G RAN stack. Based on the data collected on the different radio channels, we use domain knowledge to: 1) isolate the PING packet from other noisy data such as beam management-related control plane messages, 2) correlate the different transport channel PING related messages, and 3) synchronize (and group) the different channel events in UL and DL. Furthermore, we compute i) the time taken to send the PING data on the physical transport data channel, T_{Phy}^{Data} and ii) the time taken to send related control messages on the physical transport control channels, T_{Phy}^{Ctrl}.

Table 1. Summary of the Definitions for the Different Latency Terms Used

Delay ⇓Quantity	Delay ⇓ Definition/Breakdown	Delay in terms ⇓ UE-gNB Interactions
T_{UL}^{Ctrl}	UL Control delay in the PHY-layer	$T_{UL}^{Ctrl} = $ (U1) + (U2)
T_{UL}^{Data}	UL Data delay in the PHY-layer	$T_{UL}^{Data} = $ (U3)
T_{UL}	UL delay in the PHY-layer, $T_{UL} = T_{UL}^{Ctrl} + T_{UL}^{Data}$	$T_{UL} = $ (U1) + (U3) + (U3)
T_{DL}^{Ctrl}	DL Control delay in the PHY-layer, $T_{DL}^{Ctrl} = T_{DL}^{Ctrl1} + T_{DL}^{Ctrl2}$	$T_{DL}^{Ctrl} = $ (D1) + (D3)
T_{DL}^{Data}	DL Data delay in the PHY-layer	$T_{DL}^{Data} = $ (D2)
T_{DL}	DL delay in the PHY-layer, $T_{DL} = T_{DL}^{Ctrl} + T_{DL}^{Data}$	$T_{DL} = $ (D1) + (D2) + (D3)
T_{Phy}	UL and DL delay in the PHY-layer, $T_{Phy} = T_{DL} + T_{UL}$	$T_{Phy} = $ (U1) + (U3) + (U3) + (D1) + (D2) + (D3)
T_{5G_RAN}	Delay in the PHY-layer including 5G RAN delay of the UE	See Fig. 20
$T_{5G\_Core+Inet}$	Delay from (U1) to cloud server to (D1)	$T_{5G_Core+Inet} = $ (U1) + wired delay + (D1)
T_{E2E_RTT}	Round Trip Time from the applications	$T_{E2E\_RTT} = T_{5G\_Core+Inet} + T_{5G\_RAN}$
T_{Phy_RTT}	Round Trip Time from the PHY-layer	See Fig. 20

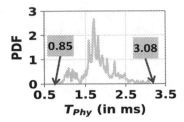
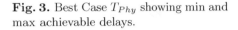

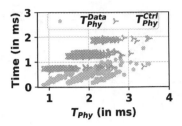

Fig. 3. Best Case T_{Phy} showing min and max achievable delays.

Fig. 4. Breakdown of T_{Phy} into Control and Data delays.

Results. We make the following observations. (1) In the best case, today's T_{Phy} delay scale, can be as low as 0.85 ms and as high as 3.08 ms (See Fig. 3). (2) Interestingly, *only* 4.43% of all our dataset samples have delays ≤ 1 ms. In other words, sub-millisecond latency occurs about $\leq 5\%$ of the time. Most delays fall between 1 ms and 2.5 ms (*i.e.,* 87.69%), and 7.83% have delays between 2.5 ms and 3.08 ms. The maximum best case T_{Phy} latency is largely unsurprising: previous studies have calculated this delay to be between 2.19±0.36ms [44]. Nevertheless, our results provide insight into today's *expected* delay scale, which can inspire new design opportunities. For example, to ensure that 5G can support latency-critical applications, sub-milliseconds PHY-layer transmission is a must. In particular, Rel 15 38.913 [3] standardized the 5G first hop (*i.e.,* PHY-layer) delay for URLLC to 1 ms. (3) A breakdown of the best case T_{Phy} delay into the control (T_{Phy}^{Ctrl}) and data (T_{Phy}^{Data}) overhead shows that the control overhead is on average 3.78 times more than the data overhead (See Fig. 4). Thus, it is clear that, today's mmWave 5G PHY-layer latency is far from enabling latency-critical applications. The question now remains, *what are the design opportunities or improvements which can favor the majority of the delay to fall below 1 ms?* To answer this question, we use Fig. 5 to dissect T_{Phy} into DL and UL delays.

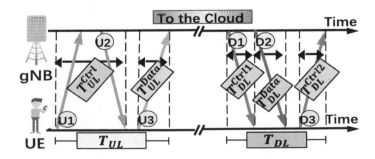

Fig. 5. PHY-layer Interaction between UE and gNB.

4.2   Dissecting DL PHY Latency

DL Transmission : As shown in Fig. 5, when data arrives at the gNB destined for a UE, the gNB first sends the data schematics via a control plane message in step $(D1)$.[5] We calculate the time taken to send this control message to the UE as T_{DL}^{Ctrl1}. The $(D1)$ message contains information for the UE to successfully decode and consume the data. This control plane message tells the UE when exactly it can expect data (*i.e.,* in which *slot* (s)), the data encoding format to decode the data, which *slot* the UE would use to send the ACK/NACK when it has successfully decoded the data, and other related information. The actual data transmission happens at step $(D2)$, and lasts T_{DL}^{Data} long. Finally, in step $(D3)$, the UE sends the ACK/NACK control plane message for the received data. This time lasts T_{DL}^{Ctrl2} long. The total DL time, $T_{DL} = T_{DL}^{Ctrl1} + T_{DL}^{Data} + T_{DL}^{Ctrl2}$ refers to the DL delay during which the gNB schedules DL resources and sends the data to the UE on the common channel.

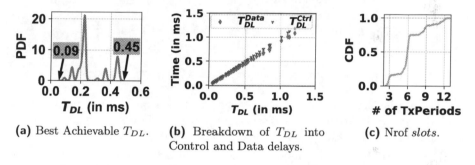

(a) Best Achievable T_{DL}.   (b) Breakdown of T_{DL} into Control and Data delays.   (c) Nrof *slots*.

Fig. 6. Dissecting the Best Case PHY-layer DL Latency.

DL Latency Results. We find that the *best* (*i.e.,* min) DL delay T_{DL} is 0.09 ms, which occurs 1.95% of the time (See Fig. 6a). This implies that $(D1)$, $(D2)$, and $(D3)$ can occur within one *slot* ($\leq$ 0.125 ms), the S *slot* in DDDSU. However, we can see that T_{DL} has multiple peaks such as 0.17, 0.22, and 0.45 ms. This is due to scheduling the 3 predefined tasks $(D1)$, $(D2)$, and $(D3)$ across *slots* and varying number of OFDM symbols within each *slot* (refer to Fig. 2). For example, when $T_{DL} = 0.45$ ms, $(D1)$, $(D2)$, and $(D3)$ span 3.6 *slots* (*i.e.,* 0.45 ms $\div$ 0.125 ms). We also find that, more than 50% of the time, the network configures the UE to wait at least 6 *slots* (0.75 ms) before it can send the ACK control message in $(D3)$ (See Fig. 6c). This time includes the processing delay on the UE side.

Impact of Physical DL Control Overheads. Figure 6b shows the breakdown of T_{DL} into control and data latency. We can notice that T_{DL} is evenly split between the control, T_{DL}^{Ctrl} and the data, T_{DL}^{Data} delays. This behavior is

---

[5] This data schematics corresponds to the DCI as shown in Fig. 2.

irrespective of the packet payload size (See Sect. 7.3) and is due to the fact that; 1) Today's mmWave 5G implements same *slot* scheduling, *i.e.*, (D1) and (D3) are in the same *slot* (as shown in Fig. 2) and, 2) the DL control ((D1) and (D3)) and DL data ((D2)) messages occupy two-to-eight and one-to-nine OFDM symbols respectively.

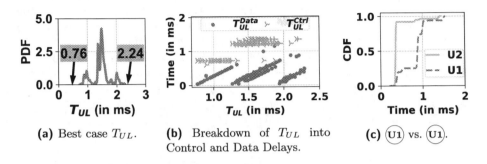

(a) Best case T_{UL}.

(b) Breakdown of T_{UL} into Control and Data Delays.

(c) (U1) vs. (U1).

Fig. 7. Dissecting the Best Case PHY-layer UL Latency.

4.3   Dissecting UL PHY Latency

UL Transmission. As shown in Fig. 5, when a UE has data to transmit, it sends a *scheduling request* to procure access to the *busy shared* radio channel as in step (U1), and waits for an explicit *grant* in step (U2). We refer to this combined time as T_{UL}^{Ctrl}, which can involve multiple unsuccessful *scheduling request* attempts due to back-offs on the *busy shared* channel. Afterward, the UE prepares and sends the data in step (U3). We refer to this time as T_{UL}^{Data}. The total time T_{UL} = $T_{UL}^{Ctrl} + T_{UL}^{Data}$ is the UL delay in the PHY-layer.

UL Latency Results. Theoretically, as per the cyclic "fixed" *slots* pattern per radio frame, the lower bound UL *slots* combination is "**UDDDS**" *i.e.*, 0.125 * 5 = 0.625 ms (See Fig. 2). This is because, the UE can request access to the *busy shared* channel ((U1)) in the U *slot*, waits to be *granted* access ((U2)) in one of the three D *slots* (-DDD-), and then sends the UL data ((U3)) in the last S *slot*. In our experiments, we find that the "best" (*i.e.*, min) PHY-layer UL delay is 0.76 ms, which corresponds to the *slots* combination U D D D S U which needed one extra slot than the theoretical bound mentioned above (See Fig. 7a for T_{UL} distribution). We can see multiple peaks in the figure, the percentage of achieving 0.76 ms is 7.46%, for 2.24 ms is 45.496%, and the mean T_{UL} = 1.46 ms. The reason for multiple peaks is two folds: 1) Within a *slot*, the UE may be scheduled varying number of OFDM symbols, and 2) UL scheduling overhead due to back-offs on the busy shared channel as we explain next.

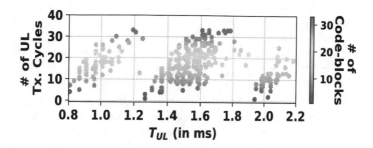

Fig. 8. Linear Relation Between the UL Latency (T_{UL}) and code-blocks.

UL Ctrl and Data Latency. We further break T_{UL} down and characterize the cost on each network communication group, *i.e.,* the control (T_{UL}^{Ctrl}) and data (T_{UL}^{Data}) overheads. Figure 7b shows that, considering a T_{UL} time of 1.5 ms as an example, the control overhead T_{UL}^{Ctrl} accounts for approximately 81% *i.e.,* 1.7 ms. Simply put, the control overhead (U1) + (U2) is responsible for the lion share of the UL delay, unlike the case for DL. This shows that the UL control overhead T_{UL}^{Ctrl} ((U1) + (U2)) takes much longer than data transmission T_{UL}^{Data} ((U3)) in the UL. This is because of two reasons: 1) We find that the UE takes more time waiting to be granted access to the busy shared channel ((U1)) than the actual grant time ((U2)) as shown in Fig. 7c. 2) A single UL transport block gets split into multiple code-blocks [Sect. 6.1.1.1 in [14]] in the UE MAC layer, which are then transmitted on the PHY-layer, and reassembled in the gNB MAC layer. In the "best" case, all the code-blocks are transmitted in one UL transmission cycle (Tx Cycle), as warranted by the allocation of network resources as specified in (U2). We define a Tx Cycle as one round of (U1), (U2), and (U3). However, when the (U2) resource allocated "grant" size is insufficient, each code-block goes through a separate UL Tx Cycles. Thus, a single UL packet can go through multiple *slots* before being completely transmitted on the PHY-layer. Figure 8 shows that T_{UL} increases linearly as the number of code-blocks increases. The number of UL Tx cycles is less than or equal to the number of code-blocks. The jumps in the figure are due to varying the number of OFDM symbols within each *slot*.

Summary and Implications: In the best-case scenario, PHY-layer latency satisfies the sub-millisecond requirement ($\leq$ 1ms) only 4.43% of the time. It can reach up to 3.08 ms [22.36% of the time]. The average PHY-layer latency is 1.79 ms. These results imply that sub-millisecond PHY-layer transmission is indeed achievable in today's commercial mmWave 5G networks. However, this minimum latency is limited by the UL scheduling in the RAN and is largely dominated by the control overhead. We believe that our results provide two incentives for enhancements or perhaps protocol re-design; 1) Implementing and adapting all 61 proposed slots scheduling interval configurations as per 3GPP [Sect. 7.3.1 in [11]], and dynamically adapting specific slot patterns for UL and DL heavy transmissions for different use cases will further reduce this latency. 2) For

UL-centric apps with heavy UL traffic demands like AR, the cyclic fixed slot configuration means that, the network is not aware of the UE-side heavy traffic demands. Therefore, we claim that, offloading some UL functions to the UE will help cap the lion share control plane overhead and further reduce latency. For example, introducing a mechanism by which a UE can signal heavy UL traffic to the network and request a UL specific slot configuration or implementing a true cross-layer signaling mechanism to anticipate and signal specific application PHY-layer latency requirements could be ways to achieve this. This might also help address variations (or instabilities) in latency, although these instabilities are largely due to channel conditions (see below).

5   Impact of Channel Conditions

Taking into account the invisibility of the network side information, we use CQI in the UL to study the impact of PHY-layer radio conditions on latency. Recall from Sect. 4 that MCS determines the number of useful bits transmitted per *slot*. A lower MCS leads to more redundant bits and fewer useful bits transmitted per *slot*, and vice versa. Fig. 9 shows the impact of CQI on MCS. On one hand, when the UE reports a high CQI value, which implies good channel conditions, the network generally selects a high MCS to be used for data encoding. On the other hand, Fig. 10 shows that a lower CQI value results in corrupted data, which leads to more ReTxs on the PHY-layer captured by the BLER. These ReTxs are transparent to the application layer, but can further increase the E2E RTT. Therefore, we quantify the impact of CQI and ReTxs on the PHY-layer latency, and further explain its impact on the E2E application perceived latency.

Methodology: Previous studies have shown the impact of HO on E2E RTT and have found that HO patches[6] occur in well-defined areas around 5G towers [30]. We leverage these findings to improve the credibility of our results by minimizing the number of HOs during our experiments: First, we conduct repeated experiments to identify the HO patches around our chosen areas. Second, we conduct controlled LoS walking experiments and do not walk beyond identified potential

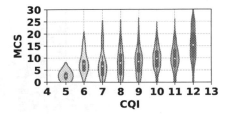

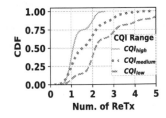

Fig. 9. Impact of CQI on Modulation Coding Scheme (MCS).

Fig. 10. Impact of CQI on Number of ReTxs.

---

[6] Defined as the area between two 5G towers A and B where HO occurs from tower A to B or vice versa.

HO areas. Third, despite these measures to ensure no HO, we still observe and discard experiments with any HO occurrences. As a way to quantify the impact of the CQI on latency, we divide the CQI values into $CQI_{low} = (6, 9]$, $CQI_{medium} = (9, 12]$, and $CQI_{high} = (12, 15]$, and refer to it as such hereafter. Note that even when the UE is in CQI_{high}, the CQI value can still change slightly between 12+ and 15, and ReTxs may occur. Thus, during our experiments, we fix the CQI range, keep all other factors constant, and investigate the impact of slight CQI changes on the PHY-layer latency.

5.1 Understanding the Impact of ReTxs on T_{Phy}

A single ReTx can Defeat the 1 ms PHY-Layer Delay: Previously, we showed that sub-millisecond T_{Phy} is indeed achievable in the best case scenario, *i.e.*, $T_{Phy} = 0.85$ ms (Sect. 4.1). However, Fig. 11 shows that when exactly one ReTx occurs (Num. ReTx = 1), the best case (*i.e.*, min) T_{Phy} is 1.33 ms and about 2.27% of the PING packets experience only 1 ReTx. We find that, the network "NACKs" corrupted received data (*i.e.*, undelivered (U3) message) by implicitly granting the UE access to the radio channel (*i.e.*,(U2)) without an explicit channel request from the UE (*i.e.*,(U1)). Practically, an example of such interaction can be: Assume the UE sends the initial corrupted data in the "U" *slot* of the previous schedule interval (*i.e.*, "**DDDSU** — DDDSU"). It has to wait and receive the implicit grant in one of the three "D" *slots* of the next scheduled interval (*i.e.*, "DDDSU — **DDD**SU") and re-transmits the data in the "S" *slot* (*i.e.*, "DDDSU — DDD<u>S</u>U"). Theoretically, this will incur an additional lower bound overhead of 0.375 ms (*i.e.*, 0.125 ms x 3 (*slots*)). Therefore, $T_{Phy} = 0.85$ ms + 0.375 ms = 1.225 ms. However, our experiments show that the actual PHY-layer delay with one ReTxs is 1.33 ms, 0.105 ms higher than the theoretical, but lower than one *slot* (0.125 ms).

Characterizing the Cost of ReTxs: To characterize the cost of ReTxs in UL and DL, we plot the latency for different numbers of ReTxs. Figure 12 shows that, unlike DL transmissions, ReTxs have a significant impact on UL transmissions due to the same theoretical analysis as explained above. Furthermore, Fig. 13

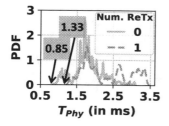

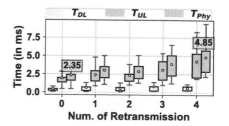

Fig. 11. 1ms T_{Phy} is defeated with one ReTx.

Fig. 12. Impact of Retransmissions on T_{DL}, T_{UL}, and T_{Phy}.

shows the impact of ReTxs on T_{Phy}^{Ctrl} and T_{Phy}^{Data}. We find that, as the number
of ReTxs increases, T_{Phy}^{Data} increases much faster than T_{Phy}^{Ctrl}; slope of line $l3$
$m_{Phy}^{Data} = 0.2072$, slope of $l1$ $m_{Phy}^{Ctrl} = 0.0219$. Hence, T_{Phy}^{Data} grows at ≈ 9.5x the
rate of T_{Phy}^{Ctrl} when the number of ReTxs increases. More specifically, T_{Phy}^{Ctrl}'s
dominance in T_{Phy} (as shown in Sect. 4.3) decreases significantly from 79.2%
to 60.1% then to 45.9% when the number of ReTxs increases from 0 to 3 to
6, respectively. This is due to two reasons; 1) for the control overhead: implicit
"NACKs" from the gNB eliminates (U1) from subsequent ReTxs and (U2) $\ll$
(U1) (See Fig. 7c), and 2) for the data overhead: we find that (U3) usually takes
between 0.0625 ms to 0.125 ms, (U2) takes on average 0.018 ms. Hence, T_{Phy}^{Data}
((U3)) overhead increases by [3.5X, 7X] faster than T_{Phy}^{Ctrl} ((U2)).

5.2   Impact of CQI on T_{UL} and T_{Phy}

We study the impact of CQI_{low}, CQI_{medium} and CQI_{high} with a fixed number of
ReTxs. Fig. 14 shows that when there is no ReTxs, there is at least an additional
2 ms overhead on T_{Phy} with poor channel conditions (*i.e.*, CQI changes from
CQI_{high} to CQI_{low}). A similar conclusion is observed for T_{UL} (See Fig. 15). This
overhead is due to a lower MCS when the CQI drops to CQI_{low}. This will cause
a decrease in the code rate *i.e.*, less useful bits are transmitted per *slot*, resulting
in more time to transmit an entire transport block. The impact of CQI on T_{DL}
is rather insignificant.

Summary and Implications: *The HARQ process is primarily used to speed
up ReTxs. The sender stores all transmitted data in its buffer and discards them
only after receiving an ACK from the receiver. The receiver also stores all erroneous packets and uses them to improve decoding [Sect. 5.4.2 in [13]]. This may
cause unavoidable latency overhead, particularly when the channel conditions
change very suddenly from CQI_{high} to CQI_{low}. This is because UL data transmission that is encoded with an MCS value suitable for the current reported CQI
value may not be suitable at a later time when there is a ReTx and the CQI
value drops. This can result in more ReTxs and higher latency, which explains*

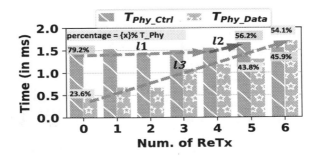

Fig. 13. Impact of ReTxs on T_{Phy}^{Ctrl} and T_{Phy}^{Data}.

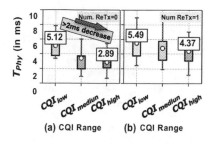
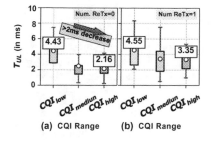

(a) CQI Range   (b) CQI Range   (a) CQI Range   (b) CQI Range

Fig. 14. Impact of CQI and Num. ReTx on T_{Phy}. We consider Num. ReTx=0 and Num. ReTx=1.

Fig. 15. Impact of CQI and Num. ReTx on T_{UL}. We consider Num. ReTx=0 and Num. ReTx=1.

why exactly one ReTx with PHY-layer latency 1.33 ms occurs about 2.27% of time. Given this, we conclude that improving the HARQ process to account for CQI to MCS mismatch, especially when channel conditions drop, can provide a remedy and perhaps eliminate the additional overhead due to more ReTxs. In the practical sense, this calls for an extensive re-design of mmWave PHY-layer operations.

6 Impact of Mobility

In this section, we address two key questions: First, what is the additional PHY-layer overhead due to UE-side activity (*i.e.*, mobility) in mmWave 5G? and second, how does mobility influence the PHY-layer latency in UL and DL?

Methodology: Similar to our experimental setup in Sect. 5, we minimize HOs and conduct clear LoS walking experiments and do not walk beyond identified potential HO patches. We study the best case *i.e.*, the UE is in CQI_{high} with slight CQI fluctuations and no ReTxs.

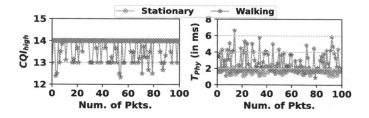

Fig. 16. Variability in T_{Phy} caused by mobility when UE is in CQI_{high} and no ReTxs.

6.1 Impact of Mobility (No HOs) on T_{Phy}

Mobility causes rapid signal quality fluctuations in mmWave which has a direct impact on T_{Phy}. In Fig. 16, the left Fig. shows the CQI fluctuations when

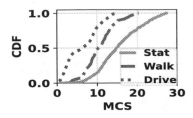

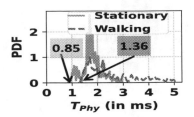

Fig. 17. Impact of mobility on MCS.   **Fig. 18.** Impact of mobility on T_{Phy}.

the UE is in CQI_{high} while walking and stationary and the Fig. on the right shows T_{Phy} while walking and stationary. We see that, even in CQI_{high}, the CQI values fluctuates frequently when the UE is walking. This is because, as shown in Fig. 17, the network adopts a lower MCS values during mobility as a way to minimize the number of ReTxs and meet the target BLER rate of <10% [Table 8.1.1-1 in [12]]. However, adopting lower MCS increases the best case (*i.e.*, min) T_{Phy} from 0.85 ms to 1.36 ms between stationary and walking, respectively, shown in Fig. 18. A difference of 0.51 ms, about 5 *slots*.

6.2   Quantifying the Impact of HOs on T_{Phy}

We aim to quantify the minimum PHY-layer latency overhead due to HOs, T_{Phy}^{HO}. Unlike the previous section, which focuses on mobility without HOs, we now study the impact of HO on PHY-layer. We conduct walking and driving experiments, ensuring that we move across 5G towers to trigger HOs. We find that the minimum additional latency overhead due to HO from one 5G tower to another 5G tower (5G → 5G HO) is 2 ms, which corresponds to 16 *slots* (See Fig. 19). Additionally, we see that when the user is driving, approximately ≥ 50% of T_{Phy}^{HO} takes at least 3 ms compared to 2 ms while walking.

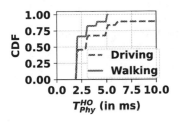

Fig. 19. Impact of 5G–>5G HOs on T_{Phy} during walking vs. Driving.

Summary and Implications: *Although, the effect of mobility causes fast and frequent instability in PHY-layer latency which are problematic for latency-critical applications like AR/VR, we argue that, it can be avoided to some extent. Here, we discuss two cases. Case 1: The additional latency due to mobility can be minimized from 1) the UE side by actively sensing and predicting blockage [21] and/or requesting more slots when blockage is unavoidable. The later approach requires more investigation and has not yet being studied. 2) from the network side by taking into account the UE-side contextual factors and/or upper layer Quality of service (QoS) when making scheduling decisions. Practically, this might require leveraging signalling messages, camera data, and cross-layer communication to* *develop mobility-aware applications. Case 2: Given mmWave's directional prop-agation and high sensitivity to obstruction, the additional delay is not avoidable in few cases. For instance, when the obstruction is due to factors beyond the con-trol of UE or network e.g., moving vehicles, people and tall building etc. Dense mmWave cell tower deployments can help in this case, however, such deploy-ments are costly and may not be the first choice for commercial carriers.*

7   E2E Application Latency

Here we break the E2E delay into the 5G RAN, including T_{Phy} and the 5G Core + Internet latency, and study the impact of the PHY-layer on the E2E delay. We aim to understand: 1) the role of server placement on E2E delay, 2) how the UE sleep cycle (*i.e.,* CDRX) incurs additional delay?, and lastly, 3) what impact do various packet payload sizes have on the PHY-layer and E2E latency?

Methodology: We deploy three VMs, each running on AWS WL, LZ, and RG edge nodes. We have verified these VMs placement relative to a UE in our two chosen locations by conducting a simple PING and traceroute experiment over mmWave 5G. The traceroute experiment reveals that, the UE is 8, 19, and 22 hops away from the WL, LZ, and RG servers respectively. A geolocation PING shows the WL and LZ in the same region as the UE. We conduct stationary clear LoS experiments, *i.e.,* the UE is in CQI_{high} with no ReTxs as follows: Three UEs send PING echo requests to the three VMs at various PING intervals (5, 8, 10, and 15 ms) using varying PING payload sizes (*i.e.,* 32, 100, 400, 900, and 1200 bytes). We enforce the reception of the PING echo reply from the server before consecutive PING echo requests. This lets us dissect the E2E delay by isolating each PING and studying the UE sleep cycle timers. We adopt varying PING payloads to mimic different application traffic patterns.

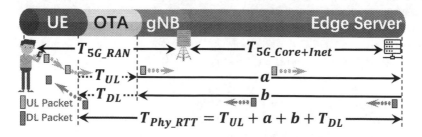

Fig. 20. Dissecting the E2E RTT into T_{5G_RAN} and $T_{5G\_Core+Inet}$.

7.1   Role of Server Placement

Dissecting the E2E Application Perceived Latency. We divide the E2E RTT delay into two components: i) The 5G RAN delay, T_{5G_RAN} defined as, the packet time spent on the PHY-layer including the processing time by the

5G RAN upper layers in the UE and ii) the 5G Core + Internet delay, *i.e.*, $T_{5G\_Core+Inet}$ defined as the time from when the UE sends the PING echo request in (U3) to when it receives the PING echo reply from the edge server on the PHY-layer in (D1). Therefore, $T_{E2E\_RTT} = T_{5G\_RAN} + T_{5G\_Core+Inet}$ (See Fig. 20). To divide the E2E RTT, we compute T_{Phy_RTT}, the physical layer RTT including $T_{5G\_Core+Inet}$ as shown in Fig. 20. Then, $T_{5G\_Core+Inet} = T_{Phy\_RTT} - (T_{UL} + T_{DL})$. From $T_{5G\_Core+Inet}$, we calculate $T_{5G\_RAN} = T_{E2E\_RTT} - T_{5G\_Core+Inet}$.

Results. As shown in Fig. 21 and Table 2, the 5G RAN delay takes on average 7.32 ms regardless of the server location. However, as the distance between the UE and the server increases, $T_{5G\_Core+Inet}$ increases dramatically to be 10 ms, 30 ms, and 35 ms (on average) across the WL, LZ, and RG servers, respectively. This signifies the importance of edge server placement on RTT. Next, we demonstrate the benefit of deploying applications on the WL, and setbacks of deploying applications on the LZ and RG servers w.r.t. a UE location.

Table 2. E2E RTT Delay Breakdown Across Edge Servers

Delay Components ⇒ ⇓ Edge Server	T_{E2E_RTT} Mean ±std. dev.	T_{5G_RAN} Mean ±std. dev.	$T_{5G\_Core+Inet}$ Mean ±std. dev.
WL	17.27 ms±1.31 ms	**7.02 ms ±3.77 ms**	10.25 ms±3.84 ms
LZ	38.15 ms±1.83 ms	**7.34 ms ±4.25 ms**	30.81 ms±4.41 ms
RG	44.08 ms±3.04 ms	**7.60 ms ±4.72 ms**	35.82 ms±4.55 ms

7.2   Impact of CDRX on T_{Phy}

mmWave 5G makes use of CDRX to achieve UE power management for efficient energy consumption and to synchronize UE wake-up timing with DL data transmission [33]. While in RRC_Connected state, the gNB configures the UE to go through active and sleep cycles. The UE CDRX behavior is determined using several timers, which we explain below. We serendipitously employ the CDRX cycles to estimate and bound the "wired" part (between the gNB and the edge server) of the E2E latency.

CDRX Sleep Timers. The CDRX cycle is controlled by the CDRX_ON and the CDRX_OFF timers – The CDRX_ON timer determines how long the UE will stay ON and the CDRX_OFF timer dictates the duration the UE will stay OFF. The CDRX ON/OFF duration cycles may be extended further on the basis of the CDRX_Inactivity timer. The CDRX_Inactivity timer determines how long the UE MUST stay ON upon reception of access to the busy shared channel (*i.e.*,(U2)), which will further extend the duration of the UE ON [1]. We observe that, both VZW and AT&T configure the CDRX _ON and CDRX _Inactivity duration as 8 ms and 30 ms, respectively.

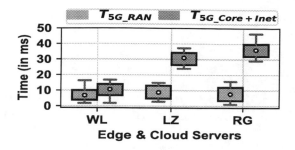

Fig. 21. Impact of Server Placement on E2E RTT Delay Breakdown.

Delay Due to CDRX. Since the CDRX_Inactivity timer starts when the UE acquires access to the busy shared channel, we therefore compute $T_{CDRX\_Overhead} = T_{PhyRTT\_CDRX}$ - 30 (CDRX_Inactivity duration), where T_{PhyRTT_CDRX} is the time between when a UE acquires access to the busy shared channel ((U2)) and receives the DCI which indicates an echo PING reply on the PHY-layer ((D1)), *i.e.*, the time from (U2)—>edge server—>(D1) in Fig. 5. We find that, in the WL case, the UE will never go to sleep before receiving the echo PING reply from the server. This is because, in the WL, T_{PhyRTT_CDRX} << 30ms (CDRX_Inactivity). However, in the LZ and RG cases, the UE goes into sleep mode (CDRX_OFF) about 60% and 97% of the time respectively before receiving the PING echo reply (See Fig. 22a). We show a detailed illustration of this behavior for each server in Fig. 23 by showing the arrival time for three sample PING echo replies w.r.t. the UE status CDRX ON/OFF. We further compute $T_{CDRX\_Overhead}$, the additional time taken before the network sends the PING echo reply to the UE when the UE is asleep (CDRX_OFF) because the CDRX_Inactivity timer has expired. We find that, $T_{CDRX\_Overhead} = 6.4$ ms (on average) (See Fig. 22b).

7.3 Impact of Packet Payload Size

By varying the PING payload size, we can understand how the amount of data sent and received affects PHY-layer latency and E2E RTT. We find that the payload size has little to no impact on T_{Phy} (See Fig. 24). We notice that, when the payload size increases, the network may schedule multiple HARQ processes that work simultaneously to carry the UE data during specific *slots*. The number of scheduled HARQ processes is sent to the UE in (U2). The UE then uses the assigned processes during scheduled UL *slot*. Simply put, when the number of HARQ processes increases, more bytes can be sent in the same *slot* without increasing the latency. We observe a maximum of 16 HARQ processes in VZW mmWave 5G, which conforms with 3GPP's specification [Sect. 5.4.2 in [13]]. This mmWave 5G design has little to no impact on the control overhead, T_{Phy}^{Ctrl}, as only one (U1) message is needed to report the UE buffer status when the data size increases. This will also have little to no impact on T_{Phy}^{Data}. However, we observe

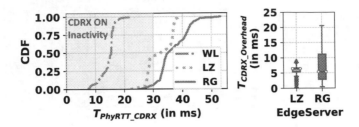

Fig. 22. Impact of CDRX and server placement on PHY-layer. a) [1] In the WL case, the UE will NEVER go to sleep. [2] In the LZ case, the UE goes to sleep 60% of the time, while [3] in the RG case, the UE will go to sleep 97% of the time. b) Additional 6.4 ms delay (on average) overhead due to CDRX.

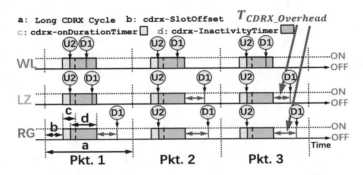

Fig. 23. Detailed illustration of how the CDRX and server placement impact the E2E RTT. Sever placement causes an additional delay due to CDRX, $T_{CDRX\_Overhead}$ in the LZ and RG edger server.

an insignificant increase in the E2E RTT (See Fig. 25). This is because both the UE and the gNB will take more time to reassemble the data chunks from all processes before forwarding it to the RAN upper layer for processing.

Summary and Implications. Although the role of CDRX in the management of UE power is paramount [24], our experiments show that there is a trade-off with the E2E latency in the LZ and RG edge nodes. Without devaluing the CDRX benefits, our experiments reveal that, the additional overhead due to CDRX (i.e., $T_{PhyRTT\_CDRX} = 6.4$ ms) is primarily due to the network side CDRX sleep timer configurations. We claim that adopting dynamic context-aware CDRX timer configuration may significantly reduce or perhaps even eliminate the latency effect due to CDRX especially in far edge nodes. For example, increasing the CDRX_Inactivity timer from 30 to 35 or 40 ms can potentially reduce the perceived latency of the E2E application by 6.4 ms on average. Additionally, it will be beneficial to customers with limited monetary resources as deploying applications on the closest edges, such as the WL node, is very expensive [45]. However, achieving this context-aware CDRX timer configurations requires a truly 5G NR *cross-layer design which perhaps calls for a protocol redesign. This approach is particularly difficult and have not yet been studied in the literature.*

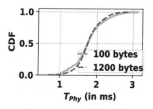

Fig. 24. Impact of Payload size on T_{Phy}.   Fig. 25. Payload size has little to no impact on T_{Phy}^{Data} and E2E RTT.

8   Related Work

We discuss the related work in two categories: **Commercial 5G Network Measurements.** Researchers have conducted several studies on commercial 5G networks since their debut in 2019. Among them, Narayanan *et al.* examines for the first time the performance of mmWave 5G on smartphones [29]. The same team also investigates 5G performance prediction [30], application QoE, and device power consumption [33]. Xu *et al.* study the coverage, performance, and energy consumption of sub-6Ghz 5G in China [44]. Rochman *et al.* compare 5G deployment in Chicago and Miami [37]. Rischke *et al.* measure 5G campus networks [36]. Pan and Claudio *et al.* examine the 5G performance on high-speed trains and in public bus transit systems respectively [22,34]. Compared to all the above studies, our work focuses on the latency of 5G networks in the context of 5G last-mile latency support for edge computing [7]– an important but under explored topic.

5G Physical Layer. There are a plethora of works on the PHY-layer foundations of 5G, including mmWave [40,42], signal propagation [41,43], beam forming [18,38], and massive MIMO [39,46], to name a few. Compared to the above works that solely tackle the E2E latency, [19,23,24,28,29,33,44] also quantify the PHY-layer UL and DL latency separately, but not both from different points of view. Almost in line with our work, Xu *et al.* quantify the latency of 5G mmWave PHY-layer in China to be 2.19±0.36 ms [44]. However, they do not state or show whether <1ms PHY-layer latency is achievable with today's mmWave 5G NR deployments. Additionally, factors that can further increase PHY-layer latency were not explored. Thus, to our knowledge, our paper is the first to systematically study and quantify the impact of several factors on PHY-layer latency, and the impact of server placement and CDRX on E2E latency. We are also the first to answer the question "Is sub-millisecond PHY-layer latency feasible with today's commercial 5G". Additionally, our paper provides insights to network operators to capitalize on which other related works lack on.

9   Discussion and Future Work

Throughout this study, we took a careful approach to quantify the impact of each factor in today's mmWave PHY-layer latency. In each section, we controlled (as best as we could) one factor at a time and carefully designed experiments to study the factor under investigation. Our approach to quantify the additional overhead per factor "in its best case scenario" revealed that, although sub-millisecond PHY-layer transmission is indeed possible in today's mmWave 5G, any slight change in each factor certainly defeats the sub-millisecond promise of mmWave 5G and the combined impact of all factors leads to a wide variability in the E2E RTT perceived by the applications. Thus, the main message is that current 5G wireless radio technology still has a long way to go to be able to achieve sub-millisecond latency.

Our results also highlighted several aspects for 5G cellular carriers to consider in order to overcome this poor latency performance such as: i) implementing and adapting all 61 proposed *slots* scheduling interval configurations as per 3GPP standards, ii) dynamically adapting specific *slot* patterns for UL and DL heavy transmissions for different use cases, and iii) improving the HARQ process to account for CQI to MCS mismatch, especially when the channel conditions drop.

However, we believe that implementing a true cross-layer designed is called for to further improve the latency performance. This cross-layer design can allow the anticipation and signaling of specific application PHY-layer latency requirements to be adapted accordingly by carriers such as: i) using a dynamic *slot* configuration based on the application traffic demand instead of a fixed configuration, ii) requesting more *slots* when blockage is sensed and predicted by the UE side, and iii) adopting dynamic context-aware CDRX timer configuration when applications are deployed on far edge nodes from the UE.

Our study is limited to PING packets and today's mmWave 5G NSA deployments. We believe that future deployments of SA will most likely use the current 5G radio access network technologies. With that assumption, 5G SA deployments might reduce the 5G Core + Internet latency, but may not affect the 5G RAN. Since our study is focused on the radio side, we believe the insights of this work reveals that the physical layer's impact on latency will still unfortunately be present in future mmWave SA 5G Deployments. Our work also sheds the light on several research directions to explore including the impact of additional factors such as: i) application traffic patterns on 5G latency and ii) the number of users within the communication range of one 5G base station or across multiple 5G base stations (given cellular carrier collaboration).

10   Conclusion

Using a commercial 5G tool to extract detailed physical channel events and messages, this study presents a first-of-a-kind comprehensive in-depth measurement study of mmWave 5G latency performance on the PHY-layer. Our findings show that the current 5G RAN-induced latency is limited by both UL scheduling and carrier configurations. To summarize Today's mmWave status quo latency: (1) In the best case scenario, the best achievable mmWave PHY-layer latency is around 0.85 ms. (2) changing any factor affecting this best case scenario, even slightly, leads the PHY-layer latency to be more than 1 ms. (3) These factors combined with the Internet (buffering and congestion) result in a wide variability in the E2E RTT perceived by the applications. (4) Finally, our study and analysis of PHY-layer latency suggest that 5G NR is indeed capable of delivering (sub)ms latency performance. However, due to inefficiencies at the 5G NR sub-layers (combined with the network stack and above), these low-latency benefits are not reflected at the application layer.

Acknowledgements. This research was supported in part by NSF under Grants CNS-1901103, CNS-1915122, CNS-2038559, CNS-21544078, CNS-2128489, CNS-2220286, CCF-2212318 and CNS-2220292 as well as a Cisco Research Award and an InterDigital gift.

References

1. 5G NR: Connected Mode DRX. https://howltestuffworks.blogspot.com/2021/04/5g-nr-connected-mode-drx.html. Accessed Nov 2022
2. Amazon web services (aws). https://aws.amazon.com/
3. 5G; study on scenarios and requirements for next generation access technologies (3gpp tr 38.913 version 14.3.0 release 14) (2017). https://www.etsi.org/deliver/etsi_tr/138900_138999/138913/15.00.00_60/tr_138913v150000p.pdf
4. https://www.gsma.com/futurenetworks/wiki/cloud-ar-vr-whitepaper/ (2019)
5. 5G SA vs 5G NSA: What are the differences? https://www.alepo.com/5g-sa-vs-5g-nsa-what-are-the-differences/ (2022). Accessed Nov 2022
6. Accuver   XCAL.   https://www.accuver.com/sub/products/view.php?idx=6&ckattempt=2 (2022). Accessed Nov 2022
7. AWS Wavelength. https://aws.amazon.com/wavelength/ (2022). Accessed Nov 2022
8. Samsung galaxy S21 5G featuring a Qualcomm snapdragon 888 5G mobile platform.   https://www.qualcomm.com/snapdragon/device-finder/samsung-galaxy-s21-5g (2022). Accessed Nov 2022
9. Speedtest by Ookla. https://www.speedtest.net/ (2022). Accessed Nov 2022
10. T-Mobile hits 3 Gbps 5G speeds without mmWave in world record production test. https://9to5mac.com/2022/06/14/t-mobile-3-gbps-5g-speeds/ (2022). Accessed Nov 2022
11. 3GPP: 5G; NR; Multiplexing and channel coding (3GPP TS 38.212 version 15.2.0 Release 15) (2018). https://www.etsi.org/deliver/etsi_ts/138200_138299/138212/15.02.00_60/ts_138212v150200p.pdf. Accessed Nov 2022
12. 3GPP: 5G; NR; Requirements for support of radio resource management (3GPP TS 38.133 version 15.3.0 Release 15) (2018). https://www.etsi.org/deliver/etsi_ts/138100_138199/138133/15.03.00_60/ts_138133v150300p.pdf. Accessed Nov 2022
13. 3GPP: 5G NR: Medium Access Control (MAC) protocol specification (3GPP TS 38.321 version 15.5.0 Release 15) (2019–05). https://www.etsi.org/deliver/etsi_ts/138300_138399/138321/15.05.00_60/ts_138321v150500p.pdf. Accessed Nov 2022

14. 3GPP: 5G; NR; Physical layer procedures for data (3GPP TS 38.214 version 16.2.0 Release 16). https://www.etsi.org/deliver/etsi_ts/138200_138299/138214/16.02.00_60/ts_138214v160200p.pdf (2020). Accessed Nov 2022

15. 3GPP: 5G; NR; Radio Resource Control (RRC); Protocol specification (3GPP TS 38.331 version 16.2.0 Release 16) (2020). https://www.etsi.org/deliver/etsi_ts/138300_138399/138331/16.02.00_60/ts_138331v160200p.pdf. Accessed Nov 2022

16. 3GPP: 5G; NR; Radio Link Control (RLC) protocol specification (3GPP TS 38.322 version 16.2.0 Release 16) (2021). https://www.etsi.org/deliver/etsi_ts/138300_138399/138322/16.02.00_60/ts_138322v160200p.pdf. Accessed Nov 2022

17. Admin, G.: News & events (2017). https://www.3gpp.org/news-events/3gpp-news/sa1-5g

18. Ahmed, I., et al.: A survey on hybrid beamforming techniques in 5G: Architecture and system model perspectives. IEEE Commun. Surv. Tutorials **20**(4), 3060–3097 (2018)

19. Corneo, L., Eder, M., Mohan, N., Zavodovski, A., BayhanZ, S.: Surrounded by the clouds. In: The Web Conference (2021)

20. Dinh, P., Ghoshal, M., Koutsonikolas, D., Widmer, J.: Demystifying resource allocation policies in operational 5G mmwave networks. In: 2022 IEEE 23rd International Symposium on a World of Wireless, Mobile and Multimedia Networks (WoWMoM), pp. 1–10 (2022). https://doi.org/10.1109/WoWMoM54355.2022.00016

21. Fang, Z., Wang, G., Xie, X., Zhang, F., Zhang, D.: Urban map inference by pervasive vehicular sensing systems with complementary mobility. Proceed. ACM Inter. Mobile Wearable Ubiquit. Technol. **5**(1), 1–24 (2021)

22. Fiandrino, C., Juárez Martínez-Villanueva, D., Widmer, J.: Uncovering 5G performance on public transit systems with an app-based measurement study. In: Proceedings of the 25th International ACM Conference on Modeling Analysis and Simulation of Wireless and Mobile Systems, pp. 65–73 (2022)

23. Ghoshal, M., et al.: An in-depth study of uplink performance of 5g mmWave networks, pp. 29–35. 5G-MeMU 2022, Association for Computing Machinery, New York, NY, USA (2022). https://doi.org/10.1145/3538394.3546042

24. Hassan, A., et al.: Vivisecting mobility management in 5G cellular networks. In: Proceedings of the ACM SIGCOMM 2022 Conference, pp. 86–100. SIGCOMM 2022, Association for Computing Machinery, New York, NY, USA (2022). https://doi.org/10.1145/3544216.3544217

25. Hassan, A., et al.: Vivisecting mobility management in 5G cellular networks. In: Proceedings of the ACM SIGCOMM 2022 Conference. pp. 86–100. SIGCOMM 2022, Association for Computing Machinery, New York, NY, USA (2022). https://doi.org/10.1145/3544216.3544217

26. Li, Y., et al.: Experience: a five-year retrospective of mobileInsight. In: Proceedings of the 27th Annual International Conference on Mobile Computing and Networking, pp. 28–41 (2021)

27. McLaughlin, R.: 5G low latency requirements (2021). https://broadbandlibrary.com/5g-low-latency-requirements/

28. Mohan, N., Corneo, L., Zavodovski, A., Bayhan, S., Wong, W., Kangasharju, J.: Pruning edge research with latency shears. In: Proceedings of the 19th ACM Workshop on Hot Topics in Networks, pp. 182–189 (2020)

29. Narayanan, A., et al.: A first look at commercial 5G performance on smartphones. In: Proceedings of The Web Conference 2020, pp. 894–905 (2020)

30. Narayanan, A., et al.: Lumos5G: mapping and predicting commercial mmWave 5G throughput. In: Proceedings of the ACM Internet Measurement Conference, pp. 176–193. IMC 2020, Association for Computing Machinery, New York, NY, USA (2020). https://doi.org/10.1145/3419394.3423629
31. Narayanan, A., Ramadan, E., Quant, J., Ji, P., Qian, F., Zhang, Z.L.: 5G tracker: a crowdsourced platform to enable research using commercial 5G services. In: Proceedings of the SIGCOMM2020 Poster and Demo Sessions, pp. 65–67 (2020)
32. Narayanan, A., et al.: A comparative measurement study of commercial 5G mmWave deployments. In: IEEE INFOCOM 2022 - IEEE Conference on Computer Communications, pp. 800–809 (2022). https://doi.org/10.1109/INFOCOM48880.2022.9796693
33. Narayanan, A., et al.: A variegated look at 5g in the wild: performance, power, and qoe implications. In: Proceedings of the 2021 ACM SIGCOMM 2021 Conference, pp. 610–625. SIGCOMM 2021, Association for Computing Machinery, New York, NY, USA (2021). https://doi.org/10.1145/3452296.3472923
34. Pan, Y., Li, R., Xu, C.: The first 5G-LTE comparative study in extreme mobility. Proceed. ACM Measure. Anal. Comput. Systems **6**(1), 1–22 (2022)
35. Ramadan, E., Narayanan, A., Dayalan, U.K., Fezeu, R.A., Qian, F., Zhang, Z.L.: Case for 5G-aware video streaming applications. In: Proceedings of the 1st Workshop on 5G Measurements, Modeling, and Use Cases, pp. 27–34 (2021)
36. Rischke, J., Sossalla, P., Itting, S., Fitzek, F.H., Reisslein, M.: 5G campus networks: a first measurement study. IEEE Access **9**, 121786–121803 (2021)
37. Rochman, M.I., et al.: A comparison study of cellular deployments in Chicago and Miami using apps on smartphones. In: Proceedings of the 15th ACM Workshop on Wireless Network Testbeds, Experimental evaluation & CHaracterization, pp. 61–68 (2022)
38. Roh, W., et al.: Millimeter-wave beamforming as an enabling technology for 5G cellular communications: theoretical feasibility and prototype results. IEEE Commun. Mag. **52**(2), 106–113 (2014)
39. Shepard, C., Blum, J., Guerra, R.E., Doost-Mohammady, R., Zhong, L.: Design and implementation of scalable massive-Mimo networks. In: Proceedings of the 1st International Workshop on Open Software Defined Wireless Networks, pp. 7–13 (2020)
40. Singh, V., Mondal, S., Gadre, A., Srivastava, M., Paramesh, J., Kumar, S.: Millimeter-wave full duplex radios. In: Proceedings of the 26th Annual International Conference on Mobile Computing and Networking, pp. 1–14 (2020)
41. Solomitckii, D., Orsino, A., Andreev, S., Koucheryavy, Y., Valkama, M.: Characterization of mmWave channel properties at 28 and 60 GHZ in factory automation deployments. In: 2018 IEEE Wireless Communications and Networking Conference (WCNC), pp. 1–6. IEEE (2018)
42. Sur, S., Pefkianakis, I., Zhang, X., Kim, K.H.: Towards scalable and ubiquitous millimeter-wave wireless networks. In: Proceedings of the 24th Annual International Conference on Mobile Computing and Networking, pp. 257–271 (2018)
43. Sur, S., Venkateswaran, V., Zhang, X., Ramanathan, P.: 60 GHZ indoor networking through flexible beams: a link-level profiling. In: Proceedings of the 2015 ACM SIGMETRICS International Conference on Measurement and Modeling of Computer Systems, pp. 71–84 (2015)

44. Xu, D., et al.: Understanding operational 5G: a first measurement study on its coverage, performance and energy consumption. In: Proceedings of the Annual Conference of the ACM Special Interest Group on Data Communication on the Applications, Technologies, Architectures, and Protocols for Computer Communication, pp. 479–494 (2020)

45. Xu, M., et al.: From cloud to edge: a first look at public edge platforms, pp. 37–53. IMC 2021, Association for Computing Machinery, New York, NY, USA (2021). https://doi.org/10.1145/3487552.3487815. https://doi-org.ezp1.lib.umn.edu/10.1145/3487552.3487815

46. Zhao, R., Woodford, T., Wei, T., Qian, K., Zhang, X.: M-cube: a millimeter-wave massive mimo software radio. In: Proceedings of the 26th Annual International Conference on Mobile Computing and Networking, pp. 1–14 (2020)

A Characterization of Route Variability in LEO Satellite Networks

Vaibhav Bhosale(✉), Ahmed Saeed, Ketan Bhardwaj, and Ada Gavrilovska

Georgia Institute of Technology, Atlanta, USA
vbhosale6@gatech.edu, {asaeed,ketan.bhardwaj,ada}@cc.gatech.edu

Abstract. LEO satellite networks possess highly dynamic topologies, with satellites moving at 27,000 km/hour to maintain their orbit. As satellites move, the characteristics of the satellite network routes change, triggering rerouting events. Frequent rerouting can cause poor performance for path-adaptive algorithms (e.g., congestion control). In this paper, we provide a thorough characterization of route variability in LEO satellite networks, focusing on route churn and RTT variability. We show that high route churn is common, with most paths used for less than half of their lifetime. With some paths used for just a few seconds. This churn is also unnecessary with rerouting leading to marginal gains in most cases (e.g., less than a 15% reduction in RTT). Moreover, we show that the high route churn is harmful to network utilization and congestion control performance. By examining RTT variability, we find that the smallest achievable RTT between two ground stations can increase by 2.5× as satellites move in their orbits. We show that the magnitude of RTT variability depends on the location of the communicating ground stations, exhibiting a spatial structure. Finally, we show that adding more satellites, and providing more routes between stations, does not necessarily reduce route variability. Rather, constellation configuration (i.e., the number of orbits and their inclination) plays a more significant role. We hope that the findings of this study will help with designing more robust routing algorithms for LEO satellite networks.

1 Introduction

Low Earth Orbit (LEO) Satellite networks are emerging as an essential part of the future of global telecommunication, with pilot networks already in deployment and more planned [8,10,11,15]. Satellites operating in a low Earth orbit provide low-latency communication, making them superior to terrestrial networks in some scenarios [38,39]. At the same time, operating in low earth orbit inherently makes the satellite network very dynamic, with satellites orbiting the Earth every 100 min to maintain their orbits [3]. As a result, a satellite is only visible for a maximum of a few minutes to any single ground station. The highly dynamic nature of LEO satellite constellations introduces significant variability in the underlying network characteristics including the topology of the network, leading to frequent changes in the path characteristics.

In this paper, we provide a thorough characterization of route variability, highlighting the benefits, downsides, causes, and potential remedies. We characterize the variability in the lengths of paths (i.e., RTT variability) and the churn it creates in the paths (i.e., rerouting frequency). Route variability can negatively impact route-adaptive algorithms (e.g., congestion control), and in turn the quality of experience of network users. In addition, high route churn complicates traffic engineering decisions. We posit that a deeper understanding of this variability can lead to better designs of the network layer and transport layer algorithms, improving the performance of satellite networks. We focus on networks equipped with inter-satellite links (ISLs), where data travel through satellite hops between a pair of ground stations, as they provide the lowest latency and constitute the future of LEO satellite networks [32,85]. We look at three constellations, leveraging publicly-available information about satellite constellations, using the Hypatia simulator [46]. Concretely, our study looks into the following three aspects of route variability in LEO satellite networks.

First, we evaluate the pervasiveness of route churn and its impact (Sect. 4). We study paths selected by the shortest-path routing algorithm (i.e., paths that were deemed the shortest between two ground stations at some point during our simulation). We find that 15% of paths selected by the routing algorithm are used for less than 10 s. Further, we show that more than 50% of paths selected by the routing algorithm are used for less than half of their lifetime. This high churn can be considered as it affords the sender the lowest possible latency to the receiver, adopting the stance of "delay is not an option" [38]. However, we observe that such rerouting decisions lead to less than 15% RTT reduction in 50% of the cases, highlighting that *this high churn in routing may be unnecessary for many applications.* Further, we show that high variability can be harmful, causing significant deterioration in the performance of path-adaptive algorithms (e.g., congestion control algorithms). This negatively impacts the quality of experience for end users. Moreover, we find that greedily minimizing path length makes some paths hotspots with all traffic between a pair of cities flocking to them, underutilizing network capacity and creating potential security vulnerabilities [34].

Second, we observe that the smallest achievable RTT between a pair of ground stations can grow by up to 2.5× as satellites move in their orbits. Further, we found that this RTT variability is predictable – it correlates with the location of ground stations, exhibiting a spatial structure (Sect. 5). In particular, we find the variability to be high only when the communicating ground stations are within 1500–3000km of each other and the travel direction between them isn't along any of the orbital planes. To better understand this structure, we examine the building blocks of LEO satellite network paths: Inter-Satellite Links (ISLs) and Ground-Satellite Links (GSLs). We show that ISLs have stable properties that are not significantly affected by the motion of satellites, with intra-orbit ISLs having much larger lengths and inter-orbit ISLs. On the other hand, GSLs exhibit significant variability in their lifetime and length, making them the main source of variability. Through this analysis, we show that drastic changes in the building blocks of a route can significantly impact its length. For example, replacing an intra-orbit ISL with an inter-orbit ISL can significantly reduce the length of a route.

Drastic changes are more likely if the travel direction between the communicating ground stations is not along any of the orbital planes. The impact of such changes is a function of the total path length (i.e., the longer the path, the smaller the impact of a change in its building blocks). Thus, we conclude that this structure is determined by the relative position of the communicating pair of ground stations (i.e., the distance and angle of travel between them).

Finally, we show that RTT variability does not necessarily decrease by increasing the number of deployed satellites (i.e., by increasing path diversity) (Sect. 6). In particular, we measure RTT variability in a constellation as we add orbital shells. Simply adding orbital shells doesn't reduce RTT variability, with variability depending on the exact configuration of each shell (i.e., the number of satellites and orbits and the inclination of orbits). To evaluate the impact of constellation configuration, we compare two Starlink constellation configurations submitted to the FCC. We find that the more recent configuration introduces more RTT variability than the abandoned configuration.

2   Background

We start with a brief discussion of relevant background on LEO satellite networks needed to follow the rest of our study.

2.1   Overview of LEO Satellite Networks

A LEO satellite network or a constellation comprises thousands of satellites orbiting the Earth at an altitude in the range of 200–1600 km [24]. Due to their closeness to earth, LEO satellite networks can provide low-latency communication, potentially outperforming terrestrial networks [38,39]. Several commercial LEO satellite networks have been announced, including SpaceX's StarLink, Amazon's Kuiper, and OneWeb. LEO satellite networks have already seen great demand with Starlink announcing they are already playing a key role as a reliable medium

Fig. 1. An illustration of the inclination angles of the first, third and fourth shells of the Starlink constellation

of communication (e.g., providing one of the most reliable means of communication in Ukraine [79] and Iran [31]). LEO satellite networks are also being considered for various purposes as part of the 3GPP's standardization effort for non-terrestrial networks (NTNs) [56]. Examples include StarLink's broadband service [10], OneWeb's mobile backhaul [9] and the agreement between Verizon and Kuiper to build a satellite-based backhaul for 5G networks [48]. Furthermore, LEO satellite networks are also opening up newer avenues such as

Table 1. Configurations of the three largest proposed constellations [50–52, 70–73, 77, 78]. Note that the configuration of StarLink's network have changed compared to those mentioned in a recent study [46], making all their orbits at an altitude of less than 600km, lowering latency and increasing topology dynamics.

	Altitude	Inclination	Orbits	Satellites
Starlink	550	53°	72	1584
	540	53.2°	72	1584
	570	70°	36	720
	560	97.6°	6	348
	560	53°	4	172
Kuiper	630	51.9°	34	1156
	610	42°	36	1296
	590	33°	28	784
	1015	98.8°	27	351
Telesat	1325	50.88°	40	1320

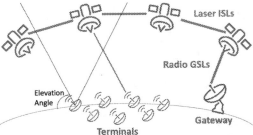

Fig. 2. An illustration of a LEO satellite network, showing the different types of links.

providing WiFi connectivity in airlines and cruise ships [13, 58, 83] The projected success of the current reincarnation of LEO satellite networks is driven by the reduced cost of building and launching such satellites [4, 22, 25, 59, 62].

In a LEO satellite network, satellites are placed in a number of shells, each consisting of a number of circular orbits or orbital planes at a constant altitude. Orbital planes are characterized by their altitude (the height above sea level), and their inclination angle (the angle at which they intersect the equator). An inclination angle of 90° refers to a polar orbit. However, most of the current constellations have smaller inclination angles to provide greater coverage to densely populated areas [70]. Figure 1 shows an example with three different orbital planes, each at a different inclination. Similar orbital planes are equally spaced to form an orbital shell. Table 1 highlights these parameters for three of the largest proposed constellations.

2.2   LEO Satellite Networks Topology

Satellites communicate with each other through laser-based Inter-Satellite Links (ISLs) and communicate with ground stations using radio-based Ground-Satellite

Links (GSLs) that operate in the Ku/Ka bands. A ground station only communicates with satellites that are visible above a certain *elevation angle* above the horizon, limiting the time traveled by the wave in the earth's atmosphere to ensure the quality of the link. Figure 2 shows an illustration of a LEO satellite network.

The LEO satellite network topology is highly dynamic in nature owing to the rapid motion of the satellites. A LEO satellite travels at about 27,000 km/hr to maintain its orbit. Thus, a satellite is visible for a maximum of 10–12 min from any point on earth. However, the satellite has to conform to the elevation angle bounds required for communication, limiting the accessibility time to a maximum of 4.5 min. The exact amount of time that a satellite remains visible from a ground station depends on the altitude of the satellite. At a higher altitude, a satellite travels at slightly slower speeds, increasing the duration of its visibility.

Currently, satellites do not rely on ISLs and use ground station gateways [5, 6]. There have been some environmental concerns regarding laser-based ISLs, leading to the initial batch of Starlink satellites being launched without ISLs [40]. However, there have been recent launches of satellites with ISLs onboard, with more launches of similar satellites planned [32]. The current plan for LEO satellite networks is to carry traffic through ISLs to the ground station closest to the destination server [38, 47]. Relying on ISLs yields high data rates and low latency, provides better resistance to weather conditions and faces no regulations and a reduced risk of jamming [41, 66]. Therefore, in this paper, we focus on ISL-based networks, where traffic is routed through the satellite network from the source terminal closest to the sender to the destination terminal closest to the receiver.

The 2018 FCC filings by Starlink indicate the presence of 4 silicon-carbide communication components on every satellite [73], with recent work identifying them to be used as ISLs [20, 38, 46]. ISLs can be dynamically configured to connect satellites, allowing for the formation of many different topologies. The setup of an ISL can take between a few tens of seconds [69] to about a minute [84], during which the link cannot be used. The setup time for Starlink ISLs might be lower because the inter-satellite distances are smaller in the Starlink constellation. However, link setup won't be instantaneous, greatly reducing the utility of these links if reconfiguration was frequent. Hence, we assume static ISL configurations that require no ISL reconfiguration operations. In particular, we assume that satellites are connected following the so-called +Grid configuration where each satellite connects to two satellites in its own orbit, and with one satellite in each of the adjacent orbits. This configuration has been selected by the earlier work as the most likely configuration to be used in practice [20, 26, 37, 38, 53, 57, 67, 68, 80, 81].

The +Grid topology has many configurations, depending on how inter-orbit links are formed. The configuration of inter-orbit ISLs depends on the phase shift of orbital planes. The phase shift is a value between zero and one, determining the relative motion of satellites in adjacent orbits. At zero, all satellites with the same index in all orbital planes cross the equator at the same time. At one, satellite n in orbital plane p crosses the equator at the same time as satellite $n+1$ in orbital plane $p + 1$. We use a phase shift of 0.5 as it very closely corresponds

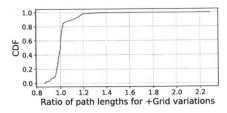
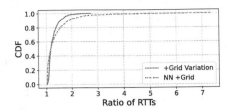

(a) The CDF for the ratio between the path lengths achieved using our +Grid variation and the nearest-neighbor +Grid

(b) The CDF for the ratio between the highest and lowest latencies observed for the two ISL variations.

Fig. 3. Characterizing the benefits of using the variation of +Grid over the nearest-neighbor +Grid ISL configuration

to the phase offset parameter used by Starlink [74] and can potentially provide good coverage of the Earth by uniformly distributing satellites in orbit [19][1].

Now consider how inter-orbit ISLs should be formed in the presence of a phase shift between orbital planes. If a satellite is connected to its nearest neighbors in adjacent orbits in the presence of phase shifts, the resulting topology will be an inclined grid, providing poor east-west paths [38]. Alternatively, prior work [19, 38,46] has intuitively argued for a slight variation of the +Grid configuration where a satellite connects with a nearest neighbor in one adjacent orbit and with a phase shifted neighbor in the other orbit. This slight variation on the +Grid topology results in shorter east-west paths. Path 2 in Fig. 16 is an example of paths created by that modified configuration. We verified this intuition with the following simulation study. We explain our simulation setup in Sect. 3.

We ran a simulation of the two +Grid variations for 100 min using the top 100 cities worldwide as source-destination pairs (total 4950 pairs). We measure the RTTs for all 4950 pairs every second to observe the variability inherent to the two choices. We first look at the ratio of the latencies observed for the two different variations at every second for all these source-destination pairs in Fig. 3a. While the nearest-neighbor +Grid configuration has shorter paths in more than 40% of the scenarios, the maximum latency gain is just 43%. On the other hand, when the nearest-neighbor +Grid configuration has longer paths, its paths can be more than 5 times longer. To better understand the performance of the nearest-neighbor +Grid configuration, we look at the ratio of the maximum RTT and the minimum RTT between every pair of cities during the course of our simulation (Fig. 3b). We observe that the nearest-neighbor +Grid configuration can have this ratio greater than 7 compared to about 2.7 for the variation to +Grid we use. Based on this simulation, we conclude that the nearest-neighbor +Grid configuration increases the magnitude and variance of the lengths of paths. Thus,

---

[1] Since the phase offset does not impact the stability of the GSL and ISL connections which we show to be the major reason for route variability in satellite networks, our results in this paper hold true for any chosen phase offset value.

for the rest of this paper, we use the +Grid variation employed in earlier work, leading to the configuration that minimizes path length variability.

2.3 Routing in LEO Satellites

Routing and traffic engineering in LEO satellite networks as a problem has seen a lot of interest over the past few decades. Earlier work has focused on providing performance guarantees, identifying paths with low latency while balancing the load between them. The typical approach is to adapt common traffic engineering techniques for the LEO satellite networks. For example, a recent proposal uses equal-cost multi-path (ECMP) techniques to distribute load between different paths, while also using obstacle-avoiding rectilinear Steiner trees (OARSTs) to ensure individual links are not overloaded [44]. Another proposal performs traffic splitting in a delay bound manner wherein a path is randomly chosen from a set of paths within a certain delay bound of the shortest path while still favoring paths with lower latency [86]. Yet another load balancing-based scheme allows a congested link to provide signals to its neighbors to find alternate shortest paths that do not consist of the congested link [76]. Another work proposes the use of multi-protocol label switching (MPLS) to improve the quality of service in satellite networks by decoupling packet forwarding from the information carried in the IP header and periodically distributing routing information to the gateways [17]. Other recent work [38,39,46,60] has also focused on using this idea of continuously computing the shortest path between destination pairs, and updating routing rules accordingly. Another strategy, towards the same goal, was to find the next hop moving toward the direction of the destination [42]. Satellite networks can also be viewed as Mobile Adhoc Networks (MANETs) with a more predictable structure. Variations of AODV [64] were proposed for satellite networks, leveraging location information to minimize delay and delay jitter [63]. All proposed algorithms covered in this brief survey rely on path length either primarily or partially in selecting routes. Thus, in this paper, we focus on shortest path algorithms which has also been the approach followed by similar studies [38,39,46].

3 Study Setup

Our study relies on simulations performed using the Hypatia framework [46] as the starting point, augmenting it with additional emulators as needed for the purposes of our study. We leverage Hypatia to generate the Two Line Element (TLE) information for satellites, a standard representation for satellite orbits containing the satellite identifier and orbit parameters [1]. Using that information, we are able to determine the ISL and GSL connectivity to conform with all the necessary physical requirements. Hypatia's routing algorithm selects the shortest path between a pair of ground stations every 100ms. We use an interval of 1s to accelerate our simulations.[2] We use the Cesium [7] (a javascript library

---

[2] It is telling that we are still able to show the impact of frequent routing even with a reduced frequency of route updates.

for visualizing 3D data and structures) interface provided by Hypatia to generate path visualizations. We do not use the packet-level simulator provided by Hypatia. Instead, we feed the delay measurements collected from Hypatia simulations into Mahimahi [61], a framework that enables running recorded traffic under emulated network conditions, to emulate route variability. Further, we use Pantheon [82], a platform developed for the evaluation and comparison of congestion control algorithms, on top of Mahimahi, allowing us to use the real implementation of all the studied transport layer algorithms. We use a modified version of Mahimahi available at [16] which allows us to vary the RTT values.

We predominantly use the first shell of the Starlink constellation, as it is the main fully-deployed constellation in practice. We also use the first shells from the Kuiper and Telesat constellations to show that our conclusions hold across constellations. We report our simulation results for a simulated period of 100 min for the Starlink and Kuiper constellations and 110 min for the Telesat constellation. Our choice of these intervals is because it allows us to capture the full orbit time of satellites in the studied constellations, where their orbit times are 96 min for Starlink, 97 min for Kuiper, and 105 min for Telesat. We assume that the TLEs remain constant for the duration of our simulations which fall in the range of 100–110 min. This is a fairly reasonable assumption since the TLEs change every few days [2]. Most of our results use the global 100 most populous cities as the ground stations and consider all possible 4950 source-destination pairs. Prior work explicitly removed source-destination pairs that are close to each other, to highlight the low latency offered by satellite networks compared to terrestrial networks [20]. We include them since we are concerned with the broader context where satellite networks are used as the main communication infrastructure (e.g., in rural and disaster-affected areas). All key parameters used in our study such as the configuration of satellites, GSLs, the ISLs (discussed in Sect. 2) are based on publicly-available information in addition to using a popular state-of-the-art SGP4 model [43] to predict the position of satellites at every timestep of our simulation.

4   Route Churn is Rife, Unnecessary, and Harmful

We start our study by assessing the extent and impact of route churn. We define a route as a sequence of satellite hops connecting a specific pair of ground stations. We define route churn as the change of routes (i.e., a change in one or more of the satellite hops forming the route). Our study considers routes that were picked by the shortest path routing algorithm (i.e., routes that were considered at some point the shortest between a pair of ground stations). Our goal is to identify the scenarios in which significant switching between paths occurs, the performance gains it leads to (if any), and its downsides. We use path and route interchangeably.

4.1   Route Churn Is Rife

We measure path churn using the following two metrics:

– *the lifetime of a path:* the duration a path remains valid (i.e., usable), allowing two specific communication ground stations to reach each other through the satellite hops of that path, and

– *the usage time of that path:* the duration a path is chosen by a routing algorithm to route traffic between the two communicating ground stations.

The lifetime of a path is determined by the topology dynamics. For instance, a satellite can remain in view of a ground station for just a few minutes, putting a cap on the lifetime of any single path. Thus, network dynamics naturally introduce churn. However, churn can be exacerbated by the routing algorithm. Consider that a routing algorithm ranks valid paths and picks the shortest path. As the topology changes, the ranks can change, leading the routing algorithm to potentially change its selected path, abandoning a valid path. Thus, a valid path might not be used for all of its lifetime. Therefore, the usage time of a path is determined by the decisions of the routing algorithm and the dynamics of the topology. Comparing the usage time and the lifetime of paths helps us paint a picture of the amount of variability in the path selection.

We look at paths used by all the source-destination pairs from the top 100 cities in the first shells of the Starlink, Kuiper and Telesat constellations. We focus on the two metrics defined above to identify any emerging patterns. Figure 4 shows the CDFs comparing the two values for the three constellations.

Looking at the lower tail of the distribution of the usage time, we observe that 15% and 20% of paths are used for less than 10 s in Starlink and Kuiper, respectively. This percentage is lower at around 8% in Telesat because it operates at a higher altitude, allowing satellites to remain in view for longer periods of time. Using paths for such a short duration can be detrimental to path-adaptive algorithms as we show later. The lifetime of paths has much higher values with the probability of the lifetime of a path being less than ten seconds is less than 5% for all constellations. Thus, it can be inferred that this volatility in path usage is actually caused by the volatility of the ranks assigned to

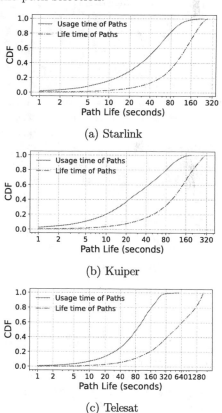

(a) Starlink

(b) Kuiper

(c) Telesat

Fig. 4. The CDF of the usage time and lifetime of paths for three different constellations

paths. We also analyze the relationship between the usage time and the lifetime of paths. In particular, we compute the ratio between the usage time and the lifetime for all studied paths (Fig. 5). The figure shows that for the three constellations, at least 50% of the paths are used for less than half of their lifetime.

4.2 Is Route Churn Necessary?

The results shown in Fig. 5 are for paths that are considered the shortest path between two ground stations at some point during their lifetime (i.e., their length/latency is not only acceptable but it's the best possible for some duration of time). This observation drove us to question the value of such high churn in paths. In other words, we try to answer the question: *is it necessary to switch between paths at a high frequency?*

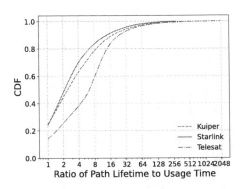

Fig. 5. The CDF for the ratio between the lifetime of a path and its usage time

High churn is justifiable if it yields significant performance improvements (i.e., a valid path is always abandoned for a much better path). If this churn leads to modest improvements in most cases, then high churn is perhaps unnecessary and routing algorithms should be designed to balance churn and performance. To assess the value of churn, we compute the maximum possible gain in performance that can be achieved by abandoning a path. Specifically, given a pair of ground stations, we evaluate the maximum achieved RTT and the minimum achieved RTT for the duration of our simulations. The minimum

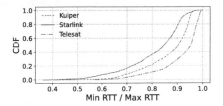

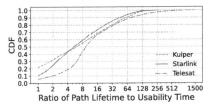

(a) The CDF for the ratio between the shortest path length and the longest path length for a pair of ground stations, highlighting that for 70% of them abandoning a path yields a maximum of 25% reduction in latency.

(b) The CDF for the ratio between usage time and lifetime of the longest shortest path for a pair of ground stations, highlighting that 70% of them are abandoned for more than than half of their lifetime.

Fig. 6. Characterizing the lifetime and benefits of abandoning longest shortest paths, showing that for the majority of cases they are abandoned for no significant gain.

RTT reflects the length of the shortest path possible between two ground stations. The maximum RTT reflects the length of *the longest shortest path*.

The longest shortest path is the longest path selected by a routing algorithm to connect a pair of ground stations. Consider that as the topology changes, the composition (i.e., hops) and length of the shortest path between any two ground stations changes. The routing algorithm always selects the shortest possible path. Amongst all these paths, we focus on the longest one, calling it as the longest shortest path. The ratio between the minimum RTT and the length of the longest shortest path reflects the highest performance gain that a routing algorithm can make when abandoning a path (Fig. 6a). The figure shows that the maximum performance gain is less than 25% for 70% of the source-destination pairs. Note that this result is fairly conservative since we focus on the best possible performance high churn can produce. In many cases, abandoning a path would lead to smaller gains.

We contrast the result in Fig. 6a with the ratio between the lifetime and usage time of longest shortest paths. Figure 6b shows that 70% of longest shortest paths are used for less than half of their lifetime (while 70% of them are only 25% longer than the best possible RTT as shown in Fig. 6a). This implies that even if longest shortest path were to be abandoned for the maximum possible gain, that gain in most cases will be modest. Achieving the lowest possible latency matters for some applications (e.g., High-Frequency Trading [65]). However, it won't impact the performance of most applications, especially given that the latency of ISL-based LEO satellite networks can be around 30% better than the latency of the terrestrial Internet [38, 39].

To better contextualize the result, we consider a concrete example. In particular, we consider the Jakarta-Bogotá route. Figure 7 shows a time series of RTT values. The thick grey line shows the actual RTTs that will be observed using the shortest path routing policy, whereas the dotted lines represent the RTT of individual paths for the time they are valid. While the first switch takes place at 17 s due to the end of the first path, the second switch takes place 5 s later due to a difference of 0.005 ms in the latencies of the second and third

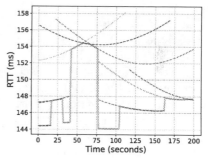

Fig. 7. The RTT of paths between Jakarta and Bogotá, showing eight path changes in 200 s. Dotted lines represent the RTT of different paths (in different colors). The solid line represents the achieved RTT.

paths, only to switch back to the second path 8 s later due to the end of the third path. Such frequent switching leads to four changes in the first 42 s, with the maximum latency gain of about 3.5 milliseconds (i.e., about 2.5% of the total RTT).

Takeaway: Path length variability causes a high churn in routes, yet the variability is very small in most cases that it doesn't warrant the high churn.

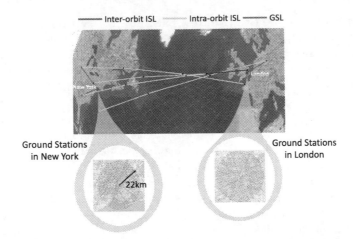

Fig. 8. An illustration of the path utilization experiment between 2000 ground stations in New York and 2000 ground stations in London. The illustration shows the available paths between the two cities.

4.3 Route Churn Can Be Harmful

Impact of Path Variability. One can argue that any improvement in latency is worth the trouble. We don't disagree. However, we show that having such a high churn rate for paths can be very harmful to performance. First, consider the impact of aggressively minimizing path length on network utilization. Our observation is that greedy selection of shortest paths drives all nodes in the same locale to flock to the same set of paths. To illustrate a problem, we create a hypothetical scenario where 2000 nodes in New York are attempting to communicate with 2000 nodes in London. The nodes in each city are

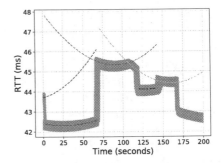

Fig. 9. The RTT of paths between New York and London. Dotted lines represent the RTT of different paths (in different colors). The width of the solid line represents the achieved the number of ground station pairs taking a path. All pairs take the same path.

uniformly distributed over a circle of 22 km radius as shown in Fig. 8.

We observe the paths taken by each of the 2000 connections and find that all connections flock to the same path, despite having other valid paths with marginally worse latency. Figure 9 shows the behavior. The thickness of the solid lines represents the number of connections with a certain RTT value. It's clear in this example that all connections are using the same paths. The purple path is abandoned by all connections for the yellow path for about half a millisecond lower RTT. All the connections abandon the yellow path for the black path for a half millisecond gain, only for all of them to reuse the yellow path after 28 s. These gains are considerably low compared to the RTT of the path (around 1–2%). In addition, the benefits of these gains may get diluted due to the inability of the transport layer to keep up with the changes.

Next, we consider the impact of path churn on the behavior of the transport layer. We consider the link utilization, the 95th percentile delay, and the power defined as the ratio of utilization to the 95th percentile delay exhibited by different congestion control protocols. We look at the route between Pune, India and Lahore, Pakistan. A path change in a LEO satellite network may end up chang-

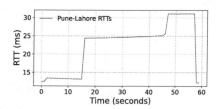

Fig. 10. The RTT of the route Pune and Lahore

ing the observed RTT and bandwidth (e.g., switching to a path with a different number of flows competing for its bandwidth). Thus, we evaluate the impact of RTT variability and bandwidth variability, separately and combined. Figure 10 shows the delays for the 60 s time interval we use for this experiment. Instead of assigning a different bandwidth value for every path, we select two bandwidth levels that we alternate between with every path change to show the impact of changing bandwidth on TCP algorithms. In particular, the bandwidth changes between 204 Mbps and 48 Mbps. We choose these values as they closely correspond to the range of bandwidth specifications for Starlink [75]. The results are shown in Table 2.

Table 2. The utilization (%), 95th percentile one-sided delay (in ms from sender to receiver), and power (defined as the ratio of utilization to the 95th percentile delay) for three different scenarios of path variability for five different congestion control algorithms. Bold reflects the best result in its row and italic reflects the worst result in the row. No single algorithm optimizes both delay and utilization.

		BBR	Cubic	PCC-Allegro	PCC-Vivace	Vegas
Constant	Utilization	**95.4**	61.8	93.5	86.8	*10.1*
Bandwidth	Delay	*18.3*	16.7	16.3	16.2	**13.6**
Variable RTT	Power	5.21	3.7	**5.74**	5.36	*0.74*
Variable	Utilization	**90.1**	55.4	70.6	64.6	*45*
Bandwidth	Delay	*29.7*	28.7	26.1	19.6	**19.5**
Constant RTT	Power	3.03	*1.93*	2.7	**3.3**	2.3
Variable	Utilization	**95.9**	68.6	71.3	73.8	*37.8*
Bandwidth	Delay	*26.4*	25.1	16.5	**16.0**	16.3
Variable RTT	Power	3.63	2.73	4.3	**4.61**	*2.32*

As expected, there is a clear tradeoff between latency and utilization, with none of the studied algorithms being able to reach a good balance between the two. For example, BBR [23] achieves high bandwidth utilization, while introducing a significant delay. On the other hand, Vegas [21] consistently achieves the lowest utilization with fairly low delays. PCC-Allegro [27] and PCC-Vivace [28] generally show utilization in the range $60 - 85\%$, while incurring fairly lower delays. This variation is further exacerbated when we look at the power values since both BBR and Vegas belong to the lower percentile of the spectrum with PCC-Allegro and PCC-Vivace outperforming on this metric. We recognize that earlier work in congestion control attempts to effectively handle bandwidth variability in datacenter networks [36,55] and wireless last miles [35]. However, these solutions are typically tailored for their target network, motivating such tailoring for LEO satellite networks.

Takeaway: High churn in routes, caused by shortest path algorithms, can cause poor path utilization and poor performance by congestion control algorithms.

---

5   Understanding RTT Variability

High churn rates for paths are caused by frequently abandoning paths to reduce route latency. We have shown that for 70% of the studied ground station pairs the gains are smaller than 25% (Fig. 6a). Route churn can be significantly reduced if the routing algorithm was made less aggressive (e.g., only abandoning a path if significant RTT gains are made). However, high churn can still happen when RTT variability is high (e.g., it is possible to improve the RTT by more than 25% if a path is abandoned). In this section, we identify the causes of high RTT variability. Our goal is to provide insights that can aid the design of better routing algorithms that can reduce route churn in the presence of RTT variability.

5.1   RTT Variability Exhibits Spatial Structure

As shown in Fig. 6a, the smallest achievable latency for the same route can exhibit a high variability potentially introducing over 2.5× higher RTT. We sought to identify any patterns in this variability and observed the presence of a spatial structure correlating to the location of the ground stations. We measured RTT variability using the ratio between the maximum RTT and the minimum RTT observed when a shortest-path routing algorithm is used. Our simulation considers RTT values observed during a period of 100 min, using the first shell of the StarLink network. We report RTT variability in paths between 2700 uniformly distributed hypothetical destination ground stations and three source ground stations: Null Island (0° latitude, 0° longitude), Kyiv ($50.4501° N, 30.5234° E$), Ukraine, and Darfur ($14.3783° N, 24.9042° E$), Sudan, each capturing a different latitude. Figure 11 shows the results, where the darker colors represent higher variability. The darkest represents cases where the max RTT is more than 2× the min RTT.

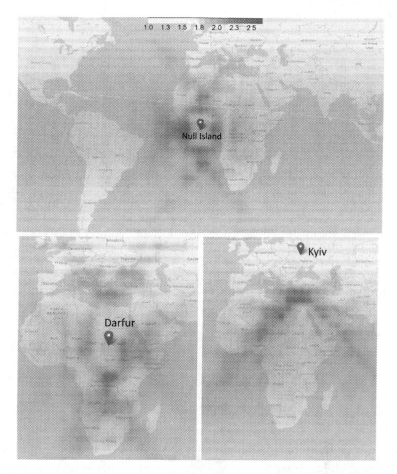

Fig. 11. Heat maps showing the ratio between max RTT and min RTT in paths between Null Island(0° latitude, 0° longitude), Darfur, and Kyiv and 2700 nodes uniformly distributed around the globe. The redder the point, the higher the ratio, indicating higher variability.

Figure 11 shows that there is a clear structure for ground station placements that would yield high variability. For example, low latitude source ground stations (e.g., Null Island and Darfur) observe high variability when communicating with ground stations placed in a ring-like structure with diagonal ribbons extending from it. On the other hand, the structure only includes the ribbons for high latitude stations (e.g., Kyiv). This structure only impacts destinations that are within 1500–3000 km from the source (geodesic distance). We found these results to hold regardless of the longitude of the source station and similar structures repeat for source stations at the same latitude.

We find that a particular route between two ground stations shows high variability when the makeup of the paths changes drastically as satellites move.

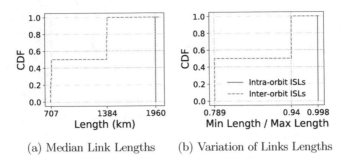

(a) Median Link Lengths   (b) Variation of Links Lengths

Fig. 12. The CDFs of different properties of ISLs

To better understand this behavior, we study the building blocks for paths and their characteristics.

5.2 Building Blocks for Paths: ISLs and GSLs

Every path from a terrestrial source to a terrestrial destination is comprised of two Ground-Satellite links (GSLs) and zero or more Inter-Satellite links (ISLs). For the +Grid topology we consider in this paper, there are two main categories of ISLs that differ significantly in their properties: inter-orbit ISLs and intra-orbit ISLs. The lifetime and length of a path are governed by the properties of its links. Thus, we take a closer look at the properties of different types of links. In particular, we examine the *length* and *lifetime* of those components.

Properties of ISLs. We record the lengths of all ISLs in a 100 min time interval for the first shell of Starlink. We observe that the lengths of ISLs are highly predictable. Figure 12a shows the CDF of the median length of ISLs, broken down based on their type.

The results show that there are two types of inter-orbit ISLs: one with a median length of about 760 km and the other at 1384 km km. The two types of inter-orbit ISLs occur alternately such that each satellite has one inter-orbit ISL of both the types. This is an outcome of the phased orbit structure we discussed in Sect. 2. On the other hand, intra-orbit ISLs are uniform with all their lengths at about 1970 km km, which is about 150% more than the first cluster of the inter-orbit ISLs and 50% more than the second. There is little variability in the lengths of ISLs. Figure 12b shows the CDF of the ratio between the minimum length and maximum length of an ISL during the 100 min period for the two types of ISLs. All intra-orbit ISLs and 50% of inter-orbit ISLs exhibit minimal length change (0.2% and 6%, respectively). The length of the other 50% of inter-orbit ISLs can change by up to 21% due to the varying distances between different orbital planes across latitudes [30,45]. The orbits are closer to each other at higher latitudes compared to the lower ones, and hence the inter-orbit ISL lengths vary accordingly.

Takeaway: The length of a single ISL is stable and there are three different types of ISLs each having significantly different lengths.

Properties of GSLs. To study the variability in GSLs, we recorded the lengths of all GSLs from a ground station placed in Tokyo as a representative example for the same 100 min interval. GSLs exhibit considerably different characteristics compared to the ISLs. They exhibit great variability in their lengths and lifetimes.

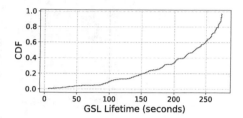

Fig. 13. The CDF of GSL lifetimes

Figure 13 shows the lifetime of different GSLs that a ground station in Tokyo can form in the 100 min period. The figure shows that the lifetime of a GSL can be as low as 6 s, with a maximum of 4.5 min.

Figure 14 shows the lengths of all the GSL lengths in the 100 min interval for Tokyo. The CDF captures the change in the length of individual GSLs as well as the variability between different GSLs. The lengths of GSLs are uniformly distributed between a minimum of 550 km to a maximum of 1254 km km, depending

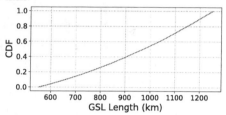

Fig. 14. The CDF of GSL lengths.

on where the satellite lies with respect to the ground station. A satellite right above the ground station will have the shortest distance whereas a satellite at the periphery of the region the ground station can communicate with will have a larger distance, and as the satellites move inside this region, their length fluctuates.

Takeaway: Due to the stability of the ISLs, the variability in the lifetime of GSLs has a greater impact on the variability in the lifetime of paths.

Path Formation. Having looked at both the components individually, we now look at how they play a part in determining the length of paths. Intra-orbit ISLs travel along the orbital planes, whereas the inter-orbit ISLs travel between them. Thus, the makeup of a path depends on the direction of travel between the two communicating ground stations.

Communicating Across Orbital Planes. We consider travel directions that crosses orbital planes. In such scenarios, the path can be made entirely of inter-orbit ISLs. Recall that the length of intra-orbit ISLs can be $2.7\times$ the length of inter-orbit ISLs. Thus, if a topology change forces replacing a single inter-orbit ISL with an intra-orbit ISL, the overall path length can change significantly.

330   V. Bhosale et al.

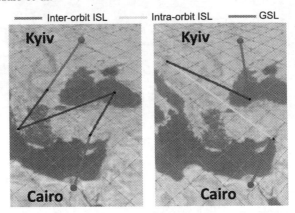

(a) A shortest path with (b) A shortest path with one
three inter-orbit ISLs   inter-orbit ISL and one intra-
                               orbit ISL

Fig. 15. An example showing that using an intra-orbit ISL when traversing across orbital planes can increase the path length

However, the impact of that change is also a function of the total length of the path. For example, replacing a single link in a path made of 20 links will result in a much lower change in total path length compared to replacing a link in a path made of two links. To illustrate this point, consider paths from Kyiv to Cairo. Figure 15 shows two paths between the two cities. Each is the shortest available path during different time intervals. Figure 15a shows a path made entirely of three inter-orbit links. Figure 15b shows a path with a smaller hop count but with a single intra-orbit link, leading to a longer path due to the larger length of intra-orbit ISLs.

> Takeaway: The length of paths communicating over short distances across orbital planes can be significantly increased by the addition of a single intra-orbit link.

Communicating Along Orbital Planes. We consider an example where the direction of travel is along an orbital place. In such scenarios, paths formed mostly by intra-orbit links yield the shortest paths. Despite having the largest lengths of all ISL types, intra-orbit ISLs help cover the distance along orbital planes along a straight line, providing shorter paths. Figure 16 shows an example for communication between Miami and Denver. Path 1 is the shortest path and it is formed exclusively by intra-orbit ISLs. We contrast with Path 2, where we picked a first hop with an orbital plane that is not parallel to the direction between the two cities. Despite being made up mostly of short inter-orbit ISLs, Path 2 is much longer than Path 1. It's important to note that the GSL hops of Path 2 are both shorter and more long living than those of Path 1.

> Takeaway: The length of paths communicating over relatively long distances along orbital paths can be significantly increased if inter-orbit communication is required.

Choosing GSLs. The choice of a GSL is not entirely a routing decision. Recall that GSLs are wireless links with SNR determining the quality of the link. The SNR depends on the length of the GSL and weather conditions among other things. Thus, the choice of GSLs can be made independent of the routing decision. We explore the impact of that choice on RTT variability. In particular, we assess the impact of the choice of GSLs, considering the worst case by examining the first hops that yield the longest paths. In particular, we compute the ratio between the length of the shortest possible path through the worst case first hop and the length of the actual shortest path. This metric measures the worst possible performance based on the choice of the first hop. We measure that metric

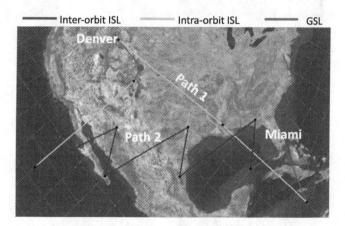

Fig. 16. An example showing the value of Intra-orbit links and the downside of not using them when applicable. Note that Path 2 is valid path but not a shortest path and is used just for illustration (i.e., never picked by a routing algorithm).

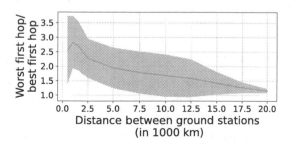

Fig. 17. The impact on the length of a path by using the worst first hop compared to the best one. The line shows the average of the ratio and the shaded part shows the standard deviation.

for four source ground stations on the 85° longitude, uniformly spaced between a latitude of 5° and 55°. Each source ground station communicates with 2700 points distributed uniformly within the coverage area of Starlink's first shell. Figure 17 summarizes the results as a function of the distance between communicating ground stations. The results show that a poorly selected first hop may double the RTT. However, with the increase in the distance between the source and the destination, this impact reduces.

Takeaway: The choice of the first hop is integral to determining and optimizing overall path length.

5.3 Darfur as a Case Study: Building Blocks in Action

As stated earlier, a particular route between two ground stations shows high variability when the makeup of the paths changes drastically.

This can include changing the first hop orbit to be closer or farther away from the destination. It can also include changing the types of ISLs. We observe that these two phenomenon may occur in tandem which can further increase the length of the path by up to 2600 km km, which could potentially double the length of the path. This also implies that the spatial structure is highly localized since the impact of changes in the makeup of a path decreases as the number of components of the path increases (i.e., as the distance between the communicating ground stations increases). Similarly, for points that are very close to each other, the path typically doesn't include any ISLs, limiting variability.

We illustrate this using two exemplary routes originating in Darfur. We choose two destinations: Isangi($0° N$, $24° E$), Democratic Republic of Congo that lies in the ring, and Muynak($44° N$, $60° E$), Uzbekistan that lies outside the ring. We look at a 200 s time interval to observe the variation in lengths and the number of times different paths are chosen (Fig. 18). The markers on each of the lines show when a path change occurred.

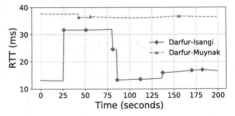

Fig. 18. The RTT variations for the two paths Darfur-Isangi and Darfur-Muynak with the markers representing path changes

The Darfur-Isangi route is a little awkwardly placed with respect to the topology of Starlink's first shell. The two ground stations are about 1600 km km away which is low enough for them to be served by a single satellite. However, as the route doesn't lie along any orbital plane, the distance isn't low enough to always be served by a single satellite. Therefore, inter-orbit ISLs will be required for this path in certain instances, leading to high variations in RTT as we discussed earlier. We show three different paths at time steps 80, 81, and 86 in Fig. 19. At time step 86, a single satellite is capable of communicating with both Darfur and Isangi and hence no other hops are needed. However, that is not the case at time step 80 and 81. At time step 80, the first hop uses an inter-orbit ISL to

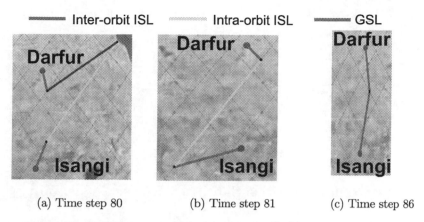

(a) Time step 80   (b) Time step 81   (c) Time step 86

Fig. 19. An example of extreme RTT variation showing three paths between Darfur and Isangi, reflecting time steps 80,81, and 86 in Fig. 18

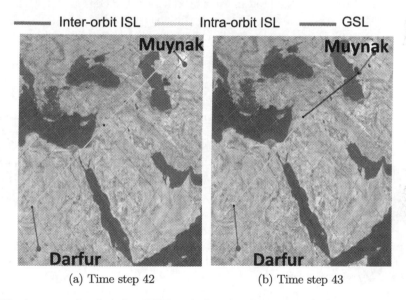

(a) Time step 42   (b) Time step 43

Fig. 20. An example of modest RTT variation showing two paths between Darfur and Muynak, reflecting time steps 42 and 43 in Fig. 18

reach the next orbit and then an intra-orbit link to finally reach the destination. Whereas at time step 80, the first hop can reach the destination with just one intra-orbit ISL making it shorter.

Since the Darfur-Muynak route is along the orbital planes for the first shell, the intra-orbit ISLs are used predominantly. We highlight the switch happening at timestep 43 in Fig. 20. In this case, even swapping out an intra-orbit ISL for an inter-orbit one doesn't lead to much change since the links are always traveling towards the destination.

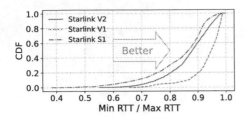

Fig. 21. The CDF of the maximum RTT variation observed by paths comparing the older and newer Starlink configurations

Table 3. The shell parameters configuration for Starlink V1

Altitude	Inclination	Orbits	Satellites
550	53°	72	1584
1110	53.2°	32	1600
1130	74°	8	400
1275	81°	5	375
1325	70°	6	450

6 Does Deploying More Satellites Reduce Variability?

We culminate our study by discussing the impact of increasing number of satellites on variability. LEO satellite network operators improve their presence and quality of coverage by launching more orbital shells. We compare the RTT variability for the first shell of Starlink with the entire Starlink constellation composed of five shells. We use both the Starlink constellation configurations released to the FCC. For brevity, we refer to the first shell as Starlink S1, and the older and newer proposals as Starlink V1 (Table 3) and Starlink V2 (Table 1) respectively. We simply analyze the impact of these configurations without claiming to have any information about the reasons for the change.

Since each satellite currently has only 4 lasers to support 4 ISLs, we assume that they are utilized to setup a +Grid leading to individual shells operating independently. ISLs only connect satellites belonging to the same shell. Different shells operate at different altitudes and their configurations include the number of orbits, the inclination of orbits, and the number of satellites per orbit. In these simulations, we use the global 100 most populous cities as the ground stations and look at all possible 4950 source-destination pairs. We record the RTT variations for both the Starlink configurations.

We consider the performance of the proposed Starlink configurations in Fig. 21. We consider the older proposal as it has four different inclination values, while the current plan has only three, creating a missed opportunity in making use of inclination diversity. Further, it demonstrates the impact of varying altitudes significantly between shells in addition to varying inclination angles. The earlier plan had the last four shells at considerably higher altitudes compared to the current plan. Deploying satellites at higher altitudes makes them visible from ground stations for longer periods of time, reducing the pace of change in the topology. Thus, higher altitude shells reduce RTT variability. This can also be observed in the results presented in Sect. 4, comparing the first shell of Starlink and the first shell of Telesat.

Thus, we can infer that simply increasing the number of satellites doesn't help solve this problem. With approximately the same number of satellites, Starlink V1 can provide improved performance over Starlink V2 due to higher altitudes and a greater diversity in the inclination angles.

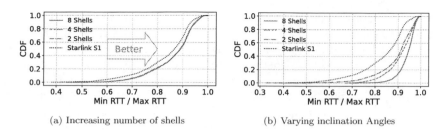

(a) Increasing number of shells   (b) Varying inclination Angles

Fig. 22. The CDF of the maximum RTT variation observed by paths for different shell configurations

In addition to comparing the two publicly available configurations by Starlink, we also tried to individually profile the number of shells and the impact of diversity in inclination angles. First, in Fig. 22a, we study the impact on RTT variation by simply increasing the number of shells with similar orbital characteristics - inclination angle, number of orbits, and number of satellites as the first shell of Starlink. We observe that adding an extra shell improves the RTT variability a little, but after that, there is no tangible difference after adding two or six more shells leading us to conclude that simply replicating the shells will provide minimal to no gains.

Second, we also considered the impact of changing the inclination angles between shells. We repeat the earlier simulation while tweaking the inclination angles. We use 53°, 27°, 72°, 13°, 40°, 62°, 82°, 53° as the inclination angles in order[3]. We observe in Fig. 22b that increasing the number of shells while varying the inclination angles can reduce RTT variability by 3× in the median. To understand the role of varying orbit inclination, consider the Darfur-Isangi (Fig. 19). Such source-destination pairs cause high RTT variability because the direction from the source to the destination does not lie on any orbital plane. Therefore, adding shells with different inclination angles reduces such occurrences, reducing RTT variability. Thus, our conclusion is that changing the inclination angle between shells yields significant benefits in reducing RTT variability.

7   Discussion

Topology Variants. As discussed earlier, our simulations use a specific variant of the +Grid topology due to its good coverage properties, making it the most likely topology to be used in practice. However, there are several other inter-satellite network topologies with desirable properties. For example, extending inter-orbit ISLs beyond adjacent orbits was shown to reduce latency and improve network throughput [20]. This approach requires more ISL reconfigurations as satellites move. In our study, the properties of ISLs were relatively stable. Thus, we posit that any such added variability in ISLs can increase path churn by adding

---

[3] Not all inclinations we used might be possible due to interference or orbital constraints. Our goal is simply to highlight the impact of that parameter.

another source of variability. Future work should explore the tradeoffs offered by such topologies, taking into account variability, latency, and throughput.

Even for the +Grid topology, we focused on a single variant. The configuration of other variants will depend on the phase shift in orbits and how inter-orbit links are formed. For example, a variant can create more uniform inter-orbit ISLs by connecting satellites to their nearest neighbors in adjacent orbits, harming latency but reducing path variability. We leave it for future work to explore the impact of such variants on route variability.

Routing Algorithm Variants. Path length is an important factor in all existing routing algorithms for LEO satellite networks. This motivated our study of path length variability and its impact on decisions made on shortest-path-routing. However, our study didn't look into the impact of path length variability on routing algorithms that use more complicated metrics. We leave such studies to future work which we hope will come as a part of new routing metric proposals that mitigate the downsides of the variability identified in this study.

Ground Relays. Our study does not take into account satellite networks that rely on ground relays. This is driven by the fact that currently deployed Starlink satellites use ground stations only to connect to the Internet directly and not to connect to each other. A network with ground relays, where ground stations and user terminals act as ground relays as described in [39], will likely exhibit a higher degree of variability than the network we studied owing to the increased number of GSLs which are a big contributor to route churn.

8 Related Work

Optimizing Delay. The domain of LEO satellite networks has seen an increased amount of interest from the networking community over the past few years. The community has been especially excited about the potential of these networks to outperform terrestrial networks. This has led to topology design proposals that aim for inter-satellite network topology providing low latency [20,38]. While these focused on ISL-based networks, others explored achieving low latency in the absence of ISLs using ground relays [39]. The goal for all of these studies is to optimize the network for low latency to outperform terrestrial fiber networks. We offer a different perspective, showing that optimizing exclusively for delay can be harmful to network utilization and path-adaptive algorithms. We also show that a slight sacrifice in delay can improve route stability. We hope that our insights will help design algorithms that can better navigate these tradeoffs. In addition, there have been multiple efforts [18,33,49] analyzing the challenges with integrating the LEO satellite network with the current internet backbone. They look at how satellites can be used to assist with inter-domain routing. While our work focuses only on intra-domain routing for the satellite network, it will help the design of such systems by providing better routing through the satellites.

Routing. A lot of work has been done in the past looking at different goals for routing such as reducing propagation delay [30,38,39,46,60], improved load balancing [76], and energy efficiency [14,45] (Sect. 2). However, most of these proposals were made for an older generation of satellites and applications. The current generation consists of a considerably larger number of satellites and also incorporates many advancements in the satellite communications domain [12]. We hope our work motivates a resurgence in research on routing algorithms in satellite networks.

Variability. Earlier work tackles the impact of variability on addressing and configuration of routing tables [54]. It proposes a rethinking of the logical network topology to better accommodate the rapid changes in the physical infrastructure. While it can reduce the variability in the logical network, it doesn't consider the causes or remedies of variability in the physical network. Our work focuses on the physical network.

9 Conclusion

In this paper, we study the variability in paths rampant in LEO satellite networks. We concretely present the amount of route churn and RTT variability, also highlighting the impact of such variability on path utilization and congestion control. We delve deeper into the reasons why this variability exists by presenting the building blocks of paths and infer that this variability exhibits a spatial structure. Our hope is that this work will provide the key insights for the design of specialized routing and perhaps, congestion control algorithms for LEO satellite networks, taking into account that when delay is an option significant gains can be made in overall network performance.

Acknowledgments. This project was partially supported by NSF grant 2212098 as well as grants and gifts from Google, Cisco, the Georgia Smart program, and VMware. We thank CloudLab [29] for providing a testbed to run our simulations.

References

1. SGP4 Propagator. https://help.agi.com/stk/11.0.1/Content/stk/vehSat_orbitProp_msgp4.htm
2. SGP4 Propagator (2016). https://help.agi.com/stk/11.0.1/Content/stk/vehSat_orbitProp_msgp4.htm
3. Popular Orbits 101 (2017). https://aerospace.csis.org/aerospace101/popular-orbits-101/. Accessed 30 Nov 2017
4. Launch Costs to Low Earth Orbit, 1980–2100 (2018). https://www.futuretimeline.net/data-trends/6.htm. ACcessed 12 Dec 2022
5. FCC Selected Application for Space Exploration Holdings, LLC. SES-LIC2019090601171 (2020)
6. FCC Selected Application for Space Exploration Holdings, LLC. SES-LIC2019021100151 (2020)

7. Cesium: The Platform for 3D Geospatial (2023). https://cesium.com/
8. OneWeb (2023). https://oneweb.net/
9. OneWeb Mobile Backhaul (2023). https://oneweb.net/solutions/carrier-enterpri
se/mobile-backhaul
10. Starlink (2023). https://www.starlink.com/
11. Telesat (2023). https://www.telesat.com/
12. Ackerman, R.K.: Technology drives new satellite communications capabilities
(2020). https://www.afcea.org/content/technology-drives-new-satellite-communic
ations-capabilities. Accessed 01 Aug 2020
13. Airlines, H.: Hawaiian Airlines to Offer Free, High-Speed Starlink Internet Connectivity on Transpacific Fleet (2022). https://newsroom.hawaiianairlines.com/
releases/hawaiian-airlines-to-offer-free-high-speed-starlink-internet-connectivity-
on-transpacific-fleet(2022/10/28)
14. Akturan, R., Vogel, W.J.: Path diversity for leo satellite-pcs in the urban environment. IEEE Trans. Ant. Propag. **45**(7), 1107–1116 (1997)
15. Alan Boyle: Amazon to offer broadband access from orbit with 3,326 satellite
'Project Kuiper' constellation (2019). https://www.geekwire.com/2019/amazon-
project-kuiper-broadband-satellite/ (2019/04/04)
16. Daigavane, A.: ameya98/mahimahi (2019). https://github.com/ameya98/mahi
mahi/
17. Berioli, M., Donner, A., Menichelli, R., Werner, M.: Mpls traffic engineering for
leo satellite constellation networks. In: 21st International Communications Satellite
Systems Conference and Exhibit, p. 2327 (2003)
18. Bhattacherjee, D., et al.: Gearing up for the 21st century space race. In: Proceedings of HotNets 2018, pp. 113–119 (2018)
19. Bhattacherjee, D.: Towards Performant Networking from Low-Earth Orbit. Ph.D.
thesis, ETH Zurich (2021)
20. Bhattacherjee, D., Singla, A.: Network topology design at 27,000 km/hour. In:
Proceedings of CoNext 2019, pp. 341–354 (2019)
21. Brakmo, L.S., O'Malley, S.W., Peterson, L.L.: TCP vegas: new techniques for
congestion detection and avoidance. In: Proceedings of ACM SIGCOMM 1994,
pp. 24–35 (1994)
22. Wang, B.: SpaceX Starlink Satellites Could Cost $250,000 Each and Falcon
9 Costs Less than $30 Million (2019). https://www.nextbigfuture.com/2019/
12/spacex-starlink-satellites-cost-well-below-500000-each-and-falcon-9-launches-
less-than-30-million.html. Accessed 12 May 2022
23. Cardwell, N., Cheng, Y., Gunn, C.S., Yeganeh, S.H., Jacobson, V.: BBR:
congestion-based congestion control. Queue (2016)
24. Allen, C.S., Giraudo, M., Moratto, C., Yamaguchi, N.: Chapter 4 - spaceflight
environment. In: Sgobba, T., Kanki, B., Clervoy, J.F., Sandal, G. (eds.) Space
Safety and Human Performance, pp. 87–138 (2018)
25. Daehnick, C., Klinghoffer, I., Maritz, B., Wiseman, B.: Large LEO satellite
constellations: will it be different this time? (2020). https://www.mckinsey.com/
industries/aerospace-and-defense/our-insights/large-leo-satellite-constellations-wi
ll-it-be-different-this-time. Accessed 12 May 2022
26. del Portillo, I., Cameron, B.G., Crawley, E.F.: A technical comparison of three
low earth orbit satellite constellation systems to provide global broadband. Acta
Astronautica **159**, 123–135 (2019)
27. Dong, M., Li, Q., Zarchy, D., Godfrey, P.B., Schapira, M.: PCC: re-architecting
congestion control for consistent high performance. In: Proceedings of USENIX
NSDI 2015 (2015)

28. Dong, M., et al.: PCC vivace: online-learning congestion control. In: Proceedings of USENIX NSDI 2018 (2018)
29. Duplyakin, D., et al.: The design and operation of CloudLab. In: Proceedings of the USENIX Annual Technical Conference (ATC), pp. 1–14 (2019). https://www.flux.utah.edu/paper/duplyakin-atc19
30. Ekici, E., Akyildiz, I.F., Bender, M.D.: A distributed routing algorithm for datagram traffic in leo satellite networks. IEEE/ACM Trans. Netw. 9(2), 137–147 (2001)
31. Woollacott, E.: Starlink terminals smuggled into iran - but how effective can they be? (2022). https://www.forbes.com/sites/emmawoollacott/2022/10/25/starlink-terminals-smuggled-into-iranbut-how-effective-can-they-be/?sh=1c2952561027. Accessed 28 Oct 2022
32. Foust, J.: SpaceX adds laser crosslinks to polar Starlink satellites (2021). https://spacenews.com/spacex-adds-laser-crosslinks-to-polar-starlink-satellites/. Accessed 26 Jan 2021
33. Giuliari, G., Klenze, T., Legner, M., Basin, D., Perrig, A., Singla, A.: Internet backbones in space. In: ACM SIGCOMM Computer Communication Review, vol. 50, pp. 25–37. ACM New York (2020)
34. Giuliari, G., Ciussani, T., Perrig, A., Singla, A.: ICARUS: attacking low earth orbit satellite networks. In: Proceedings of USENIX ATC 2021, pp. 317–331 (2021)
35. Goyal, P., Agarwal, A., Netravali, R., Alizadeh, M., Balakrishnan, H.: ABC: a simple explicit congestion controller for wireless networks. In: Proceedings of USENIX NSDI 2020 (2020)
36. Goyal, P., Shah, P., Zhao, K., Nikolaidis, G., Alizadeh, M., Anderson, T.E.: Backpressure flow control. In: Proceedings of USENIX NSDI 2022, pp. 779–805 (2022)
37. Handley, M.: Starlink revisions (2018). https://www.youtube.com/watch?v=QEIUdMiColU&ab_channel=MarkHandley
38. Handley, M.: Delay is not an option: low latency routing in space. In: Proceedings of HotNets 2018, pp. 85–91 (2018)
39. Handley, M.: Using ground relays for low-latency wide-area routing in megaconstellations. In: Proceedings of HotNets 2019, pp. 125–132 (2019)
40. Harris, M.: SpaceX Claims to Have Redesigned Its Starlink Satellites to Eliminate Casualty Risks (2019). https://spectrum.ieee.org/spacex-claims-to-have-redesigned-its-starlink-satellites-to-eliminate-casualty-risks. Accessed 21 Mar 2019
41. Hauri, Y., Bhattacherjee, D., Grossmann, M., Singla, A.: "internet from space" without inter-satellite links. In: Proceedings of HotNets 2020, pp. 205–211 (2020)
42. Henderson, T.R., Katz, R.H.: On distributed, geographic-based packet routing for leo satellite networks. In: Proceedings of GLOBECOM 2000, vol. 2, pp. 1119–1123. IEEE (2000)
43. Hoots, F.R., Roehrich, R.L.: Models for propagation of norad element sets (1980)
44. Hu, M., Xiao, M., Xu, W., Deng, T., Dong, Y., Peng, K.: Traffic engineering for software defined leo constellations. IEEE Trans. Netw. Serv. Manag. 19, 5090–5103 (2022)
45. Hussein, M., Jakllari, G., Paillassa, B.: On routing for extending satellite service life in leo satellite networks. In: Proceedings of IEEE GLOBECOM 2014, pp. 2832–2837. IEEE (2014)
46. Kassing, S., Bhattacherjee, D., Águas, A.B., Saethre, J.E., Singla, A.: Exploring the "Internet from space" with Hypatia. In: Proceedings of ACM IMC 2020, pp. 214–229 (2020)

47. Cowing, K.: Euroconsult report addresses challenges and potential of optical communications for nascent space applications market (2023). https://spaceref. com/space-commerce/euroconsult-report-addresses-challenges-and-potential-of-optical-communications-for-nascent-space-applications-market/. Accessed 31 Jan 2023

48. Ancin, K.: 5G + LEO: Verizon and Project Kuiper team up to develop connectivity solutions (2021). https://www.verizon.com/about/news/5g-leo-verizon-project-kuiper-team. Accessed 12 May 2022

49. Klenze, T., Giuliari, G., Pappas, C., Perrig, A., Basin, D.: Networking in heaven as on earth. In: Proceedings of HotNets 2018, pp. 22–28 (2018)

50. Kuiper USASAT-NGSO-8A ITU filing: USA2019-12905 (2018). https://www.itu.int/ITU-R/space/asreceived/Publication/DisplayPublication/8716

51. Kuiper USASAT-NGSO-8B ITU filing: USA2019-13020 (2018). https://www.itu.int/ITU-R/space/asreceived/Publication/DisplayPublication/8774

52. Kuiper USASAT-NGSO-8C ITU filing: USA2019-12909 (2018). https://www.itu.int/ITU-R/space/asreceived/Publication/DisplayPublication/8718

53. LeoSat: Technical Overview. https://www.leosat.com/to/media/1114/leosat-technical-overview.pdf

54. Li, Y., et al.: "internet in space" for terrestrial users via cyber-physical convergence. In: Proceedings of HotNets 2021, pp. 163–170 (2021)

55. Li, Y., et al.: HPCC: high precision congestion control. In: Proceedings of ACM SIGCOMM 2019 (2019)

56. Lin, X., Rommer, S., Euler, S., Yavuz, E.A., Karlsson, R.S.: 5G from space: an overview of 3GPP non-terrestrial networks. IEEE Commun. Stand. Maga. **5**(4), 147–153 (2021)

57. Ma, J., Qi, X., Liu, L.: An effective topology design based on LEO/GEO satellite networks. In: Yu, Q. (ed.) SINC 2017. CCIS, vol. 803, pp. 24–33. Springer, Singapore (2018). https://doi.org/10.1007/978-981-10-7877-4_3

58. Micah Maidenberg, A.S.: Delta Air Lines Tested SpaceX's Starlink Internet for Planes Delta CEO Says (2022). https://www.wsj.com/articles/delta-air-lines-tested-spacexs-starlink-internet-for-planes-delta-ceo-says-11650316287, Accessed 28 Oct 2022

59. Baylor, M.: With Block 5, SpaceX to Increase Launch Cadence and Lower Prices (2019). https://www.nasaspaceflight.com/2018/05/block-5-spacex-increase-launch-cadence-lower-prices/. Accessed 12 May 2022

60. Mohorcic, M., Werner, M., Svigelj, A., Kandus, G.: Adaptive routing for packet-oriented intersatellite link networks: performance in various traffic scenarios. IEEE Trans. Wirel. Commun. **1**(4), 808–818 (2002)

61. Netravali, R., et al.: Mahimahi: accurate {Record-and-Replay} for {HTTP}. In: Proceedings of USENIX ATC 2015, pp. 417–429 (2015)

62. Niederstrasser, C.: Small launch vehicles-a 2018 state of the industry survey. In: Proceedings of AIAA/USU Conference on Small Satellites (2018)

63. Papapetrou, E., Karapantazis, S., Pavlidou, F.N.: Distributed on-demand routing for leo satellite systems. Comput. Netw. **51**(15), 4356–4376 (2007)

64. Perkins, C.E., Royer, E.M.: Ad-hoc on-demand distance vector routing. In: Proceedings of IEEE Workshop on Mobile Computing Systems and Applications (WMCSA 1999), pp. 90–100. IEEE (1999)

65. Plac, C.: LEO speed: when milliseconds are worth $Millions... An NSR Insight (2020). https://news.satnews.com/2020/10/14/leo-speed-when-milliseconds-are-worth-millions-an-nsr-insight/. Accessed 31 Oct 2022

66. Schlicht, A., Marz, S., Stetter, M., Hugentobler, U., Schäfer, W.: Galileo pod using optical inter-satellite links: a simulation study. Adv. Space Res. **66**(7), 1558–1570 (2020)
67. Siddiqi, A., Mellein, J., de Weck, O.: Optimal reconfigurations for increasing capacity of communication satellite constellations. In: 46th AIAA/ASME/ASCE/AHS/ASC Structures, Structural Dynamics and Materials Conference, p. 2065 (2005)
68. Sidibeh, K.: Adaption of the IEEE 802.11 protocol for inter-satellite links in LEO satellite networks. Ph.D. thesis, University of Surrey (United Kingdom) (2008)
69. Smutny, B., et al.: 5.6 Gbps optical intersatellite communication link. In: Free-space Laser Communication Technologies XXI, vol. 7199, pp. 38–45. SPIE (2009)
70. SpaceX: FCC Selected Application for Space Exploration Holdings, LLC (2016). https://fcc.report/IBFS/SAT-LOA-20161115-00118/1158350.pdf
71. SpaceX: Spacex Non-Geostationary Satellite System (2019). https://fcc.report/IBFS/SAT-MOD-20190830-00087/1877671
72. SpaceX FCC Filing: SpaceX V-band Non-Geostationary Satellite System (2017). https://licensing.fcc.gov/myibfs/download.do?attachment_key=1190019
73. SpaceX Update: Spacex Non-Geostationary Satellite System (2017). https://licensing.fcc.gov/myibfs/download.do?attachment_key=1569860
74. SpaceX Update: Spacex Non-Geostationary Satellite System (2020). https://fcc.report/IBFS/SAT-MOD-20200417-00037
75. Starlink (2022). https://www.starlink.com/legal/documents/DOC-1002-69942-69. Accessed 31 Oct 2022
76. Taleb, T., Mashimo, D., Jamalipour, A., Kato, N., Nemoto, Y.: Explicit load balancing technique for ngeo satellite ip networks with on-board processing capabilities. IEEE/ACM Trans. Netw. **17**(1), 281–293 (2008)
77. Telesat: Telesat's responses - Federal Communications Commission (2018). https://licensing.fcc.gov/myibfs/download.do?attachment_key=1205775
78. Telesat: Application for Modification of Market Access Authorization (2020). https://fcc.report/IBFS/SAT-MPL-20200526-00053/2378318.pdf
79. Wadhwa,V., Salkever, A.: How Elon Musk's Starlink Got Battle-Tested in Ukraine (2022). https://foreignpolicy.com/2022/05/04/starlink-ukraine-elon-musk-satellite-internet-broadband-drones/. Accessed 12 May 2022
80. Vladimirova, T., Sidibeh, K.: Inter-satellite links in leo constellations of small satellites (2007)
81. de Weck, O.L., de Neufville, R., Chaize, M.: Staged deployment of communications satellite constellations in low earth orbit. J. Aeros. Comput. Inf. Commun. **1**(3), 119–136 (2004)
82. Yan, F.Y., et al.: Pantheon: the training ground for Internet congestion-control research. In: Proceedings of USENIX ATC 2018, pp. 731–743 (2018)
83. Young, C.: SpaceX's Starlink internet will soon be available aboard cruise ships and airplanes (2022). https://interestingengineering.com/innovation/spacexs-starlink-internet-available-cruise-ships-airplanes. Accessed 28 Oct 2022
84. Zech, H., et al.: Lct for edrs: Leo to geo optical communications at 1, 8 gbps between alphasat and sentinel 1a. In: Unmanned/Unattended Sensors and Sensor Networks XI; and Advanced Free-Space Optical Communication Techniques and Applications, vol. 9647, pp. 85–92. SPIE (2015)

85. Zech, H., Biller, P., Heine, F., Motzigemba, M.: Optical intersatellite links for navigation constellations. In: Sodnik, Z., Karafolas, N., Cugny, B. (eds.) International Conference on Space Optics (ICSO 2018), vol. 11180, pp. 370–379 (2019)
86. Zhang, S., Li, X., Yeung, K.L.: Segment routing for traffic engineering and effective recovery in low-earth orbit satellite constellations. Digital Commun. Netw. (2022)

Topology

Improving the Inference of Sibling Autonomous Systems

Zhiyi Chen$^{(\boxtimes)}$ (ID), Zachary S. Bischof (ID), Cecilia Testart (ID),
and Alberto Dainotti (ID)

Georgia Institute of Technology, Atlanta, USA
{zchen798,bischof,ctestart,dainotti}@gatech.edu

Abstract. Correctly mapping Autonomous Systems (ASes) to their owner organizations is critical for connecting AS-level and organization-level research. Unfortunately, constructing an accurate dataset of AS-to-organization mappings is difficult due to a lack of ground truth information. CAIDA AS-to-organization (CA2O), the current state-of-the-art dataset, relies heavily on Whois databases maintained by Regional Internet Registries (RIRs) to infer the AS-to-organization mappings. However, inaccuracies in Whois data can dramatically impact the accuracy of CA2O, particularly for inferences involving ASes owned by the same organization (referred to as sibling ASes).

In this work, we leverage PeeringDB (PDB) as an additional data source to detect potential errors of sibling relations in CA2O. By conducting a meticulous semi-manual investigation, we discover two pitfalls of using Whois data that result in incorrect inferences in CA2O. We then systematically analyze how these pitfalls influence CA2O. We also build an improved dataset on sibling relations, which corrects the mappings of 12.5% of CA2O organizations with sibling ASes (1,028 CA2O organizations, associated with 3,772 ASNs). To make this process reproducible and scalable, we design an automated approach to recreate our manually-built dataset with high fidelity. The approach is able to automatically improve inferences of sibling ASes for each new version of CA2O.

Keywords: AS-to-organization mapping · Sibling ASes · Whois databases

1 Introduction

Autonomous systems (ASes) are the basic constituent elements of the Internet routing system, managing routing decisions and resources (*i.e.,* IP address prefixes and routers) under a single administrative unit. An AS is uniquely identified by an Autonomous System Number (ASN), which is assigned by a Regional Internet Registry (RIR) as an identifier in the Border Gateway Protocol (BGP). Each AS is typically owned by an individual organization, and one organization may own and operate multiple ASes. ASes owned by the same organization are often referred to as *sibling ASes*. AS-to-organization mappings act as a bridge connecting AS-level and organization-level information. An accurate mapping between

A. Brunstrom et al. (Eds.): PAM 2023, LNCS 13882, pp. 345–372, 2023.
https://doi.org/10.1007/978-3-031-28486-1_15

ASes and organizations are crucial in a range of research endeavors: correct identification of AS ownership can offer insights into determining AS business type [28], and also lead to the deduction of AS relationships [23]; accurate lists of sibling ASes under the same organization can help classify events as benign when monitoring for route leaks [20,22] and BGP hijacks [27]; integrating organizations and ASes facilitates studies of organizational BGP behaviors such as IP space utilization [19], censorship evolution [25], and Internet reputation [21,26].

Despite its importance, compiling an accurate AS-to-organization mapping is still an open problem, exacerbated by a significant lack of ground truth. The Whois databases maintained by the five RIRs are the only available authoritative data sources of AS ownership data. However, they are maintained mainly for operational purposes and do not provide a consistent and up-to-date AS-to-organization mapping for registered ASNs (as discussed in Sect. 4).

The state-of-the-art dataset for inferring AS ownership is the CAIDA AS-to-Organization (CA2O) dataset [9]. CA2O leverages information from multiple fields in Whois databases to infer AS ownership and supplements it with manual input. CAIDA has incorporated the CA2O dataset into their ASRank platform [3], a tool commonly utilized by Internet researchers to determine AS ownership, relations, and size. However, the CA2O includes a number of inaccurate inferences of sibling ASes. For example, at the time of writing, AS16509 and AS14618 both belong to *Amazon.com, Inc*, while CA2O does not consider them siblings. Conversely, the owner of AS9426 is *Westpac Bank*, while CA2O maps it to an Australian telecom company *SingTel Optus* and thus it appears to be one of the 63 sibling ASes. Unfortunately, the reasons behind such problems have not been systematically studied.

In this work, we examine in detail the reasons behind the inaccuracies of sibling relations in CA2O and design a methodology to improve the inferences of sibling ASes. We make several contributions: *(i)* We start by comparing the mappings in CA2O with the corresponding Whois data and illustrate how CA2O is susceptible to wrong inferences due to inaccurate information in Whois databases in Sect. 3. *(ii)* We also inspect PeeringDB (PDB) data and find that it provides an opportunity for addressing the inaccuracies in CA2O: disagreements between CA2O and PDB on sibling relationships serve as hints of potential errors. *(iii)* In Sect. 4, we design a pipeline to automatically discover the disagreements and manually conduct a labeling process to investigate the reasons behind the inaccurate mappings. We identify two main pitfalls of Whois data and illustrate how they influence CA2O. *(iv)* Based on our analysis and manual efforts, we construct a dataset (called *reference dataset*) correcting 1,028 organizations (involving 3,772 ASes) in CA2O that include inaccurate mappings. The CA2O dataset contains 8,204 organizations that either have sibling ASes (7,573) or have a single AS according to CA2O but have sibling ASes according to PDB (631). We correct relations for 12.5% of them. *(v)* To automate the process of improving inferences of sibling ASes, in Sect. 5, we design an automatic approach to reproduce the reference dataset with high fidelity, which is reusable for each new version of CA2O. *(vi)* Finally, in Sect. 6, we present a case study of potential BGP hijacking events and show how our output dataset better identifies siblings and non-sibling related events compared to CA2O. Our improved AS-to-organization mappings provide useful context for examining hijacking events and forensic investigations. Our output dataset is publicly available to the research community[1].

2 Background, Related Work, and Datasets

2.1 Definitions of Organizations and Siblings

An organization refers to an entity with an established structure for decision-making that involves and links all its subdivisions and groups. In particular, decisions related to the Internet resources that the organization owns and operates (*e.g.,* IP addresses and ASNs) can be coordinated and managed together. Though it is possible that distinct groups within the same organization could operate different ASNs, an organization has the ability to unify and coordinate the operation if preferred. We consider all ASes legally owned and operated by a single organization as sibling ASes.

2.2 Regional Internet Registries and Whois Databases

RIRs maintain the authoritative databases related to the assignment of Internet number resources. RIRs are organizations managing the allocation and registration of resources (*i.e.,* IP addresses and AS numbers), which are obtained from the Internet Assigned Numbers Authority (IANA) [7]. Five RIRs are currently serving different regions of the world[2].

Some countries have a National Internet Registry (NIR), which allocates Internet resources to users in the corresponding economy directly from the related RIR's resource pool. When applying for Internet resources, users in those countries have the option to obtain them from either the respective RIR or the NIR. Currently, NIRs only operate in APNIC's and LACNIC's regions, seven in APNIC[3] and two in LACNIC[4]. Another important element in the hierarchy of Internet resource delegation is Local Internet Registries (LIRs), which are the organizations (usually Internet service providers or hosting providers) authorized by RIRs to sub-allocate IP addresses to the end users.

Every RIR and some NIRs maintain Whois databases containing registration information and contact details for each AS and registered organization. In general, Whois databases are organized in objects that have different fields to record AS information, where AS-objects and org-objects are central in the AS-to-organization mapping scenario. Most AS-objects are associated with an org-object with the *orgID* field. However, some ASes do not have the associated org-object, and instead, the actual owner name is stored in the *descr* field.

---

[1] https://github.com/InetIntel/Improving-Inference-of-Sibling-ASes.
[2] RIPE NCC, ARIN, APNIC, LACNIC, AFRINIC.
[3] IDNIC, CNNIC, JPNIC, KRNIC, TWNIC, VNNIC, IRINN.
[4] NIC Mexico, NIC.br.

In addition, RIRs are not responsible for integrating NIRs' Whois databases into their RIR Whois database. The structures of Whois databases vary significantly across RIRs, as they are influenced by the local RIR registration policies. More details of Whois databases for each RIR are summarized in Appendix A.

2.3   Related Work

Cai *et al.* [17] proposed the first work on AS-to-organization mappings. They emphasized the importance of an organization-level view of the AS ecosystem and presented a clustering method to generate an AS-to-organization dataset using Whois data. Their methodology was concerned with three types of Whois records: ASes, organizations, and contacts, where they clustered records using the *orgID*, *phone*, and *e-mail* fields. The authors validated their output dataset using ground truth information from a Tier-1 ISP. In addition, the authors used public documents, routing data, and Whois data to manually create AS-to-organization mappings for nine multi-AS organizations. This dataset was also used for validating their clustering methodology.

In 2012, Cai *et al.* presented a new clustering approach [18] leveraging company subsidiary information from U.S. SEC Form 10-K, which showed few false negatives and false positives compared to their preliminary work, particularly for U.S.-based companies. However, the ISI ANT lab published only one output dataset in 2012 [15] without further updates.

After the above pioneering works, CAIDA developed an inference methodology to map ASes to organizations. Similarly, they created their own objects for ASes, organizations, and contacts. They grouped the objects into families by commonalities in Whois fields. Validated with the same data of Cai's work, CA2O tuned the method and found the following 9 fields were most efficient: *aut.org_id*, *org.admin_c*, *org.tech_c*, *org.phone*, *contact.phone*, *org.org_name*, *aut.admin_c*, *aut.tech_c*, *aut.owner_c*[5]. The CA2O dataset contains two types of objects: AS-objects and org-objects. The inference methodology associates each AS object with an organization object via the *orgID* field.

The CA2O dataset is integrated into the CAIDA ASRank platform, where only the ASes with the same *orgID* are considered to be siblings. CAIDA collects bulk dumps of WHOIS databases 3-4 times per year and produces the CA2O dataset accordingly [2]. In this work, we use the CA2O dataset released in 2022-07-01, which contains 110,764 ASes.

2.4   PeeringDB and Other Data Sources

In addition to Whois databases, several datasets related to the organizational structure of ASes have emerged. PeeringDB (PDB) [4] is a freely available, user-maintained database of networks, where authorized Internet operators can register and update information about their ASes directly. For the purpose of facilitating interconnections, PDB also allows Internet Exchange Points, data centers, and other interconnection facilities to maintain information on the site.

---

[5] *aut* refers to autonomous system.

We observed that in some cases, information on PDB is more accurate than Whois and CA2O, particularly in instances of acquisitions or mergers. Since it is important for other organizations to have up-to-date information on a network, such as peering policy and contact information, one possible explanation for why Whois may be less accurate in some cases is that there are more barriers to updating records compared to PDB.

One recent example is that *Akamai Technologies* announced the acquisition of *Linode* [13] on March 21st, 2022. The PDB entry for AS63949, previously owned by *Linode*, was changed to *Akamai Technologies* on March 28th, just one week after the acquisition. However, at the time of writing, the Whois information for AS63949 has not been updated, with the latest update recorded in May 2020. Consequently, CA2O still lists the AS' organization as *Linode*.

Unfortunately, PDB has two issues that complicate the task of accurately inferring sibling ASes. First, PDB also contains outdated information. For instance, *KPN* is a Dutch landline and mobile telecommunications company that acquired *EduTel* in 2012 and *Divider B.V.* in 2017. CA2O correctly maps the included ASes as siblings, while PDB still maps AS39309 to *EduTel* and AS47628 to *Divider B.V.* The second issue with PDB is that the coverage of ASes is relatively low; PDB only contains records for 24,367 ASes, covering only about 23% of all currently delegated ASes. Despite these problems, PDB is an extremely valuable source of information, especially given the lack of ground truth.

Another data source is BGP.tools [1], which aggregates AS data from 10 different sources to provide the basic properties of ASes (*e.g.,* URL, business type) and near real-time BGP information. BGP.tools consistently updates URLs by generating possible URLs from the contact information in Whois and checking the correctness manually. Some ASes also self-report website URLs on BGP.tools. In this work, we leverage these website URLs collected by BGP.tools (Sect. 5).

3   Comparison Between Whois and CA2O

Our first step towards understanding the errors in CA2O is to quantitatively compare the similarities and differences between CA2O and the Whois data. Indeed, Whois records are the only source of data of CA2O, other than selected manual updates. We compare the CA2O-mapped organization with the Whois-associated organization for every AS, whose last modified date in Whois is no later than 2022-07-01. For ASes with the *orgID* field in Whois, we use *orgID* as an identifier to compare CA2O and Whois. For the remaining ASes that do not have the *orgID* field and the associated organizations, we compare the organization name in CA2O with the *descr* field in Whois. The results are shown in Table 1.

For APNIC, CA2O makes about 3% different inferences than Whois, while for other RIRs, the ratios of difference are all less than 1%. The discrepancies mainly come from CA2O grouping ASes into families based on the commonalities of Whois fields (*e.g., phone*) [9], where CA2O invents a new *orgID* to relate

Table 1. Results of the comparison between CA2O and Whois

RIRs	APNIC	RIPE	AFRINIC	ARIN	LACNIC
#Different inferences	602	112	1	6	108
#Candidate ASes	19,880	36,241	2,146	28,391	12,613

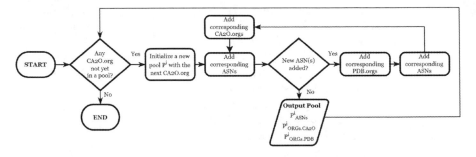

Fig. 1. Detection of *pools* of ASes and organizations that are potentially related according to CA2O and PDB.

the involved ASes (*e.g.*, @family-28933). The results demonstrate that CA2O is so consistent with the Whois mappings that Whois inaccuracies would reflect directly on CA2O (as described in Sect. 4).

To avoid relying on Whois as the single data source, we leverage PeeringDB as an extra dataset. We realize that the disagreements between PDB and CA2O are quite valuable because they help locate potential errors. For example, AS32787 and AS20940 are two famous *Akamai* ASes with big customer cones (*i.e.*, high AS ranks), but CA2O does not regard them as siblings and maps them to different org-objects (*Akamai Technologies, Inc* and *Akamai International B.V*). However, PDB disagrees with CA2O, where the two ASes are siblings under the PDB organization *Akamai Technologies*. The disagreement is a hint directing us to focus on mappings of the *involved* CA2O and PDB organizations. Consequently, we can divide the problem into individual sub-problems based on disagreements, and then conquer them by manually figuring out the real mappings.

Based on the above observations, the roadmap of our work becomes clear: discover all the disagreements between CA2O and PDB, dive into the disagreements to figure out the causes of the inaccurate Whois data (which affect the CA2O dataset), and manually correct the inaccuracies (Sect. 4). Furthermore, since repeating the manual effort is not scalable, we design an automatic approach, which is able to automatically generate a dataset containing improved inferences of sibling relations for each new version of CA2O (Sect. 5).

4   Semi-manual Investigation

In this section, we dig into the disagreements on sibling relations between CA2O and PDB. In Sect. 4.1, we design a pipeline named *Pool Detection* to automatically locate and categorize disagreements between CA2O and PDB. To identify sibling relationships and AS-to-organization mappings for each pool, we carry out a manual labeling process as explained in Sect. 4.2. In Sect. 4.3, we identify two pitfalls of the Whois data, which are the causes of inaccuracies in CA2O. In Sect. 4.4, we present the results of our investigation and illustrate how the pitfalls influence the CA2O dataset. Lastly, we briefly introduce a dataset (named reference dataset) produced by our investigation in Sect. 4.6. We refer to the whole effort as a semi-manual investigation because it combines the automatic detection of disagreements and the manual labeling process.

We collected both the CA2O and PDB datasets on 2022-07-01. Our dataset contains 104,153 ASes that were currently allocated by RIRs (i.e., *administratively alive* [24]) according to the delegation files archived on that day.

4.1   Pool Detection

We design the Pool Detection pipeline to automatically discover disagreements between CA2O and PDB in terms of AS sibling relationships. The pipeline groups potentially related ASes and organizations from both the CA2O and PDB datasets into *pools*. For each pool P^i, we use P^i_{ASNs}, $P^i_{ORGs.CA2O}$ and $P^i_{ORGs.PDB}$ to denote the set of AS numbers (ASNs), the set of organizations from CA2O, and the set of organizations from PDB, respectively. Note that it is possible for each pool to have more than one organization from each dataset, due to differences in AS-to-organization mappings between CA2O and PDB. When referring to a specific element in sets $P^i_{ORGs.CA2O}$ and $P^i_{ORGs.PDB}$, we use the notation $CA2O.org$ and $PDB.org$ respectively.

As described in Fig. 1, the Pool Detection pipeline examines all organizations in the CA2O dataset in sequence: for each unexamined organization, we initialize a new pool P^i with the organization and CA2O-mapped ASNs; then we start a discovery process to populate $P^i_{ORGs.PDB}$ with PDB-mapped organizations for the set P^i_{ASNs}. We continue the process as long as the PDB organizations include any previously unencountered ASNs. In the end, we obtain pools in which all elements are related, where the ASNs are either (or both) associated with a PDB.org or a CA2O.org. The process is repeated until every organization in the CA2O dataset has been examined.

We next categorize the results of Pool Detection based on the cardinalities of organization sets for each pool. For an output pool P^i, we identify the existence of disagreements by checking if either $|P^i_{ORGs.CA2O}| > 1$ or $|P^i_{ORGs.PDB}| > 1$. For example, if a pool contains more than one CA2O organization ($|P^i_{ORGs.CA2O}| > 1$), there must be some ASes that one of the PDB.org considers as siblings while CA2O maps them to different organizations. In contrast, if $|P^i_{ORGs.CA2O}| = 1$ and $|P^i_{ORGs.PDB}| \leq 1$, it indicates that there is no disagreement on siblings, because neither CA2O nor PDB maps any pair of ASes to different organizations.

The outcome of the Pool Detection process is as follows: initially, we identify 75,041 pools that contain a single AS ($|P^i_{ASNs}| = 1$). The ASes in these pools *do not have any sibling* according to either CA2O or PDB, while the remaining 29,112 ASes in 7,538 pools *have siblings* as per either dataset. Among these,

Class-1: P^1	Class-2: P^2	Class-3: P^3
P^1_{ASNs} : 7474, 17719, 9426, 9342, 9983, ...	P^2_{ASNs} : 2906, 40027, 55095	P^3_{ASNs} : 949, 6233, 4785, 138038, ...
$P^1_{ORGs.CA2O}$: *SingTel Optus Pty Ltd*	$P^2_{ORGs.CA2O}$: *Netflix Inc;*	$P^3_{ORGs.CA2O}$: *xTom; xTom Limited;*
$P^1_{ORGs.PDB}$: *SingTel Optus; Westpac Bank;*	*Netflix Streaming Services Inc.*	*xTom GmbH...*
Australian Broadcasting Commission...	$P^2_{ORGs.PDB}$: *Netflix*	$P^3_{ORGs.PDB}$: *xTom GmbH; Wolf Network Lab...*

Fig. 2. Real examples of pools for each class.

PDB *does not disagree* with CA2O on 19,578 ASes in 6,577 pools. There are three possible reasons why a pool may lack disagreement: 1) PDB *completely lacks* any information on all of the ASes in the pool (9,884 ASes in 3,626 pools); 2) PDB *partially agrees* with CA2O when PDB only has information on some of the ASes in a pool (8,588 ASes in 2,475 pools, with PDB having information on 2,923 ASes), or 3) PDB *fully agrees* with CA2O (1,106 ASes in 476 pools).

As the primary objective of this study is to address the disagreements in AS sibling relationships between CA2O and PDB, the remainder of our work centers on pools where PDB and CA2O have conflicting views on AS sibling relationships. This includes 961 pools comprising of 9,534 ASes (32.7% of the total sibling ASes), which are further categorized into the following three mutually exclusive classes based on the properties of each pool:

Class 1 (1:N): $|P^i_{ORGs.CA2O}| = 1$ AND $|P^i_{ORGs.PDB}| > 1$. In this case, the disagreement is that CA2O identifies all the ASes of the pool (two or more) as siblings, while PDB associates them with different organizations.

Class 2 (N:1): $|P^i_{ORGs.CA2O}| > 1$ AND $|P^i_{ORGs.PDB}| = 1$. In this case, the disagreement is that PDB identifies two or more ASes as siblings while CA2O associates them with different organizations.

Class 3 (N:M): $|P^i_{ORGs.CA2O}| > 1$ AND $|P^i_{ORGs.PDB}| > 1$. In this case, the disagreement is due to CA2O finding sibling relationships that PDB does not recognize and vice versa.

Figure 2 provides an illustration of pools belonging to each of the aforementioned classes. Table 2 summarizes the number of pools as well as the number of ASes and organizations for both CA2O and PDB in each class. For *Class-1*, each PDB organization only owns around one AS on average, which indicates PDB recognizes many single-AS or few-AS organizations as different ones from the CA2O organization. The distribution of the number of sibling ASes within CA2O is heavily skewed towards small values (*i.e.*, less than 5) with a long tail, where a total of 973 ASes are identified as siblings under the *DoD Network Information Center*. The distributions of CA2O and PDB in *Class-2* also concentrate on small values. This suggests that PDB recognizes more siblings within some "small" organizations in general, while CA2O identifies them as individual entities. The largest outlier in this class is *VeriSign Global Registry Services* which involves 338 ASes as siblings. *Class-3* shows similar skewed distributions whereas the situation is more complex because each pool contains more than one organization from both CA2O and PDB. We discuss the details of each class in Sect. 4.4.

Table 2. Statistics of the pools with disagreements.

		CA2O		PDB	
Category	#Pools	#ASes	#Orgs	#ASes	#Orgs
Class 1 (1:N)	544	5,680	544	1,506	1,312
Class 2 (N:1)	337	1,901	791	1,060	337
Class 3 (N:M)	80	1,953	292	817	336
Overall	961	9,534	1,627	3,383	1,985

So far, the Pool Detection locates 961 groups of disagreements where either CA2O or PDB may contain inaccurate mappings. To determine the root cause of inaccuracies and correctly establish AS sibling relationships, we must thoroughly examine each pool individually to identify accurate mappings and sibling relationships. To this end, we perform a manual labeling process in an attempt at obtaining ground truth.

4.2   Manual Labeling the Pools with Disagreements

In the following paragraphs, we introduce the methods we used to identify sibling relationships. We design a manual labeling process: for each pool, we first investigate the relations of every *pair of organizations* (*i.e.,* org-org) to check if they are under the same entity or not, and then we check the correctness of the *ASN-organization mappings* (*i.e.,* ASN-org) for each element in P^i_{ASNs}. It is worth mentioning that we examine all possible pairings of ASN-org, not just the mappings within CA2O or PDB datasets.

We perform four steps to verify the relationships: *(i)* check keywords in Whois names: if organizations contain the same brand name, or if an AS contains the same brand name of an organization; *(ii)* search on Google about relations between organizations (*e.g.,* merger, acquisition, trading name vs. registered name, etc.), or perhaps find the owned ASes on the website of the organization; *(iii)* directly contact operators by email; *(iv)* compare contact roles or persons.

We implement the four-step process for every pairing of elements within a pool (org-org or ASN-org) in sequence and discontinue the process if any resource indicates that two organizations are owned (or not owned) by the same entity or an ASN has an ownership relationship (or no relationship) with an organization.

In a pool, there are three possible outcomes for any two objects:

- Our labeling process confirms two organizations are *under the same entity* or an AS *is owned by* an organization. For instance, by investigating keywords of brand names, we recognize that *Netflix Inc* and *Netflix Streaming Services Inc.* are under the same entity.
- Our labeling process finds evidence that the two organizations are *owned by different entities* or an AS *does not have any relation with* an organization. For example, *Skywolf Technology* (a PDB.org) and *LSHIY Network* (a CA2O.org) are in the same pool, where CA2O maps AS7720 (SKYWOLF-AS-AP) to

LSHIY while PDB maps it to *Skywolf*. By directly contacting *Skywolf*, we confirmed that the two organizations are different, and AS7720 is not owned by *LSHIY* but owned by *Skywolf*.
- All of the four steps fail to find any evidence of an AS sibling relationship, where the brand names are different; the search engine shows no result about the relation; the operator does not reply to our email and the contact information is different. In this case, we consider two organizations are different or an AS is not owned by an organization.

By undertaking the manual labeling process, we gather the mappings and sibling relationships for each pool based on the identified outcomes of pairings, which are expected to be close to the ground truth.

4.3   Two Pitfalls of Whois: The Causes of Inaccuracies

During the manual labeling process, we identify two pitfalls of the Whois data, which are the main causes of the inaccuracies we identified in the CA2O dataset. We verify our findings by consulting the 5 RIRs and some Internet operators. Our paper is the first work that systematically analyzes and characterizes the problems of Whois data across RIRs in the context of AS-to-organization mappings.

APNIC-LIR Issue. The operation of Local Internet Registries (LIRs) varies among regions due to the diverse policies of the different RIRs. In addition to sub-allocating IP addresses and serving as the upstream of the customer ASes, LIRs under APNIC and RIPE are also responsible for applying for AS numbers on behalf of their customers [14].

In our analysis, we found that such ASN-related services might cause inaccurate Whois mappings due to the fact that certain LIRs will use their organization identifiers in the *orgID* fields of ASNs obtained on behalf of customer ASes. Consequently, CA2O *incorrectly infers the customer ASes as siblings owned by an LIR*. We consulted with contacts at the five RIRs about such practices and received confirmation that only LIRs in RIPE and APNIC are authorized to provide such ASN-related services. Moreover, only APNIC LIRs associate the AS-objects of customers with themselves: organizations can apply for AS numbers only after becoming APNIC members (*i.e.,* LIRs), while other non-member organizations (*e.g.,* some end users) need to acquire Internet number resources such as ASNs exclusively through an APNIC LIR. In this case, LIRs are responsible for registering AS-objects in the APNIC Whois database for their customers because APNIC considers LIRs as the resource holders for all Internet number resources that they apply for. For example, *LSHIY Network* is an APNIC LIR that only owns 2 ASes and applies for ASNs on the behalf of customer organizations for 26 ASes. In the CA2O dataset, these 28 ASes are all considered siblings under the *LSHIY Network* organization.

Unfortunately, APNIC does not maintain an official list of the APNIC LIRs that provide ASN services, so we need to identify APNIC LIRs ourselves.

In Sect. 4.4, we demonstrate our manual labeling process successfully identifies APNIC LIRs and discards incorrect inferences of AS sibling relationships in CA2O. In the following sections of our paper, for succinctness, we use the term APNIC LIRs to refer to the LIRs that provide ASN services in the APNIC region, which is technically a subset of all LIRs in the APNIC region.

Multi-orgID Issue. We define the multi-orgID issue as follows: CA2O splits sibling ASes into different organization objects based on different *orgIDs* in Whois. It is common for all the 5 RIRs to assign different *orgIDs* to groups, divisions, or subsidiaries under the same organization. Since CA2O carries on the Whois information, the CA2O organizations miss sibling relations between these ASes. For example, 7 Amazon ASes are associated with three different *orgIDs* (AMAZON-4, AMAZO-4, AMAZO-139) with the same org-name *Amazon.com, Inc*, where CA2O does not identify these ASes as siblings. It is also possible that one organization owns multiple ASes delegated by different RIRs, so it has to register different org-objects in different Whois databases. Even though the names of organizations are almost the same except for capitalization and punctuation, CA2O infers them as different organizations, such as *University of Guam* in APNIC (AS23676) and *UNIVERSITY OF GUAM* in ARIN (AS395400).

In addition to the above cases, the multi-orgID issue also exists in instances of mergers or acquisitions: the Whois databases may not reflect changes in legal ownership promptly after an acquisition or merger, as the process of updating records can take some time. For example, *GTT* bought *Interoute* in 2018 [6], and AS5580 changed its associated organization in Whois from *Interoute* to *GTT* in 2022. It is also possible that an operator only changes the contact email or auxiliary information (*e.g.*, *remarks* and *descr*) of involved ASes, but does not bother to change the *orgID* and *org-name*. For example, *Agrium* became *Nutrien* by a merger with *PotashCorp* in 2018 [11], and AS137945 added *Nutrien LTD APAC AS* in the *descr* field and changed the contact email, but still kept *Agrium* as the organization name. It is reasonable for operators to do so since updating contact details is enough for operational purposes. Despite this, it is important to address this issue in order to avoid missing sibling ASes in the context of AS-to-organization mappings.

4.4 Results of Investigation

In this section, we present the results of our semi-manual investigation and analyze how the two pitfalls influence the inferences of CA2O. The CA2O dataset contains 8,204 organizations either with sibling ASes (7,573) or whose ASes have siblings according to PDB (631), and we *correct relations for 12.5% of them* (1,028 organizations, which are associated with 3,772 ASes). Among the 3,772 mappings of ASes, 580 mappings are impacted by the APNIC-LIR issue and the other 3,192 mappings are impacted by the multi-orgID issue. For the remaining part of the section, we dive into each class (as shown in Fig. 3), analyze the influences of the pitfalls, and illustrate with some pools as examples.

Class-1. Our study on *Class-1* reveals that the APNIC-LIR issue is the sole cause of disagreement between CA2O and PDB. In other words, CA2O might wrongly map customer ASes to APNIC LIR organizations but does not miss siblings. Among the 544 pools, we recognize 26 pools that contain APNIC LIRs, where 375 ASes are involved. Our manual labeling process *corrects the mappings of 194* out of 375 ASes by associating the ASes to the actual owners (either PDB.orgs or organizations from *descr*), where we confirm the ownership based on the evidence found by the four-step process above.

As shown in the *Class-1* branch of Fig. 3, we first separate the pools whose P^i_{ASNs} contain more than one APNIC-delegated ASes (denoted as candidate APNIC-LIR pools) to locate the possible APNIC-LIRs (remind we do not have an official list of APNIC LIRs), because an APNIC LIR must have at least two APNIC-delegated ASes: one for itself, one for its customer. For the pools impacted by the APNIC LIR issue, CA2O incorrectly maps all *customer* ASes, while PDB is more accurate. Among the 194 mappings that we corrected, 46 ASes have information in PDB, where 42 of them are accurate. For example, *SingTel Optus* is an APNIC LIR, and CA2O considers 63 ASes to be siblings under it. Though PDB only has information for 3 out of 63 ASes, the AS-to-organization mappings are all correct: AS9342 (ABCNET-AS-AP) to *Australian Broadcasting Commission*, AS9426 (WESTPAC-AS-AP) to *Westpac Bank*, AS9438 (NETRO-AS-AP) to *Netro*. Another important observation is that the *descr* field contributes more than PDB when correcting the mappings of customer ASes: 152 out of 194 mappings are corrected based on the *descr*.

The situation is quite different for pools in which CA2O.org is not an APNIC LIR. For the other 64 candidate pools (which we confirm the CA2O.orgs are not APNIC LIRs) as well as the other non-candidate pools, CA2O is very accurate while PDB is not. We identify two problems with the PDB data. First, PDB sometimes over-divides organizations and sibling ASes. For example, PDB wrongly separates *Zettagrid* and *Conexim Australia* as two organizations and breaks the sibling relation between AS7604 (ZETTAGRID-AS) and AS37996 (CONEXIM-NET-AS-AP). Indeed, *Conexim* is a subsidiary of *Zettagrid*, and CA2O correctly identifies the two ASes as siblings. Second, we discover that the PDB information could be outdated. For example, CA2O maps AS21461 and AS44700 as siblings under *Haendle & Korte GmbH* while PDB disagrees and maps them to two organizations (*Haendle & Korte GmbH* and *Transfair-Net*). After consulting the Internet operator by email, we learned that *Haendle & Korte* bought *Transfair-Net*, and AS21461 would be disabled in near future.

To conclude, if the CA2O.org of a *class-1* pool is an APNIC LIR, the mappings of CA2O are problematic for ASes of customer organizations, while PDB is more accurate. In addition, the *descr* field in Whois can be a useful source of information. Otherwise, for the pools without APNIC LIRs, CA2O and Whois are significantly correct, while PDB tends to be inaccurate.

Class-2. For the pools in *Class-2*, the APNIC-LIR issue is unlikely to occur, but the multi-orgID issue often leads to CA2O missing many siblings. Among the

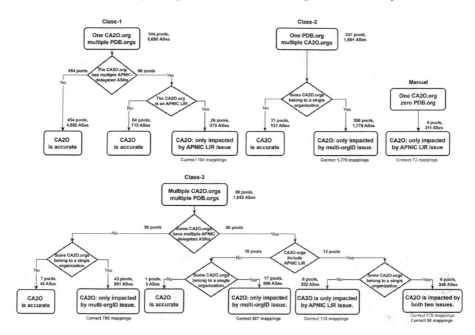

Fig. 3. Results of our semi-manual investigation. The mappings that we corrected are color-coded, with blue indicating those affected by the multi-orgID issue and red indicating those affected by the APNIC LIR issue. (Color figure online)

337 pools, we *correct 306 pools (727 CA2O.orgs, 1,770 ASes are involved)* that are impacted by the multi-orgID issue. Our manual labeling process merges the org-objects under the same entity and considers all involved ASes as siblings.

As shown in the *Class-2* branch of Fig. 3, PDB is quite accurate for the majority (∼90%) of pools, while CA2O breaks siblings into different org-objects. There are 174 pools where organizations in $P^i_{ORGs.CA2O}$ contain the same brand name in their org-names (*e.g., Netflix Streaming Services* and *Netflix Inc*). In addition, 32 pools are related to acquisitions or mergers (*e.g., Nutrien* and *Agrium*). For the remaining pools, the CA2O.orgs are groups or subsidiaries with different brand names. For example, one of the pools contains two CA2O.orgs (*VIX Route Server, ACONET*) and one PDB.org (*University of Vienna*). We directly learned from Vienna University that both *VIX* and *ACONET* are owned and operated by their Computer Center.

For the remaining 10% pools, we consider CA2O to be correct while PDB is problematic because we do not find any evidence to prove the organizations in $P^i_{ORGs.CA2O}$ operate under the same entity. We also observe that the involved organizations usually have different websites or LinkedIn profiles. For example, PDB maps AS24390 (USP-AS-AP) to *AARNet*, while CA2O maps it to *The University of the South Pacific*. We believe CA2O is correct instead of PDB because *AARNet* is an ISP providing services to the education and research communities in the Australian area.

Although CA2O might miss sibling ASes, the existing mappings within each CA2O.org (*i.e.,* ASN-org) are significantly accurate: 706 out of 791 ($\sim$90%) CA2O.orgs have ASes all with the same keyword in names. For the other 85 organizations, we also manually verify the correctness. For example, AS29697 (CNS) is correctly mapped to *BeeksFX VPS* by CA2O, because we found Beeks group acquired CNS in 2019 [12].

To conclude, the pools of *Class-2* tend to be affected by the multi-orgID issue. For most pools, PDB is correct while CA2O over-divides organizations. However, PDB is not always accurate, as it is problematic in approximately 10% of pools, while CA2O remains correct in those instances. Furthermore, the mappings within each CA2O.org are highly precise, with almost no cases of an ASN being incorrectly assigned to an organization when it actually belongs to another organization.

Class-3. The situation in *Class-3* is more entangled: the two pitfalls might exist simultaneously. Moreover, CA2O and PDB might both be inaccurate in one pool. Our manual labeling process *corrects 223 CA2O.orgs (1,422 ASes included)* that miss siblings, and *corrects 313 mappings of customer ASes* where CA2O maps them to APNIC LIRs.

For 88% of pools without any APNIC LIR (60 out of 68 pools), CA2O misses some siblings due to the multi-orgID issue. In *Class-3*, PDB may sometimes over-divide organizations, unlike in *Class-2* where PDB is always correct on the pools where CA2O is incorrect. We take the pool of *Akamai* as an example: there are 4 CA2O.orgs (*Akamai International B. V.*; *Akamai Technologies, Inc*; *Linode, LLC (APNIC)*; *Linode, LLC (RIPE)*) and 4 PDB.orgs (*Akamai Technologies*; *Asavie Technologies*; *Instart Logic, Inc*; *Nominum, Inc*), where all of the organizations actually belong to *Akamai* because of a series of acquisitions.

In addition to the case where all organizations operate under the same entity, we have observed instances where a pool without APNIC LIRs may contain two or more completely distinct organizations. Indeed, the involved organizations operate some ASes together under partnerships, whereas CA2O and PDB map these ASes differently. For instance, a pool contains 4 CA2O.orgs (*Arabian Internet & Communications*; *Saudi Telecom Company (STC)*; *London Internet Exchange Ltd*; *LINX USA Inc*) and 2 PDB.orgs (*LINX* and *Saudi Telecom Company (STC)*), where all 4 CA2O.orgs miss siblings: the first two CA2O.orgs are actually under the same entity because of an acquisition, and the latter two are subsidiaries. Interestingly, the four organizations fall in the same pool because of AS31177 (JED-IX), which PDB maps to *LINX* and Whois maps to *STC*. In fact, *LINX* and *STC* entered into a partnership to form an Internet Exchange Point called JEDIX in 2018. Our manual labeling process corrects the two organizations by finding the separated siblings and maps AS31177 to *STC* because of the contact email of this AS.

Table 3. A visual example of the reference dataset.

ASN	Reference.orgs	Sibling ASNs	CA2O.org	PDB.org
55095	PDB: Netflix, CA2O: Netflix Inc (ARIN), CA2O: Netflix Streaming Services Inc. (ARIN)	[2906, 40027]	Netflix Inc (ARIN)	Netflix

In the case of pools that contain APNIC LIRs, the main difference from *Class-1* is that some organizations obtain their ASNs from multiple APNIC LIRs, which greatly increases the size of the pools. The biggest pool in *Class-3* contains 14 CA2O.orgs, 97 PDB.orgs, and 155 ASNs. As an example, *YuetAu Network* owns AS147047 and AS138435, which are applied separately through 2 APNIC LIRs (*NEXET LIMITED* and *Aperture Science Limited*).

For the 6 pools that are impacted by both issues, we take the *xTom* pool as an example: *xTom* is a hosting provider which provides services in a wide range of regions. The pool contains 9 subsidiaries of *xTom* delegated by 4 RIRs except for LACNIC (*e.g., xTom Hong Kong Limited*; *xTom GmbH*), where the multi-orgID issue leads to missing sibling relations. Moreover, two of the subsidiaries in the APNIC region are LIRs, where CA2O also makes mistakes on the customer ASes. For example, *xTom Limited (APNIC)* helps *Wolf Network Lab* to apply for AS138038 (WOLFLAB-AS-AP), while CA2O wrongly maps AS138038 to *xTom*.

4.5   Manual Input of APNIC LIRs

During our investigation, we identify 8 APNIC LIRs (73 ASes involved), for which we do not find disagreements in their pools, because none of the customer ASes maintain any information in PDB. We manually include them to achieve a more accurate dataset, where details can be found in Appendix C.

4.6   Reference Dataset

By aggregating the results of our semi-manual investigation, we produce a dataset (denoted as reference dataset), which contains our corrections on 1,028 CA2O.orgs (3,772 ASes involved). For the remaining ASes we do not change the mappings, we directly keep the CA2O and PDB mappings in the dataset. There are four columns for each AS number: reference mapping, sibling ASes, CA2O mapping, and PDB mapping, where the first two columns record the results of our investigation. Table 3 illustrates a visual example of the dataset. We welcome corrections from owners of the involved ASes.

Since the Internet world changes rapidly, where new AS numbers could be delegated, and old AS numbers could change ownership, it is not scalable to rerun the semi-manual investigation for every new version of the CA2O dataset. Having the Whois pitfalls in mind and the reference dataset by hand, our next goal is designing an automatic approach to produce an improved dataset of AS-to-organization mappings with more accurate inferences of sibling ASes.

5   Towards Automatically Improving Inferences

In this section, we introduce our design of the automatic approach to reproduce the reference dataset. We have learned from our semi-manual investigation that matching keywords is efficient to confirm relations between organization-organization and AS-organization. Thus, we propose a clustering approach based on the keyword-matching method. In general, the approach constructs a graph for each pool, where pool elements are converted to nodes (*i.e.*, either an ASN, a CA2O.org, or a PDB.org). For each node, we collect a set of identification features and populate edges between related nodes by matching keywords. In addition, we implement different graph initialization strategies based on the knowledge of Whois pitfalls analyzed in Sect. 4. Finally, we identify clusters of each graph and output sibling relations as well as related organizations.

We present the scope of application of the approach in Sect. 5.1, and an overview of the approach in Sect. 5.2. The data preparation and strategies of graph initialization are detailed in Sects. 5.3 and 5.4. In Sect. 5.5 and Sect. 5.6, we show the methods of keyword-matching and cluster discovery. Lastly, we evaluate the ability of our automatic approach on reconstructing the reference dataset in Sect. 5.7.

5.1   Scope of Application

Similar to the investigation, we only take into account disagreements between PDB and CA2O as indications of possible mistakes, thus pools without any discrepancies fall outside the scope of our approach. As shown in Sect. 4.4, CA2O is quite accurate for pools that do not contain multiple APNIC-delegated ASes in *Class-1* (*i.e.*, a subset of non-APNIC-LIR organizations). Therefore, we simply use the CA2O mappings for these 454 pools without applying our method. As a result, we run our approach on 507 pools and 4,550 ASNs, including all pools in *Class-2* and *Class-3*, as well as the candidate APNIC-LIR pools in *Class-1*.

5.2   Method Overview

Our approach consists of five stages. Initially, we build a graph in which the nodes are the ASNs, CA2O.orgs, and PDB.orgs of a pool. Then, we conduct a three-step data preparation to extract a set of identification features for each node. To complete the graph initialization, we design and implement different strategies for different classes, including pre-populating edges and sometimes adding new organization nodes. Afterwards, we examine each pair of nodes and populate edges between them if any matching keywords are found in the two sets of features. Finally, we run a Breadth-First Search algorithm on each graph and output connected components as clusters of sibling ASes and corresponding mapped organizations.

Table 4. An Overview of Collected Attributes

Attributes	ID	Name	Alias	Descr	Admin	Website
ASN	✗	✓ *	✓ *	✓ *	✓ *	✓ *+
CA2O.org	✓ *	✓	✗	✗	✗	✗
PDB.org	✗	✓	✓ *	✗	✗	✓ *

* Not always available; + from multiple sources.

5.3 Data Preparation

In the following paragraphs, we introduce three data preparation steps in a sequence of data collection, data cleaning, and feature extraction. Upon completion of data preparation, we associate each node in a graph with a set of keywords.

Data Collection. Given that it is difficult for the automatic approach to take advantage of the Google search engine and consulting ground truths from Internet operators (as what we do in manual labeling), we partially compensate for it by leveraging more informative fields. As shown in Table 4, we collect 6 types of attributes from Whois and PDB: *ID, Name, Alias, Descr, Admin,* and *Website,* where we supplement the *website* attribute with data from BGP.tools as well.

For ASN nodes, we collect fields of *AS-name, descr,* and *admin-c* from Whois, where the *admin-c* field relates to the administrative contact, and the *descr* field contains auxiliary information (remind that the two fields could reveal the actual owners of customer ASes). In addition, we collect *alias* from the *AKA* (*i.e.,* also known as) field of PDB, where some Internet operators record aliases of ASes. This field might help identify relations between objects involved in acquisitions or mergers. At last, we collect *website URLs* from both PDB and BGP.tools (18,885 websites from PDB, 9,422 from BGP.tools), where ASes operated by different groups of an organization might use the same website URL.

For organization nodes, we collect *orgID* and *org-name* from Whois databases for CA2O.orgs. From PDB data, we collect *org-name, alias* (from *AKA* field), and *website* (13,357 websites) for PDB.orgs.

However, there are a few special cases that we should take into consideration. During the manual investigation, we notice 6 APNIC LIRs and 1 APNIC NIR register all the customer ASes with their own *admin-c*. To ensure the accuracy of our final dataset, we do not gather *admin-c* for ASes in these 7 pools (Appendix C). Such manual input of prior information requires consistent updating.

Data Cleaning. First, we convert non-English characters to English characters using Python *unidecode* package to simplify the following keyword comparison. For *descr* fields with multiple lines, we adopt the same approach as CA2O and only retain the first line, as the subsequent lines are unlikely to pertain to the names of organizations (*e.g.,* street addresses, city names, etc.).

In addition, we notice that some website URLs are not up-to-date, as they automatically redirect to a different domain. Given that new domains may reveal more information, we employ *Selenium* in Python to scrape updated website URLs. For example, AS199422 records http://rezopole.net/ as its website URL in PDB, however, this URL is redirected to https://www.lyon.franceix.net/fr/, because *Rezopole* was merged to *FranceIX* in December 2020 [10]. As a result, we updated the website information of 1,880 ASes and 241 PDB.orgs.

Feature Extraction. We define three functions to extract features from the cleaned attributes: *SLD()* is to extract the second-level domain from *website*; *Brands()* and *Acronyms()* are to extract keywords from *all other attributes*.

SLD() We use *tldextract* Python module on the websites to extract the second-level domains. For example, we extract *franceix* as a keyword of AS199422 by using the function on the website URL https://www.lyon.franceix.net/fr/.

Brands() The function is designed to extract representative keywords, especially brand names. We use regular expressions to extract a set of English keywords containing at least two characters. Then, we filter them against manually-built lists of stop-words to eliminate words without any representative information (*e.g.*, *llc, university, services*). For example, the output keywords of *Netflix Streaming Services Inc.* are {*netflix, streaming*}. We put the details of this function in Appendix B.

Acronyms() Due to different conventions of naming, it is common that an AS is named by the initials of its organization name. Thus, we extract two types of possible acronyms for organization nodes: *(i)* the concatenation of upper case English characters, *(ii)* the concatenation of the first letter of each English word split by space. For example, the acronym of organization *Internet Systems Consortium, Inc.* is *isci*.

At the end of data preparation, we group all features extracted by the three functions into a keyword set and attach it with the corresponding node.

5.4   Graph Initialization

We integrate two types of prior knowledge in the graph initialization stage. The first knowledge is *agreements of siblings* between CA2O and PDB: if in a pool, two ASes are recognized as siblings by both CA2O and PDB, we connect them with an edge between the ASN nodes. The second knowledge is from our investigation: as shown in the following paragraphs, we apply different strategies on pools from different classes based on the combinations of Whois pitfalls. Figure 4 illustrates one example of an initialized graph for each class.

Class-1. Our approach only applies to the pools with multiple APNIC-delegated ASes in *Class-1*, which are potentially impacted by the APNIC-LIR issue. Given that the mappings of CA2O on customer ASes are unreliable, we need to independently establish relationships between organizations and ASes. Consequently, we initialize each graph without any AS-organization links from CA2O. In addition,

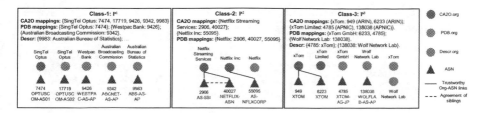

Fig. 4. Examples of graph initialization

we separate the *descr* fields from ASN nodes and initialize them as individual potential organization nodes (*i.e.*, Descr.org) according to what we learned from some APNIC LIRs in Sect. 4.3.

Class-2. The multi-orgID issue is the only potential problem in pools of *Class-2*, where CA2O may miss some relations between organizations. During the investigation, we discovered that the existing mappings within each CA2O.org are quite reliable. Thus, we need to find potential relations between different organization nodes and merge them into bigger clusters. To this end, we keep edges between AS-organization according to the CA2O mappings. By doing so, each CA2O.org and its ASes from CA2O are connected in the initialized graph.

Class-3. Though both pitfalls might exist in pools of *Class-3*, only the CA2O.orgs with multiple APNIC-delegated ASes are possibly impacted by the APNIC-LIR issue. For these CA2O.orgs, we use the same strategy as *Class-1* to discard AS-organization links of CA2O and add *Descr.orgs* as potential organizations. For the other organizations, we use the same strategy as *Class-2* to keep the CA2O mappings.

5.5   Keyword Matching

So far, we have initialized a graph with four types of nodes and some edges, where each node is associated with a keyword set. In this stage, we compare every pair of nodes (*i.e.*, ASN-ASN, ASN-Org, Org-Org) and populate an edge if there is any same keyword between the two sets. The criterion we used to compare keywords is a *keyword prefix matching*: if one word in a keyword set is equal to or is the prefix of any word in another keyword set, we consider the two nodes to be related. We do not use simple matching because it might miss some relations. For example, the *keyword prefix matching* can find relations between *Internet Systems Consortium, Inc.* and AS5277 (ISC-F-AS), since the keyword of AS5277 (isc) is the prefix of the acronym of the organization (isci). We emphasize that the risk of mismatching two randomly unrelated organizations is minimized since the Pool Detection pipeline narrows down the problem scope to related organizations according to CA2O and PDB.

Table 5. Reconstruction rate of our automatic approach, where A refers to the APNIC LIR issue and M refers to the multi-orgID issue.

	Class-1 (A)	Class-2 (M)	Class-3 (A+M)		Manual (A)	Total
Reference dataset	194	1,770	313	1,422	73	3,772
Automatic approach	194	1,649	290	1,189	73	3,395
Reconstruction rate	100%	93%	93%	84%	100%	90%

5.6   Cluster Discovery

After comparing every pair of nodes by keyword matching, the final step is to identify clusters of ASes and organizations on the graph that have been created. We define connected components (CCs) as clusters, where each CC is a set of nodes that are linked to each other by paths. To find CCs, we run a Breadth-First Search algorithm on each graph. For each ASN node, the other ASN nodes in the same cluster are its siblings, and the organizations (from CA2O or PDB or Descr) in the same cluster are the inferred organizations.

5.7   Evaluation

We evaluate the performance of our automatic approach by comparing the clustering results with our manually labeled reference dataset. We use the reconstruction rate as the metric to measure the performance of our automatic approach. In Table 5, we show the numbers of mappings corrected by the dataset and approach, and the reconstruction rate for each class. The *manual* column records the corrected mappings of the 8 APNIC LIRs for which our Pool Detection finds no disagreements. In the table, we use A to refer to corrections on the APNIC-LIR issue and use M to refer to corrections on the multi-orgID issue. As a result, the sibling relations corrected by our approach involve 3,395 ASes, where the reconstruction rate is around 90% of our manual effort (3,772 ASes involved).

Our automatic approach successfully recognizes and corrects problematic CA2O mappings influenced by the APNIC-LIR issue, where we reconstruct about 96% mappings of the reference dataset. The approach fails to identify 23 customer ASes in the biggest pool from *Class-3* and incorrectly considers them as siblings. The reason is that most of the ASes are owned by individuals in China, whose names are written by Chinese PINYIN[6], which causes our keyword-matching method to mistake relations between nodes by either keywords or acronyms.

For the multi-orgID issue, our automatic approach correctly identifies *all missing siblings* for 89% mappings of the reference dataset. The approach also partially identifies missing siblings for 56 mappings in *Class-2* and 76 mappings in *Class-3*. For example, a pool in *Class-2* contains 3 CA2O.orgs (*BeeksFX VPS USA Inc.*; *Network Foundations LLC*; *Beeks Financial Cloud Ltd*), and

---

[6] The official romanization system for Standard Mandarin Chinese in China.

our approach correctly recognizes 10 siblings in two *Beeks* organizations, only missing AS36242 (NFLLC-EQUINIX-ED) from *Network Foundations*. In fact, *Network Foundations* has another name *VDIware*, and Beeks acquired it in 2015.

The errors made by our automatic approach resulted in not identifying 354 missing siblings and mistakenly mapping 209 ASes to incorrect organizations. Out of the incorrect mappings, 193 were found in the *Class-3* pools. This is due to the fact that *Class-3* pools have a large number of ASes, and when our method incorrectly identifies the connections between organizations, it leads to a substantial amount of errors that impact a significant number of ASes. For example, a *Class-3* pool contains 3 CA2O.orgs (*DE-CIX North America Inc.*; *DE-CIX Management GmbH*; *COMNET BILGI ILETISIM TEKNOLOJILERI TICARET A.S.*), where *DE-CIX* is an organization operating Internet Exchange Points, and *COMNET* is an Internet service provider in Istanbul. Similar to the *LINX* and *STC* example, *DE-CIX* operates AS47298 (ISTIX) together with *COMNET*. Since the features of AS47298 contain keywords related to both organizations, our approach mistakes all 30 ASes in this pool as siblings.

6 Case Study: MOAS Event Analysis

In this section, we present a case study of BGP hijacking analysis to illustrate the relevance of our sibling dataset. We focus on Multiple Origin AS (MOAS) events, which are potentially linked to one type of BGP hijacking attack. A MOAS event occurs when in BGP, an IP prefix appears to be originated from more than one ASes [27]. In this context, sibling relationships between involved ASes provide key information to understand the event, the likelihood of misconfiguration and to eventually start a forensic investigation. For instance, the sibling relationship between involved ASes is an important factor when determining if an event is malicious or not. If no other suspicious behaviors are detected (*e.g.,* the AS is infiltrated by attackers), the events between sibling ASNs are highly possible to be non-malicious. As a case study, we collect all 97,975 MOAS events (containing 30,709 pairs of ASNs) monitored by the Global Routing Intelligence Platform [5] in 2021 and compare the results of using our dataset or CA2O on identifying events that happened between sibling ASes.

Using our dataset we discover more sibling-related events, also identify several non-sibling related events which CA2O identifies as sibling-related events. Both our dataset and CA2O agree on 2,076 pairs of ASes being siblings. However, our dataset additionally identifies 17% more pairs of sibling ASNs, with a total of 360 pairs and 4,219 events. We list some examples in Table 6, where the sibling relationship discovered by our dataset provides more context to the events. In addition, using our method, we identify 11 MOAS events that happened between ASes of APNIC Local Internet Registries (LIRs) and customer ASes, which CA2O considers as sibling-related events. Our dataset provides a more precise interpretation for these events: it is possible that the LIR serves as the upstream and originates the prefix in BGP for its customer. For example, our dataset identifies an event that happened between AS9658 and AS131212, where

Table 6. Examples of newfound sibling ASes in MOAS events

AS-pair	CA2O.orgs	#Occurrence
3356, 3561	Level 3 Parent LLC; CenturyLink Communications LLC	4
4755, 6453	Tata Communications Limited; TATA COMMUNICATIONS (AMERICA) Ltd	6
20115, 20001	Charter Communications; Charter Communications Inc	3
19527, 139190	Google LLC; Google Asia Pacific Pte. Ltd	3
36617, 10515	VeriSign Global Registry Services; VeriSign Infrastructure & Operations	75
16625, 20940	Akamai Technologies Inc; Akamai International B.V	28
33438, 12989	Highwinds Network Group Inc; StackPath LLC	14
8190, 3257	GTT; GTT Communications Inc	1

the former AS belongs to an LIR (*Eastern Telecommunications Philippines*), and the latter belongs to a customer AS (*Robinsons Land Corporation*). To conclude, our output dataset contributes to a more accurate understanding of BGP hijacking events and better supports potential forensic investigations.

7 Discussion and Future Work

7.1 Limitations of Our Methodology

There are some inherent limitations caused by the dependency on PDB. First of all, PDB is not specialized for the AS-to-organization mapping similar to Whois, hence there is no guarantee on the detected pools to perfectly follow our definition. For example, operators of some subsidiaries might consider their business independent, so they maintain different organizations in PDB just like the information in the Whois databases. As a result, our Pool Detection pipeline is not able to discover the relations between the involved ASes. For example, *Singtel Optus Pty Limited* (*Optus*) and *Singapore Telecommunications Limited* (*Singtel*) are two individual organizations according to both PDB and CA2O, even though *Optus* is a completely owned subsidiary of *Singtel*. As a result, our Pool Detection places them into two different pools. Another example is *vodafone*, which owns and operates networks all over the world. There are 35 and 29 different organizations containing *vodafone* as the brand name in CA2O and PDB respectively, where our Pool Detection only recognizes a few subsets of them in the same pool (*e.g.*, *Vodafone UK Limited Mobile AS* and *Vodafone UK Limited*) but neglects most of them. One possible solution to the limitation is implementing the keyword matching method on all ASes and organizations to find possible relations. However, more careful validation is needed because organizations without any relation (especially in different countries) may have exactly the same brand names.

Another limitation is that the information hidden in the natural language data of PDB (*e.g.*, the *notes* field) is hard to extract. For example, the *notes* of AS137945 in PDB records the following information: "*Nutrien operates AS137945 in APAC and AS393891 in North America; AS137900 is also operated by Nutrien APAC.*" The information about AS137900 is accurate. Indeed, AS137900 is mapped to

Ruralco Holdings Limited by Whois, where *Nutrien* acquired *Ruralco* in 2020. However, since AS137900 is not registered in PDB, and it does not have any sibling according to CA2O, our Pool Detection isolates AS137900 from the other two ASes of *Nutrien*. If the relations between ASes and organizations could be correctly extracted from the natural language data, the Pool Detection could become more precise as well as the automatic clustering approach. Towards improving this problem, leveraging natural language processing methods might be one possible solution.

Even though the knowledge in PDB is fully leveraged, some information is still not covered by the datasets we used, especially for mergers and acquisitions. There are some commercial databases such as *Crunchbase* and *Dun & Bradstreet* which contain plenty of information such as acquisition history, and subsidiary list. As for the drawbacks, the databases are neither authoritative nor directly maintained by the operators, and it is hard to validate the information.

7.2   Interaction with Internet Operators

Given that the ground truth of AS-to-organization mappings can be only obtained from Internet operators, a virtuous interaction with Internet operators is extremely beneficial. When constructing the reference dataset, we contacted 105 Internet operators. Except for 10 undeliverable email addresses, we received 12 replies in total. On the one hand, RIRs need to impose more precise supervision to ensure operators update the contact information as soon as the email changes. On the other hand, our researchers need to do more work to facilitate active and constructive interactions with Internet operators. We plan to create a website for our project about the mappings that we found different from the Whois records and welcome the authorized operators (*i.e.,* with a PDB account) to verify or modify the data, which could also help us to update our dataset and approach. Another aspect of interaction is encouraging the operators to maintain and update the information in user-maintained public databases like PDB and BGP.tools, which are extremely helpful for researchers (remind that only around 23% ASes are currently registered in the PDB database). Our approach could benefit from the higher AS coverage of PDB to attain more complete results of Pool Detection and collect more features for the automatic approach. An open question is how to motivate Internet operators to maintain the databases.

7.3   Extension the Mappings for AS-Level Analysis

Our definitions of ownership and sibling ASes mainly aim for applications related to Internet behaviors at an organizational level, which may not fit AS-level studies perfectly. For example, although *CenturyLink* acquired *Level 3* and then renamed to *Lumen* in 2020, business types between the two divisions are quite different: ASes (previously) operated by *Level 3* are mainly for transit purposes (*e.g.,* AS3356), while ASes (previously) operated by *CenturyLink* are mainly for residential Internet services (*e.g.,* AS3561). In this scenario, separating ASes of these two divisions could benefit the AS-level analysis, such as AS-type classification. One possible solution is a hierarchical structure of AS-to-organization mappings which also takes the subsidiaries and divisions into account. A preliminary but not verified structure is to organize a tree-like hierarchy for the pools impacted by the multi-orgID issue, where we place our reference organization(s) at the top level, CA2O.orgs at the middle level, and ASes at the bottom as leaves. Consequently, the AS-level analysis only focuses on the middle and bottom layers, while information on sibling relations between the subsidiaries is maintained at the top layers. We leave the evaluation of the necessity and effects of such hierarchical mappings as future work.

8   Conclusion

In this work, we aim to improve the inferences of sibling relations in AS-to-organization mappings to benefit Internet researchers. We start by comparing the state-of-the-art dataset CAIDA AS-to-organization with Whois databases and show that CA2O is susceptible to wrong inferences due to inaccurate information in Whois databases. Then we leverage PeeringDB data to find the potentially problematic mappings and conduct a meticulous semi-manual investigation. During the process, we identify two pitfalls in Whois: the APNIC-LIR issue and the multi-orgID issue, which are the main causes of the inaccuracies. We also construct a reference dataset that corrects 12.5% CA2O organizations that have sibling ASes. We further propose an automatic and scalable approach to reproduce the dataset with high fidelity, which is able to automatically improve inferences of sibling ASes for each new version of CA2O.

9   Ethics

This work does not raise any ethical issues.

A   Information of RIR/NIR Whois

APNIC. The bulk Whois data of APNIC is public, while among 7 NIRs, only JPNIC and KRNIC publish their bulk Whois data. We learned from the APNIC helpdesk that if NIRs make further assignments within the NIR-maintained whois database, they may not be reflected in the APNIC Whois database.

20,127 ASes are delegated in the APNIC region including the ones delegated by the NIRs. *aut-num* (*i.e.,* autonomous system number) and *organisation* are the AS-object and org-object in APNIC Whois, associated with the *org* field (*i.e.,* org-id of the organization) in *aut-num*. However, 8,781 ASes in APNIC do not have *org* field (*i.e.,* no related organization objects), where 99.4% of such ASes are registered in the countries of 7 NIRs. For these ASes, the *descr* (*i.e.,* description) field in AS-objects carries the name of the owner organization without association by org-id. The *descr* field is mandatory [16], and all AS-objects have such field including the ones with associated organization-objects.

RIPE NCC. The bulk Whois data of RIPE is public. 37,672 ASes are delegated in the RIPE region, which is the most among the 5 RIRs. RIPE NCC has a similar structure as APNIC that there are *aut-num* and *organization* objects associated by org-id. Though no NIR exists in the RIPE region, there is still a small amount of ASes (108 ASNs) without associated organizations, whose holder organization is in the *descr* field. Different from APNIC, the *descr* field is not mandatory and only 3,962 ASes in RIPE have this field.

AFRINIC. The bulk Whois data of AFRINIC is public. AFRINIC allocates the least AS numbers among RIRs, where only 2,168 ASes are delegated in the AFRINIC region. The Whois structure of AFRINIC is similar to APNIC and RIPE but more consistent: all *aut-num* objects have *org* fields associating with org-objects and the *descr* field is also mandatory in AFRINIC.

ARIN. The access to ARIN bulk Whois data needs an application (we get access for this work). 31,446 ASes are delegated in the ARIN region. ARIN uses its own format of Whois [8]: *ASHandle* and *OrgName* are two main objects, associated by *OrgID*. AS-objects does not have the *descr* field and every ASN-object has an associated org-object.

LACNIC. The access to LACNIC bulk Whois data needs an application (we do not get access for this work). 12,740 ASes are delegated in the LACNIC region. To compare CA2O with LACNIC Whois, we conduct a web scraping on the LACNIC official webpage for Whois to collect the Whois mappings.

B   Details of Keywords Function

We implement two lists of stop-words, where the first list contains the words that can not be used to identify an organization, while the second list might be useful for some time. The first list contains *apnic, enterprise, asn, sas, as, information, ap, pvt, university, jpnic, jsco, telecom, and, bvba, autonomous, ltda, services, for, op, backbone, telekom, based, ohg, de, gmbh, technologies, lacnic, pt, legacy, inc, company, the, technology, of, llc, sdn, organization, afrinic, com, idnic, bhd, da, international, corporation, twnic, limited, research, or, aka, pty, service, solutions, me, arin, ltd, jsc, in, org, ripe.*

The second list contains *health, communication, tecnologia, data, network, comunicacao, center, coop, hospital, australia, bank, servi, servers, sg, telecomunica, el, northern, north, net, en, me, systems, sdn, telecommunications, telecomunices, telecommunication, east, eu, uab, education, info, de, public, silva, exchange, world, serv, college, communications, eng, western, digital, hosting, apac, city, southern, yue, internet, broadband, asia, link, route, uk, consumo, provedora, networks, japan, tech, ag, west, sp, cloud, web, co, telecomunicacoes, os, servicos, ab, ix, comunica, tel, publicos, telefon, experimental, yu, europe, connect, eastern, south, computing, group, county, global.* In addition, we add the names of countries and the two-letter country codes to the second list.

For each set of extracted English keywords, we first filter out the words in the first list. Then we examine if all the remaining words exist in the second list. If so, we do not use the second list; otherwise, we use the list to filter out part of the words.

C   Manual Input Knowledge

C.1   Manual Input Pools in Sect. 4

We identified 8 CA2O.orgs during the semi-manual investigation, which are likely to be APNIC LIRs (211 ASes involved). The pool detection did not recognize them because none of the involved ASes maintain information in PDB. We list the names of them here: *REANNZ Education and Schools*; *Internet Thailand Company Ltd.*; *ePLDT Inc.*; *CS Loxinfo Public Company Limited*; *Globe Telecom (GMCR,INC)*; *Sky Internet*; *KSC Commercial Internet Co.Ltd.*; *Philippine Long Distance Telephone Co.*

C.2   Manual Knowledge of *admin-c* in Sect. 5

We identified several pools that the CA2O.orgs are very likely to be APNIC LIRs, but the involved ASes have the same *admin-c* fields. For the sake of the accuracy of our dataset, we do not add *admin-c* as a feature for the ASes in these pools:

One Pool Containing of an NIR. IRINN (Indian Registry for Internet Names and Numbers) put their org-handle (RB486-AP) in *admin-c* fields for 11 ASes. We contacted IRINN and confirmed that it was a technical glitch that the system automatically set the IRINN nic-handle on the ASes delegated by IRINN if Whois server issue happened.

Six Pools Containing APNIC LIRs. We list the names of the APNIC LIRs here: *United Information Highway*; *Eastern Telecommunications Philippines, Inc.*; *SingTel Optus Pty Ltd*; *True Internet Co.,Ltd. and TRUE INTERNET*; *Communications & Communicate Nepal Pvt Ltd*; *VOCUS PTY LTD*.

References

1. Bgp.tools. https://bgp.tools/
2. The CAIDA AS Organizations Dataset. (Downloaded on July 1 (2022)). https://www.caida.org/data/as-organizations
3. CAIDA AS Rank. https://as-rank.caida.org/
4. Daily snapshots of PeeringDB data. (Downloaded on April 4 (2022)). https://publicdata.caida.org/datasets/peeringdb/
5. Global Routing Intelligence Platform (GRIP). https://grip.inetintel.cc.gatech.edu/
6. GTT acquired Interoute in 2018. https://www.gtt.net/us-en/media-center/press-releases/gtt-to-acquire-interoute/
7. The Internet registry system. https://www.ripe.net/participate/internet-governance/internet-technical-community/the-rir-system

8. Introduction to ARIN's databases. https://www.arin.net/resources/guide/account/database/
9. Mapping autonomous systems to organizations: CAIDA's inference methodology. https://www.caida.org/archive/as2org/
10. The merge of France IX and Rezopole A.D. https://www.linkedin.com/company/france-ix
11. The merger of Nutrien in 2018. https://www.nutrien.com/investors/news-releases/2018-agrium-and-potashcorp-merger-completed-forming-nutrien-leader-global/
12. News of the acquisition of CNS by Beeks. https://beeksgroup.com/news/beeks-acquires-vps-provider-cns/
13. News of the acquisition of Linode by Akamai. https://www.akamai.com/newsroom/press-release/akamai-completes-acquisition-of-linode
14. Process of ASN application of RIPE. https://www.ripe.net/manage-ips-and-asns/as-numbers/request-an-as-number
15. The public datasets of ISI ANT lab. https://ant.isi.edu/datasets/all.html
16. Template of APNIC Whois. https://www.apnic.net/manage-ip/using-whois/guide/aut-num/
17. Cai, X., Heidemann, J., Krishnamurthy, B., Willinger, W.: Towards an AS-to-organization Map. In: Proceedings of the 10th ACM SIGCOMM conference on Internet measurement, pp. 199–205 (2010)
18. Cai, X., Heidemann, J., Krishnamurthy, B., Willinger, W.: An organization-level view of the internet and its implications (extended), p. 26 (2012)
19. Dainotti, A., et al.: Lost in space: improving inference of ipv4 address space utilization. IEEE J. Sel. Areas Commun. **34**(6), 1862–1876 (2016)
20. Jin, Y., Scott, C., Dhamdhere, A., Giotsas, V., Krishnamurthy, A., Shenker, S.: Stable and practical AS relationship inference with ProbLink, pp. 581–598 (2019). https://www.usenix.org/conference/nsdi19/presentation/jin
21. Konte, M., Perdisci, R., Feamster, N.: ASwatch: An AS reputation system to expose bulletproof hosting ASes (2015)
22. Liu, J., Yang, B., Liu, J., Lu, Y., Zhu, K.: A method of route leak anomaly detection based on heuristic rules, pp. 662–666. Atlantis Press (2017). https://doi.org/10.2991/ammee-17.2017.127. https://www.atlantis-press.com/proceedings/ammee-17/25878482. iSSN: 2352-5401
23. Luckie, M., Huffaker, B., Dhamdhere, A., Giotsas, V., claffy, k.: AS relationships, customer cones, and validation. In: Proceedings of the 2013 conference on Internet measurement conference - IMC 2013, pp. 243–256. ACM Press, Barcelona, Spain (2013). https://doi.org/10.1145/2504730.2504735. https://dl.acm.org/citation.cfm?doid=2504730.2504735
24. Nemmi, E.N., Sassi, F., La Morgia, M., Testart, C., Mei, A., Dainotti, A.: The parallel lives of Autonomous Systems: ASN allocations vs. BGP. In: Proceedings of the 21st ACM Internet Measurement Conference, pp. 593–611. IMC 2021, Association for Computing Machinery, New York, NY, USA (2021). https://doi.org/10.1145/3487552.3487838. https://doi.org/10.1145/3487552.3487838
25. Padmanabhan, R., et al.: A multi-perspective view of Internet censorship in Myanmar. In: Proceedings of the ACM SIGCOMM 2021 Workshop on Free and Open Communications on the Internet, pp. 27–36 (2021)
26. Testart, C., Richter, P., King, A., Dainotti, A., Clark, D.: Profiling BGP serial hijackers: capturing persistent misbehavior in the global routing table. In: Proceedings of the Internet Measurement Conference on - IMC 2019, pp. 420–434. ACM Press, Amsterdam, Netherlands (2019). https://doi.org/10.1145/3355369.3355581. https://dl.acm.org/doi/10.1145/3355369.3355581

27. Zhao, X., et al.: An analysis of BGP multiple origin AS (MOAS) conflicts. In: Proceedings of the 1st ACM SIGCOMM Workshop on Internet Measurement, pp. 31–35 (2001)
28. Ziv, M., Izhikevich, L., Ruth, K., Izhikevich, K., Durumeric, Z.: ASdb: a system for classifying owners of autonomous systems. In: Proceedings of the 21st ACM Internet Measurement Conference, pp. 703–719. ACM, Virtual Event (2021). https://doi.org/10.1145/3487552.3487853. https://dl.acm.org/doi/10.1145/3487552.3487853

A Global Measurement of Routing Loops on the Internet

Abdulrahman Alaraj[1,3](✉), Kevin Bock[2], Dave Levin[2], and Eric Wustrow[1]

[1] University of Colorado, Boulder, USA
abdulrahman.alaraj@colorado.edu
[2] University of Maryland, College Park, USA
[3] Prince Sattam Bin Abdulaziz University, Al-Kharj, Saudi Arabia

Abstract. Persistent routing loops on the Internet are a common misconfiguration that can lead to packet loss, reliability issues, and can even exacerbate denial of service attacks. Unfortunately, obtaining a global view of routing loops is difficult. Distributed traceroute datasets from many vantage points can be used to find instances of routing loops, but they are typically sparse in the number of destinations they probe.

In this paper, we perform high-TTL traceroutes to the entire IPv4 Internet from a vantage point in order to enumerate routing loops and validate our results from a different vantage point. Our datasets contain traceroutes to two orders of magnitude more destinations than prior approaches that traceroute one IP per /24. Our results reveal over 24 million IP addresses with persistent routing loops on path, or approximately 0.6% of the IPv4 address space. We analyze the root causes of these loops and uncover new types of them that were unknown before. We also shed new light on their potential impact on the Internet.

We find over 320k /24 subnets with at least one routing loop present. In contrast, sending traceroutes only to the .1 address in each /24 (as prior approaches have done) finds only 26.5% of these looping subnets.

Our findings complement prior, more distributed approaches by providing a more complete view of routing loops in the Internet. To further assist in future work, we made our data publicly available.

1 Introduction

Routing loops[1] are the phenomenon in which packets never reach their destination because they loop among a sequence of routers. They are the result of network misconfigurations, inconsistencies, and errors in routing protocol implementations. In addition to being a pernicious threat to Internet reliability and reachability [13,29], routing loops can even enable or exacerbate denial of service attacks [3,26,41].

---

[1] The literature is split between referring to these as "routing loops" [13,26] or "forwarding loops" [41]. We use "routing loops" to differentiate them from loops that arise from application-level redirects [8].

A. Brunstrom et al. (Eds.): PAM 2023, LNCS 13882, pp. 373–399, 2023.
https://doi.org/10.1007/978-3-031-28486-1_16

Surprisingly little is known about the true global prevalence of routing loops. Although there have been several large, longitudinal, or distributed Internet measurements to detect routing loops [2,7,29,42], they tend to make several simplifying assumptions. For instance, one of the largest studies of routing loops of which we are aware [41] tracerouted only two IP addresses (.1 and a random one) in each of about 5.5M /24 subnets—the implicit assumption being that addresses within a /24 will largely experience the same routing behavior. Unfortunately, we are unaware of any prior work validating such assumptions.

In this paper, we perform a straightforward yet illuminating experiment: we traceroute the entire IPv4 address space from two vantage points. We discover over 24 million IP addresses with routing loops: over 21× more than two concurrent, distributed traceroute scans [7,33] put together.

What allows us to scan many more addresses than prior work is that we do not perform *full* traceroutes of all destination IP addresses. Our insight is that we only need to use higher TTL values to discover routing loops; lower TTL values can largely be avoided. We use Yarrp [2], a large-scale network traceroute tool, to traceroute all 3.7 billion routable IPv4 addresses for a range of 10 TTLs per IP. To parameterize our scanning rate, we performed experiments to evaluate routers' maximum ICMP response rate, to avoid missing routing loops due to router response rate limits. By using fewer TTLs and more addresses, we are able to perform, to our knowledge, the most comprehensive study of routing loops to date.

We analyze our resulting dataset to better understand the nature of routing loops on today's Internet. In particular, we explore routing loops' root causes, locations, size, and potential impact.

Our results justify full-Internet scanning to discover routing loops: 35% of the /24 subnets in which we discovered routing loops have at most *10 IP addresses* experiencing routing loops. In addition, scanning just the .1 address in each /24 would only discover 26.5% of the 320k unique routing-loop containing /24 subnets that we find when we scan every IP. Moreover, we discover that routing loops are not evenly distributed: within a /24 subnet, routing loops occur more often at higher last-octet values than low ones.

Collectively, our results demonstrate that the common strategy of scanning only one or two IP addresses [2,15,16,21,36,41] per /24 subnet is likely to miss many routing loops. In fact, we find that the common addresses that prior approaches sample—such as gateways (typically the .1 address of a /24)—have the *least* routing loops.

Contributions. We make the following contributions:

- We perform the largest traceroute study of the Internet to date from two vantage points, tracerouting over 3.7 billion IPv4 addresses.
- We analyze this dataset to understand the prevalence (Sect. 4) and structure (Sect. 5) of routing loops in today's Internet.
- We discover that sampling at the /24 subnet granularity is often insufficient to capture routing loops within the subnet.

– We compare our results with public distributed traceroute measurements, showing that we are able to detect 21× more looping destinations than prior efforts combined.
– We uncover a new type of routing loops, namely the transport-state dependent loops that can be abused for the TCP reflected amplification attacks.

To assist in future efforts, we made our tools and data publicly available at https://github.com/RoutingLoops.

Roadmap. The rest of this paper is structured as follows: In Sect. 2, we offer a concrete definition of persistent routing loops and analyze the rate at which one can traceroute networks without getting blocked. In Sect. 3, we describe our measurement methodology. In Sect. 4, we analyze the prevalence of routing loops and validate our dataset. Then, in Sect. 5, we analyze the resulting dataset to learn about the structure of routing loops, their causes and potential impact. We review related work in Sect. 6, describe ethical considerations in Sect. 7, and conclude in Sect. 8.

2 Experiment Design

Our general goal and approach are straightforward: identifying IPv4 addresses with persistent routing loops by running partial traceroutes to every IPv4 address on the Internet. Although conceptually simple, there are several complications to doing this experiment in practice. In this section, we will describe our methodology and our experiments we used to design this approach.

To issue traceroutes, we use a modified version of Yarrp [2], a traceroute tool designed to scan large networks. To our knowledge, we are the first to use Yarrp to scan every IPv4 address; we will describe our minor modifications in Sect. 3 that enable us to use Yarrp in this way.

2.1 What Constitutes a Persistent Routing Loop?

We define a destination d as having a routing loop if our probes do not reach d (even with TTL = 255) and we observe a router that appears at two different hops in the traceroute, separated by at least two hops. In other words, we must receive a response from the same router IP for two TTL values $t_1 < t_2$, such that $\Delta t = t_2 - t_1 > 2$. We perform further analysis of this definition in Sect. 4.

Requiring a small gap between repeated hops helps insulate us against router aliasing [35]: we observed traceroutes that had apparent repeated IPs in two sequential hops, but ultimately reached other routers or their endpoint in subsequent hops, indicating no routing loop.

Finally, to detect and eliminate transient routing loops [13,39] (e.g. an apparent routing loop caused by a network change or instability during our scans) from our dataset, we perform two consecutive Internet-wide scans 5 days apart. We apply the above routing loop definition, and take the intersection of destinations that have routing loops in both scans. We mark these destinations as having *persistent* routing loops on path.

2.2   Which TTLs Should We Scan?

Traditional traceroutes start by issuing TTL-limited probes with increasing TTL values (starting at $TTL = 1$) until either the end destination is reached or a maximum TTL value is hit. To identify routing loops, however, we do not need to send so many probes. Instead, we will issue probes with ten TTL values 246–255 (inclusive).

Probing an endpoint d with such high TTL values and receiving ICMP Time Exceeded Messages indicates a routing loop on path to d. It could also indicate that d is 246–255 hops away from our scanning machine, or that there exist routers on path to d that respond with ICMP Time Exceeded Messages even if $TTL \neq 0$; however, we believe both to be rare events.

Note that like the traceroute tool itself, this approach cannot detect true infinite routing loops [3]: loops amongst routers that do not decrement the TTL (as this will never generate ICMP Time Exceeded messages).

2.3   How Fast Can We Probe?

Many routers have *rate limits* on how fast they will respond with ICMP Time Exceeded messages. For tracerouting the Internet from a single vantage point, this could result in missing data: if we probe hop-sharing routes faster than their router's rate limit, those routers may only respond to a subset of our probes, which would cause our scan to miss hops and undercount routing loops.

To determine rate limits of routers, we wrote a Golang traceroute utility to send ICMP-eliciting probes to a sample of routers repeatedly at a specific rate, and observe the speed with which they respond. We selected a sample of 10,000 random IP addresses and sent probes with a TTL limit of 15 hops. We sent each IP address approximately 50,000 probes per second (about 22 mbps) for 1 s, and recorded the response rate we received. Our goal is to momentarily saturate the ICMP response rate limit of each router, allowing us to approximate its maximum response rate. To minimize interference between responses from routers, we scanned only 5 routers in parallel during our test.

Of the 10,000 target IPs we probed, 2803 (28%) had an on-path router that responded with an ICMP Time Exceeded message. In total, we observed 5361 unique router IPs[2]. The CDF of the maximum rate we received responses from these routers is shown in Fig. 2. We observe a median rate limit of about 2,300*pps* (about 1.7 mbps), with small but clear steps around likely popular configuration such as 1,000, 2,500 or 15,000*pps*. Over 99% of routers that respond at all will respond to at least 3*pps*.

To determine our send rate for scanning the Internet, we start with a goal of averaging 3*pps* to any individual router (the 99th percentile response rate) to maximize the chance we receive a response. We observed from preliminary scans that there are over 35,000 unique router IPs at each hop we scan between 10–25

---

[2] Many targets had multiple routers that responded, due to load-balancing, ECMP, or the varying paths different probe packets take to reach their destination.

hops from us. This means that for the 3.7 billion IPs we scan, we expect to hit each router on average 108,000 times each. If we want to send a probe to each one no more than 3 times a second, our scan should take approximately 36,000 s, which equates to a scan rate of $105 kpps$. We note that it is likely possible to scan much faster than this, as many routers will not respond to our probes at all, and higher TTLs will hit even fewer routers. Nonetheless, we conservatively scan at $100 kpps$ for our full IPv4 scans, which takes approximately 10 h per TTL value.

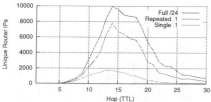

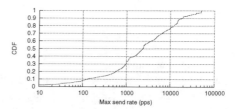

Fig. 1. Unique Router IPs per hop — We scanned 10,000 random /24 subnets for hops 1–30. For each /24, we scanned the full subnet (all 256 IPs) once (Full), as well as each gateway (.1 address) of these subnets 256 times (Repeated .1). For each hop, we count the number of unique router IPs we observe. We find that traceroutes to only the gateway (.1 address) in a given /24 fail to observe over 82% of router IPs beyond 14 hops (Single .1). This shows that scanning only a single address in a particular /24 subnet may not fully reveal all paths to addresses in that subnet. Note that the Repeated .1 scan used random destination ports.

Fig. 2. Maximum ICMP response rate — We scanned 10,000 random IPv4 addresses at a rate of $50,000 pps$ for 1 s each and observed the maximum response rate of ICMP Time Exceeded messages from the routers. The median rate was just over $2,300 pps$.

2.4   Can We Sample Subnets?

We initially hypothesized that we could significantly shorten our traceroute efforts by only scanning the gateway or a random IP per subnet. Many existing studies [2,5,15] adopt this hypothesis to only scan around 15 million IPs (one per /24) instead of 3.7 billion for a full IPv4 scan. However, we find that this hypothesis is incorrect, and that subnet level scans do not necessarily accurately represent a full IPv4 scan.

To evaluate this, we performed a short experiment using Yarrp: scanning a sample of 10,000 random /24 subnets in three different ways for TTLs (1–30) inclusive, one TTL value at a time. The goal of this experiment is to see if the gateway (.1 address) for each /24 returns a representative topology for the entire subnet.

Figure 1 shows the number of unique routers we discovered in both full /24 scans (2.56 million IPs total), and the scans for the common gateway address (.1) for each /24. In our full /24 scan, we discovered 9,990 unique router IPs at hop 14, but scanning the gateway (Single .1) address returned only 1,723 unique router IPs (17%).

We hypothesized this difference may be caused by small path variations due to different flows being load-balanced to different paths. To account for this possibility, we performed a repeated gateway scan, where we sent 256 probes to the gateway (.1) address for each /24 (Repeated .1). For this repeated scan, we disabled Paris tracerouting [1] by using different destination ports to maximize the paths our traceroutes would take. This increased the number of unique router IPs discovered (e.g. 7,812 at hop 14), but still less than the number found in our full /24 scan.

These results motivate us to scan the entire IPv4 address space to obtain an accurate view of routing loops. We further evaluate this motivation using our results in Sect. 4.

3   Scanning Methodology

Informed by the experiments in the previous section, here we detail our scanning methodology. We will issue TCP probes to every IPv4 address with the ACK flag set to port 80, with TTL values from 246 to 255 (inclusive).

3.1   Using Yarrp

While Yarrp [2] is designed to traceroute large networks, we had to make several small modifications to allow it to scan *every* IPv4 address. Internally, Yarrp has an "Entire Internet" mode, designed to handle scanning large networks. Unfortunately, the number of bits available in this mode limits the possible permutation size for scanning to just 1 probe per /24 subnet; outside this mode, Yarrp's total permutation size is limited to a domain *(IPs × max_TTL)* of size 2^{32}, still too small to scan the entire IPv4 Internet. We also discovered and fixed an integer overflow bug that prevented Yarrp from sending probes with $TTL > 127$.

To address these limitations, we provided Yarrp with a shuffled list of all 3.7 billion routable IPv4 addresses in a 50 GB file, and had it send probes to a single TTL at a time. We repeated this 10 times, for each TTL value in (246–255) inclusive. We limited Yarrp's sending rate to 100*kpps*. As Yarrp validates and logs all of the ICMP Time Exceeded messages it receives, we can construct partial traceroutes for all IP addresses for the TTL hops we scanned.

Yarrp implements Paris traceroute [1] technique by calculating the source port as a function of the destination IP address. This technique maintains the 5-tuple for every destination probed regardless of the used TTL value. This leads to a more stable routing path that is less affected by per-flow load balancers.

3.2 Vantage Points

We performed two full IPv4 scans during the month of April 2022. The first started on the 14th and completed on the 18th. The second started on the 19th and completed on the 23rd. Both scans are from our vantage point[3] in the University of Colorado Boulder (AS104).

To validate our results, we used a secondary vantage point[4] in the University of Michigan (AS36375) to run two additional consecutive scans, running during the same period as the scans from VP 1.

4   The Prevalence of Routing Loops

We begin our analysis by investigating the number and persistence of routing loops in the Internet. We also validate our use of Yarrp by performing traceroute on each of the destinations we identified as routing loops.

4.1   How Many Routing Loops Are There?

In total, we find over 24 M looping IP addresses that persisted for two consecutive scans from VP 1.

For each scan from VP 1, we received ICMP Time Exceeded messages from over 500K unique router IPs, for over 29 million unique destinations from the 3.7 billion destinations we probed. In other words, our probes did not trigger ICMP Time Exceeded messages from the on-path routers for the majority of the 3.7 billion destinations we probed, and only triggered ICMP Time Exceeded messages from at least an on-path router for 29 million unique destinations. Of these 29 million destinations, only 24 million qualified as experiencing persistent routing loops based on our definition in Sect. 2.1. Over two thirds of the non-qualifying routing loops contain a single, non-repeating router IP; and only around 23,500 contain 10 unique router IPs, suggesting that the TTL range we scan (10 hops) is sufficient to discover most routing loops on the Internet.

We also investigate how tweaking the definition of routing loops changes the number that we find. Recall that our existing definition requires that a router IP appears at (at least) two distinct hops that are more than two hops apart. We explore the impact that "two hops apart" has in Table 1. We do not find a significant difference in the number of loops found as we vary to fewer or more hops apart, suggesting that the definition of routing loops is generally robust to slight changes.

---

[3] We refer to this vantage point as VP 1 for the rest of the paper.
[4] We refer to this vantage point as VP 2 for the rest of the paper.

Table 1. Results by applying different routing loop definitions — We apply different routing loop definitions on the reconstructed traceroutes for each scan from VP 1 to find persistent routing loops. Note that our scans spanned 10 hops.

Loop definition	1st scan	2nd scan	Persistent routing loops
$\Delta t > 0$	27.07 M	27.22 M	25.66 M
$\Delta t > 1$	27.02 M	27.15 M	25.59 M
$\Delta t > 2$	26.26 M	26.36 M	**24.78 M**
$\Delta t > 3$	26.17 M	26.25 M	24.66 M
$\Delta t > 4$	24.99 M	25.09 M	23.45 M

4.2 Are These Really Loops?

To verify that the results we find from the Yarrp scans are not artifacts of our modified version of Yarrp, we used the `traceroute` utility to run TCP ACK traceroutes. This utility, however, is not designed for Internet-wide scanning: it has long timeouts, is not designed for scaling to scanning IPs simultaneously, and generally limited in speed. However, it does provide a useful check against our results.

To deal with traceroute's performance limitations, we limited its use to validating the list of 24 million looping IPs we found from VP 1 using Yarrp. We similarly limited it to the TTL range 246–255, a sending rate of 500 pps, and a timeout of 500 ms. These parameters allow us to scan the 24 million IPs in a reasonable time, but note the aggressive timeouts may result in missed hops.

Using our same routing loop definition in Sect. 2.1, traceroute confirms 18 million IPs (out of 24 million) appear to be loops. We ran follow-up traceroutes with longer timeouts on a random sample of IPs found by Yarrp but not by traceroute, and found about 75% of them do have loops, suggesting that overall traceroute confirms over 93% of the loops we find. We believe the remaining difference is largely due to network churn (the traceroute scans happened a month after our original Yarrp scans).

Overall, we believe that while there may be loops that are transient (only present temporarily or for short periods of time), the vast majority of the loops that we identify are indeed persistent routing loops.

4.3 Do These Loops Persist Across Time/Other Vantage Points?

Perspective from a Second Vantage Point. We performed two consecutive, full-Internet scans (TTLs 246–255) using Yarrp from VP 1. Simultaneously, we performed two additional scans from VP 2 which is in a different AS in the United States (located over 1,000 miles away).

Despite different locations, we find a significant overlap between the persistent routing loops found by our two vantage points. Table 2 shows the number of loops found in each scan. We apply the same routing loop definition in Sect. 2.1

Table 2. Scans Results — We count the number of IP addresses with routing loops along their path. We consider a routing loop to be persistent from a vantage point if it exists in two consecutive scans from the respective vantage point. Note that 1st Scan and 2nd Scan are back-to-back consecutive scans run from each vantage point during the same period of time.

Dataset	1st scan	2nd scan	1st scan $\cap$ 2nd scan	(Jaccard index)
VP 1	26.26 M	26.36 M	**24.78 M**	(0.8898)
VP 2	25.97 M	25.95 M	**24.59 M**	(0.8995)
VP 1 $\cap$ VP 2	24.46 M	24.47 M	**23.28 M**	(0.9076)

to find persistent loops, and find over 23 million persistent loops in common between both vantage points. Each vantage point also finds on the order of 5% of looping IPs that the other does not: VP 1 found 1.5 M loops that VP 2 did not, while VP 2 found 1.3 M not seen by VP 1.

We find that these relatively small differences are partly due to noise: for each of the 1.5 M (1.3 M) IPs discovered only by VP 1 (VP 2), we re-ran a follow-up Yarrp scan from VP 2 (VP 1). Each vantage point found over 400 K loops that it originally missed, suggesting that network noise (e.g. packet drops or ICMP rate limits) prevented us from finding these loops originally.

Perspective from Previous Scans. In addition to our two consecutive scans in April 2022, we also compare our results from two preliminary scans in October 2021 from VP 1. At the time, these scans find similar results as our later scans (roughly 24 million IPs), and we observe 19 million destination IPs that have routing loops along their paths both in the October 2021 and April 2022 scans, suggesting that these loops may be persistent over multiple months (though without longitudinal scans, we cannot rule out the possibility that these loops were fixed and later reappeared).

4.4   How Do Existing Datasets Compare?

We analyzed routing loops present in the RIPE and CAIDA Ark datasets using the same routing loop definition in Sect. 2.1. This entails that we enforce the following requirement: for a destination in the RIPE dataset to be considered experiencing a routing loop, it must exhibit a looping behavior in two consecutive scanning windows, where each window is 5 consecutive days long. We enforce this requirement to exclude transient loops and maintain consistency with our routing loop definition in Sect. 2.1. Note that we confirmed that over 98% of destinations probed in the RIPE dataset are probed in both scanning windows at least once; however, these probes are not necessarily from the same source nor necessarily traversing the same path. We do not enforce this requirement on CAIDA Ark dataset since its random nature of scanning does not permit this kind of validation during the same period of time. This means that some

Table 3. Traceroute Results — We perform partial traceroute scans (TTLs 246–255) to the entire IPv4 Internet and compare the routing loops we discover from VP 1 to other distributed traceroute datasets.

Dataset	Traceroutes	Unique destinations	Unique router IPs	Looping destinations	(%)
This paper	7,400,351,422	3,700,175,711	512,785	24,783,989	(0.66%)
RIPE atlas [33]	977,156,702	848,348	709,675	41,196	(4.85%)
CAIDA ark [7]	213,333,652	206,007,571	2,645,943	1,137,830	(0.55%)

of the routing loops we find in the CAIDA Ark dataset could potentially be transient loops. Therefore we do not compare the persistent routing loops from our Internet-wide scans with it. Table 3 compares our dataset with these three datasets. Note that the number of unique router IPs in the table excludes IPs in the RFC 1918. Note that the RIPE Atlas probes do not provide any insight on the types or codes of the ICMP messages in their traceroutes. Therefore we assume that all ICMP messages in the RIPE Atlas dataset are ICMP Time Exceeded messages, unless we manually observe otherwise. We find that perspective plays an important role in finding routing loops: For the scans dataset from VP 1, we only observe around 43% of the 41,196 routing loops in the RIPE Atlas dataset.

We manually analyze a small random sample of the persistent routing loops that are found in the RIPE Atlas dataset but not in our Internet-wide scans for the same period of time. We performed manual traceroutes from VP 1 and did not observe routing loops for almost the entire sample, suggesting these are either loops that our scans did not originally identify and yet they resolved after our scanning window, or merely not visible from VP 1. For the few ones in the random sample that looped with manual traceroutes but did not exhibit a looping behavior in our dataset, we find that their neighboring IPs in their /24s do in fact exist in our dataset, suggesting that we potentially missed these loops due to ICMP rate limiting or packet loss.

4.5   How Many Unique Routing Loops Are There?

We find over 24 million distinct IPv4 destinations with routing loops from VP 1, but many of these loops may be caused by a single misconfigured router or subnet, and could be considered as part of the same loop. For instance, if every IP address in a /24 subnet has a routing loop involving the same routers, it is natural to cluster these IPs together into a single loop, and say this single loop affects 256 addresses, rather than to consider it as 256 unique loops.

In this section, we investigate *clustering* the loops we found from VP 1 by grouping destination IP addresses into subnets, and comparing the routers involved in the loops.

Grouping Destination IPs into Subnets. While ideally a subnet (e.g. a /24) that has a single loop would show loops for all (e.g. 256) addresses, we must account for missed packets in our dataset, due to rate limits, packet drops, or other errors.

For instance, we may find that in a fully-looping /24, we only observed 230 IPs that looped, but would nonetheless want to cluster these IPs into a single /24 (and not 230 distinct /32s, or some other fragmentation of the subnet).

To do this, we heuristically group looping IPs into the largest-containing (CIDR prefix) subnet that has more than a threshold fraction of IP addresses exhibiting a loop. For instance, if we set a threshold of 50%, we would label a /24 as a loop if that subnet contained more than 128 addresses that exhibit looping behavior.

Clustering Based on Routers Involved. Another way to group individual loops together is to look at the router IPs involved in the loops. For instance if two IPs have loops involving the same pattern of routers, they may be caused by the same misconfiguration and clustered together. A naive approach to clustering would be to look for exact matches of routers, but this could easily miss clusters due to router aliasing or load balancing. While Paris-style traceroutes help keep a route stable to an individual IP address, it cannot help when comparing traceroutes to two distinct destinations. For instance, one IP address may see a loop between router A and router B, while a second IP address in the same subnet sees a loop between router A and router C due to load balancing, despite this being caused by the same misconfiguration.

To account for this, we cluster two loops together if their looping traceroute for TTLs 246–255 share a single router. Note that this can cause loops to cluster transitively: loop A-B would cluster with loop A-C, which could cluster with loop C-D. This can help handle cases where one traceroute in a subnet did not receive a response from one router due to packet loss or rate limiting. Because we only look at routers that responded in high TTLs (i.e. likely involved in the loop), we avoid clustering all traceroutes together due to routers that simply appear in many traceroutes from our vantage point (e.g. our own immediate upstream routers, or core routers in well-connected transit ASes).

Using our subnet grouping and clustering criteria, we group our 24 million looping IPs into **270,450** clusters, which contain a total of 1.8 million subnets (at a 50% threshold). Figure 4 shows the distribution of number of subnets and hops in these clusters. Most of the clusters we find have only a single subnet in them, and involve only 1 or 2 router hops in the loop.

For instance, one of the largest clusters we find comprises 65425 destination IPs, all in 159.193.0.0/16 (so we observe over 99.8% of this subnet looping). These loops involve just two hops (78.77.181.70 and 78.77.181.71).

Figure 3 shows the distribution of largest subnets we can group into, based on two thresholds of the fraction of IPs in a subnet that must be a loop to consider the subnet a loop as a whole (>50% and >75%). It also shows the distribution of subnets when we also cluster based on routers involved. The similarity of results for each of these methods suggests that it is a robust way to coalesce loops into clusters.

We find subnet groupings of nearly every size smaller than /16, suggesting that loops are not always a given size (e.g. /24). We also find many loops that are not near or similar to others, affecting only a *single IP address* (/32).

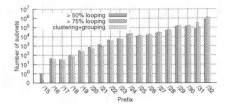

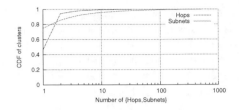

Fig. 3.   Coalesced   subnets — We examine the largest encompassing subnets of the looping IP addresses we find from VP 1. We group a set of looping IPs into their subnet if larger than a threshold fraction of the subnet's IPs exhibit looping behavior (we present 50% and 75% thresholds here). We also cluster based on the routers involved, and find similar results. We find a range of subnets that loop, from entire /16s to individual IP addresses (/32).

Fig. 4. Cluster sizes — Using clustering of loops by routers (hops) involved, and grouping by subnets, we discover 270K clusters. The majority of these clusters comprise only a single subnet, and have 1 or 2 hops involved. This suggests our clustering is accurate, and can help identify specific network misconfigurations that result in large subnets with looping IPs.

If we were to traceroute only at the subnet level, we would likely miss these loops, as discuss in Sect. 5.5.

4.6   Are We Under Counting Loops?

We analyze the scans results from VP 1 and find that we receive at least one ICMP Time Exceeded message for 29.7 M and 30 M unique destination IPs probed for the first and second scans, respectively. For the first scan, we label 3.4M reconstructed traceroutes as non-qualifying routing loops (based on our routing loop definition in Sect. 2.1), of which 2.5M have a single non-repeating router IP and 3.9K have 10 unique and non-repeating router IPs. For the second scan, we label 3.7M destination IPs based on their reconstructed traceroutes as non-qualifying routing loops, of which 2.6M have a single non-repeating router IP and 19.6K have 10 unique and non-repeating router IPs. These small numbers (3.9K and 19.6K) of routing loops with a size of more than 10 router IPs suggest that scanning the Internet for more than 10 TTL hops has diminishing returns on finding more routing loops.

5   The Structure of Routing Loops

In this section, we investigate the nature of the routing loops themselves by asking: where do we observe them, which addresses are affected, what are the root causes, and what impact might they have?

5.1   What Causes These Loops?

We adopt the general classification proposed by Xia et al. [41] and further expand
on it. We classify the routing loops we find from VP 1 into two main categories
based on the involvement of the destination AS in the loop. We argue that
this classification helps attribute the root-cause of these loops, because once
packets reach the destination AS, they are subject to the routing policies and
(mis)configurations of the destination AS. We characterize the involvement of
an AS in a routing loop as follows: Given a traceroute for a destination IP for
hops 246–255 that experiences a routing loop, if there exists at least one router
IP address that responds with an ICMP Time Exceeded message, then the AS
of that IP is involved in the loop.

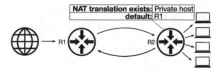

(a) We find some routing loops are
caused by misconfigured NAT devices,
which send traffic back upstream if
there is no NAT translation for the incoming packet.

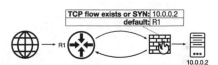

(b) We find some routing loops are
caused by middleboxes that only allow
network traffic for active TCP flows,
and forward any inactive flows back
upstream.

(c) The common misconfiguration of
network announcemnts, causing packets destined for certain subnets to
be errouneously forwarded back upstream.

Fig. 5. Examples of three types of routing loops in our dataset. We discovered the root
cause for some routing loops by directly working with network operators of affected
networks.

Loops Involving the Destination AS. We observe over 79% (19.7M) of the
routing loops we find involve the destination AS, indicating that these loops
occur at the edge of the network and closer to their destination IPs. We reached
out to several network operators for networks in which we discovered loops to
ask about their root cause. Between these discussions, and additional follow-up
experiments, we find several types of misconfigurations at the root of the looping
behavior.

First, we find a common misconfiguration at the destination AS in which ingress network traffic destined to non-allocated subnets (where the looping IP is in) is not null-routed, but rather forwarded back to an upstream provider or another router at the destination AS, causing the looping behavior. This common misconfiguration has been studied [24,41] in the past and has been shown to cause routing loops on the Internet. Figure 5 (c) shows an illustration of this kind of loops.

Traceroute to 212.106.173.213 (AS15744):	Traceroute to 144.208.106.43 (AS394994):	Traceroute to 200.205.174.82 (AS10429):	Traceroute to 180.178.163.59 (AS141361):
hop hop_ip	**hop hop_ip**	**hop hop_ip**	**hop hop_ip**
246 212.106.159.26 (AS15744)	246 38.110.25.62 (AS17077)	246 81.173.106.94 (AS12956)	246 221.120.208.150 (AS9557)
247 212.106.159.25 (AS15744)	247 38.88.11.58 (AS174)	247 *	247 *
248 212.106.159.26	248 38.110.25.62	248 *	248 221.120.208.150
249 212.106.159.25	249 38.88.11.58	249 152.255.191.213 (AS26599)	249 *
250 212.106.159.26	250 38.110.25.62	250 187.100.39.54 (AS27699)	250 221.120.208.150
251 212.106.159.25	251 38.88.11.58	251 189.44.183.251 (AS10429)	251 *
252 212.106.159.26	252 38.110.25.62	252 72.246.185.2 (AS12222)	252 221.120.208.150
253 212.106.159.25	253 38.88.11.58	253 187.120.7.53 (AS22381)	253 *
254 212.106.159.26	254 38.110.25.62	254 *	254 *
255 212.106.159.25	255 38.88.11.58	255 81.173.106.94 (AS12956)	255 *
(a) - Within dst AS	**(c) - No dst AS. Involves provider AS**	**(e) Involves 6 Ases**	**(g) No relationships can be found**
Traceroute to 45.162.174.92 (AS268527):	Traceroute to 45.224.118.229 (AS264836):	Traceroute to 156.240.40.21:	Traceroute to 198.188.178.137 (AS2152):
hop hop_ip	**hop hop_ip**	**hop hop_ip**	**hop hop_ip**
246 45.162.172.106 (AS268527)	246 84.16.11.125 (AS12956)	246 156.240.40.21	246 209.147.58.38 (AS2920)
247 187.103.120.213 (AS14840)	247 *	247 *	247 *
248 187.103.120.178 (AS14840)	248 84.16.11.125	248 156.240.40.21	248 209.147.58.38
249 45.162.172.106	249 *	249 *	249 *
250 187.103.120.213	250 84.16.11.125	250 *	250 209.147.58.38
251 187.103.120.178	251 *	251 156.240.40.21	251 209.147.58.37
252 45.162.172.106	252 84.16.11.125	252 156.240.40.21	252 209.147.58.38
253 187.103.120.213	253 *	253 156.240.40.21	253 *
254 187.103.120.178	254 84.16.11.125	254 *	254 209.147.58.38
255 45.162.172.106	255 *	255 *	255 *
(b) - Between dst AS and provider AS	**(d) - Dst AS in customer-cone of AS12956**	**(f) Involves the end-point IP**	**(h) Loops at the customer AS**

Fig. 6. Traceroute examples — We show a sample of traceroutes for the persistent routing loops we find from VP 1.

Second, we find misconfigured NAT devices in which ingress network traffic that has no translation on the NAT device is forwarded based on a configured rule instead of being dropped. The traffic, after being forwarded back upstream, eventually encounters the same NAT policy that forwards it again, creating the looping behavior. We discovered this root cause by speaking to network operators of a university network in which we discovered over 1,000 routing loops. From a network scanning perspective, there are no distinct characteristics that distinguish these loops from loops caused by the previous misconfiguration, even though they have different underlying causes. Figure 5 (a) shows an illustration of this kind of loops.

Third, transport-state dependant. We find that misconfigured middleboxes that filter traffic for TCP applications can also cause looping behavior. These middleboxes, instead of dropping outstanding TCP packets that are not part of any active TCP flow or do not initiate a new one, forward the packets based on a configured rule. These forwarded packets are then sent back towards their destination ultimately creating the looping behavior. A distinguishing feature of these routing loops is that they are dependent on the *transport state*, and that some destinations that exhibit a looping behavior for TCP ACK packets are reachable or do not exhibit any looping behavior for TCP SYN packets. To find the transport-state dependent loops, we run a full Internet scan using Yarrp with TCP SYN packets. We then calculated the set difference between the persistent loops in our original ACK scan and this SYN scan. We find over 6M looping IP addresses that did not exhibit routing loops with SYN packets. These types of routing loops can only be discovered by ACK scans (or any outstanding TCP packet that is not a SYN). Figure 5 (b) shows an illustration of this kind of loops.

Fourth, a misconfigured destination in which packets reach the destination IP but are not delivered due to some unclear misconfiguration at the destination. We observe 27K destinations in our dataset that exhibit this misconfiguration. Figure 6 (f) shows an example of this kind of loops.

Loops Not Involving the Destination AS. Over 21% (5M) of the persistent routing loops we discover from VP 1 do not involve the destination AS. Using CAIDA's dataset of AS classification [6], we classify the relationship between the AS(es) in the loop and the AS of the destination. We do not investigate the root-cause of these loops and leave this to future work.

No Apparent Relationship. For 5.81% (291K), we cannot find any relationships between the destination AS and the ASes involved in the loop based on the traceroutes in our dataset. Figure 6 (g) shows an example of this kind of loops.

Customer Relationship. We find 79.3% (3.97M) have at least one router IP belonging to an AS to which the AS of the destination is a customer. For 4.86% (244K), the destination AS is in the customer cone of one of the ASes involved. Figure 6 (d) shows an example of this kind of loops. After analyzing the relationships in that loop, we conjecture that our odd TTL probes expire at an AS (AS267699) to which the destination AS is a customer. Whereas our even TTL probes expire at an AS (AS12956) to which AS267699 (the provider AS to the destination AS) is a customer.

Provider Relationship. For 4.75% (238K), we find that the destination AS is a provider to one of the ASes involved in the loop. Figure 6 (h) shows an example of this kind of loops.

Peering Relationship. For 1.51% (76K) of loops, we find that the destination AS is in a peering relationship with at least one AS in the loop. And for 0.07% (3842), we find one of the ASes in the loop to be in the customer cone of the destination AS. For instance, the loop to 83.234.188.233 (AS20485) involves the router IP 109.196.208.113 (AS50439) which is in the customer cone of the destination AS.

No AS Announced. Finally, for around 3.66% (183K), we find that the router IPs in the loop are not announced by any AS, therefore we cannot infer any relationships

We note that it is possible that the destination AS of a given looping IP is, in fact, involved in its routing loop, but the destination AS's routers limit their

ICMP Time Exceeded responses, therefore obscuring its involvement based on the traceroutes in our dataset. It is also possible that the probes to the looping destination IPs reach their destination ASes, but are then forwarded at the layer two level (e.g., via managed switches) to an upstream provider before reaching a border router at the destination AS. In such a case, we cannot infer the involvement of the destination AS. Figure 6 (c) shows a potential example of this kind of loop, where probes never reach a router at the destination AS and rather loop between the AS's provider and another on-path AS.

5.2   Where Are These Routing Loops?

Topologically. Using the April 17, 2022 RouteViews dataset [28], we analyze the Autonomous System Number (ASN) of each of the destination IPs as well as the routers involved in the persistent routing loops we discovered from VP 1. Although other router ownership inference approaches [23] provide a better accuracy, we used the IP-to-ASN mapping approach for simplicity. We exclude router IPs that are not announced by any AS (which amount to only 0.74% of router IPs in our dataset).

Figure 7 shows the distribution of how many ASes are involved in each routing loop. While over 91% of loops contain routers within a single AS, we find many loops that include multiple ASes. For instance, we find 3 routing loops with as many as 6 distinct ASes involved in the loop. Figure 6 (e) shows one such example, involving routers from Akamai (in Miami, FL, USA), multiple ASes of Telefonica Brazil (in Sao Paulo, BR), and intermediate routers from GlobeNet.

We find that over 25% of all routing loops have at least one of the involved routers in a different AS than the destination of our probe. Meanwhile, 0.11% of routing loops *involve the destination IP itself* in the routing loop, as shown in Fig. 6 (f). We performed follow up traceroutes on a small sample of these addresses (e.g. 46.8.120.192 and 90.83.38.250) and confirmed that the round trip time for each probing packet increases with higher TTL values for these peculiar routing loop cases, which suggests a looping behavior.

Geographically. Using the April 2022 MaxMind [25] dataset, we analyze the geolocation of the destination IPs in the persistent routing loops we found from VP 1. We find 19% are in the US, followed by 6% in each of India, Brazil and Japan, followed by 5% in China.

We also find that 5% of the loops have a destination IP address in a different country than at least one of the routers in the loop. However, we note that this may simply be due to geolocation error: prior work has shown that geolocating router IPs can be complex and leads to inaccuracies [11]. We leave correcting this problem to future work, such as potentially using router hostnames to infer location [20].

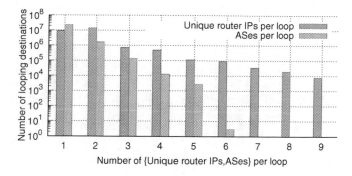

Fig. 7. Routing loops sizes and the number of ASes they span—For each persistent routing loop, we count the number of unique router IPs, and the number of unique Autonomous System Numbers by resolving the routers' IP addresses to Autonomous System Numbers using recent datasets.

5.3 How Large are Routing Loops?

Routing loops can range in size from one repeated router to containing many routers in a repeating loop. However, we measure the size of the routing loops in our dataset based on the number of unique router IPs, meaning that a routing loop could have multiple router IPs in it, yet belonging to a lesser number of physical routers. We do not perform router dealiasing [35] techniques on our dataset.

The majority (57%) of routing loops we find contain two unique router IP addresses, a result corroborated by prior work [41]. We also find larger loops—up to 9 unique IP addresses—in a small percentage of cases (0.03%). Figure 7 shows the distribution of loop sizes observed.

5.4 How Many Loops Do /24 Subnets Experience?

We find that routing-loop containing /24 subnets are limited to a small number of looping IPs in them. For each /24 subnet, we counted the number of target IP addresses that contained a routing loop in the corresponding traceroute. We expected that if a /24 subnet contained a routing loop to one IP address, it would also contain routing loops to many other IP addresses in the same subnet. Figure 8 shows the distribution of looping IP addresses per routing-loop containing /24 subnet, ranging from 1–256 loops. Over half of the /24 subnets that contained a routing loop had fewer than 25 looping IP addresses (out of 256). While it is possible that some subnets only responded to a subset of our probes, our scanning rate should have had each /24 receive a packet from us every 2 min on average, well under the ICMP rate limits for most routers (see Fig. 2).

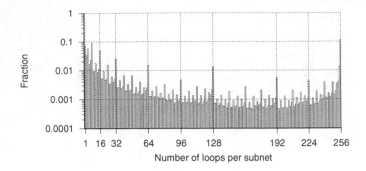

Fig. 8. Loops per /24 subnet — For each /24 subnet, we count the number of destination IP addresses whose path showed a routing loop. 35% of subnets had at most 10 IP addresses that had a loop along their path, and only about 19% had over 200 IP addresses. This demonstrates that subnet sampling is likely to miss routing loops.

5.5   Which Addresses Have Routing Loops?

A natural hypothesis is that scanning well-known addresses within a /24 subnet, such as the .1 address (e.g. 10.0.0.1), is as likely to discover routing loops as scanning other addresses. Indeed, many other studies rely on probing or scanning the .1 address of each /24, and assuming that routing topologies are largely consistent at the /24 level [2,16,21,36,41].

However, we find that this is not the case in our analysis of routing loops. Figure 9 shows the distribution of routing loops broken down by the last octet of the destination IP address. The .1 addresses reveal the *least* number of routing loops, 21% less than the maximum last octet (.255). This suggests that the .1 last octet does not act as a good *sample* for finding routing loops. This result is corroborated by prior work [10] where the authors showed that the .1 last octet is the most *responsive* last octet in an Internet census, suggesting that it is less likely to find routing loops at such addresses.

We find a general trend that higher octets are more likely to contain routing loops than lower octets, with noticeable exceptional dips after (sums of) powers of two (e.g. 64, 128, 192). The .0 octet also has, unexpectedly, a high number of routing loops.

We do not know for certain why this trend exists, but hypothesize that it may be due to the common pattern of IP allocation [10]. IP addresses are often allocated from the bottom of a subnet incrementally, and it is possible that router misconfigurations that default-route unallocated addresses may lead to more loops on higher last-octet addresses compared to the bottom of a subnet. In addition, the last address (e.g. .255 in a /24) may correspond to the broadcast address, either receiving special treatment with routers or getting sent to more devices that might retransmit the packet in a loop.

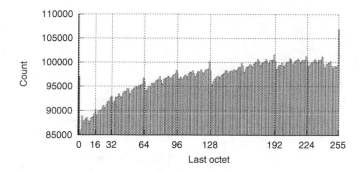

Fig. 9. Last octet distribution — We count the number of looping IP addresses for each last octet (e.g. 1.2.3.x). The .1 address contains the least number of routing loops (85,254), while the .255 contains the most (106,950), likely due to being a common broadcast address. (Note the y-axis does not start at 0)

How Many IPs per Subnet are Needed to Find Looping Subnets? A natural follow-up question is if there is any sample (short of scanning all 256 addresses) of a /24 that can be probed to find most loops?

Our dataset identifies over 320k unique /24 subnets that contain routing loops. Sending probes to only the .255 last octet in all /24 networks would have identified just over 33% of these subnets-containing loops. Adding additional last octets would help find more, but as Fig. 10 shows, it would take over 45 IPs probed per /24 to discover over 90% of the routing-loop containing /24 subnets that we find when scanning all IPs. We believe this result justifies scanning all addresses, and not sampling a handful of IPs per subnet.

5.6 Do These Loops Matter?

Prior work has already shown that routing loops can have an impact on network attacks. In 2021, researchers discovered that middleboxes could be weaponized to launch reflected amplification attacks, and that routing loops could be abused to make the attack more damaging [3]. An attacker launches the attack by spoofing their source IP address to that of their victim and sending a packet sequence that contains a request for some forbidden resource. When the middlebox responds to the seemingly forbidden request (such as by sending a block page), it will send this response to the victim, effectively amplifying the attacker's traffic. The authors found that if a vulnerable middlebox is within a *routing loop*, the middlebox can be re-triggered each time the packets circle the routing loop, significantly improving the amplification factor for the attacker (up to *infinite* amplification for infinite routing loops). In this regard alone, we believe that trying to identify routing loops is an important goal. Note that [3] examined the top 1 million amplifying hosts (by number of packets sent) from their SYN; PSH+ACK scan to identify which ones have routing loops along their path. We, however, approach this differently.

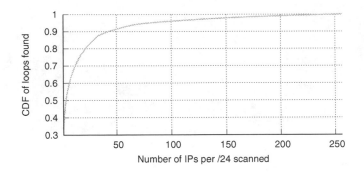

Fig. 10. Finding Loops by sampling — We measured how many unique /24 subnets that contain loops can be found as a function of the number of last-octets needed to be scanned. For instance, by only scanning the `.255`, `.127`, `.0`, and `.191` last octets (the top 4 in our dataset), one could identify over 51% of the /24 subnets that contained routing loops (compared to scanning all last octets). However, it would take scanning over 45/256 IPs per /24 to discover over 90% of unique /24s containing loops.

After we scanned the entire IPv4 Internet from VP 1 using `ACK` packets and found over 24 M destinations experiencing persistent routing loops, we now ask the question of how many of these routing loops can be weaponized in a TCP reflected amplification attack. We discussed in Sect. 5.1 that some routing loops are transport-state dependant and that scanning the IPv4 Internet with `ACK` packets reveals additional 6 M routing loops that cannot be discovered with a `SYN` scan.

We performed two *forbidden_scans*[5] on the 24 M looping destinations using two different packet sequences, namely a single `PSH+ACK`, and a `SYN` followed by `PSH+ACK` (`SYN; PSH+ACK`).

We first performed the `PSH+ACK` single packet scan. We found 273,201 looping destinations to be true amplifiers with an average amplification rate of 386.73, a median of 2.46 and a maximum of 1,414,267. We note that routing loops with an amplification rate of $\geq$ 100 are concentrated at 6601 destinations from 119 different ASes in 13 different countries.

Second, we performed the `SYN; PSH+ACK` scan. We found 1,089,457 looping destinations to be true amplifiers with an average amplification rate of 4.44, a median of 1.02 and a maximum of 1204.37.

This shows that finding and exploiting the transport-state dependant loops renders TCP reflected amplification attacks more effective.

In addition to this, we explore an avenue of the potential impact of routing loops that, to our knowledge, has not been studied before: are there any (named) services behind the destinations that experience routing loops? To answer this question, we reached out to a few AS operators for some of the looping IPs in our dataset to draw their attention to these loops and obtain ground-truth information about the root-causes of them. We received a response from a university

---

[5] https://github.com/breakerspace/weaponizing-censors.

network engineering team detailing the cause of the loops in their network. We elaborated on the root-cause of these loops in Sect. 5.1. Based on the nature of these NAT-related loops, the looping IPs in this case do not have services that otherwise could have been reachable, since the IPs are used to translate internal addresses to external, public ones. We do not know how prevalent this kind of loops is, as they do not have distinguishing characteristics. For our correspondence with other AS operators, we unfortunately have not received any response.

In an attempt to find whether any domain name resolves to a looping IP in our dataset, we used ZDNS[6] to resolve the top 5 M domain names in the tranco list [31]. We found 1256 domain names that resolve to 719 looping IPs in the dataset from our ACK scan from VP 1. Then using ZMap, we ran a SYN scan on these 719 IPs and found that 400 of them respond with SYN;ACK indicating that they do not exhibit any looping behavior when scanned with SYN packets. We also manually browsed a sample of the domains behind these 400 IPs and were able to reach and view their web content as if no loops existed along their paths. After further examination, we found that these 400 IPs experience the transport-state dependant kind of loops that we discussed in Sect. 5.1. Since the web content for the domains behind the 400 transport-state dependant looping IPs is reachable and browse-able, the impact of their loops can be dismissed; however, this kind of loop consumes their network resources unnecessarily and can be used against these domains to disrupt their service.

6 Related Work

Our work extends prior work primarily by probing many more destination IP addresses, uncovering many more routing loops than previously found, uncovering new types of routing loops that to our knowledge have not previously been known, and discovering that IP addresses within the same /24 can experience different routing loop behavior. We compare to prior work in terms of how we find routing loops, and what our findings reveal.

Identifying Routing Loops. Our overall approach to detecting routing loops—looking for repeated entries in a traceroute—is well-established in prior literature. To name a few: Paxson [29] ran periodic traceroutes between 27 sites and looked for IP addresses repeated at least three times to infer the presence of a routing loop. Paxson further differentiated routing loops as being *persistent* (they never reached the destination during the traceroute) and *temporary* (they did resolve during the traceroute, and ultimately reached the destination). Xia et al. [41] also look for repeats in traceroutes to identify persistent routing loops, and Lone et al. [19] similarly use them to infer the absence of ingress filtering.

Other studies have investigated how routing loops can be predicted by changes in BGP [38,45], how the presence of loops can indicate route leaks [18], and the dynamics of transient loops [30]. However, all of these works rely on

---

[6] https://github.com/zmap/zdns.

small-scale traceroutes of samples of the Internet, and use these to infer trends on the larger Internet.

In addition to these active techniques, routing loops have also been detected passively. Hengartner et al. [13] used packet traces from a tier-1 ISP to detect routing loops. By comparison, this method does not have as broad a view of routing loops as ours (they find only 4318 routing loops in total), but is able to detect transient routing loops—they find that most routing loops last less than 10 s.

Performing Massive Scans. Where we primarily differ from the above is the sheer scale at which we actively probe for routing loops. Prior work has used dozens [29], hundreds of thousands [42], and as many as 11M [41] destination IP addresses to discover routing loops. More recently, FlashRoute [15] presented a tool capable of tracerouting one IP per /24 subnet in a matter of minutes. Using this technique, they also discover over 16K prefixes that contain routing loops. Rüth et al. found 439K prefixes containing routing loops in 2019 using follow-up traceroutes to ZMap scans, performing 27M traceroutes [34].

In contrast to prior work, our study scans the *entire* public[7] IPv4 address space: over 3.7 billion IP addresses in total, and we find over 24 million IPs that contain a routing loop, comprising over 320K /24 subnets.

Prior work also assumed that sampling one or two IP addresses within each routable /24 would provide representative samples [2,16,21,36,41]. Our work challenges this assumption by showing that routing loops are not uniform within /24 boundaries—rather, to obtain a global view of routing loops, far more comprehensive scans are necessary.

Prior Findings About Routing Loops. Paxson [29] observed that persistent routing loops existed as early as 1996. To estimate the scale of persistent routing loops, Xia et al. [41] issued traceroutes to two IP addresses (.1 and a random one) in each of about 5.5M /24s. From this, they identified 207,891 /24s with at least one temporary routing loop; of those, they repeatedly probed the two IP addresses and found that 135,973 of the /24s had loops for each traceroute. Xia et al. assumed that if the two candidate addresses experienced routing loops, then *all* addresses in the /24 would, as well, resulting in their estimate of 135,973 * $2^8 \approx$ 35M total IP addresses with routing loops. Our work draws this assumption into question by empirically demonstrating that different IP addresses in the same /24 can exhibit different looping behavior.

Representative Scanning. Heidemann et al. [10] scanned the entire IPv4 Internet and proposed a method for generating responsive, complete and stable *hitlist*, a list of representative, alive IPv4 addresses that should suffice to represent their respective /24s during an Internet scan. We differ in this matter— we scan the Internet not to discover live hosts, but rather routing loops. We also show that the /24 granularity is not sufficient to discover all routing loops on the Internet.

---

[7] We adopt ZMap's blacklist, which excludes reserved addresses, private addresses, the loopback prefix, and the addresses reported to us to opt-out from being scanned.

Preventing Loops. There is also work on mitigating routing loops and the harm caused by them, using reconfigurable networks [37], static analysis of the data plane [22], and real-time detection of transient loops in network traffic [14, 17]. These works primarily focus on fixing or preventing loops in the first place, rather than measuring them comprehensively across the Internet as we do.

ICMP Rate-Limiting Studies. To parameterize our tool, we evaluated the maximum rate at which we could probe routers without hitting a rate limit (Sect. 2). We are not the first to do such a study. Ravaioli et al. [32] sent TTL-limited ICMP echo requests from 180 PlanetLab hosts at a rate of 1–4,000pps, with TTLs ranging from one to five. They reported that 60% of the routers exhibited rate limits. By comparison, we explored larger send rates (up to 50,000pps) and larger TTL values (1–15), but from only a single vantage point. Guo and Heidemann [12] performed a different experiment, measuring the rate-limiting of pings (not ICMP Time Exceeded responses), and observed only six out of approximately 40,000 subnets rate-limiting them on the forward path. In contrast, our study focuses on ICMP Time Exceeded messages.

Broad Implications of Loops. Persistent routing loops can be used to perform DoS attacks against the involved networks directly, by exploiting the simple fact that a single packet will get relayed multiple times [40]. But more recent work has shown how routing loops can be used to enable or exacerbate attacks indirectly as well. For instance, Bock et al. [3] detail how middleboxes can be used for DoS amplification attacks, and how routing loops around vulnerable middleboxes can worsen these attacks. Nosyk et al. [27] detail how routing loops can exacerbate DNS-based DoS attacks, finding 115 routing loops that enable high-amplification attacks. Attackers can also create or induce their own routing loops in order to amplify DoS attacks, by misconfiguring content delivery networks [8], leveraging IPv6 tunnels [26], or ARP spoofing on a wireless network [4]. Finally, Marder et al. [24] detail how loops complicate inferring outbound addresses in traceroutes, which is useful for inferring router ownership or organizations.

BGP AS Path Looping Behavior (BAPL). Loops can also be observed at the BGP level, by looking for loops in the AS paths of BGP update messages [43]. These so-called BGP AS path looping (BAPL) behavior can result in multi-AS routing loops [44].

7   Ethics

We designed our experiments to have a minimal impact on other hosts. Our IPv4 Internet-wide scans were designed such that each intermediate router would receive a packet from us at a rate of 3 packets per second, which should have a negligible impact on end hosts. To avoid overwhelming destination networks, our experiments probed addresses randomly, which spreads out traffic to any given destination network across the length of the scan. Our scanning rate should have had each /24 receive a packet from us every 2 min on average.

We follow the best practices for high speed scanning laid out by [9]. Our scanning machines we used for these experiments hosted a simple webpage on port 80 to explain the nature of our scans and provides a contact email address to request exclusion from future scans.

For our highest throughput experiments, we took additional precautions. We planned our experiment to saturate the ICMP rate limit of specific routers, we limited the experiment to a relatively small number of IP addresses (10,000). For each IP address, the experiment was limited to 1 s long and only 22 mbps.

8   Conclusion

Routing loops have long been known to exist, but their prevalence and nature have long been shrouded behind common but untested assumptions, like that all destination addresses within a /24 are likely to experience the same routing loops. In this paper, we perform a straightforward but illuminating experiment: we look for routing loops to *all* IPv4 addresses by tracerouting to a limited range of TTLs to examine the true global prevalence of routing loops. We discover over 24 million IPs with routing loops—over 21× more than three concurrent datasets combined—comprising over 500K routers. And we discuss their structure and root causes. Also, we uncover new types of routing loops that can be abused for TCP reflected amplification attacks.

Our resulting datasets confirm some prior results, but also expose unidentified biases in prior measurement efforts that may inform future studies. In particular, we find that scanning only the .1 address per /24 misses 73.5% of the routing loops we were able to find. Indeed, for 35% of the /24s in our dataset, fewer than 11 of their 256 destination addresses result in loops.

Ultimately, our results motivate full-Internet traceroutes. To assist in future efforts, we made our code and data publicly available at https://github.com/RoutingLoops.

Acknowledgments. We thank Jack Wampler for the insightful discussions. We also thank the anonymous reviewers for their helpful feedback. This work was supported in part by NSF award CNS-1943240 and NSF award CNS-1954063.

References

1. Augustin, B., et al.: Avoiding traceroute anomalies with Paris traceroute. In: ACM Internet Measurement Conference (IMC) (2006)
2. Beverly, R.: Yarrp'ing the Internet: randomized high-speed active topology discovery. In: ACM Internet Measurement Conference (IMC) (2016)
3. Bock, K., Alaraj, A., Fax, Y., Hurley, K., Wustrow, E., Levin, D.: Weaponizing middleboxes for TCP reflected amplification. In: USENIX Security Symposium (2021)
4. Brown, J.D., Willink, T.J.: A new look at an old attack: ARP spoofing to create routing loops in Ad Hoc networks. In: Ad Hoc Networks, pp. 47–59 (2018)

5. CAIDA: IPv4 Prefix-Probing Traceroute Dataset, April 2022. https://www.caida.org/data/active/ipv4_prefix_probing_dataset.xml
6. CAIDA: The CAIDA UCSD AS Classification Dataset, April 2022. https://www.caida.org/catalog/datasets/as-classification
7. CAIDA: The IPv4 Routed/24 Topology Dataset, April 2022. https://www.caida.org/data/active/ipv4_routed_24_topology_dataset.xml
8. Chen, J., et al.: Forwarding-loop attacks in content delivery networks. In: Network and Distributed System Security Symposium (NDSS) (2016)
9. Durumeric, Z., Wustrow, E., Halderman, J.A.: ZMap: fast internet-wide scanning and its security applications. In: USENIX Security Symposium (2013)
10. Fan, X., Heidemann, J.: Selecting representative IP addresses for internet topology studies. In: ACM Internet Measurement Conference (IMC) (2010)
11. Gharaibeh, M., Shah, A., Huffaker, B., Zhang, H., Ensafi, R., Papadopoulos, C.: A look at router geolocation in public and commercial databases. In: ACM Internet Measurement Conference (IMC) (2017)
12. Guo, H., Heidemann, J.: Detecting ICMP rate limiting in the Internet. In: Beverly, R., Smaragdakis, G., Feldmann, A. (eds.) PAM 2018. LNCS, vol. 10771, pp. 3–17. Springer, Cham (2018). https://doi.org/10.1007/978-3-319-76481-8_1
13. Hengartner, U., Moon, S., Mortier, R., Diot, C.: Detection and analysis of routing loops in packet traces. In: ACM Internet Measurement Workshop (IMW) (2002)
14. Holterbach, T., Molero, E.C., Apostolaki, M., Dainotti, A., Vissicchio, S., Vanbever, L.: Blink: fast connectivity recovery entirely in the data plane. In: Symposium on Networked Systems Design and Implementation (NSDI) (2019)
15. Huang, Y., Rabinovich, M., Al-Dalky, R.: FlashRoute: efficient traceroute on a massive scale. In: ACM Internet Measurement Conference (IMC) (2020)
16. Katz-Bassett, E., Madhyastha, H.V., John, J.P., Wetherall, D., Anderson, T.: Studying Black holes in the Internet with Hubble. In: Symposium on Networked Systems Design and Implementation (NSDI). USENIX Association, San Francisco, CA, April 2008. https://www.usenix.org/conference/nsdi-08/studying-black-holes-internet-hubble
17. Kučera, J., Basat, R.B., Kuka, M., Antichi, G., Yu, M., Mitzenmacher, M.: Detecting routing loops in the data plane. In: ACM Conference on emerging Networking EXperiments and Technologies (CoNEXT) (2020)
18. Li, S., Duan, H., Wang, Z., Li, X.: Route leaks identification by detecting routing loops. In: Thuraisingham, B., Wang, X.F., Yegneswaran, V. (eds.) SecureComm 2015. LNICST, vol. 164, pp. 313–329. Springer, Cham (2015). https://doi.org/10.1007/978-3-319-28865-9_17
19. Lone, Q., Luckie, M., Korczyński, M., van Eeten, M.: Using loops observed in traceroute to infer the ability to spoof. In: Kaafar, M.A., Uhlig, S., Amann, J. (eds.) PAM 2017. LNCS, vol. 10176, pp. 229–241. Springer, Cham (2017). https://doi.org/10.1007/978-3-319-54328-4_17
20. Luckie, M., Huffaker, B., Marder, A., Bischof, Z., Fletcher, M., Claffy, K.: Learning to extract geographic information from Internet Router Hostnames. In: ACM Conference on Emerging Networking EXperiments and Technologies (CoNEXT) (2021)
21. Madhyastha, H., et al.: iPlane: an information plane for distributed services. In: Symposium on Operating Systems Design and Implementation (OSDI) (2006)
22. Mai, H., Khurshid, A., Agarwal, R., Caesar, M., Godfrey, P.B., King, S.T.: Debugging the data plane with anteater. In: ACM SIGCOMM (2011)

23. Marder, A., Luckie, M., Dhamdhere, A., Huffaker, B., Claffy, K., Smith, J.M.: Pushing the boundaries with bdrmapIT: mapping router ownership at internet scale. In: ACM Internet Measurement Conference (IMC) (2018)
24. Marder, A., Luckie, M., Huffaker, B., Claffy, K.: VRFinder: finding outbound addresses in traceroute. In: Proceedings of the ACM on Measurement and Analysis of Computing Systems, vol. 4(2) (2020)
25. MaxMind: GeoLite2, October 2021. https://dev.maxmind.com/geoip/geoip2/geolite2
26. Nakibly, G., Arov, M.: Routing loop attacks using IPv6 tunnels. In: USENIX Workshop on Offensive Technologies (WOOT) (2009)
27. Nosyk, Y., Korczyński, M., Duda, A.: Routing loops as mega amplifiers for DNS-based DDoS attacks. In: Hohlfeld, O., Moura, G., Pelsser, C. (eds.) PAM 2022. LNCS, vol. 13210, pp. 629–644. Springer, Cham (2022). https://doi.org/10.1007/978-3-030-98785-5_28
28. University of Oregon: Route Views Archive Project, October 2021. http://archive.routeviews.org/bgpdata
29. Paxson, V.: End-to-end routing behavior in the Internet. In: ACM SIGCOMM (1996)
30. Pei, D., Zhao, X., Massey, D., Zhang, L.: A study of BGP path vector route looping behavior. In: IEEE International Conference on Distributed Computing Systems (ICDCS) (2004)
31. Pochat, V.L., Goethem, T.V., Tajalizadehkhoob, S., Korczyński, M., Joosen, W.: Tranco: a research-oriented top sites ranking hardened against manipulation. In: Network and Distributed System Security Symposium (NDSS) (2019)
32. Ravaioli, R., Urvoy-Keller, G., Barakat, C.: Characterizing ICMP rate limitation on routers. In: IEEE International Conference on Communications (ICC) (2015)
33. RIPE NCC Staff: RIPE Atlas: A global internet measurement network. Internet Protocol J. **18**(3), 2–26 (2015)
34. Rüth, J., Zimmermann, T., Hohlfeld, O.: Hidden treasures – recycling large-scale Internet measurements to study the Internet's control plane. In: Choffnes, D., Barcellos, M. (eds.) PAM 2019. LNCS, vol. 11419, pp. 51–67. Springer, Cham (2019). https://doi.org/10.1007/978-3-030-15986-3_4
35. Sherry, J., Katz-Bassett, E., Pimenova, M., Madhyastha, H.V., Anderson, T., Krishnamurthy, A.: Resolving IP aliases with prespecified timestamps. In: ACM Internet Measurement Conference (IMC) (2010)
36. Sherwood, R., Bender, A., Spring, N.: DisCarte: a disjunctive Internet cartographer. In: ACM SIGCOMM (2008)
37. Shukla, A., Foerster, K.T.: Shortcutting fast failover routes in the data plane. In: Symposium on Architectures for Networking and Communications Systems (ANCS) (2021)
38. Sridharan, A., Moon, S.B., Diot, C.: On the correlation between route dynamics and routing loops. In: ACM Internet Measurement Conference (IMC) (2003)
39. Wang, F., Mao, Z.M., Wang, J., Gao, L., Bush, R.: A measurement study on the impact of routing events on end to-end Internet path performance. In: ACM SIGCOMM (2006)
40. Xia, J., Gao, L., Fei, T.: Flooding attacks by exploiting persistent forwarding loops. In: ACM Internet Measurement Conference (IMC) (2005)
41. Xia, J., Gao, L., Fei, T.: A measurement study of persistent forwarding loops on the Internet. Comput. Netw. **51**(17), 4780–4796 (2007)

42. Zhang, M., Zhang, C., Pai, V., Peterson, L., Wang, R.: PlanetSeer: Internet path failure monitoring and characterization in wide-area services. In: Symposium on Operating Systems Design and Implementation (OSDI) (2004)
43. Zhang, S., Liu, Y., Pei, D.: A measurement study on BGP AS path looping (BAPL) behavior. In: International Conference on Computer Communication and Networks (ICCCN) (2014)
44. Zhang, S., Liu, Y., Pei, D., Liu, B.: Measuring BGP AS path looping (BAPL) and private AS number leaking (PANL). Tsinghua Sci. Technol. **23**(1), 22–34 (2018)
45. Zhang, Y., Mao, Z.M., Wang, J.: A framework for measuring and predicting the impact of routing changes. In: IEEE Conference on Computer Communications (INFOCOM) (2007)

as2org+: Enriching AS-to-Organization Mappings with PeeringDB

Augusto Arturi[1], Esteban Carisimo[2(✉)], and Fabián E. Bustamante[2]

[1] Universidad de Buenos Aires, Buenos Aires, Argentina
aarturi@fi.uba.ar
[2] Northwestern University, Evanston, Illinois, USA
{esteban.carisimo,fabianb}@cs.northwestern.edu

Abstract. An organization-level topology of the Internet is a valuable resource with uses that range from the study of organizations' footprints and Internet centralization trends, to analysis of the dynamics of the Internet's corporate structures as result of (de)mergers and acquisitions. Current approaches to infer this topology rely exclusively on WHOIS databases and are thus impacted by its limitations, including errors and outdated data. We argue that a collaborative, operator-oriented database such as PeeringDB can bring a complementary perspective from the legally-bounded information available in WHOIS records. We present *as2org+*, a new framework that leverages self-reported information available on PeeringDB to boost the state-of-the-art WHOIS-based methodologies. We discuss the challenges and opportunities with using PeeringDB records for AS-to-organization mappings, present the design of *as2org+* and demonstrate its value identifying companies operating in multiple continents and mergers and acquisitions over a five-year period.

1 Introduction

An understanding of the Internet topology, its properties and their evolution, is critical to a number of research questions from routing [21,40] and application performance [19,49,50] to network security [13,52,53], Internet resilience [1,17, 26,43,56], and Internet governance [28,34,39].

As a network of networks, the Internet is composed of over 73,000 Autonomous Systems (ASes) that cooperate via the Border Gateway Protocol (BGP) to exchange routing information and obtain global reachability. The connections between ASes are shaped by the business contracts between the organizations that manage them, and that define the economics and technical aspects of exchanged traffic.

Many Internet studies over the years have focused on an Internet topology defined by the ASes and their relationships, building on different heuristics to infer AS relationships from publicly available BGP routing data [16,31,40]. AS relationships fall into three broad classes: customer-provider, settlement-free peering and siblings. In a customer-provider relationship, a customer AS pays a provider for reachability to/from the rest of the Internet. In a settlement-free peering, two ASes agree to exchange traffic destined to networks they or their

A. Brunstrom et al. (Eds.): PAM 2023, LNCS 13882, pp. 400–428, 2023.
https://doi.org/10.1007/978-3-031-28486-1_17

customers own, without an associated fee. A sibling relationship exists between distinct ASes that are owned by the same organization and can exchange traffic without any cost or routing restrictions. Although seemingly straightforward, this approach ignores the relation that exists between the AS-level topology, the organizations that make up the Internet, and the rich semantic content that is key to its understanding and proper use in a range of analysis, from characterizing trends towards Internet centralization [27,32,35,42] to understanding the impact of business disputes [15], public policies [28] and legal actions [57].

In their seminal work, Cai et al. [57] define the problem of AS-to-organization mapping and present methods to generate an organization-level view of the AS ecosystem. We adopt their definition of organization as *an entity which has control over itself and is not a subsidiary of any other organization*. Organizations may include multiple ASes as a result of company merges and acquisition or to facilitate other, more complex arrangements such as different business units, or alternative routing policies for different parts of their network. An organization-level topology, thus, clusters together entities sharing common business decisions, showing two organizations as connected if there exists a relationship between at least one of their affiliated ASes.

The state-of-the-art AS-to-Organization mapping method, AS2Org [57], extracts organization information from AS registration data available on WHOIS records to identify ASes under the same management. WHOIS records, however, are known to contain inaccurate and outdated information which impact the accuracy of the inferred Internet organization-level topology (§2), ranging from the simply out-of-date records resulting from mergers and acquisitions or incongruence between commercial names and registration data, to the challenges that come from capturing the different approaches that large corporations use to structure their organizations (e.g., having independent organizations for their country-level subsidiaries).

We argue that *self-reported* information available on PeeringDB can be leveraged to boost AS-to-Organization mappings and address many of these challenges. PeeringDB (PDB) is an online open database established in 2004 to assist peering coordinators identifying potential peers and peering locations. AS operators voluntarily provide information about their networks, such as peering policies, traffic volumes and presence at various geographic locations. In the past decade, PDB has become the *de facto* public profile of Internet networks. There are a number of factors that explain the popularity of PDB, including the fact that main cloud and content providers request its peers to be listed on PDB to establish peering relationships [18,25,41]. Despite participation in PDB being voluntary with no mechanism to verify the accuracy of reported information, prior work has shown it to be mostly correct [38] and several studies have relied on it to infer the size of Hypergiants [5] and determine the relevance of peering facilities [24].

We present *as2org+*, a new framework that leverages PDB data to improve on the state-of-the-art AS-to-Organization mapping methodology. *as2org+* builds on the insight that a collaborative operator-oriented database could bring a complementary perspective to the legally-bounded information available in WHOIS records.

We face a number of challenges (§2) in leveraging PDB data including the operators' use of non-standard fields to communicate siblings, even when PDB provides an Organization Identifier (OrgID), and the use of loosely structured formats meant to be read by humans. We evaluate the contribution of PDB-based inferencing (§6) and its contribution to the AS-to-organization mapping problem (§7). We demonstrate the value of *as2org+* to derive more complete organizational structures of large transit providers (§7.2) and Hypergiants (§7.3).

In sum, our work makes the following contributions:

- We propose the use of PDB as a valuable source to enhance AS-to-Organization mappings, and present a methodology to extract self-reported siblings embedded in PDB records.
- We present *as2org+*, a new framework for AS-to-organization mapping that combines PDB-based inferences with the current WHOIS-based approach to enhance organization-level topology
- We evaluate *as2org+* contributions to the Organization level topology and discover that it provides a more complete representation of large transit networks (26 networks in CAIDA's AS-RANK TOP100) and Hypergiants, for example grouping together different subsidiaries and business units of Google (Google, Google Cloud Services and Google Fiber) and Akamai (Akamai, Prolexic and Linode).
- We apply *as2org+* to a five-year dataset and find that it enables clustering together networks as a result of mergers and acquisitions that are not visible in WHOIS-based datasets, such as GTT (AS3257) acquisition of KPN (AS286) or CenturyLink (AS209) acquisition of Level3 (AS3356).
- We contrast AS2Org's RIR-level scope with PDB's geographically-unconstrained organizations and find that *as2org+* is able to group together companies operating in multiple continents, for instance *as2org+* groups in the same cluster Yahoo's subsidiaries in the US, UK and Japan.
- We make *as2org+*[1] available to the community.

This work does not raise any ethical issues.

2   Motivation and Challenges

A more complete Organization-level topology would be a valuable resource for a wide range of disciplines. Improved AS-to-Organization mappings contribute to a better representation of private or state-owned organizations' footprint [9]. Having a more complete representation of state-owned organizations could help us to understand governments' engagements in the Internet, as a business activity, domestically and abroad. This could also be a valuable resource to identify market concentration of Internet resources at an organization level. Improved AS-to-Organization mappings can also help better understand the constant reshaping

---

[1] *as2org+* can be found at: https://github.com/NU-AquaLab/as2orgplus.

of the corporate structure of the Internet as result of mergers, de-mergers and acquisitions, such as CenturyLink's acquisition of Level3 [12] (now rebranded as LUMEN), the merger between T-Mobile and Sprint [54] or the recent de-merger between Telia's transit network (Telia Carrier, now rebranded Arelion) from the rest of the company [14].

The state-of-the-art AS-to-Organization mapping technique bases its inferences exclusively on WHOIS data. Despite providing a complete coverage and valuable information of the allocated resources, WHOIS databases have several limitations (from errors and outdated data, to entries with unstructured text formats) that impact the accuracy and coverage of methods reliant on this source. In the next paragraphs we describe some limitations and the challenges of using WHOIS data to identify networks under the same ownership.

Corporate Business Segmentation: Large corporations use different approaches to structure their organizations into *separate legal entities* running business units that include departments, divisions and subsidiaries. The lack of common practices, as well as the size and complexity of these organizations, create challenges to fully capture the business structure of these companies. Key to understanding this challenge is that network resource allocations are given to a single legal entity considering each resource holder as an independent organization. Internet access providers operating in multiple countries (*e.g.,* Orange, Deutsche Telekom or Claro) are likely to be segmented in multiple subsidiaries (a separate legal entity) with resources specifically allocated for operating each of them. Network segmentation of multinational Internet providers vary from company to company, but most approaches include a (nearly) per-country subsidiary with their own network resources. Other large corporations run a diverse portfolio of Internet businesses (*e.g.,* Internet access, content delivery) and are likely to have different companies and/or networks (and therefore network resources) for each business. This is the case, for example, of Google with Google Fiber as an Internet access provider. Claro – a mobile carrier with an extensive footprint across Latin America– offers another example. Each of Claro's country-level subsidiaries is registered as an independent organization (Claro Argentina (AS19037: `AR-CCTI1-LACNIC`), Claro Chile (AS27995: `CL-CCSA39-LACNIC`)). These business dynamics and practices are poorly captured by WHOIS records where there are no clear relationships between different assets of the same conglomerate.

(Mis)communications from Resource Holders: Despite contractual obligations requiring resource holders to maintain information up to date[2], resource holders are unlikely to contact the RIR for issues that are not regarding to renew or upgrade allocations. As a result of the lack of communication, many delegation records do not properly capture the status of the organization. In recent years, ARIN acknowledged that mergers and acquisitions create challenges to organizations to coordinate all the allocated resources to report the same information [46].

---

[2] Legacy resources [4]—allocations preceding the creation of RIRs—are also subject to different regulations [46].

RIR-Level Allocations: Corporates controlling subsidiaries in different regions are going to be treated as separate organizations for allocation purposes since RIRs' allocation policies require organizations to be an *"active business entity legally formed within the RIR service region"* [3]. The RIR-level scope of organizations included in WHOIS data limits our ability to fully capture organizations of corporations with presence in different RIRs. For example, the ASes of French-based Orange and its subsidiary in Cameroon are identified by different OrgIDs (AS5511: `ORG-FT2-RIPE`, AS36912: `ORG-OCS1-AFRINIC`).

Data Accuracy and Formats: Limitations and inaccuracies in the process of data collection and data presentation of WHOIS records limits and hinders WHOIS-based methodologies. WHOIS data schemas are not homogeneous across RIRs (and NIRs too) where syntax (field names), semantics (field content) and number of elements vary across different regions. Another methodological limitation is that WHOIS records are (mostly or exclusively) accessible through the WHOIS protocol and retrieved data is returned as loosely cohesive plain text [36]. In quarterly released AS2Org mappings, CAIDA homogenizes and structures the WHOIS data [8]. Despite these efforts to improve the quality of the data product, registration and resource allocation involves human intervention and these forms are prone to errors.

Incongruence Between Commercial Names and Registration Data. Corporations could have homogeneous brand names across subsidiaries but WHOIS databases may not capture that homogeneity since resource holders tend to fill up the registration name (`OrgName field`) with the company's legal name, which may differ from commercial names or brand names. As an example, Colombia's state-owned Internexa [9] operates in Argentina the AS262195, however, LACNIC's WHOIS reports the owner's name to be *Transamerican Telecomunication S.A.* This incongruence between commercial and registration names present barriers for analysis that uses WHOIS data to identify text similarities.

These are just examples of the limitations and challenges faced by the state-of-the-art AS-to-Organization mapping approach and partially motivate our work. Despite WHOIS-based AS-to-Organization mappings being incomplete, we believe this is a valuable data source that could be enhanced with organizational data obtained from alternative sources, such as PeeringDB.

3   Challenges and Opportunities with PeeringDB

While we argue that the growing popularity and use of PeeringDB can offer a complementary perspective to traditional WHOIS-based approaches, its use is not without challenges. For instance, the database is voluntarily and does not provide complete or uniform coverage across regions which could potentially introduce biases in AS-to-Organization mappings. We also find that despite PDB providing an Organization Identifier (OrgID), operators sometimes rely on other fields to communicate siblings, and that in some cases those siblings do not even have presence on PeeringDB (*e.g.,* Tigo-AS262206 reports AS26617 as a sibling in text fields but this network is not registered in PDB). We also find that this information is often loosely structured as it is intended to be read by human operators.

In the following paragraphs we discuss some additional challenges with using PDB to identify ASes belonging to an organization, and potential approaches to take advantage of its rich information.

3.1 PDB for AS2Orgs Mapping

A non-exhaustive set of limitations of PDB that could impact sibling inferences include its relatively limited coverage, bias in its adoption by operators, and potential issues of completeness and correctness of the database. We briefly discuss each of these limitations in the following paragraphs.

Limited Coverage: Despite PDB adoption being steadily growing, as shown in Fig. 1a, this database presents a limited visibility of the AS ecosystem where only ≈34.5% (25,767 / 74,583) of active networks[3] has registered in PDB. However, the adoption seems to be skewed towards prominent networks which we expect to have more complex organizational structures, such as large transit networks where 100% and 93.8% of CAIDA's AS-RANK [7] TOP100 and TOP1000 are registered in PDB. We also expect this number to keep growing due to some Hypergiants (HGs) requiring PDB profiles to establish peering sessions with peers [18,25,41] and government and IXP initiatives encouraging and helping local ASes to join PDB [6,45].

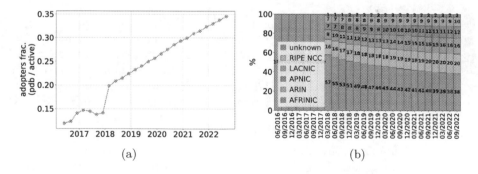

(a)   (b)

Fig. 1. PeeringDB adoption as fraction of active ASes (left) and per region (right).

Geographic Bias: PDB adoption rate may vary across countries depending on peering incentives (*e.g.*, local presence of HGs), consolidated peering ecosystems (*e.g.*, presence of large IXPs), common communication practices among local operators, *etc.*. A previous study conducted in 2013 found that RIPE is

---

[3] We refer as active ASes to Autonomous System Numbers visible in BGP routing tables.

over-represented across the networks registered at PDB, while AFRINIC and LACNIC registered networks had a small footprint [38]. We examine the *self-reported* country information of the organizations registered in PDB, as shown in Fig. 1b, and found a growing adoption at a RIR level in APNIC, and more remarkably, in LACNIC regions. Despite lacking *self-reported* country information for a fraction of the records, we observe that PDB adoption is not confined to specific regions giving us visibility of all regions.

Completeness, Correctness and Use of Fields: The fact that PeeringDB is an open and voluntary database raises questions about the accuracy and authenticity of the included data. PeeringDB uses a series of mechanics with authoritative data sources (WHOIS, RDAP [2,30], *etc.*.) to authenticate that the data source is legitimate [47]. On the other hand, the accuracy of PDB records is encouraged by the fact that inflated statistics could compromise peering agreements or harm the reputation of the networks [38].

3.2   Opportunities Using PeeringDB

We now analyze the PDB data schema (version 2) to identify elements that could potentially inform *siblings*. We investigate whether being an operation-oriented database could bring a different perspective to the sibling inference problem compared to WHOIS information, which refers as an organization to legal entities in a specific RIR. We identify two main ways organizations use to communicate the set of ASes under their management: *(i)* use of native features of PDB data schema (`org` data structure) *(ii)* custom use of plain text fields (*e.g.*, `aka`, `notes`).

Among the several data entities available in PDB, we focus on those that are more relevant for this work: organization (`org`) and network (`net`). The data entity `org` describes organizations with fields such as `name`, `also known as` (`aka`), `website`, `address`, `country`, *etc.*. However, the most important attribute of these entities is the network field which is a list of network identifiers referring to `net` entries administered by the organization The data entity `net` describes ASes with fields such as `name`, `also known as` (`aka`), `network type`, several network attributes (*e.g.*, number of IPv4 prefixes), peering, and more importantly the `organization` field referring to the organization this network belongs to. By combining both data entities using the list of bidirectional network/organization identifiers, we can directly generate AS-to-Organization mappings.

```
1  { "meta":
2    { "generated": 1601614591.736},
3     "data": [
4       {
5         "asn": 4436,
6         "website":"http://www.gtt.net",
```

```
7    "notes": "nLayer / AS4436 has been acquired by GTT
          Communications / AS3257 and is no longer directly
          peering.Please refer all peering related inquiries to
          peering [at] gtt [dot] net.",
8    "org_id": 8897,
9    "policy_url": "http://www.gtt.net/peering/",
10   "aka": "Formerly known as nLayer Communications",
11  }}}
```

Listing 1.1. Example of the **net** entry for AS4436 in the PDB snapshot of Oct. 2020.

We further investigate whether the content reported in fields of **org** and **net** could provide some information of other ASes operated by the same organization. Listing 1.1 shows an example of some fields in the **net** entry of AS4436 (nLayer) to explain how these fields could provide hints about siblings. In this specific case, nLayer was acquired by GTT in 2012 [55] and this information is available in the **notes**, where both nLayer (AS4436) and GTT (AS3257) ASNs are included. Ten year later, both networks are under different organizations in WHOIS records. The use of **aka** in this example is informative but insufficient to obtain a cluster with ASNs of both networks. In Appendix A we include an example of a **net** entry in which operators used the field **aka** to report ASes under the same management.

4 Methodology

In this section we describe our methodology to extract siblings from PDB records. This methodology offers two types of sibling inferences – *conservative* or *aggressive* – depending on the confidence level of the obtained results. Figure 2 illustrates the pipeline of the methodology before consolidation with the AS2Org's inferences. The *aggressive* part of the methodology consists of four main stages each: *(i)* feature extraction *(ii)* filters *(iii)* inspection and *(iv)* data consolidation.

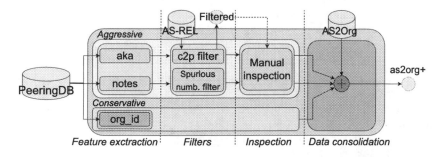

Fig. 2. Diagram of the *as2org+* framework.

The *conservative* approach only uses org_id present in the net data entity and it does not apply any heuristic to infer siblings. On the other hand, the *aggressive* approach applies heuristics to extract self-reported *siblings* ASNs embedded in either the aka field or the notes field (or both). In this approach, we create *candidate groups of ASes under the same administration* as an output and later apply filters to improve confidence. The *conservative* approach is a *zero-risk approach* since PDB applies mechanisms to authenticate the ownership of a network resource (see §3.1), preventing two non-sibling ASNs from being identified by the same org_id . The *aggressive* approach could potentially include numbers that are not *ASNs under the same managements*, though, those false positives are mitigated by the design of our framework. We give users full control of the combination of these approaches where they can choose any combination of features. Next, we describe the implementation of our heuristics.

Before starting our process, we sanitize the data from the selected inputs and normalize the text (*e.g.,* case).

4.1   Feature Extraction

Our PDB-based inference methodology uses three fields of PDB's net entity, the org_id field in the conservative approach, and notes and aka fields in the aggressive approach. In this stage, the conservative approach uses the org_id to group together all ASNs were registered by the same organization while the aggressive approach combines regular expressions (regexes) to extract groups of ASNs embedded in these fields. Next, we describe the rules applied to extract *self-reported siblings* embedded in these fields.

org_id. This feature extraction mechanism leverages the native org_id field in the PDB data schema to group together all ASes registered by the same organization.

aka. For this field, the framework applies a single regular expression that extracts numbers with 4 to 8 digits to generate the list of *candidate siblings*. We suspect that length constraints of this field (limited to 255 characters [48]) discourage operators from rich semantic statements and hence, sibling ASNs (sometimes along with AS names) are directly reported. In Appendix B we show a few examples of how operators report their networks in the aka field as well as the output of this regex. We acknowledge that this extraction method can result in wrong inferences. This rule is not capable of inferring *candidate siblings* ranging between AS1 and AS999. However, this impact is limited to missing at most 1% of the *siblings* since at the time of this submission more than 100,000 [44] have already been allocated. To be more specific, this rule lacks the semantic context of the numbers extracted, potentially leading to infer as *candidate sibling* strings such as dates and phone numbers. We apply custom filters (§4.2) to mitigate the presence of spurious numbers.

notes. We develop 37 regexes to extract *candidate lists of sibling ASes* embedded in different semantic contexts in the notes field. This is a data rich field (it is an unlimited plain text field [48]) that allows operators to include details

Table 1. Examples of simple feature extraction rules for the notes

ASN	Input	regex	output
21202	*AS21202 in the nordic region*	`AS[0-9]+`	[21202]
5462	*This as is being migrated to AS:5089*	`AS:[0-9]+`	[5089]
55818	*Operating 2 ASNS (55818 AND 45147)*	`ASNS.*`	[55818,45147]
35742	*This as will be merged soon into as 43646.*	`AS [0-9]+`	[43646]
10158	*Has 6 origin ASS: 10158, 45991, 38678, 9764, 7625, 38099*	`ASS:.*`	[10158, 45991, 38678, 9764, 7625, 38099]
54113	*Autonomous system (AS) 54113*	`[(]AS[)]) [0-9]+`	[54113]
58715	*IIG(ASN-58715) & ISP(ASN-63969)*	`ASN-[0-9]+`	[58715, 63969]

that do not fit well in any other field, including detailed descriptions or specific requirements and procedures to peer with the network. The flexibility of the field and diversity of data reported (siblings, peering policy, capacities, NOC hours, *etc..*) sets challenges to identify a *candidate list of siblings*. Moreover, there is no convention to report these features, and the text structure can vary significantly as these messages are meant to be read by human operators.

We categorize the 37 `regexes` into two groups: simple rules (21) and complex rules (16). Simple rules aim to extract ASN from simple patterns that are used to refer to ASes using prefixes such as *AS, ASN, ASNS, ASS* and *ASES*, as it is shown in Table 1. Complex rules aim to extract ASNs from notes using more complex semantic expressions. We search for common phrases used (with a maximum of three words) to report ASes under the same management, including *also manages, we administered, merging*, as it is shown in Table 2. Due to a lack of a common structure, we consider *candidate siblings* to all numbers after this template phrase. This decision comes at the risk of including numbers unrelated to ASNs, such as addresses, RFC numbers, ISO standards and others. We also acknowledge that complex rules are only capable of extracting *siblings* of records written in English. In our implementation users can select using simple, complex or both rules for sibling inferences. In Sect. 6.3 we evaluate the contribution of each of these rules.

4.2 Filters

To remove numbers misinterpreted as ASN in the previous stages, include a filtering layer in the aggressive approach pipeline. We focus on filtering out errors coming from two sources, *(i)* *spurious numbers* (*e.g.,* phone numbers, addresses, years, RFC numbers *etc..*), and *(ii)* reported-but-not-sibling ASNs. To mitigate these false positive inferences, we develop two filters: *(i)* a spurious-number filter, and *(ii)* a customer-to-provider (c2p) filter.

Spurious Number Filter. This filter mitigates the presence of *spurious numbers* (numeric expressions that are not ASNs). The feature extraction rules lack semantic context to distinguish between *spurious numbers* and actual ASNs which could potentially lead to include numeric expressions that are not ASNs.

Table 2. Examples of complex feature extraction rules for the notes

ASN	Input	Regex	output
22546	*Also manages AS10987, 16486 AND 46498.*	`Also manages.*`	[10987, 16486, 46498]
18200	*ASN behind 18200: 2198, 17480, 45345, 45461, 56055, 56089.*	`ASN behind.*`	[18200, 2198, 17480, 45345, 45461, 56055, 56089]
19750	*Criteo also manages the following ASNS: 44788, 53031, 55569*	`The following ASNS.* also manages.*`	[8613, 31672]
5413	*Merging 8613 merging 31672*	`Merging .*`	[44788, 53031, 55569]
62982	*Other ASN'S we control 62195, 133188,.133366*	`We control .*`	[62195, 133188, 133366]
28263	*We administered ASN 28263, 262272, 53126 and 265079.*	`Administered ASN .*`	[28669, 28263, 262272, 53126, 265079]
24093	*This ASN is behind 38195*	`Is behind .*`	[38195]
7303	*Other ASN under 7303 are 10481 and 10318.*	`ASN under .*`	[7303, 10481, 10318]

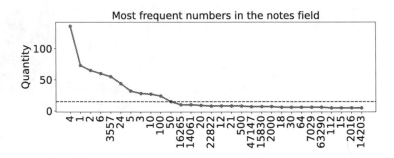

Fig. 3. Prevalence of numerical expression across the notes.

Figure 3 shows the most prevalent numeric expression across all notes of the snapshot of October 1, 2020. The most prevalent numeric expressions were extracted from notes describing protocol versions (4 and 6), maximum prefixes accepted/announced (50 or 100), and popular subnet masks (21, 22, 24 and 30 for IPv4 and 48, 64 and 80 for IPv6). The spurious-number filter includes the most prevalent number expression appearing in at least 15 notes where a knee is observed in Fig. 3.

This filter also drops numbers that range between 1970 to 2020 since these numbers tend to refer to dates such as merging dates, last update, *etc..* (*e.g.,* number of prefixes, phone numbers, addresses, years, *etc..*).

Table 3. Example of the p2c filter to filter out notes containing ASNs not related to the to network entry.

net entry	notes	inferred clustered		# c2p	decision
AS396356	*(...). Maxihost owns a Tier 3 compliant Datacenter in Sao Paulo, where its headquarter is located. We connect directly with the following ISPs, Algar (AS16735), Sparkle (AS6762), GTT (AS3257) (...)*	**396356,** (provider), (provider), (peer), 3257 (provider), 174 (provider)	16735 6762 AS3223	4	drop (✗)
AS7303	*Telecom Argentina is the major broadband and mobile provider in Argentina, with more than 4.1 MM broadband subscribers, 4 MM fixed lines and 20 MM mobile lines. Other ASN under 7303 are 10481 and 10318.*	**7303,** 10481 (provider), 10318		1	keep (✓)

We release our code[4] to allow users to make changes in these rules such as adding and removing them if they consider it necessary.

Customer-to-Provider Filter. We use AS relationships to remove ASNs that are not part of the same organization. The aggressive approach could potentially group together ASNs that do not belong to the same organization but both being present in the same note. In development stage of the project, we found networks that use their notes to describe their upstream connectivity rather than listing other networks of the same organization. We then develop a stage to filter out clusters based on customer-to-provider (c2p) relationships. In our implementation, users can specify the maximum c2p relationships allowed between ASes in the same cluster or skip this stage. In cases where this filter is applied, our PDB-based inference methodology returns a file containing the list of discarded clusters. Users manually verify these cases (§4.3) and decide to either include or exclude them from the final inference.

Table 3 show this rule in action in an example in which only one c2p relationship is allowed for two different notes. In this case, the inferred cluster for Maxihost (AS396356) is dropped because this network has more c2p relationships that the maximum allowed in this example. Indeed, as the example shows, Maxihost (AS396356) is describing its upstream connectivity. On the other hand, the cluster inferred from Telecom Argentina (AS7303) meets the criteria used for this example (only one c2p allowed) and it is then preserved.

Sibling relationships generate anomalies in the inference of AS relationships [16, 20, 40, 51]. These anomalies challenge to distinguish customer-provider relationships is between two independent companies or two companies belonging to the same conglomerate. Given that text fields can indistinctly siblings or

---

[4] *as2org+* can be found at: https://github.com/NU-AquaLab/as2orgplus.

upstreams, we leave for human inspection those clusters containing customer-to-provider relationships across members. This inspection stage is going to assess whether discarded clusters containing customer-to-provider relationships are under the same management. In the worst case scenario, this filter would discard all sibling inferences, reducing PDB-based inference capabilities through these features to zero but in any case will infer any new cluster for AS relationships data. In any case, this filter is going to use BGP-derived data to expand the sibling inferences. In Sect. 6.5, we evaluate this filter with different threshold values.

4.3   Manual Inspection

To conclude the data extraction process, the framework includes a last stage for human inspection to manually remove errors that were not filtered out in the previous automatic stages. This stage also allows users to apply their own judgment to filter out clusters generated by correctly extracting data, though from entries with mistakes (*e.g.,* typos).

The lack of authentication of the information given in text fields could be another source of erroneous inferences that requires human inspection. For example, we found that for a short period of time (from 2019 to 2020) a Bangladeshi provider called Brother Online (AS135131) was using its aka field to report "AS32934" (Meta's principal peering network) making our PDB-based inferencing method to group both networks together (see Appendix C). We are unaware whether this was an unintended or malicious event, though, this event highlights the sensitivity of *as2org+* to imprecise or unauthenticated data provided in text fields as well as the need of human inspection to rule out these cases.

4.4   Data Consolidation

After extracting and cleaning the embedded data, the framework groups together partially overlapping clusters scattered across multiple records, fields and data sources. There are some cases in which sibling information is scattered in the same field (*e.g.,* notes) across multiple records rather than being centralized. This is illustrated in Listing 1.2 where both networks report the same parent network but none of them reference each other. Another popular case is to find sibling information scattered across multiple fields (*e.g.,* notes and org_id). This stage concludes combining clusters in our PDB-based approach with clusters in the AS2Org dataset [8] to create a dataset that we call *as2org+*.

```
1  # StarHub AS10091
2  {'asn': 10091,
3   'notes': 'Please refer to as4657 PDb for Contact & Peering
            Info. Thanks.',}
4  # StarHub AS38861
5  {'asn': 38861,
```

```
6    'notes': 'Please refer to as4657 PDb for Contact & Peering
     Info. Thanks.',}
```

Listing 1.2. Example of partially overlapping clusters

5   Effectiveness of Cluster Extraction Methods

We evaluate whether our PDB-based inference framework effectively extracts all siblings' ASNs embedded in PDB records. We focus inferences generated by using `notes` and `aka` fields and exclude `org_id` from this examination since we do not rely on heuristics to extract sibling information.

Table 4. Effectiveness of the extraction methods given by true positive (*tp*), False Positive (*fp*), false negative (*fn*), True Negative (*tn*), accuracy (**A**), precision (**P**) and Recall (**R**) values.

		Predicted notes		Predicted aka	
		Positive	Negative	Positive	Negative
Actual	Positive	446	10	230	0
	Negative	16	740	4	563
		A: 0.98 P: 0.97 R: 0.98		**A: 0.99 P: 0.98 R: 1.0**	

We manually evaluate the effectiveness of the extraction methods by analyzing whether these methods successfully extracted embedded sibling ASNs in text fields. We do not evaluate the correctness of the reported data since we lack ground truth. We consider a cluster that extracts all sibling information embedded in the fields a True Positive (*tp*), a cluster that contains numbers that do not correspond to ASNs (spurious numbers, prefixes, numbers in URLs, *etc.*.) a False Positive (*fp*), a cluster that misses at least one ASN present in their corresponding text fields a False Negative (*fn*) and a text field that contains numeric expressions with no embedded siblings a True Negative (*tn*).

Table 4 shows True Positive (*tp*), False Positive (*fp*), False Negative (*fn*), True Negative (*tn*), accuracy (**A**), precision (**P**) and recall (**R**) values for the output of our inference method (using c2p threshold = 0 and without reintroducing clusters) using the snapshot of September 1, 2022. According to the results of our evaluation, our PDB-based inference framework successfully extracts embedded ASNs in text fields with values of accuracy, precision and recall of 0.98, 0.97 and 0.98 and 0.99, 0.98 and 1.0, for notes and aka, respectively.

As a result of this evaluation, we identified a list of challenges that the manual inspection stage faces to distinguish numbers corresponding to siblings. Table 5 shows some prominent examples that we gathered during this process, such as the presence of Best Current Practice (BCP) numbers, networks reporting partnership, hosting third-party resources, adoption of cloud services, among others.

Table 5. Examples generating challenges to the manual inspection stage to assess whether some networks are under the same management.

Challenge	ASN	Example
BCP	34428	*we use filtering according to BCP38*
Partnerships	19281	*We typically partner with PCH (ASN42) in IX locations*
Third-party resources	393424	*This is the TorIX Services network which includes a (...),* **AS112 node**
Cloud-hosted services	27471	*The WSS service has migrated to Google Cloud (...) peer with Google AS15169*
Numbers in URLs	50618	https://as29075.peeringdb.com (✓)
	397102	https://peeringdb.com/net/200 (✗)

6   Evaluating a PDB-Based Inferencing

We exhaustively evaluate the contribution of different components and stages of the PDB-based inferencing approach to the sibling inference problem. We evaluate the contribution of different features (§6.1), the aggressive approach (§6.2), simple and complex rules (§6.3) and the data consolidation stage (§6.6). We also investigate the prevalence of using text fields to report unregistered siblings (§6.4) and the impact of the c2p filter (§6.5).

For this evaluation, we run a longitudinal analysis using PDB snapshots from five different years (Sept. 3, 2018, Sept. 7, 2019, Sept. 1, 2020, Sept. 1, 2021, Sept. 1, 2022). To complete the framework setup, we include CAIDA's AS relationship files of each corresponding month and configure the c2p threshold = 0 (unless a different configuration is mentioned).

6.1   Unique Contribution of Features

We focus on the contribution of each feature to cluster inferences to investigate whether operators are more inclined to report *siblings* in certain fields. We evaluate the number of clusters inferred by each feature to the cluster inferences using snapshots of five different years.

We run our approach to evaluate the contribution of each feature (`notes`, `aka` and `org_id`) to sibling inferencing. Table 6 shows the number of clusters (and non-atomic clusters, *i.e.*, having more than 1 ASN, in parenthesis) obtained by each feature in different snapshots collected in the past five years. We observe that `org_id` provides more clusters than any other source, two orders of magnitude more when it is compared to results obtained by `aka` and `notes`. Narrowing our focus to *non-atomic* clusters, `org_id` still leads, however, `aka` and `notes` now

Table 6. Non-atomic ($\overline{AC}$) and total number (#) of clusters inferred per feature.

	Aka		Notes		Org	
	$\overline{AC}$	#	$\overline{AC}$	#	$\overline{AC}$	#
'18	39	128	95	229	585	12264
'19	44	160	145	289	796	14962
'20	45	188	161	338	988	18115
'21	44	208	186	400	1171	20704
'22	48	234	214	472	1384	23191

Table 7. Full overlap between clusters inferred by two given pairs of features. Numbers in brackets show the total number of clusters found per each feature.

	Notes		Aka		Org	
	Aka	Org	Notes	Org	Notes	Aka
'18	2 (95)	33 (95)	3 (39)	8 (39)	30 (585)	7 (585)
'19	3 (145)	65 (145)	3 (44)	10 (44)	48 (796)	7 (796)
'20	2 (161)	75 (161)	3 (45)	12 (45)	57 (988)	8 (988)
'21	3 (186)	88 (186)	4 (44)	12 (44)	65 (1171)	8 (1171)
'22	2 (214)	106 (214)	3 (48)	11 (48)	76 (1384)	7 (1384)

contributes 4.79% and 16.42% on average compared to org_id during this period. We expect a more prevalent use of org_id to report networks under the same management since this is a native (and compulsory) field The results also suggest that aka and notes are used to communicate relationships that are not captured by the org_id.

We further investigate partial overlaps between non-atomic clusters inferred using different features. We specifically look for cases where a cluster inferred by a field (*e.g.,* notes) is fully contained in a cluster inferred by another field (*e.g.,* org_id). By meeting this condition, the former field would provide no contribution since that information is available in the latter field. Table 7 shows the number of clusters inferred by each feature that are fully contained in clusters inferred by another feature. We observe that clusters inferred using notes and aka fields are rarely contained in each other. This is notably different when we compute the overlap between notes and aka with org_id where up to half of those clusters are contained in the org_id. We suspect that in these overlaps attempt to make sibling information available in text format at a glimpse. In any case, the low fractions in these overlaps suggests that each feature provides a unique contribution that is not visible by any other way.

We investigated the lack of partial overlap between text fields and the org_id and found that this mostly occurs after mergers and acquisitions. We suspect that this common practice allows operators to quickly communicate mergers and acquisitions rather than migrating networks to a different PDB organization. We also believe that the visibility of text fields may be more effective to inform these changes to other operators.

6.2 The Aggressive Approach

Next, we use the 5-year dataset to examine the aggressive inference approach to evaluate the contribution of the aka and notes fields to the sibling inference.

The contribution of the *aggressive approach* depends on the use of aka and notes fields to report sibling relationships. Given that these fields are occasionally used, we examine the prevalence of records with non-empty aka and notes fields. Towards the goal of extracting siblings from these fields, we investigate

Table 8. Effectiveness of the aggressive approach as a function of the number of records containing data and numeric expressions.

Field	Snapshot	# Records					
		All	Non-empty ($\bar{e}$) ($\bar{e}/all$)		w num. chars (n) (n/all)		# ASN (ASN/n)
notes	2018	13406	2034 (0.15)		1090 (0.08)		386 (0.35)
	2019	16485	2287 (0.14)		1243 (0.08)		503 (0.40)
	2020	19966	2669 (0.13)		1437 (0.07)		632 (0.44)
	2021	22892	2987 (0.13)		1622 (0.07)		743 (0.46)
	2022	25767	3326 (0.13)		1812 (0.07)		873 (0.48)
aka	2018	13406	6349 (0.47)		435 (0.03)		188 (0.43)
	2019	16485	8440 (0.51)		560 (0.03)		231 (0.41)
	2020	19966	10594 (0.53)		670 (0.03)		260 (0.39)
	2021	22892	12276 (0.54)		775 (0.03)		281 (0.36)
	2022	25767	13880 (0.54)		864 (0.03)		316 (0.37)

the prevalence of aka and notes containing numeric expressions. We then use this information to compute the average number of ASNs extracted per record containing numeric expressions

Table 8 shows the number of aka and notes fields with non-empty records ($\bar{e}$), those containing numeric expressions (n) and the number of ASNs extracted for a 5-year period. Overall, notes are rarely used—only a fraction from 0.15 to 0.13 contains data—and aka (0.47 to 0.54) is more commonly used, however, both rarely contain numeric expressions (fractions oscillate around 0.08 and 0.03 respectively). Interestingly, the ratio between fields containing numeric expressions and the total number of ASNs extracted is between 0.3 and 0.5, showing that on average fields with numeric expressions provide 0.3 to 0.5 ASNs per field. We also observe that the fraction of non-empty records, those containing numeric expressions, are stable over time while the number of ASNs embedded in notes augmented in the same period. This growth suggests that notes are being more frequently used to report other ASes under the same management.

6.3 Simple Rules, Complex Rules and Both Combined

Given the prevalence of siblings embedded in notes containing numeric expressions, we continue our evaluation looking at the contribution of simple rules, complex rules and both combined.

For this analysis we consider that a cluster is visible for both methods *iff* both outputs contain the same elements. For example, let A, B be two inferred clusters where A and B are inferred by simple and complex rules, respectively. We consider that both methods generate the same output if $\forall a_i \in A, a_i \in B \land \forall b_j \in B, b_j \in A$.

Table 9. Clusters' overlap obtained after applying simple rules, complex rules and both combined.

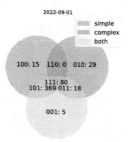

Table 10. Number of ASNs registered in PDB, number of ASNs inferred to be in clusters in the `notes` and `aka` and the number (and fraction) of those inferred ASNs in text field that have not been registered in PDB (*unregistered*).

	PDB	Notes inferences		Aka inferences	
Year	# ASN	#ASN	*Unregistered*	#ASN	*Unregistered*
2018	13406	386	36 (0.09)	188	44 (0.23)
2019	16485	503	43 (0.09)	231	46 (0.20)
2020	19966	632	43 (0.07)	260	45 (0.17)
2021	22892	743	46 (0.06)	281	43 (0.15)
2022	25767	873	51 (0.06)	316	48 (0.15)

Table 9 shows a Venn diagram with the overlap between the clusters inferred with simple rules, complex rules and both using a snapshot collected on September 1, 2022. We observe that simple rules capture 90.4% of the clusters (464/513) while the remaining clusters are observed when complex rules are applied solo or in combination of simple rules. This is a remarkable observation since simple rules have patterns that are less prone to capture spurious numbers (we recall Table 1) and they are highly successful in extracting embedded siblings. This finding also shows that despite there being no standard format to report siblings, operators mostly use similar unsophisticated patterns. A final observation is that simple and complex rules infer some identical clusters that are not visible when both rules are combined. This behavior is due to the fact that the combination of rules can create a more rich clusters in the entire dataset and some of these new enriched clusters eventual merge and create discrepancies.

6.4   Reporting Unregistered Siblings

Considering that `notes` and `aka` are free text fields, we investigate the use of these fields to report siblings that are not registered in PDB.

Table 10 shows the number of ASes registered in PDB, the number of ASNs in clusters inferred from `notes` and `aka` fields and the number of those inferred ASN that have not been registered in PDB. For the 2018–2022 period, we observe that the prevalence of unregistered ASNs is more significant in `aka` than in `notes`, ranging between 0.23 and 0.15 and 0.09 and 0.06 respectively. We also note that both trends have been declining over time, though for `aka` roughly 15% of the siblings reported are not present in PDB records. We suspect that operators sometimes report unregistered ASNs in a single record to reduce management overhead associated with registration and maintenance of multiple records. Despite being convenient, reporting ASNs that are not present in PDB lacks authentication and it is unclear whether these ASNs are in fact all under the same management.

6.5   Removing Upstream Providers

We now shift our attention to the c2p filter to investigate the impact of different c2p threshold values. In this analysis, we evaluate the trade-off between discarding false positive inferences (*i.e.*, clustering ASNs from different organizations) and discarding correctly inferred clusters (*i.e.*, an inferred c2p relationship between ASes of the same organization).

Table 11. Impact of the c2p filter on the sibling inferences as the number of filtered clusters with different threshold values. We use three posible outcomes, *(i)* positive (ASNs were not under the same management), *(ii)* negative (ASNs were under the same management) and *(iii)* neutral (ASNs were under the same management but the same information is available through the org_id. Numbers in parenthesis correspond to the fraction of clusters in that category of a c2p threshold value.

Category	c2p Threshold values					
	0	1	2	3	4	5
Positive	10 (0.04)	3 (0.08)	3 (0.14)	2 (0.15)	1 (0.09)	2 (0.29)
Neutral	125 (0.52)	11 (0.30)	5 (0.24)	2 (0.15)	1 (0.09)	1 (0.14)
Negative	104 (0.44)	23 (0.62)	13 (0.62)	9 (0.69)	9 (0.82)	4 (0.57)

We recall that the c2p filter discards clusters (before the data consolidation stage) when the number of c2p relationships across members exceeds the threshold value (§4.2). For the evaluation, we apply five different threshold values (0-5) to the snapshot of September 1, 2022. We conduct human inspection to assess whether the cluster was successfully removed based on the text provided in the notes. Table 11 shows the results for this human inspection where filtered clusters are categorized into three types: *(i)* positive (ASNs were not under the same management), *(ii)* negative (ASNs were under the same management) and *(iii)* neutral (ASNs were under the same management but the same information is available through the org_id. The results show that filtered out clusters are mostly legit siblings and a small fraction of them contain networks reporting their upstream connectivity. The overlap between notes and org_id (§6.1) partially mitigates the impact of removing valid clusters.

We manually examined the filtered clusters that contain upstream providers under different managements. We found that these networks use their notes to list their connectivity with several large transit networks (*e.g.*, Level3-3356, Telecom Italia-6762, GTT-3257) that belong to different corporations (see an example in Appendix D). This example argues in favor of implementing the c2p filter as a mechanism to prevent our approach from clustering together high-profile networks that belong to different organizations.

To summarize this analysis, the c2p filter successfully removes false positive inferences but with the cost of also discarding clusters containing siblings. The consequence of this filter is that it introduces a human examination phase to reintroduce the valid-but-removed clusters. We leave as future work a more refined filter that reduces the human interaction in the process.

6.6   Grouping Scattered Sibling Information

We conclude our evaluation by looking at the effectiveness of the consolidation stage in grouping partially overlapping clusters. We investigate the number of clusters obtained after applying extraction and filtering stages that required the consolidation stage to be grouped into single clusters.

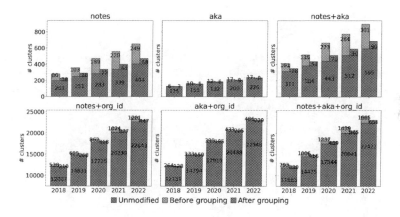

Fig. 4. Impact of the consolidation stage grouping partially overlapping clusters together.

We recall §4.3 where we describe that sibling information may be scattered across multiple PDB records. We now apply the PDB-based inferencing approach and investigate the prevalence of sibling information scattered across multiple records that creates partially overlapping clusters. Figure 4 shows the contribution of the consolidation stage counting the number of clusters before and after this stage and highlighting the number of unmodified clusters for six feature combinations in the five-year dataset. We observe that the majority of the clusters remain the same after applying this stage since the information was not scattered or they were just atomic clusters. However, for the fraction of clusters that was susceptible to be further grouped, the effectiveness of this stage is remarkable with a compression factor (number of clusters before and after the stage) between 3:1 and 4:1. This highlights the lack of uniform patterns to share sibling information as well as the prevalence of organizations without a record that aggregates all networks under control of the organization.

7   *as2org+*: Enriching the AS2Org Dataset with PeeringDB

In this section we investigate the contribution of a PDB-based inferencing approach to enhance the AS2Org' AS-to-Organization mappings. We evaluate the overall contribution to the AS-level topology (§7.1), finding that the Organization-level topology is composed by 92% single-AS clusters. For the remaining 8%, responsible for delivering the majority of Internet's traffic [22], we evaluate changes in organizations of large transit networks (§7.2) and *Hypergiants* (§7.3).

7.1   Enhancing AS2Org

In this section we investigate the contribution of PDB-based inferencing to the existing AS-to-Organization mapping techniques as a complementary source of data. *as2org+* combines the WHOIS-based AS2Org clusters with the output of our PDB-based inferencing approach.

Table 12. Contribution of PDB-based inferencing to AS2Org datasets seen in the *as2org+* output.

| | | | | Non-atomic clusters | | | | |
| | | # Clusters (AS2Org) | | # clusters | | # ASes | | |
Field	Year	All	Unmodif.	*as2org+*	AS2Org	*as2org+*	AS2Org	Migrant ASes
notes	2018	71288	70806	5529	5729	20994	21373	1518
	2019	75223	74979	5925	5932	22498	22348	759
	2020	79126	78870	6407	6424	24529	24385	815
	2021	86565	86255	6833	6856	26052	25872	1149
	2022	90508	90144	7272	7324	27771	27580	1444
aka	2018	71288	70921	5528	5729	20917	21373	1348
	2019	75223	75122	5935	5932	22413	22348	363
	2020	79126	79022	6420	6424	24446	24385	367
	2021	86565	86454	6849	6856	25936	25872	401
	2022	90508	90402	7311	7324	27635	27580	712
org	2018	71288	70382	5526	5729	21261	21373	3168
	2019	75223	74358	5946	5932	22906	22348	2659
	2020	79126	78154	6438	6424	25002	24385	2991
	2021	86565	85474	6865	6856	26561	25872	3613
	2022	90508	89251	7338	7324	28387	27580	4150

We evaluate the contribution of the PDB-based inference in *as2org+* from different perspectives. We use the AS2Org dataset as a baseline to compare it with *as2org+* to evaluate the total number of clusters that *as2org+* modifies. We then narrow the analysis and specifically examine the contribution of *as2org+* in modifying the number of non-atomic clusters. We finally contrast both datasets from the AS-level perspective and investigate the prevalence of migrant ASes, ASes that moved into a new cluster after adding the PDB-based inference.

Table 12 shows the contribution of the PDB-based inference approach to *as2org+* when different features are used in the 5-year dataset described in §6. We observe minor modifications to the number of clusters (including non-atomic clusters), independent of the snapshot and feature used. It is worth noting that we expect to see minor changes since the Internet is mostly composed of small single-AS organizations. The number of clusters in AS2Org before and after combining it with PDB-based inferences shows minor changes too due, in part, to the impact of the consolidation stages that groups together clusters when they partially overlap. Nonetheless, the number of migrant ASes reaches 4150 ($\approx$4% of the ASes in AS2Org database) using the `org_id` field in the 2022 snapshot. Despite these changes appearing negligible, it is important to examine what ASes and organizations are being modified by this contribution. In the next section, we explore some aspects of the network to put in perspective the impact of these changes.

7.2   Reshaping Large Transit Organizations

In the following paragraphs we shift our attention to the contribution of *as2org+* in drawing a more complete structure of large transit organizations and hypergiants. To put that contribution in perspective, we use CAIDA's AS-RANK [7] and investigate where there is a correlation between reshaped organizations and the transit ranking of these networks.

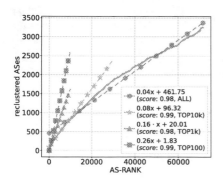

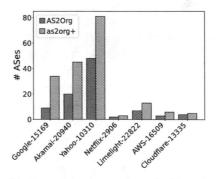

(a) Changes in the number of *siblings* inferred as a function of CAIDA's AS-RANK.

(b) Changes in the number of *siblings* in organization operating *Hygergiants*.

Fig. 5. Contribution of *as2org+* to obtain a better representation of large transit (Fig. 5a) and content delivery (Fig 5b) organzations.

We create a N-dimensional vector $v \in \{0,1\}^N$ where N is the number of ASes in the AS-RANK and the order is given the networks' ranking. We then fill that vector with either 0 or 1 where 1 means that that AS is now in a different cluster compared to the AS2Org dataset. Figure 5a shows the cumulative sum of the status vector v as well as linear regressions for the cumulative sum containing top100, top1k, top10k and all ASes in the AS-RANK. We observe that 3,254 out 71,258 ASes in the AS-RANK have moved into a different cluster comparing *as2org+* and AS2Org datasets. A linear equation describes, with a high accuracy (linear regression score: 0.98), the contribution of the PDB-based inference to reshape clusters. However, the curve is notably separated at the top of the ranking (seen at the beginning of the curve) indicating a different model for that portion. We then apply linear regression for top100, top1k, top10k ASes in the ranking and find that the slope coefficient increases when we narrow the selection of top-ranked networks. In numbers, the slope coefficient is 0.26, 0.16, 0.08 and 0.04 for linear regression including top100, top1k, top10k and all ASes in the AS-RANK. In other words, this means that 1 out of 4, 6, 12 and 25 has moved into a new cluster for different slices of the AS-RANK. This finding highlights that *as2org+* contribution is more prevalent across organizations operating large transit networks.

7.3   Impact in Hypergiant Organizations

Last, we investigate whether our PDB-based inference approach draws a more complete representation of large content providers, also known as *Hypergiants (HGs)* [5,22,33], at an organization level. We study the contribution of PDB-based inference to the 15 most prominent HGs[5] identified by recent works on that space [5,10,11].

Figure 5b shows the 7 HGs organizations that have changed when *as2org+* data is compared to AS2Org. The contribution of the PDB-based inference approach to the representation of these HGs is not homogeneous; Yahoo!, Akamai, Google, organizations have grown in 43, 25 and 25 ASNs, respectively, while Limelight, Amazon, Netflix and Cloudflare 6, 3, 1 and 1, respectively. This new organization-level representation groups together different Google's business units (*e.g.,* Google's AS15169, Google Fiber (AS16591) and Google Cloud Services (AS396982)), Akamai's subsidiaries (*e.g.,* AS20940, Prolexic-32787 and Linode-63949) and Amazon's networks (AS16509 and AS14618). This shows that *as2org+* contributes to draw a more complete representation of the organizations serving large fractions of Internet's traffic.

---

[5] The list is composed of Apple-AS714, Amazon-AS16509, Facebook-AS32934, Google-AS15169, Akamai-AS20940, Yahoo!-AS10310, Hurricane Electric-AS6939, OVH-AS16276, LimeLight-AS22822, Microsoft-AS8075, Twitter-AS13414, Twitch-AS46489, Cloudflare-AS13335 and Edgecast-AS15133.

8   Related Work

Despite the popularity of both WHOIS and PeeringDB datasets, to the best of our knowledge, there is no prior work that has combined both datasets to address the AS-to-Organization mapping problem.

Our work builds on the seminar work by Cai et al. [57] which created an automated methodology using WHOIS records to generate AS-to-organizations mappings, and Hyun *et al.* [29] which discusses of common practices in the use of multiple ASes for a single organization and introduces the idea of using WHOIS records to identify ASes under the same administration.

The WHOIS data received notorious attention given that this database offers information that is not embedded in network protocols interactions. To enable characterizations of the .com WHOIS data, Liu *et al.* [36] proposed parse and structure WHOIS query responses using a conditional random field model. For a different purpose, Livadariu *et al.* [37] examined WHOIS records to contrast the results of IP geolocation services finding partial overlaps in geolocation and delegated country fields.

A number of research efforts relied on PeeringDB as a source of topological data. Lodhi *et al.* [38] investigated the accuracy and representativeness of PDB records finding strong correlations between address space, traffic volume and geographic footprint in these records and other sources of network data. Bottger et al. [5] used several network features publicly reported in PeeringDB to identify the most prominent CDNs (Hypergiants). Other research efforts relied on PeeringDB's AS-to-facilities lists to detect ASes footprint and facilities outages [23,24]. In a recent work, Carisimo *et al.* [9] leveraged PeeringDB data to identify ASNs belonging to the same organization in the context of state-owned Internet Operators.

9   Conclusions and Future Directions

We presented *as2org+*, a new framework that leverages *self-reported* information available on PeeringDB to boost the state-of-the-art WHOIS-based methodologies, arguing that a collaborative operator-oriented database could bring a complementary perspective to the information available in WHOIS records. We conducted an in-depth study of the common practices used in PDB to report *ASes under the same management*. We apply this knowledge to design the sibling extraction rules that are at the core of the *as2org+* framework. We evaluated the contribution of this new approach and used it to carry out a preliminary analysis showing it helps yield a better representation at the Organization level of large transit networks, multinational conglomerates and merger and acquisitions.

This work suggests several promising directions for future work including the use of ML and NLP tools. These learning approaches could leverage the semantic context of the data to refine our extraction process. These techniques could be also applied to better represent complex organizations (*e.g.,* China Telecom) with multiple registration IDs in WHOIS but minimally present on PDB.

Acknowledgements. This work was partly funded by the research grant CNS-2107392.

A   Example of a aka Reporting Siblings

Listing 1.3 shows the **net** entry of Telecom Argentina's AS7303 as examples of the use of the field **aka** to report *siblings*.

```
1   {"meta":
2     {"generated": },
3     "data": [
4       {
5         "asn": 7303,
6         "website":"",
7         "notes": "Telecom Argentina is the major broadband and mobile
              provider in Argentina, with more than 4.1 MM broadband
              subscribers, 4 MM fixed lines and 20 MM mobile lines. Other ASN
              under 7303 are 10481 and 10318.",
8         "org_id": 1419,
9         "policy_url": "",
10        "aka": "FiberCorp, Cablevision (other ASN: 10481 and 10318)",
11   }}}
```

Listing 1.3. Example of the **net** entry for AS7303 in the PDB snapshot of October 1, 2020.

B   Examples of the aka Feature Extraction

Table 13 shows examples in which operators use the field **aka** to report *siblings* and the results obtained after applying the extraction rules.

Table 13. Examples of `regex` bieng applied to extract siblings from **aka** field.

ASN	Input	regex	Output
25751	*Mediaplex, Commission Junction, FastClick, Dotomi, ValueClick, SET.tv, 41041, 26762, 19834*	\d{4,8}	[41041, 26762, 19834]
24130	*9722 18398 23741 23745 17999 9894 (IX Services)*	\d{4,8}	[9722, 18398, 23741, 23745, 17999, 9894]
8100	*FKA AS29761*	\d{4,8}	[29761]
714	*Apple CDN AS6185*	\d{4,8}	[6185]

C   Example of Lack of Trust in Reported Data

Listing 1.4 shows the **net** entry of the Bangladeshi provider Brothers Online (AS135131) that was mistakenly reporting Meta's AS32934 in its aka field.

```
1   {"meta":
2    {"generated": },
3     "data": [
4       {
5        "asn": 135131,
6        "website":"http://www.brothersonlineisp.com",
7        "notes": "",
8        "org_id": 20630,
9        "policy_url": "http://www.brothersonlineisp.com",
10       "aka": "AS32934",
11   }}}
```

Listing 1.4. net entry of AS135131 in the PDB snapshot of October 1, 2020.

D   Example of a Network Reporting Transit Connectivity

Listing 1.5 shows the **net** entry of the CacheFly (AS30081) that includes in its notes ASNs that are not under the same management.

```
1   {"meta":
2    {"generated": },
3     "data": [
4       {
5     'asn': 30081,
6     'name': 'CacheFly',
7     'notes': 'AS3257/AS7922/AS1299/AS2914/AS1221 announces best anycast route at '
8              'all locations in addition to direct peering.\n'
9              '\n'
10             'Please note we only peer with local/regional carriers in each '
11             'location.',
12   }}
```

Listing 1.5. net entry of 30081 in the PDB snapshot of October 1, 2020.

References

1. Albert, R., Jeong, H., Barabási, A.L.: Error and attack tolerance of complex networks. Nature 406(6794), 378–382 (2000)
2. ARIN: Rdap: Whois for the modern world (2016). https://www.arin.net/blog/2016/05/26/rdap-whois-for-the-modern-world/
3. ARIN: Organization identifiers (org ids) (2022). https://www.arin.net/resources/guide/account/records/org/
4. ARIN: Organizations holding legacy resources (2022). https://www.arin.net/resources/guide/legacy/
5. Böttger, T., Cuadrado, F., Uhlig, S.: Looking for hypergiants in PeeringDB. ACM SIGCOMM Comput. Commun. Rev. **48**(3), 13–19 (2018)
6. CABASE: Instructivo peeringdb (2022). https://www.cabase.org.ar/wordpress/wp-content/uploads/2014/09/Alta-en-peeringDB.doc

7. CAIDA: As rank. https://catalog.caida.org/details/software/asrank_api, (Accessed 17 Jan 2022)
8. CAIDA: Mapping autonomous systems to organizations: Caida's inference methodology (2022). https://www.caida.org/archive/as2org/
9. Carisimo, E., Gamero-Garrido, A., Snoeren, A.C., Dainotti, A.: Identifying ases of state-owned internet operators. In: Proceedings of IMC (2021)
10. Carisimo, E., Selmo, C., Alvarez-Hamelin, J.I., Dhamdhere, A.: Studying the evolution of content providers in the Internet core. In: Proceedings of TMA. IEEE (2018)
11. Carisimo, E., Selmo, C., Alvarez-Hamelin, J.I., Dhamdhere, A.: Studying the evolution of content providers in IPv4 and IPv6 internet cores. Int. J. Comput. Telecommun. Industry **145**, 54–65 (2019)
12. CenturyLink: Centurylink completes acquisition of Level 3 (2017). https://news.lumen.com/2017-11-01-CenturyLink-completes-acquisition-of-Level-3
13. Cho, S., Fontugne, R., Cho, K., Dainotti, A., Gill, P.: Bgp hijacking classification. In: Proceedings of TMA, pp. 25–32 (2019). https://doi.org/10.23919/TMA.2019.8784511
14. Company T: Telia company's divestment of Telia carrier completed (2021). https://www.teliacompany.com/en/news/press-releases/2021/6/telia-companys-divestment-of-telia-carrier-completed/
15. Dhamdhere, A., et al.: Inferring persistent interdomain congestion. In: Proc. of ACM SIGCOMM, SIGCOMM 2018, pp. 1–15. Association for Computing Machinery, New York (2018). https://doi.org/10.1145/3230543.3230549
16. Dimitropoulos, X., et al.: As relationships: Inference and validation. ACM SIGCOMM Comput. Commun. Rev. **37**(1), 29–40 (2007)
17. Dolev, D., Jamin, S., Mokryn, O.O., Shavitt, Y.: Internet resiliency to attacks and failures under bgp policy routing. Comput. Netw. **50**(16), 3183–3196 (2006)
18. Facebook: Peering: Technical requirements (2022). https://www.facebook.com/peering
19. Feamster, N., Winick, J., Rexford, J.: A model of bgp routing for network engineering. In: Proceedings of ACM SIGMETRICS, SIGMETRICS 2004/Performance 2004, pp. 331–342. Association for Computing Machinery, New York (2004). https://doi.org/10.1145/1005686.1005726
20. Gao, L.: On inferring autonomous system relationships in the Internet. IEEE/ACM Trans. Netw. **9**(6), 733–745 (2001)
21. Gao, L., Rexford, J.: Stable internet routing without global coordination. Proc. of ACM Sigmetrics **28**(1), 307–317 (2000). https://doi.org/10.1145/345063.339426
22. Gigis, P., et al.: Seven years in the life of hypergiants' off-nets. In: Proceedings of ACM SIGCOMM (2021)
23. Giotsas, V., Dietzel, C., Smaragdakis, G., Feldmann, A., Berger, A., Aben, E.: Detecting peering infrastructure outages in the wild. In: Proceedings of ACM SIGCOMM (2017)
24. Giotsas, V., Smaragdakis, G., Huffaker, B., Luckie, M., Claffy, K.: Mapping peering interconnections to a facility. In: Proceedings of CoNEXT (2015)
25. Google: Prerequisites to peer with Google (2022). https://peering.google.com/#/options/peering
26. Greenlees, D., Arnold, W.: Asia scrambles to restore communications after quake - business - international herald tribune (2006). https://www.nytimes.com/2006/12/28/business/worldbusiness/28iht-connect.4042439.html

27. Holz, R., et al.: Tracking the deployment of tls 1.3 on the web: A story of experimentation and centralization. ACM SIGCOMM Comput. Commun. Rev. **50**(3), 3–15 (2020). https://doi.org/10.1145/3411740.3411742

28. Huston, G.: The death of transit and the future internet. In: ITU Workshop on Network, vol. 2030 (2018)

29. Hyun, Y., Broido, A., Claffy, k.: Traceroute and BGP AS path incongruities. Tech. rep., Cooperative Association for Internet Data Analysis (CAIDA) (2003–03)

30. ICANN: Registration data access protocol (RDAP) (2022). https://www.icann.org/rdap

31. Jin, Y., Scot, C., Dhamdhere, A., Giotsas, V., Krishnamurthy, A., Shenker, S.: Stable and practical AS relationship inference with ProbLink. In: Proceedings of USENIX NSDI (2019)

32. Kashaf, A., Sekar, V., Agarwal, Y.: Analyzing third party service dependencies in modern web services: Have we learned from the mirai-dyn incident? In: Proceedings of IMC, IMC 2020 pp. 634–647. Association for Computing Machinery, New York (2020). https://doi.org/10.1145/3419394.3423664

33. Labovitz, C., Iekel-Johnson, S., McPherson, D., Oberheide, J., Jahanian, F.: Internet inter-domain traffic. ACM SIGCOMM Comput. Commun. Rev. **40**(4), 75–86 (2010)

34. Laskowski, P., Chuang, J.: Network monitors and contracting systems: competition and innovation. Proc. ACM SIGCOMM **36**(4), 183–194 (2006)

35. Liu, E., Akiwate, G., Jonker, M., Mirian, A., Savage, S., Voelker, G.M.: Who's got your mail? characterizing mail service provider usage. In: Proceedings of IMC, IMC 2021, pp. 122–136. Association for Computing Machinery, New York (2021). https://doi.org/10.1145/3487552.3487820

36. Liu, S., Ian, Foster, Savage, S., Voelker, G., Saul, L.: Who is. com? learning to parse WHOIS records. In: Proceedings of IMC, pp. 369–380 (2015)

37. Livadariu, I., et al.: On the accuracy of country-level IP geolocation. In: Applied Networking Research Workshop, pp. 67–73 (2020)

38. Lodhi, A., Larson, N., Dhamdhere, A., Dovrolis, C.: kc Claffy: Using peeringDB to understand the peering ecosystem. ACM SIGCOMM Comput. Commun. Rev. **44**(2), 20–27 (2014)

39. Lodhi, A.H.: The economics of Internet peering interconnections. Ph.D. thesis, Georgia Institute of Technology (2014)

40. Luckie, M., Huffaker, B., Dhamdhere, A., Giotsas, V., Claffy, K.: As relationships, customer cones, and validation. In: Proceedings of IMC (2013)

41. Microsoft: Prerequisites to set up peering with Microsoft (2022). https://docs.microsoft.com/en-us/azure/internet-peering/prerequisites

42. Moura, G.C.M., Castro, S., Hardaker, W., Wullink, M., Hesselman, C.: Clouding up the internet: How centralized is dns traffic becoming? In: Proceedings of IMC, IMC 2020, pp. 42–49. Association for Computing Machinery, New York (2020). https://doi.org/10.1145/3419394.3423625

43. NCC R: Youtube hijacking: A ripe ncc ris case study (2008). https://www.ripe.net/publications/news/industry-developments/youtube-hijacking-a-ripe-ncc-ris-case-study

44. Nemmi, E.N., Sassi, F., La Morgia, M., Testart, C., Mei, A., Dainotti, A.: The parallel lives of autonomous systems: ASN allocations vs. BGP. In: Proceedings of IMC, pp. 593–611 (2021)

45. NIC.br: Collaboration between NIC.br and PeeringDB is helping improve Internet traffic exchange in Brazil (2020). https://nic.br/noticia/releases/collaboration-between-nic-br-and-peeringdb-is-helping-improve-internet-traffic-exchange-in-brazil/
46. Nobile, L., Morris, T.: Status and solutions for WHOIS data accuracy (2022). https://archive.nanog.org/sites/default/files/3_Nobile_Whois_Data_Accuracy.pdf
47. PeeringDB: Approving network (net) objects (2022). https://docs.peeringdb.com/committee/admin/approval-guidelines/#approving-network-net-objects
48. PeeringDB: Peeringdb api documentation (2022). https://www.peeringdb.com/apidocs/#operation/create%20net
49. Quoitin, B., Pelsser, C., Bonaventure, O., Uhlig, S.: A performance evaluation of bgp-based traffic engineering. Int. J. Netw. Manag. **15**(3), 177–191 (2005). https://doi.org/10.1002/nem.559, https://onlinelibrary.wiley.com/doi/abs/10.1002/nem.559
50. Spring, N., Mahajan, R., Anderson, T.: The causes of path inflation. In: Proceedings of ACM SIGCOMM, SIGCOMM 2003, pp. 113–124. Association for Computing Machinery, New York (2003). https://doi.org/10.1145/863955.863970
51. Subramanian, L., Agarwal, S., Rexford, J., Katz, R.H.: Characterizing the Internet hierarchy from multiple vantage points. In: Proceedings of IEEE INFOCOM (2002)
52. Testart, C., Richter, P., King, A., Dainotti, A., Clark, D.: Profiling bgp serial hijackers: Capturing persistent misbehavior in the global routing table. In: Proceedings of IMC, IMC 2019, pp. 420–434. Association for Computing Machinery, New York (2019). https://doi.org/10.1145/3355369.3355581
53. Testart, C., Richter, P., King, A., Dainotti, A., Clark, D.: To filter or not to filter: measuring the benefits of registering in the RPKI today. In: Sperotto, A., Dainotti, A., Stiller, B. (eds.) PAM 2020. LNCS, vol. 12048, pp. 71–87. Springer, Cham (2020). https://doi.org/10.1007/978-3-030-44081-7_5
54. USA T.M: T-mobile completes merger with sprint to create the new t-mobile (2020). https://www.t-mobile.com/news/un-carrier/t-mobile-sprint-one-company
55. Wire, B.: Gtt acquires nlayer communications, inc. (2012). https://www.businesswire.com/news/home/20120501005550/en/GTT-Acquires-nLayer-Communications-Inc
56. Wu, J., Zhang, Y., Mao, Z.M., Shin, K.G.: Internet routing resilience to failures: analysis and implications. In: Proceedings of CoNEXT, pp. 1–12 (2007)
57. Xue, X., Heidemann, J., Krishnamurthy, B., Willinger, W.: Towards an AS-to-organization map. In: Proceedings of IMC (2010)

RPKI Time-of-Flight: Tracking Delays in the Management, Control, and Data Planes

Romain Fontugne[1]([✉]), Amreesh Phokeer[2], Cristel Pelsser[3], Kevin Vermeulen[4], and Randy Bush[1,5]

[1] IIJ Research Lab, Tokyo, Japan
romain@iij.ad.jp, randy@psg.com
[2] Internet Society, Reston, USA
phokeer@isoc.org
[3] UCLouvain, Ottignies-Louvain-la-Neuve, Belgium
cristel.pelsser@uclouvain.be
[4] LAAS-CNRS, Université de Toulouse, CNRS, Toulouse, France
kevin.vermeulen@laas.fr
[5] Arrcus, Inc, San Jose, USA

Abstract. As RPKI is becoming part of ISPs' daily operations and Route Origin Validation is getting widely deployed, one wonders how long it takes for the effect of RPKI changes to appear in the data plane. Does an operator that adds, fixes, or removes a Route Origin Authorization (ROA) have time to brew coffee or rather enjoy a long meal before the Internet routing infrastructure integrates the new information and the operator can assess the changes and resume work? The chain of ROA publication, from creation at Certification Authorities all the way to the routers and the effect on the data plane involves a large number of players, is not instantaneous, and is often dominated by ad hoc administrative decisions. This is the first comprehensive study to measure the entire ecosystem of ROA manipulation by all five Regional Internet Registries (RIRs), propagation on the management plane to Relying Parties (RPs) and to routers; measure the effect on BGP as seen by global control plane monitors; and finally, measure the effects on data plane latency and reachability. We found that RIRs usually publish new RPKI information within five minutes, except APNIC which averages ten minutes slower. At least one national CA is said to publish daily. We observe significant disparities in ISPs' reaction time to new RPKI information, ranging from a few minutes to one hour. The delay for ROA deletion is significantly longer than for ROA creation as RPs and BGP strive to maintain reachability. Incidentally, we found and reported significant issues in the management plane of two RIRs and a Tier1 network.

1 Introduction

The Border Gateway Protocol (BGP [1]) is the ubiquitous inter-domain routing protocol of the Internet. Unfortunately, like the rest of the early Internet, it was designed with no thought to security. One of the main efforts to secure BGP is

© The Author(s), under exclusive license to Springer Nature Switzerland AG 2023
A. Brunstrom et al. (Eds.): PAM 2023, LNCS 13882, pp. 429–457, 2023.
https://doi.org/10.1007/978-3-031-28486-1_18

the Resource Public Key Infrastructure [2,3] (RPKI) which is an X.509-based system to share addressing and routing information assured by cryptographic methods. In the RPKI, Certificate Authorities (CAs), dominated by Regional Internet Registries (RIRs), issue to ISPs resource certificates containing a list of IP prefixes allocated to them. ISPs use these certificates to create digitally signed attestations called Route Origin Authorizations (ROAs) to certify that a particular Autonomous System (AS) may advertise these prefixes. Other ISPs' routers can then use ROAs to validate incoming BGP announcements through a process called Route Origin Validation (ROV) [4] (see right side of Fig. 1).

The RPKI (a management plane) was designed to decouple and provide data redundant to the BGP control plane, allowing validation. Since operators have to apply and assess RPKI changes before updating BGP configurations, the overall routing operations are inevitably delayed by the time it takes to update and propagate RPKI data. However, the IETF specifications were lax in not specifying, or at least strongly recommending, timing parameters for the long linear RPKI management plane protocols (see *Management plane* in Fig. 1). BGP route updates propagate in less than a minute, two at worst [5,6]. Therefore there is an expectation that propagation on the RPKI management plane is reasonably bounded; but we found that it takes on average over 25 min for APNIC and due to a bug we have reported as much as five hours for ARIN and LACNIC data to propagate; **orders of magnitude slower than BGP!** Ultimately RPKI updates should be applied as quickly as possible; long delays in the management plane increase the feedback loop for routing operations, increase the opportunities to let mistakes go unresolved, and increase the time needed to fix them [7–10]. For example, NTT has documented three common oversights that lead to discrepancies between BGP announcements and RPKI data [11]: (1) a new prefix violating the maxLength attribute of an existing ROA, (2) announcing customer prefixes while the latter has not yet updated the corresponding ROAs (also a common for DDoS and BGP hijack mitigation [12]), (3) prefix migration from one AS to another. Since these inconsistencies between the management and control plane could lead to significant traffic loss in ROV-enabled networks [13,14] the time it takes to fix ROAs and globally propagate them is of critical importance.

The goal of this paper is to measure the delays associated with the RPKI systems of the five RIRs and current ROV deployments by measuring the management, control, and data planes. We deploy experimental prefixes on the Internet and measure the management plane latency from ROA creation and subsequent publication by the RIRs to receipt by the routers, and then the resulting effects on the BGP control plane using RIPE RIS [15] data. We also measure some of the results on the data plane using RIPE Atlas [16] traceroutes; showing topological effects of ROAs, BGP path hunting, and latency shifts.

We make the following contributions:

A Method to Measure the Latency Induced by RPKI Adoption: We design an end-to-end experiment, for each of the five RIRs, to track the delay across the different steps between the creation/deletion of a ROA by the resource holder and the time in which we see the corresponding changes on the management, control, and data planes (§ 3). We deploy two experiments, one with an

AS connected mainly to ASes performing ROV (§ 4), and another one with ASes surrounded by some, but not all, ASes performing ROV to generalize our findings (§ 5.1).

A Landscape of the Impact of ROV Adoption on the Internet: With these experiments, we found that: (1) There was a significant time disparity across RIRs between the operator's input and the ROA publication delay (Table 2 and 3). (2) This observation allowed us to discover some startling anomalies (since corrected after our notification) at ARIN and LACNIC that delayed their ROA publication time by up to five hours (§ 4.1). (3) There is an important disparity in ISPs' reaction time between ROA creation and ROA deletion, ranging from minutes to an hour. ISPs take significantly more time to act on ROA deletion than ROA creation (§ 4.2); (4) We also reported anomalous behavior to a Tier1 network which quickly corrected. (5) There are vast differences between the RIRs' administrative practices seriously complicating the experiment setup, and highlighting how difficult it can be for operators to streamline their RPKI management procedures at the different RIRs (§ 6).

Extending the Findings with a Longitudinal Study: We further broaden our study with an analysis of historical RPKI and BGP data (§ 5.2) showing that the bugs reported to RIRs have been present for years and that long delays of ROA creation have been quite stable over the past four years.

Inter-RIR Differences in ROA Payloads: Our analysis of RPKI data also reveals ROA structural differences between the five RIRs, highlighting RIRs' different management of RPKI data and explaining some of their disparities (§ 5.3).

2 Background

RPKI prefix allocation follows the IANA allocation hierarchy, and each RIR maintains a separate trust anchor (TA) for the resources for which they are responsible. Certificates are issued to their members, which are then used to sign ROAs. Each RIR operates a public repository in which all RPKI objects (certs, ROAs, CRLs, manifest files [3, 17]) are stored.

Figure 1 depicts the steps performed when a resource holder queries an RIR to update RPKI information for its prefixes. Then the changes are fetched by operators performing Route Origin Validation (ROV-enabled ASes, green in Fig. 1) that use this new information to update their routers. Each step described below is common to all RIRs and ROV-enabled ASes, but each may perform these steps at different time intervals and frequency.

ROV-enabled ASes check route validity based on the information contained in ROAs. To get ROA information, routers need to connect to Relying Party (RP) software which is in charge of fetching ROAs, cryptographically validating their content, and feeding routers with Validated ROA Payloads (VRPs). Based on the VRPs, routers can then classify BGP announcements either as Valid, NotFound, or Invalid. ROV-enabled ASes typically drop the "Invalid" announcements.

432   R. Fontugne et al.

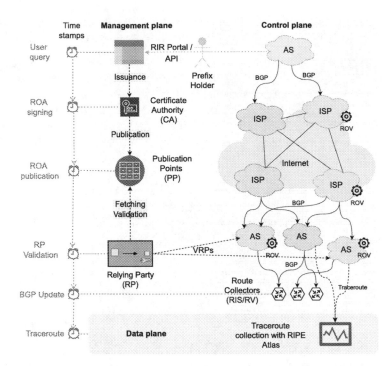

Fig. 1. Data-flow from creation of a ROA by the prefix holder to the corresponding BGP updates recorded at the route collectors (RIS / RouteViews). The red labels on the left show the points at which time measurements were taken. (Color figure online)

Each step in the provisioning process introduces delay. The aim of this study is to track and quantify these delays across RIRs and some ISPs. For this we collect timestamps at the following points:

1. ***User Query***: The most common way for resource holders to create ROAs is to query the RIR that provided the IP prefixes. The queries are either via the RIR's web portal or the RIR's REST API if available.
2. ***ROA Signing***: RIRs collect user queries, verify that they are legitimate, and pass them to certification authority software which computes ROAs and corresponding metadata information (i.e., manifest and CRL files) and creates new signed files.
3. ***ROA Publication***: Then RIRs place new ROAs and metadata files into public repositories, called Publication Points (PPs), so that Relying Party (RP) software can fetch them when desired. This seems a simple step, but RIRs must ensure that RPKI objects are consistent at all times, hence metadata files and their corresponding ROAs must be atomically published.
4. ***Relying Party (RP) Validation***: RPs are deployed by ROV-enabled ASes and their role is to periodically fetch and validate all the objects from the global RPKI repositories. After validation, they produce a list of Validated

Table 1. Summary for the two experiments presented in Sect. 4 and 5.1.

Section	RIR	Origin AS	Upstreams	Period
§4	All five RIRs	3970	ROV-enabled	Nov. 2011 to Oct. 2022
§5.1	RIPE	17660, 55722, 23676	mix	May 2022 to Oct. 2022

ROA Payloads (VRPs) which routers use to verify incoming BGP announcements. Larger ISPs often deploy multiple RPs to avoid single points of failure, and to tune the timing with which each RP visits the Publication Points.

5. **BGP Update**: ROV-enabled routers accept and advertise the *Valid* and *NotFound* announcements only and drop the *Invalid* ones based on the VRPs from the RPs. These changes propagate globally in BGP and the effects may be seen in BGP collection systems (e.g., RIS or RouteViews [15,18]).

6. **Traceroute**: These routing changes are reflected in the data plane and can be observed with measurement platforms such as RIPE Atlas [16].

3   RPKI Beacons

To measure the propagation time of RPKI data from RIRs' Certification Authorities to BGP speaking routers we automated RPKI ROA beaconing at each of the five RIRs. Each beacon is a prefix for which we switch its RPKI status daily by creating and deleting ROAs. We announce these experimental prefixes in BGP from a few locations on the global Internet and measure the beacons' effects in the management, control, and data planes.

3.1   Beacon Methodology

We perform two experiments from diverse ASes to measure the propagation time of RPKI data (Table 1): For the first experiment (§4), we obtained from each RIR a pair of IPv4 /24 prefixes and a pair of IPv6 /48 prefixes[1]. One prefix from each pair of prefixes is used as a control, while the other is the test prefix. The control prefixes are expected to be always reachable, with an always valid RPKI status. If they are not reachable then we know that the experiment is not valid for that period. For the test prefixes, the BGP announcements do not change, but we periodically add and remove a ROA to alternatively validate and invalidate the origin AS of the test prefixes' BGP data. We track changes reflected at the management (RPKI), control (BGP), and data plane (traceroute). The prefixes are announced from AS3970 , which is directly connected to AS3130 (not implementing ROV), which in turn is connected to two ROV-enabled upstream providers, NTT (AS2914) and Sprint (AS1239), and peering with a ROV-enabled route server at a large IXP, and directly with a few non-ROV IXP peers. The results for this experiment are described in Sect. 4.

---

[1] The list of all prefixes is given in appendix, Table 6.

For the second experiment (§5.1), we used three /24 prefixes (RIPE-A, RIPE-B, and RIPE-C) from the RIPE NCC and announced them from three diverse networks, including an IXP and a national ISP with 149 peer ASes. The three prefixes are used as test prefixes, meaning that we daily alternate the ROA status for all of them. The results of this experiment are described in Sect. 5.1.

3.2   ROA Toggling

In order to measure only the impact of ROV and avoid delays caused by other filtering mechanisms, we configured all filtering with the upstream providers (e.g., through the creation of Internet Routing Registry (IRR) route objects). We verified that our providers' filters accepted our prefixes and then left these mechanisms untouched.

To toggle the RPKI status of the test prefixes, each was invalidated by Pre-registering a ROA with the origin AS set to the invalid AS 666. For the first experiment our AS was primarily connected to upstream networks and IXP route servers that implement ROV, thus at the initial step, our test prefixes are dropped by ROV-mechanisms and globally unreachable, as opposed to the second experiment.

The ROA toggling consists of daily repeating the following steps for each test prefix:

1. ROA creation. At a random time between 00:00 and 06:00 UTC, we request a new ROA covering the <prefix, AS> to authorize the route to the test prefix.
2. Convergence phase 1. From 06:00 to 12:00 UTC we give sufficient time for networks to obtain the new ROA, process it, and update their routing.
3. ROA deletion. At a random time between 12:00 and 18:00 UTC, we delete the ROA created at the first step, hence letting our test prefix fall back to Invalid.
4. Convergence phase 2. From 18:00 to 00:00 UTC we again wait for all networks to converge to the new state.

In order to keep the RPKI beacons running over a long time, we automated all queries to RIRs. ARIN, RIPE, and recently LACNIC, provide APIs to ease such interactions with their services. We made all queries to these three RIRs via their APIs. AFRINIC and APNIC have no APIs for RPKI management; we could only create and delete ROAs via their web portals. To automate AFRINIC and APNIC processes we implemented Selenium [19] scripts that log in to these portals and submit web forms for ROA creation and deletion.

3.3   Data Collection

In order to measure the time for the above RPKI operations to propagate over the management, control, and data planes we collect temporal information from ROAs' payload, BGP data, and run traceroutes.

User Query. Delays are measured relative to the user query time, that is the time we request the RIRs to change RPKI (steps 1 and 3 in Sect. 3.2). This is logged by an NTP-synchronized host that automates the queries for ROA creation and deletion. We log the precise time of the confirmation from the RIR portal or API that the query was received without error.

RIR. We infer RIRs' signing and publication delays from the RPKIviews archive [20]. This archive consists of RPKI data snapshots taken every 20 min. Each snapshot contains the raw ROA files of all RPKI repositories as well as the output of a relying party software, rpki-client [21]. From this dataset, we compute the signing, publication, and RP delay (Fig. 1).

The signing delay is computed using the signing timestamp found in the ROA, more specifically in the Cryptographic Message Syntax (CMS) [22] wrapper of the signed object. As opposed to the "NotBefore" timestamp found in the ROA payload, which is used to determine at what time a ROA becomes "valid", the signing timestamp conveys the time at which the Certification Authority created the ROA. Unfortunately, the reliability of both timestamps are disputable as our results show that some RIRs set the signing and/or NotBefore timestamps arbitrarily (Sect. 4.1 and 5.3)!

The publication delay estimates the delay for an RIR to make newly created ROAs available to RPs. We infer the typical publication delay from RPKIviews snapshots. Since RPKIviews takes snapshots every 20 min and assuming that the publication of ROA is uniformly distributed over time, new ROAs appear in RPKIviews on average 10 min after their actual public availability. For ease of discussion, when reporting RPKIviews median delay publication time in Sect. 4, we subtract 10 min from the measured RPKIviews median delay. We analyze only these corrected median values, not individual delays.

Relying Party (RP). Computing Relying Party delays on the Internet is particularly challenging. The delay of RPs depends on three factors: the frequency at which they poll for new data from publication points, the downloading time, and the ROA processing time (i.e., mostly reading and decrypting files). Network operators may increase their RPs' polling frequency to fetch new data more quickly, but to reduce the burden on publication points, the recommendations are to poll for new data no more frequently than 10 min using RRDP (or as low as 1 min if there is caching infrastructure and the If-Modified-Since header value is set) and not more than every 30 min if using rsync [23]. Furthermore, past studies showed that 2 and 10 min are the most common RP polling frequencies [24] which correspond to respectively RIPE v3 validator and Routinator default values (rpki-client has no default value). As RIPE v3 validator has since been deprecated, we assume that 10 min is now a common value used by operators and attempt to estimate RP delay for RPs polling new data every 10 min.

Similarly to the publication delay, we leverage RPKIviews data to infer the typical delay experienced by an RP polling data every 10 min. Because the 20-min frequency of RPKIviews translates into a 10-min median polling delay and a 10-min polling frequency gives a 5 min median polling delay, when reporting results in Sect. 4 we correct the RP delay by subtracting 5 min from the median delay observed with RPKIviews' RP.

BGP. The ROA toggle described above affects the global reachability of our announced prefixes. They become unreachable when corresponding ROAs are deleted and reachable again when ROAs are re-created. We monitor these shifts in BGP using the RIPE Routing Information Service (RIS) data [15]. We particularly look into the BGP update messages sent from routers peering with RIS, and we record for each peer and each test prefix the time of the first announcement after creating a ROA and the time of the first withdrawal after deleting a ROA (BGP update in Fig. 1). These represent the first routing changes caused by each of our RPKI beacon events that we expect to be visible at the collector, and are accurate within seconds.

Section 4 presents delays for the RIS collectors RRC00 and RRC01. RRC00 has the advantage of being a multi-hop collector, meaning that it receives data from ASes that are located in very diverse locations. RRC01 collects data only from ASes peering at the LINX IXP which includes both upstream providers for the first experiment. Hence RRC01 allows us to investigate BGP signals from networks that make our prefixes globally reachable. In our preliminary analysis we have looked at an arbitrary set of RIS collectors (RRC03, RRC06, RRC12), but given the large amount of data, and that we see little difference across collectors, we present results only for RRC00 and RRC01. Past research has also shown a high level of redundancy between different collectors [25] which limit the benefits of using numerous collectors [26].

Traceroute. To test data plane reachability and delay of the prefixes with toggling ROAs, we performed traceroutes every 15 min from RIPE Atlas with probes in 6 different ASes. The probes were chosen to be inside the ASes that also share BGP routes with RIPE RIS at RRC00. We pick these ASes to have close vantage points for BGP and traceroutes, but there is no guarantee that the Atlas probe and the BGP collector share the same routes, so there could be some mismatch. However, we also tried a wider set of RIPE Atlas probes using Atlas geo-diverse selection of probes and observed similar behaviors, so our analysis focuses only on the traceroutes obtained with the 6 probes mentioned earlier. The measurements are public (Table 7) and traceroutes are configured to send three ICMP packets per hop.

4   Eleven Months in the Life of RPKI Beacons

We now present the results of our first experiment; over eleven months of toggling RPKI ROA beacons for prefixes from the five RIRs and announced from an AS surrounded by ROV-enabled networks (see row 1 in Table 1).

The analysis in this section follows the steps shown in Fig. 1 and is based on RIS data (RRC00 and RRC01) from November 1st 2021 until October 5th 2022, except for the LACNIC beacons that started on February 1st 2022. We rely on RPKIviews data from January 1st to October 6th 2022.

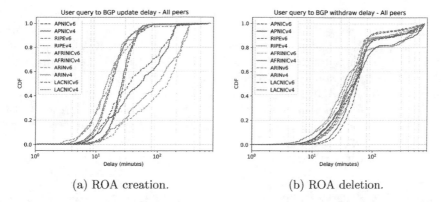

(a) ROA creation.   (b) ROA deletion.

Fig. 2. Time from user query to propagation in BGP, for all RRC00 and RRC01 peers. ARIN and LACNIC had significantly longer creation delays due to a bug related to ROAs' NotBefore timestamps. APNIC delay is typically 10 min longer than AFRINIC and RIPE. Overall the delays for ROA deletion are higher than for ROA creation.

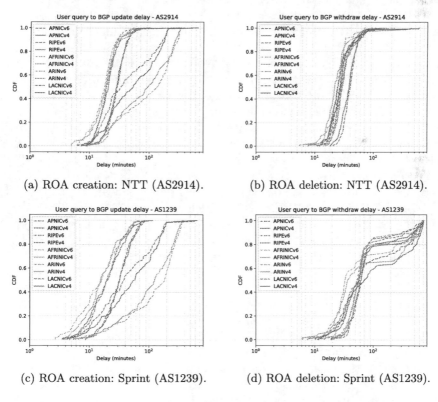

(a) ROA creation: NTT (AS2914).   (b) ROA deletion: NTT (AS2914).

(c) ROA creation: Sprint (AS1239).   (d) ROA deletion: Sprint (AS1239).

Fig. 3. Time from user query to BGP propagation (RRC00 and RRC01). Focus on the two upstream providers of our experimental AS: Sprint (AS1239) and NTT (AS2914). NTT had more consistent delays than Sprint, and Sprint had sometimes very long delays to withdraw prefixes with deleted ROAs.

Our Main Findings are that creation times vary significantly across RIRs, with medians ranging from a few minutes to over an hour for new ROAs to reach the publication points. The differences lie in the way ROAs are processed by RIRs, in batches at specific times of the day, and drastic issues we discovered at two RIRs (each applied a temporary fix). Second, deletion of ROAs takes longer to reflect in BGP as routers explore alternate routes that have not yet been invalidated. The slowest element drives the deletion time. Routers with a slow pulling cache, or redundant caches, invalidate routes late and are used by neighbors to reach the invalidated resource. Further, for ROA creation, most of the delay comes from the Relying Party pulling objects at different intervals.

4.1   ROA Creation Delay

We investigate ROA creation delay. We explore the disparity across RIRs and between upstream ASes. Figure 2a shows the per-RIR distribution of the delay between the query time to create a ROA for our test prefix and the time when reachability is first reported by each RIS peer in BGP.

AFRINIC and RIPE prefixes are seen most quickly in RIS. The median delay for an AFRINIC IPv4 prefix is 15 min (16 min for IPv6) and 18 min for RIPE prefixes for both IPv4 and IPv6. APNIC is consistently slower than AFRINIC and RIPE. The median delay for an APNIC IPv4 prefix is 26 min (28 min for IPv6). This 10-min extra delay is due to a 20-min batching process at APNIC (see Sect. 5.3). ARIN and LACNIC prefixes are susceptible to significant delays. These are due to the timezone problem described below (Publication delay and ARIN/LACNIC timezone issues). We have reported this issue to both RIRs for which ARIN deployed a workaround on 21 April 2022 and LACNIC on 12 October 2022.

For the other three RIRs delays are less than 1 h in at least 95% of the cases. We also observe some outlying values: In less than 3% of the cases, for AFRINIC, APNIC, and RIPE, the BGP delays go over 100 min. These delays are rarely visible from the two upstream providers, NTT and Sprint (Fig. 3a and 3c). Both always announce the AFRINIC prefix in less than 100 min. We cannot find consistent behaviors for the observed long delays, these could be due to unexpectedly long BGP convergence times [27]. In addition, we noticed that about half of them are related to very small ASes owned by individuals (network operators) who are active in testing new deployments (e.g., AS15562, AS35619, AS5662) so these could be the results of experiments.

We observe a large disparity across RIRs in the time elapsed between ROA creation and the effect in BGP. The same is true across our upstream ASes. In the next sections, we track the time along the different steps in Fig. 1 to understand the elements causing these disparities. We rely on Table 2, where we show the median delay for each of the steps in Fig. 1.

Table 2. ROA Creation Median Delays. Median delay in minutes from the user query to the step indicated in each column as observed for the IPv4 prefixes from the five RIRs (IPv6 results are in parenthesis). As described in § 3, delays shown in this table are either measured from ROA attributes (*) and BGP data (‡), or inferred from RPKIviews data (†).

	Sign*	NotBefore*	Publication†	Relying Party†	BGP‡
AFRINIC	0 (0)	0 (0)	3 (2)	14 (13)	15 (16)
APNIC	10 (13)	10 (13)	14 (16)	34 (38)	26 (28)
ARIN	– (–)	– (–)	69 (97)	81 (109)	95 (143)
LACNIC	0 (0)	– (–)	54 (32)	66 (42)	51 (34)
RIPE	0 (0)	0 (0)	4 (4)	14 (13)	18 (18)
After fix:					
ARIN	– (–)	– (–)	8 (9)	21 (22)	28 (23)

Certification Delay. According to the ROA signing time, AFRINIC, RIPE, and LACNIC create ROAs within a minute of receiving users' queries. APNIC's 10-min delay appears at this very first step. APNIC's signing times for our ROAs are in 20 min increments (e.g. 04:30, 04:50, 05:10) suggesting that APNIC is processing users' queries in 20-min batches, adding an average delay of 10 min.

We found that ARIN hard-codes both the ROAs signing time and NotBefore value to midnight UTC hence we are not able to compute signing delays for ARIN. LACNIC is signing ROAs immediately after the user query, but the NotBefore value in LACNIC ROAs is also hard-coded to midnight UTC.

Publication Delay and ARIN/LACNIC Timezone Issues. Before April 2022, the publication delay for ARIN and LACNIC could last several hours due to a time zone conversion problem. As mentioned above both RIRs intend to set NotBefore values to midnight, but instead, ARIN has been setting this value to 04:00 UTC or 05:00 UTC (corresponding respectively to 00:00 in Eastern Daylight Time and Eastern Standard Time) and LACNIC has been setting this value to 03:00 UTC (corresponding to 00:00 in Uruguay Standard Time). For example, a query at 01:00 UTC to create a ROA in LACNIC would create a ROA with a NotBefore value set to 03:00 UTC. Therefore, the ROA would be invalid for the two hours following its creation. Our experiment reveals that the Publication Point wisely does not publish the"not-yet-valid" ROA to the repository hence delaying its availability to RPs. The same holds for ARIN. We reported this issue to both ARIN and LACNIC.

ARIN acknowledged the problem has been present since they started their RPKI service. An interim fix for this issue was deployed on 21 April 2022, by setting the signing and NotBefore timestamps at 12:00 UTC on the day before the user query. ARIN is planning further development to properly solve this issue. Since the ARIN issue has been addressed, the publication delays for ARIN are in line with RIPE and AFRINIC at around 5 min median delay ("After fix" line in Table 2).

For LACNIC the issue is apparently only affecting ROAs created with their API, not the ones created manually on their portal. LACNIC deployed a similar fix on October 12, 2022, that sets the NotBefore timestamp at 03:00 UTC on the day before the user query. Since our LACNIC prefixes were returned on October 25, 2022, we observed the effects of this fix for less than two weeks and found that LACNIC publication delay fell in line with the other RIRs' delay (not included in Table 2 due to the small sample size). As these issues bias results for LACNIC and ARIN, the remainder of this section focuses on results from the other RIRs.

Relying Party Delay. Propagation to Relying Parties (RPs) represents the most time-consuming step observed in ROA processing. Unlike other steps where data are pushed to the next component, RPs periodically pull RPKI data from Publication Points. The delay we observe between the ROA creation and the time when an RP validates the new ROA is usually less than 15 min (38 min for APNIC). This is 10 min more than the publication delay and consists mainly of the polling interval (5 min delay on average), downloading time from all Certification Authorities (4 min), and the ROA processing time (1 min). The downloading time can be negatively impacted by Publication Points that are responding slowly. Single-threaded RPs, such as the one used by RPKIviews (rpki-client), are particularly affected by this as they sequentially visit all Publication Points and may be blocking on slow Publication Points.

BGP Updates. We usually observe BGP updates for the newly created ROAs about 3 min after the estimated RP validation time. This delay includes both the router's polling from RPs and BGP propagation time, as we are not able to measure the RP to router delay alone. As RPs signal routers when to pull, this delay should be dominated by the data transfer and the router processing of VRPs. Past work on BGP propagation estimate that a new announcement on BGP takes usually less than a minute to propagate globally [5,6], hence one can estimate the RP to routers delay should be no more than 2 min.

To further dissect delays observed at this step, we compute the BGP delay only for the two upstream providers. The BGP delay distributions of NTT (Fig. 3a) and Sprint (Fig. 3c) are similar to those observed for other peers (Fig. 2a), and their median values are all within a 4-min difference. Given that ROV is still deployed very sparsely [28], these results show that (1) the delay for ASes that are not along ROV-enabled AS paths is dictated by our upstream providers, (2) ASes beyond our upstreams that perform ROV slower would invalidate new routes. In the latter case, because we are connected to Tier1 networks, and there are many paths between Tier1 networks and RIS collectors, the effect of other ROV deployments is rarely observed.

We also compared these distributions with five other networks that are implementing ROV and announcing our prefixes to RRC00 or RRC01 (AS1299,

AS6939, AS7018, AS9002, AS14907) and found no notable differences in the distributions, meaning that these networks behave similarly to our upstreams; i.e., they are at least as fast as our upstreams to pull new RPKI data. With these data we cannot distinguish if they can fetch RPKI data faster than our upstreams as their BGP announcements are bound by the time our upstreams made the prefixes globally available. We come back to this in Sect. 5.1 with experiments announcing prefixes from very diverse locations.

A careful inspection of the delays for our two upstreams reveals that NTT is more consistent, the 10th to 90th percentile range for the IPv4 RIPE prefix corresponds to 12 and 32 min (Fig. 3a) whereas these same percentiles correspond to a range twice as large for Sprint, i.e., 7 and 47 min (Fig. 3c). Although the first quartile delay for Sprint is always better than for NTT (e.g. 12 min vs 15 min for RIPEv4), the third quartile delay for Sprint is consistently longer by 1 to 10 min for the AFRINIC, APNIC, and RIPE prefixes. We believe this is the result of a longer RP polling frequency for Sprint but a shorter RP to router delay, and we confirmed with network operators that indeed NTT is polling RPKI data more frequently than Sprint and Sprint is using faster RP software.

Using only the data after ARIN's fix we confirm the delay for ARIN prefixes improved significantly (shown in Appendix Fig. 11). The interquartile range corresponds to 13 and 33 min for IPv4 (13 and 33 for IPv6) which comes very close to RIPE and AFRINIC results for the same time period. RIPE's interquartile is 11 to 32 min for IPv4 (11 to 27 for IPv6) and AFRINIC's interquartile is 10 to 25 min for IPv4 (9 to 29 for IPv6) between 21 April 21st and May 15th 2022.

Data Plane Availability. Figure 4 shows how prefix reachability/unreachability on the data plane for IPv4 (IPv6 in Appendix, Fig. 10) is affected by ROA creation and deletion. Each row of these graphs shows a sequence of traceroutes for a different Atlas probe/prefix pair. A pack of 6 rows shows the traceroutes to the same destination, from 6 diverse RIPE Atlas probes, indexed from top (#1) to bottom (#6). The colors of the dots show whether the destination is reachable (cyan) or unreachable (black). We add to this graph the user query times for ROA creation (green dots) and deletion (red dots).

At ROA creation, the delay between the user query and data plane reachability is similar to BGP. This is represented in Fig. 4 by the time difference between a green dot and the first next cyan dot. We observe a median delay between 23 min (RIPE) and 50 min (APNIC). Given that traceroutes are run every 15 min, these delays include on average an additional 7.5 min delay from Atlas, hence we estimate the median data plane delay in our experiments to range between 15 and 43 min which is in line with the median delays observed in BGP (Table 2).

4.2   End to End ROA Deletion Delay

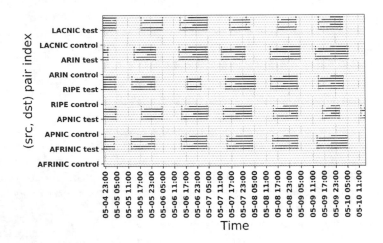

Fig. 4. Effects of ROA creation (green dots) and ROA deletion (red dots) on prefix reachability (cyan dot) and unreachability (black dot) in traceroute. Each line shows a different Atlas probe/prefix pair. Delay between ROA deletion and unreachability highly varies depending on the topology. IPv4 only, see Fig. 10 for IPv6. (Color figure online)

We investigate the ROA revocation timing along the steps in Fig. 1. In addition to longer deletion than creation due to path exploration, we show that while APNIC demonstrates longer times for the revocation to be published and to reach Relying parties, the prefixes disappear from BGP only slightly after the prefixes with ROAs hosted by other RIRs.

Certification, Publication, and Relying Party Delay.   At ROA deletion, the delays from the management plane to the RP are the same as those observed at ROA creation. The timestamps that appear in Certificate Revocation List (CRL) files usually match our user query time, and RP delays are similar across all RIRs, with the exception of APNIC which still lags 10 min behind other RIRs (Table 3).

BGP Withdraw.   BGP delays are significantly higher for ROA deletion than for ROA creation (Fig. 2b). The median BGP delay for unreachability goes up to 51 min for IPv4 and 56 min for IPv6 (Table 3). We rarely observe short BGP delays (Fig. 2b). At best the BGP delay first quartile corresponds to less than 20 min (AFRINICv4) and at worst less than 39 min (APNICv6).

There are two related causes for these high delays, one is related to BGP and the other to RPs/routers interactions. At ROA creation a prefix is announced globally in BGP by one of the prefix's upstreams as soon as either one of them fetches the new ROA. But at ROA deletion neighbors must all withdraw the

Table 3. ROA Deletion. Median delay in minutes from user query to the step indicated in each column as observed for the IPv4 prefixes from the five RIRs (IPv6 results in parenthesis). These delays are either measured from CRL files (*) and BGP data (‡), or estimated from RPKIviews data (†).

	Revocation*	Relying Party†	BGP‡
AFRINIC	0 (0)	13 (14)	34 (38)
APNIC	10 (12)	31 (36)	51 (56)
ARIN	0 (0)	14 (16)	45 (51)
LACNIC	0 (0)	18 (20)	48 (49)
RIPE	0 (0)	14 (13)	41 (50)

ROA to make it globally unreachable. Similarly, for reliability via redundancy, the RPKI-to-Router Protocol [4] allows a router to receive data from multiple Relying Party caches. This makes ASes using multiple RP caches likely to react significantly more slowly to ROA deletion than to ROA creation. This is because the BGP prefix is valid if there is a matching ROA from any of the caches. So ROA deletion is not effective until the last cache withdraws. Conversely, the first cache to receive a new ROA validates the BGP prefix, so ROA creation is seen relatively quickly.

The effect of multi-RP setups is evident for 3970s two upstream networks. Both have longer delays for ROA deletion than creation. Sprint also frequently experiences very high delays (greater than 100 min). We privately contacted the operators, and they confirmed that this delay is likely due to a reported bug in the Routinator Relying Party implementation sometimes not withdrawing ROAs (which was recently addressed in Routinator version, 0.11.2 [29]). Sprint is deploying the fix for this issue. These long delays are propagated to certain RIS peers, especially for the AFRINIC and LACNIC prefixes (Fig. 2b). This illustrates the effect caused by BGP, as only one delayed upstream kept the prefixes globally reachable for a longer period of time. Not all RIS peers are impacted though. ASes that implement ROV, or that are surrounded by ROV-enabled networks, may drop the prefix before Sprint, which is for example the case for NTT (Fig. 3b). But RIS peers that are not implementing ROV and reaching our test prefixes via Sprint are surely affected by the high Sprint delay. A mixture of both can even be observed. A good example is Deutsche Telekom AS3320 (see Fig. 5), which is highly impacted in IPv4, but not in IPv6, as the BGP paths show, it reaches the IPv6 prefixes only through NTT or through Hurricane Electric via the IXP route server, never through Sprint.

Data Plane Unreachability.   Results from traceroute provide additional insight into slow withdrawals. It is reflected in Fig. 4 by a large gap between a red dot (ROA deletion) and the next black dot, indicating a path still active after the deletion. Probe#1 and probe#4 have longer delays, on the order of hours, for all test prefixes. For probe#1, we observe that after ROA deletion,

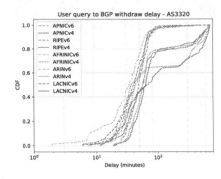
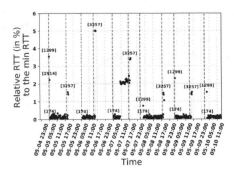

Fig. 5. ROA deletion. Time from user query to BGP withdraw for Deutsche Telekom (AS3320). IPv4 delays are impacted by Sprint late withdrawing.

Fig. 6. Effects of ROA creation/deletion on the data plane. After each ROA creation or deletion, we observe BGP path hunting with AS path changes.

the AS path between the RIPE Atlas probe and the destination changes from [Source AS, AS174 (Cogent), AS1239 (Sprint), Destination AS] to [Source AS, AS6762 (Telecom Italia), AS1239 (Sprint), Destination AS] before becoming unreachable. Since Telecom Italia is not performing ROV [30], our hypothesis is that Cogent fetches RPKI data faster than Sprint and drops the prefix while Sprint is still announcing it. BGP path hunting then selects an alternate path via Telecom Italia, until finally Sprint also drops the route and the prefix becomes unreachable. For probe#4, the delay before unreachability is similar to probe#1, but we do not observe an AS path change between ROA deletion and destination being unreachable, the AS path remaining [Source AS, AS7575 (AARNET), AS6461 (Zayo), AS1239 (Sprint), Destination AS]. Again, our hypothesis is that Sprint is slow to drop this route and keeps announcing the route to Zayo, which does not perform ROV [30], so it announces the prefix until Sprint drops it.

Impact on AS Path. Figure 6 shows the impact of ROA creation and deletion on the observed paths and illustrates BGP path hunting for one of the Atlas probe/prefix pairs. The Y axis represents the latency between the Atlas probe and the destination relative to the minimum RTT observed during the measurement period, and the X axis represents time. The vertical lines show the times of ROA creation/deletion. Each dot is a traceroute, and every time the AS path changes, we put a label above the dot with the new AS seen in paths taken by the traceroute packets.

BGP convergence and path hunting are each illustrated after ROA creation and deletion. After ROA creation, we observe a first path going through AS1299 (Telia), and then a preferred path (in the sense of BGP) going through AS174 (Cogent) is selected. This suggests that Telia was faster to integrate the new ROA than Cogent. After ROA deletion, we observe that BGP finds another path going through AS3257 (GTT), and then the destination becomes unreachable, as we see the dots stopping a short time after the red lines.

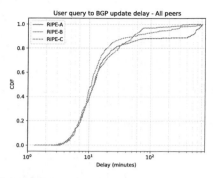 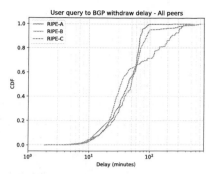

(a) ROA creation seen from RRC00 and (b) ROA deletion seen from RRC00 and RRC01 peers.   RRC01 peers.

Fig. 7. Time from user query to BGP propagation for prefixes RIPE-A, RIPE-B, and RIPE-C as observed by RRC00 and RRC01 peers.

The latency shift observed at 05-07 10:05 AM is due to an intradomain routing change within Sprint with two hops instead of one, likely not related to ROA creation/deletion, as it only appears once during our measurement time and not close to any ROA event.

5   A Bird's-Eye View of RPKI ROA Delay

The above experiment measures delays introduced by RPKI in routing using resources from all five RIRs. We discovered different handling of ROA creation at RIRs as well as the effect of different timings at ISPs when pulling RPKI data. The latter was made possible because all providers of our vantage point perform ROV. Next, we conduct a second experiment and investigate other datasets in order to generalize some of our findings.

Tier1 networks usually react to new ROAs within 20 min after the user's ROA creation query. They drop prefixes for deleted ROA within 40 min after a user's ROA deletion query; though we observe certain cases when they may take up to one hour. We discover the existence of Tier-1's that are faster than NTT and Sprint to react to ROA creation. Since the upstreams of our new prefix origins do not all perform ROV, we observe BGP collection points and traceroute vantage points with continuous connectivity to the prefixes despite the invalidation of origin ASes. Hence we show how ROV complicates the routing information propagation process and how difficult it is to predict ROV timing, especially for prefixes originated by networks that have rich and diverse connectivity. Using longitudinal datasets, we also confirm that observed delays have been stable over the past four years, and we reveal ROA structural differences between the five RIRs, highlighting RIRs' different management of RPKI information and explaining some of their disparities.

5.1   Topology Dependence

The results of Sect. 4 are constrained by the location of our originating AS in the Internet, and in particular by the way its upstream networks handle RPKI. For example, at ROA creation, the time it takes for the prefixes to become globally reachable in BGP is bounded by the reaction time of NTT and Sprint. In this section, we show that these results are representative not only for the numerous networks relying on these two Tier1 networks, but also for networks relying on other large Internet providers.

More Locations.   For this stage we obtained three /24 IPv4 prefixes (RIPE-A, RIPE-B, and RIPE-C) from RIPE NCC and three topologically diverse operators generously agreed to announce these prefixes from their networks. These three networks differ significantly from our experimental AS in the first setup; the locations are on a different continent and have different upstream providers including networks that do not implement ROV. Therefore, when running RPKI beacons for these prefixes their reachability is unaffected along paths that have no network implementing ROV. Only RIS peers that implement ROV or that are surrounded by ROV lose reachability to these prefixes.

We measured these prefixes from May 6th to October 5th 2022, and again observe that BGP delay for ROA deletion is significantly longer than it is for ROA creation (Fig. 7).

The median BGP delay for ROA creation is shorter than during the first experiment, the median ranging between 11 and 12 min (Fig. 7a) compared to the median of 18 min observed previously for our IPv4 RIPE prefix, suggesting that ROV-enabled networks between these origin ASes and RIS peers are faster than NTT and Sprint in the previous experiment (see Sect. 5.1).

On data plane reachability, we observe the expected behavior that here some probes never lose reachability, because they find a route via a provider that does not enforce ROV, as opposed to the probes in the first experiment (Fig. 4).

ROV by Tier1.   We leverage this experiment to measure the BGP delays of Tier1's that peer with RIS and implement ROV. Since these three prefixes are announced in places that are not entirely surrounded by networks performing ROV we assume the prefixes remain continuously reachable by a large fraction of the Internet. Hence, well-connected networks, i.e., Tier1s, are likely to adopt new paths for these prefixes based on their ROV mechanisms, not owing to a change in BGP reachability.

Starting with a list of Tier1 networks (CAIDA's peering clique of ASes [31]), we select six networks that are peering with RIS (RRC00 and RRC01) and that are known to implement ROV [28]. Figure 8 shows the measured BGP delay for these six networks. Comparing the delays at ROA creation with the RIPE IPv4 results of the previous experiment (Fig. 3a) confirms the stable delays for NTT and the higher variability of Sprint (AS1239) for these additional prefixes.

We also notice that NTT (AS2914) is consistently 5 to 10 min slower than AT&T (AS7018), Telia (AS1299), and PCCW (AS3491). This suggests that these

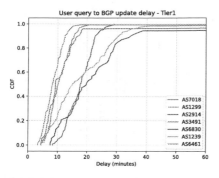
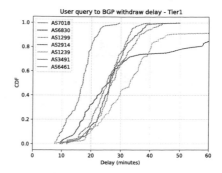

(a) ROA creation: ROV-enabled Tier1.   (b) ROA deletion: ROV-enabled Tier1.

Fig. 8. User query to BGP delay for prefixes RIPE-A, RIPE-B, and RIPE-C as observed by Tier1 networks implementing ROV.

networks fetch RPKI data more frequently than NTT, which we confirmed with operators of two of these networks. This difference may also explain the 7 to 8 min difference between the median delay for the RIPE prefix in the previous experiment (Fig. 2a) and the three prefixes used here (Fig. 7a).

The delay at ROA deletion is higher than at ROA creation for all monitored networks as seen in Fig. 8b. As we expect these networks to drop the prefixes as soon as they get in sync with RPKI, the slower deletion of ROAs is the result of RP redundancy, i.e. the ROA deletion is not effective until the last cache withdraws the ROA (Sect. 4.2). The anomaly in Sprint ROA deletion was confirmed to be due to the Routinator bug.

5.2   Delay Analysis from Historical Data

Are these results consistent over time? We investigate historical ROA and BGP data and compute the delay between the *BGP withdrawal* time t_1, of an RPKI-invalid prefix and the NotBefore time of the ROA t_0 that invalidates the <prefix, origin> pair. In this experiment, we track the occurence of BGP Withdraw (W) messages instead of BGP Announcements (A), as we cannot affirmatively say whether a ROA creation triggered an update (A). BGP updates (A) can happen both when the routes are tagged as "RPKI-valid" or "RPKI-notfound". However, withdrawals (W) following the creation of ROAs are more likely due to the routes being tagged as "RPKI-Invalid" and being dropped by ROV-enabled ASes.

Furthermore, as opposed to our active measurements, we do not have access to the user ROA query time and hence we rely on the NotBefore time as a proxy. The NotBefore time indicates when a ROA becomes valid and therefore actionable for ROV. A quick analysis of the current RPKI repository shows that 77% of ROAs have a signing time equal to their NotBefore time, except for ARIN and LACNIC where the NotBefore time is not reliable as explained in Sect. 4.1. We observe that for AFRINIC, RIPE and APNIC, there is almost no time difference between the signing time and NotBefore time, except for a

Table 4. Data processed for historical analysis (IPv6 in parentheses)

Date	# RIB entries	# VRPs	# Invalids	# Withdrawals
2018-05-22	786361	52421	17435 (1079)	1344 (–)
2019-05-01	853149	83221	20854 (1467)	2765 (86)
2020-05-15	923715	149075	21689 (2624)	2827 (351)
2021-05-02	1010201	247858	28203 (2764)	3837 (1751)
2022-05-13	1078454	342199	34604 (4688)	5918 (4191)

few exceptional cases with AFRINIC ($< 10\%$) where the NotBefore time is set before signing time. This provides confidence that the NotBefore time is usually a good estimator of the signing time for AFRINIC, RIPE and APNIC but not for ARIN and LACNIC. We also confirmed from our active measurements that the NotBefore time for RIPE and AFRINIC is usually within a minute of our query time and on average 10 min later for APNIC.

Below is the process to calculate BGP delay using historical data:

1. **VRP data:** We first collect a list of VRPs (Validated ROA Payloads) from the RIPE RPKI archive [32], which provides historical RPKI data organized by TA (Trust Anchor). Each repository contains the certificates and ROAs classified by date and also provides a list of VRPs for each day. We extract the NotBefore time (t_0) and route (prefix, origin) for each VRP.
2. **RIB files:** We select from RIS RRC00 collector a RIB dump on a randomly selected day in May every year from 2018 to 2022.
3. **BGP update messages:** we extract the BGP update messages from RIS update files and look for BGP withdrawals at time t_1 that correspond to a VRP's prefix and where t_1 is between t_0 and $t_0 + 1\,h$.
4. **BGP delay:** We calculate the BGP delay as $t_1 - t_0$.

Table 4 provides detail about the volume of longitudinal data processed from the RRC00 collector and from the RIPE RPKI archive. It shows the total number of RIB entries, the number of invalid routes and the corresponding number of withdrawals found in BGP data.

Figure 9a shows an overview of the BGP delay for all data points collected between 2018 and 2022. There is no major difference in median propagation delay between IPv4 and IPv6, but there is greater variability in IPv6. We observe that AFRINIC, APNIC and RIPE had consistently shorter median delays over time while ARIN and LACNIC had higher delays for IPv4. The reason for higher delays for ARIN and LACNIC may be caused by the anomaly in the publication process (see 4.1). However, as we can see from Fig. 9b, the median delay remained usually around 20 min between 2019 and 2022. The numbers for 2018 are slightly higher but overall these results suggest that the Certification Authority to BGP delays at ROA creation have been stable over the past four years.

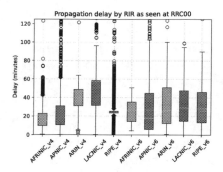

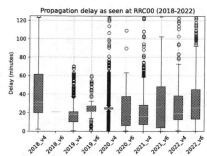

(a) Median propagation delay across all RIRs (2018-2022).

(b) Median propagation delay excluding ARIN and LACNIC (2019-2022).

Fig. 9. Median propagation delay retrieved from historical data.

Table 5. Number of unique ROA objects, routes, and signing timestamps from a snapshot on December 31st 2021 of ROAs created in 2021.

	# ROA object	# Route	# Signing time
AFRINIC	134	207	134
APNIC	5213	74349	5162
ARIN	29213	31307	311
LACNIC	5071	1 6536	2484
RIPE	25691	145950	22279

5.3 ROA Anatomy

Finally, this section describes the differences between the ROA payloads generated by the different RIRs and how these can impact ROA publication delay.

Signing Time Distribution. The first notable difference between the ROA payloads of different RIRs is the distribution of signing and NotBefore timestamps. As mentioned in Sect. 4.1 we found that ARIN is using a hardcoded value for the signing and NotBefore timestamps. Looking at a snapshot of all ROAs on December 31st 2021, we found that the 29213 ROA objects that ARIN signed in 2021 contain only 311 unique signing timestamps (Table 5), which is roughly equal to the number of days in 2021 minus weekends where we rarely see new ROAs. We have also confirmed that this behavior is present since ARIN started its RPKI service in September 2012.

For LACNIC, the results are not as clear. We do observe an abnormally high number of ROAs with the NotBefore time set to 03:00 UTC but not all. This is because it affects only the API, which was released in 2021, and thus only recently used in the LACNIC region.

Unified ROA (APNIC, RIPE). The second difference is the number of routes encapsulated in each ROA object. RFC6482 [33] specifies that a ROA object has only one ASN but a list of prefixes and corresponding maximum length attributes. Hence for prefixes of a single authorized ASN, the RIR can maintain one unified ROA with all prefixes or multiple ROAs with one prefix each.

Grouping multiple prefixes in a single ROA object has the advantage of a simpler file management as there is a single file for each (organization, ASN) pair. The ROA snapshot from 31st December 2021 shows that APNIC and RIPE have opted for this unified ROA management. To illustrate this, Table 5 depicts the number of published ROA objects and the number of corresponding routes (prefix, origin ASN). APNIC has on average 12 routes per ROA (5 routes on average for RIPE), whereas ARIN has mostly ROAs with 1 route. This difference is also visible on RIR portals and APIs. For example, APNIC and RIPE only require the route and max-length value to create a ROA, whereas other RIRs have more specific requirements, including a ROA unique identifier.

Although APNIC and RIPE unified ROAs provide simpler file management, they substantially complicate ROA signing and revocation mechanisms. For example, given a single ROA authorizing two prefixes originated by AS65536, If an organization requests the creation of a ROA for a new prefix for AS65536, then the Certification Authority has to revoke the previous ROA and create a new ROA including all three prefixes. Similarly, if someone requests the revocation of one of the prefixes, the Certification Authority has to revoke the ROA and create a new ROA with the remaining prefixes. Thus, in both cases, involving two cryptographic operations for a single query. This may explain why APNIC has a 20 min batch to allow it to collect multiple user queries and produce a single ROA file.

6   Discussion

Setting up these experiments and maintaining them over several months was an eye-opener to the challenges that operators face with RPKI and RIRs.

First, the procedures and requirements to obtain resources, activate RPKI, and manage ROAs for the five RIRs are all quite different. In addition, the lack of APIs to manage RPKI resources for APNIC and AFRINIC makes automation a lot more challenging. We implemented Selenium scripts for AFRINIC and APNIC beacons, which is not trivial given the security measures employed by RIR portals (e.g., two-factor authentication and password renewal) and need adjustments whenever portals are updated.

Second, the need for continued monitoring of the management, control, and data planes is crucial to ensure proper operation of all components involved and impacted by RPKI. For example, one of our AFRINIC beacons failed for multiple days because one of the ROA was left un-revoked by the Certification Authority, even though our deletion query succeeded and it had disappeared from the AFRINIC web interface. We only noticed this problem in our data plane measurements thanks to the prefix visualization. APNIC also automates the creation/deletion of an IRR route object corresponding to RPKI operations which had painful effects on our experiments, and likely to cause pain to operators.

Third, the use of redundant RPs is obvious for a commercial ISP but inevitably slows the responsiveness of routers withdrawing prefixes for deleted ROAs. This may be an unexpected behavior that requires operators to experiment with different configurations.

Fourth, the RPKI ecosystem is rapidly evolving. During the course of these experiments, popular RPs had numerous bug fixes, including fixes that may impact the measured delays. It is however hard to track when operators are applying these updates. The RIRs' services have also been evolving, for instance APNIC has recently started experimenting with an API for managing RPKI [34].

Finally, less obvious but still very important is the use of a synchronized clock in the UTC timezone. Certification Authorities, Relying Parties, and any software that deals with ROA creation/deletion/validation should run their operations using a single timezone, UTC as used by the hardware security modules, to prevent delays and mismatches in ROA management as observed in Sect. 4.1.

7   Related Work

As RPKI deployment is gaining more traction in network operations, understanding the end-to-end delay of the ROV supply chain is extremely important. Previous research has focused mostly on measuring the deployment and adoption of RPKI [14,35,36] or on the security of the underlying infrastructure [37,38], rather than on operational considerations, especially the propagation time.

Recommendations of timing parameters such as Relying Party refresh time are briefly mentioned in RFCs [39]. Other delay factors between the user query and the corresponding impact on BGP have not yet been well investigated. There are currently no BCP (Best Current Practice) documents on how to maintain reasonable RPKI end-to-end delay, aside from a currently inactive Internet-draft [23], which provides some, possibly overly liberal, high-level guidance on the frequency and refresh time intervals for Relying Party software.

One recent study from Kristoff et al. [24] collected access log information from both hosted and delegated RPKI Certification Authorities. This study analyzed the refresh intervals and observed the somewhat erratic fetching behavior of Relying Parties (RPs) - potentially affecting the overall propagation delay. In our study, we go a step further by understanding the end-to-end delay between the user ROA creation and the impact on BGP. We collected data from the RPKI management plane, the BGP control plane, as well as the data plane.

Finally, a study by Hlavacek et al. [40], performed data-plane experiments, in addition to the control plane, to evaluate ROV on the Internet. They analyzed and correlated the results of their study to identify the number of ASes enforcing ROV but no delay characterization was performed.

8   Conclusion

In this paper, we designed wide-ranging experiments to measure the timing and effects of the propagation of ROAs on the management, control, and data planes. This enabled us to track how ROAs are disseminated - starting from the moment creation is triggered through the RIRs' API/portals, then signed by the hosted Certificate Authorities, published at their respective Publication Points, to the moment they are fetched and validated by RPs, consequentially seeing routers announcing new routes in BGP, and then affecting delay and reachability on the data plane. We found ROA management issues for two RIRs and discovered that RIRs usually publish new RPKI information within 5 min, except APNIC which is 10 min slower. For ISPs, we observe disparate behaviors in the control and data planes between when routes are validated or invalidated by a ROA creation or deletion. At the ISP level, we observed that the reaction time following a ROA deletion is much longer due to BGP and multi-RP deployment that require complete ROA withdrawals on all RPs for a route to be withdrawn. Predicting prefix reachability and the BGP convergence time is getting even harder as it requires insights about which networks are implementing ROV and how quickly each reacts to RPKI changes. This study reveals some of the complexity added by RPKI to basic routing operations.

Ethics. This work does not raise ethical issues. It is focussed on the reachability of experimental prefixes delegated to us by the RIRs specifically for the time of the experiment. These prefixes were cleared for advertisements by our providers and documented in the IRR databases. A webpage describing the experiment was available throughout the experiment (https://github.com/romain-fontugne/rov-timing). In addition, our work does not involve personal identification data.

Acknowledgments. We thank the anonymous reviewers and our shepherd, Kyle Schomp, for their helpful comments. This research was supported in part by the MANRS Fellowship Program. We would like to thank the five RIRs for providing experimental prefixes to carry out this study. Special thanks to the engineers from ARIN and LACNIC to have responded in a timely manner to our queries with regards to the issues discovered in the ROA signing time, and to the network operators who helped confirm our hypotheses and details of their operations.

A   Appendix

A.1   Data Plane Availability in IPv6

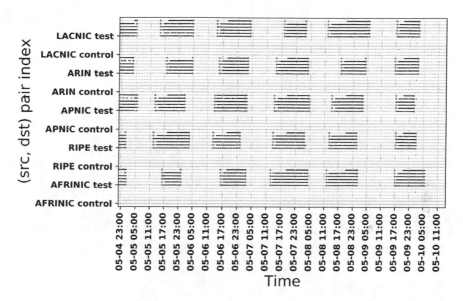

Fig. 10. IPv6: Effects of ROA creation (green dots) and ROA deletion (red dots) on prefix reachability (cyan dot) and unreachability (black dot) in traceroute. Each line shows a different Atlas probe/prefix pair. Delay between ROA deletion and unreachability highly varies depending on the topology. (Color figure online)

A.2   BGP Update Delay after ARIN Fix

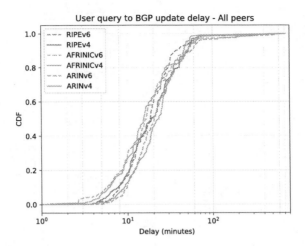

Fig. 11. ROA creation after ARIN's fix. RRC00 and RRC01 peers from April 21st to May 15th 2022. APNIC and LACNIC are not plotted to improve readability. ARIN's user query to BGP delay distributions became similar to the ones of AFRINIC and RIPE.

A.3   Reproducibility

Our experimental data is publicly available in order to make the results of this work entirely reproducible. Our source code and logs of user query time are available at https://github.com/romain-fontugne/rov-timing.

The list of experimental prefixes obtained from the five RIRs are shown in Table 6.

Table 6. IP prefixes used for our first experiment.

RIR	Type	IPv4	IPv6
AFRINIC	Control	102.218.96.0/24	2001:43f8:df0::/48
AFRINIC	Test	102.218.97.0/24	2001:43f8:df1::/48
APNIC	Control	103.171.218.0/24	2001:DF7:5380::/48
APNIC	Test	103.171.219.0/24	2001:DF7:5381::/48
ARIN	Control	165.140.104.0/24	2620:9E:6000::/48
ARIN	Test	165.140.105.0/24	2620:9E:6001::/48
LACNIC	Control	201.219.252.0/24	2801:1e:1800::/48
LACNIC	Test	201.219.253.0/24	2801:1e:1801::/48
RIPE	Control	151.216.4.0/24	2001:7fc:2::/48
RIPE	Test	151.216.5.0/24	2001:7fc:3::/48

Table 7. RIPE Atlas measurement IDs corresponding to traceroute data analyzed in this study.

ID	Target	RIR	Type
40388150	103.171.218.1	APNIC	Control
40388151	103.171.219.1	APNIC	Test
40388152	2001:DF7:5380::1	APNIC	Control
40388153	2001:DF7:5381::1	APNIC	Test
40388154	151.216.4.1	RIPE	Control
40388155	151.216.5.1	RIPE	Test
40388156	2001:7fc:2::1	RIPE	Control
40388157	2001:7fc:3::1	RIPE	Test
40388158	102.218.96.1	AFRINIC	Control
40388159	102.218.97.1	AFRINIC	Test
40388160	2001:43f8:df0::1	AFRINIC	Control
40388161	2001:43f8:df1::1	AFRINIC	Test
40388162	165.140.104.1	ARIN	Control
40388163	165.140.105.1	ARIN	Test
40388164	2620:9E:6000::1	ARIN	Control
40388165	2620:9E:6001::1	ARIN	Test
40388166	201.219.252.1	LACNIC	Control
40388167	201.219.253.1	LACNIC	Test
40388168	2801:1e:1800::1	LACNIC	Control
40388169	2801:1e:1801::1	LACNIC	Test

The list of RIPE Atlas measurement IDs corresponding to the traceroute measurements for this study are in Table 7.

References

1. Rekhter, Y., Hares, S., Li, T.: A Border Gateway Protocol 4 (BGP-4). RFC 4271, January (2006)
2. Lynn, C.: X.509 Extensions for Authorization of IP Addresses, AS Numbers, and Routers within an AS. Internet-Draft draft-clynn-bgp-x509-auth-00, Internet Engineering Task Force
3. Lepinski, M., Kent. S.: An Infrastructure to Support Secure Internet Routing. RFC 6480, February (2012)
4. Mohapatra, P., Scudder, J., Ward, D., Bush, R., Austein, R.: BGP Prefix Origin Validation. RFC 6811, January (2013)
5. Mao, Z.M., Bush, R., Griffin, T.G., Roughan, M.: BGP beacons. In: Proceedings of the 3rd ACM SIGCOMM conference on Internet measurement, pp. 1–14 (2003)

6. Garcia-Martinez, A., Bagnulo, M.: Measuring bgp route propagation times. IEEE Commun. Lett. **23**(12), 2432–2436 (2019)

7. Al-Musawi, B.: Common pitfalls in RPKI deployment and how to avoid them, Apr (2021)

8. Hlavacek, T.: DISCO: Sidestepping RPKI's deployment barriers. In: Network and Distributed System Security Symposium (NDSS) (2020)

9. Iamartino, D., Pelsser, C., Bush, R.: Measuring BGP route origin registration and validation. In: Mirkovic, J., Liu, Y. (eds.) PAM 2015. LNCS, vol. 8995, pp. 28–40. Springer, Cham (2015). https://doi.org/10.1007/978-3-319-15509-8_3

10. Candela, M.: A One-Year Review of RPKI Operations, RIPE 84, May (2022)

11. Candela, M.: One Does Not Simply "Deploy RPKI", MANRS blog, July (2022)

12. Sermpezis, P., Kotronis, V., Gigis, P., Dimitropoulos, X., Cicalese, D., King, A., Dainotti, A.: ARTEMIS: Neutralizing BGP hijacking within a minute. IEEE/ACM Trans. Netw. **26**(6), 2471–2486 (2018)

13. Kimura, T.: Long Chopsticks in Heaven - When Packets Dropped Using ROA, May (2019)

14. Gilad, Y., Cohen, A., Herzberg, A., Schapira, M., Shulman, H.: Are we there yet? on RPKI's deployment and security. Cryptology ePrint Archive (2016)

15. RIPE NCC. Routing Information Service (RIS), May (2022)

16. RIPE NCC. RIPE Atlas, May (2022)

17. Boeyen, S., Santesson, S., Polk, T., Housley, R., Farrell, S., Cooper, D.: Internet X.509 Public Key Infrastructure Certificate and Certificate Revocation List (CRL) Profile. RFC 5280, May (2008)

18. University Oregon. Route Views, September (2022)

19. Selenium. Selenium webdriver, September (2022)

20. Job Snijders. RPKIviews, May (2022)

21. OpenBSD. rpki-client, May (2022)

22. Housley, R.: Cryptographic Message Syntax (CMS). RFC 5652, September (2009)

23. Bush, R., Borkenhagen, J., Bruijnzeels, T., Snijders, J.: Timing Parameters in the RPKI based Route Origin Validation Supply Chain. Internet-Draft draft-ietf-sidrops-rpki-rov-timing-06, Internet Engineering Task Force, February 2022. Work in Progress

24. Kristoff, J.: On Measuring RPKI Relying Parties. In: Proceedings of the ACM Internet Measurement Conference, IMC '20, pp. 484–491, New York, NY, USA, 2020. Association for Computing Machinery

25. Alfroy, T., Holterbach, T., Pelsser, C.: MVP: Measuring Internet routing from the most valuable points. In: Proceedings of the 22nd ACM Internet Measurement Conference, IMC '22, pp. 770–771, New York, NY, USA, 2022. Association for Computing Machinery

26. Fontugne, Romain, Shah, Anant, Aben, Emile: The (thin) bridges of as connectivity: measuring dependency using as hegemony. In: Beverly, Robert, Smaragdakis, Georgios, Feldmann, Anja (eds.) PAM 2018. LNCS, vol. 10771, pp. 216–227. Springer, Cham (2018). https://doi.org/10.1007/978-3-319-76481-8_16

27. Ongkanchana, P., Fontugne, R., Esaki, H., Snijders, J., Aben, E.: Hunting BGP zombies in the wild. In: Proceedings of the Applied Networking Research Workshop, pp. 1–7 (2021)

28. Cloudflare. Is BGP safe yet? No., May (2022)

29. Routinator.: Changelog (v0.11.2), April (2022)

30. Fontugne, R.: The Routing Game: Hunting Invalid Routes., November (2021)

31. Luckie, M., Huffaker, B., Dhamdhere, A., Giotsas, V., Claffy, KC.: AS relationships, customer cones, and validation. In: Proceedings of the 2013 Conference on Internet Measurement Conference, pp. 243–256 (2013)
32. RIPE NCC. RIPE NCC's RPKI repository archive, May (2022)
33. Lepinski, M., Kong, D., Kent, S.: A Profile for Route Origin Authorizations (ROAs). RFC 6482, February (2012)
34. Harrison, T.: APNIC Registry API, APNIC blog, March (2022)
35. Reuter, A., Bush, R., Cunha, I., Katz-Bassett, E., Schmidt, T.C., Wählisch, M.: Towards a rigorous methodology for measuring adoption of rpki route validation and filtering. ACM SIGCOMM Comput. Commun. Rev. **48**(1), 19–27 (2018)
36. Chung, T., et al.: RPKI is coming of age: A longitudinal study of RPKI deployment and invalid route origins. In: Proceedings of the Internet Measurement Conference, pp. 406–419 (2019)
37. Gilad, Y., Sagga, O., Goldberg, S.: Maxlength considered harmful to the RPKI. In: Proceedings of the 13th International Conference on Emerging Networking EXperiments and Technologies, pp. 101–107 (2017)
38. Hlavacek, T., Jeitner, P., Mirdita, D., Shulman, H., Waidner, M.: Stalloris: RPKI downgrade attack. In: 31st USENIX Security Symposium (USENIX Security 22), Boston, MA, August (2022) USENIX Association
39. Bush, R.: Origin validation operation based on the Resource Public Key Infrastructure (RPKI). IETF RFC7115 (January 2014)
40. Hlavacek, T.,Herzberg, A., Shulman, H., Waidner, M.: Practical experience: Methodologies for measuring route origin validation. In: 2018 48th Annual IEEE/IFIP International Conference on Dependable Systems and Networks (DSN), pp. 634–641. IEEE (2018)

Security and Privacy

Intercept and Inject: DNS Response Manipulation in the Wild

Yevheniya Nosyk[1]([✉]), Qasim Lone[4], Yury Zhauniarovich[2], Carlos H. Gañán[2,5],
Emile Aben[4], Giovane C. M. Moura[2,3], Samaneh Tajalizadehkhoob[5],
Andrzej Duda[1], and Maciej Korczyński[1]

[1] Univ. Grenoble Alpes, CNRS, Grenoble INP, LIG, Grenoble, France
{yevheniya.nosyk,andrzej.duda,maciej.korczynski}@univ-grenoble-alpes.fr
[2] TU Delft, Delft, The Netherlands
[3] SIDN Labs, Arnhem, The Netherlands
[4] RIPE NCC, Amsterdam, The Netherlands
[5] ICANN, Los Angeles, CA, USA

Abstract. DNS is a protocol responsible for translating human-readable domain names into IP addresses. Despite being essential for many Internet services to work properly, it is inherently vulnerable to manipulation. In November 2021, users from Mexico received bogus DNS responses when resolving whatsapp.net. It appeared that a BGP route leak diverged DNS queries to the local instance of the k-root located in China. Those queries, in turn, encountered middleboxes that injected fake DNS responses. In this paper, we analyze that event from the RIPE Atlas point of view and observe that its impact was more significant than initially thought—the Chinese root server instance was reachable from at least 15 countries several months before being reported. We then launch a nine-month longitudinal measurement campaign using RIPE Atlas probes and locate 11 probes outside China reaching the same instance, although this time over IPv6. More broadly, motivated by the November 2021 event, we study the extent of DNS response injection when contacting root servers. While only less than 1% of queries are impacted, they originate from 7% of RIPE Atlas probes in 66 countries. We conclude by discussing several countermeasures that limit the probability of DNS manipulation.

Keywords: DNS · Root servers · DNS manipulation · DNS censorship · BGP route leaks

1 Introduction

The Domain Name System (DNS) [41, 42] is one of the core Internet protocols. It was introduced to translate human-readable domain names (e.g., example.com) into IP addresses (e.g., 2001:db8::1234:5678), but has gone far beyond this basic service. It is now a large-scale distributed system comprising millions of recursive resolvers and authoritative nameservers—the two main components of the DNS infrastructure. It was designed in a hierarchical manner so that no single entity stores the data about the entire domain name space. Each authoritative

© The Author(s), under exclusive license to Springer Nature Switzerland AG 2023
A. Brunstrom et al. (Eds.): PAM 2023, LNCS 13882, pp. 461–478, 2023.
https://doi.org/10.1007/978-3-031-28486-1_19

nameserver is only responsible for a subset of the domain tree and it is the role of recursive resolvers to follow the chain of delegations and find authoritative query responses.

Nonetheless, DNS is prone to manipulation. The original specification does not ensure data integrity or authentication, allowing on-path entities (Internet Service Providers, national censors, attackers, etc.) to intercept plain-text DNS traffic and inject responses (whether bogus or not). A latter standard, Domain Name System Security Extensions (DNSSEC) [55], provides data integrity, but its usage and deployment remain optional and far from being universal [10,17].

In November 2021, Meta engineers reported that users in Mexico were receiving bogus A records when querying `whatsapp.net` and `facebook.com` [15]. A closer look revealed that those queries were routed to the local China-located anycast instance of the `k-root`, despite having several other points of presence nearby [1]. As the Great Firewall of China (GFW) is known to inject bogus responses when detecting sensitive domains [28], Mexican users might have experienced collateral damage from DNS censorship. The `k-root` operator (RIPE NCC) later confirmed that a Border Gateway Protocol (BGP) route leak made the local root server instance globally available. This outage stemmed from a series of unfortunate events but nevertheless rendered both domains unavailable. The Internet has already seen similar events in the past [56,59] and researchers reported on detecting DNS root manipulation [21,32,35,44]. However, the prevalence of this phenomenon has not been systematically analyzed across all the root server letters over a long period of time.

In this paper, our contribution is two-fold. First, we leverage built-in RIPE Atlas [54] measurements to identify probes affected by the November 2021 route leak. We show that at least two months prior to be reported by Meta, the Chinese `k-root` instance had already been accessible from 32 autonomous systems (ASes) in 15 countries. Second, we set up a nine-month DNS measurement campaign and observe the same problem in the wild, although this time mostly over IPv6. More broadly, the DNS manipulation experienced by Mexican clients motivates us to study the extent of DNS response injection when contacting root servers. We reveal that even though less than 1% of queries are affected, they originate from 7% of probes located in 66 countries.

2   Manipulating Root DNS Traffic

2.1   Background on DNS Root Server System

DNS namespace is organized in a tree-like manner with the root zone at the very top. It is served by 13 root servers each referred to by letters "a" to "m" (`[a--m].root-servers.net.`). Despite being managed by 12 different organisations, each is contracted to provide an identical copy of the zone file, maintained by the Internet Assigned Numbers Authority (IANA). Every root server letter, in turn, can be accessed at its IPv4 and IPv6 addresses, both deployed using anycast (i.e., the same BGP prefix is announced from multiple anycast sites across the globe). This ensures that the root DNS service remains highly available.

As of October 2022, there are 1,575 anycast instances accessible either world-wide (global) or only within a limited range of networks (local) [1]. In the latter case, local network operators typically limit the propagation of BGP routes by using NO_EXPORT or NOPEER BGP community attributes [37]. DNS queries are then routed to the nearest anycast locations based on the routing tables. As BGP is latency agnostic, it may eventually map clients to instances from another continent, even when closer ones are available [43].

To assist in troubleshooting, root servers support DNS queries that identify individual anycast instances. This is achieved by one of the CHAOS-class TXT queries [18] (e.g., id.server, hostname.bind) or the NSID option [8]. The latter does not require issuing a separate query because the nameserver identifier provided in the OPT resource record is stored in the Additional section of a DNS response packet.

2.2   Previous Route Leaks

Root traffic manipulation has been previously reported twice. In both cases, a BGP route leak made China-located local instances globally available. Even though root servers themselves were legitimately run by their operators, the GFW or other interceptors were likely present in transit. In the first case in 2010, clients located in the USA and Chile had their queries for three domains (twitter.com, facebook.com, and youtube.com) answered with bogus IP addresses. Upon further investigation, it was found that original queries were sent towards the i-root instance in Beijing [59]. Similarly, in 2011 the clients in Europe and the USA were directed towards the f-root instance in Beijing [56], although no response injection was reported at that time.

2.3   November 2021: Mexico Event

In November 2021, whatsapp.net and facebook.com became inaccessible for some clients located in Mexico [15]—an event closely resembling those happening in 2010 and 2011. Figure 1 describes the course of events as reproduced by Meta engineers. A RIPE Atlas probe from Mexico was instructed to resolve the IP address of d.ns.facebook.com (one of the Meta nameservers) by contacting the k-root server directly. As it would not provide an authoritative answer for such a query, the injected response (202.160.128.195—an IP address belonging to *Twitter*) demonstrated that the DNS request was intercepted. To identify where the query was routed, Meta engineers configured the same probe in Mexico to send an id.server CHAOS TXT query. The response pointed to the Guangzhou instance in China (ns1.cn-ggz.k.ripe.net)—a *legitimate* k-root server as confirmed by its operator RIPE NCC. A traceroute measurement to k-root's anycast IP address demonstrated that the seven penultimate hops went through AS4134—the Chinese telecommunication operator. As previously, the local root server instance should have been announced only to clients in China, but nevertheless leaked to the whole Internet.

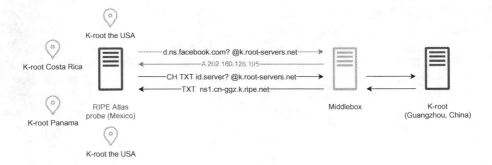

Fig. 1. DNS traffic seen on the RIPE Atlas probe from Mexico. A middlebox intercepts the DNS query and injects the bogus response for `d.ns.facebook.com`. The `CHAOS`-class `TXT` query for `id.server` confirms that the request was routed towards the Chinese instance of the `k-root`.

Extending Meta's initial analysis, we further investigated the issue by analyzing built-in `id.server` measurements from *all* the ~13K RIPE Atlas probes active between September 1, 2021, and November 30, 2021. We identified 57 probes from 32 ASes in 15 countries reaching the local Guangzhou instance of the `k-root` at least once prior to the leak being reported on November 6, 2021. Consequently, the instance became reachable outside China for some time before the `k-root` BGP leak was noticed and fixed in November 2021. Interestingly, we saw one probe allegedly located in the USA reaching the Guangzhou instance between September 2021 and July 2022, thus after the leak was fixed. It is only since August 2022 that the probe would be routed to the `ns1.ar-bue.k.ripe.net` site in Argentina. We referred to the historical RIPE Atlas dataset with the metadata for all the probes and confirmed that the aforementioned probe was located in China until August 2022 and was then moved to the USA. Therefore, that case does not constitute a BGP route leak.

3   Characterizing DNS Manipulation in the Wild

The events described in Sect. 2.2 and Sect. 2.3 demonstrate the cases when queries directed to certain DNS root servers resulted in response injection. In this section, we set out to characterize the extent of this phenomenon for all the root letters. We identify the response injectors and factors influencing such manipulation. We analyze more than 1 billion DNS RIPE Atlas measurements issued between February and October 2022.

3.1   Measurement Setup

Figure 2 shows the series of queries we issue on each RIPE Atlas probe, directed to all the root servers on their IPv4 and IPv6 anycast addresses. We explicitly request them not to perform recursion by setting the Recursion Desired (`RD`) flag

Fig. 2. DNS queries issued by each RIPE Atlas probe every 12 h. We send queries to all root servers to resolve A/AAAA records of google.com, facebook.com, and ripe.net over two transport protocols (TCP/UDP) and both IP versions (IPv4/IPv6).

to false, even though correctly operating root servers would not do it anyways. Each root server is requested to resolve A and AAAA records of three domain names (google.com, facebook.com, and ripe.net) over TCP and UDP. The first two domains are known to trigger censorship middleboxes [48], while the third one (ripe.net) is a control domain. In addition, we request to include the NSID string in all the responses to learn which anycast instance (if any) answers our queries. In total, each available probe performs 312 DNS lookups every 12 h.

3.2 The Guangzhou K-Root Instance

We first check whether the local Guangzhou-located instance of the k-root was still reachable outside China after the BGP leak was fixed. We experimentally verified and confirmed with RIPE NCC that the server's id.server string is identical to the NSID identifier (ns1.cn-ggz.k.ripe.net). We then extracted the latter from all the DNS responses received during the 9 months of our measurements. As expected, the instance was mainly accessible locally, but 12 probes outside mainland China (from Russia, Israel, Mexico, Denmark, and Hong Kong) would also reach it. We then verified that those probes had k-root sites in neighboring countries and most of the time would be routed there. For example, the probe from Hong Kong would we routed to the ns1.vn-han.k.ripe.net instance in Vietnam, while the probe from Russia would go to Russia itself (ns1.ru-led.k.ripe.net) and ns1.kz-pwq.k.ripe.net in Kazakhstan. Yet, during one day both probes were exceptionally reaching the Guangzhou-located instance of the k-root. We shared these findings with the k-root operator and they explained that sporadic route leaks do occasionally happen, but are then fixed quickly.

Interestingly, 11 probes out of 12 would reach the local China-located instance of the k-root over IPv6. Those probes received *bogus* responses for facebook.com queries containing, among others, IP addresses of Dropbox and Twitter. In IPv4, only one probe would reach the Chinese instance of the k-root. However, the event lasted a single day and no injected response was received. Overall, DNS injection is not persistent—the 12 aforementioned probes would occasionally reach the local k-root instance in Guangzhou without receiving rewritten responses even for sensitive domains.

Table 1. The number of injected responses per domain name and response type.

Domain	A	AAAA	URI	SOA	CNAME
ripe.net	726,993	486,111	0	0	0
google.com	3,573,083	2,156,859	13,512	0	4,536
facebook.com	2,730,047	1,456,150	29,065	6,687	0
Total:	7,030,123	4,099,120	42,577	6,687	4,536

3.3 Injected Responses

We now analyze all the DNS responses received on probes when sending queries to the 13 root servers. Recall that root servers do not directly answer queries for second-level domains, such as example.com. Instead, they point to authoritative DNS servers of top-level domains. Therefore, we refer to each measurement result as either *non-injected* (the answer section of the DNS response is empty) or *injected* (the answer section contains the response). In the collected dataset, over 9M responses (0.82%) were *injected* and contained more than 11M individual resource records of different types. Table 1 presents the response types received per domain name:

- A: maps a domain name to an IPv4 address—the most common response type received on 1,005 probes. As expected, the two sensitive domain names (facebook.com and google.com) triggered significantly more injected responses than ripe.net. The distribution of the returned IPv4 addresses is diverse—29 were private, 517 were from 120 globally routable ASes, and 1.8K belonged to Google and Facebook. Globally routable IPs are known to be injected by national censors [28] so that it complicates the detection of injection. Interestingly, 49% of facebook.com and 89.6% of google.com responses contained valid IP addresses of Facebook and Google, respectively. Therefore, the response injection did not prevent access to those domain names at the DNS level.
- AAAA: maps a domain name to an IPv6 address, received on 678 RIPE Atlas probes. Similarly to aforementioned A type responses, google.com and facebook.com—the two sensitive domains—experience significantly more injection than ripe.net. Overall, injected responses contained 3.2K unique IPv6 addresses—1.7K from reserved IP address ranges, 3 globally routable (belonging to Russian, German, and American telecommunication operators), and the remaining 1.4K addresses from Facebook and Google. The ratio of valid responses for sensitive domains was even higher than in IPv4—98.3% of google.com and 64.4% of facebook.com responses were correct. Once again, despite being injected, the majority of the DNS responses contained genuine IP addresses of the requested domains.
- URI: maps domain names to Uniform Resource Identifiers. We located 15 probes in Iran that received URI resource records in response to google.com and facebook.com. The responses contained 6-character strings (one for each domain name), but did not appear to be meaningful for external observers.

- SOA: contains administrative information about a DNS zone. One probe from the USA received SOA records for facebook.com queries as if they came from Facebook's authoritative nameservers. However, the nameserver and maintainer names revealed the true originator—a DNS content filter [20]. As no valid IP address of facebook.com was returned, end users would not be able to access the domain name.
- CNAME: maps one domain name to another. We found 4,536 aliases that pointed google.com to forcesafesearch.google.com—the service [25] to exclude explicit content (e.g., pornography, violence) from search results. It is configured by adding a CNAME record to local DNS configurations. All the six affected probes (located in Spain, the USA, the Netherlands, and Russia) received corresponding A or AAAA resource records along with CNAMEs. Apart from one probe that received a bogus IP address, others would still access google.com, although some parts of search results would be filtered.

Overall, DNS injection impacted only 0.82% of all the queries issued during nine months in 2022. Figure 3 further demonstrates that the weekly ratio of response injection never exceeded 1%, yet proving that it is constantly present in the wild. Interestingly, response injection does not necessarily prevent access to requested domains at the DNS level - the majority of all the injected responses were not bogus. Therefore, if not coupled with other filtering techniques, such as HTTP(S) interception or destination IP address blocking, DNS manipulation would stay transparent to end users.

3.4 Identifying Injectors

The injected responses demonstrate that DNS queries originated from RIPE Atlas probes must have encountered middleboxes on the way to root servers. Such devices were shown to serve different purposes. Transparent forwarders [45] only relay incoming DNS requests to alternative resolvers, such as public or network's internal DNS resolvers. Importantly, they do not inject spoofed responses, but rather let those alternative resolvers respond to end clients directly. More intrusive DNS interceptors, such as national censors, impersonate intended query destinations and actively inject bogus responses [38]. DNS interception is often accomplished at Customer Premises Equipment [51] and can be detected by issuing CHAOS-class or other DNS queries with the NSID option enabled.

We thus leverage the nameserver identifier option (NSID) to fingerprint services that provided responses to RIPE Atlas probes. We extracted and manually analyzed more than 12K unique NSID strings from over 1 billion measurements. We consulted the web pages of root server operators, online documentation, and issued additional DNS queries to validate our assumptions. We then generated regular expressions to match each identified service. Finally, we contacted root server operators and six of them (including Verisign that manages a-root/j-root with the same pattern) responded confirming the validity of our mappings.

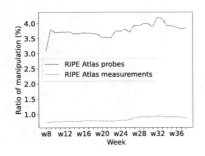
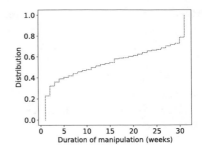

Fig. 3. Ratio of probes and measurements experiencing response injection per week.

Fig. 4. Distribution of probes by the duration of DNS response manipulation in weeks.

Table 2 in Appendix provides the list of services and examples of corresponding nameserver identifiers. Apart from root server instances, we got responses from 4 public DNS providers (Cloudflare DNS, Google DNS, OpenDNS, Quad9), one DNS filtering service (CleanBrowsing), and other unknown entities. In most cases, we could deduce service names (e.g., `cmh1.groot`), airport codes (e.g., `a1.us-mia.root`), and city/country codes (e.g., `ua-kiv-aa`) from returned `NSID` strings. Other identifiers, e.g., `114m93` for Cloudflare DNS, could not be easily mapped to originators. We had to additionally issue queries directly to predefined addresses such as `1.1.1.1` (the IP address of Cloudflare public resolver) to prove the hypothesis.

As expected, none of the injected responses contained valid nameserver identifiers of root servers—78% of `NSID`s were empty and the remaining ones included public resolvers, DNS filtering, and other undetermined services. Naturally, valid (i.e., empty) DNS responses were mostly returned by genuine root servers—they account for 95% of all the extracted `NSID`s. As for the remaining 5%, we assume the presence of transparent forwarders. Additionally, we may have encountered middleboxes serving the root zone locally [21], thus not possessing the identifiers of root servers. Overall, our findings show that one can rely on nameserver identifiers to understand whether queries were answered by genuine root servers.

3.5 Participating Probes

We leveraged 14,335 RIPE Atlas probes from 177 countries and 4,132 ASes. A great majority of them did not experience DNS manipulation, but a smaller fraction (1,010 or 7.05%) received injected responses—a substantial increase since 2016 when less than 1% of RIPE Atlas probes were reported to be intercepted when contacting DNS root servers [44]. We compute the fraction of affected probes per country in Table 3 and plot the results on Fig. 6 in Appendix. Overall, the manipulation ratio remains low—113 countries do not host a single probe experiencing DNS injection. On the contrary, some of the other 66 countries have a significant ratio of manipulated probes - 97.1% in Iran, 83.15% in China,

66.67% in Palestine, 50% in Yemen, and 50% in Saint Barthélemy. As for the remaining countries (see Table 3 in Appendix), the ratio of manipulated probes does not usually exceed 30%. The autonomous system distribution is much more diverse, but more than half of the ASes host only a single probe. Overall, 5.61% of ASes only host probes experiencing manipulation, 88.92% only host probes that do not, and the remaining 5.47% have probes of both types.

RIPE Atlas probes are not constantly available and may get occasionally disconnected, which makes it non-trivial to run longitudinal measurements. However, Fig. 3 shows that the proportion of probes experiencing manipulation to all the participating probes per week remains stable (the corresponding proportion of measurements exhibits the same behavior). Figure 4 additionally shows that roughly 20% of probes (mostly located in Iran, China, the USA, and Russia) experienced response manipulation during all the weeks of the experiment.

We emphasize that DNS interception and injection may happen anywhere in transit between RIPE Atlas probes and DNS root servers. Therefore, we refer to countries and networks as those *hosting* probes that experience injection. We do not assume that those entities are necessarily responsible for manipulating with DNS traffic of their clients.

3.6 Factors Driving DNS Manipulation

We leverage a generalized linear mixed-effects model (see Appendix for more details) to quantify whether the following variables make certain DNS requests more prone to response injection: query type (A, AAAA), the use of a sensitive domain name (google.com, facebook.com), transport protocol (UDP, TCP), IP version (IPv4, IPv6), and the queried root server. Figure 5 in Appendix shows that three variables significantly affect the probability of getting an injected response. As expected, the queried domain name is the factor that has the highest impact. Domain names such as facebook.com and google.com are 5.99 and 4.49 times, respectively, more likely to be manipulated than ripe.net. The second factor that impacts most the probability of DNS response injection is the transport protocol used in the DNS request. Requests over UDP are 3.50 times more likely of getting manipulated than requests over TCP. Similarly, AAAA requests are 0.70 times less likely to get manipulated than A requests. We also analyze the odds of DNS response injection when querying different root servers. While some root servers present marginally statistically significant increase of the probability of getting injected response compared to the a-root, only queries to the k-root were 0.72 times less likely of getting manipulated.

3.7 Limitations

We acknowledge that the presented measurement study has certain limitations. Using two sensitive domains would not trigger all the existing censorship middleboxes. Yet, domains from other categories (e.g., gambling or adult content) would potentially put the owners of RIPE Atlas probes in danger as those could break local laws. We thus consider this limitation acceptable and suggest the reader to interpret the reported results as a lower-bound estimation of the problem. We also note that we only study the extent of interception and injection when sending DNS queries to root servers. Other filtering mechanisms, e.g., IP-blocking, may eventually block access to domain names at the network level.

4   Countermeasures

Some techniques presented below can effectively reduce the risks of DNS injection. However, a deliberate interceptor, especially when located close to the query source, is capable of monitoring all the client activity and reacting accordingly:

- **BGP Communities**: Li et al. [36] proposed to encode geographic coordinates of anycast sites in BGP announcements so that routers could choose the closest location. If deployed by DNS root operators, the client from Mexico could have detected nearby k-root instances and privilege those routes over the one from China. This would eventually avoid DNS middleboxes that injected bogus responses. While it is relatively easy to include coordinates in BGP announcements, many routers worldwide would require additional configuration to parse those geographic hints.
- **DNS Query Name Minimisation:** recursive resolvers usually include a full query name in requests to authoritative nameservers [26]. While in some cases it could reduce the total number of packets sent, query names may trigger keyword-based filtering. The client from Mexico could have issued a minimal necessary request (.net instead of whatsapp.net) [14] to the k-root server located in China—it would be still intercepted, but it might have not triggered keyword-based response injection. Queries to root servers can be avoided altogether when serving the root zone locally [34]. At some point, the resolver will be forced to issue a DNS request with a full query name, but if the path to the authoritative nameserver is not under interception, the response injection will not happen.
- **Encrypted DNS:** making DNS exchanges private effectively hides the communication for on-path observers. Such techniques (DNS-over-TLS [30], DNS-over-QUIC [31], and DNS-over-HTTPS [29]) are getting slowly but steadily adopted [6,40] between end clients and recursive resolvers. Yet, securing the communication link between resolvers and authoritative nameservers is still a work in progress [24]. Once standardized, it will effectively prevent middleboxes from sniffing plain-text domain names and injecting responses, as it happened for the client in Mexico. While DNS encryption is a promising technique, note that unsolicited TCP connections can be trivially torn down with injected RST packets [12], provided encrypted DNS is using a dedicated well-known port (e.g., port 853 for DoT and DoQ).
- **DNS Security Extensions (DNSSEC):** originally designed to fight cache poisoning attacks, DNSSEC [55] helps ensure that received responses are genuine. While it is an effective mechanism to detect bogus responses (e.g., a Twitter IP address returned in response to facebook.com query), it requires

the domain names in question to be cryptographically signed and recursive resolvers to be able to perform validation—the two criteria not met for Mexican clients. Generally, DNSSEC signing and validation are far from being deployed universally [10,17].

5   Ethical Considerations

Measurement research must be designed extremely carefully so that it minimizes any risk for involved parties but maximizes the probable benefits, as outlined in The Menlo Report [9]. This is especially important in censorship studies, which usually involve actively generating traffic to trigger censors. A rich body of research [47,48,50,57,58] performed experiments similar to ours, in particular using RIPE Atlas infrastructure [2,13], and reported that no evidence suggested that any harm was caused. We further received a formal approval from the institutional review board (IRB) of our institution. They judged our research as the one complying with all the ethical requirements.

Our choice of the measurement platform was dictated by several reasons. RIPE Atlas is an opt-in service where all the participants accept the Terms and Conditions [52]. In particular, probe hosts agree that i) the permission to install probes was obtained (§5.1), ii) other users can perform measurements on probes, in particular for research (§5.4, §4.5), iii) probes may be disabled one month after a written request is received (§8.4), and iv) measurement results will be made public either fully or in the aggregated form (§4.2). Our measurements comply with these terms and in this paper, we do not expose sensitive information about individual probes, even when allowed (§4.3).

All the RIPE Atlas probes regularly perform a set of built-in measurements [53] for different protocols. More than half of 242 recurring DNS measurements (running every 4 min to 12 h) are destined to root servers. Moreover, each probe is also requesting A records of popular domain names every 10 min. Consequently, the traffic we generate for this experiment does not stand out from the normal operation of RIPE Atlas probes. Two out of three domain names that we query, namely google.com and facebook.com, are the first and the third most popular worldwide respectively [49]. Thus, queries to such domains are challenging to link to particular end hosts when observed in the wild.

6   Related Work

DNS middleboxes were previously known to interfere with root DNS traffic. In 2013, Fan et al. [21] reported that 1.75% of 64K vantage points worldwide would encounter DNS proxies, rogue root servers, and other unusual behavior when sending requests to the f-root. Moreover, some of the queries for www.facebook.com would be answered directly. Jones et al. [32] further formalized the phenomenon as *DNS root manipulation*. Measurements towards the b-root from 8K RIPE Atlas probes revealed 10 DNS proxies and one root server replica in China. Moura et al. [44] identified 74 RIPE Atlas probes (less that 1%

of all the 9K probes at that time) that would have root server queries answered by third parties. More recently, Li et al. [35] found that some of the queries originated inside China to `k-root` root server instances located inside the country would also result in hijacking. In our paper, we present a nine-month longitudinal study that characterizes the extent of DNS response injection across all the root server letters. We show that the ratio of affected probes has significantly risen compared to previous studies.

More broadly, various types of DNS manipulation have been extensively studied in the literature. Censors [7,23,27,46–48,50,57,58], transparent forwarders [33,45], rogue DNS servers [19], and middleboxes [16,38,51,60,61]—all interfere with the normal DNS resolution process. Particular attention has been paid to the GFW of China [3–5,11,22,28,39], known to intercept DNS traffic and inject bogus responses. Hoang et al. [28] provided the most complete picture of DNS manipulation by the GFW to date. The authors issued queries for 534M domain names from outside China to controlled servers inside the country. Their measurements triggered the GFW, suggesting that it indeed operates on the traffic coming from outside. As witnessed during the November 2021 route leak, middleboxes were shown to inject globally routable IP addresses in their bogus responses. These findings are in line with the previous study of the anonymous researcher [3], showing that the GFW is acting on the traffic that is barely traversing Chinese ASes. Overall, the existing research suggests that clients from Mexico were affected by the operation of the GFW.

7 Conclusions

In this paper, we explored the November 2021 BGP route leak that resulted in DNS response injection as a side effect. We identified 32 ASes worldwide that would reach the Guangzhou instance of the `k-root` and potentially encounter injecting middleboxes on the way. While this particular problem was quickly fixed, our longitudinal measurements revealed that DNS injection is omnipresent. Queries to DNS root servers are constantly getting intercepted and may result in injected responses, especially when involving sensitive domain names.

We also revealed that the Guangzhou `k-root` instance became reachable outside mainland China several months before it was reported. As it is crucial to identify such events early enough before the impact on end users becomes apparent, RIPE NCC deployed BGP community attributes identifying each `k-root` server instance. Therefore, such leaks are now detectable.

Acknowledgments. We thank root server operators for validating the nameserver identifiers. This work was partially supported by RIPE NCC, Carnot LSI, the Grenoble Alpes Cybersecurity Institute (under the contract ANR-15-IDEX-02), and the French Ministry of Research (PERSYVAL-Lab project under the contract ANR-11-LABX-0025-01 and DiNS project under the contract ANR-19-CE25-0009-01).

Appendix

Generalized Linear Mixed-Effects Model

To determine which factors make DNS queries more susceptible to manipulation, we fit a generalized linear mixed-effects model (GLMM) assuming a binomial distribution with logit link function (logistic regression) while accounting for the country-level random effects, i.e., with the response variable as a logit transformation of DNS response state: 1 (manipulated) or 0 (not manipulated). With the inclusion of country effects, we account for observable and unobservable factors specific to queries executed within a country such as state-level filtering factors, which potentially influence DNS response manipulation. We describe the results in odds ratios, indicating the change in the odds of DNS queries getting manipulated. The modeling results are presented in Fig. 5 and discussed in detail in Sect. 3.6.

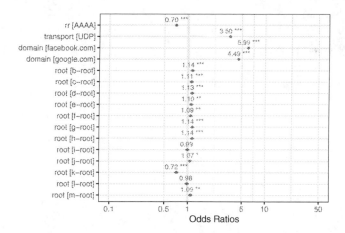

Fig. 5. Odds ratios of DNS injection survival. Values above 1 (in blue) indicate that the corresponding variables increase the chances of DNS injection, while ratios below 1 (in red) decrease the chances of DNS injection. The 95% confidence limits are delimited by horizontal lines. Those that do not cross the zero line correspond to variables that affect DNS injection more significantly. (Color figure online)

Table 2. Services identified from 12,150 unique `NSID` strings.

Name	Example	Name	Example
A/J-root	`a1.us-mia.root`	Empty string	–
B-root	`b4-iad`	Unclassified	–
C-root	`jfk1b.c.root-servers.org`	Cloudflare DNS	`114m93`
D-root	`jbsa4.droot.maxgigapop.net`	Google DNS	`gpdns-waw`
E-root	`p01.atlc.eroot`	CleanBrowsing	`CleanBrowsing v1.6a [...]`
F-root	`abq1f.f.root-servers.org`	OpenDNS	`r2.fra`
G-root	`cmh1.groot`	Quad9	`res760.qfra3.rrdns.pch.net`
H-root	`001.hkg.h.root-servers.org`		
I-root	`s1.pnh`		
K-root	`ns2.gb-lon.k.ripe.net`		
L-root	`ua-kiv-aa`		
M-root	`M-NRT-DIXIE-1`		

Fig. 6. The ratio (in %) of probes that experienced response injection to all the probes participating in our measurements. We did not receive any results for countries highlighted in grey. (Color figure online)

Table 3. The ratio of RIPE Atlas probes experiencing manipulation to all those hosted in a particular country. This table only includes countries with at least one probe experiencing manipulation.

Rank	Country	Ratio (%)	Rank	Country	Ratio (%)
1	Iran	97.1%	34	Malaysia	6.67%
2	China	83.15%	35	Ireland	6.56%
3	Palestine	66.67%	36	Uruguay	6.25%
4	Yemen	50.0%	37	Poland	6.01%
5	Saint Barthélemy	50.0%	38	Brazil	5.77%
6	Indonesia	34.18%	39	Slovakia	5.45%
7	Venezuela	33.33%	40	Romania	5.38%
8	Myanmar	25.0%	41	Armenia	5.0%
9	Russia	20.57%	42	South Africa	4.85%
10	Mexico	20.41%	43	Argentina	4.76%
11	Israel	15.38%	44	Belgium	4.74%
12	Albania	14.81%	45	Lithuania	4.44%
13	Tanzania	14.29%	46	Hungary	4.35%
14	Cameroon	14.29%	47	Austria	4.17%
15	Colombia	13.04%	48	Canada	4.11%
16	Egypt	12.5%	49	The UK	4.07%
17	Ukraine	12.0%	50	The Philippines	3.85%
18	Saudi Arabia	11.11%	51	Belarus	3.85%
19	Benin	11.11%	52	Taiwan	3.57%
20	Türkiye	9.59%	53	Finland	3.38%
21	France	8.25%	54	Bulgaria	3.03%
22	Hong Kong	8.16%	55	Denmark	2.9%
23	Portugal	7.79%	56	Estonia	2.7%
24	Italy	7.77%	57	Greece	2.68%
25	New Zealand	7.5%	58	Panama	2.22%
26	Chile	7.5%	59	Luxembourg	2.08%
27	Spain	7.46%	60	Czechia	1.93%
28	Australia	7.22%	61	The Netherlands	1.91%
29	Thailand	7.14%	62	Singapore	1.57%
30	Cyprus	7.14%	63	Kazakhstan	1.39%
31	India	7.1%	64	Sweden	1.32%
32	Norway	6.96%	65	Germany	1.24%
33	The USA	6.88%	66	Switzerland	1.04%

References

1. Root Server Technical Operations Association (2022). https://root-servers.org
2. Anderson, C., Winter, P., Ensafi, R.: Global censorship detection over the RIPE Atlas network. In: USENIX FOCI (2014)
3. Anonymous: The Collateral Damage of Internet Censorship by DNS Injection. SIGCOMM Comput. Commun. Rev. 42(3), June 2012
4. Anonymous: Towards a Comprehensive Picture of the Great Firewall's DNS Censorship. In: USENIX FOCI (2014)
5. Anonymous, Niaki, A.A., Hoang, N.P., Gill, P., Houmansadr, A.: Triplet censors: demystifying great firewall's DNS censorship behavior. In: USENIX FOCI (2020)
6. APNIC: Encrypted DNS World Map, January 2023. https://stats.labs.apnic.net/edns
7. Filastò, A., Appelbaum, J.: OONI: open observatory of network interference. In: USENIX FOCI (2012)
8. Austein, R.: DNS Name Server Identifier (NSID) Option. RFC 5001 (2007)
9. Bailey, M., Kenneally, E., Maughan, D., Dittrich, D.: The menlo report. IEEE Secur. Privacy 10(02), 71–75 (2012)
10. Bayer, J., Nosyk, Y., Hureau, O., Fernandez, S., Paulovics, I., Duda, A., Korczyński, M.: Study on Domain Name System (DNS) abuse : technical report. Appendix 1. Publications Office of the European Union (2022). https://doi.org/10.2759/473317
11. Bhaskar, A., Pearce, P.: Many roads lead to Rome: how packet headers influence DNS censorship measurement. In: USENIX Security (2022)
12. Bock, K., Alaraj, A., Fax, Y., Hurley, K., Wustrow, E., Levin, D.: Weaponizing middleboxes for TCP reflected amplification. In: USENIX Security (2021)
13. Bortzmeyer, S.: DNS Censorship (DNS Lies) As Seen By RIPE Atlas, December 2015. https://labs.ripe.net/author/stephane_bortzmeyer/dns-censorship-dns-lies-as-seen-by-ripe-atlas/
14. Bortzmeyer, S., Dolmans, R., Hoffman, P.E.: DNS query name minimisation to improve privacy. RFC 9156 (2021)
15. Bretelle, M.: [dns-operations] K-root in CN leaking outside of CN, November 2021. https://lists.dns-oarc.net/pipermail/dns-operations/2021-November/021437.html
16. Chung, T., Choffnes, D., Mislove, A.: Tunneling for transparency: a large-scale analysis of end-to-end violations in the internet. In: IMC (2016)
17. Chung, T., van Rijswijk-Deij, R., Chandrasekaran, B., Choffnes, D., Levin, D., Maggs, B.M., Mislove, A., Wilson, C.: A Longitudinal. USENIX Security, End-to-End View of the DNSSEC Ecosystem. In (2017)
18. Conrad, D.R., Woolf, S.: Requirements for a Mechanism Identifying a Name Server Instance. RFC 4892 (2007)
19. Dagon, D., Lee, C., Lee, W., Provos, N.: Corrupted DNS resolution paths: the rise of a malicious resolution authority. In: NDSS (2008)
20. DNSFilter: DNS Threat Protection (2022). https://www.dnsfilter.com
21. Fan, X., Heidemann, J., Govindan, R.: Evaluating anycast in the domain name system. In: IEEE INFOCOM (2013)
22. Farnan, O., Darer, A., Wright, J.: Poisoning the well: exploring the great firewall's poisoned DNS responses. In: WPES (2016)
23. Gill, P., Crete-Nishihata, M., Dalek, J., Goldberg, S., Senft, A., Wiseman, G.: Characterizing Web censorship worldwide: another look at the OpenNet initiative data. ACM Trans. Web 9(1), 1–29 (2015)

24. Gillmor, D.K., Salazar, J., Hoffman, P.E.: Unilateral Opportunistic Deployment of Encrypted Recursive-to-Authoritative DNS. Internet-Draft draft-ietf-dprive-unilateral-probing-02, Internet Engineering Task Force, September 2022. work in Progress
25. Google: SafeSearch (2022). https://safety.google/products/#search
26. Hilton, A., Deccio, C., Davis, J.: Fourteen years in the life: a root server's perspective on DNS resolver security. In: USENIX Security (2023)
27. Hoang, N.P., Doreen, S., Polychronakis, M.: Measuring I2P censorship at a global scale. In: USENIX FOCI (2019)
28. Hoang, N.P., Niaki, A.A., Dalek, J., Knockel, J., Lin, P., Marczak, B., Crete-Nishihata, M., Gill, P., Polychronakis, M.: How Great is the Great Firewall? USENIX Security, Measuring China's DNS Censorship. In (2021)
29. Hoffman, P.E., McManus, P.: DNS Queries over HTTPS (DoH). RFC 8484 (2018)
30. Hu, Z., Zhu, L., Heidemann, J., Mankin, A., Wessels, D., Hoffman, P.E.: Specification for DNS over Transport Layer Security (TLS). RFC 7858 (2016)
31. Huitema, C., Dickinson, S., Mankin, A.: DNS over Dedicated QUIC Connections. RFC 9250 (2022)
32. Jones, B., Feamster, N., Paxson, V., Weaver, N., Allman, M.: Detecting DNS root manipulation. In: PAM (2016)
33. Kührer, M., Hupperich, T., Rossow, C., Holz, T.: Exit from hell? reducing the impact of amplification DDoS attacks. In: USENIX Security (2014)
34. Kumari, W.A., Hoffman, P.E.: Running a Root Server Local to a Resolver. RFC 8806 (2020)
35. Li, C., Cheng, Y., Men, H., Zhang, Z., Li, N.: Performance analysis of root anycast nodes based on active measurement. Electronics 11(8), 1194 (2022)
36. Li, Z., Levin, D., Spring, N., Bhattacharjee, B.: Internet Anycast: Performance, Problems, & Potential. SIGCOMM (2018)
37. Lindqvist, K.E., Abley, J.: Operation of Anycast Services. RFC 4786 (2006)
38. Liu, B., Lu, C., Duan, H., Liu, Y., Li, Z., Hao, S., Yang, M.: Who is answering my queries: understanding and characterizing interception of the DNS resolution path. In: USENIX Security (2018)
39. Lowe, G., Winters, P., Marcus, M.L.: The Great DNS Wall of China. New York University, Technical report (2007)
40. Lu, C., et al.: An end-to-end, large-scale measurement of DNS-over-encryption: how far have we come? In: IMC (2019)
41. Mockapetris, P.: Domain names - concepts and facilities. RFC 1034 (1987)
42. Mockapetris, P.: Domain names - implementation and specification. RFC 1035 (1987)
43. Moura, G.C.M., et al.: Old but gold: prospecting TCP to engineer and live monitor DNS anycast. In: PAM (2022)
44. Moura, G.C.M., et al.: Anycast vs. DDoS: evaluating the November 2015 root DNS event. In: IMC (2016)
45. Nawrocki, M., Koch, M., Schmidt, T.C., Wählisch, M.: Transparent forwarders: an unnoticed component of the open DNS infrastructure. In: CoNEXT (2021)
46. Niaki, A.A., et al.: ICLab: a global, longitudinal internet censorship measurement platform. In: IEEE S&P (2020)
47. Pearce, P., Ensafi, R., Li, F., Feamster, N., Paxson, V.: Towards continual measurement of global network-level censorship. In: IEEE S&P (2018)
48. Pearce, P., et al.: Global measurement of DNS manipulation. In: USENIX Security (2017)

49. Le Pochat, V., Van Goethem, T., Tajalizadehkhoob, S., Korczyński, M., Joosen, W.: Tranco: a research-oriented top sites ranking hardened against manipulation. In: NDSS (2019)
50. Raman, R.S., Stoll, A., Dalek, J., Ramesh, R., Scott, W., Ensafi, R.: Measuring the deployment of network censorship filters at global scale. In: NDSS (2020)
51. Randall, A., et al.: Home is where the hijacking is: understanding DNS interception by residential routers. In: IMC (2021)
52. RIPE Atlas: Legal (2020). https://atlas.ripe.net/legal/terms-conditions/
53. RIPE Atlas: Built-in Measurements (2022). https://atlas.ripe.net/docs/built-in-measurements/
54. RIPE Ncc: RIPE Atlas (2022). https://atlas.ripe.net
55. Rose, S., Larson, M., Massey, D., Austein, R., Arends, R.: DNS Security Introduction and Requirements. RFC 4033 (2005)
56. Snabb, J.: F.ROOT-SERVERS.NET moved to Beijing? https://seclists.org/nanog/2011/Oct/12, October 2011
57. Sundara Raman, R., Shenoy, P., Kohls, K., Ensafi, R.: Censored planet: an internet-wide, longitudinal censorship observatory. In: CCS (2020)
58. VanderSloot, B., McDonald, A., Scott, W., Halderman, J.A., Ensafi, R.: Quack: scalable remote measurement of application-layer censorship. In: USENIX Security (2018)
59. Vergara Ereche, M.: [dns-operations] Odd behaviour on one node in I root-server (facebook, youtube & twitter), March 2010. https://lists.dns-oarc.net/pipermail/dns-operations/2010-March/005263.html
60. Weaver, N., Kreibich, C., Nechaev, B., Paxson, V.: Implications of Netalyzrs DNS Measurements. In: SATIN (2011)
61. Weaver, N., Kreibich, C., Paxson, V.: Redirecting DNS for Ads and Profit. In: USENIX FOCI (2011)

A First Look at Brand Indicators for Message Identification (BIMI)

Masanori Yajima[1]($\boxtimes$), Daiki Chiba[2], Yoshiro Yoneya[3], and Tatsuya Mori[4]

[1] Waseda University, Tokyo, Japan
y-masa22@nsl.cs.waseda.ac.jp
[2] NTT Security (Japan) KK, Tokyo, Japan
daiki.chiba@ieee.org
[3] Japan Registry Services Co., Ltd., Tokyo, Japan
yoshiro.yoneya@jprs.co.jp
[4] Waseda University/NICT/RIKEN AIP, Tokyo, Japan
mori@nsl.cs.waseda.ac.jp

Abstract. As promising approaches to thwarting the damage caused by phishing emails, DNS-based email security mechanisms, such as the Sender Policy Framework (SPF), Domain-based Message Authentication, Reporting & Conformance (DMARC) and DNS-based Authentication of Named Entities (DANE), have been proposed and widely adopted. Nevertheless, the number of victims of phishing emails continues to increase, suggesting that there should be a mechanism for supporting end-users in correctly distinguishing such emails from legitimate emails. To address this problem, the standardization of Brand Indicators for Message Identification (BIMI) is underway. BIMI is a mechanism that helps an email recipient visually distinguish between legitimate and phishing emails. With Google officially supporting BIMI in July 2021, the approach shows signs of spreading worldwide. With these backgrounds, we conduct an extensive measurement of the adoption of BIMI and its configuration. The results of our measurement study revealed that, as of November 2022, 3,538 out of the one million most popular domain names have a set BIMI record, whereas only 396 (11%) of the BIMI-enabled domain names had valid logo images and verified mark certificates. The study also revealed the existence of several misconfigurations in such logo images and certificates.

Keywords: BIMI · Email · Measurement

1 Introduction

As promising countermeasure technologies against phishing emails, sender authentication techniques such as Sender Policy Framework (SPF) [38], Domain-based Message Authentication, Reporting & Conformance (DMARC) [26], and DNS-Based Authentication of Named Entities (DANE) [23] have been standardized and have become widespread. In addition to these technologies,

A. Brunstrom et al. (Eds.): PAM 2023, LNCS 13882, pp. 479–495, 2023.
https://doi.org/10.1007/978-3-031-28486-1_20

the standardization of Brand Indicators for Message Identification (BIMI) [16] is underway. The idea behind BIMI is to display the trademarked logo of a company or organization, along with information regarding its certification, in an email message. The recipient of the email can visually verify the legitimacy of the email sender by checking for the existence of a brand logo image with which they are familiar. BIMI technology has gained popularity since receiving official support from Google in July 2021.

For SPF, DMARC, and DANE, which are already widely used, many measurement studies have been conducted on the adoption, misuse, and misconfiguration of technologies. However, to the best of our knowledge, there have been no comprehensive measurement studies conducted on BIMI. Given this background, we set the following research questions to identify best practices and open research questions regarding the BIMI operation:

- *How widespread is BIMI currently?*
- *How do DNS administrators configure the BIMI records for their domain names?*
- *Is BIMI configured with other DNS-based email security mechanisms?*
- *What are the typical misconfigurations of BIMI?*
- *Are there any cyberattacks exploiting BIMI?*

To address these research questions, we conducted the first large-scale measurement study of BIMI in the wild. We examined the presence and configuration of BIMI records for a list of one million popular domain names. We collected logo images and Verified Mark Certificates (VMC) for BIMI records and verified the validity of each setting. In addition, we examined the domain names extracted from 114,915 phishing emails collected by our spam trap and the open database of phishing websites and investigated whether there are any attack cases that exploit BIMI.

The contributions and findings of this study are as follows:

- This is the first large-scale measurement study of the adoption and operation of BIMI in the wild.
- Of the one million popular domain names, 3,538 have BIMI records.
- Of the 3,538 domain names with a BIMI configuration, only 11% had a valid logo image and VMC.
- In domain names that had set up a VMC for BIMI, DMARC was set up in 99.5% of the domain names.
- We found 16 BIMI misconfigurations/violations in BIMI records, 1,224 in logos, 58 in VMCs, and 14 in the DMARC configuration.
- We found 45 domain names having differences between the images contained in the VMC and the images provided on the server.
- In this study, we found no cases of attacks exploiting BIMI.

2   Background

In this section, we first review the email security mechanisms. We then describe the specification of BIMI. For reference, we present the survey results of BIMI implementations for major mail user agents in Appendix.

2.1   DNS-Based Email Security Mechanisms

In the following, we present the overview of the major DNS-based email security mechanisms, except BIMI, which will be described in the next subsection.

The **Sender Policy Framework** (SPF) [38] is a mechanism used to verify the legitimacy of the sender of an email based on IP addresses. By registering SPF information in the DNS TXT record, mail server administrators can explicitly specify IP addresses that are allowed to send emails to the domain name in question.

DomainKeys Identified Mail (DKIM) [25] is a mechanism used to achieve authentication by adding a digital signature when sending email. To use DKIM, the domain name administrator must set up a public key for digital signatures on the DNS server. In addition, by setting a label called a selector, multiple public keys can be operated with a single domain name.

Domain-based Message Authentication, Reporting & Conformance (DMARC) [26] is a mechanism to verify the legitimacy of an email sender by referring to SPF and DKIM records. Like SPF, DMARC can be used by setting a TXT record on the authoritative DNS server of the domain name of the mail sender.

MTA-STS is a mechanism used to enforce STARTTLS on the sender of email, where STARTTLS [22] is a mechanism for encrypting the sending and receiving of email.

DNS-based Authentication of Named Entities (DANE) [15] is a mechanism used to guarantee the authenticity of mail destinations and the confidentiality of mail. DNSSEC [33–35] is used to determine the legitimacy, and STARTTLS is used to achieve confidentiality. To use DANE, a TLS public key must be set up on the email server.

TLS Reporting (TLSRPT) In MTA-STS and DANE, mail may not be delivered because of a failed authentication process. TLSRPT [29] is a function reporting such failures.

2.2   BIMI Specifications

BIMI presents an email to a user with an authenticated brand logo. This allows email recipients to visually distinguish the legitimacy of the email sender without having to look at the subject line or body of the email. The widespread use of BIMI is expected to reduce the success rate of phishing emails. However, for BIMI to be effective, the brand logo displayed by BIMI must be recognized by users [4,5,7]. As with DKIM, multiple logos can be set for a single domain name by setting the selector.

Table 5 in appendix summarizes the DNS records that must be set for each of the security mechanisms described above. "Configure" indicates who needs to configure the record.

BIMI Record: To enable BIMI for a domain name, the following data must be added to the TXT record of the domain name of the MX server:

    v=BIMI1;l=<logo link>;a=<vmc link>,

where `logo link` describes the brand logo link and `vmc link` describes the link for the VMC. Among these links, only `https` is allowed as a schema.

Logo Image: The brand logo images used by BIMI must be provided in the SVG file format defined in RFC 6170 [36]. SVG Tiny P/S, currently proposed as an Internet Draft [17], sets the following restrictions:

- A title tag must be included (64 characters or less is recommended).
- The following attributes must be set in an svg tag:
xmlns="http://www.w3.org/2000/svg",
version="1.2",
baseProfile="tiny-ps".
- The inclusion of a desc tag is also recommended.
- The size of the logo is recommended to be less than 32 KB.

VMC: VMC is a digital certificate used to certify the ownership of a logo. Currently, DigiCert and Entrust are two CAs that can issue a VMC [14].

DMARC: In DMARC, the domain name owner can set a policy regarding what action should be taken by the email recipient when the source authentication by SPF or DKIM fails. The three policies are as follows:

- "none" indicates that no specific action will be taken.
- "quarantine" indicates that the email recipient will treat as suspicious email that fails the DMARC mechanism check. The email recipient must take action, such as placing the email in the spam folder or conducting further investigations.
- "reject" indicates that an email that fails the DMARC mechanism check is rejected.

DMARC allows one domain name and its subdomain names to be independently configured. A pct is a field that allows the domain name administrator to gradually implement the DMARC mechanism. By setting the pct, it is possible to apply a strong denial policy with a certain probability; otherwise, the next-strongest denial policy is applied. To use BIMI, domain name administrators must fully implement the DMARC mechanism. When using BIMI, "none" should not be applied.

Vetting Process. In order to use BIMI, it is necessary to obtain a valid VMC for the target logo as an email client will test both BIMI record and VMC. A user wishing to obtain a VMC for their logo submits the trademarked logo and information verifying the identity of the user to the VMC-issuing CA. The CA will review the submitted information and also conduct a video conference with the user. If no problems are found, a VMC associated with the logo will be issued. The two VMC-issuing CAs clearly describe in their Certification Practice Statement (CPS) that they meet the official security requirements for issuing the VMC [6,8,9]. They are subject to an external audit in order to conduct the business of issuing VMCs. This audit is similar to the external audit that CAs issuing server certificates in Web PKI undergo.

3   Measurement Method

In this section, we present the list of domain names we target for our analysis and the data collection methodology.

3.1   Target Domain Names

In this study, we adopt the domain names used for popular websites, those of phishing email senders, and those of phishing websites as our research target domain names.

Tranco: We adopted the one million domain names published by Tranco [13] on February 20, 2022. To ensure that these Tranco domain names contained enough legitimate targets for phishing, we conducted a preliminary study. Specifically, we determined how many of the 382 brands targeted by phishing sites listed on OpenPhish [10] between January 22, 2022 and February 20, 2022 were included in these Tranco domain names. As a result, 96% ($= 365/382$) of the brands were included in them. This indicates that Tranco domain names are a reasonable target for our BIMI study.

Phishing Email Sender: We analyzed the phishing emails received by our spam trap, and extracted domain names from the email address of the email sender. We collected the domain names of email addresses in the From and Received headers of emails received on April 1 – April 28, 2022. Random sampling resulted in 84,730 unique domain names.

Phishing Website: We employed domain names published by OpenPhish [10] as the domain names of the phishing sites. We obtained this list of domain names on May 2, 2022. A total of 30,221 domain names were examined.

3.2   Data Collection Methodology

This section describes how to determine whether a domain name employs BIMI and other DNS-based email security mechanisms described in Sect. 2.1.

We first send a query to each domain name to look up the BIMI, SPF, DKIM, DMARC, MTA-STS, TLSRPT, or DANE records. Queries were sent using dnspython [32]. We recorded the response to each query and determined that each mechanism is operational if the responses matched the signatures listed in Table 5. In the following, we describe specific notes on collecting data for each security mechanism.

BIMI: In a BIMI study, we adopted `default` as the selector. We downloaded data from the URLs of the logo image and the VMC listed in the BIMI record. In this study, we defined three levels of operation in BIMI, as listed in Table 1.

SPF: In our SPF study, we covered both TXT and SPF records.

Table 1. The levels of BIMI configuration.

Level	Description
1	Has a valid BIMI record shown in Table 5
2	Has a valid logo available for download
3	Has valid logo and VMC available for download

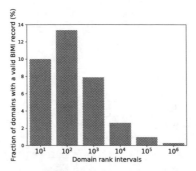

Fig. 1. Fractions (%) of the domain names with valid BIMI records. 10^n represents the logarithmic rank interval ranging from the $10^{n-1}+1$ th domain to the 10^n th domain.

DKIM: In the DKIM survey, we used `default` and `key1` as the selectors.
DANE: In the DANE study, the domain names listed in the MX records were targeted. If at least one of the domain names listed in the MX record supports DANE, the domain name is determined to have adopted DANE.

4   Understanding BIMI in the Wild

In this section, we report on our measurement study of the adoption of BIMI in the wild and its correlation with other DNS-based email security mechanisms described in Sect. 2. We also investigate cases where BIMI has been used in attacks.

4.1   Adoption of BIMI

Among the Tranco one million domain names examined, 3,581 domain names with BIMI records existed (Level 1). We obtained logos from 3,034 domain names (Level 2). However, surprisingly, only 396 of these domain names had a valid VMC available for download (Level 3). We believe that the reason why so few domain names today have had their VMC correctly set up is due to the high cost of obtaining a VMC. To obtain a valid VMC, a brand logo must be registered as a trademark, and a certificate must be issued by a third-party organization based on an examination. We expect that the fact that the cost of operating BIMI is not low will serve as a barrier to attacks that exploit BIMI using fake logos.

Figure 1 presents the number of BIMI-compatible domain names (Level 1 and above) in each rank interval expressed in logarithms, where the rank indicates the popularity of the website corresponding to the domain name on the Tranco

Table 2. Correlations of the email security mechanisms: BIMI vs. other mechanisms. The rows indicate other email security mechanisms and the columns indicate the BIMI setting level. The numerical values in the table indicate the number of domain names.

	Total	BIMI level 1	BIMI level 2	BIMI level 3
All	1,000,000	3,581	3,034	396
MX-enabled	745,746	3,552	3,012	392
SPF	600,672	3,529	2,993	392
DKIM	107,633	3,72	309	14
DMARC	194,123	3,450	2,929	394
MTA-STS	1,310	182	163	23
DANE	8,219	58	50	2
TLSRPT	2,187	249	218	35

list. As expected, the higher the ranking of a domain name, the higher the rate of BIMI adoption; for the top-100 domains, more than 10% of domain names have configured a valid BIMI record. On the other hand, we can see that a certain number of domain names with low rankings have also adopted BIMI, suggesting that the use of BIMI is spreading. For reference, we analyzed the breakdown of the domain names that have configured BIMI. The results are shown in Appendix.

4.2 Correlations Between BIMI and Other DNS-Based Email Security Mechanisms

We analyzed the correlation between BIMI and other DNS-based email security mechanisms, i.e., whether they are simultaneously employed. Table 2 presents the results. "MX-enabled" indicates that the results are restricted to only domain names for which MX records existed. As described in Sect. 2.1, if an email recipient retrieves BIMI data for a domain name, the domain name must pass the DMARC authentication, and the configured policy must be "quarantine" or "reject." Therefore, a high percentage of BIMI-enabled domain names have adopted SPF and DMARC.

We found that the number of domain names configuring BIMI is larger than those of MTA-STS and TLSRPT. This result suggests that BIMI is attracting the attention of more domain name administrators despite being a relatively new security mechanism. If a domain name operates BIMI with Level 3 and DANE, the domain name has an extremely high security level. We found that only two domain names meet these criteria. DANE requires DNSSEC [18,28,31,33–35] settings, which are difficult to configure.

4.3 Attacks Exploiting BIMI

We applied BIMI record lookups on the domain names of phishing emails and websites, which we describe in Sect. 3.1. We found no BIMI records for 114,915 domain names in the two datasets combined; that is, as of today, we have not observed any phishing attempts that exploit BIMI records. We expect that this observation is due to the fact that the trademark registration process contributes to raising barriers to BIMI record operations. However, there is no assurance that BIMI-abusing domain names will not appear in the future, and it is therefore necessary to keep a close watch on this aspect.

5   Incorrect BIMI Configurations

In this section, we present a measurement study focused on the typical incorrect configurations of BIMI records, logo images, and VMC.

5.1   BIMI Record

We first study the inherent configuration errors we found with respect to the format of the BIMI records collected. It is meaningful to summarize such information and share explicit knowledge of the mistakes that administrators are prone to make.

Logo Setting: Two of the domain names did not have a field to set the logo. In one of these two cases, only a link to the certificate existed. In addition, although 11 domain names had a field for setting a logo, the content was empty, where the empty content in the logo setting field indicates that the domain name in question explicitly refuses to participate in BIMI.

Use of HTTP: There are five domain names whose logo URLs used `http` instead of `https`. None of the five domain names has a URL for the certificate. Similarly, one domain name was used `http` in the URL pointing to the certificate. The URL pointed to the Let's Encrypt server and not the certificate.

Typos: Six domain names were incorrectly used `I=` instead of `l=` as the field for setting the logo. The certificate link did not exist for any of the six domain names.

Unnecessary Parentheses: One domain name existed in which the domain name was described as `l=[<logo link>]` when setting the logo. The domain name in question does not contain a certificate link set.

Invalid String: Two domain names existed, in which invalid character strings were set in records that should describe the URLs.

These misconfigurations were found in domain names that had set only a logo or had not set a logo at all.

5.2   Brand Logo Image

We analyzed logo images in SVG format retrieved from the URLs listed in the BIMI records. A total of 3,034 logo images were analyzed. In the following, we show the cases that violated the mandatory and recommended conditions described in the Internet Draft [17] of SVG shown in Sect. 2.2. Of the domain names with VMC configured, only five domain names failed to configure SVG in the correct format.

Title Tag—*mandatory:* There were 1,008 (33%) logo images without title tags. Two images with empty title tags are found.

Table 3. Frequencies of issuers.

Issuer	Count
Entrust, Inc	166
Digicert, Inc	225
Sectigo Limited	2
Let's Encrypt	3

Table 4. BIMI configuration policies for the target domain (rows) vs. subdomains (columns).

	Reject	Quarantine	None
Reject	258	6	**4**
Quarantine	2	114	**2**
None	**0**	**0**	**6**

SVG Tag—*mandatory:* There were 1,224 (40.3%) logo images that did not conform to the svg tag format.

Desc Tag—*recommended:* A total of 2,905 (95.7%) logo images did not contain a desc tag.

Image Size—*recommended:* In total, 241 (7.9%) logo images exceeded the recommended 32 KB.

Aspect Ratio—*recommended:* Logos displayed on email clients are often circles or squares. It is therefore recommended that the aspect ratio of the logo be 1:1 [1], and 496 (16.3%) of the logo images do not have this aspect ratio.

5.3   VMC

We analyzed VMCs obtained from the URLs listed in the BIMI records. The analysis covered 396 certificates collected from domain names with Level 3 BIMI settings, as shown in Table 1.

Certificate Issuer: Table 3 shows a breakdown of the issuers of the collected certificates. Currently, certificates issued by parties other than Entrust and Digicert are invalid for BIMI, among which there are five such cases. These certificates did not contain logo images, whereas all certificates issued by Entrust and Digicert contained image data.

Certificate Validity Period: We analyzed the validity period of the collected certificates. As a result, 13 certificates had expired. One of these is the domain name `entrustdatacard.com`, which was used by Entrust. The domain name redirects https://www.entrust.com/. However, BIMI records, logos, and certificate links are still accessible.

Legitimacy of Images Extracted from the VMC: We verified whether the 391 logo images extracted from the collected VMCs matched the logos collected from the URLs listed in the BIMI records. We found 45 domain names for which there was a difference between the two logo images. The differences included the use of completely different images, the presence of line breaks in the files, differences in the image size, and differences in the SVG titles.

5.4   Violation of DMARC Policy

We analyzed DMARC policies for 396 domain names using Level 3 BIMI settings. Of the 396 cases, four domain names did not have DMARC configurations. Table 4 presents the results of the analysis of the DMARC policy settings. The rows represent the configuration policies for the target domain names, and the columns represent configuration policies for the subdomain names. In the table, bold numbers indicate the number of policy violations, 12 of which were present.

6   Discussion

6.1   Current Status of BIMI

Here, we discuss three perspectives on the current status of BIMI as revealed by our results.

Prevalence of BIMI: Compared with other security mechanisms, BIMI has a relatively high adoption rate despite its novelty (see Sect. 4.2). This is because BIMI is relatively easy to set up, and includes setting up the BIMI records and registering the SVGs. However, our results show that only a small fraction of domain names are correctly configured up to VMC. This is because setting up a VMC increases the difficulty of setting up BIMI and incurs certain financial costs.

Misconfiguration of BIMI: Currently, many documents on the Web introduce BIMI settings, and we assume that domain name administrators refer to these documents to set up BIMI. However, it is highly likely that the SVG conversion tool [2] and the BIMI configuration check tool [4,5,7] are not correctly introduced in such documents since misconfiguration of BIMI exists. In the future, further dissemination of these tools is essential to reduce BIMI misconfiguration by domain name administrators and to enable them to self-check whether the correct settings have been made.

Abuse of BIMI: The results of our study show that there is still no evidence of BIMI abuse in phishing emails or in the domain names of phishing sites. BIMI is not yet fully deployed, even for well-known services, and end users are not yet familiar with BIMI. Thus, there is no advantage for attackers in configuring BIMI. However, there is no guarantee that attackers will not continue to implement BIMI abuse in the future. It is therefore necessary to continuously monitor the existence of BIMI abuses.

Challenges for BIMI to Scale: Our measurement study revealed that the adoption of BIMI is not high at the present time. In the following, we discuss approaches that may be effective in increasing the adoption of BIMI. We examined information about MUAs that have implemented BIMI and the categories of domain names that have registered BIMI (see Appendix for detials.) First, we found that there are MUAs that do not currently support BIMI. Although we surveyed major MUAs, there were cases where MUAs did not support BIMI. We hope that MUA vendors will understand the effectiveness of BIMI for protecting their users and implement it in the near future. It is also important for MUAs to provide a usable interface for displaying BIMI so that end-users can recognize and utilize BIMI correctly. In addition, in order to increase the number of BIMI compliant domain names, it would be effective to reduce the cost of setting up BIMI [42]. We expect that the availability of open tools and knowledge of the procedures required to register BIMI will increase its popularity.

6.2 Limitations

Our study has the following three limitations. First, in our study, we sent only a minimum number of queries (up to three) to avoid overloading the target. This means that if the target server was offline during our study, the data might not have been correctly retrieved. Second, our study only investigated the specific selectors for BIMI and DKIM. Therefore, if the target of our survey is to use individual selectors for each sending destination, it may be judged as unsupported in our study. Finally, our study did not clarify the current status of BIMI from the viewpoint of administrators and email recipients. To investigate the current issues in setting up BIMI and the effectiveness of BIMI from the viewpoint of the recipients, it is necessary to conduct an interview study.

6.3 Possibility of Registering Fake Logos

To register a brand logo with BIMI and obtain a legitimate certificate, it must be registered as a trademark. This is expected to make the registration of fake logos more difficult. By contrast, approximately 90% of the domain names that currently have BIMI records operate BIMI without valid certificates. It has also been pointed out that some email clients display BIMI brand logo images without certificate validation [3]. Based on this background, we investigated whether there were any cases of fake logos registered with BIMI. We employed a perceptual hash (pHash) [11], which calculates the similarity between two images. In addition, pHash is widely used to detect a copyright infringement. The analysis revealed several cases in which the same logo was used for multiple domain names. Most of these cases involve the use of several different TLDs for the same service, such as amazon.com and amazon.co.uk. By contrast, there was one domain name using the digicert logo for a completely different service, which we concluded was a misconfiguration. At this point, no obviously fake logos have been found, although we plan to monitor this situation closely.

6.4 Ethical Considerations

Our measurement study discovered several domain names with incorrect BIMI settings. As an ethical consideration, we decided to notify the administrators of those domain names to prevent their misuse. In particular, we are in the process of making a responsible disclosure to the administrators of domain names with VMC configured but with some misconfiguration. We also plan to notify the administrators of domain names that have only SVG configured.

7 Related Work

Several measurement studies have been conducted on DNS-based email security mechanisms. This section divides such studies into two broad categories: those that focus on SPF, DKIM, and DMARC, and those focusing on other areas.

SPF, DKIM, and DMARC: In 2011, Mori et al. conducted an early study on SPF implementation by investigating the existence of SPF and the errors found in SPF policies [30]. In 2015, Durumetric et al. measured email servers supporting SPF, DKIM, and DMARC by analyzing SMTP connections on Google's email servers [20]. In 2015, Foster et al. investigated the prevalence of SPF and DMARC from the perspective of email providers [21]. Hu et al. studied the states of support for SPF, DKIM, and DMARC in 35 email providers in 2018, and conducted a phishing email measurement with end-users [24]. Deccio et al. measured the latest status of SPF, DKIM, and DMARC on several email servers in 2021 [19]. Tatang et al. continuously investigated the status of SPF, DKIM, and DMARC support for domain names listed in multiple top lists in 2021 for a period of 1.5 years [40]. Wang et al. conducted measurements of DKIM deployments using a 5-year Chinese Passive DNS dataset from 2015 to 2020 and server logs of an Chinese email provider in 2020 [41].

Others: In addition, measurement studies were conducted to elucidate other individual protocols (see Sect. 2.1). Scheitle et al. were the first to examine the number of CAAs deployed in 2018 [37]. In 2020, Lee et al. conducted an extensive study to determine how widely DANEs are spread and managed at both the server and client sides [27]. Tatang et al. conducted the first large-scale measurement study of MTA-STS adoption in 2021 [39]. Yajima et al. measured the adoption rates of DNSSEC, DNS Cookies, CAA, SPF, DMARC, MTA-STS, DANE, and TLSRPT, which are security mechanisms that can be implemented in 2021 [42].

None of the studies above mentioned any quantitative results for BIMI, which is just beginning to spread, and our study is the first BIMI measurement approach as of November 2022.

8   Conclusion

In this study, we conducted the first large-scale measurement of BIMI in the wild. We investigated the prevalence of BIMI in one million domain names and found that 3,538 already had BIMI records, despite the BIMI mechanism having only recently begun to be used. We also found that there are intrinsic misconfiguration patterns and specification violations in BIMI records, logos, VMCs, and DMARCs. In addition, no evidence of BIMI abuse was found during our investigation. For the coming widespread use of BIMI, future work includes development of a tool that enables domain name administrators to configure BIMI settings easily and properly, conducting interviews with both domain name administrators and email users on the incentives of adopting/leveraging BIMI, and continuously measure the adoption status of BIMI. We hope that the findings we derived through our measurement study of the BIMI will contribute to its further spread and help thwart the damages caused by phishing attacks.

A   BIMI Implementations of Major Mail User Agents

Table 5. DNS records used for configuring mail security mechanisms.

	Configure	Target domain name	RR	Signature
BIMI	sender	<selector>._bimi.<domain name>	TXT	v=BIMI1...
SPF	sender	<domain name>	TXT	v=spf1...
DKIM	sender	<selector>._domainkey.<domain name>	TXT	v=DKIM1...
DMARC	sender	_dmarc.<domain name>	TXT	v=DMARC1...
MTA-STS	receiver	_mta-sts.<domain name>	TXT	v=STSv1...
DANE	receiver	_25._tcp.<mail server domain name>	TLSA	n/a
TLSRPT	receiver	_smtp._tls.<domain name>	TXT	v=TLSRPTv1...

Table 6. BIMI adoption status of major MUAs. ✓ indicates that the valid BIMI logo was correctly displayed on the corresponding MUA.

MUAs (Webmail + browser)	Website 1 (Perfect)	Website 2 (Presence of logo)
Gmail (Chrome 107.0.5304.87)	✓	–
Fastmail (Chrome 107.0.5304.87)	✓	✓
Yahoo Mail (Chrome 107.0.5304.87)	✓	–
MUAs (Email apps)	Website 1 (perfect)	Website 2 (presence of logo)
Apple Mail (iOS 16)	✓	–
Gmail 6.0.221016 (iOS 16)	✓	–
Gmail 2022.09.18.479203120 (Xperia Z4, Android 6)	✓	–
Gmail 2022.09.18.479203120 (Galaxy S6 edge, Android 7)	✓	–
Microsoft Outlook (Windows 10, version 2202)	–	–
Thunderbird (Windows 10, version 102.3.3)	–	–

In the following, we summarize the current support status of BIMI by the major Mail User Agents (MUAs) – both webmail services and application-based email clients. As webmail services, we adopted Gmail, Fastmail, and Yahoo Mail. We used Google Chrome to study the BIMI adoption status of these webmail services. As email client apps, we adopt Apple Mail, Microsoft Outlook, and Thunderbird. For Gmail in particular, we checked Gmail apps that work on iOS and Android.

We picked up the two popular websites operated with the following BIMI-compatible domain names.

- Website 1 (perfect): Both VMC and logo are correctly registered.
- Website 2 (valid logo): Only logo is correctly registered. VMC is not properly configured.

Note that since our goal is not to expose the level of BIMI operation for specific institutions, and since the BIMI configuration status is likely to be updated in the future and is not invariant, we decided to refrain from naming the respective websites. In addition, since the purpose of this study is to evaluate the BIMI compatibility of MUAs, the type of website does not matter as long as the BIMI setting on the domain name side is consistent.

We registered email accounts on the two websites, where we used different email accounts for each MUA. Emails sent from each website were received by the MUAs used in the experiment to study the adoption of BIMI by MUAs.

Table 6 presents the results of studying whether or not each MUA displays the BIMI logo for emails sent from website 1 and website 2. The behavior of a correctly developed BIMI implementation is to display the logo for website 1, which has perfectly configured BIMI, and not for website 2, which has registered BIMI records but has incomplete VMC. The study revealed that, for webmail-based MUAs, Gmail and Yahoo Mail, accessed with Chrome, correctly implemented BIMI. Fastmail displays the BIMI logo for correctly configured domain names, but does not validate the VMC. Considering the risk of the above-mentioned fact being exploited in a phishing attack, we are currently in the process of making a responsible disclosure to Fastmail. In the email apps, Apple Mail and the all the versions of the Gmail apps correctly implemented BIMI. As of November 2022, Outlook and Thunderbird do not support BIMI.

B   Categorization of Domain Names Adopting BIMI

We have categorized domain names that have adopted BIMI. To this end, we leveraged SimilarWeb [12], which is a commercial database that collects web traffic statistics and compiles website information collected from million-order devices deployed around the world. We made use of SimilarWeb to identify categories of domain names, both for those with BIMI records present, and for those with VMC set in addition to BIMI records. Table 7 presents the aggregated

Table 7. Top-10 categories of domain names with BIMI configuration. Level 1 (left) and Level 3 (right).

	Level 1		Level 3	
Rank	Category	Count	Category	Count
1	Computers and Electronics	697	Finance	66
2	Unknown	406	Computers and Electronics	59
3	Finance	373	Lifestyle	29
4	Business and Consumer Services	269	Business and Consumer Services	28
5	Science and Education	197	E-commerce and Shopping	26
6	Health	158	Arts and Entertainment	26
7	Lifestyle	155	Health	25
8	E-commerce and Shopping	140	News and Media	20
9	Travel and Tourism	133	Food and Drink	17
10	Food and Drink	127	Travel and Tourism	15

results for the top-10 categories for domain names with BIMI configuration of Level 1 and Level 3. Majority of Level-1 websites were dominated by Computers and Electronics, Finance, and Business uses. Note that "Unknown" indicates that the category of the website with that domain name was not identified in SimilarWeb. For the Level-3, the breakdown of the websites was different from the above, with Finance topping the list. This observation suggests that since financial websites are often the target of phishing attacks, there is an incentive for them to eagerly take measures using BIMI.

References

1. Creating BIMI SVG Logo Files (2020). https://bimigroup.org/creating-bimi-svg-logo-files/
2. SVG Conversion Tools Released (2020). https://bimigroup.org/svg-conversion-tools-released/
3. Fastmail now supports BIMI (2021). https://www.spamresource.com/2021/04/fastmail-now-supports-bimi.html
4. BIMI Inspector (2022). https://bimigroup.org/bimi-generator/
5. BIMI Record Checker - BIMI Record | EasyDMARC (2022). https://easydmarc.com/tools/bimi-lookup
6. DigiCert Certificate Policy/ Certification Practices Statement for Private PKI Services (2022). https://www.digicert.com/content/dam/digicert/pdfs/legal/digicert-private-pki-cp-cps-v3-9.pdf
7. Email Sender Identity Verification, Authentication & Security Solutions | Valimail (2022). https://domain-checker.valimail.com/bimi/
8. ENTRUST CERTIFICATE SERVICES Certification Practice Statement (2022). https://www.entrust.com/-/media/documentation/licensingandagreements/entrust-certificate-services-cps-3-11.pdf?la=en&hash=EA7E3B4CDEB02433939E7F7AB2762E60
9. Minimum Security Requirements for Issuance of Verified Mark Certificates Version 1.4 (2022). https://bimigroup.org/resources/VMC_Requirements_latest.pdf
10. OpenPhish (2022). https://openphish.com/
11. phash (2022). https://www.phash.org/
12. SimilarWeb (2022). https://www.similarweb.com/
13. Tranco (2022). https://tranco-list.eu/
14. VMC Issuer Information (2022). https://bimigroup.org/vmc-issuers/
15. Barnes, R.: Use Cases and Requirements for DNS-Based Authentication of Named Entities (DANE). RFC 6394, October 2011. https://doi.org/10.17487/RFC6394
16. Blank, S., Goldstein, P., Loder, T., Zink, T., Bradshaw, M., Brotman, A.: Brand Indicators for Message Identification (BIMI). Internet-Draft draft-brand-indicators-for-message-identification-01, Internet Engineering Task Force, April 2022. https://datatracker.ietf.org/doc/html/draft-brand-indicators-for-message-identification-01, work in Progress
17. Brotman, A., Adams, J.T.: SVG Tiny Portable/Secure. Internet-Draft draft-svg-tiny-ps-abrotman-03, Internet Engineering Task Force, April 2022. https://datatracker.ietf.org/doc/html/draft-svg-tiny-ps-abrotman-03, work in Progress
18. Chung, T., et al.: A longitudinal, end-to-end view of the DNSSEC ecosystem. In: Proceedings of USENIX Security Symposium (2017)

19. Deccio, C.T., et al.: Measuring email sender validation in the wild. In: Proceedings of the International Conference on emerging Networking EXperiments and Technologies (CoNEXT) (2021). https://doi.org/10.1145/3485983.3494868
20. Durumeric, Z., et al.: Neither snow nor rain nor MITM...: an empirical analysis of email delivery security. In: Proceedings of the ACM Internet Measurement Conference (IMC) (2015). https://doi.org/10.1145/2815675.2815695
21. Foster, I.D., Larson, J., Masich, M., Snoeren, A.C., Savage, S., Levchenko, K.: Security by any other name: On the effectiveness of provider based email security. In: Proceedings of the ACM Conference on Computer and Communications Security (CCS) (2015). https://doi.org/10.1145/2810103.2813607
22. Hoffman, P.E.: SMTP Service Extension for Secure SMTP over Transport Layer Security. RFC 3207, February 2002. https://doi.org/10.17487/RFC3207
23. Hoffman, P.E., Schlyter, J.: The DNS-Based Authentication of Named Entities (DANE) Transport Layer Security (TLS) Protocol: TLSA. RFC 6698, August 2012. https://doi.org/10.17487/RFC6698
24. Hu, H., Wang, G.: End-to-end measurements of email spoofing attacks. In: Proceedings of the USENIX Security Symposium (2018). https://www.usenix.org/conference/usenixsecurity18/presentation/hu
25. Kucherawy, M., Crocker, D., Hansen, T.: DomainKeys Identified Mail (DKIM) Signatures. RFC 6376, September 2011. https://doi.org/10.17487/RFC6376. https://www.rfc-editor.org/info/rfc6376
26. Kucherawy, M., Zwicky, E.: Domain-based Message Authentication, Reporting, and Conformance (DMARC). RFC 7489, March 2015. https://doi.org/10.17487/RFC7489
27. Lee, H., Gireesh, A., van Rijswijk-Deij, R., Kwon, T., Chung, T.: A longitudinal and comprehensive study of the DANE ecosystem in email. In: Proceedings of the USENIX Security Symposium (2020). https://www.usenix.org/conference/usenixsecurity20/presentation/lee-hyeonmin
28. Lian, W., Rescorla, E., Shacham, H., Savage, S.: Measuring the practical impact of DNSSEC deployment. In: Proceedings of the USENIX Security Symposium (2013)
29. Margolis, D., Brotman, A., Ramakrishnan, B., Jones, J., Risher, M.: SMTP TLS Reporting. RFC 8460, September 2018. https://doi.org/10.17487/RFC8460
30. Mori, T., Sato, K., Takahashi, Y., Ishibashi, K.: How is e-mail sender authentication used and misused? In: Proceedings of the Collaboration, Electronic messaging, Anti-Abuse and Spam Conference (CEAS) (2011). https://doi.org/10.1145/2030376.2030380
31. Müller, M., Chung, T., Mislove, A., van Rijswijk-Deij, R.: Rolling with confidence: managing the complexity of dnssec operations. IEEE Trans. Netw. Serv. Manage. (2019). https://doi.org/10.1109/TNSM.2019.2916176
32. Nominum: dnspython (2022). https://github.com/rthalley/dnspython
33. Rose, S., Larson, M., Massey, D., Austein, R., Arends, R.: DNS Security Introduction and Requirements. RFC 4033, March 2005. https://doi.org/10.17487/RFC4033
34. Rose, S., Larson, M., Massey, D., Austein, R., Arends, R.: Resource Records for the DNS Security Extensions. RFC 4034, March 2005. https://doi.org/10.17487/RFC4034
35. Rose, S., et al.: Protocol Modifications for the DNS Security Extensions. RFC 4035, March 2005. https://doi.org/10.17487/RFC4035
36. Santesson, S., Housley, R., Rosenthol, L., Bajaj, S.: Internet X.509 Public Key Infrastructure - Certificate Image. RFC 6170, May 2011. https://doi.org/10.17487/RFC6170. https://www.rfc-editor.org/info/rfc6170

37. Scheitle, Q., et al.: A first look at certification authority authorization (CAA). Comput. Commun. Rev. (2018). https://doi.org/10.1145/3213232.3213235
38. Schlitt, W., Wong, M.W.: Sender Policy Framework (SPF) for Authorizing Use of Domains in E-Mail, Version 1. RFC 4408, April 2006. https://doi.org/10.17487/RFC4408
39. Tatang, D., Flume, R., Holz, T.: Extended abstract: A first large-scale analysis on usage of MTA-STS. In: Proceedings of the Detection of Intrusions and Malware, and Vulnerability Assessment (DIMVA) (2021). https://doi.org/10.1007/978-3-030-80825-9_18
40. Tatang, D., Zettl, F., Holz, T.: The evolution of dns-based email authentication: measuring adoption and finding flaws. In: Proceedings of the International Symposium on Research in Attacks, Intrusions and Defenses (RAID) (2021). https://doi.org/10.1145/3471621.3471842
41. Wang, C., et al.: A large-scale and longitudinal measurement study of DKIM deployment. In: Proceedings of the USENIX Security Symposium (2022)
42. Yajima, M., Chiba, D., Yoneya, Y., Mori, T.: Measuring adoption of DNS security mechanisms with cross-sectional approach. In: Proceedings of the IEEE Global Communications Conference (GLOBECOM) (2021). https://doi.org/10.1109/GLOBECOM46510.2021.9685960

A Second Look at DNS QNAME Minimization

Jonathan Magnusson[1]([✉]) [iD], Moritz Müller[2] [iD], Anna Brunstrom[1] [iD], and Tobias Pulls[1] [iD]

[1] Karlstad University, Karlstad, Sweden
{jonathan.magnusson,anna.brunstrom,tobias.pulls}@kau.se
[2] SIDN Labs, Arnhem, The Netherlands
moritz.muller@sidn.nl

Abstract. The Domain Name System (DNS) is a critical Internet infrastructure that translates human-readable domain names to IP addresses. It was originally designed over 35 years ago and multiple enhancements have since then been made, in particular to make DNS lookups more secure and privacy preserving. *Query name minimization* (qmin) was initially introduced in 2016 to limit the exposure of queries sent across DNS and thereby enhance privacy. In this paper, we take a look at the adoption of qmin, building upon and extending measurements made by De Vries *et al.* in 2018. We analyze qmin adoption on the Internet using active measurements both on resolvers used by RIPE Atlas probes and on open resolvers. Aside from adding more vantage points when measuring qmin adoption on open resolvers, we also increase the number of repetitions, which reveals *conflicting resolvers* – resolvers that support qmin for some queries but not for others. For the passive measurements at root and Top-Level Domain (TLD) name servers, we extend the analysis over a longer period of time, introduce additional sources, and filter out non-valid queries. Furthermore, our controlled experiments measure performance and result quality of newer versions of the qmin-enabled open source resolvers used in the previous study, with the addition of PowerDNS. Our results, using extended methods from previous work, show that the adoption of qmin has significantly increased since 2018. New controlled experiments also show a trend of higher number of packets used by resolvers and lower error rates in the DNS queries. Since qmin is a balance between performance and privacy, we further discuss the depth limit of minimizing labels and propose the use of a public suffix list for setting this limit.

Keywords: DNS · Privacy · QNAME minimization · Measurements

1 Introduction

The *Domain Name System* (DNS) is a global hierarchical key/value-store that maps domain names to *Resource Records* (RRs) on the Internet [13,14]. One of the most common use-cases for DNS is performing lookups for RRs containing IP addresses. While privacy and security on the Internet has been a common area

© The Author(s) 2023
A. Brunstrom et al. (Eds.): PAM 2023, LNCS 13882, pp. 496–521, 2023.
https://doi.org/10.1007/978-3-031-28486-1_21

of research for the past decades, these topics were less prevalent when DNS was implemented over 35 years ago. The early Internet was relatively small, where everyone knew each other, and the focus was on getting data from point A to point B. Similar to other areas of the Internet, this has resulted in multiple proposals to improve DNS privacy and security as an afterthought. By encrypting DNS traffic with TLS, HTTPS, or QUIC [9–11], it is possible to achieve transport confidentiality. By signing sets of RRs and building chains of trust using DNSSEC [1], it is possible to prove integrity of the data. Due to the hierarchical structure of DNS, the top two levels of servers—root and Top-Level Domain (TLD)—are observing a large portion of non-cached requests on the Internet. From a privacy perspective, it is important that the information sent here is the minimum needed for each task. This is known as the fundamental privacy principle of *data minimization* [6]. The DNS resolvers may strip unnecessary labels for each query in the lookup process. This privacy feature is referred to as *query name minimization* (qmin) and is at present standardized in RFC 9156 [4].

The aim of this study is to measure the adoption of qmin. To do so, we build upon the experiments of De Vries *et al.* [23], who took a first look at qmin adoption in 2018. We considerably extend the experiments, consider an additional source of passive measurements, and include an additional open-source resolver for the controlled experiments. Our contributions are as follows:

1. Extended active measurements from 2018 up until October 2022 show that the adoption of qmin has increased from 2.5k resolvers used by RIPE Atlas probes in 2018 to 14k. We also show that the adoption of qmin has increased using active measurements on open resolvers, from 18k open resolvers categorized as qmin-enabled in 2018 to 80k in 2022.
2. Extended passive measurements at root and TLD name servers show an increase of qmin adoption from 0.6% in 2018 to 2.5% at one root server and from 35.5% in 2019 to 57.3% at the .nl TLD. We also observe that a significant amount of noise is removed when filtering out invalid labels at root.
3. Up-to-date performance and error-rate measurements of four open source resolvers (Bind, Knot, PowerDNS, and Unbound) show that while error-rates have been significantly reduced for all resolvers, the number of packets have gone both up (Bind and Unbound) and down (Knot).
4. Grounded in our findings, we discuss the trade-off between privacy and performance of minimizing queries, and propose that a promising solution may be to set the depth limitation of qmin using a public suffix list.

The rest of the paper is structured as follows. Section 2 provides background with regards to DNS and qmin as well as related work on qmin. We present active measurements surveying qmin adoption from the client-side perspective in Sect. 3. Section 4 presents passive measurements surveying qmin adoption from the name server perspective. Controlled experiments measuring the performance and error rates of resolvers with qmin implemented are shown in Sect. 5. Section 6 discusses our findings, focusing on the observed resolver behavior and the depth limit of minimizing queries. Finally, Sect. 7 concludes the paper.

2   Background and Related Work

2.1   The Domain Name System

In order for computers to communicate on the Internet, they need to indicate where a packet of data should be sent. This is solved by assigning addresses to devices within the Internet Protocol (IP) using IP addresses [18]. In order for end users to navigate on the Internet, names are mapped to IP addresses. For ARPANET, the Internet's predecessor, this mapping was originally maintained in a file on each computer. With the explosive growth of machines on the network, it quickly became unfeasible to maintain such a file. In 1985 a hierarchical system of names was introduced called the *Domain Name System* (DNS) [13,14]. DNS is responsible for mapping a domain name to a *Resource Record* (RR). The most common use of DNS is to request the associated `A` or `AAAA` RR of a domain, corresponding to the IPv4 and IPv6 addresses, respectively. Other common RRs include `MX` for identifying mail servers for a domain, `TXT` for associating arbitrary text with a domain, and `NS` for referring a resolver to the authoritative name servers for the requested zone. The distributed hierarchy is divided into "zones" to allow for local maintenance. The zones are connected in a tree hierarchy and each zone is served by multiple authoritative name servers: *root* name servers, *Top-Level Domain* (TLD) name servers, etc.

When querying for the IPv4 address of a domain name, a DNS client stub resolver sends a query to a recursive DNS resolver, requesting the `A` RR for the specified domain. Using the client-server model, the DNS resolver sends a query to one of thirteen[1] root name servers. Instead of responding with the `A` record containing the requested IP address, the root name server sends a referral with an `NS` record containing the IP address of the matching TLD name server. TLDs include generic TLDs (e.g., `.com`, `.net`, `.org`), country-code TLDs (e.g., `.se`, `.nl`, `.us`) and sponsored TLDs (e.g., `.edu`, `.gov`, `.mil`). The DNS resolver then sends the query to the specified TLD name server. Yet again, the DNS resolver will not get the `A` record requested, but instead a referral with the `NS` record to another name server. Depending on the number of delegations, this will continue until the correct RR (in this case an `A` record IP address) is obtained from the name server that is authoritative for that record. When the recursive DNS resolver has obtained the RR, it will forward the response to the client stub resolver that initiated the process. Resolvers are also able to cache responses for a time in order to improve performance and reduce the amount of DNS traffic.

2.2   Query Name Minimization

There is no added functional value when sending a query containing all labels to the root. This was the fundamental idea of RFC 7816 *query name minimization* (`qmin`) specified in March 2016 [3]. A `qmin`-enabled DNS resolver querying the domain name `www.example.domain` will only send a query for the right-most label (`.domain`) to the root name server. This minimizes the amount of information being leaked. When the resolver receives the `NS` RRs

---

of the TLD name servers for `.domain` it appends one additional label to the query (`example.domain`) and sends it to the TLD name server. The resolver will then receive the address to the authoritative name server for `example.domain` and finally append the third and last piece of the domain name (`www.example.domain`), send the last request and, hopefully, get the requested RR in return.

The default implementation of `qmin` in RFC 7816 has two main challenges. Firstly, the standardized RR type for queries when using `qmin` is the NS RR, which could cause some name servers to not respond or result in an error if no such RR is found for a minimized query. This behavior is not according to the standard, but an error on the name server side. Secondly, a domain name with many labels creates additional traffic, which could be abused for Denial-of-Service (DoS) attacks. If the DNS zone `example.domain` contains a RR for `a.b.c.d.example.domain`, a `qmin`-enabled resolver would send multiple queries to `example.domain` name servers before asking for the final RR. This has led to alternative implementations of `qmin` in the wild, which includes requesting A RRs instead of NS and iteratively adding *multiple* labels after the second-level label instead of one at a time.

In November 2021, RFC 7816 was obsoleted by RFC 9156 [4], which combined the results and recommendations from De Vries *et al.* with experiences from implementing `qmin` in the wild. Updated implementation details were presented to reduce error rates and improve performance while keeping a reasonable level of privacy. The NS RR was discarded in favor of A and AAAA RRs when sending minimized queries. Fallbacks for specific error codes were specified and two tunable parameters for incrementally adding labels were introduced. The RR types used for queries in standard DNS, RFC 7816 and RFC 9156, respectively, are shown in Table 1.

Table 1. DNS queries and responses of Standard DNS, RFC 7816 and RFC 9156.

Standard DNS	qmin RFC 7816	qmin RFC 9156
a.b.foo.bar. A → .	bar. NS → .	bar. A → .
bar. NS ← .	*bar. NS ← .*	*bar. NS ← .*
a.b.foo.bar A → bar.	foo.bar NS → bar.	foo.bar A → bar.
foo.bar NS ← bar.	*foo.bar NS ← bar.*	*foo.bar NS ← bar.*
a.b.foo.bar A → foo.bar.	b.foo.bar NS → foo.bar.	b.foo.bar A → foo.bar.
a.b.foo.bar A ← foo.bar.	*b.foo.bar NS ← foo.bar.*	*b.foo.bar NS ← foo.bar.*
	a.b.foo.bar NS → foo.bar.	a.b.foo.bar A → foo.bar.
	a.b.foo.bar NS ← foo.bar.	*a.b.foo.bar A ← foo.bar.*
	a.b.foo.bar A → foo.bar.	
	a.b.foo.bar A ← foo.bar.	

There are two modes called "relaxed" and "strict" when enabling `qmin` on a resolver [2,17]. In "relaxed mode", the resolver will fall back to querying for the full query name to potentially broken name servers. In contrast, the "strict mode" will not, and it therefore results in more non-resolved domains.

2.3 Related Work

A first measurement study of the adoption of `qmin` was done by De Vries *et al.* [23], where they measured from April 2017 to October 2018. By carrying out both active and passive measurements they could conclude that there was a slow but steady adoption of `qmin`, which resulted in noticeable improvements of query privacy at root and TLD name servers. Between two active measurements they discovered an improved method to measure `qmin` adoption. A `qmin`-enabled resolver might forward the query to a not `qmin`-enabled resolver. If a minimized query is cached at the latter, it could incorrectly be classified as a `qmin`-enabled resolver. A wildcard label was therefore introduced to make each query in the subsequent active measurements unique. Fingerprinting the resolver algorithms showed that the implementation of `qmin` in the wild differed from the details in RFC 7816 [3] in order to reduce error rates and improve performance. Further, controlled experiments with three open source resolvers measured the error rates and performance of using `qmin` in different modes. From the results in the study, new implementation recommendations were designed by combining the best practices observed in the wild.

ICANN (Internet Corporation for Assigned Names and Numbers) has been doing measurements on root traffic to analyze leaks, patterns and characteristics of resolvers [12]. They classify a query at the root as minimized if it consists of only one single label and clarify that non-valid queries (TLDs) are filtered out. A resolver is only classified as `qmin`-enabled if *all* requests originating from it are minimized.[2] The passive measurements of root traffic by ICANN is used to categorize resolvers by counting the number of labels for each query. The passive measurements of root traffic in Sect. 4.2 in this study is not for classifying resolvers, but instead for observing the total share of minimized queries over time.

A report from CZ.NIC, the domain registry for the `.cz` ccTLD, measured and analyzed `qmin` support in the `.cz` DNS ecosystem [7]. They introduce a new method of classifying `qmin`-enabled resolvers with machine learning. While the new method is promising, they noted a couple of circumstances where the prediction could be distorted. There could be multiple resolvers behind one single IP address, and sometimes there are too few queries from a single resolver to make a good enough prediction. A two label query at the TLD name server does also not necessary mean that the query is minimized. This limitation is true for this study as well. A resolver could be falsely classified as a `qmin`-enabled resolver when the fully-qualified domain name only has two labels. The passive measurements of TLD traffic by CZ.NIC is used to categorize resolvers using machine learning. The passive measurements of TLD traffic in this study is for validating queries from already classified resolvers (Sect. 4.1) and for observing the total share of minimized queries over time (Sect. 4.2).

---

[2] https://ithi.research.icann.org/about-m3.html#M3Res.

3   Active Measurements

The goal of the active measurements is to query resolvers on the Internet in order to observe the adoption of qmin based on their responses. The active measurements consist of two parts: resolver adoption over time (Sect. 3.1) and adoption by open resolvers (Sect. 3.2). The former classifies the resolvers used by RIPE Atlas probes [21] and the latter classifies resolvers from a list generated by scanning the IPv4 address space for servers listening on UDP port 53 [20]. The purpose of the first active measurement is to see the adoption trend of qmin over time and to observe characteristics of the resolvers adopting qmin. The purpose of the second active measurement is to classify open resolvers and then use these results in the passive measurements (Sect. 4.1) to enhance the classification accuracy. We also observe the adoption of qmin on open resolvers since the previous qmin adoption study by De Vries *et al.*.

3.1   Resolver Adoption over Time

Method. In this study, the Internet-wide active measurement technique introduced by De Vries *et al.* to identify support for the qmin feature in recursive DNS resolvers was employed. The method leverages the fact that resolvers without qmin will transmit the complete request to the authoritative name server, while resolvers with qmin-enabled will iteratively add labels to the request.

To detect qmin support, two authoritative name servers, both running mainstream server implementations, were specially configured to behave in the following way, as illustrated in Fig. 1. When a non-minimizing resolver is queried for the TXT record at a.b.example.domain (Fig. 1(a)), it sends a query with the full query name and type TXT to server ns1. In this case, ns1 responds with an authoritative answer containing a TXT RR with the text "NO"; ns2 is never queried. However, when a minimizing resolver is queried for the same name (Fig. 1(b)), it sends a query with query name b.example.domain and type NS or A to server ns1. In this case, ns1 responds with a referral to the server ns2. Server ns2 responds with a TXT RR containing "HOORAY". This setup makes it possible to detect the qmin functionality of a resolver from the client-side (see Fig. 2).

Since the first look at qmin by De Vries *et al.*, active measurements using RIPE Atlas probes [21] have been continued by NLnet Labs[3] and the measurement results have been presented as part of DNSThought [16].

In Sect. 3.1 we do not conduct any active measurements of our own, but analyze and discuss already available data. Specifically, we utilize qmin measurement data collected by NLnet Labs using RIPE Atlas and made available for analysis on the DNSThought website. The graphs in this study that are generated from this data are annotated thus: "(data source: DNSThought)".

---

[3] https://nlnetlabs.nl/.

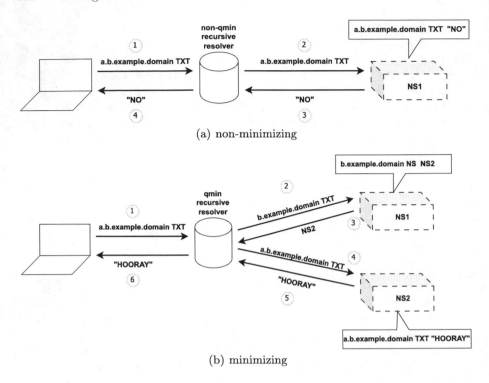

(a) non-minimizing

(b) minimizing

Fig. 1. Example diagram of detecting a (non-)minimizing resolver from the client-side using two authoritative name servers.

Results. Figure 3 shows the current trend of qmin adoption from the client-side (RIPE Atlas probes) perspective. Green represents the number of qmin-enabled resolvers and orange the number of not qmin-enabled resolvers. The gray in turn shows the resolvers which are not answering to the qmin measurements, but still responds to other queries done as part of DNSThought. The RIPE Atlas probes are churned daily in batches and a bug in the locking system of the measurement caused newly added probes to not query for qmin. This caused a steady increase of gray resolvers from early 2020 to early 2022. With the help of NLnet Labs we contacted RIPE NCC and the bug was fixed on the 6th of April 2022.

In order to see the relative adoption of qmin-enabled resolvers we created Fig. 4, based on the assumption that the out-churned probes are not correlated with the qmin adoption of their resolvers. We see that 64% of the resolvers used by RIPE Atlas probes in 2022 have enabled qmin compared to 10% around the time of the report of De Vries *et al.* at the end of 2018. When going back to Fig. 3, we still see the slight increase of qmin-enabled resolvers in April 2018 that was pointed out by De Vries *et al.* in the original study and attributed to Cloudflare enabling qmin on their DNS resolvers by default. There has been a steady increase of qmin-enabled resolvers since then, until a spike in January 2020 after which the adoption was seemingly slowing down. But looking at Fig. 4,

```
$ dig @1.1.1.1 a.b.qnamemintest.net TXT +short
"HOORAY - QNAME minimisation is enabled on your resolver :)!"

$ dig @8.8.8.8 a.b.qnamemintest.net TXT +short
"NO - QNAME minimisation is NOT enabled on your resolver :("
```

Fig. 2. Using dig to query resolvers for qmin.

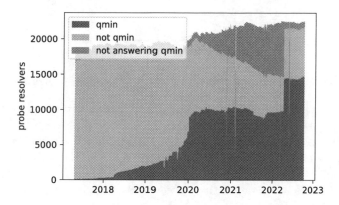

Fig. 3. Adoption of qmin over time (data source: DNSThought [16]).

we know that the relative adoption of qmin-enabled resolvers is actually still going up. While only a small fraction of resolvers were using qmin at the time of the study by De Vries *et al.*, our results suggest that a majority of resolvers are today qmin enabled.

The sudden spike of adoption in 2020 prompted a deeper dive into the characteristics of the qmin-enabled resolvers observed by DNSThought. Looking at the top ten ASNs of qmin-enabled resolvers (see Fig. 5), we observe that Google has become the biggest ASN of qmin-enabled resolvers since January 2020.

The RIPE Atlas probes used in DNSThought have been using the zone a.b.qnamemin-test.internet.nl for measuring qmin adoption. This means that the improved method of using a wildcard label in order to mitigate cached delegations (see Sect. 2.3), is *not* utilized. Some resolvers may therefore have a cached minimized query from a previously forwarded request and show up as qmin-enabled at DNSThought. By contacting NLnet Labs, a new zone was set up for measuring the adoption by open resolvers in Sect. 3.2 using this improved method.

3.2   Adoption by Open Resolvers

Method. In the initial study by De Vries *et al.*, a list of 8 million addresses from Rapid7 was used [20] to query open resolvers for qmin adoption. Rapid7 generated this list by scanning the Internet for servers responding on UDP port

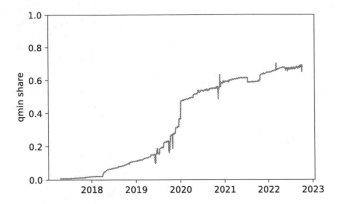

Fig. 4. Share of `qmin` over time (data source: DNSThought [16]).

53. For the active measurements, requests for a `TXT` RR were sent to a zone under NLnet Labs' control through each of the resolvers on the list to classify them as either `qmin`-enabled or not. The flowchart in Fig. 6 shows the process of the classification. First a query is sent to the resolver, which will either respond or timeout. If it does not timeout the answer is checked for errors. If the response is free from errors the next check is for a correct answer. A correct answer is a `TXT` record that contains either "HOORAY" or "NO". Finally the response is classified as either of those two. The results from the previous study are included in Sect. 3.2 to allow for comparison.

For this study we used the Rapid7 list from February 2022 since access to the list was later restricted.[4] The list contains 6 million addresses and was used in April 2022 to send queries from North Virginia, Tokyo, and Frankfurt using EC2 instances on Amazon Web Services to see if the geographical location had any effect on the results. We sent 100 queries to each resolver to collect more data points and get a more comprehensive view of each resolver. However, the system described previously has the following limitation. The delegation (i.e., the NS records from the referral response) from a test might be cached by a resolver that performs `qmin`, such that the outcome of a subsequent test to the same resolver favors `qmin`. To overcome this limitation, we developed a custom authoritative server that behaves similarly to the other system, but additionally allows custom query names, the referrals for which are synthesized, based on the query. This allows us to send unique query names in close proximity by using a wildcard label, avoiding the effects of cached delegations. For example, a query for `a.tokyo-00.qnamemintest.net` (corresponding to the first iteration of queries from Tokyo) results in a query of `tokyo-00.qnamemintest.net` to ns1 by a qmin resolver. In response, ns1 is able to refer the resolver to ns2 for `tokyo-00.qnamemintest.net`. When the next iteration of queries from Tokyo is sent, `tokyo-01.qnamemintest.net` will not be found in the cache.

---

[4] https://web.archive.org/web/20220414114758/https://www.rapid7.com/blog/post/2022/02/10/evolving-how-we-share-rapid7-research-data-2/.

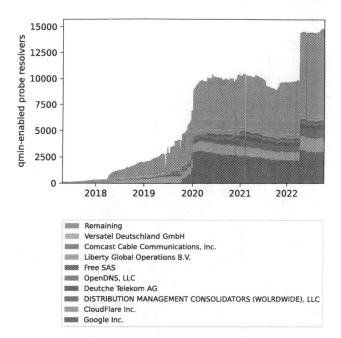

Fig. 5. Top ten `qmin`-enabled resolver ASNs (data source: DNSThought [16]).

Table 2. Categorized responses from open resolvers.

Year	Geo	#resolv	#queries	Resp	Noerr	Correct	qmin
2018	Netherlands	8M	8M	64%	32%	72%	1.6%
2022	Nvirginia	6M	600M	70.82%	19.46%	78.12%	16.43%
2022	Tokyo	6M	600M	70.71%	19.45%	78.32%	16.42%
2022	Frankfurt	6M	600M	70.78%	19.45%	78.21%	16.42%

Results: Over Time and Location. Table 2 shows the results for our measurements (2022) from North Virginia, Tokyo, and Frankfurt as well as the earlier results from 2018 by De Vries *et al.*. Our results are calculated from all 100 queries to each of the 6 million resolvers. The values therefore represent the fraction of queries and *not* the fraction of resolvers. The columns `year` and `geo` indicate which study and which geographical location the queries were sent from. The `#resolv` column shows the size of the list from Rapid7 and the `#queries` shows the total number of queries sent. The `resp` column shows the percentage of queries that did not timeout. The column named `noerr` shows the percentage of queries *from responding resolvers* that did not contain any errors (e.g., `SERVFAIL`, `NXDOMAIN` and `REFUSED`). The `correct` column shows the percentage *of noerror responses* that contained a correct `TXT` RR reply, which means that the response was either "HOORAY" or "NO". The last column, `qmin`, shows the percentage of "HOORAYs" out of the total number of correct responses.

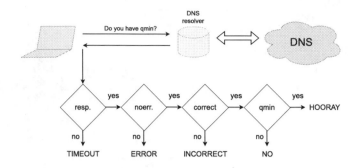

Fig. 6. Flow-chart of categorizing `qmin` query responses from resolvers.

The share of minimized queries in 2018 was 1.6% and in 2022 this number increased to about 16%, measured from three different geographical locations. Comparing the geographical locations we observe minimal deviations in the results. The Rapid7 scan on UDP port 53 in February 2022 resulted in 6 million addresses, which is a decrease of 25% from 2018, and the active measurements of this study using that list shows that the share of non-timeouts has increased to almost 71% from 64%. Another interesting observation is that the share of `NOERROR` replies had gone down from 32% to around 19% and more than 90% of the errors are `REFUSED`. The reason could be that some resolvers are configured to only handle queries from clients within a specified subnet. The share of correct `TXT` responses have increased from 72% to 78% and finally the share of queries classified as minimized have increased from 1.6% to 16%. So while we only got correct responses from a small fraction of the open resolvers, we see a ten-fold increase in the use of `qmin` also in this data set.

Results: Conflicting Resolvers. The original study by De Vries *et al.* sent a single query to each resolver and classified each resolver based on the response. In this study we queried each address on the Rapid7 list 100 times, which revealed additional information when classifying the resolvers. First, the resolvers that did not respond with a single correct `TXT` RR were filtered out (5.27M). All responses from these resolvers were a mix of timeouts, errors and incorrect `TXT` RRs. Incorrect `TXT` responses contained: nothing, validation tokens, notifications about the domain being expired or disabled, and replies such as: "txt", "this is a txt record", "hello, dns!", "OK" and "pong". The remaining more interesting resolvers contained at least one correct answer, which could either be a HOORAY or a NO reply. Our analysis of these 730k resolvers found that 87.3% responded correctly to between 80–100 queries, while the remaining 100k resolvers responded correctly to 1–79 queries. Further research is needed to determine the reasons for this discrepancy and its potential impacts on the overall quality of replies from open resolvers.

One interesting observation is that a subset of the resolvers did not consistently respond with only HOORAY or only NO, but responded with at least one of each

Table 3. Comparing share of classified resolvers

Year	#resolv	qmin (%)	Not-qmin (%)	Conflicting (%)
2018	8M	18.8k (0.2%)	1.1M (13.7%)	N/A
2022	6M	80.2k (1.3%)	539.3k (8.9%)	120.8k (2%)

during the 100 queries. So in addition to the list of *qmin-enabled resolvers* and the list of *not qmin-enabled resolvers*, we consider a list of resolvers which sometimes answered HOORAY and at other times NO. This list is called *conflicting resolvers*. A resolver is classified as qmin-enabled if at least one query resulted in a HOORAY and none of the queries resulted in a NO. A resolver is classified as not qmin-enabled if at least one query resulted in a NO and none of the queries resulted in a HOORAY. Finally, a resolver is classified as conflicting if at least one query resulted in a HOORAY and at least one query resulted in a NO.

In the original study by De Vries *et al.* 0.2% of 8 million resolvers were classified as qmin-enabled (see Table 3). In this study we classified 1.3% of 6 million resolvers as qmin-enabled. In the original study 13.7% of resolvers were classified as not qmin-enabled, whereas 8.9% of resolvers were classified as not qmin-enabled in this study. Additionally 2% were classified as the new category of conflicting in this study.

Table 4. Share of conflicting resolvers, top 10 countries.

Country	CN	RU	US	BR	ID	AU	UA	IR	PL	ZA
Share	26.8%	11.4%	5.5%	4.5%	3.6%	3.4%	3.0%	2.4%	2.3%	2.1%

The minimum number of correct replies in a conflicting resolver is two: one HOORAY and one NO. This results in a 50% share of qmin. However, when 100 queries are sent, the ratio of HOORAY and NO responses can range from 1:99 to 99:1. Our analysis showed that out of approximately 109k conflicting resolvers, 80k (73.4%) had a qmin share of less than 50%. Approximately 8k resolvers (7.4% of the total) had a qmin share of more than 90%. Additionally we looked into the geographical location of ASes containing the conflicting resolvers. Table 4 shows the top 10 countries according to their share of 120.8k conflicting resolvers based on ASN whois lookups. China, Russia and the United States dominate this list.

We also wanted to see if the conflicting resolvers were more or less short-lived compared to the resolvers categorized as qmin-enabled and not qmin-enabled. Five months after the initial measurements (September 2022) we observed that 33.1% of the qmin-enabled resolvers no longer responded. We also got timeouts from 38.2% of the not qmin-enabled resolvers and 35.5% of the conflicting resolvers. Thus slightly more than a third of the resolvers were no longer reachable, but we could not observe any major difference in lost resolvers across our categories.

Results: Unexpected Google. Given the rapid adoption of qmin-enabled resolvers from the Google ASN since 2020 seen in Fig. 5, it was unexpected to see that the Google Public DNS resolvers were classified as *not* qmin-enabled in the active measurements of open resolvers above. We performed additional queries to verify this behavior of the 8.8.8.8 and 8.8.4.4 Google Public DNS resolvers using three different zones: a.b.qnamemin-test.nlnetlabs.nl, a.b.qnamemin-test.internet.nl, and a.b.qnamemintest.net.

The first zone is a set of subdomains under the second-level domain of NLnet Labs that was used for measuring qmin adoption in the study by De Vries *et al.*. The second zone is the official name for measuring qmin after the publication of the original study.[5] This is also the zone used by DNSThought at NLnet Labs. The third zone was set up in early 2022 for this study, using the label wildcard cache mitigation technique, which neither of the other two zones implemented. All of these zones are using the same method when measuring qmin from the client-side. When using Google Public DNS resolvers, only a.b.qnamemin-test.internet.nl responded with HOORAY (see Fig. 7), which is the name used for the RIPE Atlas qmin adoption measurements in DNSThought.

```
$ dig @8.8.8.8 a.b.qnamemin-test.nlnetlabs.nl TXT +short
"NO - QNAME minimisation is NOT enabled on your resolver :("

$ dig @8.8.8.8 a.b.qnamemin-test.internet.nl TXT +short
"HOORAY - QNAME minimisation is enabled on your resolver :)!"

$ dig @8.8.8.8 a.b.qnamemintest.net TXT +short
"NO - QNAME minimisation is NOT enabled on your resolver :("
```

Fig. 7. Using dig to query a Google Public DNS resolver (8.8.8.8) for qmin.

By contacting NLnet Labs we were told that Google had reached out in May 2020 in regards to qmin. They wrote that they had implemented qmin but with a depth limitation that stops after two labels. This would result in a partial qmin that sends minimized labels to the roots and TLDs but not to Second-Level Domains (2LDs) such as co.uk. They also said that they would like to extend it to public suffix plus one label in the future. As a result, the Google Public DNS does not show up as minimizing queries on DNSThought at all, which is why they added an exception to the depth limitation for a.b.qnamemin-test.internet.nl to reflect that the resolvers do minimize queries (up to a point). They did not want to "cheat" the system, but still get credit for the privacy benefit of minimizing queries at the root and TLD level. This brings to question what an adequate level of minimizing queries is in regards to performance and privacy, which is further discussed in Sect. 6.

---

[5] https://web.archive.org/web/20220428083123/https://labs.ripe.net/author/wouter_de_vries/making-the-dns-more-private-with-qname-minimisation/.

4   Passive Measurements

In this section we show how qmin has evolved in the years between the study by De Vries *et al.* and October 2022 on a larger scale. As the previous study, we rely on data collected at the root servers as well as the .nl ccTLD. Furthermore, we improve the measurement technique, dive deeper into qmin adoption, showing who drives qmin and who lags behind, and find that qmin-enabled resolvers can leak information occasionally.

4.1   Method

In order to identify minimized queries and qmin-enabled resolvers in our passive data sets, we rely on a similar methodology as De Vries *et al.* but extend and improve it further.

Identifying Minimized Queries. We count queries as minimized if they contain one label at the root and two at .nl. De Vries *et al.* already mentioned the fact that the data from the root might be influenced by queries to non-existing, single-label, domain names caused by Google's Chrome browser. Including these queries in our analysis would lead to overestimating the number of minimized labels at the root.[6] For this reason we filter out these queries by considering only queries with one and, respectively, two labels for existing domain names.

The DITL (a Day In The Life of the Internet) data collected by DNS-OARC[7] (Operations Analysis and Research Center) does not contain DNS responses. For this reason, we verify for each query that contains only one label whether the queried label belongs to a registered top level domain. The data sets of .nl contain both DNS queries and responses. This allows us to filter for queries that result in a DNS response with response code NOERROR.

Identifying qmin-Enabled Resolvers. In order to single out resolvers that have enabled qmin, we again extend the methodology proposed by earlier work. Here, we use traffic from resolvers that we identified as qmin-supporting in the previous section as ground truth. The fact that we now also differentiate between conflicting resolvers allows us to identify qmin-enabled resolvers in passive data with a smaller error margin. To address possible biases from our Dutch vantage point, we now also take data from the Swedish ccTLD .se into account.

Figure 8 and Fig. 9 show the share of minimized queries of resolvers in the different categories to the name servers of the two ccTLDs. Only resolvers with a minimum of ten observed queries at each ccTLD that date were included.

The share of minimized queries for qmin-enabled resolvers is over 90% (median) and is in stark contrast with resolvers that have not enabled qmin. Those resolvers send less than 20% of their queries minimized. As expected, the conflicting resolvers show more diverse behaviour. For the remainder of

---

[6] For more details we refer to the bug report [8] and to Verisign [22].

[7] https://www.dns-oarc.net/.

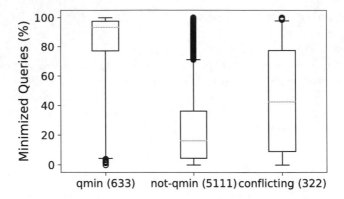

Fig. 8. Minimized queries to the `.nl` ccTLD. Whiskers at 5th and 95th percentiles.

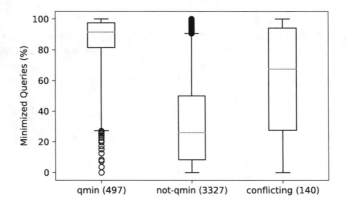

Fig. 9. Minimized queries to the `.se` ccTLD. Whiskers at 5th and 95th percentiles.

this section, we classify resolvers as `qmin`-enabled if they send at least 77.2% of their queries minimized to name servers of 2nd level domain names (25% quartile in Fig. 8). The chosen threshold reduces the number of wrongly classified resolvers, since it is above the 95th percentile of minimized queries of non-`qmin` enabling resolvers and above the 75th percentile of minimized queries of conflicting resolvers in the `.nl` data set.

4.2   Results

Since 2019, `qmin` adoption has improved significantly, at least from the perspective of TLDs. Figure 10 shows the share of queries sent to the K-Root servers and to three of the four `.nl` authoritative name servers. The blue color indicates the share of queries regardless of whether the domain name exists or not. The yellow color marks measurements that include only minimized queries to existing domain names.

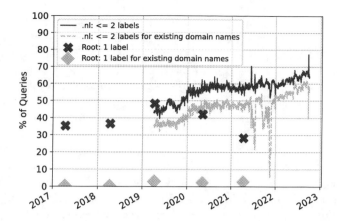

Fig. 10. Minimized queries to the `.nl` ccTLD and K-Root over time.

The increase in minimized queries at `.nl` is clearly visible and has now reached 64% (compared to 43% in 2019). Adoption raises regardless of whether or not we filter out queries for non-existing domain names. Occasional drops in minimized queries are caused by random events, for example crawlers or misconfigurations. The picture at the root is, however, less clear.

Results: Impact of Non-existing Domain Names. If we look at queries for all domain names at the root, then adoption of `qmin` has even decreased in the last years. In 2017, 35.2% of queries would have been minimized compared to 28.3% in 2021. This shows that filtering out queries to non-existing domain names is important when measuring `qmin` at the root. When doing so the share of minimized queries at the root decreases drastically. In 2021, the share drops from 28.3% to 2.7%.

In 2021, we can see clearly what causes the high number of potentially minimized queries. Then, the number of queries with one label decreased from 42% to 28%. This drop correlates with the rollout of a new Chromium version for Android in November 2020. From then on, the feature responsible for sending out the random subdomain queries has been disabled. Root server operators noticed this rollout [22]. This shows that the numbers reported by De Vries *et al.* were indeed heavily influenced by Chrome's behaviour.

Omitting queries to non-existing domain names paints a clearer picture of the deployment of `qmin`. When doing so the share of minimized queries at the root increases from 0.4% in 2017 to 2.7% in 2021.

Results: Qmin Adoption in Detail. Not everyone benefits equally from the rising `qmin` adoption. Already 2021 the root traffic exhibits strong local variations. The K-Root site in Bhutan receives 17.8% of its queries minimized, while at the site in Tajikistan only 0.1% of the queries fall into this category.

We dive deeper into this phenomenon relying on data collected at the .nl name servers on October 4 2022.[8] We map each IP address to its corresponding country and autonomous system (AS) using the Maxmind database. On this date, we observe 2.9B queries from 1.4M unique IP addresses from 236 countries and 38,469 ASes. We count an IP address as a qmin-enabled resolver if the share of existing queries is above the threshold defined above. This reflects the top 75% resolvers that have enabled qmin in our ground truth data set (see Fig. 8).

By Country. Only countries from which queries have been received from at least 100 unique IP addresses are taken into account. This leaves us with IPs from 159 countries. Interestingly, the country with the highest share of minimized queries is Yemen (see Table 5). This high share of minimized queries is mainly driven by large providers. Here, 10% of resolvers have qmin enabled, but those are responsible for a large share of queries from this country. We explore the influence of single networks in the next section. Overall, however, these countries only account for a small fraction of total traffic at .nl.

Table 5. Countries with most minimized .nl queries.

Country	.nl query share	Minimized queries	Qmin enabled resolvers
Yemen	0.01%	89.2%	10.0%
Afghanistan	0.01%	85.7%	19.5%
Iraq	0.01%	84.5%	45.3%
Benin	0.01%	82.2%	22.0%
Finland	1.0%	81.9%	33.6%

The adoption rate is lower when we look at the countries from which .nl receives the most queries. Table 6 summarizes the results. For these countries, the share of minimized queries vary between 1% for China and 59.5% for Great Britain. Also the share of qmin-enabled resolvers is the highest in Great Britain, followed by the Netherlands.

Table 6. Deployment of qmin from the top 5 origins of .nl queries.

Country	.nl query share	Minimized queries	Qmin enabled resolvers
US	35.3%	32.3%	19.2%
Netherlands	20.6%	41.6%	28.9%
Germany	9.2%	14.4%	25.8%
China	4.6%	1.0%	4.4%
Great Britain	3.2%	59.5%	30.9%

By Network. Within one country there are significant differences. As an example, we have a closer look at networks with IP addresses located in the Netherlands,

---

[8] We also carried out our analysis two months earlier, with similar results.

and focus especially on networks of Internet Service Providers (ISPs). We rely on a community maintained list of ISPs[9] to identify relevant networks. ISPs serve especially many human users, who would potentially benefit the most from qmin.

In our dataset, 23 networks belong to an ISP and send queries from at least 10 distinct addresses. Of those, less than half (10 networks, 43.5%) send their queries through qmin enabled resolvers most of the time. Networks that use qmin include Freedom Internet (AS 206238), an ISP that positions itself as an especially secure and "free" ISP. Also T-mobile Netherlands (AS 13127), one of the largest ISPs in the Netherlands, appears to have qmin enabled. The former incumbent KPN (ASes 1136, 8737, and 15879) does not appear to have enabled qmin on their resolvers (minimizing resolvers send only 0.3% of the queries).

Qmin in the Context of Other Internet Standards. Qmin has became best common practice. Overall, resolvers that have enabled qmin show more support for "modern" Internet standards and DNS best practices. We compare resolvers that send queries to the .nl name servers via IPv6, that indicate support for DNSSEC[10], and that indicate a EDNS(0) buffer size of 1,232 bytes[11] with resolvers that do not follow these best practices.

Table 7 shows that resolvers that have enabled IPv6, show support for DNSSEC, and set the recommended buffer sizes also support qmin in most cases. These resolvers reflect 3.7% of all resolvers observed in our dataset. In contrast, only a minority of resolvers that do not follow any of these best practices have enabled qmin (4.8% of all resolvers in our dataset). The largest group of resolvers do indicate support for DNSSEC, but rely on legacy IPv4, and signal a different buffer size. Of those, 16.4% send minimized queries (63% of all resolvers in our dataset).

Table 7. Qmin support per resolver by support of modern standards and best common practices.

Standard supported	IPv6	DNSSEC	Recommended buffer size	All
✓	35.5%	26.4%	48.4%	54.4%
✗	18.7%	8.1%	18.6%	6.4%

Results: Qmin Imperfections. Already De Vries *et al.* have shown that qmin-enabled resolvers send queries with three or more labels to the authoritative servers of the .nl TLD occasionally. The observations at .nl and .se, as shown in Fig. 8 and Fig. 9, confirm this finding. When neglecting queries to domain names and records for which .nl are authoritative (e.g., the domain names of the .nl name servers [ns1-ns4].dns.nl), we find that 77% of qmin-enabled resolvers send queries with more than two labels occasionally. In 55.1% of these

---

[9] https://bgp.tools/tags/dsl.csv.

[10] By setting the DO-flag in the query.

[11] As recommended by the 2020 DNS Flag day: https://www.dnsflagday.net/2020/.

cases the queries result in NXDOMAIN responses, signalling that the queried domain name does not exist. We could not find when exactly resolvers would fall back to sending the full query name, but this shows that even with qmin enabled, information about lower labels can leak. We could also observe this behaviour at resolvers of Google Public DNS and we reached out to their operators for clarification. Unfortunately, they could not explain to us what causes these occasional queries for fully-qualified domain names.

5   Controlled Experiments

The purpose of the controlled experiments is to look at the most recent versions of popular open source resolvers and look at how they handle minimized queries in regards to performance. In the controlled experiments by De Vries *et al.*, four open source resolvers were considered due to their popularity: Bind, Unbound, Knot Resolver, and PowerDNS. Only the first three resolvers had implemented qmin in their most recent version at the time, which meant that PowerDNS was excluded. PowerDNS has since then implemented and enabled relaxed qmin by default in version 4.3.0 and is therefore included in this study.[12] The versions of each resolver for the controlled experiments in this study were: Unbound 1.14.0, Bind 9.16.24, Knot Resolver 5.4.4 and PowerDNS 4.6.0. DNSSEC was turned off and the resolvers were configured to have the same size of caches.

5.1   Method

Just as in the original study, we use the Cisco Umbrella Top 1M list [5] for domains to query in the performance and error-rate measurements. The list contains the most popular queries based on passive DNS usage on their Umbrella global network. This list does not only contain browser-based HTTP user requests, but takes other protocols and non-end-users into account. Like in the study by De Vries *et al.*, domain names were aggregated from a timespan of two weeks (April 4th until April 19th, 2022) to avoid daily and weekly fluctuations and patterns. This resulted in 1.3M domain names with a mean of 3.26 labels, a median of 3 labels, a min of 1 and a max of 104 labels. This list of domains was sorted in four different orders to even out caching effects.

As mentioned in Sect. 2, there are two modes when enabling qmin on resolvers (i.e., relaxed and strict). These modes dictate whether the resolver should fall back to full query names when receiving NXDOMAIN or other unexpected responses from potentially broken name servers. For the controlled experiments in this study, both Unbound and Bind had the option to turn qmin off, run it in relaxed mode, or run it in strict mode. PowerDNS could either turn qmin off or turn it on in relaxed mode. Knot did not have any option to turn off qmin and only runs in relaxed mode. We used all the possible configurations in the experiments and compared the results to the results from the controlled experiments by De Vries *et al.*.

---

[12] https://doc.powerdns.com/recursor/settings.html#qname-minimization.

5.2   Results

As seen in Table 8, Unbound 1.14.0 is sending more packets compared to Unbound 1.8.0 when using `qmin` regardless of mode. The error-rate has decreased for all queries regardless of settings, and strict mode still have a higher error-rate than relaxed due to the extra `NXDOMAIN` responses from potentially broken name servers. Bind 9.16.24 is also sending out more packets compared to Bind 9.13.3 regardless of configuration.

Table 8. Resolver performance and result quality

Mode	#packets	Error
Unbound 1.8.0 (2018)		
Off	5.70M	12.6%
Strict	6.71M	15.9%
Relax	6.82M	12.6%
Knot 3.0.0 (2018)		
Relax	5.94M	13.5%
Bind 9.13.3 (2018)		
Off	5.07M	16.6%
Strict	5.84M	21.6%
Relax	6.39M	17.1%
Unbound 1.14.0 (2022)		
Off	5.93M	6.8%
Strict	8.50M	8.4%
Relax	8.68M	6.8%
Knot 5.4.4 (2022)		
Relax	3.14M	7.0%
Bind 9.16.24 (2022)		
Off	7.09M	11.2%
Strict	7.73M	11.2%
Relax	7.69M	11.2%
PowerDNS 4.6.0 (2022)		
Off	3.35M	7.0%
Relax	3.56M	7.0%

When looking closer at the traffic for Unbound and Bind we discovered that Unbound always resolves all name servers received and Bind is establishing TCP connections to the root servers. The error-rates for Bind have also decreased and there is no difference between strict and relaxed mode, which is unexpected. We have not been able to identify why relaxed mode showed no advantage. Knot is running relaxed `qmin` without any option to turn it off. The number of packets and the error-rate have decreased significantly in version 5.4.4 compared to version 3.0.0. The large decrease in number of packets is the opposite trend of Unbound and Bind. For PowerDNS the number of packets were similar when comparing relaxed `qmin` and no `qmin`, which was unexpected since `qmin` should produce more packets. Since PowerDNS enables `qmin` with the relaxed mode, the similar error-rates seen with and without `qmin` enabled was expected. This is true for Unbound and Bind as well. As the error-rates of all resolvers have decreased since 2018, regardless of qmin and mode, this could be a change on the name server side and not necessarily on the resolvers themselves.

The controlled experiments showed that the error-rate decreased for all resolvers compared to the original study, but the number of packets and the error-rate varied depending on the specific resolver and mode used. The qmin feature is tightly correlated with the number of packets, as a fully complete domain name typically requires fewer queries to resolve than a minimally built query that is iteratively resolved. Our results suggest that the performance of recursive DNS resolvers with qmin enabled has improved since the previous study, but further investigation is needed to fully understand the effects on each resolver. The number of packets can be an important factor in evaluating the performance of a resolver, as it can indicate the resources and communication required to process queries and retrieve responses. While a lower number of packets may indicate efficiency, other metrics such as latency and response accuracy should also be considered when assessing the performance of a resolver.

6   Discussion

In this section we summarize the results from our measurements and analyze the general adoption of qmin. Then we look at the improvements of the measurement methods as well as discuss the balance between performance and privacy.

6.1   Analysis of the Results

Looking at the summary of the measurement results compared to the results by De Vries *et al.* in Table 9 we can see that the active measurements (RIPE/open) show an increase in the adoption of qmin. The relatively high qmin share of RIPE suggest that the RIPE Atlas probes may be biased. People running RIPE Atlas probes in their network are likely technically adept and administrating resolvers with up-to-date security and privacy features. They may therefore not be representative of the average resolver on the Internet, but we see that the adoption of qmin has grown. The active measurements on the open resolvers paints perhaps a more accurate picture of qmin, but keep in mind that over 80% of the responding resolvers replied with an error, out of which over 90% are REFUSED. As mentioned earlier, this could be resolvers configured to only send queries on behalf of certain clients.

Table 9. Results of RIPE Atlas probe resolvers, open resolvers, K-Root and .nl ccTLD

Year	RIPE	Open	K-Root	.nl ccTLD
2018	10%	1.6%	0.6%	35.5%
2022	64%	16.42%	2.5%	57.3%

(.nl ccTLD numbers available are from 2019 and onwards.)

For the passive measurements at the root and the TLD we filtered out the invalid labels that affected the results of De Vries *et al.*. Here we also see a positive trend of minimized queries which matches the relative growth in the RIPE Atlas active measurements, a sixfold increase. The .nl TLD passive measurements also show an increase of `qmin`, but already in 2019 the share of incoming minimized queries was high. The resolvers querying domains at .nl are likely less representative of all DNS resolvers on the Internet, and instead point to the early adoption of privacy features in dutch DNS infrastructure. The results from the active and passive measurements show a clear and consistent increase in the adoption of `qmin`-enabled resolvers when comparing to the previous study. While the actual level of `qmin` adoption varies between the measurements, as they capture the behavior of different sets of resolvers from different vantage points, this is a positive development for Internet privacy.

6.2   Improvements of Measurements Methods

Our work builds heavily on the methods used by De Vries *et al.*, but also brings new insights based on enhancements to the methods. In the active measurements on open resolvers we observed that there were no significant differences between the three geographical locations, something that could not be inferred based on the measurements from a single location in the original study. The original study also classified open resolvers based on a single response. In this study we queried each open resolver 100 times, which revealed additional information when classifying the resolvers. In relation to improved measurement methods, we also set up a new domain using a wildcard label to mitigate cached delegations which was used when querying open resolvers in the second active measurements. DNSThought is currently not using a domain with a wildcard label, which means that some of the responses in the first active measurements could be cached false positives.

Some of the open resolvers were classified as conflicting resolvers in this study. With the use of a wildcard label we are able to mitigate any cached delegation happening, i.e., querying a non-minimizing resolver that has cached a recent minimized query from a `qmin`-enabled forwarding resolver. The most likely culprits are DNS load-balancers distributing query load across a pool of resolvers. According to Randall *et al.* [19], some DNS load-balancers could be using different software packages for their backend resolvers, which could be a cause of the conflicts that we observe. We also observed that 73% of the conflicting resolvers are responding with more NO than HOORAY, which is similar to the ratio of resolvers classified as `qmin`-enabled and not `qmin`-enabled.

6.3   Qmin Depth Limitation

The client-side active measurements at DNSThought are measuring `qmin` at the fourth-level domain. This means that the number of resolvers minimizing queries at lower levels (e.g., TLD and root) could be even higher. The Google Public DNS resolvers were classified as not `qmin`-enabled in the active measurements on open resolvers using a separate domain in Sect. 3.2. This was unexpected since the resolvers have been minimizing queries since 2020 according to DNSThought. Additional queries using different domains showed that the Google Public DNS resolvers were consistently responding differently based on domain. This was because Google wanted to get credit for minimizing queries at the root and TLD level, which originally did not show on DNSThought statistics.

Even though a resolver is not implementing `qmin` beyond the 2LD, a lack of data minimization within an authoritative DNS zone is less serious compared to fully disclosed query names at the root and TLD level. An organization registering a 2LD is most likely aware of their subdomains, so no harm would come from exposing those labels to their own name servers. Some organizations register domains under e.g., `.ac.uk` or `.co.jp` and it is therefore not as simple as to only minimize until the 2LD. We propose setting the depth limit using the Public Suffix List (PSL) [15] with one additional label (PSL+1). The PSL is a list maintained by Mozilla mainly used for restricting cookie setting. It contains effective TLDs (e.g., `.com` and `.net`) including those with more than one label (e.g., `.ac.uk` and `co.jp`.) A `qmin`-enabled resolver using the PSL+1 approach and looking up a RR for `a.b.example.ac.uk` should send `uk` to the root, `ac.uk` to the `.uk` ccTLD and then `example.ac.uk` to the name server of `.ac.uk`. The resolver would then stop minimizing and send `a.b.example.ac.uk` to the name server of `example.ac.uk` which is most likely the authoritative DNS zone. Since `ac.uk` is in the PSL, we refer to `example.ac.uk` as PSL+1.

7   Conclusion

We measured the adoption of query name minimization using active measurements from the client-side and passive measurements from the name server side. In addition we also performed controlled experiments on four open source resolvers to measure performance and error rate. We built the study on the methods of De Vries *et al.*, extended them, and included additional sets of data for the passive measurements. The extension of the methods includes measuring from multiple geographical locations and sending multiple queries to the resolvers instead of one. The latter revealed that some of the resolvers are sending both positive and negative responses, which was not observable with the previous method. The value of doing this replicated study comes from observing changes over time in the DNS ecosystem, improving the measurement methods and getting a picture of the `qmin` adoption shortly after the publication of RFC 9156, which builds on the result from the previous `qmin` adoption study.

The results of the active measurements of `qmin` adoption over time shows a positive trend with a rapid increase in 2020 when the resolvers in Google's ASN started minimizing queries. Plotting the share of `qmin`-enabled resolvers over time shows that 64% of the resolvers used by RIPE Atlas probes are minimizing queries. This is a significant adoption compared to 10% at the time of the previous study by De Vries *et al.*. The data used for the first active measurements with RIPE Atlas probes are displayed as part of DNSThought and our work has helped improve the probing for qmin adoption. With some communication with NLnet Labs and RIPE Atlas, a bug was fixed where new probes used by DNSThought were not querying for qmin. When looking closer at the Google Public DNS we observed that client-side active measurements using these resolvers seem to be highly dependent on specific domain names. With the help of NLnet Labs we found out that Google's resolvers have a qmin depth limitation, except for the domain used by DNSThought. This exception was done in order to get credit for minimizing at the root and TLD levels. In the controlled experiments using four open source resolvers we observed that the error-rates are decreasing. This is likely due to RFC 9156 which switched RR query types, specified fallbacks on certain errors, and added labels more dynamically and thus obsoleted the previous implementation of qmin in RFC 7816. But it could also be a change on the name server side. The number of packets are going up for two of the resolvers while it is decreasing or rather low for the other two, and it is still unclear why. We discussed the adequate level of minimizing query names in regards to both performance and privacy, where we argue that the privacy risks of leaking sensitive subdomains decrease after the authoritative DNS zone. We therefore look at the Public Suffix List as a possible resource for configuring the minimization depth limit.

Research Artifacts

To enable a third look at qmin in the future we provide whatever scripts used (https://github.com/Arcnilya/qmin2022) beyond what was already available by De Vries *et al.* [24]. The RIPE Atlas measurements by NLnet Labs are also accessible at RIPE [21].

Ethical Considerations

In this work we thought carefully about the ethical aspects of our measurements and disclosure. We used a list of open resolvers from third-party scans instead of doing the scan of the IPv4 address space on our own, thus avoiding adding more unnecessary load on the networks. We also spread out our active measurements in a round-robin style to not put too much load on single resolvers in a short span of time.

Acknowledgement. This work was founded by the Swedish Internet Foundation. The Day-in-the-live of the Internet dataset was kindly provided by DNS-OARC and the root server operators. We would like to thank Ulrich Wisser and Johan Stenstam for expertise within DNS, Roger Murray for help with querying .se ccTLD data, and Willem Toorop for understanding DNSThought and setting up the active measurements. We would also like to thank the reviewers and our shepherd Casey Deccio for valuable feedback.

References

1. Arends, R., Austein, R., Larson, M., Massey, D., Rose, S.: DNS security introduction and requirements. RFC 4033, RFC Editor, March 2005. http://www.rfc-editor.org/rfc/rfc4033.txt
2. Bind: Bind documentation: options. https://bind9.readthedocs.io/en/v9_18_3/reference.html#options-statement-definition-and-usage. Accessed June 2022
3. Bortzmeyer, S.: DNS query name minimisation to improve privacy. RFC 7816, RFC Editorm March 2016
4. Bortzmeyer, S., Dolmans, R., Hoffman, P.: DNS query name minimisation to improve privacy. RFC 9156, RFC Editor, November 2021
5. Cisco: Cisco umbrella top 1m list. http://s3-us-west-1.amazonaws.com/umbrella-static/index.html. Accessed 12–25 Feb 2022
6. Cooper, A., et al.: Privacy considerations for internet protocols. RFC 6973, RFC Editor, July 2013
7. CZ.NIC: Measuring qname minimisation support. https://adam.pages.nic.cz/reports/adam/qname-minimisation-en/. Accessed Nov 2021
8. Google: Issue 1090985: Disable Intranet Redirect Detector by default. https://bugs.chromium.org/p/chromium/issues/detail?id=1090985. Accessed June 2020
9. Hoffman, P., McManus, P.: DNS queries over HTTPS (DoH). RFC 8484, RFC Editor, October 2018
10. Hu, Z., Zhu, L., Heidemann, J., Mankin, A., Wessels, D., Hoffman, P.: Specification for DNS over transport layer security (tls). RFC 7858, RFC Editor, May 2016
11. Huitema, C., Dickinson, S., Mankin, A.: DNS over Dedicated QUIC Connections. RFC 9250m May 2022. https://doi.org/10.17487/RFC9250, https://www.rfc-editor.org/info/rfc9250
12. ICANN: M3: DNS root traffic analysis. https://ithi.research.icann.org/graph-m3.html. Accessed Mar 2022
13. Mockapetris, P.: Domain names - concepts and facilities. STD 13, RFC Editor, November 1987. http://www.rfc-editor.org/rfc/rfc1034.txt
14. Mockapetris, P.: Domain names - implementation and specification. STD 13, RFC Editor, November 1987. http://www.rfc-editor.org/rfc/rfc1035.txt
15. Mozilla Foundation: Public suffix list. https://publicsuffix.org/. Accessed 5 June 2008
16. NLnet Labs: DNSThought. https://dnsthought.nlnetlabs.nl/#qnamemin. Accessed 14 Oct 2018
17. NLnet Labs: Unbound documentation: qmin strict. https://unbound.docs.nlnetlabs.nl/en/latest/manpages/unbound.conf.html?highlight=relaxed%20qname#term-qname-minimisation-strict-yes-or-no. Accessed May 2021
18. Postel, J.: Internet protocol. STD 5, RFC Editor, September 1981. http://www.rfc-editor.org/rfc/rfc791.txt
19. Randall, A., et al.: Trufflehunter: cache snooping rare domains at large public DNS resolvers. In: Proceedings of the ACM Internet Measurement Conference, pp. 50–64 (2020)
20. Rapid7 Labs: UDP scans. https://opendata.rapid7.com/sonar.udp/. Accessed Jan 2022
21. RIPE Atlas: RIPE Atlas measurement. https://atlas.ripe.net/measurements/8310250/. Accessed 20 Apr 2017
22. Verisign: Chromium's Reduction of Root DNS Traffic. https://blog.verisign.com/domain-names/chromiums-reduction-of-root-dns-traffic/. Accessed Jan 2021

23. de Vries, W.B., Scheitle, Q., Müller, M., Toorop, W., Dolmans, R., van Rijswijk-Deij, R.: A first look at QNAME minimization in the domain name system. In: Choffnes, D., Barcellos, M. (eds.) PAM 2019. LNCS, vol. 11419, pp. 147–160. Springer, Cham (2019). https://doi.org/10.1007/978-3-030-15986-3_10
24. de Vries, W.B., Scheitle, Q., Müller, M., Toorop, W., Dolmans, R., van Rijswijk-Deij, R.: A first look at qname minimization in the DNS, datasets. https://www.simpleweb.org/wiki/index.php/Traces#A_First_Look_at_QNAME_Minimization_in_the_Domain_Name_System. Accessed Oct 2022

DNS

How Ready is DNS for an IPv6-Only World?

Florian Streibelt[1], Patrick Sattler[2], Franziska Lichtblau[1], Carlos H. Gañán[3], Anja Feldmann[1], Oliver Gasser[1], and Tobias Fiebig[1(✉)]

[1] Max Planck Institute for Informatics, Saarbrücken, Germany
{fstreibelt,rhalina,anja,oliver.gasser,tfiebig}@mpi-inf.mpg.de
[2] TU München, Munich, Germany
sattler@net.in.tum.de
[3] TU Delft, Delft, The Netherlands
c.hernandezganan@tudelft.nl

Abstract. DNS is one of the core building blocks of the Internet. In this paper, we investigate DNS resolution in a strict IPv6-only scenario and find that a substantial fraction of zones cannot be resolved. We point out, that the presence of an `AAAA` resource record for a zone's nameserver does not necessarily imply that it is resolvable in an IPv6-only environment since the full DNS delegation chain must resolve via IPv6 as well. Hence, in an IPv6-only setting zones may experience an effect similar to what is commonly referred to as lame delegation.

Our longitudinal study shows that the continuing centralization of the Internet has a large impact on IPv6 readiness, i.e., a small number of large DNS providers has, and still can, influence IPv6 readiness for a large number of zones. A single operator that enabled IPv6 DNS resolution–by adding IPv6 glue records–was responsible for around 20.3% of all zones in our dataset not resolving over IPv6 until January 2017. Even today, 10% of DNS operators are responsible for more than 97.5% of all zones that do not resolve using IPv6.

1 Introduction

With the recent exhaustion of the IPv4 address space, the question of IPv6 adoption is gaining importance. More end-users are getting IPv6 prefixes from their ISPs, more websites are reachable via IPv6, hosting companies start billing for IPv4 connectivity or give discounts for IPv6-only hosting and IoT devices further push IPv6 deployment. Yet, one of the main entry-points for Internet services—the DNS—is suffering from a lack of pervasive IPv6 readiness. While protocols such as Happy Eyeballs [41, 45] help to hide IPv6 problems, they complicate detection and debugging of IPv6 issues. Indeed, the threat of DNS name space fragmentation due to insufficient IPv6 support was already predicted in RFC3901, over 18 years ago [18]. Hence, in this paper, we measure the current state of IPv6 resolvability in an IPv6-only scenario.

© The Author(s) 2023
A. Brunstrom et al. (Eds.): PAM 2023, LNCS 13882, pp. 525–549, 2023.
https://doi.org/10.1007/978-3-031-28486-1_22

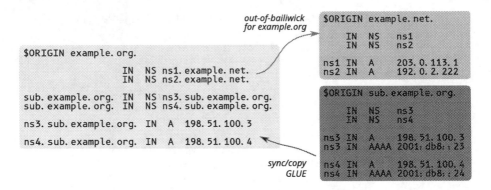

Fig. 1. Broken IPv6-delegation for `example.org` (missing `AAAA` resource records in `example.net` for NS) and `sub.example.org` (missing IPv6-GLUE in parent).

In Fig. 1 we show two common misconfigurations, which prevent DNS resolution over IPv6 and lead to an effect similar to what is commonly called lame delegation. Note, that RFC8499 [26] defines lame delegation as incorrect NS entries or nameservers *not responding properly*. While the observed behaviour might look the same, the underlying misconfiguration, e.g., missing `AAAA` or GLUE for IPv6, often is different. Hence, in this paper we use the term broken IPv6-delegation to avoid unnecessary ambiguity and distinguish the case of zones that are not IPv6 ready, e.g. show no intent to support IPv6 by not having any `AAAA` records, and zones that appear to intend supporting IPv6, Sect. 2.

In the first example, the external nameservers ("out-of-bailiwick") of `example.org` do not have `AAAA` records and, thus, the resolution via IPv6 is impossible. In the second example, the zone `example.org` misses the `AAAA` glue records. These glue records make the `A`/`AAAA` records available for resolution if they have to be resolved from the zone being delegated, i.e., the names of the NS `{ns3,ns4}.sub.example.org` are in-bailiwick.

These examples highlight (a) that it needs cooperation between multiple parties for proper configuration, i.e., `sub.example.net` cannot be resolved via IPv6 even though it is correctly configured; (b) that dual-stack hides issues, i.e., both examples work for dual-stack enabled hosts where the `AAAA` records for `ns3` and `ns4` are resolvable. This demonstrates how working IPv4 resolution hides broken IPv6-delegation for dual-stack DNS recursors.

To be IPv6 *ready*, DNS resolution must work in IPv6-only scenarios. In this paper, we leverage passive DNS data—the Farsight SIE dataset [17]—to identify scenarios in which the DNS delegation chain breaks when only IPv6 is available. Our main contributions can be summarized as follows:

– We identify common broken IPv6-delegation scenarios and point out the importance of checking the full delegation chain.
– We show that big players have a major impact on the number of zones affected by broken IPv6-delegation. Today, 10 DNS providers are responsible for about 24.8% of IPv6-only-unresolvable domains we observe. Just by adding correct

glue records, in Jan. 2017 one single provider fixed the IPv6-only name resolution of more than 45.6 M domains (20.3% of the domains in the dataset).
- Resilience mechanisms often hide misconfigurations. For example, broken IPv6-delegation is hidden by the combined efforts of DNS resilience and Happy Eyeballs. Correctly configuring ones own DNS zone is not sufficient and dependencies are often non-obvious.
- Additionally, we conduct a thorough validation of our methodology. We assess the coverage of the Farsight SIE data in comparison to available ground-truth zonefile data, finding it to provide sufficient coverage for our analysis. Furthermore, we cross-validate our passive measurement results using active measurements, again finding our results to be robust.
- We implemented a DNS measurement tool instead of using, e.g., ZDNS [29], as we need IPv6 support which ZDNS does not (yet) support. The dataset from our active measurements and an implementation of our scanning methodology, including a single-domain version operators can use to evaluate IPv6 support for their own domains, are publicly available at: https://github.com/mutax/dns-v6-readyness

2   Broken IPv6 Zone Delegation

In this section, we briefly recap DNS zone delegation, and sketch common DNS resolution failure scenarios.

2.1   Background: DNS Zone Delegation

The DNS is organized in a hierarchical structure where each node represents a zone that can be operated separately from its parent or child zones. For a zone to be resolvable, NS resource records have to be set in two places. First, the parent of the zone has to explicitly delegate the zone to authoritative nameservers via NS resource records. If an authoritative server has a domain name within the delegated zone itself or a child zone, i.e., if it is "in-bailiwick" [26], the parent zone must also contain A and AAAA resource records for this name, called GLUE, that are returned in the ADDITIONAL section of the DNS responses whenever the NS record is returned. This process breaks the circular dependency in the resolution chain. Furthermore, the zone itself must contain appropriate NS records as well as A and AAAA records if they are in-bailiwick. If the name in an NS record is not within the zone itself or a child zone, i.e., it is out-of-bailiwick, then the zone of the NS' name must also resolve for the initial zone to be resolvable.

2.2   Reasons for Broken IPv6 Delegation

In this paper, we focus on a subset of DNS misconfigurations. In an IPv6-only scenario these misconfigurations can lead to effects similar to what is commonly referred to as lame delegation. To avoid ambiguity, we use the term broken IPv6-delegation referring to any set of misconfiguration specific to IPv6, that breaks the DNS delegation chain of a zone and prevents any of its records from resolving in an IPv6-only scenario. Other issues where a zone does not resolve due to, e.g., DNSSEC problems or unresponsive nameservers, i.e., the strict definition of "lame delegation" (see RFC8499 [26]) are out-of-scope. The issues we discuss can also occur in IPv4 DNS resolution, but are usually quickly discovered given the currently still large number of sites with IPv4-only connection to the Internet, that will not be able to resolve the affected zones.

For a zone to be IPv6-resolvable —i.e., resolvable using IPv6-only— the zones of the authoritative nameservers have to be resolvable via IPv6 and at least one nameserver must be accessible via IPv6. This has to be the case *recursively*, i.e., not only for all parents of the zone itself but also for all parents of the authoritative nameservers in such a way that at least for one[1] of the authoritative nameservers of a zone a delegation chain from the root zone exists, that is fully resolvable using IPv6. We identify the following misconfigurations which can cause broken IPv6-delegation in an IPv6-only setting:

- **No AAAA records for NS names:** If none of the NS records for a zone in their parent zone have associated AAAA records, resolution via IPv6 is not possible.
- **Missing GLUE:** If the name from an NS record for a zone is in-bailiwick, i.e., the name is within the zone or below [26], a parent zone must contain an IPv6 GLUE record, i.e., a parent must serve the corresponding AAAA record(s) as ADDITIONAL data when returning the NS record in the ANSWER section.
- **No AAAA record for in-bailiwick NS:** If an NS record of a zone points to a name that is in-bailiwick but the name lacks AAAA record(s) in its zone, IPv6-only resolution will fail even if the parent provides GLUE, when the recursive server validates the delegation path. One such example is Unbound [35] with the setting `harden-glue: yes`–the default.
- **Zone of out-of-bailiwick NSes not resolving:** If an NS record of a zone is out-of-bailiwick, the corresponding zone must be IPv6-resolvable as well. It is insufficient if the name pointed to by the NS record has an associated AAAA record.
- **Parent zone not IPv6-resolvable:** For a zone to be resolvable via IPv6 the parent zones up to the root zone must be IPv6-resolvable. Any non-IPv6-resolvable zone breaks the delegation chain for all its children.

The above misconfigurations are not mutually exclusive. For example, if the NS sets between parent and child differ, a common misconfiguration [42], the NS in the parent may not resolve due to missing GLUE (as they are in-bailiwick) *but also* the NS in the child may not resolve due to having no AAAA for their names, if they are out-of-bailiwick. In this paper we investigate the prevalence of these misconfigurations to evaluate the IPv6 readiness of the DNS ecosystem.

3   Datasets and Methodology

In this section, we present our choice of datasets as well as our active and passive measurement methodology for identifying DNS misconfigurations that break IPv6-only resolution.

---

[1] RFC2182 [21] suggests to avoid such single points of failure.

Table 1. List of data fields in the Farsight SIE dataset.

Field	Description	Example
count	# of times the tuple <rrname, rrtype, bailiwick, rdata> has been seen	12
time_first	Unix timestamp of the first occurrence of the unique tuple during the data slice	1422251650
time_last	Unix timestamp of the last occurrence of the unique tuple during the data slice	1422251650
rrname	Requested name in the DNS	example.com
rrtype	Requested RRtype of the query	NS
bailiwick	Zone authoritative for the reply	com
rdata	List of all responses received in a single query.	["ns1.example.com", "ns2.example.com"]

3.1 DNS Dataset: Farsight SIE

For our evaluation we are looking for a dataset that enables us to (a) perform a longitudinal study, (b) detect IPv6 DNS misconfigurations, (c) analyze not just top level domains (TLDs) but *also* zones deeper in the tree, and (d) focus on zones that are used in-the-wild. As such we select the Farsight SIE dataset for our study.

The *Farsight Security Information Exchange* (SIE) dataset [17] is collected by Farsight Inc. via globally distributed sensors, co-located with recursive DNS resolvers. Each sensor collects and aggregates all DNS cache misses that the recursive DNS resolver encounters, i.e., the outgoing query and the received answer. By only recording cache-misses and providing aggregates, Farsight reduces the risk of exposing Personally Identifiable Information (PII). Cache-misses occur when a recursive DNS resolver does not have a DNS record for a specific domain name in its cache (or the record's TTL has expired). The recursive resolver then has to ask the authoritative nameserver for the requested name, which is then recorded by Farsight SIE. Farsight does not share the exact number and location of its sensors for business confidentiality reasons. Farsight's SIE dataset has been used in previous research [22,27,32] and its efficacy, coverage, and applicability for research has been demonstrated in the past [23]. We discuss ethical considerations of using this dataset in Sect. 3.5.

We use monthly aggregates from January 2015 to August 2022, containing unique tuples of: requested name, requested RRtype, bailiwick of the response, and returned data record, also for the additional sections, see Table 1. Thus, the Farsight dataset contains essential information for us, as it also records additional data as entries with the bailiwick of the parent. In addition, the Farsight dataset reaches deeper into the DNS hierarchy than, e.g., OpenINTEL [36], as it monitors DNS requests in the wild instead of resolving a set of names below zones sourced from TLD zone files.

Farsight Global Zone Coverage. A common question when using a passive dataset like the one provided by Farsight is how well it actually covers zones on the Internet. In order to determine the coverage of the Farsight dataset, we evaluated the overlap of the second-level domains (SLDs) observed in the

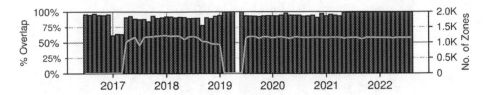

Fig. 2. Zone coverage of Farsight data and number of zones used for the evaluation. We used available zone files to determine the share of covered second level domains by Farsight's dataset. Please note the dip in the graph from February to August 2019, where our zone file collection was limited, i.e., we only collected few zones with high coverage (February - April and July, including .com), or no data at all (May and June).

dataset with ground-truth data, i.e., the names extracted from available zone files. Specifically, we are comparing to .com, .net, and other gTLD (generic TLD) zone files starting from mid of 2016. Additionally, from April 2017 onward, we also obtained CZDS (ICANN Centralized Zone Data Service) zone file data for all available TLDs. Moreover, we use publicly available zone file data from .se, .nu, and .ch for the coverage analysis. In total, this allows us to compare Farsight's data to more than 1.1k zones as of August 2022.

Looking at coverage over time, we find a significant overlap between the Farsight dataset and the number of actually delegated zones based on zone files, see Fig. 2. Coverage averages above 95% from 2019 onwards, with especially since May 2021, our coverage reaches over 99%. Furthermore, we find a reduced average coverage in the beginning of 2017. A closer investigation revealed that these relate to the introduction of various vanity gTLDs with an overall small size, i.e., below 100 delegated zones in the TLD. This implies that missing coverage for just a few zones would lead to a significant reduction in aggregate coverage. Nevertheless, our analysis shows that a significant share of zones is covered in the Farsight dataset. Hence, we the Farsight dataset–especially due to the historic perspective it provides–is ideal to investigate our research questions.

Despite this high coverage, we still face the drawback of the Farsight dataset relying on real-world usage. As such, a missing record in the passive dataset does not necessarily indicate non-existence. Hence, we independently corroborate all major findings with data from TLD zone files for a specific period to check for missing glue records in the zone file, see Sect. 5.4.

3.2   Domain Classification

There are many ways to cluster DNS domains into subgroups. For example, one may look only at the *Top Level Domains* as specified by ICANN [28], or use the *Public Suffix List (PSL)* provided by the Mozilla Foundation [34] to identify second level domains. The PSL is used by browser vendors to decide if a domain is under private or public control, e.g., to prevent websites from setting a *super-cookie* for a *domain* such as .co.uk. Based on matching monthly samples of the ICANN TLDs and the PSLs we identify *TLDs* as well as 2nd *Level Domains*, and *Zones Below 2nd Level*, i.e., all zones *below* 2nd Level Domains.

Another way of grouping DNS domains is to use the Alexa Top-1M list [3]. Using, again, matching monthly samples, we distinguish between the Top 1K, Top 1K–10K, Top 10K–100K, and Top 100K–1M domains. We note that there are limitations in the Alexa Top List [39,40], but compared to other toplists such as Tranco [31], the Alexa list is available throughout the measurement period.

3.3   Misconfiguration Identification

Here, we describe how we identify whether zones can be resolved only via IPv4, only via IPv6, via IPv4 and IPv6, or not at all from the dataset.

1. Per Zone NS set Identification: We first identify all zone delegations by extracting all entries with rrtype = NS. Next, for all names used in these delegations, we find all associated IPs by extracting all A and AAAA records. We do not consider CNAMEs since they are invalid for NS entries, see RFC2181 [20].

We then iterate over all zones, i.e., names that have NS records, to create a unique zone list. In this process, we record the NS records for each bailiwick sending responses for this zone observed in the dataset, and for each NS name all AAAA and A type responses, again grouped by bailiwick from which they were seen. This also captures cases where parent and child return *different* NS sets.

2. Per Zone DNS Resolution: We consider a zone to be resolvable via IPv4 or IPv6 if *at least one* of the NS listed for the zone can be resolved via IPv4 or IPv6 respectively. Hence, to check which zones can be resolved using which IP protocol version we simulate the DNS resolution, starting at the root, i.e., we assume the Root zone . to be resolvable by IPv4 and IPv6. We then iterate over the zone set with attached NS and A/AAAA data. For each zone, except the root zone, we initialize an empty state marking the zone as not resolving.

We then attempt to resolve each zone. For that, we first check if the zone's parent has been seen.

If so we check for each NS of the zone we are trying to resolve as listed in the parent whether its name resolves via IPv4 and/or IPv6. This is the case if:

1. The NS is outside the zone we are trying to resolve, the NS' zone has been recorded as resolving in the zone state file (via IPv4 and/or IPv6), and there are A/AAAA records with that zone's bailiwick for the NS.
2. The NS is in the zone we are resolving and there is an A/AAAA glue record for the name with the bailiwick of the zone's parent (only if an in-bailiwick NS is listed in the parent).

Algorithm 1. Resolve Zones from Passive Data

1: $zone\_res \leftarrow \{\}$
2: $ns\_res \leftarrow \{\}$
3: $prev\_res\_zones \leftarrow -1$
4: $cur\_res\_zones \leftarrow 0$
5:
6: **while** $!prev\_res\_zones == cur\_res\_zones$ **do**
7:       $prev\_res\_zones \leftarrow cur\_res\_zones$
8:       $cur\_res\_zones \leftarrow 0$
9:       **for** $zone$ in $input$ **do**
10:           **if** $zone\_res[zone.parent][res]$ **then**
11:               $glue\_resolve \leftarrow false$
12:               $zone\_resolve \leftarrow false$
13:               **for** NS in $glue$ **do**
14:                   **if** NS in ns_res || (NS in $zone$ && $zone.parent$ has $NS.ip$) || ($zone\_res[ns\_zone][res]$ && ns_zone has $NS.ip$) **then**
15:                       **if** $zone\_res[ns\_zone][res]$ && ns_zone has $NS.ip$ **then**
16:                           $ns\_res[NS] \leftarrow true$
17:                       $glue\_resolve \leftarrow true$
18:               **for** NS in $zone$ **do**
19:                   **if** NS in ns_res || (NS in $zone$ && $zone$ has $NS.ip$) || ($zone\_res[ns\_zone][res]$ && ns_zone has $NS.ip$) **then**
20:                       **if** $zone\_res[ns\_zone][res]$ && ns_zone has $NS.ip$ **then**
21:                           $ns\_res[NS] \leftarrow true$
22:                       $zone\_resolve \leftarrow true$
23:               $zone\_res[zone][glue\_res] \leftarrow glue\_resolve$
24:               $zone\_res[zone][zone\_res] \leftarrow zone\_resolve$
25:               **if** $glue\_resolve$ && $zone\_resolve$ **then**
26:                   $zone\_res[zone][res] \leftarrow true$
27:                   $cur\_res\_zones \leftarrow cur\_res\_zones + 1$

To ensure full resolution, we also have to check that the NS listed in the child resolve. For NS with names under the zone this is the case if the NS listed for this zone in the parent can be reached via IPv4/IPv6, see above, and they have A/AAAA records with the bailiwick of the zone itself. For out-of-bailiwick NS, this is again the case if their own zone resolves and they have A/AAAA records.

A single iteration of this process is not sufficient, as zones often rely on out-of-bailiwick NS. Hence, we continue iterating through the list of zones until the number of unresolved zones no longer decreases. For a simplified pseudo-code description, see Algorithm 1.

3.4   Active Measurement Methodology

To validate our passive measurement results, we implemented a resolver in python. While, technically, Izhikevich et al. presented ZDNS, a tool for this purpose, ZDNS does not provide sufficient support for IPv6 resolution for our use-case. Our measurement methodology follows essentially the same algorithm as our passive resolution. For each zone, we start at the root, and iterate through the DNS tree. From there, we query all authoritative nameservers recorded in the parent on each layer of the DNS hierarchy using IPv4 and IPv6 where possible for the NS of that zonelayer. Furthermore, we try to obtain any possibly available GLUE (A and AAAA) for in-bailiwick NS. For out-of-bailiwick NS, we try to resolve the NS, again starting from the root. If there is an inconsistency between parent and child, i.e., if we discover additional NS when querying the NS listed in the parent, we also perform all queries for this layer against these, noting that they were only present in the child.

To limit the amount of queries sent to each server, our implementation follows the underlying principles of QNAME minimization as described in RFC7816 [5]. By using the NS resource record type to query the parent zones we can directly infer zonecuts and store GLUE records from the additional section, if present. Note that RFC8020 [6] is still not implemented by all nameservers, thus we cannot rely on NXDOMAIN answers to infer that no further zones exist below the queried zone. Our measurement tool will retry queries using TCP on truncation and disable EDNS when it receives a FORMERR from the upstream server.

To further limit the number of queries sent, all responses, including error responses or timeouts, are cached. We limit the number of retries (4) as well as the rate (20 s wait time) at which they are sent. To further enrich the actively collected dataset, we query all authoritative nameservers of a zone for the NS, TXT, SOA and MX records of the given zone as well as the version of the used server software using the *version.bind* in the CHAOS class. Queries and replies are recorded tied to the NS that provided them.

We ran these measurements between October 10th to 14th and 22nd to 24th 2022 against the Alexa Top1M from August 15th 2022 containing 476,242 zones, collecting responses to a total of 32M queries sent via IPv4 and 24M queries sent via IPv6. Our active measurement dataset (101GB of json data), and a tool implementing our measurement toolchain are publicly available at: https://github.com/mutax/dns-v6-readyness.

3.5   Ethical Considerations

The *Farsight Security Information Exchange* (SIE) dataset [17] used in this work is collected by Farsight Inc. at globally distributed vantage points, co-located to recursive DNS resolvers. These sensors collect and aggregate DNS cache misses they encounter, i.e., outgoing queries of the recursors and the received answers. Only collecting cache misses is a conscious choice by Farsight to ensure PII is protected. The dataset also does not contain which sensors collected a specific entry. We specifically use a per-month aggregated version of the dataset, see Sect. 3.1. For details on the fields in the dataset, see Table 1. Data has been handled according to best practices in network measurement data handling as outlined by Allman and Paxson [2].

Before running the active measurements for validation purposes (cf. Section 3.4), we consult the Menlo report [30] as well as best measurement practices [19]. We limit our probing rate, send only well-formed DNS requests, and make use of dedicated servers which have informative rDNS names set. Additionally, we run a webserver providing additional information and contact details on

the IP as well as on the rDNS name. We also focused our measurements on the
Alexa Top 1M, i.e., sites for which the impact of additional requests at the scale
of our measurements is not significant, while also limiting repeated requests using
caching. During our active measurements, we did not receive any complaints. In
summary, we conclude that this work does not raise any ethical issues.

4   Results

Here, we first provide an aggregate overview of the Farsight dataset. Subsequently, we present the results of our analysis of broken IPv6-delegation based on
passive measurement data. Finally, we validate our passive measurement results
against active measurements run from 10th to 24th of October 2022.

4.1   Dataset Overview

Our passive dataset spans 7 years starting on January 1st, 2015 and ending on
August 31st, 2022. During this period, the number of unique zones increased
from 126 M to 368 M. Similarly, the number of PSL 2nd level domains increased
from 116 M to 326 M. For a visualization see the gray line in Fig. 3 (right y-axis).
To highlight our findings, we present results for selected subsets of domains only.
The full results for all domain subsets are in shown in Appendix A.

4.2   IPv6 Resolution in DNS over Time

In Fig. 3 we show how the fraction of zones that is resolvable via IPv4-only,
IPv6-only, both protocols, or fails to resolve, changes across time. We also show
how the total number of zones changes (gray line). The figure shows data for
all zones, the ICANN TLDs, PSL 2nd domains, zones deeper in the tree, Alexa
Top-1K and Alexa Top-1M.

Overall, see Fig. 3a, we find that 11.4% of all zones are IPv6-resolvable in
January 2015. This is significantly higher than the sub 1% reported by Czyz
et al. [13] in 2014. However, they only accounted for glue records, which does
not consider zones with out of bailiwick NS. Over time IPv6 adoption steadily
increases, with 55.1% of zones resolving via IPv6 in August 2022. A notable
increase of IPv6 resolvable zones by 17.3% occurs in January 2017. Further
investigation we find, that this increase relates to two major DNS providers—a
PaaS provider and a webhoster—adding AAAA glue for their NS.

For ICANN TLDs, see Fig. 3b, we find that the majority of zones is
IPv6-resolvable. Throughout our observation period nearly all TLDs are IPv6-
resolvable. The remaining not IPv6-resolvable zones are several vanity TLDs as
well as smaller ccTLDs.

While PSL 2nd level domains, see Fig. 3c, mirror the general trend of all
zones, we find that zones deeper in the tree (Fig. 3d) are generally less likely to
be IPv6-resolvable. Still, we observe an upward trend. We attribute this to the
fact that the process of entering such domains into TLDs for 2nd level domains

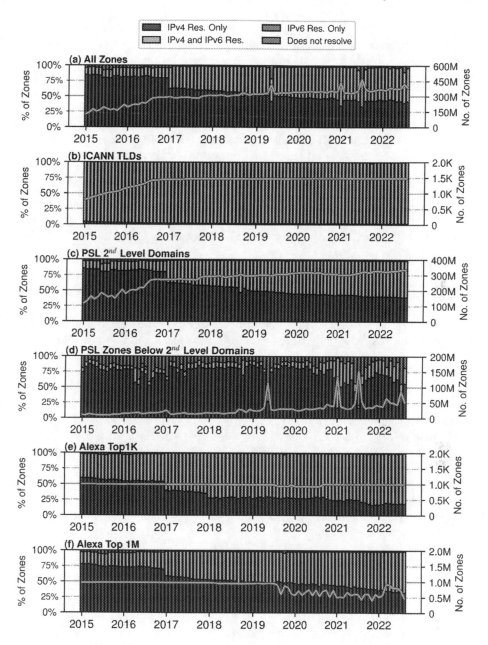

Fig. 3. Per month: # of zones (gray line–right y-axis) and IPv4/IPv6 resolvability in % (left y-axis).

still receives oversight by NICs, e.g., regarding the RFC compliant use of at least two NS in different networks [21], while zones below 2nd level domains can be freely delegated by their domain owners. Also, for sub-domains, we observe three distinct spikes in Fig. 3d which correspond to the spikes seen for all domains, recall Fig. 3a. These spikes occur when a single subtree of the DNS spawns millions of zones. These are artifacts due to specific configurations and highlight that lower layer zones may not be representative for the overall state of DNS.

Finally, comparing PSL 2nd level domains, see Fig. 3d, to the Alexa Top-1K domains, see Fig. 3e, we find that IPv6 adoption is significantly higher among popular domains, starting from 38.9% in 2015 and rising to 80.6% in 2021. There are two notable steps in this otherwise gradual increase, namely January 2017 and January 2018. These are due to a major webhoster and a major PaaS provider enabling IPv6 resolution (2017), and a major search engine provider common in the Alexa-Top-1K enabling IPv6 resolution (2018).

Comparison with Active Measurements: Evaluating zone resolvability from our active measurements, see Sect. 3.4, we find that 314,994 zones (66.14%) support dual stack DNS resolution, while 159,166 zones (33.42%) are only resolvable via IPv4.

A further 2066 zones (0.43%) could not be resolved during our active measurements, and 16 zones ($\leq$0.01%) were only resolvable via IPv6. In comparison to that, our passive measurements–see also Fig. 3f–map closely: We find 66.18% (+0.04% difference) of zones in the Alexa Top 1M resolving via both, IPv4 and IPv6, and 32.23% (−1.19% difference) of zones only resolving via IPv4. Similarly, 1.16% (+0.73%) of zones do not resolve at all, and 0.42% (+0.42% difference) of zones only resolve via IPv6 according to our passive data. Hence, overall, we find our passive approach being closely aligned with the results of our active measurements for the latest available samples. The, in comparison, higher values for non-resolving and IPv6 only resolving zones are most likely rooted in the visibility limitations of the dataset, see Sect. 5.4. Nevertheless, based on the low deviation between two independent approaches at determining IPv6 resolvability of zones we have confidence in the results of our passive measurements.

4.3   IPv6 Resolution Failure Types

Next, we take a closer look at zones that show some indication of IPv6 deployment, yet, are not IPv6-resolvable. These are zones where an NS has an AAAA record or an AAAA GLUE. To find them we consider NS entries within the zone as well as NSes for the zone in its parent. In Fig. 4 we show how their absolute numbers evolve over time (gray line) as well as the failures reasons (in percentages).

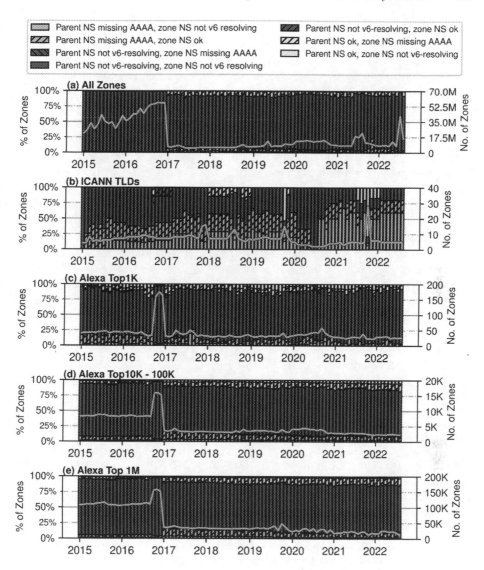

Fig. 4. Per month: # of zones not IPv6-resolvable with `AAAA` or GLUE for `NS` (gray line–right y-axis) and causes for IPv6 resolution failure in % (left y-axis).

We find that for all four subsets of zones shown—all zones, ICANN TLDs, Alexa Top-1K, Alexa Top-10K–100K—the most common failure case is missing resolution of `NS` in the parent. This occurs mostly when the `NS` is out-of-bailiwick and *does* have `AAAA` records, but the `NS`'s zone itself is not IPv6-resolvable. Furthermore, there is a substantial number of zones per category—especially in the

Alexa Top-1K—where the NS in the parent lacks AAAA while the NS listed in the zone has AAAA records, commonly due to missing GLUE. We also observe the inverse scenario, i.e., GLUE is present but no AAAA record exist for the NS within the zone itself. Both cases can also occur if NS sets differ between the parent and its child [42].

We see a major change around January 2017, i.e., a sharp increase in zones that are IPv6-resolvable, which is also visible in Fig. 3: For all zones as well as for the Alexa Top 10K–100K, we observe that several million zones not resolving via IPv6 since the start of the dataset but having NSes with AAAA records, now are IPv6-resolvable. The reason is that a major provider added missing glue records. Interestingly, we do not see this in the Alexa Top 1K.

In the Alexa Top 1K, and to a lesser degree in the Alexa Top 10K-100K, we observe a spike of zones that list AAAA records for their NS but are not IPv6-resolvable in Oct. 2016. This is the PaaS provider mentioned before, first rolling out AAAA records for their NS, and then three months later also adding IPv6 GLUE. Operationally, this approach makes sense, as they can first test the impact of handling IPv6 DNS queries in general. Moreover, reverting changes in their own zones is easier than reverting changes in the TLD zones–here the GLUE entries. Again, the major webhoster is less common among the *very* popular domains, which is why its effect can be seen in Figs. 4a and 4d, but not in Fig. 4b. Also, this operator had AAAA records in place since the beginning of our dataset, as seen by the plateau in Fig. 4d. These observations have been cross-confirmed by inspecting copies of zonefiles for the corresponding TLDs and time-periods.

4.4   Centralization and IPv6 Readiness

Finally, we focus on the nameservers hosting most non IPv6-resolvable zones. We first identify the top NS sets in terms of the number of hosted zones, aggregating NS names to their PSL 2nd level domain and known operators' NS under a multiple well-patterned zones. Then, we compute a CDF over the number of zones per NS set for each time bin. Figure 5 shows how this CDF changed across time and highlights the impact of centralization within the DNS providers. Over 97.5% of the non-IPv6-resolvable zones are hosted by the Top 10% of NS sets.

Again, we see the impact of a change by a major webhoster in January 2017—it is the top NS set among all zones (Fig. 5a). Similarly, the PaaS provider is pronounced among the Alexa Top-1K, i.e., part of the Top 10 of NS sets (Fig. 5c) and the top NS set for the Alexa Top-10K–100K (Fig. 5d). Finally, the major search engine operator's impact can especially be seen among TLDs (Fig. 5b) and the Alexa Top-1K (Fig. 5c), where—in both cases—this operator is the top NS set for non IPv6-resolvable zones.

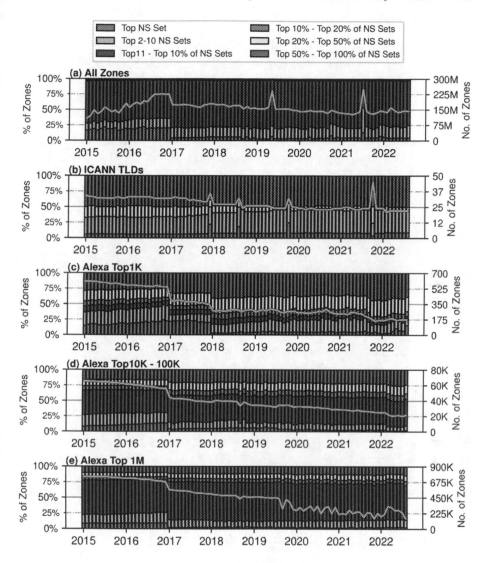

Fig. 5. Per month: # of zones not IPv6-resolvable (gray line–right y-axis) and distribution of zones over NS sets in % (left y-axis).

4.5   Resolvability and Responsiveness of NS in Active Measurements

During our active measurements, we also had the opportunity to validate whether NS records listed in zones did actually reply to DNS requests or not. During our evaluation of the Alexa Top 1M, we discovered a total of 176,207 NS records, of which 212 had A or AAAA records associated that were invalid, as for example : : as a AAAA record. Of the remaining 175,995 records, 116,504 needed glue, i.e., they were in-bailiwik NS for their own. Among these, 19,310 NS were dual-stack, while 94,192 only had A records associated with them, and a further 108 NS only had associated AAAA records. Furthermore, 85,213 (90.47%) of A-only NS needing glue had correct glue set. For dual-stack configured NS, 14,072 (72.87%) have complete (A and AAAA) glue. A further 3,932 (20.36%) NS only has A glue records, while 24 (0.12%) NS only have AAAA glue, despite generally having a dual-stack DNS configuration. Finally, of the 108 NS records only having AAAA records associated, 70 (64.81%) NS have correctly set AAAA glue.

Moving on to the reachability of these NS, we find that of the total number of NS that have an A record (169,547) *and* are reachable is at 164,255, i.e., 96.88% actually responds to queries. For IPv6, these values are slightly worse, with 30,193 of 32,285 NS (93.52%) responding to queries via IPv6. This highlights a potential accuracy gap of 3–6% for research work estimating DNS resolvability from passive data. Notably, this gap is larger for IPv6.

5 Discussion

In this section, we first state our key-findings, and then discuss their implications.

5.1 The Impact of Centralization

Centralization is one of the big changes in the Internet over the last decade. This trend ranges from topology flattening [4,7] to the majority of content being served by hypergiants [8] and—as we show—also applies to the DNS. An increasing number of zones are operated by a decreasing number of organizations. As such, an outage at one big DNS provider [44]—or missing support for IPv6—can disrupt name resolution for a very large part of the Internet as we highlight in Sect. 4. In fact, out-of-bailiwick NS not being resolvable via IPv6 is the most common misconfiguration in our study, often triggered by missing GLUE in a single zone. Given that *ten* operators could enable IPv6 DNS resolution for 24.8% of not yet IPv6 resolving zones, we claim that large DNS providers have a huge responsibility for making the Internet IPv6 ready.

5.2 IPv6 DNS Resolution and the Web

In general, as we travel down the delegation chain we find more misconfigurations and a smaller fraction of IPv6-resolvable zones. Given that common web assets–JavaScript, Style Sheets, or images–are often served from FQDNs further down the DNS hierarchy, we conjecture that this may have a another huge, yet still hidden, impact on IPv6 readiness for web. We encourage operators to be mindful of this issue, and study its effect in future work.

5.3   Implications for Future Research

Our findings demonstrate that it is not sufficient to test for the presence of AAAA records to asses the IPv6 readiness of a DNS zone. Instead, measurements have to assess whether the zones are IPv6-resolvable. The same applies to email setups and websites.

Furthermore, given the centralization we observe in the DNS, network measurements of IPv6 adoption should consider and quantify the impact of individual operators. More specifically, researchers should distinguish between effects caused by a small number of giants vs. the behavior of the Internet at large. Artifacts that can occur temporarily should be recognized and then excluded.

5.4   Limitations

Since our dataset relies on DNS cache misses, we are missing domains that are not requested or not captured by the Farsight monitors in a given month. Moreover, our use of monthly aggregates may occlude short-term misconfigurations. To address this, we support major findings on misconfigurations with additional ground-truth data from authoritative TLD zone files.

Similarly, we use the Alexa List with its known limitations [39, 40]. Thus, we cluster the Alexa list into different rank tiers, which reduces fluctuations in the higher tiers. Furthermore, we only assess zones' configuration states, and not actual resolution, i.e., "lame delegation" for other reasons is out of scope.

Furthermore, we cannot make statements on whether the zones we measure *actually* resolve, e.g., if there is an authoritative DNS server listening on a configured IP address returning correct results. Still, we have certainty that zones we measure as resolvable are at least sufficiently configured for resolution. Similarly, we can not assess the impact of observed DNS issues on other protocols, e.g., HTTPs. To further address this limitation of our passive data source, we conducted active measurements, which validated the observations from our passive results and added further insights on the actual reachability of authoritative DNS servers for zones.

Naturally, our active measurements also have several limitations that have to be recorded. First, we conducted our measurements from a single vantage point. Given load balancing in CDNs via DNS [43], this may have lead to a vantage point specific perspective. Nevertheless, we argue that misconfigurations [14] are likely to be consistent across an operator, i.e., the returned A or AAAA records may change, but not the issue of, e.g., missing GLUE. Furthermore, DNS infrastructure tends to be less dynamic than A and AAAA records.

Second, our measurements were only limited to the Alexa Top 1M and associated domains. We consciously made this choice instead of, e.g., running active measurements on *all* zones in the Farsight dataset to reduce our impact on the Internet ecosystem.

In summary, our study provides an important first perspective on IPv6 only resolvability. We suggest to complement our study with active measurements of IPv6 only DNS resolution and the impact of broken IPv6-delegation on the IPv6 readiness of the web due to asset dependencies as future work.

6   Related Work

Our related work broadly clusters into two segments: *i)* Studies on IPv6 adoption and readiness, and *ii)* Studies about DNS and DNS misconfigurations.

6.1   IPv6 Adoption and Readiness

With the exhaustion of the IPv4 address space [38], IPv6 adoption has been a frequent topic of study. In 2014, Czyz et al. [13] conducted a primer study on IPv6 adoption, taking a multi-perspective approach that also covered DNS. Our measurements shed light on the time after their measurements which concluded in 2014. Furthermore, they estimate IPv6 adoption in DNS by only surveying `AAAA` glue records in `net.` and `com.`, while we consider the full resolution path. Work by Foremski et al. [24] and Plonka & Berger [37] investigate IPv6 adoption at the edge, which is orthogonal to our work. In recent years, various researchers took country and domain specific perspectives on IPv6 adoption, e.g., [12,25,33].

6.2   DNS and DNS Misconfiguration Studies

Since DNS is a core component of the Internet, it has been studied regularly over the past decades, including studies regarding the adoption of new protocol features, e.g., [9–11,15,16,43]. Such studies use various active datasets, e.g., OpenINTEL [36], as well as passive datasets, e.g., the Farsight SIE dataset which we rely on, to, e.g., study operational aspects of the DNS [23]. More specifically focusing on DNS (mis)configuration, Sommese et al. [42] study inconsistencies in parent and child NS sets and Akiwate et al. [1] work on lame delegation. However, contrary to our work, the latter two either do not consider the IP part of DNS delegation (Sommese et al.), or explicitly focus on IPv4 (Akiwate et al.). More recently, Izhikevich et al. presented ZDNS, a tool for large-scale studies of the DNS ecosystem in the Internet [29]. Unfortunately, ZDNS is tailored towards IPv4 and does not support querying authoritative nameservers over IPv6. Therefore, we cannot make use of ZDNS in our study. Instead we perform active DNS measurements with our own implementation of a DNS resolution methodology, which implements IPv6 resolution.

6.3   Summary

We expand on earlier contributions regarding IPv6 adoption. We provide a more recent perspective on the IPv6 DNS ecosystem and take a more complete approach to asses the IPv6 readiness in an IPv6-only scenario. This focus on IPv6 is also our novelty in context to earlier work on DNS measurements and DNS misconfigurations, which did not focus on how IPv6 affects DNS resolvability. Additionally, our active measurements for validating our passive measurement results also highlight that the presence of `AAAA` records does not necessarily imply IPv6 resolvability. Instead, to measure IPv6 resolvability, the resolution state of provided IPv6 resources has to be validated.

7   Conclusion

In this paper, we present a passive DNS measurement study on root causes for broken IPv6-delegation in an IPv6 only setting. While over time we see an increasing number of zones resolvable via IPv4 and IPv6, in August 2022 still 44.9% are not resolvable via IPv6. We identify not resolvable NS records of the zone or its parent as the most common failure scenario. Our recommendations to operators include to explicitly monitor IPv6 across the entire delegation chain.

Additionally, we conducted a dedicated validation of our results using active measurements. This validation broadly confirmed our results from the passive measurements and further highlighted the importance of not only relying on the presence of specific records, as nameservers for which IPv6 addresses are listed in the DNS may not actually be responsive.

We plan to provide an open-source implementation of our measurement methodology along with the paper. Furthermore, we will provide a reduced implementation of our measurement toolchain which will enable operators to explicitly check a given zone or FQDN for IPv6-resolvable. Similarly, we will provide the results of our active measurements as open data.

For future work we suggest to systematically expand our active measurement campaign to assess resolvability, e.g., for websites including all web assets. Using active measurements, one can explicitly resolve a hostname and run active checks on the delegation chain, validating the responses of all authoritative nameservers and find inconsistencies not only between a zone and its parent but also within the NS set. We conjecture that–especially given the widespread use of subdomains for web assets–the reduced IPv6 resolvability we observe may have a significant impact on the IPv6-readiness of the web, i.e., a website using assets on domains that do not resolve via IPv6 is not IPv6 ready.

Acknowledgments. We thank Farsight Security, Inc. (now DomainTools) for providing access to the Farsight Security Information Exchange's passive DNS data feed. Without this data, the project would not have been possible. The authors express their gratitude to the anonymous reviewers for their thoughtful and encouraging input during the reviewing process. manner. This work was partially funded by the German Federal Ministry of Education and Research under the project PRIMEnet, grant 16KIS1370, and 6G-RIC, grant 16KISK027. Any opinions, findings, and conclusions or recommendations expressed in this material are those of the authors and do not necessarily reflect the views of Farsight Security, Inc., DomainTools, the German Federal Ministry of Education and Research or the authors' host institutions and further affiliations.

A   DNS Resolution Overview

See Fig. 6.

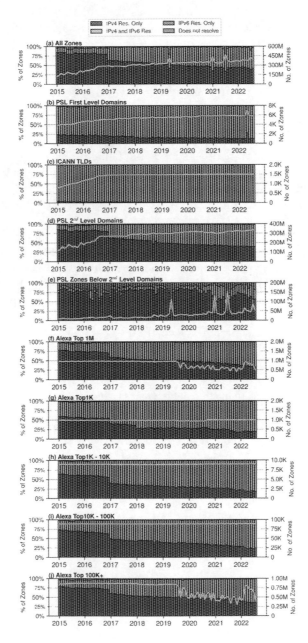

Fig. 6. Total number of zones in the dataset per month (gray line) and resolvability

B   IPv6 only Resolution Failures

See Fig. 7.

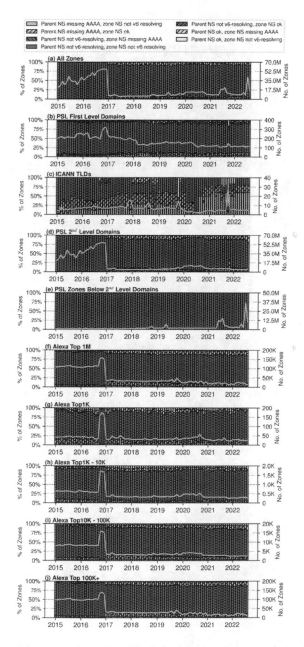

Fig. 7. Zones unable to resolve using IPv6, but with `AAAA` records in GLUE or zone apex (gray line), by resolution failure.

C   Zones Without IPv6 Resolution per NS set

See Fig. 8.

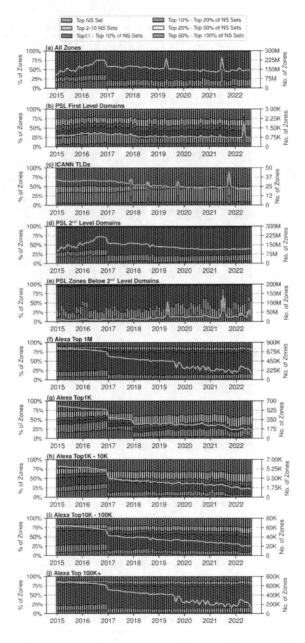

Fig. 8. Distribution of zones not resolving via IPv6 over NS sets.

References

1. Akiwate, G., et al.: Unresolved issues: prevalence, persistence, and perils of lame delegations. In: Proceedings of the Internet Measurement Conference (IMC), pp. 281–294. ACM (2020). https://doi.org/10.1145/3419394.3423623
2. Allman, M., Paxson, V.: Issues and etiquette concerning use of shared measurement data. In: Proceedings of the Internet Measurement Conference (IMC), pp. 135–140. ACM (2007). https://doi.org/10.1145/1298306.1298327
3. Amazon.com Inc: Alexa Top Sites. https://www.alexa.com/
4. Arnold, T., et al.: Cloud provider connectivity in the flat Internet. In: Proceedings of the Internet Measurement Conference (IMC), pp. 230–246. ACM (2020). https://doi.org/10.1145/3419394.3423613
5. Bortzmeyer, S.: DNS query name minimisation to improve privacy. RFC 7816 (Experimental), March 2016. https://www.rfc-editor.org/rfc/rfc7816.txt, obsoleted by RFC 9156
6. Bortzmeyer, S., Huque, S.: NXDOMAIN: there really is nothing underneath. RFC 8020 (Proposed Standard), November 2016. https://www.rfc-editor.org/rfc/rfc8020.txt
7. Böttger, T., et al.: Shaping the internet: 10 years of IXP growth. arXiv (2019). https://doi.org/10.48550/ARXIV.1810.10963, https://arxiv.org/abs/1810.10963
8. Böttger, T., Cuadrado, F., Tyson, G., Castro, I., Uhlig, S.: A hypergiant's view of the internet. ACM Comput. Commun. Rev. (CCR) **47**(1) (2017)
9. Calder, M., Fan, X., Hu, Z., Katz-Bassett, E., Heidemann, J., Govindan, R.: Mapping the expansion of Google's serving infrastructure. In: Proceedings of the Internet Measurement Conference (IMC), pp. 313–326. ACM (2013). https://doi.org/10.1145/2504730.2504754
10. Chhabra, R., Murley, P., Kumar, D., Bailey, M., Wang, G.: Measuring DNS-over-HTTPS performance around the world. In: Proceedings of the Internet Measurement Conference (IMC), pp. 351–365. ACM (2021). https://doi.org/10.1145/3487552.3487849
11. Chung, T., et al.: Understanding the role of registrars in DNSSEC deployment. In: Proceedings of the Internet Measurement Conference (IMC), pp. 369–383. ACM (2017). https://doi.org/10.1145/3131365.3131373
12. Colitti, L., Gunderson, S.H., Kline, E., Refice, T.: Evaluating IPv6 adoption in the internet. In: Krishnamurthy, A., Plattner, B. (eds.) PAM 2010. LNCS, vol. 6032, pp. 141–150. Springer, Heidelberg (2010). https://doi.org/10.1007/978-3-642-12334-4_15
13. Czyz, J., Allman, M., Zhang, J., Iekel-Johnson, S., Osterweil, E., Bailey, M.: Measuring IPv6 adoption. In: Proceedings of the 2014 ACM SIGCOMM Conference (SIGCOMM), pp. 87–98. ACM (2014). https://doi.org/10.1145/2619239.2626295
14. Dietrich, C., Krombholz, K., Borgolte, K., Fiebig, T.: Investigating system operators' perspective on security misconfigurations. In: Proceedings of the 25th ACM SIGSAC Conference on Computer and Communications Security (CCS), pp. 1272–1289. ACM (2018)
15. Doan, T.V., Fries, J., Bajpai, V.: Evaluating public DNS services in the wake of increasing centralization of DNS. In: IFIP Networking Conference (2021). https://doi.org/10.23919/IFIPNetworking52078.2021.9472831
16. Doan, T.V., Tsareva, I., Bajpai, V.: Measuring DNS over TLS from the edge: adoption, reliability, and response times. In: Hohlfeld, O., Lutu, A., Levin, D. (eds.) PAM 2021. LNCS, vol. 12671, pp. 192–209. Springer, Cham (2021). https://doi.org/10.1007/978-3-030-72582-2_12

17. DomainTools, formerly Farsight Security: Farsight Security Information Exchange (SIE). https://www.farsightsecurity.com/solutions/security-information-exchange/ (2022)
18. Durand, A., Ihren, J.: DNS IPv6 transport operational guidelines. RFC 3901 (Best Current Practice), September 2004. https://www.rfc-editor.org/rfc/rfc3901.txt
19. Durumeric, Z., Wustrow, E., Halderman, J.A.: ZMap: fast Internet-wide Scanning and its security applications. In: Proceedings of the 31th USENIX Security Symposium (USENIX Security), pp. 605–620. USENIX Association (2022)
20. Elz, R., Bush, R.: Clarifications to the DNS specification. RFC 2181 (Proposed Standard), July 1997. https://www.rfc-editor.org/rfc/rfc2181.txt, updated by RFCs 4035, 2535, 4343, 4033, 4034, 5452, 8767
21. Elz, R., Bush, R., Bradner, S., Patton, M.: Selection and operation of secondary DNS servers. RFC 2182 (Best Current Practice), July 1997. https://www.rfc-editor.org/rfc/rfc2182.txt
22. Fiebig, T., Borgolte, K., Hao, S., Kruegel, C., Vigna, G.: Something from nothing (there): collecting global IPv6 datasets from DNS. In: Kaafar, M.A., Uhlig, S., Amann, J. (eds.) PAM 2017. LNCS, vol. 10176, pp. 30–43. Springer, Cham (2017). https://doi.org/10.1007/978-3-319-54328-4_3
23. Foremski, P., Gasser, O., Moura, G.C.: DNS observatory: the big picture of the DNS. In: Proceedings of the Internet Measurement Conference (IMC), pp. 87–100. ACM (2019)
24. Foremski, P., Plonka, D., Berger, A.: Entropy/IP: uncovering structure in IPv6 addresses. In: Proceedings of the Internet Measurement Conference (IMC), pp. 167–181. ACM (2016). https://doi.org/10.1145/2987443.2987445
25. Han, C., et al.: Insights into the issue in IPv6 adoption: a view from the Chinese IPv6 Application mix. Concurr. Comput. Pract. Exp. **28**(3), 616–630 (2016). https://doi.org/10.1002/cpe.3327
26. Hoffman, P., Sullivan, A., Fujiwara, K.: DNS terminology. RFC 8499 (Best Current Practice), January 2019. https://www.rfc-editor.org/rfc/rfc8499.txt
27. Houser, R., Hao, S., Li, Z., Liu, D., Cotton, C., Wang, H.: A comprehensive measurement-based investigation of DNS hijacking. In: Proceedings of the 40th International Symposium on Reliable Distributed Systems (SRDS), pp. 210–221. IEEE (2021)
28. ICANN: List of Top-Level Domains. https://www.icann.org/resources/pages/tlds-2012-02-25-en
29. Izhikevich, L., et al.: ZDNS: a fast DNS toolkit for internet measurement. In: Proceedings of the Internet Measurement Conference (IMC). ACM (2022)
30. Kenneally, E., Dittrich, D.: The Menlo report: ethical principles guiding information and communication technology research. Available at SSRN 2445102 (2012)
31. Le Pochat, V., Van Goethem, T., Tajalizadehkhoob, S., Joosen, W.: TRANCO: a research-oriented top sites ranking hardened against manipulation. In: Proceedings of the 26th Network and Distributed System Security Symposium (NDSS). Internet Society (ISOC) (2019)
32. Liu, B., et al.: A reexamination of internationalized domain names: the good, the bad and the ugly. In: Proceedings of the 48th IEEE/IFIP International Conference on Dependable Systems and Networks (DSN), pp. 654–665. IEEE (2018)
33. Livadariu, I., Elmokashfi, A., Dhamdhere, A.: Measuring IPv6 adoption in Africa. In: Odumuyiwa, V., Adegboyega, O., Uwadia, C. (eds.) AFRICOMM 2017. LNICST, vol. 250, pp. 345–351. Springer, Cham (2018). https://doi.org/10.1007/978-3-319-98827-6_32

34. Mozilla Foundation: Public Suffix List. https://publicsuffix.org/
35. NLnet Labs: Unbound nameserver documentation. https://unbound.docs.nlnetlabs.nl/en/latest/reference/history/requirements.html
36. OpenINTEL project: The OpenINTEL measurement platform. https://openintel.nl/
37. Plonka, D., Berger, A.: Temporal and spatial classification of active IPv6 addresses. In: Proceedings of the Internet Measurement Conference (IMC), pp. 509–522. ACM (2015). https://doi.org/10.1145/2815675.2815678
38. Richter, P., Allman, M., Bush, R., Paxson, V.: A primer on IPv4 scarcity. ACM Comput. Commun. Rev. (CCR) **45**(2), 21–31 (2015). https://doi.org/10.1145/2766330.2766335
39. Rweyemamu, W., Lauinger, T., Wilson, C., Robertson, W., Kirda, E.: Clustering and the weekend effect: recommendations for the use of top domain lists in security research. In: Choffnes, D., Barcellos, M. (eds.) PAM 2019. LNCS, vol. 11419, pp. 161–177. Springer, Cham (2019). https://doi.org/10.1007/978-3-030-15986-3_11
40. Scheitle, Q., et al.: A long way to the top: Significance, structure, and stability of Internet top lists. In: Proceedings of the Internet Measurement Conference (IMC), pp. 478–493. ACM (2018)
41. Schinazi, D., Pauly, T.: Happy eyeballs version 2: better connectivity using concurrency. RFC 8305 (Proposed Standard), December 2017. https://www.rfc-editor.org/rfc/rfc8305.txt
42. Sommese, R., et al.: When parents and children disagree: diving into DNS delegation inconsistency. In: Sperotto, A., Dainotti, A., Stiller, B. (eds.) PAM 2020. LNCS, vol. 12048, pp. 175–189. Springer, Cham (2020). https://doi.org/10.1007/978-3-030-44081-7_11
43. Streibelt, F., Böttger, J., Chatzis, N., Smaragdakis, G., Feldmann, A.: Exploring EDNS-client-subnet adopters in your free time. In: Proceedings of the Internet Measurement Conference (IMC), pp. 305–312. ACM (2013). https://doi.org/10.1145/2504730.2504767
44. ThousandEyes Blog, Cisco: The DDoS attack on Dyn's DNS infrastructure. https://www.thousandeyes.com/blog/dyn-dns-ddos-attack/
45. Wing, D., Yourtchenko, A.: Happy eyeballs: success with dual-stack hosts. RFC 6555 (Proposed Standard), April 2012. https://www.rfc-editor.org/rfc/rfc6555.txt, obsoleted by RFC 8305

TTL Violation of DNS Resolvers in the Wild

Protick Bhowmick[1], Md. Ishtiaq Ashiq[1], Casey Deccio[2], and Taejoong Chung[1(✉)]

[1] Virginia Tech, Blacksburg, USA
{protick,iashiq5,tijay}@vt.edu
[2] Brigham Young University, Provo, USA
casey@byu.edu

Abstract. The Domain Name System (DNS) provides a scalable name resolution service. It uses extensive caching to improve its resiliency and performance; every DNS record contains a time-to-live (TTL) value, which specifies how long a DNS record can be cached before being discarded. Since the TTL can play an important role in both DNS security (e.g., determining a DNSSEC-signed response's caching period) and performance (e.g., responsiveness of CDN-controlled domains), it is crucial to measure and understand how resolvers *violate* TTL.

Unfortunately, measuring how DNS resolvers manage TTL around the world remains difficult since it usually requires having the cooperation of many nodes spread across the globe. In this paper, we present a methodology that measures TTL-violating resolvers using an HTTP/S proxy service, which allows us to cover more than 27 K resolvers in 9.5 K ASes. Out of the 8,524 resolvers that we could measure through at least five different vantage points, we find that 8.74% of them extend the TTL arbitrarily, which potentially can degrade the performance of at least 38% of the popular websites that use CDNs. We also report that 44.1% of DNSSEC-validating resolvers incorrectly serve DNSSEC-signed responses from the cache even after their RRSIGs are expired.

1 Introduction

The Domain Name System (DNS) provides a scalable name resolution service. It uses extensive caching to improve its resiliency and performance with a time-to-live (TTL) value that specifies how long a DNS record can be cached before being discarded [22]; the TTL value is assigned by the DNS authoritative servers. DNS consumers (e.g., DNS resolvers) can cache the DNS responses during the TTL so that the future requests can be fulfilled locally without sending extra DNS queries to the DNS authoritative server.

Due to its resiliency and efficiency, DNS has evolved from simply providing a mapping between human-readable names and network-level IP addresses, to providing security features for other protocols (e.g., MTA-STS [19], TLSA [13], and BIMI [4] for email protocols) or better performance by delegating its control

A. Brunstrom et al. (Eds.): PAM 2023, LNCS 13882, pp. 550–563, 2023.
https://doi.org/10.1007/978-3-031-28486-1_23

to another entity (e.g., CDN). For example, an email server can publish its certificate information as a DNS record (i.e., TLSA) so that a sender can cross-check the certificate. Thus, the service operators have to manage the DNS records and their security information in a synchronous way. When they update (i.e., rollover) their credential information such as public key, they usually publish the updated DNS records in advance [13,19] and wait at least for the TTL (or twice of TTL), *expecting that DNS resolvers clear the old cache after then*. However, it is unclear how DNS clients follow such practice; for example, a DNS resolver may cache DNS responses longer than its TTL to reduce DNS requests towards authoritative servers. This may bring a negative impact on both security and performance; for example, DNS resolvers that *extends the TTL value* may impair the performance of CDNs, which typically uses a lower TTL value to improve their resilliency and responsiveness [9].

However, it is challenging to understand how such TTL violations exist in the wild without access to devices or users in affected networks; for example, it is not straightforward to understand if a local DNS resolver in an ISP extends TTL without deploying a vantage point in the ISP. To address this challenge, there have been several successful prior approaches to measuring DNS TTL violations by using datasets collected from DNS authoritative servers [15], residential networks [7], or using active probes such as RIPE Atlas [20]. While these approaches have identified a number of resolvers that violates the TTL value in DNS records, but it is typically difficult for others to replicate and often to scale [16,20], and mostly focus on public DNS resolvers [16].

In this paper, we explore an alternative approach to detecting DNS TTL violations of resolvers using a residential proxy service called, BrightData, which allows us to achieve measurements from over 274,570 end hosts and their 27,131 resolvers across 9,514 ASes in 220 countries. We discovered the TTL violation is prevalent; for example, we find 745 (8.74%) resolvers that extends TTLs. Furthermore, we find that another form of TTL violation that can happen to *DNSSEC-signed* records; we find that 285 DNSSEC-validating resolvers that return expired DNSSEC-signed responses when the TTL does not expire yet.

We make our analysis code and data public to the research community at

https://ttl-violation-study.github.io

2   Background and Related Work

2.1   Related Work

There have been a long thread of work focusing on TTL violations in DNS resolvers, using different datasets and methodologies. Early in 2004, Pang et al. [15] used DNS logs collected from a large CDN, Akamai, to measure TTL violations and reported that 47% of clients used the expired DNS record, which indicates the prevalent violation of the TTL. Similarly, Callahan et al. [7] found 13.7% of user connections measured from residential network across 90 homes used expired DNS records in 2013.

Schomp et al. [16] took an active measurement-based approach by sending DNS queries to open resolvers from 100 PlanetLab nodes and found that 81% of open resolvers did not consistently return the correct TTL values.

Some studies [3,12] found that TTL violations are more likely to happen with small TTLs (e.g., 20 s); for example, Flavelet al. reported that 2% of users used stale DNS responses with 20 s TTL even after 15 min and Almeida et al. [18] found similar patterns in the traffic measured from a European mobile network operator.

Recently, RIPE labs used 9,119 unique RIPE Atlas probes reported that 4.1% of the measured resolvers increased the TTL value and 1.97% of the measured resolvers decreased the TTL value [20].

While these studies have identified several different TTL violations, it is still challenging to provide the overall TTL violation on the Internet as each of them used a different approach (e.g., passive vs. active) to focus on a different type of DNS resolvers (e.g., local vs. public resolver). Our goal is to develop an approach that achieves the same goal, but without having privileged access (e.g., CDN logs), and without having to spend significant effort to deploy software or hardware for users to install.

2.2   BrightData

In this work, we use BrightData, a residential proxy service, to characterize the behavior of resolvers. BrightData, formerly known as Luminati, is the paid HTTP/S proxy service that routes traffic via residential nodes (called exit nodes), who installed *Hola Unblocker* [14]. In order to route traffic, the client needs to send a HTTP request to a BrightData server, called the *super proxy*; the super proxy then forwards the request to an exit node. The exit node can perform the HTTP request and return the response back to the client via the super proxy.

BrightData offers options that can be passed with HTTP request to control exit nodes. Figure 1 shows the overview of how the BrightData platform works.

Exitnode Preference: BrightData allows clients a measure of control over which exit node is chosen to forward the traffic. The client can select the country or autonomous system (AS) that the exit node is located in by adding a -country-XX (where XX is the ISO country code) or a -asn-YY (where YY is AS number) parameter to the HTTP request. The client is also allowed to choose the same exit node for subsequent requests by adding a -session-XX (where XX is a random number) to the HTTP request. Within 60 s, the client can choose the same exit node by using the same session number.

Exitnode Persistence: The client can find the hash of the exit node's IP address in the HTTP response header, x-luminati-ip. By adding the -ip-XX option to the HTTP request (where XX is the hash of the IP address), the client can use the same exit node if available. This option is extremely useful to measure the TTL violation behavior of the resolvers; we can still measure the same resolvers

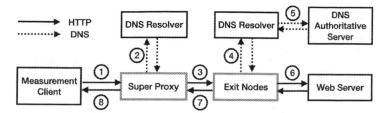

Fig. 1. Timeline of a request in BrightData: the client sends an HTTP request to the super proxy ①; the super proxy makes a DNS request for the sanity check and forward the request to an exit node ②–③; the exit node uses its DNS resolver and fetch the HTTP response ④–⑥ and forward it back to the super proxy ⑦, which return it to the client ⑧. Brightdata controls the Super Proxy and exit nodes (shown with blue boxes). (Color figure online)

(used by the same exit node) by finding the same exit node after a TTL with a longer period of time (e.g., 60 min) expires.

DNS Request Location: By default, DNS resolution is done and cached at the super proxy's end; however, the client can specify the `dns-remote` option to the HTTP request to make DNS resolution done by the exit node (using the exit node's DNS server). In out experiment, we do so as we want the resolution to be done at the client's end.

   With these options, we use BrightData to let exit nodes send HTTP requests to our domains; the exit nodes will also send DNS requests to our DNS authoritative server through their resolvers, which gives an opportunity to understand their behavior. In the following section, we introduce our experiment methodology and its challenges.

3   TTL Extension in the Wild

In this section, we describe how we use BrightData to understand how DNS resolvers *extend* TTL in the DNS responses.

3.1   Methodology

At first glance, measuring and identifying resolvers that extend the TTL seems straightforward: we pick one exit node and request it fetch the domain that resolves IP_1. After its TTL expires, we update its A record to IP_2 and let the same exit node fetch the same domain to see if they connect to IP_1. However, in practice it more difficult, because the client may use multiple DNS resolvers that have many upstream resolvers, thus it may receive multiple DNS responses; this behavior is common mainly to improve the performance; modern public DNS servers usually have multiple caches with complex caching hierarchy [1,28]. However, we are not allowed to see which DNS response the exit node actually

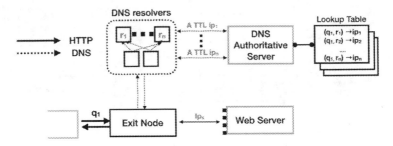

Fig. 2. Our methodology that extends the BrightData platform in Fig. 1. We control the DNS authoritative and web server (shown with green boxes); for the same `qname`, our DNS authoritative server now returns a different `A` record to each different resolver so that we can infer which DNS response the exit node used by monitoring the incoming IP address of HTTP request. (Color figure online)

used, making it hard for us to identify who has extended the TTL. To address these issues, we return *a different A record to each different resolver* so that we can identify which DNS resolver's response the exit node has used by monitoring the incoming IP address of the HTTP request for a certain domain. More specifically, we proceed our experiments as follows as illustrated in Fig. 2.

(a) As the first phase (P_1), we first let an exit node fetch a unique subdomain, `http://<<UID>>.m.com`. We extract the `x-luminati-ip` value from the HTTP response header so that we can choose the same exit node after the TTL expires.

(b) At our authoritative nameserver, for each resolver that looks up the same `qname`, we pick an IP address that has never been used for the `qname` and dynamically generate an `A` to serve the request. Then, we create an entry that maps a tuple of `qname` and the resolver's IP address to the served IP address and insert it to the mapping table. If we observe more DNS resolvers for the same `qname` than N, we discard the exit node from further analysis.

(c) From the webserver, we examine the destination of the IP address of the HTTP request to find the matched DNS resolver's IP address in the mapping table. This allows us to find the DNS resolver that the exit node used.

(d) Then, we immediately *retract* all DNS entries from the DNS authoritative name server to ignore all subsequent DNS requests, and we wait for TTL to let the cached DNS responses expire.

(e) Once TTL expires, we set our authoritative name server to serve `A` that points to the IP address (IP_{new}) that has never been assigned to any DNS resolver. We then use `-ip-XX` option in the HTTP request to choose the same node and let it fetch `http://<<UID>>.m.com` again. We call this step the second phase.

In our experiment, we use 8 (N) different IP addresses based on the observation where 99.9% of HTTP requests incur less than 9 DNS requests.

Ethical Consideration: First of all, we adhere to the Terms of Service of Bright-Data; our experiment followed their terms and condition and only used the commercial services provided by Brightdata network. The peers are always explicitly asked with a clear consent screen to opt-in the proxy network. Additionally, we do not collect any PII of the exit nodes' users and the exit nodes agreed to allow Brightdata to route traffic through themselves in exchange for their free VPN services. Our experiments only involve generating HTTP and DNS queries to the DNS authoritative servers and HTTP servers that we control. Moreover, we do not send any other queries to other domains that we do not control. Thus, we believe that the experiments do not introduce any harm to the proxy service or the exit nodes.

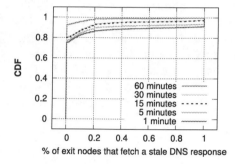

Fig. 3. CDF of the fraction of the exit nodes that use the the stale response for each resolver.

Table 1. Validation results with direct probing and ProxyRack

		Ours	
		Honor.	Ext.
Direct scan	Honor.	197	0
	Ext.	0	16
Proxy rack	Honor.	381	1
	Ext.	0	62

3.2 Results

During our measurement period, we are able to send 2,068,686 unique HTTP queries served by 274,570 unique exit nodes and their 27,131 resolvers[1] in 9,514 ASes across 220 countries.

We also run our experiment with five different TTLs (1, 5, 15, 30, and 60 min) to investigate how TTL values impact on a DNS resolver's caching behavior.

Identifying potential TTL-extending resolvers is straightforward; when we observe an exit node that still connects to the webserver with the old IP address, we can find it by looking up the mapping table and label it as a potential TTL-extending resolver. However, when we observe an exit node that uses the new IP address (IP_{new}), we cannot simply mark all resolvers in the second phase as TTL-honoring resolvers because some resolvers only show up in the first phase. Thus, we mark resolvers as the potential TTL honoring resolvers only when they appear in both the first and second phase.

Since we use exit nodes as a proxy to understand DNS resolvers behavior, we cannot blindly use the results to characterize the DNS resolvers; for example, a

---

[1] Since we are only permitted to observe the only egress resolver IPs querying our authoritative servers, we label each querying IP as a resolver.

stub resolvers on the exit node may extend the TTL making their resolvers look like TTL-extending ones. Thus, we focus on the resolvers where we have at least 5 exit nodes, this sample size allows us to draw strong inferences to characterize their behaviors; this leaves us 9,031 resolvers, and their 234,605 exit nodes across the different TTL setups. Then, for each resolver, we calculate the fraction of the exit nodes that connect to the IP_{old}; Fig. 3 shows the results and we make a number of observations. First, we find that there is a clear separation between TTL-extending resolvers and TTL-honoring resolvers. For example, when we set our TTL values to 60 min, 4,147 (92.5%) resolvers perfectly honor the TTL while 14 (0.31%) resolvers extend TTL; the others (7.1%) show mixed behaviors, which could be due to the stub or other frontend resolvers that we could not measure. Second, we find that *the* number of TTL extending resolvers constantly grows as we decrease the TTL value; for example, the percentage of TTL extending resolvers increases from 14 (0.31%) to 129 (2.53%), 161 (2.87%), 414 (6.53%), and 745 (8.74%) as we decrease the TTL value from 60, 30, 15, 5 and 1 min. Surprisingly, we also find that the set of TTL extending resolvers that we measured with TTL_x is *always* a subset of what we measure with TTL_y if TTL_x is less than TTL_y. This strongly suggests that some resolvers use a default minimum TTL value; this could be due to reduce their resolution load; for example, popular DNS software such as PowerDNS [26], KnotDNS [17] and Unbound [29] has an option for this.

3.3   Cross-validation

We now attempt to cross validate our methodology by focusing on the resolvers that *always* honor (or extend) the TTL with 1 min, which leaves us 7,160 resolvers. For each resolver, we first attempt to directly send DNS queries to test whether they respond, and if so, if they extend the TTL by looking up our domain twice with a time gap of TTL. Since this is likely to allow us to measure public resolvers, we also leverage another residential proxy service, ProxyRack [27] to cover local resolvers as well; the coverage is limited (less than 2+ million residential proxies), but it permits to send an arbitrary UDP traffic so that we can send a DNS request to its local resolver. For each of the rest of the resolvers, we attempt to find exit nodes that share the same AS with the resolver and send DNS requests. Table 1 shows the result; surprisingly, we find that *all 212 resolvers that we could measure show the consistent behaviors our observation.* From the ProxyRack experiment, all 443 resolvers except one show the consistent behavior; we found one resolver that our methodology and a ProxyRack experiment disagree, but could not find the cause.

Interestingly, when we consider the number of TTL extending resolvers, we see more TTL-violating resolvers in ProxyRack experiments than the direct scanning (i.e., 14.0% vs. 7.5%). Since direct scanning only allows us to measure the public resolvers, it may indicate that the local resolvers are more likely to extend TTLs; we will explore this in the following section. In summary, we confirm that our methodology can accurately find the TTL-extension policy of DNS resolvers.

3.4   Macroscopic Analysis

To obtain a macroscopic view of TTL extension phenomena, we first map ASes to ISPs (as one ISP may operate many ASes) and countries using CAIDA's AS-organizations dataset [8]. Next, we group exit nodes according to country and AS, and focus on the groups where we have at five exit nodes. We first notice that the exit nodes that fetch expired DNS responses are widely spread across the globe; Table 2 shows the top 15 countries sorted by the fraction of exit nodes that use TTL-extending resolvers. For example, we found that in Togo, more than 85% of exit nodes we measured experienced TTL extension.

Table 2. Top fifteen countries sorted by the fraction of exit nodes that use TTL-extending resolvers

Rank	Country	Exit nodes		Ratio
		w/ TTL-extended	Total	
1	Togo	91	106	85.84%
2	China	1,514	2,425	62.43%
3	Réunion	112	189	59.26%
4	Jamaica	175	481	36.38%
5	Sint Maarten	137	455	30.12%
6	France	81	329	24.62%
7	Ivory Coast	68	288	23.61%
8	Cayman Islands	105	461	22.77%
9	Ireland	347	1,726	20.1%
10	Switzerland	141	704	20.02%
11	Spain	489	2,603	18.79%
12	Myanmar	136	762	17.85%
13	Germany	36	226	15.93%
14	Finland	300	1,912	15.69%
15	Russia	8,808	57,283	15.38%

Now, we focus on individual DNS resolvers; as we have observed from the validation results, local resolvers tend to have more TTL-extending resolvers than that of the public ones. Now, we try to find local resolvers by grouping exit nodes by the DNS resolver.

Again, to minimize potential client side impact, we focus on those where we observe at least 5 exit nodes using the DNS resolver.

We then identify ISP-provided DNS servers as ones where all exit nodes and the DNS server belong to the same ISP. With this method, we have identified 6,871 ISP-provided DNS resolvers in our measurement. Table 3 shows the top 15 local resolvers, *all of which exit nodes always receive the old, TTL-expired,*

Table 3. Table showing the top 15 local resolvers that extend TTLs.

Country	ISP	DNS servers	Exit nodes
Russia	PSJC Vimpelcom	16	366
	PSJC Rostelecom	12	124
	Net By Net	8	58
	TIS Dialog	6	108
	MTS PSJC	4	69
	MSK-IX	4	36
China	China Telecom	13	125
	China Mobile	7	39
	Tianjin Provincial	5	50
	China Unicom	4	27
South Africa	MTN SA	6	49
	Neology	5	97
Cayman Islands	Cable & Wireless	7	88
Hong Kong	HGC Global Communications	4	38
Trinidad and Tobago	Columbus Comm	6	115
Turkey	Netonline Billisim	5	84

responses. The majority of these ISPs and DNS resolvers are in Russia and China; for example, we measure 13 local resolvers in China Telecom, *all of which extend TTL*; this strongly suggests that the TTL extension is imposed by the ISP.

3.5 Impact of TTL Extension: Case Study of CDNs

It is known that CDN typically uses short TTLs for performance (e.g., load-balancing) or security reasons [11,23]; for example, if a PoP (Point of Presence) experiences outages, a short TTL can help them rapidly direct traffic to a different one. Thus, TTL-extending resolvers may hurt their responsiveness; for example, Moura et al. [21] found that A records have relatively shorter TTLs than other record types due to dynamic changes of server addresses in clouds and CDNs. We now focus on Tranco 1M domains [25] and try to identify domains that use CDNs. We note that most CDNs use DNS-based redirection scheme such as Akamai [23] to redirect users to CDN infrastructures by using Canonical Name (CNAME) records; for example, when a user requests a domain, www.reddit.com, it will redirect to another domain controlled by Fastly, so that they can handle the request as shown below.

```
$ dig www.reddit.com
...
;; ANSWER SECTION:
www.reddit.com.          3600    IN  CNAME   reddit.map.fastly.net.
reddit.map.fastly.net    60      IN  A       151.101.1.140
```

Table 4. Top 10 CDNs and their TTL of expanded A records used by most of their domains

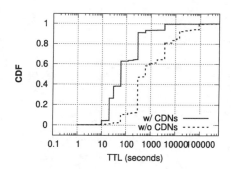

Fig. 4. CDF of TTLs in the Tranco top 1 million domains

CDN	TTL	Domains
Akamai	20	12,247 (99.9%)
CloudFlare	300	10,736 (98.7%)
Cloudfront	60	9,642 (99.8%)
Fastly	30	6,237 (98.6%)
Google	300	2,759 (98.8%)
Azure	10	2,536 (47.0%)
Netlify	20	1,531 (98.2%)
XCDN	20	99 (47.8%)
Alibaba	120	91 (58.7%)
CDN77	15	68 (91.8%)

We use a OpenINTEL dataset [24] that collects A records of Tranco Top 1M domains including full CNAME expansion. For each domain, we focus on whether a CNAME record exists in its lookup and whether the CNAME record was used to direct traffic to popular CDNs; in order to do so, we manually compiled the list of CNAME patterns for popular CDNs (e.g., e[1-9]*.a.akamaiedge.net for Akamai), which contains 38 CDNs in total.[2] Fig. 4 shows the CDF of the TTL of the A records after their CNAMEs are expanded. We immediately notice that the TTL of A records from CDN is much shorter than the rest of domains; for example, 38% of TTLs from CDNs is less than 60 s. Considering that we have found that 8.74% of resolvers extend the TTL when it is less than or equal to 60 s (Sect. 3.2), this indicates that these resolvers will extend the TTLs for more than 38% of CDN-managed websites, which potentially hurt their responsiveness. For example, we find that Akamai sets the TTL to 20 s for 99.9% of their domains; Table 4 shows the TTL values for the top 10 CDNs in terms of the number of domains they serve and we can find that most of them use very short TTLs (e.g., 10 s for Azure).

---

[2] Our methodology can miss domains that delegate its name server to CDNs by replacing their NS records with CDN's ones. We could potentially identify them by checking whether both of their web server and DNS server are managed by the same CDN. However, some companies (e.g., Alibaba and Google) also provide VPS hosting service, which will cause false-positive (e.g., the domain owner manages both servers within the same VPS), thus we only focus on the CNAME expansion information.

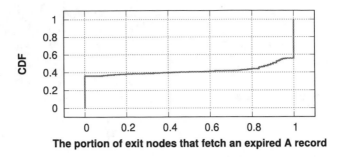

Fig. 5. 44.1% of resolvers serve expired (thus invalid) DNS responses.

4   TTL Violation in DNSSEC

When it comes to DNSSEC, the TTL in a DNS response is not the only attribute that determines the caching period; a DNSSEC-signed response can come with its signature, which is called `RRSIG` records. `RRSIG` records also carry `inception` and `expiration dates` that limits its validity, thus DNSSEC-supporting resolvers *must evict DNS responses of which `RRSIG`s are expired from the cache, even if their TTL is not expired yet* [2]. Now, we also examine whether DNSSEC-supporting resolvers in the wild correctly honor TTL values for signed DNS records by expanding our methodology.

Experiment Settings: We follow the similar methodology as presented in Sect. 3.1. Additionally, we make our domain name fully signed (e.g., uploading a `DS` record to the parent zone) and provide DNS responses of which signature expires earlier than its TTL. More specifically, we set our TTL value to 60 min for `A` records and other DNSSEC-related records, and their corresponding `RRSIG`s to be invalidated in 30 min. After sending the first request, we make the second request after the `expiration date`, *but within TTL* to see whether the resolver fetches a fresh `A` from the authoritative server.

Results: We run our measurement from October 27th, 2022 to Nov 1st, 2022 and obtain 91,634 exit nodes and 13,679 DNS resolvers. For the rest of this section, we now focus on DNS resolvers where we observed at least 5 exit nodes to minimize the potential client-side impacts, which leaves us 5,274 (38.5%) resolvers with 75,684 (82.6%) exit nodes.

DNSSEC-Validating Resolvers: DNSSEC-validating resolvers must specify `DO` ("DNSSEC OK") bit in the EDNS prseudorecord so that the DNS authoritative servers can provide the `RRSIG`s and other DNSSEC-related records. In our measurement, we find 4,917 (93.2%) resolvers covering 94% (71,242) of exit nodes enabled `DO`, which indicates that the majority of DNS resolvers *seem* to support DNSSEC. However, not all DNS resolvers with `DO` correctly support DNSSEC. For example, a study [6] found that 82% do not validate the response even though they have requested and received `RRSIG` records. To consider the only DNSSEC-validating resolvers, we make exit nodes to send another HTTP requests, which is incorrectly signed (i.e., the RRSIG of A record is cryptographically invalid); thus, if an exit node can only fetch the correct record, it indicates that its DNS resolver actually performs DNSSEC validation. With the additional step, we find 646 (13.1)% resolvers covering 6,001 (8.4%) exit nodes perform validation.

DNSSEC-Validating Resolvers with TTL Violation: We now calculate the percentage of exit nodes that fetch an expired DNS record for each resolver. As shown in Fig. 5, we find that 475 (73.6%) resolvers show consistent behavior among the exit nodes; 190 (29.4%) resolvers (with 1,505 exit nodes) have fetched the DNS response again from our authoritative server, which indicates that the resolvers evicted the DNS responses with expired RRSIGs. However, 285 (44.1% of considered) resolvers (with 2,645 exit nodes) have served the second client request from its cache without making the second request to the authoritative server, which is a direct violation of the DNSSEC standard [2].

5   Concluding Discussion

In this paper, we have leveraged a residential proxy network, BrightData, to measure TTL violations in resolvers. BrightData manages millions of exit nodes, which potentially opens an opportunity for researchers to understand DNS resolvers in the wild. However, since we are not permitted to directly send DNS requests to DNS resolvers, we developed a methodology to pinpoint which DNS response an exit node uses and which DNS resolver disregard TTL; we identified 745 resolvers that extend TTL values and 285 DNSSEC-validating resolvers that do not consider validity period in cache. Before concluding the paper, we wish to discuss our limitation and measuring resolvers that shorten the TTL.

Limitation: If an exit node uses a DNS resolver that leverages a multi-layer distributed caching infrastructure like Cloudflare [28], our methodology can only measure the backend caching DNS resolvers because we can only monitor the incoming DNS requests to the authoritative server. This makes it hard for us to determine where the TTL violation exactly happens; it could be due to the frontend caches, stub resolvers, or middleboxes. Thus, we have only focused on the resolvers that we are able to measure at least from five exit nodes that show consistent behavior, which provides more confidence on our inference, but costs us to lose the number of resolvers that we could analyze.

TTL Shortening in the Wild: A DNS resolver may cache the DNS response shorter than the TTL; unlike TTL extension, however, caching DNS records shorter than the TTL is not any violation of the DNS standard since RFC 2181 [10]. We can use a similar methodology to detect resolvers that cache DNS records shorter than the TTL set by the authoritative server; for example, some resolvers may have a parameter that determines the maximum TTL mainly not to trust very large TTL values for security purpose [29] [5]. However, resolvers can also decide to evict the cached DNS response depending on its cache size and eviction policy, which makes it a bit hard to consistently capture DNS resolvers that always cache shorter than the TTL. By making the second request earlier than the TTL, we are able to measure 49 (0.99%, out of 4,965) resolvers that *always* shorten the TTL and 4653 (93.7%) resolvers that always preserve the original TTL, but we also find 263 (5.3%) resolvers showing mixed behaviors, which suggests that their eviction policy might have impacted on, and eventually, makes it hard for us to further investigate.

Acknowledgments. We thank the anonymous reviewers and our shepherd, Paul Schmitt, for their helpful comments. We also thank BrightData for their credits to use the service. This research was supported in part by NSF grants CNS-2053363 and CNS-2051166, and 4-VA, a collaborative partnership for advancing the Commonwealth of Virginia.

References

1. Amit, K., Haya, S., Michael, W.: Counting in the Dark: DNS caches discovery and enumeration in the internet. IEEE Comput. Soc. DSN (2017)
2. Arends, R., Austein, R., Larson, M., Massey, D., Rose, S.: DNS security introduction and requirements. RFC 4033, IETF (2005). http://www.ietf.org/rfc/rfc4033.txt
3. Alzoubi, H.A., Rabinovich, M.I., Spatscheck, O.: The anatomy of LDNS clusters: findings and implications for web content delivery. In: WWW (2013)
4. Blank, S., Goldsten, P., Loder, T., Zinkn, T., Bradshaw, M.: Brand indicators for message identification (BIMI). In: IETF (2021)
5. BIND max-cache-ttl. https://bind9.readthedocs.io/en/v9_18_7/reference.html?highlight=max-cache-ttl
6. Chung, T., et al.: A longitudinal. End-to-end view of the DNSSEC ecosystem, In: USENIX Security (2017)
7. Callahan, T., Allman, M., Rabinovich, R.: On modern DNS behavior and properties. CCR **43**(4) (2013)
8. CAIDA ASOrganizations Dataset. http://www.caida.org/data/as-organizations/
9. DNS based load-balancing. https://www.cloudflare.com/learning/performance/what-is-dns-load-balancing/
10. Elz, R., Bush, R.: Clarifications to the DNS specification. RFC 2181, IETF (1997)
11. Edge and Browser Cache TTL. https://developers.cloudflare.com/cache/about/edge-browser-cache-ttl/
12. Flavel, A., Mani, P., Maltz, D.A.: Re-evaluating the responsiveness of DNS-based network control. In: LANMAN (2014)
13. Hoffman, P., Schlyter, J.: The DNS-based authentication of named entities (DANE) transport layer security (TLS) protocol: TLSA. RFC 6698, IETF (2012)
14. Hola VPN. http://hola.org/
15. Jeffrey, P., Aditya, A., Anees, S., Balachander, K., Srinivasan, S.: On the responsiveness of DNS-based network control. In: IMC (2004)
16. Kyle, S., Tom, C., Michael, R., Mark, A.: On measuring the client-side DNS infrastructure. In: IMC (2013)
17. cache-min-ttl in KnotDNS. https://knot-resolver.readthedocs.io/en/stable/daemon-bindings-cache.html

18. Mario, A., Alessandro, F., Diego, P., Narseo, V.-R., Matteo, V.: Dissecting DNS stakeholders in mobile networks. In: CoNEXT (2017)

19. Margolis, D., Risher, M., Ramakrishnan, B., Brotman, A., Jones, J.: SMTP MTA strict transport security (MTA-STS). RFC 8461, IETF (2018)

20. Moura, G.: DNS TTL violations in the wild - measured with RIPE atlas. https://labs.ripe.net/author/giovane_moura/dns-ttl-violations-in-the-wild-measured-with-ripe-atlas

21. Moura, G., Heidemann, J., Schmidt, R.D.O., Hardaker, W.: Cache me if you can: effects of DNS time-to-live. In: IMC (2019)

22. Mockapetris, P.: Domain Names - Concepts and Facilities. RFC 1034, IETF (1987)

23. Nygren, E., Sitaraman, R.K., Sun, J.: The Akamai network: a platform for high-performance internet applications. OSR **44**(3) (2010)

24. OpenINTEL. https://www.openintel.nl/

25. Pochat, V.L., Goethem, T.V., Tajalizadehkhoob, S., Korczyński, M., Joosen, W.: TRANCO: a research-oriented top sites ranking hardened against manipulation. In: NDSS (2019)

26. minimum-ttl-override option in PowerDNS. https://doc.powerdns.com/recursor/settings.html#minimum-ttl-override

27. ProxyRack. https://www.proxyrack.com

28. Randall, A., et al.: Trufflehunter: cache snooping rare domains at large public DNS resolvers. In: IMC (2020)

29. Cache-min-ttl, Cache-max-ttl option in Unbound. https://nlnetlabs.nl/documentation/unbound/unbound.conf/

Operational Domain Name Classification: From Automatic Ground Truth Generation to Adaptation to Missing Values

Jan Bayer[1]([✉]), Ben Chukwuemeka Benjamin[1], Sourena Maroofi[2],
Thymen Wabeke[3], Cristian Hesselman[3,4], Andrzej Duda[1],
and Maciej Korczyński[1]

[1] Univ. of Grenoble Alpes, CNRS, Grenoble INP, LIG, Grenoble, France
{jan.bayer,ben.benjamin,andrzej.duda,
maciej.korczynski}@univ-grenoble-alpes.fr
[2] KOR Labs Cybersecurity, Grenoble, France
[3] SIDN Labs, Arnhem, The Netherlands
[4] University of Twente, Enschede, The Netherlands

Abstract. With more than 350 million active domain names and at least 200,000 newly registered domains per day, it is technically and economically challenging for Internet intermediaries involved in domain registration and hosting to monitor them and accurately assess whether they are benign, likely registered with malicious intent, or have been compromised. This observation motivates the design and deployment of automated approaches to support investigators in preventing or effectively mitigating security threats. However, building a domain name classification system suitable for deployment in an operational environment requires meticulous design: from feature engineering and acquiring the underlying data to handling missing values resulting from, for example, data collection errors. The design flaws in some of the existing systems make them unsuitable for such usage despite their high theoretical accuracy. Even worse, they may lead to erroneous decisions, for example, by registrars, such as suspending a benign domain name that has been compromised at the website level, causing collateral damage to the legitimate registrant and website visitors.

In this paper, we propose novel approaches to designing domain name classifiers that overcome the shortcomings of some existing systems. We validate these approaches with a prototype based on the COMAR (COmpromised versus MAliciously Registered domains) system focusing on its careful design, automated and reliable ground truth generation, feature selection, and the analysis of the extent of missing values. First, our classifier takes advantage of automatically generated ground truth based on publicly available domain name registration data. We then generate a large number of machine-learning models, each dedicated to handling a set of missing features: if we need to classify a domain name with a given set of missing values, we use the model without the missing feature set, thus allowing classification based on all other features. We estimate the

A. Brunstrom et al. (Eds.): PAM 2023, LNCS 13882, pp. 564–591, 2023.
https://doi.org/10.1007/978-3-031-28486-1_24

importance of features using scatter plots and analyze the extent of missing values due to measurement errors.

Finally, we apply the COMAR classifier to unlabeled phishing URLs and find, among other things, that 73% of corresponding domain names are maliciously registered. In comparison, only 27% are benign domains hosting malicious websites. The proposed system has been deployed at two ccTLD registry operators to support their anti-fraud practices.

Keywords: DNS · Domain name abuse · Classification · Phishing · Malicious domain registration · Compromised websites

1   Introduction

Attackers have traditionally used domain names to spread malware, ensure reliable communication between malicious command-and-control (C&C) servers and botnets using domain generation algorithms (DGAs), or to launch spam or phishing campaigns. A domain name can be registered for a legitimate purpose by a benign registrant or with malicious intent by an attacker. A benign domain name can also be compromised at the hosting, domain, or website level, and involved in malicious activities later in its lifetime.

With more than 350 million active domain names[1] and at least 200 thousand newly registered domains per day,[2] it is technically and economically challenging for top-level domain (TLD) registries and registrars to scrutinize them at the time of registration and accurately assess whether they are benign or likely registered with malicious intent. Furthermore, once a domain name is involved in a malicious activity, and the abusive URL is blacklisted, or reported to the operator's helpdesk, an investigator must gather evidence on whether the domain name is attacker-owned (i.e., registered by a malicious actor) or has been compromised (and possibly how) before deciding on the type of the mitigation action. While a maliciously registered domain name can be suspended, a benign and subsequently hacked domain name generally cannot be blocked because it may cause collateral damage to the harmless domain name owner and regular visitors of legitimate websites available under the benign domain name. Instead, the webmaster or the hosting provider should remove the malicious content (e.g., malware or phishing website) from the server and patch the vulnerable application to prevent future intrusions [48].

The problem of DNS abuse and domain names being a vehicle for delivering malicious content [5,27,28,36,47] motivates the development and implementation of automated methods to support investigators in assessing domain name maliciousness as well as appropriate and prompt mitigation of security threats. To address these challenges, several research studies proposed domain name reputation systems based on machine learning (ML) to distinguish between benign

---

[1] https://www.verisign.com/assets/domain-name-report-Q22022.pdf.
[2] https://zonefiles.io.

registrations and the malicious ones [4,6,7,15,16,20,24,31,33,45] as well as compromised domain names and those owned by attackers [10,29,34].

However, building a fully automated domain name classification system that can be effectively used and deployed in an operational environment requires meticulous design: from feature engineering and acquiring the underlying data to handling missing values resulting from measurement and data collection errors. The design flaws of existing classifiers may make them unsuitable in operational environments despite their high theoretical accuracy. Even worse, incorrect classification may lead to misguided decisions by intermediaries such as the suspension of a benign domain name, causing collateral damage to their legitimate users and the painstaking process of reclaiming the domain by its rightful registrant.

Most of the proposed systems make use of privileged, closed, or pay-walled data (e.g., passive DNS, non-public registration information, retail pricing of domain names, or search engine results). Therefore, building such classifiers can be costly or complicated for those involved in DNS operations to assess and mitigate domain name abuse and challenging for researchers to replicate previous scientific results.

Furthermore, since the domain name classifiers often use supervised machine learning methods, researchers strive for high-quality ground truth data to train robust models. Their sources vary from one study to another: some rely on third-party sources such as Google Safe Browsing [24], some others on website or domain popularity ranking lists [4,24], or blacklists [4,20,24], while lacking insight into the underlying proprietary methodology used by their providers. Another approach to obtain high-quality ground truth data is to manually label the dataset [10,34]. However, it is a time-consuming process requiring expert knowledge and the datasets may quickly become outdated.

Another design issue is related to handling missing values in ground truth and unlabeled data. Previous methods tended to impute missing values using statistical methods (e.g., the mean of a group [13,31]). Maroofi et al. [34] proposed another approach to deal with missing values: use other available data for selected features (e.g., estimating the domain registration date based on privileged passive DNS). However, not all proposed methods can be applied to different types of features. Moreover, as models are often trained and evaluated on data with a complete feature value vector, the domain names with missing values arising from, for example, measurement errors, may not be classified. The number of unclassified cases may be significant and can affect the operational utility of the deployed domain classifier.

In this paper, we propose novel approaches to designing domain name classifiers that overcome the shortcomings of existing systems. We present a method to automatically generate ground truth based on publicly available domain name registration data. We generate a large number of ML models, each dedicated to handling a set of missing features: if we need to classify a domain name with a given set of missing values, we use the model without the missing feature set thus supporting classification based on all other features. The proposed design principles apply to any domain name classifier.

We validate these approaches with a prototype based on the COMAR (COm-promised versus MAliciously Registered domains) system [34] focusing on its careful design, automated and reliable ground truth generation, feature selection, the analysis of the extent of missing values resulting from measurement errors, and on its extensive evaluation.

We also apply the implemented classifier to 20 months of phishing data, study selected characteristics of the domain names of malicious URLs, and analyze their distribution across different types of TLDs. The system has shown its suitability for efficiently classifying compromised and maliciously registered domain names as two country-code TLD (ccTLD) operators have deployed it to support their DNS anti-abuse practices.

Our contributions can be summarized as follows:

- We develop a novel technique for automatically generating ground-truth data for compromised (benign) and maliciously registered domains. It consists of measuring the mitigation actions on abusive domains by TLD registries, registrars, and hosting providers.
- We propose a visualization method to assess the importance of features using scatter plots and analyze the features most likely to be missing due to measurement errors.
- We propose an approach based on multiple trained models to account for missing values, as opposed to traditional methods based on imputing missing values using statistical methods.
- We apply the COMAR classifier to domain names extracted from phishing URLs and find that while for legacy gTLDs and ccTLDs between 27% and 31% of abused domains are benign but possibly exploited at the website level, the vast majority of new gTLD domain names are maliciously registered.
- As many as 66.1% of the maliciously registered domain names have no specific technology on their homepages. In comparison, 52.2% of compromised domains use more than five different frameworks and plugins to build the website, making them more susceptible to web application attacks.

2 Background and Related Work

Several researchers proposed domain name classifiers to address the problem of domain name abuse [4,6,7,10,15,16,20,24,29,31,33,34,45]. Many studies provided domain name reputation scores indicative of whether they are malicious (i.e., registered by a miscreant for cybercriminal purposes) or benign (i.e., registered by a benign user for legitimate purposes) [4,6,7,15,16,20,24,31,33,45]. Some recent work proposed distinguishing between maliciously registered and benign but compromised domain names [10,29,34]. The last type corresponds to the domains taken over by attackers, for example, through vulnerabilities in libraries or frameworks such as content management systems used to build websites. In this section, we identify the key challenges in domain name classification and discuss how the existing methods address them.

2.1   Data and Feature Selection

After formulating the classification problem and the outcomes (i.e., labels), one of the starting points in designing any domain name classifier is the selection of data sources and *features* for distinguishing between two groups of domain names (e.g., benign and malicious).

The primary criterion for selecting data sources is their availability. Datasets used in DNS reputation systems can be either publicly or non-publicly available. The privileged or commercial sources such as the passive DNS data used in the Exposure [6,7], Notos [4], or Predator [20] are only limited to those who have access to such data. Historical data raise a similar problem (e.g., historical WHOIS data used in the takedown of Avalanche [31]). Furthermore, reproducibility and performance validation of the systems relying on non-publicly available data by independent researchers may be difficult or impossible.

On the other hand, systems based on publicly available data sources do not have the problems raised by non-public data sources and can still achieve high accuracy. Moreover, they are more likely adopted by the involved operators, not only DNS intermediaries but also, for example, law enforcement agencies [31].

The Mentor [24] and Domain Classifier [29] systems used public data sources and demonstrated high accuracy. De Silva et al. [10] combined public and non-public (passive DNS data from Farsight [14]) data sources to achieve 97.2% accuracy. COMAR [34] used both publicly and non-publicly available data to distinguish between compromised and maliciously registered domain names and concluded that when removing the non-publicly available passive DNS, it achieves an accuracy of up to 97%.

In Sect. 3.2, we critically revisit relevant features and select those that do not use privileged or commercial data sources.

2.2   Feature Importance

Feature importance refers to techniques that assign a score to input features (e.g., domain name popularity, domain name age, etc.) based on the extent to which they contribute to the prediction of the target variable (e.g., classification of benign versus maliciously registered domain names). Ranking features according to their importance shows which features are irrelevant and can be omitted. It reduces the dimensionality of the model, its complexity, the need to collect data, and makes it possible to estimate the impact of missing features on the system.

In the DNS reputation systems we reviewed, only Hao et al. [20], Maroofi et al. [34], and Le Pochat et al. [31] documented feature importance of the proposed models. Note that even the most important feature, if it is missing from the dataset (and its value cannot be estimated), cannot contribute to the prediction of the target variable. Therefore, we analyze the extent of missing values resulting from measurement errors in Sect. 3.4, discuss feature importance in Sect. 3.6, and show how missing values of selected features affect the classification of domains using scatter plots.

2.3   Ground Truth

The reviewed systems use classifiers to distinguish between malicious, compromised, and benign domain names. The quality and quantity of ground truth data largely determines the ability to train and evaluate a classifier correctly. Table 1 shows different approaches to building ground truth datasets used in previous work. Some of them rely on third-party services such as Google Safe Browsing (GSB) [18], PhishLabs [41], McAfee SiteAdvisor [43], or Alexa [2], some leverage publicly available datasets created by other work [8]. Some others create their ground truth datasets by manually labeling domain names.

Table 1. Comparison of ground truth datasets in different DNS reputation systems (T: Total, M: Malicious, B/C: Benign or Compromised).

Proposed system	Ground truth source	T	M	B/C
Predator [20]	McAfee SiteAdvisor [43], Spamhaus [44] URIBL [50] Internal spam trap	769,464	512,976	256,488
Domain Classifier [29]	PhisLabs [41], DeltaPhish [8]	10,150	9,475	675
De Silva et al. [10]	Manual labeling	3,278	1,889	1,389
COMAR [34]	Manual labeling	2,329	1,199	1,130
Mentor [24]	GSB [18], https://malwaredomains.com/, https://malwaredomains.com/, Alexa [2]	1,430	930	500
Notos [4]	SURBL [46], Alexa [2]	–	–	–

The advantage of third-party services is their availability, ease of use, and timeliness. However, researchers do not have full insight into the proprietary methods used by third-party vendors to label the data. Therefore, such datasets cannot be fully trusted. For instance, Le Page et al. investigated phishing URLs that, according to PhishLabs, were most likely using compromised domains and found instances of obviously maliciously registered domains [29]. Another approach is to use GSB to generate ground truth data. Since the ultimate purpose of GSB is to protect end users from accessing malicious content regardless of the domain state, the dataset cannot be used 'as is' to label malicious registrations.

With manual labeling, researchers carefully select the source and methodology for such data. However, it requires expert knowledge and a considerable amount of time. In some cases, the labeling process is not trivial (the expert is unable to make a reliable assessment of the maliciousness of a domain name). It can introduce inaccuracies (if the domain is incorrectly labeled) or biases (if such corner cases are skipped and not included in the model). Furthermore, its time-consuming nature often discourages researchers from updating ground truth data and retraining models. A similar problem can arise when using data from previous work—it may be outdated, and thus, it may not include evasion techniques recently used by attackers. Therefore, in Sect. 3.1, we propose a novel approach to automatically generate ground truth data for such systems. It consists of measuring the mitigation actions on abusive domain names by TLD registries, registrars, and hosting providers and can be applied to different domain classification problems.

2.4   COMAR System

We validate the proposed approaches with a prototype that extends COMAR (COmpromised versus MAliciously Registered domains) [34]—a domain name classification system that distinguishes domain names from blacklisted URLs as compromised or maliciously registered with an accuracy of 97%. It consists of three modules: a data collection module, a feature extraction module, and a classification module. The data collection module acquires data on domain names from phishing and malware delivery blacklists. The feature extraction module extracts 38 features, grouped into seven categories: lexical features, ranking and popularity features, passive DNS features, content-based features, WHOIS and TLD-based features, TLS certificate features, and active DNS features. The classification module uses a trained Logistic Regression model to predict the output class (compromised or maliciously registered domain name).

We have chosen COMAR as it combines new features with those proposed by earlier systems, demonstrates high accuracy, and we have access to its implementation. In contrast to its initial design and performance evaluation, we train multiple models on automatically generated ground truth data to account for missing values and extensively evaluate its performance. Finally, we apply COMAR to unlabeled data and present selected statistics for domain names extracted from phishing URLs over a 20-month period.

3   Methodology

In this section, we discuss in detail the methodology to generate ground truth data automatically, the prototype implementation of the classifier, and the practical approach to overcoming the problem of missing values.

3.1   Automated Generation of Ground Truth

The automated ground truth generation method takes advantage of the type of mitigation actions undertaken by the relevant intermediaries involved in domain registration and hosting. After a domain name is involved in malicious activity and the abusive URL is blacklisted or reported to the operator, the TLD registry or registrar must first collect evidence of whether the domain has been maliciously registered or compromised before deciding on the type of mitigation action. A malicious domain name can be blocked at the DNS level. In contrast, a benign and later hacked domain name cannot be blocked without interrupting benign services related to the domain name. In this case, the webmaster or hosting provider (possibly a reseller) should only remove the malicious content from the server, such as a malware download or a phishing site, and patch the vulnerable application to prevent future intrusions. Based on these generally accepted mitigation practices [11], we design the measurement setup to automatically distinguish between compromised and malicious domains.

Maliciously Registered Domains. The most common mitigation action for a malicious domain used by registries or registrars consists of removing the domain name from the zone, which makes the domain effectively nonexistent (`NXDOMAIN`). While technically this procedure is sufficient to make the domain name and hosted services inaccessible via the public DNS, it is also essential to prevent re-registration of the domain name at the registry/registrar level. Therefore, it is necessary to change its registration status through the Extensible Provisioning Protocol (EPP) [21] indicating that the domain name is not only taken down but unavailable for any change. This effect is achieved by setting the EPP domain registration status code to `clientHold` (set by the registrar) or `serverHold` (set by the TLD registry) [22].

To generate a list of maliciously registered domain names automatically, we collect registration information using either the Registration Data Access Protocol (RDAP) [38] or WHOIS [9] protocols for domains that appeared in the Anti-Phishing Working Group (APWG) [3] or PhishTank [49] URL blacklists between January 2021 and September 2022. We extract the creation and expiration dates of the domain name, and the EPP status codes. Six months later, we again collect the registration information data for domains expected to be active (i.e., the expiration date is after the date of the second measurement). A recent study shows that the uptime of malicious domain names (i.e., the time between URL blacklisting and mitigating abuse) in all TLDs does not exceed three months [5]. We select the conservative interval between two measurements to six months to ensure that relevant intermediaries have enough time to identify abuse, assess the maliciousness of the registered domain name, and proceed with the appropriate mitigation action. If the EPP status code of the domain name is `clientHold` or `serverHold`, we automatically label such a domain as maliciously registered and conclude that the accredited registrar or TLD registry has suspended the domain name. Note that Alowaisheq et al. [1] excluded domain names with one of the two hold status codes and `pendingDelete`, `redemptionPeriod`, or `autorenewPeriod` in their algorithm for identifying domain delisting. However, we argue that these status codes should not appear before the expiration of benign domains. We analyzed our ground truth data set and found only 2 out of 12,179 records flagged with one of the three status codes alongside the hold status. After a manual investigation of these samples registered at two different registrars, we found that both were maliciously registered and were in `redemptionPeriod` while not yet expired.

Finally, it is important to verify that the domain name creation date for both measurements (i.e., at the time of blacklisting and six months later) remains unchanged to ensure that the mitigation action is related to the activity of the original registrant. If it is not the case, it might be possible that such a domain was blacklisted, removed from the zone, later became available for registration, and re-registered.

Compromised Domain Names. To generate the ground truth dataset for compromised domain names, we first use browser emulation to collect the content and the title of the index page hosted at the root directory of the apex domain and the corresponding URL reported by APWG and Phistank at the time of blacklisting. For instance, for a given URL `https://a.example.com/_boa/login.html`, we visit the index page of the registered domain name (`https://example.com`) and keep track of the HTTP status code and the title of the webpage. We deliberately choose to visit the index page hosted at the registered domain name rather than at the subdomain level. As the DNS-level takedown actions target registered domain names, our system does not consider content hosted on subdomains relevant for assessing the maliciousness of the registered domain.

Six months later, we fetch the content of the originally blacklisted URL using browser emulation. We only keep URLs returning a 404 HTTP status code, i.e., the pages whose content is not available anymore (it was taken down). Note that the use of browser emulation is important at this stage as some malicious websites use bot evasion techniques [52] and we need to eliminate the URLs that seem to be unavailable as the result of cloaking. During this measurement, we also extract the title of the index page of the registered domain. We choose the domains whose index page is available (HTTP status code 200) and whose title stayed unchanged for six months. We are aware that such an approach is conservative; however, it can only lead to a decrease in the size of the ground truth dataset. We observed many cases where the content hosted at the URL was taken down at the web hosting level (e.g., webpage indicating the website was not found), but the status code of the HTTP response remained 200. The combination of these conditions guarantees that the malicious content had been taken down by the webmaster or hosting provider but the domain webpage stayed intact as it represents the benign part of services served under the domain name and thus indicating that the website was compromised.

After excluding public apex domains belonging to legitimate services such as URL shorteners,[3] dynamic DNS, or subdomain providers,[4] we have identified 3,632 compromised and 12,179 maliciously registered domain names. One of the reasons for the imbalance between the two datasets is the conservative approach we have chosen for labeling compromised domains. We have decided to inspect whether the title of each domain homepage has changed within six months, excluding all domains that modified their titles. For instance, we have observed changes in which webpage administrators prepend/append characters to the titles of the benign domain names: `Example - Homepage` became

---

[3] https://github.com/korlabsio/urlshortener.

[4] https://github.com/korlabsio/subdomain_providers.

Example - Homepage ### and thus, the page was automatically excluded
from the compromised dataset even though the title still contains the original
string.

3.2   Feature Selection

We next critically revisit 38 proposed features originally used by the COMAR
system [34], exclude features that use privileged or unavailable data and remove
irrelevant features.

1. Bing search engine results. As discussed by the authors of the COMAR system, it is a paid service, therefore, we exclude it.
2. Features depending on passive DNS. The access to passive DNS data is privileged and related features proved to have a negligible impact on the performance [34].
3. TLD maliciousness index.[5] It is calculated by Spamhaus [44] and is not available for commercial use.
4. The relationship between the domain name and the hosted content. Original
   COMAR extracts keywords from the domain name and generates their syn-
   onyms using a commercial API. They then determine if the domain name is
   related to its content based on the occurrence of the keywords and their syn-
   onyms in the text of the home page. Since the API is not publicly available
   at the time of writing, we decided to remove this feature.
5. Quantcast ranking system is not publicly available anymore.
6. TLS certificate price. It is not trivial to distinguish between free and paid
   certificates since some certificate authorities (e.g., Comodo CA1) offer both
   paid and free certificates.
7. Presence of a TLS certificate. We exclude the presence of the Transport Layer
   Security (TLS) certificate from our features since the use of TLS certificates
   among malicious and benign but compromised domains used in phishing is
   comparable (see Sect. 4.1).
8. Valid TLS certificate. For shared hosts, if a certificate is not valid (e.g., wrong
   host error), we cannot conclude if the malicious actor issued a wrong certificate or if the certificate belongs to another domain on the same (shared)
   hosting service. Therefore, this feature is not suitable for operational deployments.
9. TLD price. The TLD price is not unique among all registrars and resellers,
   and changes over time. In addition, special offers from registrars or domain
   resellers can drastically reduce the price for a specific TLD. It is also difficult
   to collect such data at scale.

Based on this analysis, we remove 13 features and train the model with the
remaining 25 features using Logistic Regression. We analyze the coefficients and
remove features that are not important for the model. We present the final set

---

[5] https://www.spamhaus.org/statistics/tlds/.

of the 17 remaining features in Table 2. Note that the *is_in_alexa* (F14) feature was only available before the termination of service announced by Alexa in May 2022.[6] Since this feature is unavailable for only three of the twenty months of phishing data collected, we keep it and use the method of handling missing values as explained in Sect. 3.3. However, it can be replaced by the Tranco top sites ranking [30] in future work. For *has_famous_brand_name* (F2), we used the list of target brand names provided by PhishTank. We consider this binary feature to be true if a domain name contains one of these trademarks. We use a similar method to the one proposed by Kintis et al. [25]. However, as our work does not only focus on combo squatting, we consider this feature to be true even for some of the five typosquatting models of Wang et al. [51] (e.g., the value of this feature for domain `facebookk.com` with trademark `facebook` would be true even if it would not be marked as *combosquatted* by the method proposed by Kintis et al. [25]).

Table 2. List of selected features with their corresponding feature sets.

F	Feature	Description	F-set	Set name
F1	digit_ratio	Number of digits over the length of the domain name	FS1	Lexical
F2	has_famous_brand_name	If the domain name contains a famous brand name	FS1	Lexical
F3	level_of_subdomain	Number of subdomains in the fully qualified domain name	FS1	Lexical
F4	special_keywords	If there is a special keyword used in the domain name	FS1	Lexical
F5	num_hyphen	Number of hyphens used in the domain name	FS1	Lexical
F6	diff_create_blacklist_time	Difference between domain creation and blacklisting time	FS2	WHOIS
F7	content_length	Content length of the homepage of the domain name	FS3	Content length
F8	has_index_page	Default webserver index page?	FS5	Index page
F9	is_use_redirection	If there is a redirection to another domain	FS4	Home page redirect
F10	is_default_homepage	If there is a default installation of a famous CMS	FS5	Index page
F11	has_vulnerable_tech	If there is a vulnerable technology (e.g., WordPress) used	FS6	Technologies
F12	num_of_tech	Number of distinct libraries used in the homepage	FS6	Technologies
F13	is_self_resolving	The domain name is self resolving	FS7	DNS (Self resolving)
F14	is_in_alexa	If the domain name is in the Alexa list	FS8	Alexa
F15	num_internal_hyperlinks	Number of working internal hyperlinks on the homepage	FS9	Hyperlinks
F16	num_external_hyperlinks	Number of working external hyperlinks on the homepage	FS9	Hyperlinks
F17	num_captured_wayback	Number of saved pages in the Wayback machine	FS10	Wayback machine

3.3   Measuring the Extent of Missing Values

Regardless of the importance of a feature, if it cannot be collected, it cannot contribute to the prediction of the target variable. Therefore, we first evaluate the occurrence of missing values per feature for the unlabeled dataset (see Sect. 4 for more details). Only 36.5% of domain names have a complete feature vector (i.e., have no missing values). Table 3 shows the percentage of missing values per feature. Some features are always available as they do not depend on any measurements (i.e., lexical features such as domain name digit ratio or the number of hyphens in the domain name) or whose measurements are generally easy to perform such

---

[6] https://support.alexa.com/hc/en-us/articles/4410503838999-We-retired-Alexa-com-on-May-1-2022.

as DNS-related features. However, some features suffer from missing values either due to measurement or parsing errors, or the unavailability of data.

For instance, the difference between domain creation (registration) and domain blacklisting time, also referred to as domain name age [34] (F6), is a feature derived from WHOIS/RDAP data and is missing for 22.29% of domain names. However, for some TLDs (e.g., .de TLD), there is no information about the domain registration date in WHOIS. For other TLDs, it is not feasible to collect WHOIS information at scale since either there is no conventional WHOIS server (e.g., for .gr TLD) or the access is restricted to authorized IP addresses (e.g., .es TLD). Moreover, extracting WHOIS information relies on manual creation of parsing rules and templates for individual registrars, and is by nature limited in scope and susceptible to changes in data representation [32]. The RDAP protocol [38] overcomes the problem of parsing but it is not universally deployed.

Table 3. Percentage of missing values for each feature.

Name	F-set	Missing %
digit_ratio	FS1	0.00%
num_hyphen	FS1	0.00%
special_keywords	FS1	0.00%
level_of_subdomain	FS1	0.00%
has_famous_brand_name	FS1	0.00%
is_self_resolving	FS7	0.00%
num_captured_wayback	FS10	1.42%
is_in_alexa	FS8	15.18%
content_length	FS3	15.22%
num_of_tech	FS6	15.35%
has_vulnerable_tech	FS6	15.35%
diff_create_blacklist_time	FS2	22.29%
is_use_redirection	FS4	26.27%
has_index_page	FS5	26.53%
is_default_homepage	FS5	26.53%
num_internal_hyperlinks	FS9	47.53%
num_external_hyperlinks	FS9	47.53%

While the features related to the page content play an essential role in classification [34], our results show that the values for these features are often missing (up to 47.5% for Hyperlinks). The reason is that data collection related to web content requires significant resources (e.g., browser emulation in our case) and its results highly depend on the page load time and implementation. For instance, poorly maintained websites may result in timeout or measurement errors. Domain redirection is another reason for the missing values of content-related features. URLs that use domain redirection (i.e., HTTP 3XX status code or JavaScript redirection) will load the content of the destination domain name (i.e., different from the original domain). In such cases, we consider these features as missing.

3.4   Handling Missing Values with Multiple Models

Applying simple techniques to handle missing values such as median or mean imputation might generate biased results [12]. Maroofi et al. [34] proposed an imputation method that infers the missing value of one feature from others. For example, a domain name age (i.e., the difference between domain creation and URL blacklisting time) that can be estimated based on the first appearance in the Internet Archive [23], Google Certificate Transparency logs [17], and privileged passive DNS data. However, such an approach cannot be applied to all types of features as many of them are independent of each other (e.g., the number of external hyperlinks cannot be estimated using other features).

To handle missing values, we propose a new approach—we design a multiple-model system that makes use of models trained on different combinations of features. The idea is to generate a large number of models, each dedicated to handling records with missing values of a specific subset of features: if we need to classify a domain name with missing values for features X and Y, we can use the model trained without features X and Y thus allowing classification based on all other features.

Based on our observations of missing values shown in Table 3, we group the features into 10 different sets as illustrated in Table 2. The features in each set are either all available or all missing. For example, the Lexical feature set (FS1) contains 5 features (F1: digit ratio, F2: has famous brand name, F3: level of subdomain, F4: special keywords, F5: number of hyphens). They are always available since they do not rely on active measurements or external third-party services. As soon as the system receives the input URL, it can generate these features. However, the Technologies feature set (F11: has vulnerable technology, F12: number of technologies) heavily depends on the availability of the HTML content of the domain homepage and HTTP headers. Note that our method of grouping features into feature sets is supported by the empirical assessment of missing value rates shown in Table 3, as opposed to Maroofi et al. [34] who grouped features into feature sets only based on their categories.

With eight feature sets with possible missing values (FS2-FS10), we calculate the number of models to be trained using the following formula:

$$number\ of\ models = \sum_{n=0}^{8} \binom{9}{n}, \tag{1}$$

where n is the number of removed feature sets, and 8 is the maximum number of removed feature sets. We create 511 models.

Based on the results of our previous work and the successful implementation of the Logistic Regression method in the operational COMAR system, we use the same classification method. LR uses a combination of weighted input feature values to predict output probabilities, making it easier to interpret (especially when considering multiple models) and assess the maliciousness of registered domains based on the most significant features. Therefore, its interpretability is not only important at the design stage for system tuning and evaluation. It can also play an essential role for operators at helpdesks who need a good understanding of classification results and the underlying models.

Therefore, we train the 511 models using Logistic Regression and use two sources of ground truth data. First, we use automatically generated data using methods described in Sect. 3.1 and refer to it as *Ground Truth 1* (GT1). This data represents labeled real-world samples of domain names with possibly missing values as quantified and detailed in Sect. 3.3. As the second source, we use manually labeled data provided to us by Maroofi et al. [34]. This dataset has no missing values and can bring corner cases into the training and testing. We refer to it as *Ground Truth 2* (GT2).

We use these two ground truth data sets in the following way. We train distinct models in 511 iterations. Each iteration represents a subset of feature sets after removing one to eight chosen feature sets at a time. We then use the feature vector of the iteration to train and evaluate each model. For instance, the feature vector of one of the iterations covers the feature sets without WHOIS (FS2), i.e., only FS1 and FS3 to FS10 are used. We train the complete model using the records with a complete feature vector from both GT1 and GT2. For other models with removed feature sets, we use the domain names from GT1 and GT2 in which all values of the remaining features are present.

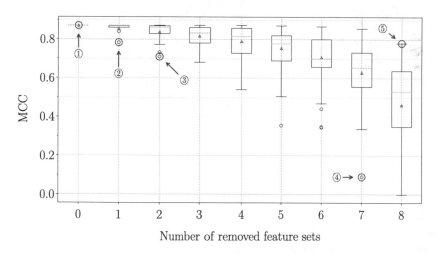

Fig. 1. Boxplot showing the MCC of models grouped by the number of removed features at a time. Triangles and horizontal lines represent the mean and median of MCC for each group of models, respectively.

Training of 511 models takes approximately 20 min on a personal computer (Intel Core i5-8265U CPU @ 1.60 GHz, 16 GB RAM), which may increase the cost compared to systems based on one model only, but overall, it remains low. More importantly, the cost of training is mainly related to the time required to generate ground truth, which is low compared to manual labeling. Therefore, the here-proposed method significantly reduces the overall cost and can label more samples for training. Given the automated approach for ground-truth generation, we could consider regular active learning. However, it would require future work to evaluate if static models exhibit high performance over time.

3.5   Performance Evaluation

To evaluate the models, we used Stratified K-fold Cross-Validation (SKCV) [26] with $K = 10$. While the standard K-fold Cross-Validation splits the dataset into the training and testing data in each iteration randomly by the predefined ratio, SKCV ensures that each fold keeps the same proportion of classes (i.e., malicious and compromised labels in our case) as in the original distribution. As our ground truth dataset is imbalanced, we have chosen this method to evaluate the models more accurately.

Table 4. Distribution of top ten models (combinations of removed feature sets) with the highest coverage of samples in the unlabeled dataset.

Missing F-sets	Coverage (%)	Model MCC	Model FNR
None	36.5	0.87	0.08
FS4, FS5, FS9	10.5	0.87	0.11
FS9	10.2	0.87	0.10
FS2	7.7	0.78	0.14
FS8	5.8	0.86	0.09
FS3, FS4, FS5, FS6, FS9	4.6	0.80	0.23
FS2, FS4, FS5, FS9	3.7	0.79	0.20
FS2, FS3, FS4, FS5, FS6, FS9	3.1	0.65	0.41
FS3, FS6, FS9	3.1	0.82	0.20
FS8, FS9	2.7	0.86	0.12

During the following evaluation, we use common metrics to evaluate the performance of models. For details, we refer the reader to Appendix A. Figure 1 shows a boxplot summarizing the distribution of Matthews Correlation Coefficient (MCC) for the 511 models. The MCC of the full model (①) is 0.87 with a 93.67% accuracy. The model without the WHOIS feature set (②) is the most significant outlier (MCC: 0.78, FNR: 14.2%) for the models with one removed feature set at a time. This result confirms that the domain age at the time of blacklisting is a strong feature and its absence causes a significant decrease in performance. Similarly, the model without the FS2 and FS10 feature sets (③) is the most significant outlier (MCC: 0.71, FNR: 17.9%) for the group of models with two removed features at a time. If we remove the WHOIS (FS2) and Wayback machine (FS10) feature sets, the performance of the model is highly impacted. As expected, one of the worst models ④ (MCC: 0.09, FNR: 98%) lacks all previously discussed feature sets (FS2, FS10), but also the remainder of the important features (FS3, FS5, FS6, FS8, and FS9). We discuss the implications of these findings for operational classification later in this section.

Note that even if MCC is a suitable method to evaluate the performance of binary classification with an unbalanced distribution of classes, it is still essential to consider other metrics, such as the false negative and false positive rates. For instance, we carefully monitor the false negative rate to avoid compromised domains incorrectly classified as malicious, which may lead to the blocking of a benign domain causing collateral damage to the legitimate registrant. Therefore, model ⑤ that only uses the domain name age (F6) calculated based on WHOIS has a high MCC (0.78) but it has to be used with caution as its FNR is high (26.1%).

As described in Sect. 3.3, our system consists of models trained on combinations of incomplete feature vectors and handles the classification of domain names with missing values. Table 4 shows ten of such combinations that appeared the most in our unlabeled dataset. For instance, 10.2% of domains that have missing values for FS9 (Hyperlinks) can still be classified using a model with good overall performance (MCC: 0.87, FNR: 10%), similar to the model with no missing values. We observed that 36.5% of domain names in our unlabeled dataset (see Sect. 4) do not have any missing values and therefore, they can be classified using the complete model with all 10 feature sets present. The remaining 63.5% of domain names have at least one missing value and cannot be classified using a single-model approach (assuming that other methods to handle missing values are not implemented). The 501 remaining models cover 12.1% of samples. These models are necessary for the system to handle missing values resulting from measurements related to each feature set.

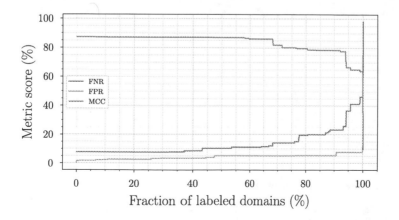

Fig. 2. Empirical cumulative distribution function of performance metrics.

A system that can be used by investigators should offer a way of tailoring it to different use cases. If an investigator needs precise classification at the expense of an increased number of remaining domain names that need to be manually verified, she could only use models with good performance metrics such as MCC ≥ 0.85 and FNR $\leq 10\%$ covering 43.2% of unlabeled data. However, if the investigator needs the classification results for informative purposes only (to observe general trends regarding abusive domain names), she can choose more relaxed requirements (e.g., MCC ≥ 0.7 and FNR $\leq 20\%$ covering 80.6% of the dataset). Therefore, we propose a systematic approach for selecting the models and metrics based on the desired coverage of unlabeled data and performance, for example, by DNS operators to support their anti-abuse practices. Figure 2 shows the dependency between the chosen metrics and the fraction of automatically classified domains. While FPR stays below 10% for all 511 models, the percentage of automatically labeled domains has a more significant impact on FNR. If investigators want to label 100% of domain names, only 0.01% of domain names will be classified using the worst model with 97.9% FNR. If the coverage of 80% of the dataset is required, the worst model will suffer from 20% FNR. For the results presented in Sect. 4, we choose models with MCC ≥ 0.8 resulting in 76.3% of labeled domain names.

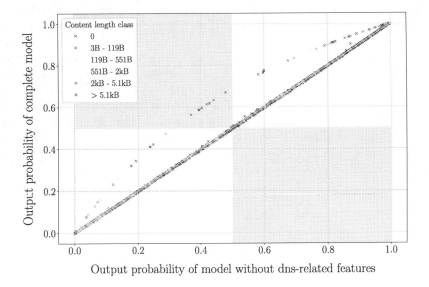

Fig. 3. Scatter plot of probability changes between the full model and the model without DNS-related features (FS7).

3.6   Feature Importance

Hao et al. [20] and Maroofi et al. [34] assessed the feature importance by excluding feature sets one by one from the system and comparing the calculated metrics of these models. In this section, we present a post hoc method for fine-grained visualization of the feature importance using scatter plots based on similar principles as in their methods. Out of the 511 models, we select those trained with only one feature set missing (9 models as we do not consider lexical features as possibly missing). We choose a sample of 10,000 domain names with no missing values and we classify them first with the complete model and then with 9 models with one removed feature at a time. We present the results for selected feature sets in Figs. 3 and 4. Each point in the graph represents one domain name. The y-axis is the predicted probability of a domain being compromised when classified with the complete model. The x-axis is the probability predicted by a model without one of the feature sets. Each point is colored based on the category (content length or domain age). The output probability of points laying on the line $x = y$ remained unchanged after a feature set elimination. Points for which $x > y$ (increase in output probability), became "more compromised" after feature set removal. Similarly, points for which $x < y$ (decrease in the output probability), became "more malicious". Note that the red zone at the top left and bottom right corner highlight the points that could potentially change labels. For instance, Fig. 3 shows that the output probability of a small fraction of domains was impacted by removing the DNS-related features (FS7). Therefore, this feature set does not have a high impact on the classification results.

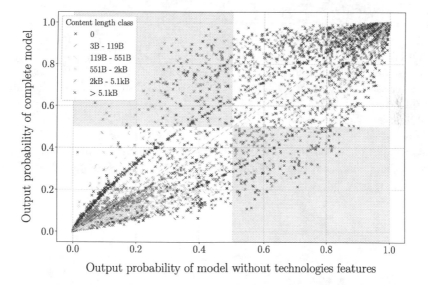

Fig. 4. Scatter plot of probability changes between the full model and the model without feature set FS6 (web technologies).

On the other hand, Figs. 4, 10, and 11 (in Appendix B) demonstrate that feature sets FS2 (WHOIS), FS8 (Alexa), and FS9 (Hyperlinks) strongly influence the output of our system as many data points moved horizontally after eliminating a feature set (i.e., became more malicious or more compromised).

However, it is important to note that especially the most important features can lead to misclassification if manipulated by attackers. An attacker may generate long content, deploy multiple technologies on the index page of a registered domain name, or avoid registering domain names with special keywords. However, manipulating COMAR features also requires additional effort and can be costly. Since we based our prototype on the original COMAR system, the individual features share the same characteristics regarding robustness and possible evasion. We refer interested readers to our initial study for a detailed discussion of possible evasion techniques for each feature [34].

3.7 Ethical Considerations

To collect data, we perform active measurements, particularly browser emulation via HTTP requests and active DNS lookups. Ethical issues that may arise mainly concern the possible overloading of the scanned infrastructure. To address this issue, we limited the number of simultaneous scans to twenty during the browser emulation phase, representing negligible traffic that should not significantly affect web servers. We used the Google public DNS resolver for DNS scans, adhering to the restrictions specified in the official documentation.[7]

4   Classification Results

In this section, we apply the prototype classifier to 218,806 unlabeled unique domain names from APWG [3], OpenPhish [39], and PhishTank [49] URL blacklists collected between January 2021 and September 2022. We study four selected characteristics of the domain names of malicious URLs and analyze their distribution across different types of TLDs.

The overall classification results show that 73% of phishing domain names were registered for malicious purposes, and 27% were classified as registered by benign users but have been compromised. If the domain names were compromised at the hosting rather than at the DNS level, they should not be blocked by TLD registries or registrars.

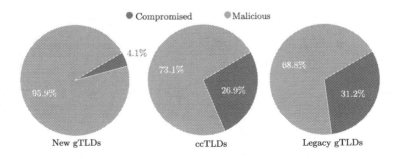

Fig. 5. Top level domain distribution.

---

[7] https://developers.google.com/speed/public-dns/docs/isp.

Figure 5 shows that almost 96% of domain names of blacklisted phishing URLs in new generic TLDs (e.g., .top, .pharmacy, .xyz) are likely to be maliciously registered, 69% for legacy gTLDs (e.g., .com, .net, .org), and about 73% for country-code TLDs (e.g., .br, .no, .jp). The question arises: why is the fraction of domains registered for malicious purposes in new gTLDs compared to compromised ones much higher than in ccTLDs and legacy gTLDs? Previous studies [19,28] showed that, in general, for new gTLDs, a relatively large proportion of domain names are either parked or contain no content (DNS or HTTP errors) compared to legacy gTLDs. Intuitively, only domain names containing content are likely to be vulnerable to certain types of exploits and thus can be exploited at the website level. It might be a plausible explanation for why only a tiny fraction of domain names of new gTLDs are likely to be compromised. However, this hypothesis requires systematic future research because no recent studies have conducted such a comparative analysis.

The presented results should be merely seen as trend indicators and may be influenced by the blacklist bias as well as short-term trends in the choices made by attackers. For example, some blacklists may be more effective in detecting maliciously registered domain names (e.g., based on suspicious keywords), while others may be more effective in detecting compromised sites. Some domain registrars, accredited by a TLD registry, may offer low registration prices for a short period to attract new customers. Malicious actors may take advantage of such special offers and register domain names on a large scale, which may affect the observed percentage of compromised and maliciously registered domains.

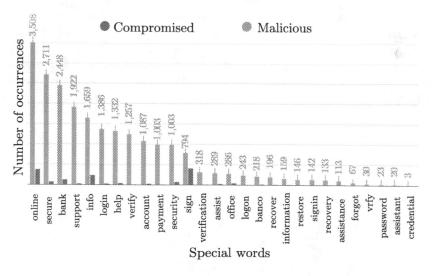

Fig. 6. Distribution of popular keywords in domain names of compromised and maliciously registered domains. (Color figure online)

4.1   Analysis of the Selected Features

We now explain how the compromised and maliciously registered domain names distinguished by our system differ in terms of four selected features: popular terms in domain names, the number of web technologies used, the domain name age, and the use of TLS certificates.

The features indicating that a cybercriminal (rather than a benign user) has registered a domain name include specific keywords such as 'verification', 'payment', 'support', or brand names (e.g., paypal-online-support.com). Figure 6 presents a word frequency analysis of the phishing dataset for both domain names automatically classified as maliciously registered (orange) and those classified as compromised (blue).

We can observe that cybercriminals tend to incorporate such words into domain names to lure victims into entering their credentials. The most frequently used keywords by malicious actors are 'online', 'secure', 'bank', 'support, 'info', 'login', and 'help'. On the other hand, the domain name of compromised sites rarely contains such specific keywords.

One of the used features is the *number of web technologies* (F12): a count of the JavaScript, Cascading Style Sheets (CSS), or Content Management System (CMS) frameworks and plugins used to build the *homepage* of a registered domain name. The higher number of technologies used for developing a website could reflect the amount of effort and time its designer spent to create a fully-functional website. While this is true for benign (compromised) domain names, malicious actors tend to put little effort into deploying multiple technologies when designing websites on maliciously registered domain names, as it is not critical to the success of phishing attacks. Figure 7 shows the results for compromised and maliciously registered domain names. As many as 52.2% of compromised domains use more than five different (potentially vulnerable) technologies, frameworks, and plugins to build the website. In comparison, 66.1% of the maliciously registered domain names have no specific technology on their homepage. We have noticed that many maliciously registered domains either have no homepage (showing the default directory index served by the web server), redirect to

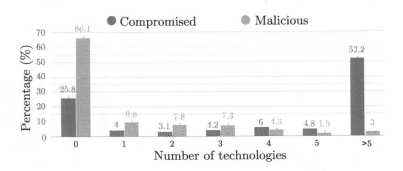

Fig. 7. Distribution of the number of technologies between compromised and registered domains.

another domain (e.g., the landing page of a phishing attack), or display a custom error message (e.g., forbidden page). Instead, they frequently serve the phishing page either on a URL path or a subdomain level.

The age of a domain name (F6), defined as the time between the registration of the domain name and its appearance on the blacklist, is one of the important features of our classifier. Intuitively, the older the domain name, the more likely it is to have been registered by a benign user but subsequently compromised. On the other hand, cybercriminals tend to use a domain name for malicious activities soon after registration. Figure 8 shows the age of domain names for all TLDs that provide the registration date as part of their WHOIS data: "0" means that registration and blacklisting occurred on the same day, "1" – the difference between the registration date and the blacklisting date is at most one year, and ">5" means that the difference between the domain registration date and the blacklisting date is greater than five years. For 93.6% of maliciously registered domain names, the difference between the domain registration date and the blacklisting date is less than a year, and for 11.3% of them, the domains were blacklisted on the same day the domain was registered. For compromised domain names, about 51.4% of them were registered at least six years before being blacklisted. A possible explanation for this phenomenon is that websites hosted on older domain names are more likely to use outdated technologies or content management systems (e.g., vulnerable versions of CMS such as WordPress), making them easier to compromise.

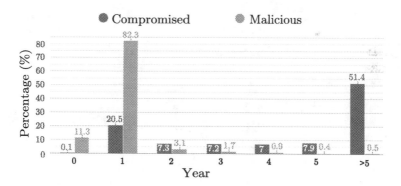

Fig. 8. Distribution of domain ages between maliciously registered and compromised domain names in percentage.

In some sporadic cases, malicious actors may "age" registered domains, waiting weeks or sometimes months before abusing them, or compromise domain names shortly after their registration [34]. However, as our system is fully automated and performs classification based on multiple features (the domain name age is just one of them), it is more resistant to manipulation (e.g., domain aging).

While we explain in Sect. 3.2 why we avoid using TLS certificate features, we analyze their use by owners of compromised versus maliciously registered domain names. According to a PhishLabs report [40], three quarters of all phishing sites used HTTPS (HTTP over TLS) in 2020 *"to add a layer of legitimacy, better mimic the target site in question, and reduce being flagged or blocked from some browsers."* However, the report conflates compromised and maliciously registered domain names. Therefore, to establish whether cybercriminals increasingly use TLS certificates, we need to distinguish between compromised and maliciously registered domain names and analyze the use of TLS only in the latter group. Otherwise, it is unclear whether the TLS certificate was issued at the request of a criminal for a maliciously registered domain to enhance the website's credibility or at the request of a legitimate domain owner for a benign domain name that was later compromised and abused by a criminal.

Figure 9 shows the statistics of TLS certificates issued for malicious and benign (and later compromised) domains involved in phishing attacks. The use of TLS certificates is less widespread among phishers than for benign (but compromised) domain names. 63.9% of phishing attacks using compromised domains take advantage of TLS certificates issued at the request of benign domain owners while 55.2% of maliciously registered domains use TLS certificates deliberately deployed by malicious actors to lure their victims. Surprisingly, 15.5% of maliciously registered domains used most likely paid TLS certificates. We further investigate these domains and find that 48.7% of them had a TLS certificate issued by Sectigo [42]. The majority of these domains were registered with Namecheap [37] which offers a cheap all-in-one hosting package including a domain name registration, hosting, and a one-year valid TLS certificate issued by Sectigo [42].

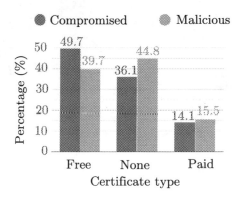

Fig. 9. TLS use by maliciously registered and compromised domain names in percentage.

5   Conclusions and Future Work

Domain reputation systems are of great importance for Internet intermediaries to accurately assess whether domain names are benign, likely to have been maliciously registered, or have been compromised and used to distribute malicious content or ensure the proper functioning of malicious infrastructures. Developing a domain name classification system suitable for deployment in an operational environment requires careful design. To address the shortcomings of some existing systems, we first proposed an approach to automatically generate ground truth data based on mitigation actions undertaken by the relevant intermediaries involved in domain registration and hosting. We carefully selected publicly available features to ensure that our system can be implemented by different actors: from DNS operators and hosting providers to law enforcement agencies. We carefully measured the extent of missing values stemming from measurement and parsing errors, since even the most important features have no real value if they cannot be collected and used in classification. Our results show that for 36.5% of domain names, we can use a complete feature vector to classify domain names. To handle missing values, we proposed a new approach based on multiple models as an alternative to simple statistical techniques. Since the performance of different models varies, we propose a systematic approach to choosing models based on the expected rate of classified domain names and the performance required by DNS operators to support their anti-abuse practices.

We applied the prototype classifier to blacklisted URLs over a 20-month period and explored selected characteristics of abused domain names and their distributions across different types of TLDs. We found that approximately one-quarter of domain names used to launch phishing campaigns are compromised and generally cannot be blocked at the DNS level. The percentage of domains registered with malicious intent to compromised domains in new gTLDs (96%) is much higher than in ccTLDs (73%) and legacy gTLDs (69%). The results also indicate that malicious actors usually put little effort into deploying multiple technologies when designing websites on maliciously registered domain names and typically use them shortly after registration.

The proposed design approaches can be applied to any domain name classification problem, and the designed prototype has demonstrated its utility in an operational environment, as two ccTLD registries have adopted it to support their DNS anti-abuse practices.

We plan to use the proposed classifier to perform a longitudinal analysis on phishing URLs to observe the changes in attackers' behavior over time such as the use of popular keywords in maliciously registered domain names. Finally, since the training cost is low and mainly related to automated truth data generation, we can apply active learning to the proposed system, adapting it to new trends and techniques used by attackers over time.

Acknowledgments. We thank Benoît Ampeau, Marc van der Wal (AFNIC) and the anonymous reviewers for their valuable feedback, Anti-Phishing Working Group, OpenPhish, and PhishTank for providing access to their URL blacklists. This work has been carried out in the framework of the COMAR project funded by SIDN, the .NL Registry and AFNIC, the .FR Registry. It was partially supported by the Grenoble Alpes Cybersecurity Institute (under contract ANR-15-IDEX-02), and the French Ministry of Research (PERSYVAL-Lab project under contract ANR-11-LABX-0025-01, and DiNS project under contract ANR-19-CE25-0009-01).

Appendix

A   Machine Learning Metrics

$$Accuracy = \frac{TP + TN}{TP + TN + FP + FN}$$

$$FPR = \frac{FP}{FP + TN} \qquad FNR = \frac{FN}{FN + TP}$$

$$MCC = \frac{TP \times TN - FP \times FN}{\sqrt{(TP + FP)(TP + FN)(TN + FP)(TN + FN)}}, \tag{2}$$

where TN, TP, FN, and FP represent the numbers of true negative, true positive, false negative, and false positive, respectively. We refer to compromised domains as positives and to maliciously registered ones as negatives. Accuracy is the proportion of correctly predicted labels among all samples. We also make use of a Matthews Correlation Coefficient (MCC) as defined in Eq. 2 [35]. This metric was developed to evaluate the quality of a binary classification and its values vary between –1 and +1, where +1 means perfect prediction (the best score), 0 is equivalent to random results, and –1 shows that all samples were misclassified (the worst score). In contrast to accuracy, MCC provides a more realistic metric for imbalanced datasets such as ours.

B   Scatter Plots of Probability Changes

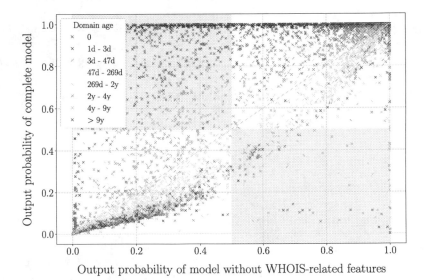

Fig. 10. Scatter plot of probability changes between the full model and the model without features related to WHOIS data (FS2).

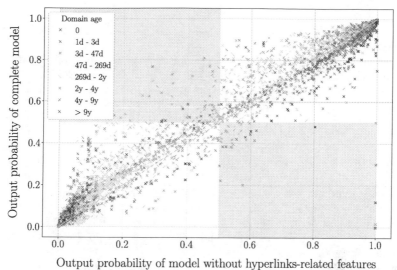

Fig. 11. Scatter plot of probability changes between the full model and the model without features related to hyperlinks (FS9).

References

1. Alowaisheq, E., et al.: Cracking the wall of confinement: understanding and analyzing malicious domain take-downs. In: Proceedings of NDSS (2019)
2. Amazon: Alexa: SEO and Competitive Analysis Software (2022). https://www.alexa.com/
3. Anti-Phishing Working Group: Global phishing survey: Trends and domain name use in 2016 (2016). https://docs.apwg.org/reports/APWG_Global_Phishing_Report_2015-2016.pdf
4. Antonakakis, M., Perdisci, R., Dagon, D., Lee, W., Feamster, N.: Building a dynamic reputation system for DNS. In: Proceedings of USENIX Security, p. 18 (2010)
5. Bayer, J., et al.: Study on domain name system (DNS) abuse: technical report. arXiv preprint arXiv:2212.08879 (2022)
6. Bilge, L., Kirda, E., Kruegel, C., Balduzzi, M.: EXPOSURE: finding malicious domains using passive DNS analysis. In: Proceedings of 18th NDSS (2011)
7. Bilge, L., Sen, S., Balzarotti, D., Kirda, E., Kruegel, C.: Exposure: a passive DNS analysis service to detect and report malicious domains. ACM Trans. Inf. Syst. Secur. **16**(4) (2014)
8. Corona, I., et al.: DeltaPhish: detecting phishing webpages in compromised websites. arXiv:1707.00317 (2017)
9. Daigle, L.: Whois protocol specification. Technical report, RFC Editor (2004)
10. De Silva, R., Nabeel, M., Elvitigala, C., Khalil, I., Yu, T., Keppitiyagama, C.: Compromised or attacker-owned: a large scale classification and study of hosting domains of malicious URLs. In: Proceedings of USENIX Security, pp. 3721–3738 (2021)
11. DNS Abuse Framework. https://dnsabuseframework.org/

12. Donders, A.R.T., van der Heijden, G.J., Stijnen, T., Moons, K.G.: Review: a gentle introduction to imputation of missing values. J. Clin. Epidemiol. **59**(10), 1087–1091 (2006)
13. Emmanuel, T., Maupong, T., Mpoeleng, D., Semong, T., Mphago, B., Tabona, O.: A survey on missing data in machine learning. J. Big Data **8** (2021)
14. Farsight Security: Passive DNS Historical Internet Database: Farsight DNSDB (2022). https://www.farsightsecurity.com/solutions/dnsdb/
15. Felegyhazi, M., Kreibich, C., Paxson, V.: On the potential of proactive domain blacklisting. In: Proceedings of 3rd USENIX LEET (2010)
16. Frosch, T., Kührer, M., Holz, T.: Predentifier: detecting botnet C&C domains from passive DNS data. In: Zeilinger, M., Schoo, P., Hermann, E. (eds.) Advances in IT Early Warning, pp. 78–90. AISEC (2013)
17. Google: Certificate Transparency. https://certificate.transparency.dev/
18. Google Safe Browsing. https://safebrowsing.google.com/
19. Halvorson, T., Der, M.F., Foster, I., Savage, S., Saul, L.K., Voelker, G.M.: From academy to.zone: an analysis of the new TLD land rush. In: Proceedings of IMC, pp. 381–394 (2015)
20. Hao, S., Kantchelian, A., Miller, B., Paxson, V., Feamster, N.: PREDATOR: proactive recognition and elimination of domain abuse at time-of-registration. In: Proceedings of ACM SIGSAC, pp. 1568–1579 (2016)
21. Hollenbeck, S.: Extensible Provisioning Protocol (EPP) Domain Name Mapping. RFC 3731, RFC Editor (2004)
22. ICANN: EPP Status Codes — What Do They Mean, and Why Should I Know? https://www.icann.org/resources/pages/epp-status-codes-2014-06-16-en
23. Internet Archive: Wayback Machine. https://archive.org/web/
24. Kheir, N., Tran, F., Caron, P., Deschamps, N.: Mentor: positive DNS reputation to skim-off benign domains in botnet C&C blacklists. In: Cuppens-Boulahia, N., Cuppens, F., Jajodia, S., Abou El Kalam, A., Sans, T. (eds.) SEC 2014. IAICT, vol. 428, pp. 1–14. Springer, Heidelberg (2014). https://doi.org/10.1007/978-3-642-55415-5_1
25. Kintis, P., et al.: Hiding in plain sight. In: Proceedings of ACM SIGSAC (2017)
26. Kohavi, R.: A Study of Cross-Validation and Bootstrap for Accuracy Estimation and Model Selection. In: Proceedings of 14th IJCAI, vol. 2, pp. 1137–1143 (1995)
27. Korczyński, M., Tajalizadehkhoob, S., Noroozian, A., Wullink, M., Hesselman, C., van Eeten, M.: Reputation metrics design to improve intermediary incentives for security of TLDs. In: Proceedings of IEEE Euro SP (2017)
28. Korczyński, M., et al.: Cybercrime after the sunrise: a statistical analysis of DNS abuse in new gTLDs. In: Proceedings of ACM ASIACCS (2018)
29. Le Page, S., Jourdan, G.-V., Bochmann, G.V., Onut, I.-V., Flood, J.: Domain classifier: compromised machines versus malicious registrations. In: Bakaev, M., Frasincar, F., Ko, I.-Y. (eds.) ICWE 2019. LNCS, vol. 11496, pp. 265–279. Springer, Cham (2019). https://doi.org/10.1007/978-3-030-19274-7_20
30. Le Pochat, V., Van Goethem, T., Tajalizadehkhoob, S., Korczyński, M., Joosen, W.: Tranco: a research-oriented top sites ranking hardened against manipulation. In: Proceedings of NDSS. Internet Society (2019)
31. Le Pochat, V., et al.: A practical approach for taking down avalanche botnets under real-world constraints. In: Proceedings of 27th NDSS (2020)
32. Liu, S., Foster, I., Savage, S., Voelker, G.M., Saul, L.K.: Who is.Com? learning to parse WHOIS records. In: Proceedings of IMC, pp. 369–380 (2015)

33. Ma, J., Saul, L.K., Savage, S., Voelker, G.M.: Beyond blacklists: learning to detect malicious web sites from suspicious URLs. In: Proceeding of 15th ACM SIGKDD ICKDDM, pp. 1245–1254. KDD (2009)
34. Maroofi, S., Korczyński, M., Hesselman, C., Ampeau, B., Duda, A.: COMAR: classification of compromised versus maliciously registered domains. In: Proceedings of IEEE EuroS&P, pp. 607–623 (2020)
35. Matthews, B.: Comparison of the predicted and observed secondary structure of T4 Phage Lysozyme. Biochimica et Biophysica Acta (BBA) - Protein Struct. **405**(2), 442–451 (1975)
36. Moura, G.C.M., Müller, M., Davids, M., Wullink, M., Hesselman, C.: Domain names abuse and TLDs: from monetization towards mitigation. In: Proceedings of IFIP/IEEE, pp. 1077–1082 (2017)
37. Namecheap. https://www.namecheap.com/
38. Newton, A., Hollenbeck, S.: Registration data access protocol (RDAP) query format. Technical report, RFC Editor (2015)
39. OpenPhish. https://openphish.com/
40. PhishLabs: Abuse of HTTPS on Nearly Three-Fourths of all Phishing Sites (2020). https://www.phishlabs.com/blog/abuse-of-https-on-nearly-three-fourths-of-all-phishing-sites/
41. PhisLabs: https://www.phishlabs.com/
42. Sectigo Limited: Sectigo®Official - SSL Certificate Authority & PKI Solutions. https://sectigo.com/
43. SiteAdvisor, M.: https://www.siteadvisor.com/
44. Spamhaus. https://www.spamhaus.org/
45. Spooren, J., Vissers, T., Janssen, P., Joosen, W., Desmet, L.: Premadoma: an operational solution for DNS registries to prevent malicious domain registrations. In: 35th ACSAC, pp. 557–567 (2019)
46. SURBL. https://surbl.org/
47. Tajalizadehkhoob, S., Böhme, R., Gañán, C., Korczyński, M., Eeten, M.V.: Rotten apples or bad harvest? what we are measuring when we are measuring abuse. ACM Trans. Internet Technol. **18**(4) (2018)
48. Tajalizadehkhoob, S., et al.: Herding vulnerable cats: a statistical approach to disentangle joint responsibility for web security in shared hosting. In: Proceedings of ACM SIGSAC, pp. 553–567 (2017)
49. Ulevitch, D.: PhishTank Join the fight Against Phishing (2006). https://phishtank.org/
50. URIBL. https://www.uribl.com/
51. Wang, Y.M., Beck, D., Wang, J., Verbowski, C., Daniels, B.: Strider typo-patrol: discovery and analysis of systematic typo-squatting. In: Proceedings of USENIX Association, vol. 2, p. 5 (2006)
52. Zhang, P., et al.: CrawlPhish: large-scale analysis of client-side cloaking techniques in phishing. In: Proceedings of IEEE S&P, pp. 1109–1124 (2021)

Web

A First Look at Third-Party Service Dependencies of Web Services in Africa

Aqsa Kashaf[1]($\boxtimes$) (ORCID), Jiachen Dou[1], Margarita Belova[2], Maria Apostolaki[2], Yuvraj Agarwal[1] (ORCID), and Vyas Sekar[1]

[1] Carnegie Mellon University, Pittsburgh, USA
{akashaf,jiachend,yuvraja,vsekar}@andrew.cmu.edu
[2] Princeton University, Princeton, USA
{margarita.bel,apostolaki}@princeton.edu

Abstract. Third-party dependencies expose websites to shared risks and cascading failures. The dependencies impact African websites as well *e.g.,* Afrihost outage in 2022 [15]. While the prevalence of third-party dependencies has been studied for globally popular websites, Africa is largely underrepresented in those studies. Hence, this work analyzes the prevalence of third-party infrastructure dependencies in Africa-centric websites from 4 African vantage points. We consider websites that fall into one of the four categories: *Africa-visited* (popular in Africa) *Africa-hosted* (sites hosted in Africa), *Africa-dominant* (sites targeted towards users in Africa), and *Africa-operated* (websites operated in Africa). Our key findings are: 1) 93% of the *Africa-visited* websites critically depend on a third-party DNS, CDN, or CA. In perspective, *US-visited* websites are up to 25% less critically dependent. 2) 97% of *Africa-dominant*, 96% of *Africa-hosted*, and 95% of *Africa-operated* websites are critically dependent on a third-party DNS, CDN, or CA provider. 3) The use of third-party services is concentrated where only 3 providers can affect 60% of the Africa-centric websites. Our findings have key implications for the present usage and recommendations for the future evolution of the Internet in Africa.

Keywords: DNS · Certificate authorities · Third-party dependency · Availability · CDN · Africa Internet

1 Introduction

The websites we use everyday offload critical services such as name resolution (DNS), content distribution (CDN), and certificate issuance/revocation (CA) to third parties for key services *e.g.,* AWS Route 53 for DNS, Akamai for CDN, DigiCert for CA. As a result, the availability and security of these websites, and thus of our data and operations, depend on the availability and security of those third parties. The effects of such dependencies are routinely observed in the Internet today. For example, a dependency on DNS resulted in the downtime of multiple websites (more than 100K) for several hours together with their DNS provider (Dyn) which was attacked by a Mirai Distributed Denial of Service

© The Author(s), under exclusive license to Springer Nature Switzerland AG 2023
A. Brunstrom et al. (Eds.): PAM 2023, LNCS 13882, pp. 595–622, 2023.
https://doi.org/10.1007/978-3-031-28486-1_25

(DDoS) attack [24]. Similarly, users of multiple websites lost access to their accounts for weeks, because a single CA issued an incorrect revocation of a certificate in 2016 [22].

To gauge the security risk that such dependencies entail, one needs to understand the prevalence of third-party dependencies across the websites that are important for users all over the world. While such studies exist [25, 26, 28, 33, 47, 55], their target users/websites are particularly skewed towards North America and Europe. The geographical bias of the datasets used in previous studies of third-party dependencies creates a critical gap as distinct regions exhibit unique characteristics, needs, and opportunities that are effectively ignored. Naively assuming that observations generalize across regions, entails risks as it underestimates the practicality of certain attacks and creates false assurance of the security of critical region-specific websites (*e.g.,* those related to government or health insurance in those countries). This is also recognized by the Internet Society's Measuring Internet Resilience in Africa (MIRA) project [46].

To bridge this gap, in this paper we study third-party dependencies of websites in Africa. Our study is motivated by the increasing number of DDoS attacks in Africa [21], the increasing popularity of third-party services, the low cyber readiness of African users and businesses [40]. These are exemplified by various recent attacks. For example, in July 2022, Afrihost, one of the major hosting and DNS providers in South Africa, went down for 30 h due to load shedding which caused a cooling equipment failure in one of Afrihost's datacenters. Moreover, the relative scarcity of local providers urges website operators to rely often solely on global service providers such as Amazon, Akamai, and Cloudflare whose outages also affect users, and websites from Africa.

Beyond raising awareness of the unique security challenges that African users and operators face, our study contributes to the resilience of the Internet in Africa. Concretely, we aim to provide stakeholders and operators with more tailored insights, to help them avoid common pitfalls in using third-party dependencies, understand their attack surface, and optimize their defense strategies towards the most pressing needs.

To investigate third-party dependencies in African websites, we focus on websites which are *Africa-centric*: websites that are popular in Africa (*Africa-visited*), or predominantly targeted towards Africans (*Africa-dominant*), or are hosted in Africa (*Africa-hosted*), or are operated in Africa (*Africa-operated*). We investigate their dependencies using four measurement vantage points in Africa (Nigeria, Rwanda, South Africa, and Kenya). Specifically, our measurement study focuses on answering the following questions: First, how prevalent are third-party dependencies in the *Africa-visited*, *Africa-hosted*, *Africa-operated*, and *Africa-dominant* websites? Second, how centralized are third-party dependencies among providers used in *Africa-visited*, *Africa-hosted*, *Africa-operated*, and *Africa-dominant* websites? Finally, how does the dependence on third parties in Africa compare to the US? Since prior work [28] studies third-party dependencies from a US vantage point, hence, in this work, we use the US as a baseline.

Our main findings are as follows: First, third-party dependencies are 5% to 12% more prevalent in Africa as compared to the US. Moreover, for more popular sites, this gap increases up to 25%. Second, 93% of *Africa-visited*, 97% of *Africa-dominant*, 96% of *Africa-hosted*, and 95% of *Africa-operated* websites are critically dependent on a third-party DNS, CDN, or CA provider. Second, all vantage points in Africa are equally critically dependent on third-party DNS, CDN, and CA providers. Third, the top-three DNS, CDN or CA providers for *Africa-centric* websites serve as sole providers for up to 60% of the websites. Finally, the top providers for *Africa-visited* websites are mainly global providers (*e.g.,* Cloudflare, Amazon, etc.). However, for the hosted, dominant and operated sets, we observe some local providers among the top providers.

Our findings have key implications for the present usage and recommendations for the future evolution of the Internet in Africa. The high degree of centralization of providers and third-party dependencies make African websites vulnerable to various exploits, and availability attacks. While these dependencies mirror trends in other countries such as the US, there are some unique threats. First, Africa has unreliable Internet infrastructure which makes outages more commonplace [10,42,45] as observed in the Afrihost outage due to load-shedding [15]. Secondly, African website operators and service providers lack cyber expertise [40], due to which it can take longer for them to recover from an outage. By studying this issue in the African context, we highlight the need to build a more resilient Internet infrastructure in Africa.

2 Preliminaries

Before we formally define our measurement goals, we define a set of actionable metrics that we use throughout our analysis. These metrics have been taken from Kashaf et al. [28]. We also articulate several research questions, that we aim to answer in this study.

2.1 Dependency Metrics

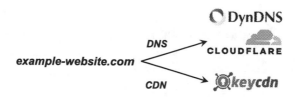

Fig. 1. *example-website.com* has a dependency on CloudFlare DNS and Dyn DNS. Moreover, it has a dependency on KeyCDN for CDN services. Since it uses a single CDN provider, it has a critical dependency on KeyCDN. However, it is redundantly provisioned with respect to DNS as it is using two DNS providers.

When a website uses another entity for a particular service (*e.g.*, DNS), we say that the website has a **third-party dependency** on that service provider, making it a third-party provider as opposed to having a private provider which belongs to the website itself as defined by Kashaf *et al.* [28]. We illustrate this in Fig. 1. Here, *example-website.com* uses an entity other than itself for a particular service (here DNS and CDN). Therefore, *example-website.com* has a third-party DNS dependency on Cloudflare and Dyn DNS, and it has a third-party CDN dependency on KeyCDN. *example-website.com* in Fig. 1 uses only a single CDN provider. Hence, it has a **critical dependency** on KeyCDN. However, since *example-website.com* uses two DNS providers, it is **redundantly provisioned** with respect to DNS and does not have a critical dependency on Cloudflare or Dyn DNS.

For DNS and CDN, we measure critical dependency by analyzing if a given website is redundantly provisioned or not. However, in the case of CA dependency, a website is critically dependent on a CA if it does not support Online Certificate Status Protocol (OCSP) stapling. If OCSP stapling is enabled, the user accessing a given website does not have to contact the OCSP server to check the website certificate for revocation. Instead, an OCSP response signed by the certificate authority comes stapled from the website server itself, thus removing the dependence on OCSP server [4].

Concentration of a Service Provider. The number of websites dependent on a service provider gives the concentration of that service provider.

Impact of a Service Provider. This gives the number of websites critically dependent on a service provider.

2.2 Taxonomy of Websites

To systematically study third-party service dependencies in Africa-centric web services, we create a taxonomy of websites (Table 1) based on *(i)* who visits them; *(ii)* who operates them; *(iii)* where are they hosted; and *(iv)* who are their dominant users. Below, we define these classes precisely at the granularity of a country.

Users of a website are the people who visit the website. A website may be used primarily by people from a single country (geolocation) or from multiple countries. We define u_C as the Internet user, who is geographically located in country C.

Owner/Operator of a website is the entity or person that builds and manages the website, makes security decisions, defines its privacy policy, etc. A website may have operators in a single country or in multiple countries. We define o_C as the website operator in country C.

Host of a website is the country (or countries) in which the servers running the website are. We use the notation h_C to specify that the hosting location of the website is in the country C.

Dominant country for a website is the country that has the majority traffic share for that website. We use d_C to denote the dominant country for a website.

Table 1. We consider three sets (categories) of websites for our analysis which differ in the location of their users (usage), the location in which they are hosted (hosting), and their audience.

Who uses it?	Who operates it?	Who hosts it?	Who is it for?	Website sets
u_C	–	–	–	$W_C^{visited}$
–	h_C	–	–	W_C^{hosted}
–	–	o_C	–	$W_C^{operated}$
–	–	–	d_C	$W_C^{dominant}$

Using this taxonomy, we define the following website sets:

***Country-Visited* Websites** $W_C^{visited}$**:** This set is composed of websites that are used/visited by users u_C of country C. In other words, this includes websites that are popular in the country C. For example, *facebook.com* is among the top 1K websites in Kenya.

***Country-Dominant* Websites** $W_C^{dominant}$**:** These websites have the majority of their users in country C. They may be operated or hosted by single or multiple countries. These websites are specifically targeted toward a particular demographic. Studying this set is important because it includes websites that may not be very popular but are essential for African users such as government websites, and hospital websites. This set is different from the $W_C^{visited}$ websites. While the $W_C^{visited}$ set contains websites that are popular in a country, *e.g.*, *facebook.com* is popular in Kenya, however, the $W_C^{dominant}$ set contains websites which are primarily targeting the Internet users of Kenya. *facebook.com* is not primarily targeting Kenyans, while the website *kenyanmusic.co.ke* is primarily targeting Kenyans with its majority traffic from Kenya[1].

***Country-Operated* Websites** $W_C^{operated}$**:** This set comprises of websites operated by country C. These websites may have users from single or multiple countries and may be hosted by single or multiple countries. Studying this set facilitates investigating the implications of third-party dependencies from the perspective of African website operators.

***Country-Hosted* Websites** W_C^{hosted}**:** This set comprises of websites that are hosted in country C. Each of these websites may have users from single or multiple countries and may be operated in single or multiple countries. Studying this set is important because it often contains sensitive websites which need to remain local such as banking websites, hospital websites, etc.

2.3 Research Questions

Given these definitions, we now define the main research questions that we answer in this paper.

- How prevalent are third-party critical CDN, DNS, and CA dependencies in Africa-centric websites?

---

[1] https://www.similarweb.com/website/kenyanmusic.co.ke/#geography.

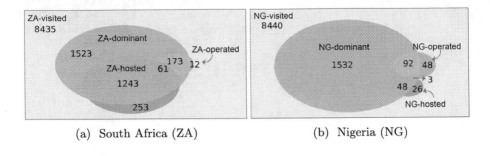

(a) South Africa (ZA)   (b) Nigeria (NG)

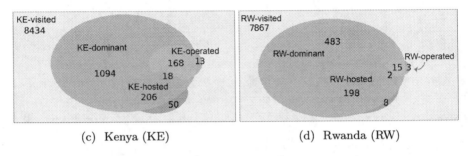

(c) Kenya (KE)   (d) Rwanda (RW)

Fig. 2. The figure shows the relationship between different website sets for all four countries. The visited set is the super-set of all the other sets according to our methodology described in Sect. 3.

- How centralized are third-party dependencies among providers that serve Africa-centric websites?
- How does the state of third-party service dependencies in African countries compare to the US? We compare with the US to use it as a baseline, as the prior work [28] looks at the prevalence of third-party dependencies from a vantage point in the US.

3   Dataset

To perform measurements, first, we pick four vantage points located in Kenya (KE), Rwanda (RW), South Africa (ZA), and Nigeria (NG). We choose these countries as they provide us with a vantage point in each of South, East, West, and Central Africa. Moreover, we found it extremely hard to get physically located servers (using VPN or cloud providers) in more African countries. Many VPN providers do not have physically located servers [60], and cloud providers are largely scarce. Next, we prepare country-specific website sets for each country, and then use the same country as a vantage point to carry out measurements. For example, we study *NG-visited* websites from NG. This section explains our methodology for collecting websites for each country and sets of interest.

One could look at all existing websites that belong the categories we defined in Sect. 2. To make the sets more tractable and focus on the most impactful websites, we start from the popular websites in each African country which constitutes the *country-visited* set $W_C^{visited}$. This helps in identifying websites that can impact the African Internet users, website operators, and the Internet economy of African countries the most.

We use the Chrome User Experience Report (CrUX) dataset [23] to get the top 10K popular websites in each selected African country. This dataset is curated monthly by aggregating browsing data of Chrome and Chromium users who have opted in for browser history and usage statistic reporting.This opt-in requirement may introduce bias and the list may not truly reflect popular websites in a region, however, prior work has evaluated the Google CrUX dataset and found it to be quite reliable with respect to popularity [53]. Moreover, Chrome and Chromium browsers constitute more than 80% traffic in our countries of interest [56]. CrUX is ranked by the number of completed page loads.

The CrUX dataset is aggregated by web origin (e.g., https://google.com). For DNS analysis, we need domain names, and using web origin may result in multiple entries for the same domain. Hence, we normalize this dataset by grouping web origins by domain names and choosing the smallest rank value as the rank for each domain. This same normalization technique has been previously done in prior work [53] and is shown to be accurate at capturing popular websites. [53] also shows that CrUX is better at capturing popular websites than other top lists as defined by visit and visitor metrics. In addition, most top lists only give popular websites in the world. However, for this analysis, we need regional popular websites and found that the CrUX dataset is a good source for that. We build our website sets based on the CrUX dataset for August 2022 and the definition of website sets can be found in Table 1.

Dataset for *Country-Visited* Websites: We use the CrUX dataset of the top 10K websites, for NG, RW, KE, ZA, and US. We normalize this dataset for each country, by grouping web origins by domain names as mentioned above. This gives us the *country-visited* $W_C^{visited}$ dataset for each country.

The *country-dominant*, *country-hosted*, and *country-operated* website sets are built from this dataset with the relationship shown in Fig. 2 for all countries. We describe our methodology below:

Dataset for *Country-Dominant* Websites: As defined in Sect. 2, *country-dominant* websites are made for users located in the corresponding African country. A naive approach to collecting such a list is to filter websites by their country code top-level domain (ccTLD) [8]. However, this approach would result in many false positives because some domain registrars give .ccTLD domains to anyone. For example, `parse.ly` has the Libyan ccTLD, but the website is not made for or visited by Libyan users[2]. Therefore, we combine multiple heuristics to collect the *country-dominant* websites. Concretely, a website belongs to the *country-dominant* set, if it belongs to *country-visited* set which is the top 10K visited websites and satisfies one of three requirements. First, we pick websites with ccTLDs that belong to that particular country. Observe that this filtering is

---

[2] https://www.similarweb.com/website/parse.ly/#geography.

different from the previous heuristic as we require that the website is popular in that country and has the ccTLD of the same country. Second, the website hostname contains Africa or the name of an African country. Again, while this heuristic would alone cause false positives *e.g.,*`ancient-egypt.org`[3] intersecting it with the popular sites in Africa considerably decreases those cases. Finally, we look at the website content of the landing page, and the website URLs referred to in the landing page to get the phone number associated with the website. We only consider a website to belong to a particular country if all the phone numbers mentioned on it have the country code of that country. This technique reduces false positives resulting from websites containing multiple phone numbers, not necessarily belonging to the website. For example, the website *viagogo.com* contains phone numbers of multiple countries including South Africa but its dominant country is actually Brazil[4]. To conclude, we define *country-dominant* websites $W_{dom-afr}$ as:

$$W_C^{dominant} = (W_C^{ccTLD} \cup W_C^{substr} \cup W_C^{phone}) \cap W_C^{visited}$$

Dataset for *Country-Hosted* Websites: To find websites hosted in an African country, we perform an IP geolocation lookup using the Maxmind Geo-Lite database [39], and the `ipinfo.io` [27] database for IPs missing in the Max-Mind database. Instead of performing IP geolocation lookup on all existing websites, here also we only look at websites that are hosted in the corresponding country, and are also popular in it *i.e.,* are in the $W_C^{visited}$ set. IP geolocation databases have certain limitations. Particularly, these databases tend to erroneously geolocate IPs that belong to ASes with global presence and IPs that change ownership due to merger and acquisition as observed by prior work [37]. This may misclassify some websites as not being hosted in Africa.

Dataset for *Country-Operated* Websites: To find websites operated in a given country, we look at the privacy policy and terms and conditions of websites to identify the country of interest. For example, in *murukali.com*, their terms and conditions page mentions, "These Terms of Service and any separate agreements whereby we provide you Services shall be governed by and construed in accordance with the laws of Rwanda." We use the Python Geography library [50] to extract geolocation mentions in the privacy policy or terms. We include only those websites for which we get a single country name, to decrease the number of false positives in classifying a website as being operated in a given country.

4 Methodology

We are interested in measuring the third-party dependencies of *Africa-centric* websites on authoritative Domain Name Servers, Content Delivery Networks, and Certificate Authorities for revocation information (OCSP servers and certificate revocation list (CRL) distribution points).

---

[3] https://www.similarweb.com/website/ancient-egypt.org/#geography.
[4] https://www.similarweb.com/website/viagogo.com/#geography.

To capture dependencies as observed by African users, we need to measure from multiple locations in Africa. Yet, accessing servers in various locations within Africa is challenging, due to the limited offered coverage from cloud service providers. To address this challenge, we combine the limited cloud presence with VPN services (PrivateVPN [48], ExpressVPN [20]) whose true location we diligently verified. We perform our measurements in October 2022 using four vantage points in Africa, scattered in East, West, South, and Central Africa. Particularly, our vantage points are in South Africa, Nigeria, Kenya, and Rwanda. For the South Africa vantage point, we use Amazon AWS, while all others are VPNs. To verify the location of the VPN server, we ping the server from different locations to identify the location with the smallest ping using online services like *ping.pe*, we also perform traceroute and we separately also reached out to the VPN provider to confirm the location of the VPN.

DNS Measurements: Given a website, we find out, 1)Does the website has a dependency on a third-party DNS provider? If so, 2) Is the website critically dependent on that DNS provider, or is it redundant? To find out the authoritative name servers, we use dig [17] (Domain Information Groper) which is a command-line tool to fetch the NS (nameserver) records which give the records for authoritative nameservers of a given website. To identify third-party nameservers, we follow the methodology documented in Kashaf *et al.* [28]. Particularly, we use top-level domain (TLD) matching [32], subject alternate name (SAN) lists [54], and start-of-authority (SOA) DNS record [6] to classify an NS as a third party. Particularly, we check if the second-level domain (SLD) and top-level domain (TLD) of the website and the NS match (*e.g.*, website *www.example.com* and its NS *ns1.example.com* have same SLD+TLD *i.e., example.com*) or if the SLD+TLD of the NS exists in the SAN list of the website, we classify it as private. If the SOA of the website and the NS do not match or if the concentration of the NS exceeds 50, we classify it as a third party. Kashaf *et al.* [28] shows that these heuristics can accurately classify providers as private or third-party. We get 12825 distinct (website, nameserver) pairs for *KE-visited*, 12287 pairs for *NG-visited* and 12792 pairs for *RW-visited*, and 14336 for *ZA-visited* websites of which 3% remain uncategorized as third-party or private for ZA, 4% for RW, 3% for NG and 2% for KE, and 3% from US. Hence, we conservatively exclude the websites involving them from our analysis. After identifying the third-party nameservers, we need to check if a website is redundantly provisioned. To do this, we group the nameservers of the websites by TLD and SOA records as documented in Kashaf *et al.*. Nameservers in the same group are considered to belong to the same provider. We observe 1010 distinct nameservers for KE, 1170 for NG, 1078 for RW and 980 for the ZA, and 1274 for US.

Certificate Revocation Measurements: Given a website, we are interested in knowing, 1)If the website has a dependency on a third-party CA provider. If yes, 2) Is the website critically dependent on that CA, or has it enabled OCSP stapling? We extract the CRL distribution points (CDP) and OCSP server information from the SSL certificate of the website. To fetch certificates, we first send a SYN on TCP port 443 to see if the website supports HTTPS. If we receive a Connection Refused error, then it means the website does not support HTTPS. Next, we initiate an HTTPS connection with it and fetch the SSL certificates. In the *NG-visited* websites, 94.0% support HTTPS, 95.7% support HTTPS in *KE-visited*, and 94.3% support HTTPS in the *RW-visited*, 95.2% in *ZA-visited* and 94.6% in *US-visited*. We observed 22 distinct CAs for NG, 26 distinct CAs for RW, 24 distinct CAs for KE, 23 distinct CAs for ZA, and 23 distinct CAs for US. We classify the CAs as a third party, again using TLD matching, SAN list, and SOA records [28].

Certain private CAs issue certificates and provide revocation checking for their own domains only, e.g., Microsoft, etc. Therefore, we use the same heuristics as mentioned for DNS to classify whether OCSP servers and CDPs are private or third parties as in [28]. Particularly, we classify a CA as private if the SLD+TLD of the website matched the SLD+TLD of the OCSP server, or if the SLD+TLD of the OCSP server exists in the SAN list of the website. Moreover, we classify the CA as third-party if the SOA of the OCSP server and the website differ. Next, to see if a website has a critical dependency on OCSP servers, we check if it has enabled OCSP stapling using OpenSSL [61]. If enabled, the certificate's revocation status comes stapled from the webserver when a user visits the website, requiring no online revocation check from the OCSP server.

CDN Measurements: To find CDNs used by a website, we look at the canonical name (CNAME) redirects for the internal resources of a webpage. If the website is using a CDN for a particular resource, the CNAME of that resource will point to the CDN. First, we render the landing page of the website using Puppeteer [49] and record the URL of all the resources retrieved by a website. Then, if the SLD + TLD of the resource matches that of the website or it exists in the website's SAN list, we classify it as an internal resource [28]. Then, we query the CNAME record for all internal resources of the webpage and use the CNAME-to-CDN map from the prior work [28], which we verified and extended to include African CDNs. Then we classify a CDN as a private or third party by using the same SLD+TLD matching, SAN Lists, and SOA records as done in the case of DNS and CA and in [28]. We find that 18.5%, 23.9%, 19.6%, 22.0%, and 40.4% use CDN for *NG-visited*, *RW-visited*, *KE-visited*, *ZA-visited* and *US-visited*. We observe 56 CDNs for NG, 59 CDNs for RW, 59 CDNs for KE, 55 CDNs for ZA, and 60 CDNs for the US.

4.1   Limitations

– Our analysis considers only four vantage points in Africa. It is possible that the dependencies in countries for which we do not have more vantage points vary greatly. While we accept this limitation, however, getting vantage points in some of the African countries is extremely hard due to the lack of mature Internet infrastructure, including VPN server presence.
– We only look at popular websites. While this may overlook certain websites, studying all possible websites is not feasible. We argue that this is a reasonable compromise as popular websites will be the ones that impact African users and businesses the most.

- Our heuristics for *Africa-dominant* websites may have false positives and negatives. However, the correct way to find *Africa-dominant* websites would be to choose the websites which have the largest traffic share from Africa. We had to use these heuristics because the data for per country traffic share of a website is not available.
- We inherit the limitations of Kashaf *et al.* [28] as we use their methodology.
- We describe OCSP revocation checking as a critical dependency from a website's point of view. However, the online revocation behavior of browsers differs. For example, many existing browsers circumvent online revocation checking by using other mechanisms like CRLsets in Chrome [12]. Similarly, Safari performs online revocation checking in case of revoked certificates. Many browsers also consider failures in revocation checking as a soft-fail. Note that some browsers allow users to enable online revocation checking. Moreover, the system's TLS stack at the user in some cases always performs online revocation checking no matter what browser is used [12]. Hence, we focus on the dependency from the website side while keeping in mind that at the user end, there may be other accommodations that make the dependency not critical.

5 Findings

In this section, we first analyze third-party dependencies in *Africa-centric* websites and use the US as a baseline. Next, we analyze provider concentration to identify single points of failure in the African web ecosystem. Note that for all the findings below, we show comparisons using percentage point difference.

5.1 Third-Party Dependencies

Observation 1: *93% of Africa-visited websites are critically dependent on third-party CAs, CDNs, or DNS. In perspective, US-visited websites are up to 25% less critically dependent.*

Figure 3 illustrates the portion of *US-visited*, *ZA-visited*, *NG-visited*, *RW-visited* and *KE-visited* websites that are critically dependent or redundantly provisioned as a function of the particular service and as measured by vantage points that are in the corresponding region. Concretely, Fig. 3a shows the percentage of critically dependent websites on DNS in African countries and the US. We observe that for DNS, critical dependency in *US-visited* is 5% to 7% less as compared to the African countries. Interestingly, when we look at more popular websites (top 1K), this gap further increases (6% to 10%) as shown in Fig. 3a. This means that web users from the US are comparatively less vulnerable, especially if they are visiting more popular websites, as compared to African users. This result indicates that more popular websites in the US may care more about availability as compared

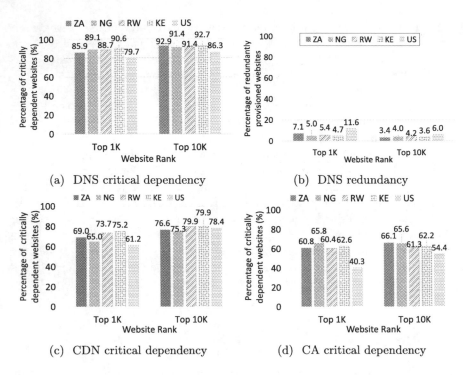

(a) DNS critical dependency   (b) DNS redundancy

(c) CDN critical dependency   (d) CA critical dependency

Fig. 3. (a) Critical DNS dependency for top 10K *US-visited* sites when measured from a US vantage point is 5% to 7% less than the top 10K *Africa-visited* websites. This gap in critical dependency increases to 6% to 10% in the more popular (top 1K) websites. (b) The percentage of websites that are redundantly provisioned is slightly higher (2%) in the *US-visited* websites as compared to the *Africa-visited* websites. However, when we look at more popular websites (top 1K), for *US-visited*, the percentage of redundantly provisioned websites is 5% to 7% higher than the *Africa-visited* websites. (c) Critical CDN dependency for the top 10K *US-visited* sites is similar to the top 10K *Africa-visited* websites. However, for more popular websites, *US-visited* sites are 4% to 15% less critically dependent than *Africa-visited* sites. (d) Critical CA dependency for the top 10K *US-visited* sites, when measured from a US vantage point, is 7% to 12% less than the top 10K *Africa-visited* websites. This gap in critical dependency increases to 20% to 25% in the more popular (top 1K) websites.

to the popular websites in African countries, making African Internet users more vulnerable.

Figure 3b illustrates the percentage of redundantly provisioned websites in DNS. We observe that there is not much difference (2%) between *US-visited* websites and *Africa-visited* websites. However, when we look at more popular websites (top 1K), the gap increases by 5% to 7% from 2%. At the same time, we find that the use of private DNS is only 3% to 4% higher in *US-visited* websites (not shown) and becomes 2% to 5% when we look at more popular websites (also not shown). This means that critical dependency in more popular *US-visited* websites is reduced because of an increase in redundancy instead of the use of Private DNS. However, for *Africa-visited*, there is not much significant increase in redundancy for more popular websites, except South Africa.

In case of CDN dependency, 22%, 18%, 23% and 19% websites use a CDN in *ZA-visited*, *NG-visited*,*RW-visited* and *KE-visited* websites respectively, while in *US-visited*, 40% websites use CDN (not shown here). Fig. 3c compares the critical CDN dependency in *US-visited* with *Africa-visited* websites. In the top 10K, critical CDN dependency in *US-visited* is comparable to the *Africa-visited* websites. We find the number of redundantly provisioned websites is also similar (not shown here). When we look at more popular websites (top 1K), the critical CDN dependency in *US-visited* is 4% to 14% less than *Africa-visited* websites while the CDN adoption in the top 1K websites is almost double in the US (44.6%) than African countries (20% to 27%). The use of private CDN remains negligible in *US-visited* and *Africa-visited* websites (not shown here). Moreover, the percentage of redundantly provisioned websites in the top 1K is 5% to 15% higher for the *US-visited* as compared to the *Africa-visited* websites. The reduced critical dependency as we move towards more popular websites in *US-visited* websites is because of an increase in redundancy.

Figure 3d shows the percentage of websites critically dependent on a CA in the *US-visited* and *Africa-visited* websites. The number of websites that support HTTPS is similar in *US-visited* and *Africa-visited* websites (not shown). Recall that for CAs, critical dependency is measured in terms of whether a website supports OCSP stapling or not. We find that *US-visited* websites are 6% to 12% less critically dependent on CAs compared to *Africa-visited*. Moreover, as we move to more popular websites (top 1K), the gap in critical dependency between *US-visited* and *Africa-visited* websites further increases to 20%–25%. This low adoption of OCSP stapling may be an indicator of low cyber readiness in Africa. Furthermore, in the US there have been many efforts to promote OCSP stapling, particularly by popular CDN providers such as Cloudflare, Amazon Cloudfront, and Akamai. Since the adoption of CDNs in *Africa-visited* websites is low, this could explain the lower adoption of OCSP stapling.

Observation 2: *Critical DNS dependency in Africa-centric websites is extremely prevalent (92% to 97%), leaving users highly exposed. Third-party critical DNS dependencies are higher in more popular websites compared to less popular ones.*

To further investigate the results of Figs. 3a and 3b, Fig. 4a also shows critical dependency and redundancy of websites in a third-party DNS provider but distinguishes them between visited, hosted, dominant, and operated website sets. For the set of visited websites, the critical DNS dependency is very high 91% to 93%, and stable across countries. This shows that users in Africa from these countries are equally vulnerable to the side effects of DNS third-party dependencies. If we look at the hosted websites, the *NG-hosted* websites are less critically dependent compared to other African countries. Concretely, the third-party DNS dependency is only 84% in *NG-hosted* websites. This is due to two key reasons. First, many

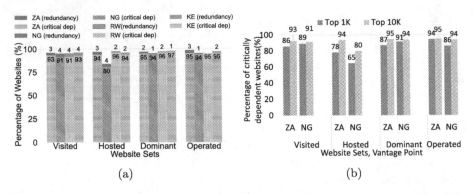

(a)   (b)

Fig. 4. (a) We show the percentage of critically dependent websites on third-party DNS providers with the percentage of redundantly provisioned websites stacked on it. The height of the bar stack shows the percentage of websites using a third-party DNS provider. Third-party critical DNS dependency is highly prevalent (more than 90%) in Africa-centric websites when measured from all four vantage points. (b) For each website set, we show how the critical dependency varies as we move from more popular (top 1K) websites to less popular (top 10K) ones for ZA and NG. Across all website sets, less popular websites are more critically dependent than more popular ones.

websites belonging to Meta (*e.g.,* facebook.com, freebasics.com, whatsapp.com, etc.) are locally hosted in Nigeria, and these websites use private DNS. Indeed, we confirmed their hosting by pinging them from Nigeria. Second, the *NG-hosted* sets contain only a small number of websites (Fig. 2) making the Meta associated domains statistically significant.

For dominant website sets, critical dependency for all African websites is very high, concretely 94% to 97%. In fact, the websites that predominantly target African Internet users are more vulnerable than *Africa-visited* websites, with a difference of 2% to 5%. There is almost negligible redundant provisioning in this set. For operated websites, again the critical dependency is 94% to 95% with negligible redundant provisioning. This trend in general shows that no matter where in Africa users are, or what they visit, they are highly vulnerable to the side effects of third-party DNS dependencies. Moreover, the fact that the trend persists across all African countries that we studied shows that the situation is dire for the entire continent. In fact, the countries for which we have results have relatively more developed Internet infrastructure.

Across countries, we observe that for ZA, critical dependency (though very high), and redundancy remain similar across different website sets. For NG and RW, with the exception of the *NG-hosted* websites, critical dependency in the specialized (dominant, hosted, operated) sets is larger than the corresponding *visited* set. In NG, this is because of a decrease in redundancy, while in RW this is because of a decrease in redundancy and a decrease in the use of private providers. KE has similar trends to RW and NG as shown in Fig. 4a. All in all, specialized sets have reduced redundancy except for ZA.

Figure 4b shows the critical dependency for the top 1K and top 10K websites for ZA and NG. As we move towards more popular websites (top 1K), the critical

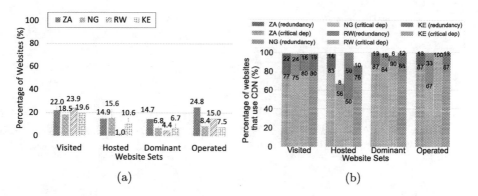

Fig. 5. (a) We show the percentage of websites that use CDN in different website sets for each country. CDN usage is less in the specialized sets such as hosted, dominant, and operated as compared to the visited set except for ZA. (b) We show the percentage of critically dependent websites on third-party CDN providers with the percentage of redundantly provisioned websites stacked on it. The height of the bar stack shows the percentage of websites using a third-party CDN provider. Critical dependency on CDNs for Africa-centric websites is less prevalent as compared to critical DNS dependency.

dependency decreases across all website sets for both ZA and NG. This is partly because of an increase in the number of websites using Private DNS (not shown). For example, for ZA, third-party dependency decreases by 4% for *ZA-visited*, and *ZA-dominant*. For *ZA-hosted* it decreases by 8%, while for *ZA-operated* it remains the same. In addition to the increase in private DNS, we also observe an increase in redundantly provisioned websites. For example, in the case of ZA, redundantly provisioned websites increase from up to 4% in the top 10K, to 6%-12% in the top 1K. We observe a similar trend in NG, KE, and RW. While the increase in redundancy for more popular websites is encouraging, it is still far from ideal. Even for more popular websites, third-party dependencies are highly prevalent. Across different website sets, we see more encouraging trends. For example, the hosted websites in the top 1K are far less critically dependent than the other website sets. However, this trend is only for ZA and NG and does not appear in KE and RW where it is more similar to the other sets. In NG, this decrease in critical dependence is primarily because of the use of Private DNS. For ZA, however, this is because some of the websites using global providers are using multiple providers, and also because all the websites using TENET South Africa as DNS, are redundantly provisioned.

Observation 3: *Among the websites that use CDN, critical dependency is prevalent (75% to 80%); although less compared to DNS. Third-party critical dependencies in CDN are higher in more popular websites compared to less popular ones.*

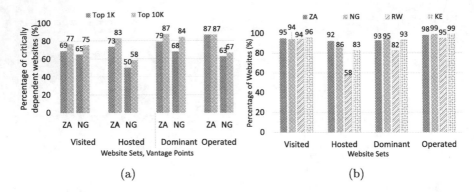

Fig. 6. (a) For each website set, we show the change in critical dependency as we move from more popular (top 1K) websites to less popular (top 10K) ones for ZA and NG. Critical CDN dependency is lower for more popular websites, as compared to the less popular ones. (b) The percentage of HTTPS support in websites is very high in Africa-centric websites, with the exception of the *RW-hosted* set.

Figure 5b shows the critical dependency and redundancy in websites that use CDN for different website sets. Here, the sum of critical dependency and redundancy gives the total third-party dependency. The number of websites using a CDN in each set is shown in Fig. 5a. In the visited sites, 18.5% to 23.9% use a CDN. In general, we observe a decrease in critical dependency as compared to DNS. In the case of visited websites, *ZA-visited* and *NG-visited* are slightly less critically dependent and are slightly more redundantly provisioned as compared to *RW-visited* and *KE-visited* websites. The use of private CDN across all vantage points of the visited set is less than 1%, which is not surprising. For the hosted set, *NG-hosted* has a higher percentage of websites with private CDN (100−58+8). This is because the websites affiliated with Meta use a private CDN. We ignore the trend in *RW-hosted* websites, as only 1% (2 websites) use CDN. *KE-hosted* websites are less critically dependent than *KE-visited* websites; this is also because of the private CDN using Meta domains, which become statistically significant because not many *KE-hosted* websites use CDN. For *ZA-hosted* websites, the critical dependence is higher than *ZA-visited* websites. It is unclear why this is the case as the CDN providers for both sets are similar.

For the dominant website set, all the countries have more critical dependence compared to the visited set. This means websites that predominantly target African users are more vulnerable. However, as shown in Fig. 5a, only a very small number of the dominant websites use a CDN. In the case of operated websites, the critical dependency is high for *ZA-operated*, *KE-operated*, and *RW-operated* websites. We do not see a specific reason for which the *NG-operated* are less critically dependent. The adoption of CDN in the specialized sets of hosted, operated, and dominant is very less to have a significant impact.

All in all, across countries, critical CDN dependency in the specialized set is higher than the visited set for ZA due to decreased redundancy. RW and KE follow the same trend with the exception of the hosted set. For NG, hosted, and

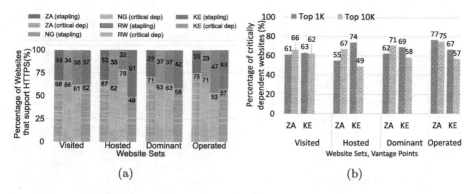

(a)   (b)

Fig. 7. (a) We show the percentage of critically dependent websites on CA providers with the percentage of websites having stapling enabled stacked on them. Third-party CA critical dependency is less prevalent in Africa-centric websites as compared to DNS dependency. Moreover, KE and RW are less critically dependent in the hosted, dominant, and operated sets as compared to ZA and NG. (b) For each website set, we show the change in critical CA dependency as we move from more popular (top 1K) websites to less popular (top 10K) ones for ZA and KE. Increase in popularity does not reduce critical CA dependency in Africa-centric websites. In fact, for KE (and also NG and RW), critical CA dependency increases as we move towards more popular websites.

dominant sets have reduced critical dependency compared to the visited set, while the operated set has increased critical dependency.

Figure 6a shows the change in critical CDN dependency as we move from more popular (top 1K) websites to less popular websites (top 10K). For example, for ZA, the critical dependency for more popular websites is 8% to 10% lower than less popular ones (except the operated set). We observe a similar trend for RW and KE. This reduction in critical dependency for more popular websites is because they are more redundantly provisioned. The use of private CDN remains negligible for the top 1K and top 10K websites (not shown here).

Observation 4: *In the case of CA critical dependency, 40% to 75% of the Africa-centric websites are critically dependent. For the hosted, dominant, and operated website sets, more popular websites are more critically dependent.*

Figure 6b shows the number of websites that support HTTPS. HTTPS adoption is in general very high in Africa-centric websites, which is encouraging. However, there are a few notable exceptions. For example, HTTPS adoption is low particularly in the *RW-hosted* websites. It is also low for *NG-hosted* and *KE-hosted* when compared to the visited websites. For RW, the *RW-dominant* website set also has lower HTTPS adoption as compared to other countries.

Figure 7a shows the percentage of critically dependent websites among all HTTPS-supporting websites. In general, critical dependency on CAs is less compared to DNS. In the visited website set, 33% to 38% of the websites that support HTTPS, also support OCSP stapling. In the case of hosted websites, the trend remains largely similar for ZA and NG. For RW, which already has only 58% HTTPS (Fig 6b supported websites in *RW-hosted* website set, for the remaining websites, only 22% support OCSP stapling. Hence, the *RW-hosted* websites leave African users particularly vulnerable. More alarming is the fact that more than half of these critically dependent websites are government websites ending with *.gov.rw*. For KE, 51% of the *KE-hosted* websites support OCSP stapling, which is encouraging. OCSP stapling support in KE is in general better for all website sets as compared to other countries. In the case of RW, OCSP stapling support is also good except for the *RW-hosted* websites. OCSP Stapling support for ZA is not very encouraging compared to other African countries. The *ZA-operated* and *ZA-dominant* websites are particularly more vulnerable than the respective sets in other countries. This means that ZA Internet users are vulnerable to the side effects of third-party CA dependency. In the case of NG, the *NG-operated* websites are more vulnerable compared to other website sets for NG.

Overall, critical CA dependency in the specialized sets for ZA is higher than in the visited set. For KE, the trend is the opposite. For NG, all sets have a similar critical dependency with the exception of the *NG-operated* set. For RW, critical dependency is higher for the hosted and dominant set, while lower for the operated set when compared to the visited websites.

Figure 7b shows the change in critical dependency as we move from more popular (top 1K) websites to less popular (top 10K) websites. For ZA, the critical CA dependency follows the same trend as in the case of DNS and CDN, where more popular websites are less critically dependent (except for *ZA-operated* websites). However, for KE, critical dependency actually increases in more popular websites (top 1K). We observe a similar trend for NG and RW. It is unclear why this is the case. Nevertheless, it is not encouraging and implies that more popular hosted, dominant, and operated websites are more vulnerable to the side effects of third-party CA dependency including outages, performance degradation, etc.

6   Provider Concentration

In this section, we first look at the concentration among providers for *Africa-visited* websites and use *US-visited* websites as a baseline. Then we closely look at Africa, for different website sets.

Observation 5: *The concentration of providers in Africa-visited websites is slightly higher than US-visited websites for DNS and CA.*

Figure 8 shows the cumulative fraction of websites for a given number of DNS, CDN, and CA providers. To compare the degree of concentration between

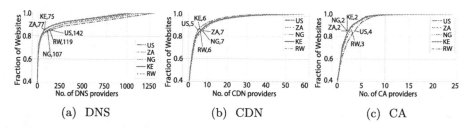

Fig. 8. The CDF of websites against the number of DNS, CDN, and CA providers for African countries and the US is shown. (a) Concentration of DNS providers in *ZA-visited* and *KE-visited* is slightly higher than *RW-visited*, *NG-visited* and *US-visited* websites. (b) The concentration of CDN providers in *Africa-visited* and *US-visited* websites is largely similar, with the concentration in *US-visited* websites being slightly higher. (c) The concentration of CA providers in *Africa-visited* websites is slightly higher than the *US-visited* websites.

Africa-visited and *US-visited* websites, we plot the fraction of websites served by a given number of providers. We label the number of providers that cover 85% of the websites for each country. In general, we observe a similar degree of concentration in *US-visited* and *Africa-visited* websites. Figure 8a shows the fraction of websites served by a given number of DNS providers. For *ZA-visited* and *KE-visited* websites, the concentration is slightly higher than *US-visited* websites. In general, a single DNS provider critically serves more than 40% of *Africa-visited* websites, while in the case of *US-visited*, a single provider critically serves 34% of the websites. Interestingly, the top 5 providers for *US-visited*, *NG-visited*, *RW-visited*, and *KE-visited* websites are the same global DNS providers (Amazon, Cloudflare, GoDaddy, NS1, Akamai). However, for *ZA-visited* websites, we do find local providers like Xneelo and Afrihost.

Figure 8b shows the fraction of websites served by a given number of CDN providers. We observe high concentration in *Africa-visited* as well as *US-visited* websites. Moreover, top CDN providers in *Africa-visited* and *US-visited* websites are also the same and are all global providers. Although *US-visited* websites have higher CDN adoption, the concentration among providers remains the same, which means websites are using the same few CDN providers. Figure 8c shows the fraction of websites served by a given number of CA providers. CA providers are more concentrated for *Africa-visited* as compared to *US-visited* websites. While the top providers in *US-visited* and *Africa-visited* websites are similar, we observe some minor differences. For example, Let's Encrypt and Sectigo are more popular in *Africa-visited* websites as compared to *US-visited* websites where Amazon is more popular. In general, DigiCert is the major provider in all.

Overall, we observe that African users are as vulnerable to the side effects of third-party dependencies as US users. Note that this is not encouraging or alleviating because Africa faces more challenges with respect to cyber security expertise, reliable infrastructure, etc., and hence single points of failure in Africa can have more severe consequences.

Observation 6: *Approximately 60% of the total African-visited sites are critically dependent on the top 3 DNS, CDN, or CA providers.*

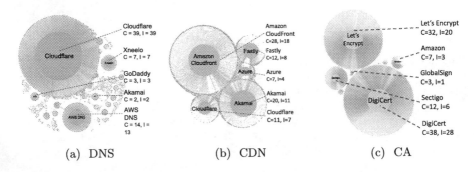

(a) DNS   (b) CDN   (c) CA

Fig. 9. Fig. 9a shows the dependency graph of the *ZA-visited* websites on third-party DNS providers, Fig. 9b shows the dependency graph of *NG-visited* websites on third-party CDNs, and Fig. 9c shows the dependency graph of *KE-visited* websites on third-party CAs. The size of a node in the dependency graph is proportional to its in-degree (signifying a dependency on the provider). We label the concentration C and impact I of the top 5 providers in terms of the percentage of total websites. (a) Cloudflare and Amazon serve most of *ZA-visited* websites and have higher concentration and impact than other third-party DNS providers. (b) Amazon Cloudfront and Akamai have a slightly higher concentration and impact as CDN providers for *NG-visited*. (c) DigiCert and Let's Encrypt serve the largest number of *KE-visited* websites and have a higher concentration and impact than other CA providers.

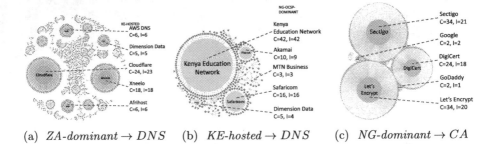

(a) *ZA-dominant → DNS*   (b) *KE-hosted → DNS*   (c) *NG-dominant → CA*

Fig. 10. (a) Africa local providers like Afrihost and Xneelo show up in the top 5 DNS providers for *ZA-dominant* websites. (b) Kenya Education Network provides DNS service for the largest number of *KE-hosted* websites. (c) Sectigo, Let's Encrypt, and DigiCert provide CA services to almost the same number of *NG-dominant* websites. The three providers also have similar concentration and impact.

Figure 9 shows the dependency graph for *Africa-visited* websites. The size of a node is proportional to its in-degree which is the number of websites dependent on it. We also label the concentration (C) and impact (I) of each provider as described in Sect. 2 in terms of the percentage of websites. Figure 9a shows the dependency graph for DNS providers for *ZA-visited* websites. We find that Cloudflare alone critically serves 39% of the *ZA-visited* websites. In general, the top 3 DNS providers critically serve 59% of the websites. We observe the same trends for other countries. For example, for *RW-visited* websites, the top 3 DNS providers critically serve 60% of the websites, 62% for *NG-visited*, and 58% for *KE-visited* websites. Moreover, the top 2 providers in all the countries are the same, namely Cloudflare and AWS DNS. For NG, we do not observe any local DNS provider in the top 10 DNS providers. For Kenya, we observe the Kenya Education Network (KENET) as one of the major DNS providers. For Rwanda, we observe AOS.rw as one of the major local providers. For ZA, we observe many local DNS providers in the top 10, namely Xneelo, Dimension Data, DiaMatrix, and Afrihost. For more popular websites (top 1K), the local DNS providers also come in the top 3 providers, for example, Kenya Education Network (KENET) for top 1K *KE-visited* websites, AOS.rw for top 1K *RW-visited* websites, and Dimension Data for top 1K *NG-visited* websites. However, websites using these local providers have almost zero redundant provisioning.

In the case of CDN providers, Fig. 9b shows the CDN dependency graph for *NG-visited* websites. The top 3 providers in *NG-visited* websites critically serve 37% of the websites that use CDN. We observe similar trends for other countries. For example, for *RW-visited* websites, the top 3 CDN providers critically serve 47% of the websites, 39% for *ZA-visited*, and 44% for *KE-visited* websites. Importantly, we find no local CDN provider being used by our African websites. Moreover, the top CDN providers remain similar for all African countries, even for more popular websites (top 1K).

In the case of CA providers, Fig. 9c shows the CA dependency graph for *KE-visited* websites. The top 3 CA providers critically serve 54% of the *KE-visited* websites. We observe similar trends for other countries. For example, for *NG-visited* and *ZA-visited* websites, the top 3 CDN providers critically serve 57% of the websites that support HTTPS, and 51% for *RW-visited* websites that support HTTPS. The top CA providers across all countries remain the same. There are again no local providers.

For the *Africa-dominant* websites, many local providers dominate. For example, Fig. 10a shows the DNS dependency graph for *ZA-dominant* websites. The concentration of DNS providers is evident: the top 3 DNS providers critically serve 47% of the *ZA-dominant* websites. More importantly, the top providers include many local providers such as Afrihost, Xneelo, and Dimension Data. *KE-dominant* websites have similar trends in DNS dependency, where KENET, Safaricom, and Kenya Web Experts are among the top providers. Similarly, for RW, local providers such as AOS.rw, Kaneza, and Afriregister are among the top providers. However, for *NG-dominant*, we do not see any local DNS provider.

Overall, there is concentration in *Africa-dominant* websites across all services. For example, in the top 3 DNS providers for *Africa-dominant*, the concentration remains between 48% to 58%. In the case of CDN dependency, the concentration of top 3 CDN providers for *Africa-dominant* websites remains around approximately 50% to 63%. Similarly, for CA dependency in *Africa-dominant* websites, the concentration of top 3 CA providers for *Africa-dominant* websites remains around approximately 52% to 62%. In the case of CDN and CA dependency, we do not see any local providers across all website sets. For example, Fig. 10c shows the CA dependency graph for *NG-dominant* websites.

In the case of *Africa-hosted* websites as well, there is concentration across all services. Figure 10b shows the DNS dependency graph for *KE-hosted* websites. A large number (42%) of these websites are served by Kenyan Education Network (KENET), which is a not-for-profit service provider that primarily serves universities, research institutes, government websites, and hospitals. Overall, the top 3 DNS in *Africa-hosted* websites critically serve 42% for ZA, 44% for NG, 68% for KE, and 91% for RW. For RW, only a single DNS provider AOS.rw critically serves 87% of the *RW-hosted* websites. In the case of CDN, only 3 CDN providers critically server 56% to 58% of *Africa-hosted* websites. Similarly, only 3 CA providers critically serve 45% for KE, 49% for NG, 75% for RW, and 60% for ZA in the hosted websites. For Rwanda, Digicert alone serves 63% of the *RW-hosted* websites, and for ZA, Let's Encrypt alone serves 42% of the *ZA-hosted* websites.

In addition to this, the providers for *Africa-operated* websites are also highly concentrated. For example, for *NG-operated* websites, Cloudflare serves as a DNS provider for more than half of the websites. We observe similar trends in CDN and CA providers and across countries. The high degree of concentration in the specialized sets also points towards the vulnerability of African users to single points of failure. Moreover, the existence of local providers in the specialized sets while encouraging also raises questions about the resilience of these websites. The high concentration among these local providers makes them single points of failure, where their expertise to defend against attacks and security incidents is not determined as compared to global providers like Amazon.

7   Discussion

In light of our findings, now we present some implications and recommendations for African users, website operators, and service providers.

High Concentration: We find that there is a great degree of concentration in the use of third-party DNS, CDNs, and CAs in the Africa-centric websites. This high concentration creates even more single-points-of-failure which are already prevalent in Africa [45]. Naturally, the third-party dependencies in combination with the problematic intermittent connectivity [15,42,45] hinder the growth of the digital economy in Africa, which would require reliable communication among users and businesses. Hence, it is of paramount importance that the websites are redundantly provisioned so that the outage of service providers does not affect the websites and that the website operators are trained to effectively handle outages and recover from failures.

Highly Prevalent Third-Party Dependencies: While the concentration of third-party dependency in Africa-centric websites risks their availability, it also creates opportunities. Indeed, third-party providers have certain benefits such as better quality of service, higher capacity, better security expertise, etc. which small websites cannot afford on their own. Hence, using third-party providers is not necessarily bad, but critically depending on it is.

Sparse Local Providers: We find that on all Africa-centric websites, the number of local providers is very small, except for South Africa. This is problematic in two ways. First, the lack of local providers questions the cyber-autonomy of Africa-centric websites and reduces the diversity of providers available to Africa-centric websites. Indeed, governments could and have tried to rectify that. For example, in Rwanda, with the help of Korea Telecom, the Government of Rwanda created a service provider AOS.rw that serves many Rwanda-centric websites. Even, not-for-profit initiatives like KENET, and South Africa TENET which provide DNS, and web hosting services among others to websites, are often supported by the government. Second, the use of non-local providers in some cases can also increase the cost of Internet access in Africa, if it implies content loading from outside Africa. Africa has one of the highest transit costs [51], hence accessing remote content also makes Internet access expensive for Africans. In our data, we find that most websites are hosted outside of Africa. Therefore, there is an incentive for policymakers to promote local hosting of content so that local providers and infrastructure are promoted.

Higher Critical Dependency in the Specialized Sets: In our analysis, we find that the prevalence of third-party critical dependency is higher in the specialized website sets, which are the *hosted*, *dominant*, and *operated* sets, as compared to the *visited* set. This is particularly more evident in the *dominant* and *operated* set for all services and countries. This is not an encouraging trend. This indicates that websites targeting Africans (dominant set) and websites being operated in Africa (operated set) are not paying enough attention to reliability, making them more vulnerable to the side effects of third-party dependencies.

8   Related Work

A huge body of work exists that performs dependency analysis. Some of those analyze dependencies on the country, or/and ISP. For example, Simeonovski *et al.* analyzes dependencies with respect to global scale threats where bad actors can be a country, an autonomous system, or a service provider like an Email server, DNS *etc.* [55]. Similarly, NSDMiner discovers network service dependencies such as ISPs, from passively observed network traffic [43]. Zembruzki *et al.* [62] looks at centralization among hosting providers. Hsiao *et al.* [25] analyzes the cyber-autonomy of government websites of the G7 countries. Dell *et al.* [16] studies third-party DNS dependency using a passive DNS dataset. WebProphet measures the internal backend infrastructure of websites for performance [35]. Similarly, Ikran *et al.* studies dependency chains in third-party web content [26].

Many studies try to understand CDNs and hosting infrastructure [1,11,31, 38,57]. These are complementary to our work. Other work analyzes the critical paths to understand how content affects the page load time (e.g., [59]), or focuses on the privacy implications of the tracking services (e.g., [30,34,52]). However, our work is orthogonal as it focuses on the infrastructure services at a higher level than individual websites. Kumar et al. [32] study HTTPS adoption and Podins et al., [47] measure the implementation of Content Security Policy, among third-party web content. Other efforts (e.g., [41,44]) analyze third-party web content for attacks. Ager *et al.* identifies and classifies content hosting and delivery infrastructures across the world [1]. Zmap [19] and Censys [18] present tools to scan the Internet at scale to find vulnerabilities like heartbleed. Our focus on web infrastructure is complementary to this work. Other work has analyzed the use of TLS, the certificate ecosystem, and the use of Certificate Revocation in the wild (e.g., [13,14,29,32,36,58,63]). These suggest potential attacks that could be executed via the third party services we analyze here.

There have been many efforts to understand the African Internet Ecosystem. For example, Akanho *et al.* measures the EDNS and TCP compliance in the nameservers for African websites [2]. Chavula *et al.* analyzes the location of cloud hosting providers in Africa for latency [9]. Calandro *et al.* analyzes the hosting of African news websites [7] to determine the fraction of local content. Similalry Brinkman *et al.* [5] discusses the interweaving connection in the Internet due to dependencies and tries to seek what constitutes "African websites", which we provided a definition for in our work. Arouns *et al.* looks at the DNS landscape for African ccTLDs [3]. Our work is complementary to these efforts as we also try to understand the resilience of the Internet in Africa.

9   Conclusion

In this work, we analyze third-party DNS, CDN, and CA dependencies in Africa-centric websites in an effort to bridge the gap between previous works, and offer region-specific actionable insights to African users and operators. Particularly, we study the prevalence of third-party dependencies on *Africa-visited*, *Africa-dominant*, *Africa-operated*, and *Africa-hosted* websites. We find that *Africa-centric* websites are highly vulnerable to the side effects of third-party dependencies. In addition, we find that there is a high degree of concentration in the use of third-party service providers, meaning that a handful of providers serve a large portion of the websites. Our findings have implications for the current usage and recommendations for the future evolution of the Internet in Africa.

10   Availability

Our code is publically available[5]. Our work does not raise any ethical concerns.

---

[5] https://github.com/synergylabs/Web-Dependencies.git.

Acknowledgements. We thank Amreesh Phokeer for their feedback and insights. Furthermore, we greatly appreciate the anonymous reviewers and our shepherd Oliver Gasser for their feedback and comments. We would like to acknowledge the support from the Bill and Melinda Gates Foundation through the Upanzi network. This work was also partially supported by NSF Awards TWC-1564009 and SaTC-1801472 and the Carnegie Mellon CyLab Security and Privacy Institute.

References

1. Ager, B., Mühlbauer, W., Smaragdakis, G., Uhlig, S.: Web content cartography. In: Proceedings of the 2011 ACM SIGCOMM Conference on Internet Measurement Conference, pp. 585–600 (2011)
2. Akanho, Y., Alassane, M., Houngbadji, M., Phokeer, A.: African nameservers revealed: characterizing DNS authoritative nameservers. In: Zitouni, R., Phokeer, A., Chavula, J., Elmokashfi, A., Gueye, A., Benamar, N. (eds.) AFRICOMM 2020. LNICST, vol. 361, pp. 327–344. Springer, Cham (2021). https://doi.org/10.1007/978-3-030-70572-5_20
3. Arouna, A., Phokeer, A., Elmokashfi, A.: A first look at the African's ccTLDs technical environment. In: Zitouni, R., Phokeer, A., Chavula, J., Elmokashfi, A., Gueye, A., Benamar, N. (eds.) AFRICOMM 2020. LNICST, vol. 361, pp. 305–326. Springer, Cham (2021). https://doi.org/10.1007/978-3-030-70572-5_19
4. Bock, H.: The problem with OCSP stapling and must staple and why certificate revocation is still broken (2017). https://blog.hboeck.de/archives/886-The-Problem-with-OCSP-Stapling-and-Must-Staple-and-why-Certificate-Revocation-is-still-broken.html
5. Brinkman, I., Merolla, D.: Space, time, and culture on African/diaspora websites: a tangled web we weave. J. Afr. Cult. Stud. **32**(1), 1–6 (2020)
6. Butkiewicz, M., Madhyastha, H.V., Sekar, V.: Understanding website complexity: measurements, metrics, and implications. In: Proceedings of the 2011 ACM SIGCOMM Conference on Internet Measurement Conference, pp. 313–328 (2011)
7. Calandro, E., Chavula, J., Phokeer, A.: Internet development in Africa: a content use, hosting and distribution perspective. In: Mendy, G., Ouya, S., Dioum, I., Thiaré, O. (eds.) AFRICOMM 2018. LNICST, vol. 275, pp. 131–141. Springer, Cham (2019). https://doi.org/10.1007/978-3-030-16042-5_13
8. Country domains: a comprehensive ccTLD list. https://www.ionos.com/digitalguide/domains/domain-extensions/cctlds-a-list-of-every-country-domain/
9. Chavula, J., Phokeer, A., Calandro, E.: Performance barriers to cloud services in Africa's public sector: a latency perspective. In: Mendy, G., Ouya, S., Dioum, I., Thiaré, O. (eds.) AFRICOMM 2018. LNICST, vol. 275, pp. 152–163. Springer, Cham (2019). https://doi.org/10.1007/978-3-030-16042-5_15
10. Chege, K.G.: Measuring internet resilience in Africa, November 2020. https://www.internetsociety.org/blog/2020/11/measuring-internet-resilience-in-africa/
11. Choffnes, D., Wang, J., et al.: CDNs meet CN an empirical study of CDN deployments in china. IEEE Access **5**, 5292–5305 (2017)
12. Chromium, G.: Crlsets. https://www.chromium.org/Home/chromium-security/crlsets/
13. Chung, T., et al.: Measuring and applying invalid SSL certificates: the silent majority. In: Proceedings of the 2016 Internet Measurement Conference, pp. 527–541 (2016)

14. Chung, T., et al.: Is the web ready for OCSP must-staple? In: Proceedings of the Internet Measurement Conference 2018, pp. 105–118 (2018)
15. Comment, D.S.: Load shedding in South Africa causes cooling system failure at MTN data center, July 2022. https://www.datacenterdynamics.com/en/news/load-shedding-in-south-africa-causes-cooling-system-failure-at-mtn-data-center/
16. Dell'Amico, M., Bilge, L., Kayyoor, A., Efstathopoulos, P., Vervier, P.A.: Lean on me: mining internet service dependencies from large-scale DNS data. In: Proceedings of the 33rd Annual Computer Security Applications Conference, pp. 449–460 (2017)
17. Dig: DNS lookup utility. https://linux.die.net/man/1/dig
18. Durumeric, Z., Adrian, D., Mirian, A., Bailey, M., Halderman, J.A.: A search engine backed by internet-wide scanning. In: Proceedings of the 22nd ACM SIGSAC Conference on Computer and Communications Security, pp. 542–553 (2015)
19. Durumeric, Z., Wustrow, E., Halderman, J.A.: ZMAP: fast internet-wide scanning and its security applications. In: Presented as Part of the 22nd USENIX Security Symposium (USENIX Security 13), pp. 605–620 (2013)
20. ExpressVPN: High-speed, secure and anonymous VPN service — expressVPN (2016). https://www.expressvpn.com/
21. Global, S.: Latest research shows DDoS attacks up by 300% in Africa since (2019). https://seacom.com/media-centre/latest-research-shows-ddos-attacks-300-africa-2019/
22. Globalsign certificate revocation issue, 13 October 2016. https://www.globalsign.com/en/status. Accessed 23 May 2020
23. Google: Chrome UX report. https://developer.chrome.com/docs/crux/
24. Hilton, S.: Dyn analysis summary of Friday October 21 attack, 26 October 2016. http://dyn.com/blog/dyn-analysis-summary-of-friday-october-21-attack/. Accessed 23 May 2020
25. Hsiao, H.C., et al.: An investigation of cyber autonomy on government websites. In: The World Wide Web Conference, pp. 2814–2821 (2019)
26. Ikram, M., Masood, R., Tyson, G., Kaafar, M.A., Loizon, N., Ensafi, R.: The chain of implicit trust: an analysis of the web third-party resources loading. In: The World Wide Web Conference, pp. 2851–2857 (2019)
27. Comprehensive IP address data, IP geolocation API and database - IPinfo.io. https://ipinfo.io/
28. Kashaf, A., Sekar, V., Agarwal, Y.: Analyzing third party service dependencies in modern web services: have we learned from the mirai-dyn incident? In: Proceedings of the ACM Internet Measurement Conference, pp. 634–647 (2020)
29. Kotzias, P., Razaghpanah, A., Amann, J., Paterson, K.G., Vallina-Rodriguez, N., Caballero, J.: Coming of age: a longitudinal study of TLS deployment. In: Proceedings of the Internet Measurement Conference 2018, pp. 415–428 (2018)
30. Krishnamurthy, B., Wills, C.: Privacy diffusion on the web: a longitudinal perspective. In: Proceedings of the 18th International Conference on World Wide Web, pp. 541–550 (2009)
31. Krishnamurthy, B., Wills, C., Zhang, Y.: On the use and performance of content distribution networks. In: Proceedings of the 1st ACM SIGCOMM Workshop on Internet Measurement, pp. 169–182 (2001)
32. Kumar, D., Ma, Z., Durumeric, Z., Mirian, A., Mason, J., Halderman, J.A., Bailey, M.: Security challenges in an increasingly tangled web. In: Proceedings of the 26th International Conference on World Wide Web, pp. 677–684 (2017)

33. Kumar, R., Asif, S., Lee, E., Bustamante, F.E.: Third-party service dependencies and centralization around the world (2021). https://doi.org/10.48550/ARXIV.2111.12253, https://arxiv.org/abs/2111.12253
34. Lerner, A., Simpson, A.K., Kohno, T., Roesner, F.: Internet jones and the raiders of the lost trackers: an archaeological study of web tracking from 1996 to 2016. In: 25th USENIX Security Symposium (USENIX Security 16) (2016)
35. Li, Z., Zhang, M., Zhu, Z., Chen, Y., Greenberg, A.G., Wang, Y.M.: Webprophet: automating performance prediction for web services. In: NSDI, vol. 10, pp. 143–158 (2010)
36. Liu, Y., et al.: An end-to-end measurement of certificate revocation in the web's PKI. In: Proceedings of the 2015 Internet Measurement Conference, pp. 183–196 (2015)
37. Livadariu, I., et al.: On the accuracy of country-level IP geolocation. In: Proceedings of the Applied Networking Research Workshop, pp. 67–73 (2020)
38. Matic, S., Tyson, G., Stringhini, G.: Pythia: a framework for the automated analysis of web hosting environments. In: The World Wide Web Conference, pp. 3072–3078 (2019)
39. Maxmind, L.: Geoip country database
40. Moyo, A.: Africa found wanting on cyber crime preparedness, December 2019. https://www.itweb.co.za/content/4r1lyMRoaVAqpmda
41. Mueller, T., Klotzsche, D., Herrmann, D., Federrath, H.: Dangers and prevalence of unprotected web fonts. In: 2019 International Conference on Software, Telecommunications and Computer Networks (SoftCOM), pp. 1–5. IEEE (2019)
42. Mutiso, R., Hill, K.: Why hasn't Africa gone digital? Scientific American, August 2020. https://www.scientificamerican.com/article/why-hasnt-africa-gone-digital/
43. Natarajan, A., Ning, P., Liu, Y., Jajodia, S., Hutchinson, S.E.: NSDMiner: automated discovery of network service dependencies. IEEE (2012)
44. Nikiforakis, N., et al.: You are what you include: large-scale evaluation of remote Javascript inclusions. In: Proceedings of the 2012 ACM Conference on Computer and Communications Security, pp. 736–747 (2012)
45. Phokeer, A.: The Gambia's internet outage through an internet resilience lens, January 2022. https://pulse.internetsociety.org/blog/the-gambias-internet-outage-through-an-internet-resilience-lens
46. Phokeer, A., Chege, K., Chavula, J., Elmokashfi, A., Gueye, A.: Measuring internet resilience in Africa (Mira). Internet Soc. (2021)
47. Podins, K., Lavrenovs, A.: Security implications of using third-party resources in the world wide web. In: 2018 IEEE 6th Workshop on Advances in Information, Electronic and Electrical Engineering (AIEEE). pp. 1–6. IEEE (2018)
48. PrivateVPN: Privatevpn: The world's most-trusted private VPN provider. https://privatevpn.com/
49. Puppeteer: Puppeteer, May 2022
50. Rakshit, S.: geograpy3: Extract countries, regions and cities from a URL or text, October 2022. https://pypi.org/project/geograpy3/
51. Rao, N.: Bandwidth costs around the world, August 2016. https://blog.cloudflare.com/bandwidth-costs-around-the-world/
52. Roesner, F., Kohno, T., Wetherall, D.: Detecting and defending against third-party tracking on the web. In: Presented as Part of the 9th USENIX Symposium on Networked Systems Design and Implementation (NSDI 12, pp. 155–168 (2012)
53. Ruth, K., Kumar, D., Wang, B., Valenta, L., Durumeric, Z.: Toppling top lists: evaluating the accuracy of popular website lists. In: Proceedings of the 22nd ACM Internet Measurement Conference, pp. 374–387 (2022)

54. SAN Certificates: Subject Alternative Name – Multi-Domain (SAN). https://www.digicert.com/faq/subject-alternative-name.htm
55. Simeonovski, M., Pellegrino, G., Rossow, C., Backes, M.: Who controls the internet? Analyzing global threats using property graph traversals. In: Proceedings of the 26th International Conference on World Wide Web, pp. 647–656 (2017)
56. SimilarWeb: Top browsers market share - most popular browsers in August 2022 — similarweb. https://www.similarweb.com/browsers/
57. Singh, R., Dunna, A., Gill, P.: Characterizing the deployment and performance of multi-CDNs. In: Proceedings of the Internet Measurement Conference 2018, pp. 168–174 (2018)
58. VanderSloot, B., Amann, J., Bernhard, M., Durumeric, Z., Bailey, M., Halderman, J.A.: Towards a complete view of the certificate ecosystem. In: Proceedings of the 2016 Internet Measurement Conference, pp. 543–549 (2016)
59. Wang, X.S., Balasubramanian, A., Krishnamurthy, A., Wetherall, D.: Demystifying page load performance with WPROF. In: Presented as Part of the 10th USENIX Symposium on Networked Systems Design and Implementation (NSDI 13), pp. 473–485 (2013)
60. Weinberg, Z., Cho, S., Christin, N., Sekar, V., Gill, P.: How to catch when proxies lie: verifying the physical locations of network proxies with active geolocation. In: Proceedings of the Internet Measurement Conference 2018, pp. 203–217 (2018)
61. Young, E.A., Hudson, T.J., Engelschall, R.: OpenSSL: the open source toolkit for SSL/TLS (2011)
62. Zembruzki, L., Sommese, R., Granville, L.Z., Jacobs, A.S., Jonker, M., Moura, G.C.: Hosting industry centralization and consolidation. In: NOMS 2022–2022 IEEE/IFIP Network Operations and Management Symposium, pp. 1–9. IEEE (2022)
63. Zhu, L., Amann, J., Heidemann, J.: Measuring the latency and pervasiveness of TLS certificate revocation. In: Karagiannis, T., Dimitropoulos, X. (eds.) PAM 2016. LNCS, vol. 9631, pp. 16–29. Springer, Cham (2016). https://doi.org/10.1007/978-3-319-30505-9_2

Exploring the Cookieverse:
A Multi-Perspective Analysis of Web Cookies

Ali Rasaii[1]([✉]), Shivani Singh[2], Devashish Gosain[1,3], and Oliver Gasser[1]

[1] Max Planck Institute for Informatics, Saarbrücken, Germany
{arasaii,oliver.gasser}@mpi-inf.mpg.de
[2] New York University, New York, USA
shivani.singh@nyu.edu
[3] KU Leuven, Leuven, Belgium
dgosain@esat.kuleuven.be

Abstract. Web cookies have been the subject of many research studies over the last few years. However, most existing research does not consider multiple crucial perspectives that can influence the cookie landscape, such as the client's location, the impact of cookie banner interaction, and from which operating system a website is being visited. In this paper, we conduct a comprehensive measurement study to analyze the cookie landscape for Tranco top-10k websites from different geographic locations and analyze multiple different perspectives. One important factor which influences cookies is the use of cookie banners. We develop a tool, *BannerClick*, to automatically detect, accept, and reject cookie banners with an accuracy of 99%, 97%, and 87%, respectively. We find banners to be 56% more prevalent when visiting websites from within the EU region. Moreover, we analyze the effect of banner interaction on different types of cookies (*i.e.,* first-party, third-party, and tracking). For instance, we observe that websites send, on average, 5.5× more third-party cookies after clicking "accept", underlining that it is critical to interact with banners when performing Web measurements. Additionally, we analyze statistical consistency, evaluate the widespread deployment of consent management platforms, compare landing to inner pages, and assess the impact of visiting a website on a desktop compared to a mobile phone. Our study highlights that all of these factors substantially impact the cookie landscape, and thus a multi-perspective approach should be taken when performing Web measurement studies.

1 Introduction

Web cookies serve various purposes, like keeping the user logged in or storing a user's website settings. However, other than their originally intended use, cookies have been exploited for commercial activities like user tracking and advertisement targeting [1, 4, 17, 18, 59]. As a consequence, various data protection laws have been enacted in the past few years, *e.g.,* the General Data Protection Regulation

(GDPR) [19] in the EU and the California Consumer Privacy Act (CCPA) [8] to regulate the use of cookies.

Numerous studies shed light on the complex ecosystem of sharing users' personal information across various third parties [6,26,43,44,64] and to what extent GDPR mitigates such abuse [74]. However, most of this research was conducted from a single or a limited number of vantage points (VPs). Thus, in this work, we characterize the cookie landscape from diverse geographic locations spanning six continents—North America, South America, Europe, Africa, Asia, and Australia. We complement the existing research by globally analyzing the following aspects of the cookie landscape:

Interaction with Cookie Banners: Most research involving GDPR does not consider interaction with cookie banners (*e.g.,* clicking accept/reject buttons) [1,18,45,74]. Thus, we develop the automated tool *BannerClick* to automatically detect, accept and reject cookie banners with an accuracy of 99%, 97%, and 87%, respectively (see Sect. 3). With *BannerClick* we automatically detect banners on about 47% of the Tranco top-10k websites in the EU region whereas in non-EU regions we find banners on less than 30% of websites (see Sect. 4). Furthermore, we analyze the difference in the number of cookies before and after interacting with a cookie banner and find an increase of 5.5× for third-party cookies.

Impact of Geographic Locations: To assess the effectiveness of GDPR, we compare observed cookies (especially third-party and tracking cookies) between EU and non-EU vantage points (cf. Section 5). We find that without banner interaction, 43% of websites send more tracking cookies when accessed from non-EU regions compared to the EU. Even after accepting a banner, 83% of websites send more tracking cookies in non-EU countries compared to EU countries. This percentage increases to 96% when rejecting banners. Our findings indicate a positive impact of GDPR on reducing the number of TP and tracking cookies.

Consistency of Websites: For cookie analysis, it is essential to observe that when a website is accessed multiple times, it sets a consistent number of cookies. If the variation in the number of cookies is high, then one cannot have statistically significant deductions about cookie characteristics (*e.g.,* number of third-party cookies). Thus we perform two statistical tests: First, we use the coefficient of variation to test for intra-location consistency, *i.e.,* how consistent the cookie landscape is when visiting a website multiple times from the same location. Second, we use the Mann-Whitney U test [47] to test for inter-location consistency, *i.e.,* how consistent is the cookie landscape when visiting a website from different locations. Our results show that websites are more consistent within the EU and that we find the most statistically significant differences between EU and non-EU countries (cf. Section 6).

Cookie Differences Between Landing and Inner Pages: We also explore the difference in cookies between the landing and inner pages of a website (see Sect. 7). As shown by previous work, the structure and content of landing pages differ substantially from inner pages [3]. Similarly, some websites may not send cookies on landing pages but may send them on inner pages. Hence, we quantify the difference between cookies on the landing and the inner pages of a website. For instance, at our United States VP, we find that 32% of websites send more third-party cookies on the landing compared to inner pages. Similarly, 29.7% of websites send more third-party cookies on inner pages when accessed from Germany. Overall, we find that 27.4% and 15.7% of websites exhibit different third-party and tracking cookie behavior on all VPs. Thus, studies analyzing *only* the landing pages may not present the full picture of the cookie landscape.

Cookie Differences When a Website is Accessed from Desktop and Mobile Browsers: As mobile Web browsing is becoming more popular and overtaking desktop browsing [23,70], it is important to study its cookie differences. This is underlined by the fact that websites often have mobile-specific versions that could lead to a difference in cookies. Thus, we conduct measurements to quantify the cookie differences between mobile and desktop (cf. Section 8). For instance, our US East VP sees more third-party cookies on desktop compared to mobile for 28% of all websites. Contrarily, when accessing websites from Brazil, 28% set more third-party cookies on mobile. Overall, 14.6% and 9% of websites show different third-party and tracking cookie behavior on all VPs. Therefore, future research investigating cookie behavior needs to take desktop as well as mobile websites into account.

Additionally, we analyze the *impact of the Brazilian and Californian privacy laws* [8,65] on Web cookies. Since these laws came into effect recently (*i.e.,* in 2020), the analysis of their impact is still in its early days [9,53]. Following California's privacy law, other US states are also considering adopting online privacy laws [78]. Thus it becomes necessary to draw insights from the enactment of these existing laws on the cookie landscape. In Sect. 9, we show that CCPA does not have a direct positive impact on Web cookies. Instead, we find that websites publicly adhering to CCPA tend to send more third-party and tracking cookies compared to others.

Overall, our measurement study highlights that factors like banner interaction, client location, landing vs. inner pages, and desktop vs. mobile substantially impact Web cookies. Thus, future research should incorporate these factors when analyzing the cookie landscape. To encourage reproducibility, we open-source our code [58] and release our data and analysis scripts [57] at bannerclick.github.io.

2   Background

In this section, we provide background information on different privacy laws and Web measurement platforms.

2.1   Privacy Laws Regarding Web Tracking

General Data Protection Regulation (GDPR): The European Union's GDPR—which came into effect in May 2018—is considered to be one of the most comprehensive laws safeguarding user privacy online.

The GDPR mandates that the storage and exchange of personal information (*e.g.,* cookies) is allowed only after a user has explicitly consented.

The only exception is for "strictly necessary" cookies that are essential for a website's operation, *e.g.,* storing user credentials. According to the GDPR, websites must obtain users' consent concisely and transparently. This results in websites showing *cookie banners*, informing users about the cookies being collected by the websites and third parties. Some banners explicitly ask for users' consent (*e.g.,* with *accept* or *reject* buttons), and some assume users' continued website use as implied consent. In this research, we study the impact of GDPR on cookie characteristics across the globe.

California Consumer Privacy Act (CCPA): CCPA is a state statute enacted by the California state assembly in June 2018. CCPA has similar goals as GDPR: it intends to protect the privacy of the residents of California. CCPA enables California residents to know what personal data is being collected (*e.g.,* their IP address), whether it is being sold to third parties, and the right to refuse to share their data. All companies operating in California with at least an annual revenue of $25 million must comply with the law. Importantly, even if these companies are not headquartered in California (or even the US), they still come under the purview of the CCPA.

Brazil's General Personal Data Protection Law (LGPD): Similar to the EU, Brazil also introduced a privacy law "Lei Geral de Proteção de Dados Pessoais" (LGPD) [39,65] that was enforced on September 2020. LGPD is again similar to GDPR. It also focuses on personal data and users' rights. Moreover, it states that website publishers must obtain consent before storing the personal data of clients (in the form of cookie banners).

To the best of our knowledge, in this work, we take the first step to empirically quantify the impact of CCPA and LGPD on Web cookies.

2.2   Web Privacy Measurement Platforms

There exist a variety of Web privacy measurement platforms, *e.g.,* OpenWPM [17], FPdetective [2], Chameleon [7] and Common Crawl [11].

OpenWPM is built using Python and uses the Firefox Web browser to visit websites through the Selenium automation tool [67]. OpenWPM is feature-rich, provides speed and scalability for large-scale measurements [17], and has been used by a plethora of Web measurement studies [79]. Thus in our research, we use and extend OpenWPM to collect, store, and analyze measurement data.

3   Data Collection and Approach

We now present our VP locations, target websites, and our approach to studying the cookie landscape in detail.

3.1   Location Diversity and Target Websites

We use AWS cloud instances at the following locations as our VPs: Frankfurt (Germany), Stockholm (Sweden), Ashburn (US East), San Francisco (US West),

Mumbai (India), São Paulo (Brazil), Cape Town (South Africa), and Sydney (Australia). We select these vantage points to have two VPs inside GDPR countries (Germany and Sweden), two VPs in the US (of which one is in the CCPA state California), one in Brazil (that has LGPD), one in Africa, one in Australia, and one in Asia.

In our measurement study, we use the global Tranco top-10k [42] as target websites for our analysis. The popularity of these websites is measured considering the actual Web traffic of users [63]. Other counterparts like the Cisco Umbrella list [31] and the Majestic Million list [46] are created using indirect sources like DNS queries and URLs embedded in website ads.

Additionally, for some experiments that require repeated measurements (*e.g.,* consistency tests), we use a subset of Tranco top-10k websites; we select three sets of websites: Tranco top-100, 1001–1100, and 9901–10k. These sets include websites from the top, middle, and bottom of the Tranco top-10k websites and hence represent different website tiers. We call this subset the "tiered Tranco list". In order to identify a suitable OpenWPM configuration, we perform multiple small-scale test runs. Table 1 shows an overview of our final large-scale measurement runs. The longest measurement takes 20 days, in which the Web can change substantially. In order to keep results comparable, we ensure that each website is crawled at a similar time from all vantage points. In the case of failure in one vantage point the website would be excluded from the final result. Moreover, we run OpenWPM in stateless mode and ensure that the browser does not block tracking when accessing websites [54].

As already mentioned, we completely automate our measurement campaign and access the Tranco websites using OpenWPM. We now explain our approach to detecting and interacting with cookie banners on our target websites.

Table 1. Overview of different measurement types.

Measurement Type	Start Date	Duration	Target Websites
Banner Interaction	Jan 20, 2022	20 days	Tranco Top 10k
Consistency Tests	Feb 9, 2022	10 days	Tranco tiered 300
Landing vs. Inner	Mar 8, 2022	4 days	Tranco tiered 300
Desktop vs. Mobile	Feb 27, 2022	10 hours	Tranco tiered 300
Impact of CCPA	Mar 13, 2022	10 hours	Tranco tiered 300

3.2 Automated Banner Detection and Interaction

Due to the EU ePrivacy Directive [20] and GDPR [19], many popular websites explicitly show cookie banners when accessed from within the EU [48]. These banners must inform the user about what user data will be collected by the website (using cookies). Moreover, they must provide a clear choice to users on whether to accept or reject these cookies.

To test whether websites respect the users' consent or not, (1) we detect the banners, (2) interact with them (*e.g.,* accepting/rejecting the banner policies), and (3) throughout the whole process collect all cookies. We completely automate this process by developing our tool called "*BannerClick*". We now explain how our tool detects and interacts with cookie banners using Selenium browser automation [67].

To detect banners, we first create a corpus of English words that very likely exist in banners by manually inspecting 50 random websites from Tranco top-100 domains. The corpus has eight unique English words *i.e.,* cookies, privacy, policy, consent, accept, agree, personalized, and legitimate interest. We translate these words into 11 different languages (German, Swedish, Spanish, Italian, Portuguese, Chinese, Russian, Japanese, French, Turkish, and Persian) and append the translated words to the corpus, increasing the corpus size to 80 words. We later show that with these words, we achieve an accuracy of about 99% for detecting banners.

Banner Detection: On a website's HTML page, *BannerClick* first searches all elements that contain a word from our corpus. As an example, the element `<p>` (shown in blue in Fig. 1) contains a banner-related word.[1]

Next, it traverses up in the DOM hierarchy towards the HTML element that has either a *positive z-index* or a *fixed position* attribute. Generally, cookie banners are either displayed on top of the webpage content (positive z-index) or maintain the same position on the webpage (fixed position). The element with these properties very likely contains the banner. We call this the "anchor" element (see the green `<div>` element in Fig. 1). If *BannerClick* fails to find such an element, it considers the `<body>` element as the div anchor element.

The anchor element contains the banner, but the banner may still be fully contained within some sub-element of the anchor. To find this most-specific element, *BannerClick* traverses down again in the DOM, starting from the anchor element. It uses the following heuristic: the visible elements contained inside the anchor (*e.g.,* banner title, description, and buttons) should also be contained entirely within the more-specific candidate element. Following this heuristic, *BannerClick* continues traversing down the DOM tree until it finds an element that does not completely contain all visible banner elements anymore. This implies that the parent of this element is the most-specific banner-containing element. This is shown as the red `<div>` element in the DOM tree in Fig. 1.

Some websites might include banners as `iframes`, which are outside the regular website's DOM. In cases where *BannerClick* fails to locate the desired element that contains the banner, it specifically iterates over all visible `iframes`. The above steps are once again repeated inside each `iframe` to detect the banner.

Efficacy of Banner Detection: We test our banner detection approach on the Tranco top-1k websites. We manually inspect and confirm that a total of 518

---

[1] We take extra precautions to filter out unlikely banner elements. For instance, if an element has a word from our corpus, but the element is set as *invisible*, we discard the element (as the banner should be visible to the user). See Appendix A for details.

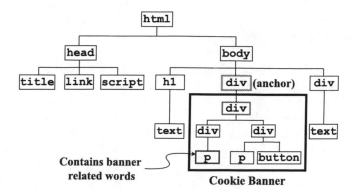

Fig. 1. An HTML Document Object Model (DOM) containing a banner.

websites show banners. Using *BannerClick*, we are able to correctly detect banners on 513 websites. Therefore, only 5 websites show a banner, but *BannerClick* fails to detect them. The reasons include the presence of a shadow DOM [50] on the website (godaddy.com) and banners having words not present in our corpus (washington.edu). Similarly, only 4 websites do not show any banner, but *BannerClick* incorrectly detects a banner. For example, allaboutcookies.org has cookie-related words in its DOM, but does not show a banner. Overall, *BannerClick* detects banners with more than 99% accuracy and extremely low FPR (0.008) and FNR (0.009).

Banner Interaction: After successfully detecting a banner, *BannerClick* can also interact with it. It can both "accept" and "reject" cookies in an automated manner. To do so, it relies on a corpus of words that are frequently used in cookie banners to indicate acceptance or rejection of cookies. This corpus consists of three categories of words indicating "accept", "reject", and "settings" (see Appendix B for more details on how we create the corpus). After successfully detecting the banner and identifying these words, *BannerClick* automatically clicks the identified button. Throughout all our experiments we use three modes to interact with websites *i.e.*, "No interaction" (we do not click any button on the banner), "Accept" (we click accept related words), and "Reject" (we click reject related words).

BannerClick first detects the banner and then identifies those HTML elements of the banner that contain words belonging to the said corpus. If it identifies multiple such elements, it first prioritizes <button> elements and then selects the one with the minimum number of words. For instance, in a banner, a <p> element may contain the text, "To accept all cookies, please click the button below", and another <p> element simply has the word "accept". Our tool selects the latter, as it is likely the button to provide consent.[2]

---

[2] One can simply detect the <button> tags and search for words inside them. However, we observe that banner buttons are not always implemented in this manner. Instead, many websites use other types of tags like <input> or <div> to implement buttons.

To provide consent for cookies, *BannerClick* searches for words belonging to the "accept" category in the corpus. When it finds a match, it clicks on the identified element. The process of rejecting cookies is similar: *BannerClick* searches for words inside the banner belonging to the "reject" category in the corpus. However, if it fails to find such words, it attempts to reject the banner policies using the Never-Consent browser extension [60]. Never-Consent searches for different functions provided by Consent Management Platforms (CMPs) to reject the banner policies (*e.g.,* OneTrust CMP's function `OneTrust.RejectAll()`).

However, if *BannerClick* still fails to reject the banner, it searches for the third category of words *i.e.,* "settings". This is because very often, the option to reject cookies is present inside a banner's settings. On a successful match, it clicks on the element containing the "settings" word. If the click is successful, the settings dialogue opens, and *BannerClick* again searches for words belonging to the "reject" category inside this dialogue. Using this approach, *BannerClick* can successfully detect, accept, and reject banners on websites.

Efficacy of Banner Interaction: As previously mentioned, 518 websites of Tranco top-1K websites show a banner. We manually confirm that 444 of these offer an explicit accept option. The remaining 74 websites do not give the option to explicitly accept (*e.g.,* the banner just has a close button, or there is an implicit accept[3]). *BannerClick* does not click accept button on any of these 74 websites.

In our research, we just consider explicit accept when interacting with banners. This is because, according to GDPR, websites must take users' consent explicitly. Later, for such websites, we quantify the increase in cookies after clicking the accept button. With *BannerClick*, we successfully click accept on 430 out of 444 banners with explicit accept. However, amongst the remaining 14, *BannerClick* clicks the incorrect button on 13 websites. The banners of these websites contain buttons with words that negate the semantic meaning of accept, *e.g.,* "NOT Accept" (which is essentially a reject). Since *BannerClick* does not consider the text's semantics, it incorrectly classifies them as the accept. Lastly, only one website shows a banner with words that we do not have in our corpus. Thus *BannerClick* failed to click the button for that single website. Overall *BannerClick* successfully clicks the button with more than 97% accuracy.

Finally, we calculate *BannerClick*'s reject accuracy by manually checking the screenshots for the Top-1k websites. *BannerClick* successfully reject banners on 377 out of 524 websites and finds that 81 banners do not provide a reject option, resulting in an accuracy of 87.4%. The majority of unsuccessful rejections come from 38 websites that use multi-select mechanisms to reject cookies.

3.3   Cookie Classification

Classifying cookies as first-party or third-party requires identifying the domain of the website as well as the received cookies. Thus, we use the public suffix

---

[3] Some websites show banners that do not overtly show the "accept" option. For instance banner on `bitly.com`, just states that "By continuing to use this site you are giving us your consent to do this".

list [52] to identify the domain of (1) the website and (2) the URL in the *domain attribute* of the cookies. Then for each of the received cookies, we compare its domain with the website's domain. On a successful match, we classify the cookie as first-party; otherwise, we consider it a third-party.

Next, similar to Götze *et al.* [28], we use the justdomains blocklist [36] to identify tracking cookies. This list contains entries from various popular tracking lists *viz.* EasyList, EasyPrivacy, AdGuard, and NoCoin filter lists, only if the *complete domain* is identified as tracking. If the cookie domain matches one of the domains in the justdomains list, we classify it as a tracking cookie. To ensure the correct classification of tracking cookies, we perform a small-scale validation: We identify the top 100 websites sending the most tracking cookies and then we manually inspect the tracking cookie domain. We confirm that well-known tracking domains are indeed sending these cookies (*e.g.,* `doubleclick.net`).

3.4   OpenWPM Measurement Setup

We use Amazon EC2 instances in eight different geographic locations. These instances have four CPU cores and are provisioned with 16GB RAM. For our measurements, we use OpenWPM v0.18.0 running Firefox in stateless mode [55] with the following configuration. In each run, we execute 7 browser instances in headless mode, with a 60s Selenium timeout[4]. Empirically, we observe the vast majority of websites to be loaded within these 60s. Moreover, we set the sleep time to 30s, which we experimentally find to be a suitable value. The sleep timer starts when the on-load event is triggered, ensuring that OpenWPM remains on the website for this time period. This is necessary because some cookies are still being set even after the page has finished loading. Furthermore, we set the OpenWPM timeout[5] to 360s (six times larger than the Selenium timeout). *BannerClick* starts detecting the banner (and interacting with it if configured) in three attempts at 0, 10, and 20 s after the sleep time has started. We see that more than 94% of banners are detected just on the first try. To aid in manual verification of measurements, *BannerClick* takes a screenshot of the website before interaction, the detected banner, the clicked buttons, and the website after each click.

For the banner interaction measurements from the VP in Germany, which consists of 150,000 separate crawls (10k domains each with 5 repetitions and 3 different modes of interaction), 138,018 are reachable, 946 and 455 exceed Selenium's and OpenWPM's timeout, respectively, for 10,175 the domain is unreachable, 406 trigger exceptions (*e.g.,* due to the lack of a `<body>` tag or page reloading during banner detection). In total, we consider 135,307 successfully completed measurements from all 8 vantage points in our analysis.

---

[4] Selenium timeout indicates the duration that Selenium waits for a website to be loaded by the browser.

[5] OpenWPM timeout forces the current website crawl to stop upon expiration. That is useful, as Selenium freezes during the loading of some websites (*e.g.,* `bet365.com`).

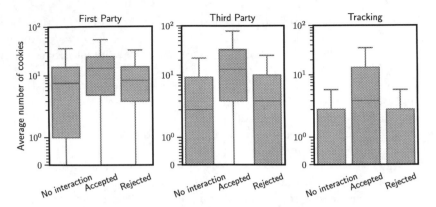

Fig. 2. Cookie differences between no interaction, accept, and reject from the Germany VP.

3.5   Ethical Considerations

Before conducting our Web measurements with OpenWPM, we incorporate proposals by Partridge and Allman [56] and Kenneally and Dittrich [37] and follow best measurement practices [16]. The AWS nodes are used only for measurement purposes, they are set up with informative rDNS names, they host a website with information about the measurements, and we offer the possibility for network administrators to be added to a blocklist. We run OpenWPM similarly as any regular user when visiting websites with a normal browser. During our measurement period, we did not receive any complaints.

4   Effect of Cookie Banners

As most research involving GDPR does not consider banner interactions (*i.e.,* clicking accept/reject buttons) [1,18,45,74], we develop *BannerClick* to automatically interact with banners.

We run *BannerClick* on the Tranco top-10k websites [42] to analyze the effect of cookie banners. First, we investigate how many websites we can detect and interact with banners. From the vantage point in Germany, we can successfully detect banners on about 47% out of all accessible websites. *BannerClick* is then able to click on Accept and Reject buttons of the banner for around 40% and 30% of all websites, respectively. Next, Fig. 2 shows how interacting with banners can substantially impact cookie distribution. After accepting a banner, the number of first-party (FP) cookies increases by more than 1× and the number of third-party (TP) cookies increases by 5.5× on average. As for tracking cookies, the average increase from zero to 7 which shows a significant impact. Also, the minimum number of cookies set by 75% websites (lower quartile) increases from 1 to 4 and 1 to 3 for FP and TP cookies, respectively; for tracking cookies it remains 0. Moreover, we observe a jump in the maximum number of cookies set, which for third-party cookies, and consequently tracking cookies, is quite

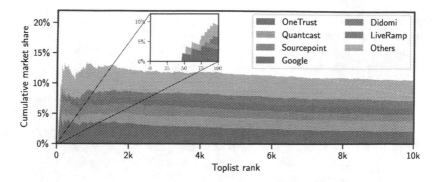

Fig. 3. CMP distribution depending on the Tranco rank from the Germany VP.

noticeable. As for the rejection impact on first-party cookies, we can also see a slight increase in the number cookies. This might be because of cookies that are being set to keep the state of rejection for future website access. This is further corroborated, as we do not see this trend for third-party cookies. Furthermore, we see that the number of tracking cookies is quite low (near zero) when the banner is not accepted, which indicates the effectiveness of GDPR to reduce tracking. Overall, we find that banner interaction has a large influence on the number of cookies, and it is therefore imperative to use tools like *BannerClick* to take banner interactions into account.

While accessing these websites with *BannerClick*, we also analyze the distribution of Consent Management Providers (CMPs). CMPs are platforms that offer cookie consent handling as a service, *i.e.*, websites can include a ready-to-use, yet configurable banner instead of developing their own cookie banner solution. The IAB Europe Transparency and Consent Framework (TCF) is a GDPR-compliant consent solution that specifies the overall behaviors of CMPs [33]. As mentioned in the specification of TCFv2 [32], all CMPs need to implement a `__tcfapi()` function which allows third parties to have access to the users' selected preferences and act accordingly. In *BannerClick* we use this function to record the name of the CMP while crawling a website. We observe that—contrary to the specification— not all websites with CMP banners actually implement the `__tcfapi()` function. This specification violation is not limited to a specific CMP. To obtain a better and more comprehensive distribution for CMPs, we additionally incorporate results from the Never-Consent browser add-on [60] into our data. Never-Consent leverages custom APIs which some CMPs implement in addition or instead of `__tcfapi()`. These custom APIs allow for interaction with CMPs to fetch user-related data or can even trigger a *reject all* event.

In Fig. 3 we show the cumulative market share of different CMPs for the Tranco top-10k websites. As we can see, in total within the top-1k websites around 13% of websites use CMPs. The CMP deployment remains almost constant with increasing rank, hinting at a consistent CMP deployment between ranks 2k and 10k. The CMP ecosystem is dominated by four companies (OneTrust, Quantcast, Sourcepoint, and Google) which are responsible for more than half of all CMP banners. Interestingly, we can not find a single website in the top 46 websites using a CMP and there is a generally much lower CMP deployment among top-ranked websites (see zoomed-in figure). This can be attributed to the fact that large Internet companies tend to avoid relying on third parties for handling privacy-sensitive data.

Throughout our study, we see a slight increase in CMP usage: From 95 websites out of the top-1k in July 2021 to 107 websites in January 2022. Therefore, it seems that CMPs will continue to play an important role in the cookie ecosystem, which future research should take into account.

As for other VPs, we see fewer CMPs detected on average. This is due to some CMPs not implementing their APIs (*i.e.,* `__tcfapi()` or custom ones), when they do not show a banner, which happens more for non-EU VPs. There is also an increase in the share of CMPs in the category "Others", which underlines that popular CMPs are less likely to provide APIs if no banner is shown.

Finally, we also compare our CMP results to previous work [29]. Their results for CMPs following TCFv1 are similar to our results for the new TCFv2 standard.

5   Impact of Geographical Location

We examine the effect of geographical location on banner interaction and Web cookies to observe if websites behave differently (*e.g.,* set a different number of cookies) in different regions. We crawl the Tranco Top-10k websites from eight geographically diverse vantage points (see Sect. 3.1 for more details). While accessing the websites, we interact with the banners in three modes: no interaction, accept, and reject. Figure 4 depicts the impact of geographic location on banner detection and interaction. In non-EU countries, we detect banners on less than 30% of websites, whereas, in EU countries we observe more banners (*i.e.,* on about 47% of the Tranco top-10k). This is a banner increase of 56% from non-EU compared to EU. Also, across all locations, *BannerClick* is able to accept more banners (blue + orange) than reject them (only blue).[6] This indicates that banners are biased towards showing more accept than reject options.

To analyze the effect of geographical location on cookies, we visit each website five times in each mode and record the number of cookies. If a website is not accessible in five of the iterations at any location, we exclude it from our geographical location analysis. We now report the cookie trends observed at different locations in different modes.

No Interaction Mode: In the no interaction mode, 63% of sites set a different number of TP cookies in at least one location. Of these websites, 56% follow a trend where they set the highest number of TP cookies in either the US East or the US West and the least in Germany and Sweden. We also confirm that in the EU region, about 56% of websites set TP cookies and 30% set tracking

---

[6] The slightly lower number of rejects in Sweden compared to Germany is due to a lack of Swedish reject-related words in our corpus.

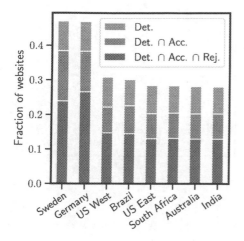

Legend:
- Det.
- Det. ∩ Acc.
- Det. ∩ Acc. ∩ Rej.

Fig. 4. Effect of location on banner detection, accept, reject.

cookies even in the no-interaction mode. In non-EU regions, a larger proportion of websites set TP (64%) and tracking cookies (43%). This indicates that GDPR has a positive impact on the reduction of TP and tracking cookies, but still many websites set these cookies without the users' consent. Setting TP (especially tracking) cookies before taking users' approval is a clear violation of GDPR.

Accept Mode: When analyzing the accept mode, we focus on those websites where we can successfully detect and accept banners at all VPs (*i.e.,* 18% of Tranco top-10k). This ensures that banner presence and different banner languages due to varying VPs do not influence our analysis. Amongst them, 21% of websites send precisely the same number of TP cookies at all locations; examples include `truecaller.com`, `ghostery.com`, and `deepmind.com`. These websites represent an ideal case where users from different regions receive the same number of TP cookies after consenting to the banner. This is noteworthy as even users who reside in regions without strong data protection laws (*e.g.,* India) experience similar privacy standards to those that live in the regions protected by such laws (*e.g.,* EU).

To further assess the impact of GDPR on TP and tracking cookies, we now consider those websites that offer banners *only* in the EU and on which *BannerClick* is able to click the accept button (*i.e.,* 37.6% of the total). For such websites, we observe that the variation in TP cookies is nearly identical for both VPs in the EU. We find a similar trend across the rest of the VPs in non-EU regions. Thus, we aggregate the data points per website for VPs in the EU, and separately for all non-EU ones.

In Fig. 5 we show an ECDF of the number of TP and tracking cookies for both EU (in blue) and non-EU regions (in orange). It is evident from the figure that, before interaction, about 60% of websites in the EU region set, on average at most 5 TP cookies, and about 80% of websites set, on average at most 4 tracking cookies. On the contrary, in non-EU regions, 60% of the websites set at most 20 TP cookies, and 80% set at most 40 tracking cookies *i.e.,* an increase compared to the EU region by a whole magnitude. Interestingly, 65% and 83% websites set fewer TP and tracking cookies respectively, even after accepting the banner policies in the EU, compared to no interaction at non-EU VPs. This shows that GDPR has a noticeable impact on the number of TP cookies. However, as expected, we find that GDPR does not impact FP cookies: 70% of websites set more or an equal number of cookies after accepting the banner compared to no interaction at the non-EU VPs.

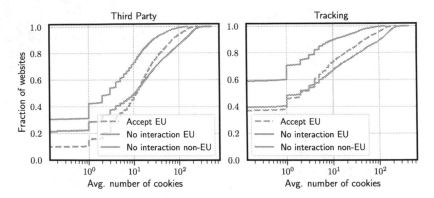

Fig. 5. ECDF plot with the average number of TP (left) and tracking (right) cookies for websites on which *BannerClick* is able to click accept only in the EU.

Reject Mode: For the reject mode analysis, we again select websites that again show banners only in the EU, and for which we are able to click the reject button (*i.e.*, 23.7% of the total). We find that 87% and 96% of these, set fewer TP and tracking cookies respectively in the EU after rejecting the banner compared to the no interaction mode at non-EU VPs. We observe a similar trend for FP cookies: 72% of these websites set fewer FP cookies in the same scenario.

Overall, our results indicate that GDPR has a positive impact on reducing the number of TP and tracking cookies, but we do not find any measurable effect of other privacy laws (*i.e.*, LGPD and CCPA) on TP and tracking cookies. This observation holds good for banner detection as well; we detect a maximum number of banners in the EU countries.

6   Website Cookie Consistency

Next, we analyze the consistency of website cookie behavior, in order to learn how consistently websites send a certain number of cookies. This is important to ensure, that what we measure is not influenced by website randomness, *i.e.*, due to excessively changing third-party content. For statistical consistency analysis, we visit each website of the tiered Tranco top-10k (100 websites each in three different rank tiers) 100 times for each of the three different interactions (no banner interaction, accept, reject).

Intra-location Consistency: To draw meaningful conclusions about cookie characteristics, one must ensure that a website sends a similar number of cookies when accessed multiple times from the same location. *E.g.*, if a website, when accessed for the first time, sends only five cookies, but when accessed the second time, sends hundreds of cookies, it should be classified as inconsistent. For such websites, it is non-trivial to draw meaningful conclusions from the measurements.

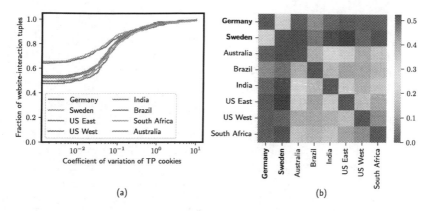

(a)   (b)

Fig. 6. (a) Intra-location consistency of third-party cookies. (b) Inter-location statistically significant differences of third-party cookies (EU VPs in bold).

From each of the VPs (in eight countries), we measure the intra-location consistency using the coefficient of variation (CoV) as a metric. The CoV is calculated by dividing the standard deviation by the mean. The smaller the CoV, the more consistent the cookie behavior is, when looking at it from each VP separately. We visit each website of the tiered Tranco list from each location and then calculate the CoV based on the number of cookies the website sends. Figure 6 (a) shows the ECDF of CoV for third-party cookies. We can clearly see two groups of websites in the plot: EU (Germany and Sweden) on the top and non-EU below that. It seems that when visiting websites from within the EU, they exhibit a more consistent cookie behavior. However, this difference is influenced mainly by the number of websites that send exactly zero third-party cookies which result in a CoV of zero: More websites when visited from within the EU send exactly zero third-party cookies, compared to when visited from a non-EU VP. This in turn leads to the ECDF curves of EU countries starting higher than non-EU countries, exhibiting a shifted, but the similar curve and later even merging. This is another indicator of the effect of the VP's geographical location in combination with GDPR on cookie behavior, as pointed out in Sect. 5. Overall, we find that 75–80% of websites are consistent with a CoV of less than 0.1 (*i.e.,* the standard deviation is at most 10% of the mean). For first-party cookies (not shown) we see a more similar picture across VPs.

Inter-location Consistency: To find statistically significant differences in the number of observed cookies depending on the VP location we use the Mann-Whitney U (MWU) test [47][7]. Again, we crawl websites from the tiered Tranco list 100 times for each interaction (no interaction, accept, reject) from each VP.

---

[7] The MWU test is a statistical post hoc test, *i.e.,* it allows to find differences in the cookie distribution between all pairs of VP locations. Our setup fulfills the MWU assumptions, *i.e.,* all test samples from both groups are independent of each other, the samples are ordinal. The distributions of both populations are identical under H_0 and not identical under H_1.

Then we apply the MWU test with Holm p-value correction [30] and choose a p-value of 0.05 to determine statistical significance. In Fig. 6(b) we show a heatmap depicting the statistical differences. In the figure, we see two main clusters, *i.e.*, EU vs. non-EU and non-EU vs. non-EU. We find that the majority of differences occur between EU (bold label) and non-EU locations, with more than half of all website-interaction tuples showing a statistically significant difference. On the other hand, if both locations are either in the EU or both outside the EU, we see fewer differences. Moreover, we also confirm that the Tranco rank tier does not affect the differences. An example of such a website is `nytimes.com`, which sends on average 5 TP cookies when visited from Germany or Sweden, 10 TP cookies from Brazil, and more than 80 TP cookies from other countries.

In conclusion, when visiting a website from a GDPR country compared to a non-GDPR country, there is a significant difference in third-party cookies being sent by most websites. For first-party cookies (not shown) we see a similar picture across VPs, although with fewer differences in total.

7   Landing vs. Inner Pages

When users access a website, they often not only access the website's main landing page but navigate through other inner pages of the website as well. For instance, people visiting the landing page https://www.bbc.com/ could access the article on the inner page https://www.bbc.com/sport/football/58920223. Thus, it is important to study the differences between cookies for landing and inner pages for a given website. We use a simple criterion to classify a link as an inner page (corresponding to a given landing page). An inner page link must begin with the landing page's fully qualified domain name (FQDN). For instance, https://www.bbc.com/sport/football/58920223 is the inner page of https://www.bbc.com/.

We intended to use the Hispar list [3] (which contains links to seemingly inner pages) for our analysis. However, we find that many inner pages mentioned in the list either do not begin with the FQDN of the landing page or redirect to completely different domains. For instance, `mail.google.com` is classified as an inner page of `google.com`, which in practice it is not. In general, we observe that more than 50% of inner pages (corresponding to a landing page) in the Hispar list are actually not inner pages. Thus, we use our own automated approach to access a given website's landing and inner pages. For our analysis, we select 10 random inner pages for each landing page as follows.

We first access the landing page of the given website (*e.g.*, https://www.bbc.com/). The obtained HTML page contains Web links to inner as well as non-inner pages. Next, we select a link by crawling for `<a>` elements and check whether it is a potential inner page or not. As already mentioned, we simply check that the inner page link must begin with the landing page's FQDN. Using Selenium, we visit this link and extract the final link (which might have changed due to redirection). If the link is an inner page, we append it to the list of inner pages. If the link is already present in the list, we ignore it and proceed with the

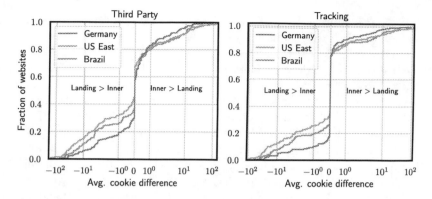

Fig. 7. Average number of TP cookies comparing landing vs. inner pages.

remaining ones. Finally, we stop searching for inner pages when either 10 inner pages are found or a total of 50 links (present on the landing page) have been tested. We repeat the same process for all tiered Tranco websites.

In total, we obtain 2273 inner pages corresponding to 300 Tranco websites. We access the set of landing and inner pages from all VPs. Like our other experiments, we visit each webpage (landing and inner) five times in each mode (no interaction, accept, reject) and record the average number of cookies per webpage. Figure 7 shows the ECDF of the difference of average TP and tracking cookies from the ten inner pages compared to the corresponding landing page (in the no interaction mode). The negative difference on the x-axis (left part of the figure) corresponds to the fraction of websites where we observe more cookies on a landing page than on inner pages (shown as Landing > Inner). Zero means the same number of cookies is found for both categories. Positive values (right part of the figure) correspond to the fraction of websites where more cookies are sent on inner pages than the landing page (represented as Inner > Landing). Figure 7 depicts this difference for three VPs *i.e.*, US East, Brazil, and Germany. We show only these three VPs because we observe nearly the same trend for US East and US West; observations in Brazil are quite similar to India, South Africa, and Australia; the trend in EU countries is almost the same.

At all of our VPs, we find that 12.7% and 8% of websites set more TP and tracking cookies, respectively, on the landing page than on the inner page (*e.g.*, `amazon.com`, `vk.com`, and `youtube.com`). Looking at VPs separately, the proportion of such websites is the highest in US East (32% TP and 24% tracking) and the lowest in Sweden (21% TP) and Germany (12.3% tracking). Moreover, our analysis reveals that 87% of these websites set at least 10 more TP cookies on average on the landing page at all locations. One possible explanation for this trend could be that many websites show more content on the landing page, include more third-party content, and thus set more TP cookies.

Similarly, we observe that 14.7% and 7.7% of websites set more TP and tracking cookies respectively on inner pages across all VPs (*e.g.*, `cnn.com`, `bbc.com` and `reddit.com`). When investigating each VP separately, the proportion of such websites is the highest in Germany (29.7% TP) and South Africa (19.3 tracking), and the lowest in US East (22% TP) and Brazil (15.3% tracking). It is interesting to note that, although GDPR discourages the use of third parties without consent, a substantial fraction of websites prioritize setting TP cookies on inner pages. This could also facilitate user profiling [1] as third-party services could better characterize users' viewing habits and choice of content at a more fine-grained granularity. Overall, our results indicate that studying *only* the landing page provides a partial picture of the TP cookies a user might get. In total, 49.3% and 27.3% of websites set a different number of TP and tracking cookies respectively on landing and inner pages at all our VPs.

Banners on Inner Pages: We check for banner presence as a potential contributing factor. Although we find a small number of websites with different banner behavior (*e.g.*, www.colorado.edu/map), we generally see a similar number of banners on landing and inner pages. Overall, using *BannerClick*, we detect banners on 22% (US East), 51% (Germany), and 30% (Brazil) of the landing pages of the tiered Tranco list. Correspondingly, we detect banners on 25% (US East), 50% (Germany), and 31% (Brazil) of the inner pages.

8 Mobile vs. Desktop

We look into the effect of visiting websites from browsers in desktop vs. mobile environments to understand how websites and third parties behave in this context. To visit a website from a mobile browser, we modify the default OpenWPM user agent[8] and the screen size[9]. We manually confirm that modifying these parameters change the appearance of most websites[10] and we see both desktop and mobile versions of the same website. Interestingly, even with these minimal changes, we observe substantial differences between measurements conducted from desktop vs. mobile. We crawl the 300 tiered Tranco websites 5 times in each mode of interaction from all VPs with desktop and mobile configurations.

Figure 8 shows the difference between the average number of TP and tracking cookies measured per website when visited from a browser on desktop vs. mobile in the no interaction mode. We subtract the number of cookies observed on mobile from what we observe on desktop. Hence, websites that set more cookies on the desktop yield a positive cookie difference on the x-axis. Vice-versa, if a website sets more cookies on mobile, the cookie difference is negative on the x-axis. We observe that the TP and tracking cookies variation is nearly the same

---

[8] Desktop: "Mozilla/5.0 (X11; Linux x86_64; rv:95.0) Gecko/20100101 Firefox/95.0"; mobile: "Mozilla/5.0 (Android 12; Mobile; rv:68.0) Gecko/68.0 Firefox/93.0".

[9] Desktop: 1366 × 768; mobile: 340 × 695.

[10] In some cases this also changes the URL, *e.g.*, by prepending `m.` or `mobile.` to the domain name.

for US East and US West. The data from the VPs in the EU are alike, and the data from the remaining VPs are similar to each other. Hence, we plot the TP and tracking cookies per website for US East, Germany, and Brazil representing their respective classes.

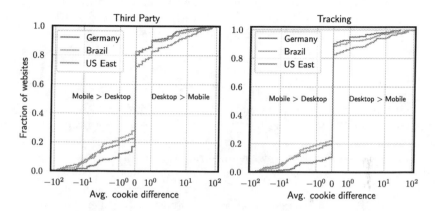

Fig. 8. Average number of TP cookies comparing mobile vs. desktop.

At all VPs, we find that 7.3% and 2.7% of websites set more TP and tracking cookies, respectively, when visited from a desktop (*e.g.,* `bing.com`, `twitch.tv`). On investigating VPs independently, we find that the proportion of such websites is the highest in US East (28% set TP and 17% set tracking cookies) and the lowest in Brazil (17% set TP cookies) and Sweden (9% set tracking cookies). From our analysis, we note that 7% of websites set at least 10 more TP cookies when being visited from a desktop from US East. These facts can be attributed to some websites having more content and hence more embedded third parties on desktop than on mobile. Many websites, when designed for mobile, decrease the number of advertisements and limit the content to what is visible without scrolling. This reduces data usage and improves the user's viewing experience.

We also observe that 7.3% and 6.3% of websites set more TP and tracking cookies, respectively when viewed from the mobile environment across all VPs (*e.g.,* `nytimes.com`, `livestream.com`). Distinct VP analysis shows that the proportion of such websites is the highest in Brazil (28% set TP cookies, 22% set tracking cookies) and the lowest in Sweden (15% set TP cookies) and in Germany (10% set tracking cookies). Our analysis shows that 4% of websites set at least 10 more cookies when visited from mobile from non-EU VPs. As users are increasingly spending more time on their mobile devices [23], some third parties seem to be prioritizing placing more cookies when sites are visited from mobile for better targeting. It becomes imperative that measurements from mobile environments also be considered for a real-world analysis of cookies.

Overall, we observe that 14.6% websites set a different number of TP cookies when accessed from desktop and mobile environments at all our VPs.

Furthermore, our findings show a higher degree of similarity between desktop and mobile compared to previous work [81], which did not consider banner detection or interaction at all.

Banners on Websites Browsed from Mobile: We check for banner presence as a potential contributing factor in this experiment as well. Using *BannerClick* we detect a similar number of banners on websites when visited from desktop and mobile ($\approx 21\%$ US East, 46% Germany, and 26% Brazil).

9   Impact of CCPA

The California Consumer Privacy Act (CCPA) came into effect in January 2020. In the context of CCPA, selling personal information in the form of TP cookies has been a widely debated topic [5]. Thus, we take the first step to studying how CCPA-compliant websites deal with third-party cookies. To analyze the cookie landscape of such websites, we first need to find which websites are overtly complying with CCPA. For this, we use a straightforward approach. Websites covered by CCPA must include a conspicuous hyperlink on their homepage with the text "Do Not Sell My Personal Information" (DNSMPI) [78]. We crawl the tiered Tranco list and identify websites that contain this hyperlink.[11]

Out of 300 tiered Tranco websites, we identify that 39 websites contain DNSMPI links from our US West vantage point, 29 websites from US East, and 21 from Germany. This indicates that a user's location impacts whether or not the DNSMPI link is shown. Interestingly, this applies to different locations within the US as well, *i.e.,* we see 11 websites that only show the DNSMPI link to clients from California but not when visiting the website from the US East.

To observe the impact of CCPA on TP cookies, we compare the TP cookies of websites containing DNSMPI links with websites that do not include said links. We select our US West (*i.e.,* California) VP for this analysis. First, we classify the 39 websites with DNSMPI links into three sets belonging to Tranco top-100, 1001–1100, and 9901–10k, respectively. For instance, we obtain 12 websites that belong to the first set. Thus, to have a fair comparison, we randomly select the same number of websites without a DNSMPI link from the Tranco top-100 websites only. We repeat the same process for the other two sets as well. In the end, we compare websites in the same Tranco rank tier. In total, we compare 39 websites with DNSMPI links with the same number of websites without DNSMPI links. This approach ensures that differences in TP cookies are not due to differences in Tranco rank.

Similar to previous experiments, we crawl each website five times and record the number of TP cookies. Figure 9 illustrates the variation in average TP cookies for DNSMPI and non-DNSMPI websites (without cookie banner interaction). We can see that websites without DNSMPI (blue line) set a lower number of TP cookies than the websites with DNSMPI (orange line). For example, 42%

---

[11] We use 8 different phrases for searching DNSMPI hyperlinks (*e.g.,* "do not sell my info") as suggested by Van Nortwick *et al.* [78].

of non-DNSMPI websites set on average just two or fewer TP cookies, whereas the same fraction of DNSMPI websites send 30 or fewer cookies. For tracking cookies, the trend is the same as TP cookies.

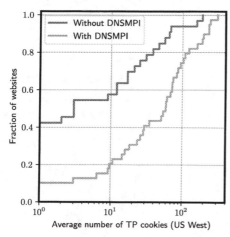

Fig. 9. Effect of CCPA on cookies: Websites with DNSMPI links send more TP cookies.

We further extend our analysis to Tranco top-10k websites, where we identify a total of 1373 websites with DNSMPI links from the US West. We observe a similar trend as we see with the tiered Tranco list. This shows that CCPA does not have a positive impact on TP cookies by default. On the contrary, websites overtly adhering to CCPA send, on average more TP cookies than non-DNSMPI websites. Furthermore, users need to manually look for the often well-hidden (*e.g.,* in website footers) DNSMPI links and click them to get any real benefit. When it comes to reducing the number of cookies, CCPA seems much less effective than GDPR or similar legislation.

We check if banner presence could be contributing to the TP cookie differences for DNSMPI and non-DNSMPI websites. To our surprise, we find that DNSMPI websites are twice as likely to show a banner compared to non-DNSMPI websites. As a result, DNSMPI websites show a banner more often but still send more TP cookies.

10   Discussion

Cookie Banner Automation: Since GDPR [19] and similar privacy legislation came into effect, cookie banners have become more and more prevalent on the Web. Moreover, during our measurements, we also see a wide variety of different banners. This not only makes automated detection and interaction more challenging for research purposes, but it also hinders browser and extension developers to effectively interact with banners in an automated fashion. These often rely on manually curated rules, do not have the option to reject cookie consent [38], or are no longer maintained [60]. Efforts to offer a general easy-to-use mechanism to refuse all tracking cookies such as HTTP's "Do Not Track" header [49], have not been adopted by the advertising industry and were therefore abandoned. The deployment of Consent Management Platforms (CMPs) could be leveraged as a standardized API for application developers to automate banner interaction. Unfortunately, we confirm previous findings [29] that many CMP websites do not properly implement these standardized APIs, which makes it difficult to make use of them. Moreover, CMPs are almost non-existent for very popular websites, which again leads to a lack of standardization potential for websites most visited by users. Additionally, many cookie banners make it purposefully difficult for people to reject all cookies [68]. As a prominent example, Google has been fined 150 million € for not providing users a choice to reject all cookies and was consequently forced to update their cookie banner [15]. All these factors hinder effective banner automation and it is unlikely that the situation will improve without a joint push by browser developers, advertising companies, and lawmakers.

Looking Ahead: In order to improve user privacy, browser vendors have recently started to block third-party cookies at various degrees. Mozilla introduced "Enhanced Tracking Protection" in 2019 [80] and is now moving towards completely isolated cookie stores per website [51]. Apple has introduced by-default TP cookie blocking in 2020 [24,71]. Google has long touted its desire to get rid of TP cookies and proposed a myriad of different possible replacements [10,25,66,72,77]. Getting rid of TP cookies is likely not the end of user tracking, as different techniques such as Local Storage, IndexedDB, Web SQL, or browser fingerprinting [41] can easily replace TP cookie functionalities [12]. Finally, privacy regulations such as GDPR are not specifically limited to cookies, but require informed consent for any shared user data, irrespective of the used technology. Cookie banners will therefore likely remain a prominent sight in the future, even if the underlying technology might change.

Limitations: Even though we cover a wide range of factors in our work, there are natural limitations to our approach. First, since our banner detection approach leverages words from 12 languages, we might not be able to detect banners on websites using other languages. Second, we use OpenWPM which uses the Firefox browser to access websites. Websites could exhibit different cookie behavior when being accessed from a different browser, such as Chrome or Safari. Third, we solely focus on HTTPS when accessing websites. Since many browsers use an HTTPS-first approach and most websites do support HTTPS [22], we think this focus is warranted. Websites can also be accessed via QUIC, which is not yet widely deployed [82], and we thus do not consider it in our study. Fourth, to classify third-party cookies as tracking cookies, we rely on tracking cookie lists. In order to limit false positive tracking classifications, we use the conservative approach by Götze et al. [28]. Therefore, our identified tracking cookies serve as a *lower bound*. Fifth, to obtain the mobile version of the websites, we modify the OpenWPM user agent and screen size (see Sect. 8). Although for most websites, we see the mobile version, for some websites these simple changes are not enough to load the mobile version [81].

11   Related Work

To regulate the use of cookies, various data protection laws such as the GDPR [19] in the EU or CCPA [8] in California have been enacted in the last years. A large body of previous work attempts to quantify the efficacy of such laws. Dabrowski *et al.* [13] reported less persistent cookie usage for EU users in comparison to US users with Alexa top-100k websites as targets. On the contrary,

Sanchez *et al.* [61] claimed that the US appears to approach cookie regulations similar to the EU. We do, however, observe a lower number of TP cookies in the EU when compared to non-EU VPs (see Sect. 5).

Furthermore, to check whether website publishers adhere to the EU cookie laws, Trevisan *et al.* [74] developed the tool "CookieCheck" [75]. They reported that half of the websites they tested ($\approx 35k$) from an Italian VP, violate the law *i.e.*, they install profiling cookies[12] before the user's consent. In contrast, we observe that in the no-interaction mode, "only" about 30% of websites set tracking cookies at our EU VPs. This might indicate that website publishers are adhering more to privacy laws over time.

While studying tracking, Iordanou *et al.* [34] identified the geographic locations of the tracking servers. They found that around 90% of the tracking flows originating in the EU terminate at tracking servers hosted within the EU itself. Additionally, there are multiple measurement studies that highlight how trackers use cookies for user profiling [6,17,21,26,43,44,64]. As an example, Englehardt *et al.* [18] demonstrated that adversaries could reconstruct up to 73% of a user's browsing history using only the collected cookies.

Linden *et al.* [45] took a different direction; they conducted a longitudinal study to assess privacy policies adopted by website publishers before and after GDPR went into effect. They reported that GDPR has a positive impact on privacy policies. Post-GDPR, not only the visual (and textual) representation of policies have improved, but the coverage of important topics *e.g.,* data retention, has also increased. Degeling *et al.* [14] also made similar observations *i.e.,* after GDPR, many websites have added and updated their privacy policies and now show cookie banners to the users. Sørensen *et al.* [69], rather than analyzing the privacy policies, found that after the introduction of GDPR, the number of third parties on EU websites has declined. They noted, however, that it cannot be concluded with certainty that this decline is solely due to GDPR. Kretschmer *et al.* [40] conducted a comprehensive survey of the existing research (> 70 research papers), describing the legal as well as technical aspects of GDPR. They report that the enactment of GDPR has resulted in a decline in third-party tracking, increase in cookie banners, and privacy policies in the EU region.

Santos *et al.* [62] studied cookie banners to analyze how clearly they explain privacy policies. They manually analyzed 400 cookie banners on English language websites that are popular in the EU. They report that 61% of banners used vague language and violated the specificity purpose. Utz *et al.* [76] rather than only focusing on the text of the banners, also studied other factors that could influence user consent decisions (*e.g.,* positioning of the banners on the website). The authors partnered with an e-commerce website in Germany and reported that changing the position of the banner or the text has a significant impact on the users' consent decisions. For instance, if the banner is shown in in the lower left part of the screen, users are more likely to interact with it.

---

[12] These are cookies that are managed by Web trackers to identify users and are clearly subject to explicit consent according to the GDPR.

More recently, Chen *et al.* [9] conducted a user survey of Californian consumers to study, to analyze how well they understand privacy policies of popular websites. They reported a significant variance in how websites interpret CCPA. Thus, privacy policy disclosures (mandated by CCPA) seem ambiguous to end-users. To this end, Connor *et al.* [53] performed a study to specifically analyze how websites implement "right to opt-out of the sale of users' personal information". They observed that websites implement this mandate in ambiguous ways, which deters the users' motivation to opt-out.

Finally, other research specifically analyzes cookie banners themselves *e.g.*, how clearly they specify privacy policies [62] or the impact of banner location on user consent [76]. Jha *et al.*'s [35] work is closest to our research. Similar to our work, the authors also attempted to interact with the banners in an automated manner to observe differences in cookies. However, their tool only accepts the privacy policies (of the banner), whereas our tool *BannerClick* has the capability to accept as well as reject a banner's consent.

12 Conclusion

In this paper, we performed a multi-perspective analysis of Web cookies. We developed *BannerClick* to automatically detect, accept, and reject cookie banners with an accuracy of 99%, 97%, and 87%, respectively. Then we ran measurements from 8 geographic locations on 5 continents and identified substantial differences between these vantage points. We found 56% more banners on websites when visited from an EU vantage point. Moreover, we quantified the effect of banner interaction: websites sent 5.5× more third-party cookies on average after clicking "accept". Accordingly, we observed a similar trend for tracking cookies as well. Finally, we also identified differences in cookies depending on the visited page on a website (inner vs. landing) and the client platform (desktop vs. mobile).

A   HTML Elements Not Part of Cookie Banners

While detecting banners, if an element has words from our corpus (see Sect. 3.2), and one of the following properties applies, we simply discard the element and move to the next one: (1) If the element is set as *invisible*, the banner is not visible to users, and they can therefore not interact with it. (2) An element with a *negative z-index* is behind some other objects on the page. Thus it cannot contain a banner as the banner should be on top of every object in order to be visible by the user. (3) The banner should be within the user's visible area of a web page. An element *outside the viewport* cannot contain the banner. (4) The GUI part of a banner is generally not implemented using *JavaScript*. Thus even if it contains cookie-related words, we simply discard them.

We use additional heuristics *e.g.*, if the cookie-related words are present in a `table` element, we simply ignore them as well. We make our code publicly available [58], along with detailed information about these additional heuristics.

B   Corpus of Words Used for Banner Interaction

To create the corpus of the "accept", "reject", and "settings" words, we access the Tranco top-10K websites and detect the banners on them. We proceeded with those Tranco websites, for which we successfully detect the banner. Next, we identify the language of each of these websites using Google's `cld3` library [27].[13] We observe that 4215 of these websites are in 12 languages; English alone is the language of more than 77% of those.

To detect commonly used words in a given language, we adopt a simple approach. For example, we select all banners in the English language, identify the `<buttons>` and their associated words in the banner, and count the frequency of such words. We separate out the words that individually appear in at least 1% of the banners. Figure 10 shows examples for such words. Examples for such words are "Accept", "Settings", "Reject", "Options", or "Agree".

For non-English languages (*e.g.,* German), we repeat the same process, but we additionally translate each of these words to English. We then manually check if they are semantically similar to any one of the following three categories: accept, reject, or settings. If the tested word is closer to any of these, we append the word to the appropriate category. We repeat the same process for each of the 11 non-English languages. At the end, we have 172 words in 12 different languages belonging to the three different categories.

C   Comparison With Priv-Accept Web Crawler

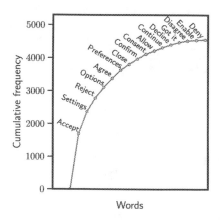

Fig. 10. Select English words appearing at differing frequencies inside the buttons of cookie banners.

Recently Jha *et al.* [35] proposed the tool Priv-Accept [73], which automatically attempts to "accept" privacy policies mentioned in a banner. They create a corpus of "accept" related words and compare them with the words present in the DOM of the website. If Priv-Accept finds the accept button, clicks it and compares the website behaviour before and after the click (*e.g.,* page load time).

We compare *BannerClick* with Priv-Accept. First, Priv-Accept is unable to identify and click reject buttons. Second, unlike *BannerClick*, Priv-Accept does not detect the banners but instead inspects the complete

---

[13] `cld3` at its core uses neural networks to detect the language of any given document. We manually select 20 websites belonging to 10 different languages (*i.e.,* two websites for each language). We identify the language of these websites using `cld3` library and find it to be 100% accurate.

DOM for accept-related words and, on a successful match, attempts to click the element containing the word. As a result, it can encounter multiple failures before actually clicking the desired accept button on the banner. On the contrary, *BannerClick* first detects the banner and searches for words contained within the banner. Third, *BannerClick* can click on accept related elements in 12 popular languages whereas, Priv-Accept only searches for English words. There are other differences, *e.g., BannerClick* looks for banners within the iframes, but Priv-Accept ignores iframes.

We compare both tools on the Tranco top-1k websites. With Priv-Accept, we can click accept on 451 websites, whereas with *BannerClick*, the number is 430. Websites where Priv-Accept could click accept but not *BannerClick* are 66, and vice-versa 59 websites. The vast majority of the former set are websites that do not show an explicit accept option. These are not considered to be explicit accepts by *BannerClick*, however Priv-Accept considers them. Additionally, Priv-Accept also clicks on the incorrect accept button for 11 websites. The latter group contains websites where Priv-Accept is unable to identify the correct button, *BannerClick* detects banners in iframes, or the website is in a non-English language.

References

1. Acar, G., et al.: The web never forgets: Persistent tracking mechanisms in the wild. In: CCS 2014
2. Acar, G., et al.: FPDetective: dusting the web for fingerprinters. In: CCS 2013
3. Aqeel, W., et al.: on landing and internal web pages: the strange case of Jekyll and Hyde in web performance measurement. In: IMC 2020
4. Bangera, P., Gorinsky, S.: Ads versus regular contents: dissecting the web hosting ecosystem. In: IFIP Networking 2017
5. Bateman, R.: CCPA: does Using Third-Party Cookies Count as Selling Personal Information? https://www.termsfeed.com/blog/ccpa-third-party-cookies-selling-personal-information/
6. Cahn, A., et al.: An empirical study of web cookies. In: WWW (2016)
7. Chameleon Crawler contributors: Chameleon crawler. https://github.com/ghostwords/chameleon
8. Chau, E., Hertzberg, R.: California consumer privacy act. https://leginfo.legislature.ca.gov/faces/billTextClient.xhtml?bill_id=201720180AB375
9. Chen, R., et al.: Fighting the fog: evaluating the clarity of privacy disclosures in the age of CCPA. In: WPES 2021
10. Chromium blog: potential uses for the privacy sandbox. https://blog.chromium.org/2019/08/potential-uses-for-privacy-sandbox.html
11. Common crawl: common crawl. https://commoncrawl.org/
12. Cookiebot: google ending third-party cookies in Chrome. https://www.cookiebot.com/en/google-third-party-cookies/
13. Dabrowski, A., et al.: Measuring cookies and web privacy in a post-GDPR world. In: PAM 2019
14. Degeling, M., et al.: We value your privacy... now take some cookies: measuring the GDPR's impact on web privacy. In: NDSS 2019

15. Dillet, R.: Google to update cookie consent banner in Europe following fine. https://techcrunch.com/2022/04/21/google-to-update-cookie-consent-banner-in-europe-following-fine/
16. Durumeric, Z., et al.: ZMap: fast internet-wide scanning and its security applications. In: USENIX Security 2013
17. Englehardt, S., Narayanan, A.: Online tracking: a 1-million-site measurement and analysis. In: CCS 2016
18. Englehardt, S., et al.: Cookies that give you away: The surveillance implications of web tracking. In: WWW 2015
19. European Commission: the general data protection regulation (GDPR) in EU. https://ec.europa.eu/info/law/law-topic/data-protection/
20. European Parliament: European ePrivacy directive. https://eur-lex.europa.eu/eli/dir/2009/136/2020-12-21
21. Falahrastegar, M., et al.: The rise of panopticons: examining region-specific third-party web tracking. In: TMA 2014
22. Felt, A.P., et al.: Measuring HTTPS adoption on the web. In: USENIX Security 2017
23. Gibbs, S.: Mobile web browsing overtakes desktop for the first time. https://www.theguardian.com/technology/2016/nov/02/mobile-web-browsing-desktop-smartphones-tablets
24. GlobalData thematic research: apple block on third party cookies will change digital media forever. https://www.verdict.co.uk/apple-halts-third-party-cookies/
25. Goel, V.: Get to know the new topics API for privacy sandbox. https://blog.google/products/chrome/get-know-new-topics-api-privacy-sandbox/
26. Gonzalez, R., et al.: The cookie recipe: untangling the use of cookies in the wild. In: TMA (2017)
27. Google: CLD3 on GitHub. https://github.com/google/cld3
28. Götze, M., et al.: Measuring web cookies in governmental websites. In: WebSci (2022)
29. Hils, M., et al.: Measuring the emergence of consent management on the web. In: IMC (2020)
30. Holm, S.: A simple sequentially rejective multiple test procedure. Scand. J. Statist. **6**, 65–70 (1979)
31. Hubbard, D.: Cisco umbrella 1 million. https://umbrella.cisco.com/blog/2016/12/14/cisco-umbrella-1-million/
32. IAB Europe: What is TCF v2.0? https://iabeurope.eu/tcf-2-0/
33. IAB Europe: what is the transparency & consent framework (TCF)? https://iabeurope.eu/transparency-consent-framework/
34. Iordanou, C., et al.: Tracing cross border web tracking. In: IMC (2018)
35. Jha, N., et al.: The internet with privacy policies: measuring the web upon consent. TWEB **16**(3), 1–24 (2021)
36. Justdomains: Domain-only filter lists. https://github.com/justdomains/blocklists
37. Kenneally, E., Dittrich, D.: The Menlo report: ethical principles guiding information and communication technology research. SSRN (2012). https://doi.org/10.2139/ssrn.2445102
38. Kladnik, D.: I don't care about cookies. https://www.i-dont-care-about-cookies.eu/
39. Koch, R.: What is the LGPD? Brazil's version of the GDPR. https://gdpr.eu/gdpr-vs-lgpd/
40. Kretschmer, M., et al.: Cookie banners and privacy policies: measuring the impact of the gdpr on the web. TWEB 15(4)

41. Laperdrix, P., et al.: Browser fingerprinting: a survey. TWEB **14**(2), 1–33 (2020)
42. Le Pochat, V., et al.: Tranco: a research-oriented top sites ranking hardened against manipulation. In: NDSS (2019)
43. Lerner, A., et al.: Internet jones and the raiders of the lost trackers: an archaeological study of web tracking from 1996 to 2016. In: USENIX Security (2016)
44. Li, T.C., et al.: Trackadvisor: taking back browsing privacy from third-party trackers. In: PAM (2015)
45. Linden, T., et al.: The privacy policy landscape after the GDPR. PoPETS (2020)
46. Majestic: the majestic million. https://majestic.com/reports/majestic-million
47. Mann, H.B., Whitney, D.R.: On a test of whether one of two random variables is stochastically larger than the other. Annal. Math. Stat. **18**(1), 50–60 (1947)
48. Matte, C., et al.: Do cookie banners respect my choice? measuring legal compliance of banners from IAB Europe's transparency and consent framework. In: S&P (2020)
49. Mayer, J., et al.: Do not track: a universal third-party web tracking Opt Out. https://datatracker.ietf.org/doc/html/draft-mayer-do-not-track-00
50. Mozilla: MDN: using shadow DOM. https://developer.mozilla.org/en-US/docs/Web/Web_Components/Using_shadow_DOM
51. Mozilla: new year, new privacy protection for firefox focus on android. https://blog.mozilla.org/en/mozilla/new-privacy-protection-for-firefox-focus-on-android/
52. Mozilla: public suffix list. https://publicsuffix.org/
53. O'Connor, S., et al.: (Un) clear and (In) conspicuous: the right to opt-out of sale under CCPA. In: WPES (2021)
54. OpenWPM: OpenWPM not using tracking blocking. https://github.com/openwpm/OpenWPM/issues/101
55. OpenWPM: openWPM stateful vs stateless crawls. https://github.com/openwpm/OpenWPM/blob/master/docs/Configuration.md#stateful-vs-stateless-crawls
56. Partridge, C., Allman, M.: Ethical considerations in network measurement papers. CACM **59**(10), 58–64 (2016)
57. Rasaii, A.: Analysis scripts and raw data for BannerClick web measurements. https://doi.org/10.17617/3.1MUYFX
58. Rasaii, A.: BannerClick on GitHub. https://github.com/bannerclick/bannerclick
59. Razaghpanah, A., et al.: Apps, trackers, privacy, and regulators: a global study of the mobile tracking ecosystem. In: NDSS (2018)
60. Robin, M.K.: Never-Consent on GitHub. https://github.com/MathRobin/Never-Consent/
61. Sanchez-Rola, I., et al.: Can i opt out yet? GDPR and the global illusion of cookie control. In: CCS (2019)
62. Santos, C., et al.: Cookie banners, what's the purpose? analyzing cookie banner text through a legal lens. In: WPES 2021 (2021)
63. Scheitle, Q., et al.: A long way to the top: significance, structure, and stability of internet top lists. In: IMC (2018)
64. Schelter, S., Kunegis, J.: Tracking the trackers: a large-scale analysis of embedded web trackers. In: ICWSM (2016)
65. Schreiber, A.: Right to privacy and personal data protection in Brazilian law. In: Data Protection in the Internet (2020)
66. Schuh, J.: Building a more private web. https://www.blog.google/products/chrome/building-a-more-private-web/
67. Selenium: browser automation using selenium. https://www.selenium.dev/
68. Soe, T.H., et al.: Circumvention by design-dark patterns in cookie consent for online news outlets. In: NordiCHI (2020)

69. Sørensen, J., Kosta, S.: Before and after GDPR: the changes in third party presence at public and private European websites. In: WWW (2019)
70. Statista: percentage of mobile device website traffic worldwide from 2015 to 2021. https://www.statista.com/statistics/277125/share-of-website-traffic-coming-from-mobile-devices/
71. Statt, N.: Apple updates Safari's anti-tracking tech with full third-party cookie blocking. https://www.theverge.com/2020/3/24/21192830/apple-safari-intelligent-tracking-privacy-full-third-party-cookie-blocking
72. Temkin, D.: Charting a course towards a more privacy-first web. https://blog.google/products/ads-commerce/a-more-privacy-first-web/
73. Trevisan, M.: Priv-Accept on GitHub. https://github.com/marty90/priv-accept
74. Trevisan, M., et al.: 4 years of EU cookie law: results and lessons learned. PoPETS 2019
75. Trevisan, M., et al.: Cookiecheck tool on github. https://github.com/CookieChecker/CookieCheckSourceCode
76. Utz, C., et al.: (un) informed consent: Studying GDPR consent notices in the field. In: CCS (2019)
77. Vale, M.: Privacy, sustainability and the importance of "and". https://blog.google/products/chrome/privacy-sustainability-and-the-importance-of-and/
78. Van Nortwick, M., Wilson, C.: Setting the bar low: are websites complying with the minimum requirements of the CCPA? In: PoPETS 2022
79. WebTAP at Princeton University: studies using OpenWPM. https://webtap.princeton.edu/software/
80. Wood, M.: Firefox blocks third-party tracking cookies and Cryptomining by default. https://blog.mozilla.org/en/products/firefox/todays-firefox-blocks-third-party-tracking-cookies-and-cryptomining-by-default/
81. Yang, Z., Yue, C.: A comparative measurement study of web tracking on mobile and desktop environments. In: PoPETS (2020)
82. Zirngibl, J., et al.: It's over 9000: analyzing early QUIC deployments with the standardization on the horizon. In: IMC (2021)

Quantifying User Password Exposure to Third-Party CDNs

Rui Xin, Shihan Lin$^{(\boxtimes)}$, and Xiaowei Yang

Duke University, Durham, US
{rui.xin926,shihan.lin}@duke.edu, xwy@cs.duke.edu

Abstract. Web services commonly employ Content Distribution Networks (CDNs) for performance and security. As web traffic is becoming 100% HTTPS, more and more websites allow CDNs to terminate their HTTPS connections. This practice may expose a website's user sensitive information such as a user's login password to a third-party CDN. In this paper, we measure and quantify the extent of user password exposure to third-party CDNs. We find that among Alexa top 50K websites, at least 12,451 of them use CDNs and contain user login entrances. Among those websites, 33% of them expose users' passwords to the CDNs, and a popular CDN may observe passwords from more than 40% of its customers. This result suggests that if a CDN infrastructure has a vulnerability or an insider attack, many users' accounts will be at risk. If we assume the attacker is a passive eavesdropper, a website can avoid this vulnerability by encrypting users' passwords in HTTPS connections. Our measurement shows that less than 17% of the websites adopt this countermeasure.

Keywords: HTTPS · CDN · Password · Security · Measurement

1 Introduction

Content Distribution Networks (CDNs) [37, 45] play an important role in improving the performance and security of web services. A CDN caches web pages at servers near end users to reduce retrieval latency. It also blocks malicious requests to defend a web server against various attacks [20]. Currently, many websites employ CDNs provided by third-party companies such as Akamai [1], Cloudflare [3], and Fastly [4].

However, third-party CDNs introduce a considerable security and privacy risk when they serve websites that enable HTTPS [15,17]. HTTPS uses a certificate to certify the domain name of a website. Thus, to make the web pages appear as if they come from the original site, a website has to share its TLS private key [15] or TLS session keys [51] with the CDN. In both cases, a third-party CDN can observe the content of all connections between a website and its users.

In this work, we aim to raise awareness of this security and privacy risk and quantify its severeness from a user's perspective. We choose to measure the extent to which users' website login passwords are exposed to CDNs due to the HTTPS key sharing practice. Although prior research has shown that private key sharing is prevalent on the Internet [15] and HTTPS termination weakens connection security of a great portion of the Internet [17], it is not clear whether websites have taken preliminary countermeasures such as client-side encryption (see Sect. 2) to protect users' passwords in the case of a passive attacker.

We conduct a measurement on Alexa top 50K sites [2] to quantify password exposure to CDNs during the user login procedures. We also measure the deployment of client-side password encryption on websites to understand websites' treatment of users' passwords. Such a large-scale measurement is technically non-trivial, because we need to automate the login procedures on websites with diverse structures to inspect login requests. Thus, we design and implement a framework for automatic login. The framework can detect login elements on a website and collect login requests when it submits credentials to websites.

Our main contributions and findings can be concluded as the following:

- We propose an open-source framework for automatic login[1], which can be applied to other research such as the measurement of authentication methods.
- Our measurement presents that 33.0% of websites that employ CDNs and contain login entrances expose users' passwords in plaintext to their CDNs.
- We find that two popular CDN providers, Cloudflare and Akamai, can observe users' passwords from 44% and 25% of their customers, respectively.
- We find prevalent password exposure in most website categories, including websites whose user accounts should be carefully protected, such as websites related to finance and health. Retail websites substantially benefit from CDNs, but most of them (58%) expose passwords to CDNs.
- Our result shows that less than 17% of the websites encrypt users' passwords when transferring login requests to CDNs, and the top 1,500 websites are more likely to adopt client-side password encryption.

Overall, our measurement points out potential security issues caused by password exposure to CDNs. Even though websites trust CDNs, users may concern about their privacy when CDNs can monitor their private data including passwords. Moreover, CDNs have never been secure enough. Prior work has shown that an attacker can trick some CDNs to cache and reveal other users' private data [19,38,39]. Thus, private data leakage to CDNs may turn into a disaster when attackers or malicious insiders exploit vulnerabilities of CDNs.

2   Background

In this section, we briefly introduce CDNs and HTTPS, and we analyze the security issues when a website with HTTPS employs a CDN. We also discuss two countermeasures adopted by websites in practice to address such issues.

2.1   HTTPS on CDNs

A CDN reduces web retrieval time by directing a client's request to an *edge server* which is hosted by the CDN and geographically close to the user. The edge server

---

[1] The code is available at https://github.com/SHiftLin/PAM2023-CDNPassword.

responds to the client with cached content. If the requested content is not cached, the edge server may fetch the content from the *origin server* which is hosted by the website (the CDN's *customer*) and is the initial source of all content. CDNs do not cache private data, as they are usually dynamic.

Modern CDNs are used not only to speed up page loading but also to provide an effective shield against attacks such as DDoS and code injections [20]. A CDN enlarges the serving capability of its customers to prevent volumetric DDoS attacks. It also applies techniques such as IP blocking and rate limiting to block attacks when DDoS happens. For example, Akamai protected its customers from 38,905 separate DDoS attacks from 2014 to 2019 [50]. CDNs also inspect the content of requests and use Web Application Firewall (WAF) to filter out malicious requests such as XSS injection [59] and SQL injection [24].

Unfortunately, CDNs have become a source of vulnerabilities in the HTTPS ecosystem in recent years [15,17]. If a website employs a CDN to represent it to respond to clients' HTTPS requests, it has to share its private key with the CDN. With the private key, the CDN can build HTTPS connections with clients, and clients cannot differentiate between the CDN and the origin server. When a client requests for private data, the CDN will forward the request by terminating the HTTPS connection and building another HTTPS connection with the origin server. Therefore, the CDN becomes a man in the middle when a user's private data are transmitted between the client and the origin server [15].

2.2   Countermeasures in Practice

Two instant but imperfect countermeasures have been deployed by some websites. First, a website can bypass the CDN and send the private requests to the origin server directly. In this countermeasure, a website should use a separate domain or subdomain for the private data, because the CDN possesses the private key of the original domain. We refer to this method as *"CDN bypassing"* in this paper. This method will not affect CDNs' benefit of page loading acceleration, since the private data are not cached by CDNs. However, it eliminates the benefit of having the origin server shielded against DDoS attacks, because the IP address of the origin server is exposed to the public. When attackers can connect to the origin server directly, it is much easier to launch DDoS attacks since the origin server usually cannot construct a DDoS defense as effectively as CDNs [22,54]. Besides DDoS, the CDN cannot inspect the private content to filter out malicious requests, and thus the origin server may suffer from attacks such as code injections.

Another countermeasure is to encrypt private data inside HTTPS connections. The website generates another key pair and delivers the new public key to the client. The client uses the public key to encrypt the private data to be sent out. Therefore, when a CDN forwards the request, the private data are invisible to the CDN. We refer to this method as *"client-side encryption"* in our paper. We observe some websites use this method to protect users' passwords only, as encrypting all private data may introduce too much overhead. However, the client-side encryption only defends against a passive attacker as described in Sect. 3. Besides, secure public key delivery is non-trivial when HTTPS connections are already intercepted by a CDN [35]. Delivering another certificate differing from the HTTPS certificate is useless, because a website has to use JavaScript to conduct encryption in current browsers, and the JavaScript code cannot obtain the root certificates of a client to verify a certificate. Without a certificate, if the public key is delivered by a CDN, a CDN with an active attacker (defined in Sect. 3) inside can launch the man-in-the-middle attacks by replacing the public key. If the public key is delivered by the origin server, the origin server is exposed to the public and under the threat of DDoS. In practice, websites use an asynchronous JavaScript call [6] to request for a public key from the origin server and encrypt passwords by JavaScript code.

Despite the defects of these two methods, they preserve users' privacy to some extent. Moreover, if the origin server builds its own DDoS defense or a CDN is assumed to be a passive attacker, these two countermeasures can provide sufficient protection. However, it is unclear about the deployment of these two countermeasures on websites. Thus, we investigate the password exposure to provide a profile of their deployment.

3 Threat Model

We use the threat model proposed by the prior work [35]. We consider the private data in a website as the data can only be accessed by a authenticated user. The users can be authenticated by the traditional password, one-time password (OTP), OAuth [25], certificates, etc. The credentials for authentication are considered as private data as well. We focus on the measurement of the traditional password in this paper.

We considered two types of attackers defined in the prior work [35].

- **Passive attacker:** A CDN behaves honestly to serve the requests, but an attacker inside the CDN may eavesdrop on the transmitted messages. For example, a malicious administer of a CDN cannot change the CDN's behavior but may peek at the transmitted traffic and record users' passwords. Client-side encryption can protect users' password under a passive attacker.
- **Active attacker:** An attacker insider CDN may launch arbitrary attacks including eavesdropping and tampering. Thus, it is more capable than a passive attacker. For example, a CDN may modify or corrupt the cached HTML or JavaScript to disable the client-side encryption so that it can observe users' passwords in the login requests. This may happen when attackers exploit a vulnerability of a CDN. As previously mentioned, CDN-bypassing can defend against an active attacker inside a CDN, but it introduces the vulnerability of DDoS to the origin server.

4 Method

To detect the password exposure, we should inspect a website's login request and the destination. Thus, we need a framework for automatic login in a large-scale measurement. Currently, a website may adopt multiple authentication methods, such as text passwords, OAuth [25], one-time password (OTP). In our measurement, we only consider the method of text passwords.

Based on the existing frameworks [31,47,48], we designed and implemented an automatic login framework that copes with more web pages with diverse structures. In our work, we do not need to successfully log into a website, so the framework merely triggers a failed login and collects the login request. We elaborate on the design and implementation of such a framework in the appendix.

Besides the automatic login framework, we use the method in the prior work [15,27,32,33,35] to discover the CDN usage of a website. This method also helps to inspect the destination of the collected login requests to determine whether the requests are sent to a CDN server.

Some cloud providers will provide both hosting service and CDN service, such as AWS and Azure. In our method, when a request is sent to such a cloud provider, we cannot determine whether the website is using the CDN service or the hosting service. If the password is sent to a hosting service, it should not be considered as an exposure to a CDN. Since our goal is to provide an underestimation of password exposure, our CDN list does not include a CDN service provider that also provides hosting service. As a result, our CDN list contains 9 popular CDNs, namely Cloudflare, Akamai, Fastly, Highwinds, Edgecast, Incapsula, Quantil, CDNetworks, and Limelight.

We collected 50k websites from the Alexa ranking list [2] and ran our experiments of automatic login and CDN discovery in Oct. 2020. In our future work, we will set up our experiments as a monitoring platform to observe the evolution of password exposure behavior.

Ethical concerns: We respect user privacy, and our work does not raise ethical concerns. The method of CDN discovery only used public data from the Internet, such as Registration Data Access Protocol (RDAP) [43]. As for the automatic login framework, since we do not require a successful login, we use a randomly generated fake account that is nearly impossible to coincide with existing ones. We skip the websites that require a test of the account existence before submitting the login credentials. We only conduct the login trial once for each website, so we do not overload the websites in our test.

5   Password Exposure

We only consider HTTPS-enabled websites because a website without HTTPS apparently contains major vulnerabilities. In Alexa top 50K sites [2], 42,502 of them enable HTTPS. We run the framework to automatically log into these websites. If the framework submits the fake credentials to a website, we consider it performs a login. The framework performs 17,111 logins in total. In this paper, we focus on these 17,111 websites and call them "login-detected websites".

We detect CDNs employed by these websites according to Sect. 4. Our result shows that 12,451 websites employ CDN service, and we call them "CDN-enabled websites" in this paper. By inspecting their login procedures, we find that 4,114

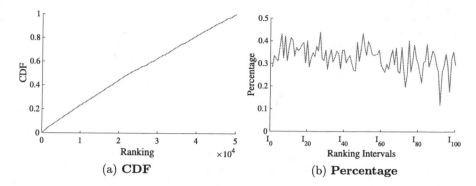

Fig. 1. (a) Distribution of login-detected websites. (b) Percentages of password-exposed websites among CDN-enabled websites across different ranking intervals. We divide 50K websites into 100 ranking intervals. Each interval contains 500 websites. The x-axis ticks at every 20 intervals.

websites send the login requests with users' passwords in plaintext or Base64 encoding to CDNs. We denote these websites as "password-exposed websites". We discovered that 33% of CDN-enabled websites expose users' passwords to CDNs, demonstrating a potential privacy issue. In this section, we present the results in detail.

5.1   Distribution over Rankings

Since our framework may fail to detect the login forms of some websites, the dataset of login-detected websites is a sample set of all websites that enable logins. We first investigate the distribution of these samples over rankings.

Figure 1a shows the distribution of login-detected websites. A linear relationship between the CDF and ranking shows a uniform distribution of the websites. Therefore, the logins detected by our framework are unbiased in the rankings.

To investigate the relationship between websites' rankings and their preference for password exposure, we divide the rankings into 100 intervals. For an interval I_j, it contains 500 websites ranking in the range of $[1+500*(j-1), 500*j]$. For each interval, we count the password-exposed websites and the CDN-enabled websites, and we compute the percentage of password-exposed websites in CDN-enabled websites.

Figure 1b presents the percentage variation across the intervals. Given the result of unbiased detection in Fig. 1a, we can examine the distribution of password exposure on website rankings through Fig. 1b. Even though some fluctuations exist, the percentages are overall above 20%, meaning that the password exposure is common across all rankings. Besides, we can find that the most popular websites in the first two intervals have relatively low password exposure percentage. It is because that the top websites are more likely to deploy defense mechanisms, which can be justified by our analysis in Sect. 6.

Table 1. Distribution across CDN providers (a) and website categories(b). The "Percent" column denotes the percentage of password-exposed websites in CDN-enabled websites. We mark notable data with red color.

(a) **CDN providers**

CDN provider	CDN-enabled	Password-exposed	Percent
Cloudflare	6356	2803	44%
Akamai	3280	818	25%
Fastly	1631	291	18%
Highwinds	504	26	5%
Edgecast	241	16	7%
Incapsula	216	142	66%
Quantil	161	10	6%
CDNetworks	32	3	9%
Limelight	30	5	17%

(b) **Website categories**

Category	CDN-enabled	Password-exposed	Percent
Retail	304	175	58%
Internet	231	69	30%
Business	225	72	32%
Entertain	213	76	36%
News	181	62	34%
Finance	159	60	38%
Technology	155	42	27%
Education	145	14	10%
Society	99	31	31%
Travel	79	34	43%
Science	50	18	36%
Sports	49	15	31%
Health	43	17	40%
Reference	36	13	36%

5.2   Distribution over CDN Providers

We also consider how password-exposed websites are distributed among the CDN providers. Table 1a presents the number of password-exposed websites in each CDN provider. As shown in the table, Cloudflare and Akamai are the two most popular CDNs in the world, and they observe the most users' passwords from their customers' requests. More than 40% of Cloudflare's customer websites in our dataset share users' passwords to Cloudflare, and Akamai observes passwords from 25% of its customers. Besides, 66% of websites that use Incapsula expose passwords to the CDN. Some CDNs only observe a small fraction of sensitive traffic, such as Highwinds and Edgecast.

Compared to the other CDN providers, a much larger portion of Cloudflare and Incapsula customers are affected by password exposure. For Cloudflare, the reason may be the difference in request redirection methods. Cloudflare uses anycast for request redirection by default [14], while the other CDNs use DNS redirection [37,45]. As discussed in [35], to enable anycast redirection, a website needs to use Cloudflare as the DNS provider. Such a practice will transfer a website's all DNS records to Cloudflare DNS service, including the resolution to the domain of the login request (*e.g.* DNS A record of login.example.com). Cloudflare will conduct anycast redirection for the transferred domains by default. Therefore, the login request is very likely to be terminated by Cloudflare. We verify this inference by checking the DNS provider of password-exposed websites using Cloudflare. We find that 63% of websites that transferred their DNS providers to Cloudflare expose their passwords to Cloudflare, while 83% of websites that use Cloudflare CDN service without transferring their DNS providers do not suffer the password exposure.

As for Incapsula, such a high percentage (66%) may originate from the dynamic content caching provided by Incapsula [8]. Such a service will cache the dynamic content for a short period to improve the performance of webpage loading, which is not enabled by the other CDN providers. Websites using Incapsula may employ this service to cache the dynamic content including the login responses, leading to password exposure.

It is reasonable for websites to trust famous CDN providers and employ their defense against attacks. However, it does not necessarily mean users should also trust CDNs. From the users' perspective, they may be concerned about their private data when it is shared with a third-party CDN. The results also imply a risk of the single point failure of popular CDNs: a malicious insider in a popular CDN may divulge the users' passwords of more than 40% of its customer websites, leading to a large-scale user data leakage.

We reported our findings to three CDN providers, Cloudflare, Akamai, and Fastly. All of them replied to us. They acknowledged the implication of password exposure and claimed that they are trustworthy and will follow the privacy policy [7,10] to secure customers' data. Akamai also explained that they must terminate the TLS connections including those transmitting private data in order to provide protections such as WAF for customers.

5.3   Distribution over Website Categories

We investigate the practice of exposing passwords among different website categories. We collect the website category data from Alexa Top Sites by Category [2]. In 12,451 CDN-enabled websites, 2,010 of them can be classified by the Alexa data. In our dataset, three categories (Government, Recreation, and Home) contain less than 20 CDN-enabled websites, so we consider the dataset is not representative enough for these three categories. Thus, we only use the rest of the 14 categories in our analysis in this section.

Table 1b presents the statistics of CDN usage and password exposure across 14 website categories. As we can see, retail websites employ most CDNs because they need to display many pictures of their products, and CDNs notably accelerate the picture delivery . However, most retail websites (58%) also expose passwords to CDNs. Besides retail websites, more than 40% of websites of travel and health expose users' passwords. We note that a large portion (38%) of finance and health websites which are usually considered to require sophisticated defense divulges users' passwords to CDNs. Moreover, education websites have the least percentage of password exposure. Our results point out that password exposure is prevalent within a wide range of categories, while retail, travel, and health are the most affected website categories.

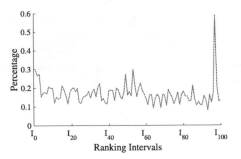

Fig. 2. Percentages of password-encrypted websites among CDN-enabled websites across different ranking intervals. We divide 50K websites into 100 intervals. Each interval contains 500 websites. The x-axis ticks at every 20 intervals.

6   Countermeasures

In this section, we first present the measurement of the countermeasures against password exposure used by current websites. We also discuss possible countermeasures that websites and users can adopt.

6.1   Client-Side Encryption and CDN Bypassing

In our measurement, we observe that some websites indeed adopt client-side encryption discussed in Sect. 2.2 to protect users' passwords. For example, `baidu.com`, `dropbox.com`, and `chase.com` deliver public keys by their origin servers. However, such a solution is rarely adopted by the websites. In our measurement, if our framework submits the credentials but cannot find the password in plain text or Base64 encoding in the login request, we consider that the website encrypts the password. Since our framework may fail to login, we have an upper-bound estimation of the deployment of client-side password encryption. Therefore, in our dataset, at most 2,057 (16.5%) out of 12,451 CDN-enabled websites adopt such a solution. We call these websites "password-encrypted websites". This result demonstrates that password encryption is a rare practice on the web.

We investigate the relationship between a website's ranking and password encryption deployment. We used the same method and intervals in Fig. 1b, and the results are shown in Fig. 2. As we can see, even for the websites that rank top 1,500 (I_0, I_1, and I_2), less than 30% of them encrypt users' passwords. Nevertheless, when compared with other websites with lower ranks, they have a relatively higher percentage of password encryption. However, an outstandingly high percentage exists around the intervals of quite low rankings. We manually inspected websites located in that interval. We found 13 websites of all 20 password-encrypted websites are subdomains of `tmall.com` for different retailers, such as www.kfc.tmall.com and www.lenovo.tmall.com. Once a user attempts to sign into these subdomain sites, they all direct the user to `tmall.com`. This website is a top electronic shopping website, and it adopts password encryption.

We note that as a preliminary defense, client-side encryption can only defend against passive attackers as described in Sect. 3. However, our measurement shows that most websites including top ones cannot even prevent a passive attacker. If an active attacker exists, CDN bypassing can protect users' privacy, but it exposes origin servers' IP addresses and leave servers at the risk of DDoS. In our measurement, we cannot verify whether the destination of a login request is the origin server through RDAP. We leave the further measurement of CDN bypassing as future work.

6.2 Possible Countermeasures

Besides client-side encryption and CDN bypassing, Password Authenticated Key Exchange (PAKE) [13,21] also prevents password exposure. PAKE protocols, such as SRP [60] and OPAQUE [29], authenticate users without the requirement of revealing passwords in login requests. Moreover, it is proven to be secure during login even when CDNs can launch active attacks. However, PAKE protocols require trust on first use (TOFU), meaning that a secure channel is required during account registration. Therefore, PAKE solves the password exposure issue for web services that do not allow online registration. For example, it can be used in banking industry, as users are required to open a bank account physically at branches. Nevertheless, PAKE is almost never used by websites [21]. The reason may be the difficulty of understanding and implementing PAKE protocols for developers. It may also be because developers usually trust third-party CDNs and are not aware of such a password exposure issue.

From the users' perspective, a user can use OAuth [25] such as using a Google account to sign in to other websites. Because leading tech companies such as Google and Facebook have built their own CDNs, a user's password will not be exposed to a third party during the login. However, more OAuth practices may lead to a severe single-point failure if a user's password of the Google account is leaked. Besides OAuth, users can also adopt two-factor authentication. Even though two-factor authentication cannot prevent passwords from being exposed to third-party CDNs, it prevents accounts from being compromised even when the passwords are exposed to attackers.

These countermeasures can only protect users' passwords. However, users' private data stored on a website may also be divulged to a CDN during the transmission. As private data are much more complicated and diverse than the passwords, developing countermeasures would be harder. Thus, private data leakage may be much more prevalent than password leakage. We leave the measurement of private data leakage as future work.

7 Discussion and Future Work

Our measurement quantifies password exposure to CDNs and suggests potential security issues in current web ecosystem. In this section, we provide suggestions to the security community, users, and the industry.

We need further research on the solutions. As presented in Sect. 2.2, the preliminary strategies of CDN bypassing and client-side encryption can be easily deployed but contain vulnerabilities. Proposed techniques such as Keyless SSL [18,40,51], certificate delegation [34], and mcTLS [42] are ineffective in preserving user privacy. The SGX-based solutions [26,41] can provide comprehensive protection, but it is hard to be deployed on CDNs. InviCloak [35] can achieve the goal of DDoS defense, privacy protection, and instant deployment simultaneously, but it disables the Web Application Firewall (WAF) of CDNs. Therefore, further research on this area is critical to a more secure Internet.

We recommend users adopt two-factor authentication. Two-factor authentication provides additional protection for an account even when the password is stolen by a hacker. Adopting OAuth is debatable as it may lead to the single point of failure although it prevents password exposure as discussed in Sect. 6.2.

Websites should adopt preliminary defense. The results shows that many websites do not apply the minimal defense against password exposure. Despite the preliminary strategies are vulnerable to some attacks, they provide basic protection for users' privacy. Since it is acceptable to assume a passive CDNs in most cases, the client-side encryption usually provides a sufficient protection.

CDN providers should involve in developing and deploying advanced solutions. The widespread of Keyless SSL on Cloudflare demonstrates that a CDN provider plays an important role in the security community [51]. Cooperation from CDN providers can validate researchers' ideas and advance further research. CDNs can also guide their customers to deploy a defense mechanism.

This paper presents the preliminary results of password sharing to third-party CDNS. We propose the following directions as the future work.

1. Augment the existing CDN discovery method to differentiate the hosting service and the CDN service of a cloud provider, as mentioned in Sect. 4.
2. Quantify the adopted or available countermeasures besides the client-side encryption in websites, including CDN bypassing, OAuth, one-time password, two-factor authentication, etc., as mentioned in Sect. 6.
3. Measure private data leakage in websites to understand the security impact of TLS private key sharing from users' perspectives, as mentioned in Sect. 6.
4. Survey the users and website developers to understand their awareness of private data leakage to thrid-party CDNs. Such a survey helps to figure out the reason why countermeasures are not widespread.

8   Related Work

Password security. Password security has attracted attention from many researchers. Lu *et al.* analyzed how websites deploy measures to prevent online password cracking [36]. Wang *et al.* manually inspected 188 websites to characterize the login process and built an extension to inform users of potential password leakage caused by the lack of HTTPS [56]. Acker *et al.* studied the security of password input fields among the Alexa top 100K sites, and they found that 62.8% of the websites with a login page are vulnerable to basic man-in-the-middle attacks [53]. Bonneau *et al.* surveyed the proposals for replacing passwords and pointed out the difficulty of replacing passwords [12]. Peng *et al.* explored how passwords are spread after they are divulged by phishing sites [47]. In addition, many prior works investigated the prevalence of the password reuse problem [28,46,49,57] and its countermeasures [55].

CDN security. Researchers have shown the existence of a wide range of vulnerabilities in CDNs. Mirheidari *et al.*'s measurement shows that private data can be divulged by CDNs through web cache deception [19,38,39]. Nguyen *et al.* presented an attack of poisoning CDN cache with error pages, and five CDN services were vulnerable to such an attack [44]. Besides CDN cache, researchers also presented approaches to disclosing the IP addresses of origin servers hidden behind CDNs, demonstrating insufficient DDoS protection of CDNs [30,54]. Moreover, attackers may utilize a CDN to launch DoS to an origin server or to the CDN itself [16,23,52]. In addition, Durumeric *et al.*'s measurement shows that the HTTPS interception on CDNs may downgrade the TLS version or cipher suites and thus reduce connection security [17].

Solutions to TLS key sharing. A line of research focuses on building keyless CDNs. Cloudflare, Akamai, and Modadugu *et al.* proposed similar solutions called "Keyless SSL", respectively [18,40,51]. Certificate delegation [34] and mcTLS [42] enable a client to recognize the CDN as a delegation of the website. Wei *et al.* [58] and Ahmed *et al.* [11] adopted Trust Executive Environment (TEE) on CDNs for private key management. However, these strategies only prevent the TLS private key sharing, while users' private data are still visible to CDNs. Phoenix [26] and mbTLS [41] extend TEE solutions to fully protect users' private data. However, deploying TEE-based solutions on CDNs may take a long time as it requires upgrades of hardware and operating systems. Invi-Cloak [35] protects users' private data with an additional encryption channel and low overhead, but its adoption by websites in the future remains unclear.

9   Conclusion

In this paper, we conduct a large-scale measurement to quantify user password exposure to third-party CDNs in the web ecosystem. Our results show that 33.0% of CDN-enabled websites expose users' passwords to the CDNs during the login procedures. Retail websites substantially benefit from CDNs but also tend to expose passwords to CDNs. Besides, client-side password encryption is adopted by less than 17% of websites, even though it is simple and effective to a certain extent. Overall, our results suggest that current websites excessively trust CDNs, leading to potential security issues when attackers exploit CDNs' vulnerabilities. We publicly released the code to facilitate future research [9].

Acknowledgements. We sincerely thank our shepherd Georgios Smaragdakis and anonymous reviewers for their helpful comments. This work is supported in part by the Duke CS+ summer research program and NSF award CNS-1901047.

Appendix

We present the detail of our auto-login framework in this section. For each web page, the framework applies four steps to the HTML elements: filtering, classifying, scoring, and submitting credentials. The framework first filters the elements based on tag names and locations. Then it uses keyword frequency as the features to classify filtered elements into three classes: login entrances, account inputs, and password inputs. In each class, it assigns a score to each element according to features extracted from the HTML code. Finally it fills and submits credentials if the login form is found, or it clicks on the login entrance to visit the login page. The elements to interact with are chosen by their scores in each class. The followings paragraphs introduce each step in detail.

1. **Filtering**: When the framework arrives at a page, it starts with filtering out elements that are considered irrelevant to login. Specifically, it selects elements containing one of the following tag names: "input", "button", "label", "a" and "iframe". To reduce element candidates, we assume that a login entrance or a login form should be shown within the area of one and a half of the viewport height from the top of a web page. The rationale of this assumption is that a website should place login elements at positions that are easily accessible to users.
2. **Classifying**: To classify an element into the classes mentioned above, the framework extracts strings from HTML properties and the inner text of the element. It then splits strings into words by camel case and non-word characters. It computes the frequencies of some keywords in the string. The keyword frequencies are regarded as a feature of the element. The framework classifies the element based on these features and heuristic rules. We manually select eleven keywords and construct rules for classification after examining Alexa top 100 sites. One example of the rules is that a login entrance should contain at least one of the keywords related to "login", "account", or "email". To improve the detection accuracy, we also apply some deprecation keywords such as "user guide" and "policy". An element is discarded if it contains any of the deprecation keywords.
3. **Scoring**: While a website usually contains only one login entrance, the framework may classify multiple elements into the login class. Thus, our framework assigns scores to elements. For each element, the framework extracts other features besides keywords, such as the length of inner text and the visibility of element. The framework uses the features to assign a score to each element according to the rules we construct manually. For example, in the class of login entrance, a visible and interactive element receives a higher score than ones that are not. The frequency of a keyword in an element is also factored in the scores. Finally, the framework sorts elements in each class according to their scores.

4. **Submitting Credentials**: If the framework obtains any input element in the account class or the password class, it fills each input element with credentials. Then it uses the keyboard signal, ENTER, to submit fake credentials. If no input field is detected, the framework clicks on the login element with the highest score and repeats the presented steps on the new web page to detect input fields. The framework collects the login request once it considers a credential submission happens.

Overall, our framework uses heuristic rules to detect login entrances and input fields of credentials. We implement the framework by using Selenium Web-Driver [5] to control Chrome. We test our framework on 100 random-selected websites of which 52 enable the login. The results show that our framework successfully submits credentials to 45 of 53 websites, meaning a recall of 84.9%. The framework ignores all 47 websites without a login entrance, meaning a false positive of 0%. The overall detection accuracy is (45+47)/100=92.0%.

Existing automatic login frameworks: Browsers such as Chrome and Firefox can help users automatically fill in the credentials on some web pages. We do not use this function because it relies on the existence of the "autocomplete" attribute in HTML elements, and thus it cannot handle the websites that do not enable this attribute in HTML. Besides the automation of browsers, Peng *et al.* implemented a framework to log into phishing websites automatically [47]. Our framework can handle issues that are common in legitimate sites but rare in phishing sites, such as confusion caused by sign-up forms and pop-ups. Jonker *et al.*. also proposed a framework for post-login security analysis [31]. Our framework shares many similarities with theirs but adds the capability to operate in the presence of HTTP Authentication and reCAPTCHA.

References

1. Akamai (2020). https://www.akamai.com/
2. Alexa Top Sites (2020). https://www.alexa.com/topsites
3. Cloudflare (2020). https://www.cloudflare.com/
4. Fastly (2020). https://www.fastly.com/
5. SeleniumHQ Browser Automation (2020). https://www.selenium.dev/
6. AJAX (2022). https://developer.mozilla.org/en-US/docs/Web/Guide/AJAX
7. Certifications and Compliance Resources (2022). https://www.cloudflare.com/trust-hub/compliance-resources/
8. Global CDN and Optimizer - Introduction (2022). https://docs.imperva.com/bundle/cloud-application-security/page/introducing/global-cdn-optimizer.htm
9. PAM2023-CDNPassword (2022). https://github.com/SHiftLin/PAM2023-CDNPassword
10. Security Measures (2022). https://docs.fastly.com/en/guides/security-measures
11. Ahmed, R., Zaheer, Z., Li, R., Ricci, R.: Harpocrates: giving Out Your Secrets and Keeping Them Too. In: Proceedings of IEEE/ACM Symposium on Edge Computing (SEC), pp. 103–114. IEEE (2018)
12. Bonneau, J., Herley, C., Van Oorschot, P.C., Stajano, F.: The quest to replace passwords: a framework for comparative evaluation of web authentication schemes. In: Proceedings of S&P, pp. 553–567. IEEE (2012)

13. Boyko, V., MacKenzie, P., Patel, S.: Provably secure password-authenticated key exchange using diffie-hellman. In: Preneel, B. (ed.) EUROCRYPT 2000. LNCS, vol. 1807, pp. 156–171. Springer, Heidelberg (2000). https://doi.org/10.1007/3-540-45539-6_12

14. Calder, M., Flavel, A., Katz-Bassett, E., Mahajan, R., Padhye, J.: Analyzing the performance of an anycast CDN. In: Proceedings of International Media Conference (IMC), pp. 531–537 (2015)

15. Cangialosi, F., et al.: Measurement and analysis of private key sharing in the HTTPS ecosystem. In: Proceedings of Computer and Communications Security (CCS), pp. 628–640. ACM (2016)

16. Chen, J., et al.: Forwarding-loop attacks in content delivery networks. In: Proceedings of the Network and Distributed System Security Symposium (NDSS). ISOC (2016)

17. Durumeric, Z., et al.: The security impact of HTTPS interception. In: Proceedings of Network and Distributed System Security Symposium (NDSS). ISOC (2017)

18. Gero, C.E., Shapiro, J.N., Burd, D.J.: Terminating SSL Connections without Locally-Accessible Private Keys (2013). u.S. Patents, No. 9,647,835

19. Gil, O.: Web Cache Deception Attack (2017). https://omergil.blogspot.com/2017/02/web-cache-deception-attack.html

20. Gillman, D., Lin, Y., Maggs, B., Sitaraman, R.K.: Protecting websites from attack with secure delivery networks. Computer **48**(4), 26–34 (2015)

21. Green, M.: Let's Talk About PAKE (2018). https://blog.cryptographyengineering.com/2018/10/19/lets-talk-about-pake/

22. Guo, R., et al.: Abusing CDNs for fun and profit: security issues in CDNs' origin validation. In: Proceedings of 2018 IEEE 37th Symposium on Reliable Distributed Systems (SRDS), pp. 1–10. IEEE (2018)

23. Guo, R., et al.: CDN Judo: breaking the CDN DoS protection with itself. In: Proceedings of 2020 Network and Distributed System Security Symposium (NDSS). ISOC (2020)

24. Halfond, W.G., Viegas, J., Orso, A., et al.: A classification of SQL-injection attacks and countermeasures. In: Proceedings of International Symposium on Secure Software Engineering. vol. 1, pp. 13–15. IEEE (2006)

25. Hardt, D.: The OAuth 2.0 authorization framework. Internet Engineering Task Force (IETF) (2012)

26. Herwig, S., Garman, C., Levin, D.: Achieving Keyless CDNs with Conclaves. In: Proceedings of Security Symposium, pp. 735–751. USENIX (2020)

27. Huang, C., Wang, A., Li, J., Ross, K.W.: Measuring and evaluating large-scale CDNs. In: Proceedings of the 8th ACM SIGCOMM conference on Internet measurement (IMC), pp. 15–29. ACM (2008)

28. Ion, I., Reeder, R., Consolvo, S.: "... no one can hack my mind": Comparing expert and non-expert security practices. In: Proceedings of Symposium On Usable Privacy and Security (SOUPS), pp. 327–346. USENIX (2015)

29. Jarecki, S., Krawczyk, H., Xu, J.: OPAQUE: an asymmetric PAKE protocol secure against pre-computation attacks. In: Nielsen, J.B., Rijmen, V. (eds.) EUROCRYPT 2018. LNCS, vol. 10822, pp. 456–486. Springer, Cham (2018). https://doi.org/10.1007/978-3-319-78372-7_15

30. Jin, L., Hao, S., Wang, H., Cotton, C.: Your remnant tells secret: residual resolution in DDoS protection services. In: Proceedings of 2018 48th Annual IEEE/IFIP International Conference on Dependable Systems and Networks (DSN), pp. 362–373. IEEE (2018)

31. Jonker, H., Karsch, S., Krumnow, B., Sleegers, M.: Shepherd: a generic approach to automating website login. In: Proceedings of NDSS Workshop on Measurements, Attacks, and Defenses for the Web. ISOC (2021)
32. Krishnamurthy, B., Wills, C., Zhang, Y.: On the use and performance of content distribution networks. In: Proceedings of International Media Conference (IMC), pp. 169–182. ACM (2001)
33. Levy, A.: CDNs and Privacy Threats: A Measurement Study. Ph.D. thesis, Princeton University (2017)
34. Liang, J., Jiang, J., Duan, H., Li, K., Wan, T., Wu, J.: When HTTPS meets CDN: a case of authentication in delegated service. In: Proceedings of IEEE Symposium on Security and Privacy (S&P), pp. 67–82. IEEE (2014)
35. Lin, S., Xin, R., Goel, A., Yang, X.: InviCloak: an end-to-end approach to privacy and performance in web content distribution. In: Conference on Computer and Communications Security (CCS). ACM (2022)
36. Lu, B., Zhang, X., Ling, Z., Zhang, Y., Lin, Z.: A measurement study of authentication rate-limiting mechanisms of modern websites, In: Proceedings of the 34th Annual Computer Security Applications Conference (ACSAC), pp. 89–100 (2018)
37. Maggs, B.M., Sitaraman, R.K.: Algorithmic nuggets in content delivery. ACM SIGCOMM CCR **45**(3), 52–66 (2015)
38. Mirheidari, S.A., Arshad, S., Onarlioglu, K., Crispo, B., Kirda, E., Robertson, W.: Cached and confused: web cache deception in the wild. In: Proceedings of Security Symposium, pp. 665–682. USENIX (2020)
39. Mirheidari, S.A., Golinelli, M., Onarlioglu, K., Kirda, E., Crispo, B.: Web cache deception escalates! In: Proceedings of Security Symposium. Boston, MA, pp. 179–196. USENIX (2022)
40. Modadugu, N., Goh, E.J.: The Design and Implementation of WASP: A Wide-Area Secure Proxy. Stanford University, Tech. rep. (2002)
41. Naylor, D., Li, R., Gkantsidis, C., Karagiannis, T., Steenkiste, P.: And then there were more: secure communication for more than two parties. In: Proceedings of CoNEXT, pp. 88–100 (2017)
42. Naylor, D., et al.: Multi-context TLS (mcTLS): enabling secure in-network functionality in TLS. In: Proceedings of Proceedings of the 2015 ACM Conference on Special Interest Group on Data Communication (SIGCOMM), pp. 199–212. ACM (2015)
43. Newton, A., Hollenbeck, S.: RFC7482: registration data access protocol (RDAP) query format. Internet Engineering Task Force (IETF) (2015)
44. Nguyen, H.V., Iacono, L.L., Federrath, H.: Your cache has fallen: cache-poisoned denial-of-service attack. In: Conference on Computer and Communications Security (CCS), pp. 1915–1936. ACM (2019)
45. Nygren, E., Sitaraman, R.K., Sun, J.: The akamai network: a platform for high-performance internet applications. SIGOPS OSR **44**(3), 2–19 (2010)
46. Pearman, S., et al.: Let's go in for a closer look: observing passwords in their natural habitat. In: Proceedings of Conference on Computer and Communications Security (CCS), pp. 295–310. ACM (2017)
47. Peng, P., Xu, C., Quinn, L., Hu, H., Viswanath, B., Wang, G.: What happens after you leak your password: understanding credential sharing on phishing sites. In: Proceedings of the 2019 ACM Asia Conference on Computer and Communications Security (AsiaCCS), pp. 181–192 (2019)
48. Senol, A., Acar, G., Humbert, M., Borgesius, F.Z.: Leaky Forms: a study of email and password exfiltration before form submission. In: Proceedings of Security Symposium. Boston, MA, pp. 1813–1830. USENIX (2022)

49. Shay, R., et al.: Encountering stronger password requirements: user attitudes and behaviors. In: Proceedings of Symposium On Usable Privacy and Security (SOUPS), pp. 1–20. USENIX (2010)
50. Sparling, C.: 5 Years of Fighting DDoS with the Power of Akamai (2019). https://blogs.akamai.com/2019/07/5-years-of-fighting-ddos-with-the-power-of-akamai.html
51. Sullivan, N.: Keyless SSL: The Nitty Gritty Technical Details (2014). https://blog.cloudflare.com/keyless-ssl-the-nitty-gritty-technical-details/
52. Triukose, S., Al-Qudah, Z., Rabinovich, M.: Content delivery networks: protection or threat? In: Backes, M., Ning, P. (eds.) ESORICS 2009. LNCS, vol. 5789, pp. 371–389. Springer, Heidelberg (2009). https://doi.org/10.1007/978-3-642-04444-1_23
53. Van Acker, S., Hausknecht, D., Sabelfeld, A.: Measuring login webpage security. In: Proceedings of the Symposium on Applied Computing (SAC), pp. 1753–1760. ACM (2017)
54. Vissers, T., Van Goethem, T., Joosen, W., Nikiforakis, N.: Maneuvering around clouds: bypassing cloud-based security providers. In: Conference on Computer and Communications Security (CCS), pp. 1530–1541. ACM (2015)
55. Wang, K.C., Reiter, M.K.: How to end password reuse on the web. In: Proceedings of Network and Distributed System Security Symposium (NDSS). ISOC (2019)
56. Wang, X.S., Choffnes, D., Gage Kelley, P., Greenstein, B., Wetherall, D.: Measuring and predicting web login safety. In: Proceedings of SIGCOMM Workshop on Measurements up the Stack, pp. 55–60 (2011)
57. Wash, R., Rader, E., Berman, R., Wellmer, Z.: Understanding password choices: how frequently entered passwords are re-used across websites. In: Proceedings of Twelfth Symposium on Usable Privacy and Security (SOUPS), pp. 175–188. USENIX (2016)
58. Wei, C., Li, J., Li, W., Yu, P., Guan, H.: STYX: a trusted and accelerated hierarchical SSL key management and distribution system for cloud based CDN application. In: Proceedings of the 2017 Symposium on Cloud Computing (SoCC), pp. 201–213. ACM (2017)
59. Weinberger, J., Saxena, P., Akhawe, D., Finifter, M., Shin, R., Song, D.: A systematic analysis of XSS sanitization in web application frameworks. In: Atluri, V., Diaz, C. (eds.) ESORICS 2011. LNCS, vol. 6879, pp. 150–171. Springer, Heidelberg (2011). https://doi.org/10.1007/978-3-642-23822-2_9
60. Wu, T.D., et al.: The secure remote password protocol. In: Proceedings of Network and Distributed System Security Symposium (NDSS). vol. 98, pp. 97–111. Citeseer (1998)

Correction to: An In-Depth Measurement Analysis of 5G mmWave PHY Latency and Its Impact on End-to-End Delay

Rostand A. K. Fezeu ⓘ, Eman Ramadan ⓘ, Wei Ye ⓘ,
Benjamin Minneci ⓘ, Jack Xie, Arvind Narayanan ⓘ,
Ahmad Hassan ⓘ, Feng Qian ⓘ, Zhi-Li Zhang ⓘ,
Jaideep Chandrashekar ⓘ, and Myungjin Lee ⓘ

Correction to:
Chapter "An In-Depth Measurement Analysis of 5G mmWave PHY Latency and Its Impact on End-to-End Delay" in: A. Brunstrom et al. (Eds.): *Passive and Active Measurement*, LNCS 13882, https://doi.org/10.1007/978-3-031-28486-1_13

In the originally published version of chapter 13, the presentation of Jaideep Chandrashekar's affiliation was misleading. This has been corrected.

The updated original version of this chapter can be found at
https://doi.org/10.1007/978-3-031-28486-1_13

Author Index

Printed in the United States
by Baker & Taylor Publisher Services